BASIC
Programming
Inside & Out

Bomanns

Abacus
A Data Becker Book

Second Printing, July 1991
Printed in U.S.A.
Copyright © 1990, 1991

Abacus
5370 52nd Street SE
Grand Rapids, MI 49512

Copyright © 1988, 1989, 1990, 1991

Data Becker GmbH
Merowingerstrasse 30
4000 Duesseldorf, West Germany

```
Library of Congress Cataloging-in-Publication Data
Bomanns, H.J. (Heinz Josef), 1958-
        BASIC programming : inside and out / H.J. Bomanns.
                p.  cm.
        "A data Becker book."
        Includes index.
        ISBN 1-557-55084-0 : $34.95
        1. BASIC (Computer program language)  I. Title
QA76.73.B3B66 1990
005.26'2--dc20                                    90-39928
                                                  CIP
```

ISBN   1-55755-084-0

Table of Contents

vi

1. Introduction

1.1   A Few Words about this Book

Even though you've probably heard such negative comments as "BASIC is only for beginners," "BASIC is spaghetti code" and "Structured programming is impossible with BASIC," you've obviously decided to learn more about BASIC. Despite these types of comments, no programming language is easier to learn, as widely distributed and requires as little program development time than BASIC. Because of this, GW-/PC-BASIC has become the standard on the PC.

Throughout the years I've used GW-/PC-BASIC to implement programs on various PCs ranging from small utilities to large inventory control systems. On some computers, the documentation for the GW-/PC-BASIC consisted of three words for each command. On other computers the documentation was more comprehensive but still didn't provide enough information. To find answers to various questions, I had to look through numerous books. This gave me the idea to compile my experiences and information into a book.

A review of GW-/PC-BASIC is presented in the first part of this book. This review is organized chapter by chapter, according to the applications area. In the second part of the book, there is valuable information for professional programming with GW-/PC-BASIC. A brief reference table, with pointers to detailed explanations, enables you to quickly find the syntax of the commands and functions. In the Appendix you'll find additional information arranged in an easy-to-understand overview concerning GW-/PC-BASIC. Finally, a comprehensive Index ensures that you can easily find specific information without having to look through the entire book.

Before working through the following chapters, you should be familiar with the functions of your computer system and any special features. You should also be familiar with the reference manuals for your computer and MS-DOS.

Heinz-Josef Bomanns

1.2   Chapter Overview

Chapter 1

This chapter contains an introduction to GW-/PC-BASIC.

Chapter 2

In this chapter you'll discover what GW-/PC-BASIC is, how it works and the structure of a program.

Chapter 3

This chapter tells you everything you need to know in order to work with GW-/PC-BASIC or the integrated editor.

Chapter 4

In this chapter all the commands and functions provided by GW-/PC-BASIC are presented, with many examples, according to the applications area.

Chapter 5

In this chapter we'll demonstrate how the PC can be a musician.

Chapter 6

This chapter presents the GW-/PC-BASIC capabilities that can be used for programming graphic material.

Chapter 7

In addition to the standard commands and functions presented in Chapter 4, this chapter discusses the special capabilities of GW-/PC-BASIC.

Chapter 8

Starting with this chapter, we present information for advanced programmers and professionals. We also discuss the assembler and GW-/PC-BASIC.

Chapter 9

In this chapter we will present ways to simplify the input of programs.

Chapter 10

You shouldn't begin to program unless you have a plan. This chapter shows you what is important and offers some useful tools.

Chapters 11 and 12

Since the screen and the keyboard enable the user to communicate with a program, they require special attention during programming. These chapters show how to write professional looking programs and how to implement user interfaces.

Chapter 13

An important subject of data processing is sorting data. In this chapter we present the common sort algorithms and discover which routine is the most useful for a certain application.

Chapter 14

This chapter demonstrates how to implement a fast and convenient file retrieval system for larger file inventories.

Chapter 15

In this chapter we present capabilities for universal printer control and formatting of printed output.

Chapter 16

Most programs now have a Help function and sophisticated error correction capabilities. However, many programmers try to avoid this subject because it supposedly creates extra work. But actually it's rather simple.

Chapter 17

This chapter introduces you to the implementation of graphics for business.

Chapter 18

Compilers are important for professional or commercial programming. In this chapter you will discover what compilers do, their features and how to use them.

Chapter 19

In this chapter you will find an index of all the commands and functions, with their respective parameters, listed according to application area and sorted alphabetically.

Appendix

The Appendix presents information on error codes, BIOS/DOS interrupts, mouse function calls, ASCII codes and PC character sets, and other valuable information.

1.3   Important Suggestions

Before beginning an in-depth study of GW-/PC-BASIC, you should read the following suggestions. They'll help you avoid many problems.

Graphics

GW-/PC-BASIC can only be used with a color graphic card (CGA/EGA). If your PC has a monochrome graphic card, you can't use the graphic commands and functions of GW-/PC-BASIC without experiencing problems. You have a monochrome card when the characters on the screen are green on black, amber on black or (rarely) black on white. You'll need to install either a color graphic card and color monitor on your PC or use the utility programs found in Chapter 17 before you can use the GW-/PC-BASIC graphic.

Versions

As you know, there are many personal computer manufacturers. Some of these manufacturers purchase licensed versions of GW-/PC-BASIC from the developer, Microsoft, and adapt it to their own PCs. Unfortunately, because of this, some of these versions lack certain commands or functions, or do not function like the standard GW-/PC-BASIC. So, if something doesn't execute on your system as described in this book, please remember that, due to the countless PC manufacturers, we cannot test every version for potential differences. However, if we know of any differences, we'll indicate them.

Compatibility

Originally IBM developed the PC as a computer for programmers; its success in the home and business markets wasn't anticipated. As this success became apparent, other companies quickly "copied" the successful concept of the PC and manufactured devices which appeared to be similar and generally performed in the same manner as the original PC. However, an exact imitation wasn't possible because this would be a violation of patent law. So, the imitations only resemble the original. This resemblance is called *compatibility*. The more the copy is similar to the original, the more the "clone" is compatible.

The compatibility determines whether a program can execute on a copy (compatible). Each software manufacturer develops its programs on an original IBM PC to ensure program compatibility. If you're using a compatible PC and any of the examples, routines or utilities from this book don't execute as described, it's possible that this is caused by your PC's incompatibility.

1.4   BASIC's Many Names

You've probably seen the terms GW-BASIC, PC-BASIC, MS-BASIC or BASICA and wondered how they were different. However, these are simply different names for the same concept:

MS-BASIC

Originally developed by the Microsoft Corporation for CP/M computers, the predecessors of the PC, MS-BASIC is the ancestor of all BASIC interpreters.

GW-BASIC

This is an enhanced MS-BASIC specifically designed for the MS-DOS computers (Personal Computer) dominating the market today.

BASICA

BASICA, a special version of GW-BASIC, is designed for the special requirements of the IBM PC. We'll discuss this subject in more detail later in the book.

PC-BASIC

PC-BASIC is merely a generic name for the various versions mentioned above. Therefore, every interpreter that runs on a PC, whether it's an IBM or compatible, can also be designated as PC-BASIC.

Throughout this book we'll only refer to PC-BASIC. You may have heard of QuickBASIC or Turbo-BASIC. This is a compiler allowing the conversion of a PC-BASIC program into a program (.EXE) that can be executed under MS-DOS. The interpreter is not required for the program to execute. We'll fully discuss this subject in more detail in Chapter 18.

1.5   How to Use this Book

While outlining and writing a book, an author tries to please as many potential readers as possible. This isn't easy to do, especially with technical books. So, some compromises must be made. Therefore this book is divided into two parts.

The first part, which includes Chapters 2 to 7, is designed as a review of PC-BASIC. You will find explanations and many examples on such topics as calling the interpreter and controlling the editor. The topics are organized by applications areas and many illustrations are provided. At the same time, this part of the book also serves as a guide into the new BASIC environment for former users of Commodore or Atari home computers. The advanced user can use this section as a comprehensive reference tool.

The second part of the book, which includes Chapters 8 to 19, is designed for the advanced and professional PC-BASIC programmers. In this section professional and commercial programming are described. Also, we will demonstrate how to accelerate and enhance programs and discuss what aspects must be considered during the development and organizational phase or what problems can occur while printing data.

The Appendix, which includes information that has been collected about PC-BASIC, can be used as a general reference source during programming.

2. About PC-BASIC

2.1 What is PC-BASIC?

The "heart" of your computer is a 8088, 8086, 80186, 80286 or 80386 *microprocessor*, which is located within the Central Processing Unit or *CPU*. The CPU controls the computer system and the devices interfaced to it. *Peripheral controllers* help the CPU perform its tasks by controlling the keyboard, screen, disk drives or hard disks and other devices.

The CPU "understands" a series of commands (instructions), passed to it as binary numbers in a *command register*. The dialog between the CPU and the assistants also occurs through binary numbers, which are passed to the command registers of these controllers. On the lowest level, the code for these communications is the *machine language*.

When programmers communicate on this level with the CPU, it's a very complicated procedure, but the program will be executed very rapidly. For example, assume that you are taking a vacation in India and, in order to talk with a native person, you have to hire a translator. Since everything must be translated by the interpreter, the conversation will take more time than if you were speaking directly to the person.

Programmers usually assign abbreviations to the individual commands when working on this level. The CPU or a peripheral controller understands these abbreviations are known as *mnemonics*. They consist of three to five letters and are used by programmers in the *source program*. This source program is passed to an *assembler*. The assembler is responsible for creating an executable machine language program from the source code.

Using our example of a vacation in India, we can demonstrate how this works. Now you would pass a list of questions to the interpreter. He would translate the questions and then read them to the native. The native responds to each question serially, which speeds up the conversation. The list of questions is similar to the source program; the translator performs the work of an assembler.

The complexity of this type of programming can be easily understood. For example, in order to print out a single character, about 15 individual commands for the CPU are needed.

This changed, however, when John Kemeny and Thomas Kurtz from Dartmouth College in New Hampshire discovered a way to simplify the entire process. Tasks, such as displaying output on the screen, reading input from the keyboard and saving files on the disk or hard disk, are often the same in various programs.

These and similar tasks constantly appear in every program. The individual commands are grouped together, depending on the task, in order to complete routines which are assigned a name and are capable of using variable additional parameters. The collection of these routines results in an *interpreter* which is easier to use and more convenient than the previously mentioned assembler. A small increase in the execution time of these programs is the only negative effect. A single character displayed on the printer appears as follows:

```
LPRINT "A"
```

It soon became obvious that this type of programming was very valuable because the programs were easily learned and could be tested and changed immediately. These are ideal qualities for making programming accessible to everyone. This type of programming quickly became *BASIC* (Beginners All Purpose Symbolic Instruction Code or Beginners All Purpose SymbolIc Computing language).

Through the years the interpreter has become more powerful and user-friendly. Microsoft has made advances in this field resulting in the PC-BASIC interpreter. The acronym *GW* represents *Graphic & Window*. This means that this interpreter is capable of presenting graphic material and can divide the screen for output in various windows.

2.2   How does PC-BASIC operate?

In the previous section we found that, in BASIC, routines for a certain task can be called with a corresponding name, called *commands*. There are also some routines which return a result, after their call, in the form of a value or other information. These routines are called *functions*. Sometimes commands without parameters are called *statements*. However, we'll refer to commands without parameters as commands. These commands and functions must be passed parameters in order to perform their assignments.

For example, suppose someone tells you: "The sky is blue." You look up at the sky. Then the person says: "The sky behind the tree and to the right is blue". Again you follow the directions and look to the right and behind the tree. The phrase "behind the tree and to the right" could be called a *parameter* because it describes the assignment in more detail.

Now you will become a function when the person asks you: "What color is the sky?" If you reply "blue," you have returned a result as a function does. Parameters can also be used with functions, for example, "What color is the sky behind the tree and to the right?"

As we have demonstrated, the interpreter translates our commands and functions. As a result, it returns a value from a function or the result of a command. Together commands and functions form statements which the interpreter understands. This appears visually as follows:

```
                    ┌──────────> PC-BASIC line
            ┌───────┤
            │       │
    PRINT DATE$
            │       └─> function: The current date
            └─> statement: print on the screen
```

Fig. 1: Statement/Function

As we can see, a parameter can be passed to the command as a function. A parameter can also be an *expression*.

```
                    ┌──────────> PC-BASIC line
            ┌───────┤
            │       │
    PRINT 3*8+4
            │       └─> expression: the result of this calculation
            └─> statement: print on the screen
```

Fig. 2: Statement/Expression

9

2.3   Structure of a BASIC Program

In the previous section you learned that the PC-BASIC interpreter converts our statements into results. A program for the solution of a certain problem must contain several statements. Because these statements should be executed by the interpreter in a certain sequence, they must be arranged in a certain order. This occurs by dividing the program into individual *program lines* to store the statements. Every program line starts with a sequential number. This clearly shows how the interpreter gets the sequence for the execution of the statements. A small program could appear as follows:

```
10 CLS
20 INPUT "Input your name:";INAME$
30 PRINT "On this date ";
40 PRINT DATE$;
50 PRINT " your name was ";
60 PRINT INAME$;
70 PRINT " input"
```

The previous example shows seven program lines containing statements. After the statements of one program line are executed, the interpreter executes the next line. Because of the way the program lines are numbered, the interpreter knows the sequence in which the statements should be executed. As we shall see later, the sequence can change by using special statements. This means that, depending on the requirements, the interpreter can execute another program line instead of the line that is next in order.

To summarize, a program consists of program lines. A program line consists of a line number and statements. A statement consists of a *keyword* (also called *reserved word*), command, expression, function or argument. It may also contain parameters required for functions and commands.

```
50 PRINT "This is the current date: ";DATE$
 |   |                        |          └─> Function
 |   |                        └─> Parameter for the command
 |   └─> Keyword
 └─> Line number
```

Fig. 3: Program Line

In the above example, you see the program lines consist of one keyword. In PC-BASIC, it's possible to combine several keywords in one line. You must use a colon (:) to separate a statement from the next keyword:

```
10 CLS:PRINT "Hello":PRINT DATE$;
```

When you use a colon as a separator, it can be at the end of a line or as the only character in a line. You can use spaces before and after the colon for a more organized listing:

```
10 CLS  :  PRINT "Hello"  :  PRINT DATE$;
```

Random Access Memory (RAM)

Throughout this book we'll use the term *random access memory (RAM)*. Simply, this is where PC-BASIC stores your programs. RAM can be compared to a piece of note paper on which you collect ideas and information.

2.4   Programming Style

Programming style is the manner in which you construct your programs or input them through the editor. The first step is to analyze the problem to be solved. Usually a PEP (Program Execution Plan) or flowchart is created listing all the execution steps. Using a PEP allows you to create a well structured program. Screen templates and printer listings are created on 8 x 11 inch paper or, for large flowcharts, on a poster sized sheet. Implementing the program according to this chart should be simple.

If you simply entered a program without a PEP, you may eventually achieve the desired results but it would require extra time and effort. A routine could be missing or an overlooked command must be added to a line. If you're unsure of the structure of a program, examine the program listings in this book or from the accompanying disk.

These differences are also demonstrated in the individual program lines. Although you can increase the amount of available RAM by placing 10 statements in a single line, the program will be almost impossible to read. For example, even an experienced programmer could be confused by the following program line:

```
53 A=B/12:N1$=MID$(N$,10,15)+RIGHT$(N3$,4)+"BLABLABLA"+LEFT$(MG5$,5): IF
   B+3>A+1 THEN 243 ELSE MG$="MIST":A=1:GOSUB 5283:GOSUB 3481:GOTO 1827
```

It's better to split the statements in several lines. As you can see, the following example is clearer, easier to follow and easier to find syntax or other errors:

```
50 MONTHPAY=YEARPAY/12:'determine monthly pay
60 LASTNAME$=MID$(ADDRESS$,10,15):'assign last name
70 and so on .....
```

Tips on Programming Style

By using the following suggestions, you will be able to write programs that won't be described as "Spaghetti Code" or "Chaos".

*   Use meaningful variables.

*   Instead of using "MP" for the amount of monthly pay, simply use "Monthpay".

*   Avoid GOTO statements. Place a REM (') behind it to be safe.

```
10 IF INPUT$="" THEN GOTO 100 'If no input, continue in the next field
```

Use REM (') as often as possible:

```
10 X$=INKEY$:IF X$="" THEN 10 'Check keyboard until a key has been struck
20 IF X$=CHR$(27) THEN CLS:END 'When the <Esc> key is activated, End
```

3. Working with PC-BASIC

3.1 Loading the PC-BASIC Interpreter

You'll need to create a work disk for the work we'll be performing in this book. Besides the interpreter, you'll also save the test programs and files on this disk. We'll also modify the AUTOEXEC.BAT file so that it automatically starts the interpreter. To do this, first format a disk with the MS-DOS command FORMAT.

```
FORMAT A: /S /V
```

Refer to your MS-DOS manual if you're unfamiliar with any of the DOS commands mentioned in this book.

Name the disk PC_BASIC. Once the disk is formatted it will contain the system files and COMMAND.COM (command processor). Since the system files are the "hidden files", don't be alarmed if the DIR command only displays the COMMAND.COM. You'll need the ANSI driver called ANSI.SYS for some tests. You'll also need the configuration file CONFIG.SYS for the configuration. We also need the GWBASIC.EXE interpreter and the line editor EDLIN.COM. Copy these files to our test disk with the COPY command. If you use a keyboard driver, such as KEYBGR.COM, you should also copy this to our test disk. Under certain circumstances some files may be recorded on your system disk under a different name. Obtain the valid names from your user reference manual and convert them as needed.

If it isn't already, the ANSI driver must be included in the CONFIG.SYS file. Call this file with EDLIN and insert the line:

```
device= ansi.sys
```

If your system disk doesn't contain the ANSI.SYS file, omit this change for now and obtain the file from your computer dealer. The tests won't produce the correct results until you have this file.

For foreign keyboard users; some manufacturers don't deliver the keyboard driver as EXE or COM files, so it must be included in the CONFIG.SYS file as a *device*. For more information refer to your DOS user manual.

You should see the following lines in the CONFIG.SYS file:

```
buffers= xx
files= yy
```

13

If you don't see these lines, enter xx=20 and yy=10. This tells the operating system how many disk buffers are needed and how many files can be opened simultaneously. We will discuss this in more detail in Chapter 4. After CONFIG.SYS has been changed and saved, we can create the AUTOEXEC.BAT file by entering the following lines with EDLIN. Don't enter the semicolon or the text shown after it. These are only our comments to explain the data that was entered.

```
1: date          ;input date
2: time          ;input time
3: <name>        ;call Interpreter
```

Note: For <name> input the program name of your interpreter. This can be BASICA, GWBASIC or simply BASIC. As already mentioned, this depends on which name the interpreter has on your system disk. Date and time could be left out, if necessary, but you will not know the last time a file was created or changed.

When the AUTOEXEC.BAT file is saved, we have finished creating our disk. Perform a reset from the keyboard in order to include any changes in the operating system that occurred in the CONFIG.SYS file. To reset from the keyboard, press the key combination <Ctrl><Alt><Del>. This produces the same effect as switching the computer off and on again. You should only do this when the computer is "frozen" and no longer reacts to input from the keyboard.

The interpreter will be loaded after you enter the date and time. You will discover what happens next in the following chapter.

You could also call the interpreter directly from the system disk. Enter:

```
GWBASIC
```

or the name which the interpreter has on your disk. Press the <Return> key.

During the call some parameters can be passed to PC-BASIC. We'll discuss these on the next page. If you cannot remember the rules for the syntax of a command, refer to Section 3.4 of this chapter.

The numeric parameters can be entered as decimal (xx), hexadecimal (&Hxx) or octal (&Oxx).

Calling PC-BASIC

```
"GWBASIC [<filespec>]
[< <STDIN>] [>[>]<STDOUT>]
[/C:<buffer>]
[/D]
[/F:<files>]
[/M:[<address>][<blocks>]]
[/S:<buffer>]
[/I]"
```

Note: The parameters < <STDIN>, >[>] <STDOUT> and /I depend on the implementation and are not available in all versions of PC-BASIC. You may use BASICA instead of GWBASIC.

<filespec>

Use this to automatically execute a specific BASIC program after the interpreter is loaded. If you don't indicate <filespec>, the interpreter loads so you can immediately write or edit a program.

< <STDIN>

After the call of the interpreter, the input is expected from the keyboard as usual. If you indicate a filename for <STDIN>, the input is expected from an ASCII file instead of the keyboard. All key activations that are required for program control must be stored in this file. In this way BASIC programs can be executed, for example, in BATCH files. A complete explanation can be found in the MS-/PC-DOS reference manual under "Input/Output Redirection" or "Redirection".

> [>] <STDOUT>

After the call of the interpreter, the display usually appears on the screen. If you indicate a filename for <STDOUT>, the display is saved in this file in ASCII format. In this way, input masks can be saved for later inclusion in a text file. If you place two angle brackets (>>) before the filename and the file is already in existence, the output is attached to the end of this file.

/C:<buffer>

You can reserve a buffer for the RS232 interface. As a normal value, PC-BASIC uses 256 bytes for the size of the buffer. You can indicate a maximum of 32,767 bytes for the buffer.

/D

With this parameter, PC-BASIC is forced to perform the calculation of specified functions with double precision.

/F:<files>

Determines the maximum number of files which can be accessed at the same time. PC-BASIC requires 4 of these files. With *files= 10* in CONFIG.SYS, only 6 files can be used for your applications.

/M:<address>,<blocks>

PC-BASIC can control one segment (64 Kbytes) with data and stack. If you also need space for assembler routines, *address* must be used to set the highest available memory address which is available to PC-BASIC. Then you can safely save the routines. If you need more than 64 Kbytes for PC-BASIC and routines, you must indicate this with *blocks*. */M:,&H1010* reserves 64 Kbytes for PC-BASIC (1000H=4096*16) and 256 bytes (10H=16*16) for routines. The number of bytes can be calculated with <blocks>*16. If you're working with the SHELL command, it may also be necessary to reserve the required space for the programs to be called with blocks.

/S:<buffer>

When working with random files a buffer is required for transmitting data. PC-BASIC uses 128 bytes as a preset value. You can indicate the size of the buffer as a maximum of 32,767 bytes. A record length which deviates from 128 bytes must be indicated in some versions. Some of the other versions automatically increase the buffer when the program contains the correct statement.

/I

With this switch you reserve the memory space, required for the switch /F and /S, immediately after the call. Without the /I, the memory available for the program and data is divided with the buffers. Sometimes during an access to the data, the "OUT OF MEMORY" error could occur.

Don't worry about entering countless parameters. Since all standard values are selected, PC-BASIC can be called without parameters. You only need to provide parameters when you want or must deviate from the standard settings.

3.2   The PC-BASIC Editor

You'll be in the editor after the call of PC-BASIC. Although the term "editor" isn't really accurate, we use it because you can input, change or delete program lines, similar to a word processor.

A message appears on the screen indicating the version and manufacturer of PC-BASIC. The message should look similar to this:

```
GW-BASIC 2.01
(C) Copyright Microsoft 1984

Genie 16 Personal Computer - PC-BASIC Rev. 2.01
********************************************

61098 Bytes free
Ok
```

The Direct Mode

Since we are now in the *direct mode* of the interpreter, everything we enter as statements will be immediately executed. From this point on, whenever we indicate that you should enter something on your keyboard, you should press the <Return> key at the end of your input.

Enter the following line:

```
PRINT DATE$
```

The current date appears on the screen; the statement PRINT DATE$ was immediately executed. With "O.K.", the interpreter indicates that the statement was executed and additional inputs can be made. Perhaps you even encountered your first SYNTAX ERROR:

```
PRIMT DATE$
SYNTAX ERROR
Ok
```

The interpreter informs you that the input wasn't correct. In this case a "M" was entered instead of a "N". Check your input and try again. Throughout this book you will encounter many other error messages.

Entering a Program Line

Now enter the line:

```
10 PRINT DATE$
```

Although nothing appears on the screen, the line number (10) informs the interpreter that this is a program line and should be assigned to RAM. The interpreter verifies if a line 10 exists in RAM. If so, the interpreter replaces the old line 10 with the new line 10. It stores the lines in the correct sequence in RAM to avoid "overloading" the interpreter during program execution. So, line 10 is stored before line 11 and after line 9.

You now know how the direct mode works. Next we'll discuss how to get into the program mode. We already have entered a one line program. Next enter the following in direct mode:

    CLS

to clear the screen. Now enter:

    RUN

and the current date will be displayed. The program was executed in the program mode.

Use the RUN command to inform the interpreter that you want to execute the program. It begins with the first line of a program and processes all statements in this and all subsequent lines until all the program lines have been executed.

To summarize, each item that has a line number is assigned, by the interpreter, to a program. Everything else is immediately executed.

Note: If you enter an incorrect statement in direct mode, the interpreter immediately detects this as a programming error and displays a corresponding error message. Any errors in program mode are only detected when the program is executed with RUN.

Processing programs

To create complete programs, we'll be entering, changing and deleting program lines using the editor. You just learned how to input a program line. Now enter:

    20 PRINT TIME$

Nothing seems to happen but the line is added to the program. To see it, enter:

    LIST

This command lists every program line, which, in our case here, consists of only lines 10 and 20. The LIST command lists in sequential order the current content of the working memory.

Changing a program line

Changing a line is quite simple. With the cursor keys position the cursor in line 10 on the "D" of DATE$. Press the <Ins> key and enter the following, exactly as shown:

```
"date: ";
```

You must press the <Return> key for the interpreter to accept the change. Press the <Ctrl> and <L> keys simultaneously. The screen is cleared. After entering:

```
LIST
```

you can verify the changes in line 10. You've also just been introduced to the first edit key of the PC-BASIC editor with <Ctrl> <L> keys. This will be discussed in more detail in Section 3.3.

When we made this change, we inserted data in line 10. We could also remove data from a line using the same method. List line 10 again. Position the cursor on the first quotation mark (") and activate the <Del> key. Each time this key is pressed, a character will be deleted from the line. Erase all the characters, including the semicolon and press the <Return> key. Line 10 will return to its original content again.

Erasing Program Lines

To erase an entire line from the program, you don't have to individually delete all characters with the <Del> key. Simply enter the line number:

```
10
```

After a LIST, our program consists of only line 20.

The input line

New program lines or statements must be entered in an empty screen line during direct mode. The BASIC editor is *screen oriented*. This means that the cursor can be moved to any position on the screen. All changes to program lines are accepted where they occur. In the course of this book you'll learn to appreciate the advantages of this because other editors operate *line oriented*. This means that the line to be changed is called and must be entered again with the changes. In order to be compatible with other editors, PC-BASIC provides, with the EDIT command, a variant of this editing capability.

So far you have learned how to input, change and delete a program line. All of these tasks are made easier through the function keys, which we'll discuss in the next section, and special commands for creating a program, which will be presented in Section 3.4.

3.3   The Function and Edit Keys

Depending on which version of PC-BASIC you have, it's possible that the function and edit keys on your computer will produce results different than those described in this book. Any differences that we know of will be indicated. For example, in the section on the edit keys you will find several key combinations that produce the same result. Since some manufacturers may have omitted some features, you'll have to try the examples yourself and see if they work.

The Function Keys

When you call PC-BASIC, besides the system message "Ok", called the *prompt*, the assignment of the function keys is displayed in the 25th line. The function keys are assigned commands for the program input. This makes your work easier when you are programming because the commands can be activated by pressing a single key. For example, the function key <F1> is assigned the LIST command. <F2> immediately executes a program with RUN. <F3> displays "LOAD" on the screen, so you can simply add a program name in order to load a program.

Unfortunately, the key assignment for these keys can differ among computers, so don't be alarmed if you don't receive the same results. If you want to switch off the display, press <Ctrl><T> or enter the following command in direct mode:

```
KEY { ON | OFF }
```

KEY OFF switches the display off and KEY ON switches it on again.

Assigning/Redefining Function Keys

The function keys can be temporarily reassigned with commands or functions you frequently use. Each key can contain a maximum of 15 assigned characters. Control characters, such as the <Return> key, can be included in these 15 characters.

The following example should demonstrate this:

```
KEY 1,"LIST"+CHR$(13)
       │    │        └─> control-character [return-key]
       │    └─> command
       └─> number of the function-key
```

Fig. 4: The Key Command

The previous example assigns the LIST command and the control character for the <Return> key to the function key <F1>. This means the LIST command is immediately executed when you press <F1>. Be careful when using the control characters for the <Return> key. If the cursor is located within the text and you press <F1>, this can lead to unpleasant consequences, such as immediate program execution. You'll find a detailed description of the KEY command in Chapter 4.

The Edit Keys

PC-BASIC provides a series of edit keys that can be used for editing programs. The expression <Cursor> represents one of the cursor control keys. The <Return> key and the <Backspace key> can also be used.

Note: As mentioned in the introduction, different versions may produce different results than the ones shown below.

<Ctrl> <Cursor right>

Moves the cursor to the first word to the right.

<Ctrl> <Cursor left>/<Ctrl> <B>

Moves the cursor to the first word to the left.

<Ctrl> <Home>/<Ctrl> <L>

Clears the screen and moves the cursor to the top left corner.

<End>/<Ctrl> <N>

Moves the cursor to the end of the program line.

<Ctrl> <End>/<Ctrl> <E>

Erases the program line contents located after the cursor.

<Ins>/<Ctrl> <R>

Toggles between insert and overwrite mode. Depending on the version, the cursor changes its appearance to indicate the current condition.

<Del>

Deletes the character located under the cursor. The remainder of the program line contents move to the left.

<Tab>/<Ctrl> <I>

All 8 character tab positions are set in the editor. Use the <Tab> key to move the cursor to the next tab position.

<Backspace>/<Ctrl> <H>

Deletes the character to the left of the cursor.

<Esc>

Deletes the entire line, including line number, where the cursor is currently located and moves the cursor to the beginning of the line.

<Ctrl> <Return>/<Ctrl> <J>

Inserts a blank line in the program line.

<Ctrl> <Z>/<Ctrl> <PgDn>

Clears the screen from the current cursor line down.

<Return>/<Ctrl> <M>

Accepts the program line into the RAM.

<Ctrl> <P>/<Ctrl> <PrtSc>

All input/output entered is immediately directed to the printer. Pressing these keys again turns this mode off.

<Shift> <PrtSc>

Sends current screen display to the printer.

<Ctrl> <X>/<Ctrl> <Cursor up>

The program listing scrolls down.

<Ctrl> <Y>/<Ctrl> <Cursor down>

The program listing scrolls up.

<Ctrl> <T>

The function key display in the 25th line is switched on/off.

<Home>/<Ctrl> <K>

Moves the cursor into the top left corner. The screen isn't cleared.

<Ctrl> <PgDn>

Deletes the program text starting at the cursor position to the next colon (:) or the next space.

<Ctrl> <C>/<Ctrl> <Break>

Terminates the edit mode. Does not save any changes. In the program mode the entire program is terminated and PC-BASIC returns to the direct mode again.

<Ctrl> <NumLock>

Stops the output of a listing on the screen. Press any key to continue listing.

3.4   Syntax

Before we discuss the commands and functions, we'll briefly examine the *writing syntax*, which you may remember from your DOS user manual.

[ ] Square Brackets

The parameters contained in square brackets are optional and do not have to be entered.

< > Angle Brackets

The expression contained in angle brackets must be entered. For example, for <filename> you would enter the name of the file.

{ } Braces

The parameters contained in braces must be entered. For example, in KEY {ONIOFF} you must enter either ON or OFF.

| Vertical Line

Represents *"or"*. You can choose among the parameters. For example, in KEY {ONIOFF} you must enter either ON or OFF.

... Three Dots

Indicate that a parameter or an expression can be repeated as often as necessary.

..... Five Dots

In an example program they indicate that this is a program fragment for illustration purposes and cannot be executed by itself.

Dr:

Any drive. Replace with *A:, B:* etc.

Pathname

Name of the subdirectory you want to address.

File

Represents the first 8 characters of the filename.

.EXT

Represents the last 3 characters (extension) of the filename.

Filename

Consists of the name of the file and .EXT.

Filespec

The filespec(ification) is composed of the Dr: pathname, filename or parts of the named parameters.

3.5 Commands for Program Input

The most important capabilities to continue writing or executing a program is to be able to save a new program or load a program previously saved.

SAVE

```
SAVE <filespec> [,A |,P]
```

We can send the program from RAM to the disk or hard disk with the SAVE command. Besides the file specifications, a parameter to determine how the program should be saved can also be given. PC-BASIC automatically attaches the .BAS extension if you don't attach an extension to the filename.

With the ",A" parameter, the program will be saved as an ASCII file. This is important, for example, for the MERGE command or for later processing with a compiler.

The ",P" parameter causes PC-BASIC to save the program as a protected file. This file cannot be listed or changed after it's loaded (an "Illegal function call" error is displayed on the screen). The protection is achieved through a mark in the file header or through encrypting the entire program according to a certain algorithm. We'll discuss this in Chapter 9.

If you don't provide a parameter, or the ",P" parameter, the program is saved in compressed form. This means that every command and every function is saved as a *token*. For example, a number that represents PRINT is saved instead of the word "PRINT". The program is also saved in this form in the RAM. By using the LIST command, these numbers are replaced with the proper text again. This saves space in the RAM and on the disk.

LOAD

```
LOAD <filespec> [,R]
```

The LOAD command reads the program from the disk into RAM. This command deletes the program that is currently in memory so save the current program before using LOAD. Files which are still open will be closed by LOAD. If you don't indicate an extension in the filename, LOAD automatically adds .BAS.

The program can automatically execute using the [,R] parameter after loading. You can also use the RUN command to perform automatic execution. The [,R] parameter does not close open data files.

RUN

```
RUN <filespec> [,R]
```

The program currently in memory is deleted and all open files are closed. If you indicate the ",R" parameter, the files remain open and can be immediately used by the newly loaded program.

Program Input

Besides the function and edit keys, PC-BASIC offers a series of commands which make program input easier. These commands can be used in the direct mode and (if it makes sense) in the program mode. At this point, we are interested in the commands which we can use in the direct mode to make our work easier.

Modifying RAM

NEW

```
NEW
```

This command must be used before entering a new program. NEW erases a program which is currently in memory and resets all internal pointers and temporary storage areas of PC-BASIC. Before using NEW, use the SAVE command to save the previous program if you need to. Otherwise that program will be lost.

Note: If you were working on a program and forgot to use NEW before entering a new program, the recently entered program lines are added to the existing program. The existing lines are replaced with new ones that contain the same line number. This creates a "program salad" of old and new lines. After using NEW, always use LIST to ensure that program lines no longer remain in RAM.

CLEAR

```
CLEAR[,<address>][,<Stack>]
```

CLEAR erases all internal pointers, intermediate memory, variables and definitions. Also, with <address> the highest memory address available to PC-BASIC can be determined. This address can only be changed through another call of PC-BASIC. With <stack>, the area for the stack (see Section 3.65) can be determined. The indication is in bytes. Unlike using NEW, the program in memory isn't deleted.

AUTO

```
AUTO [<line-number>][,<increment>]
```

There is a method of avoiding the need to enter the line number for each line. PC-BASIC will perform this task for you with the AUTO command. Suppose that the program to be entered starts with line 10 and is programmed in increments of 10 steps. With the input:

```
AUTO 10,10
```

PC-BASIC provides the correct line numbers, you only have to enter the program text. For line number, indicate the line from which increments should be automatically made. With increment, indicate the distance between the lines. If you omit the line number, PC-BASIC assumes line 0 is the first line number. When you omit increment, PC-BASIC assumes the value 10 as increment. An omitted parameter should be marked with a comma (,). You can indicate the last line to be processed with a period (.) as a parameter. AUTO is disabled when you press <Ctrl><Break>.

For example:

AUTO ,20
Proceeds from line 0 in steps of 20: 0,20,40,60,80 etc.

AUTO 100,
Proceeds from line 100 in steps of 10: 100,110,120,130,140 etc.

AUTO .,10
Proceeds from the last line processed in steps of 10: 25,35,45,55 etc.

PC-BASIC places an asterisk (*) behind the indicated line number if that line already exists in the program. With <Return>, you leave the line unchanged and PC-BASIC proceeds to the next line. The input of program text overwrites the existing line.

RENUM

```
RENUM [<New_line-number>] [,<Old_line-number>] [,<increment>]
```

With this command you can reorganize your program or make room for a new group of lines. As you add lines to your program, you'll frequently need to insert or delete lines. So, the line numbering could be as follows: 10,11,16,21 etc.

27

Enter the following program for a small test of the RENUM command and save it under the name RENUM.TST:

```
10 'RENUM-Test
20:
30 CLS
40 INPUT "Your name: ";INAME$
42 PRINT "Your name is: ";INAME$
55 INPUT "Your age: ";AGE$
63 PRINT "Your age is: ";AGE$
```

Before the following exercises, you'll need to load RENUM.TST before each RENUM command example; otherwise the line numbers cannot be found:

RENUM

Without parameter, the program is renumbered, starting at line 10, in steps of 10.

RENUM 50,42,10

The lines 42 to 63 are renumbered in steps of 10 after line 50.

RENUM 100,10,20

The entire program is renumbered, after line 10 in steps of 20, with the new line number 100.

Use the LIST command to see the results for each example. Also, the omitted parameter can be marked with the comma (,), or the current line indicated with the period (.). Now try some of your own exercises. If you indicate the wrong line sequence, PC-BASIC will inform you with the message, "Illegal Function Call".

DELETE

```
DELETE [<from_line>]-[<to_line>]
```

Deleting individual program lines has already been discussed. To delete several lines (line areas), use the DELETE command. DELETE erases all lines including <from_line> and <to_line>. For example:

DELETE 20-50

Deletes all lines beginning with line 20 and ending with line 50 inclusive.

DELETE -100

Deletes every line to 100 inclusive.

DELETE 100-

Deletes lines starting with line 100 through to the end of the program.

DELETE 125

Deletes only line 125.

PC-BASIC always returns to the direct mode after the DELETE command. DELETE also accepts the period (.) as a parameter for the line last processed. A wrongly defined line area or unavailable lines cause either the error message "Illegal Function Call" or "Undefined line number".

Note: In some versions, DELETE without a parameter erases the entire program without confirmation check. Therefore, be careful when using DELETE without parameters.

LIST

```
[L]LIST [<from_line>]-[<to_line>]
```

With the LIST command we can output lines or line areas on the screen. The line areas are defined exactly as in the DELETE command. Even the use of the period (.) to list the last processed line is possible.

Unfortunately, PC-BASIC doesn't offer editing in a program like a word processor. However, a lot can be done with line oriented scrolling by using the edit keys <Ctrl> <Cursor Up/Down> or <Ctrl> <X/Y>. If it's difficult to read the listing for a large program, perhaps the following suggestion can help. Save the program with the ",A" parameter as an ASCII file. Then leave the interpreter and load the program into your word processor. Here you can page through it and make any necessary changes. For example:

LIST 100-150

Lists the lines 100 to 150.

LIST .

Lists the last line processed. A line is also considered the last processed line if an error is detected by the program. The line containing the error is immediately displayed for you to correct the error(s).

LIST -120

Lists from the program start to and including line 120.

LIST 500-

Lists from line 500 to the end of the program.

LLIST

Lists to printer.

Press <Ctrl><NumLock> to temporarily stop the program listing. The listing continues by pressing any key (we recommend simultaneously holding down <Ctrl> with the left hand and then alternately pressing the <NumLock> and <Backspace> keys).

RUN and GOTO

```
RUN [<line-number>]
```

or

```
GOTO <line-number>
```

Sometimes, especially if you write large programs, you may want to test only certain portions of these programs. This can be done with the RUN command and a line number. PC-BASIC executes the program starting at that line number. Remember that variables defined before a line number are meaningless, since RUN ignores the contents of all variables. Insert a STOP after the variable definition (this is described shortly) if you need the variables for this program portion. Then use the GOTO command, instead of the RUN command, with the appropriate line number.

Any files which may be open are closed by RUN. For the RUN command you can use the period (.) for the last processed line. For example:

RUN 50

Executes the program in memory starting at line 50. All variable content is erased.

GOTO 100

Executes the program in memory starting at line 100. The variables retain their assigned values.

If a nonexistent line is indicated as a line number, PC-BASIC sends either the message "Undefined line number" or "Illegal Function Call".

FILES

```
FILES [<dr:>] [<Path-Name>] [<file-name> | <Mask>]
```

Obviously you cannot remember all the file and program names on your disks. Use the FILES command to check the program names. This command displays the filenames in the form of DIR/W command. In the mask you can indicate, as in DOS, the wildcards * and ? with filenames and/or extensions. This command can also be used in the program mode.

However, it isn't possible to print out the list either in the program or the direct mode. The screen may be scrolled up with disks containing several small programs. In Chapter 8 you'll find a user-friendly program that replaces the FILE command. For example:

FILES "A:"

Displays all files from the disk in drive A.

FILES ".BAS"*

Displays all files with the extension *.BAS* on the disk in the active drive.

FRE

```
FRE(0) or FRE("")
```

As your program listing grows, you'll need to check the amount of free memory available with the PRINT FRE(0) statement. After the call, depending on the PC-BASIC version and installed RAM, between 30 Kbytes and 62 Kbytes will be available. PC-BASIC performs a "garbage collection" to clean out the memory before it displays the available memory. All variable content, which is no longer required, is released for program text or new variables. Depending on the variables in your program, this process may take a few seconds. Some computer experts can tie up a computer for several minutes by using innumerable variables and comprehensive string processing. So don't be surprised if your computer freezes for awhile.

You can minimize the time "garbage collection" requires with a frequent call of the X=FRE("") statement. To help avoid error 14, "Out of string space", and error 7, "Out of Memory" insert the X=FRE("") statement at a specific location in your program (i.e., a frequently called subroutine).

SYSTEM

```
SYSTEM
```

Use the SYSTEM command to return to MS-DOS after completing your programming work. This returns you to the COMMAND.COM command processor.

Remember that programs must be saved with SAVE in order to be executed or revised at a later time because all open files are closed before the return to DOS. Your program is lost as soon as you leave the interpreter. The only way to retrieve it is with LOAD.

Note: You should always use the END command instead of SYSTEM in the test phase of a program. If you use SYSTEM in the program mode, it terminates both the program and the interpreter.

END

```
END
```

The program is terminated as soon as PC-BASIC encounters the END command in a program. PC-BASIC returns to the direct mode and displays the "Ok" prompt and the program remains unchanged in memory. Don't forget to input the NEW command before entering a new program.

The program is automatically terminated when there isn't an additional line available following the current line. Although this practice is often used to end a program, a properly written program should always include an END command to make the structure clearer.

STOP

```
STOP
```

This command was already mentioned during our discussion of the RUN/GOTO command. It causes an interruption in the execution of a program. PC-BASIC displays the following message during the STOP command:

```
BREAK IN <line-number>
```

Since you can set several STOP commands, PC-BASIC indicates the line number where STOP was executed. You can, as described with the RUN/GOTO command, test a subroutine or view variable content with the PRINT command. By using several STOP commands with the CONT command (see below), a program can be executed in steps in order to check variable content during the STOP or analyze program reactions. Many computer experts discuss a "trap" or "breakpoint" when using the STOP command. Unfortunately, PC-BASIC doesn't offer a DUMP command that displays all variable contents. The contents must be selected with PRINT, which is a tedious job when many variables are involved.

It's helpful to access a subroutine with a GOTO command. This subroutine should use a high line number, for example 50000, so it can't interfere with the main portion of your program; otherwise the call must be changed. The subroutine outputs all variable content with PRINT and ends with a STOP:

```
50000 '----- DUMP-Subroutine -----
50010 :
50020 CLS:KEY OFF
50030 PRINT <Variable>:GOSUB 55000
50040 PRINT <Variable>:GOSUB 55000
50050 PRINT <Variable>:GOSUB 55000
50060 PRINT <Variable>:GOSUB 55000
```

```
50070 PRINT <Variable>:GOSUB 55000
50080 FOR DUMP= 1 TO 50
50090   PRINT <ARRAY(DUMP)>
50100   IF CSRLIN>= 20 THEN GOSUB 55000:CLS
50110 NEXT DUMP
... etc.
55000 '----- Wait for any key -----
55010 :
55020 IF CSRLIN < 24 THEN RETURN
55030 IF INKEY$="" THEN 55030 ELSE RETURN
```

This routine must be modified each time you use a new variable or a new array. In the program, place a GOTO 50000 at the correct place and the DUMP is ready.

CONT

CONT

This command continues program execution after a STOP was executed. As previously described, several STOP commands can be set to check the variables and continue the program with CONT.

The CONT command is useless if you're using a subroutine for the output of the variable content because there are no program lines following the STOP command. A subroutine, which is accessed with GOSUB before every STOP, can be used in this situation. After it completes its task, it ends with a RETURN and then encounters the STOP.

Remember that the CONT command cannot be used after the change of a line because the line address may have changed. PC-BASIC informs you of this with the message "Can't continue".

MERGE

MERGE <filespec>

You'll find, as you work with PC-BASIC and create larger programs, that certain subroutines are the same or at least similar in all programs. For example, subroutines for keyboard queries and printer output would be similar in different programs. Therefore, you should enter these routines only once and add them in various programs. The MERGE command enables you to do this.

Note: The <filespec> must be a BASIC program in ASCII format. To create such a file, use the SAVE command with the [,A] parameter. If you attempt to "merge" a file that wasn't saved with the [,A] parameter, PC-BASIC notifies you with the message "Bad File Mode".

Enter the following two programs and save them under the name indicated in the first line with the [,A] parameter.

```
10 'MERGE_1.TST
20 :
30 CLS
40 PRINT "This is the first program"
50 PRINT "for the MERGE-Test"
60 PRINT


100 'MERGE_2.TST
110 :
120 PRINT "This is the second program"
130 PRINT "for the MERGE-Test"
140 PRINT
150 PRINT "That's how simple it is....."
```

Remember to enter the line numbers as they are shown. After saving both programs, use NEW to clear the memory. Then use LOAD to load the first program and examine it with LIST. With the following input:

```
MERGE "MERGE_2.TST"
```

we can attach the second program to the first. Use LIST to see the results. As you can see, the complete program now consists of the two connected single programs. With the RUN command we can see that this creates an executable program.

For the next exercise clear the memory again with NEW command, load the first program with LOAD and enter:

```
RENUM 105,10,10
```

The LIST command shows that the line numbers are now 105, 115, 125, 135, 145 and 155. Use the same MERGE command as in the previous exercise to combine the programs again and then use LIST to see the results. You can imagine what happened! For that reason you must be careful to use different line numbers in the second program.

Use NEW to clear the memory and use LOAD to load the first program. Using the RENUM command:

```
RENUM 100,10,10
```

we now have the necessary format. Now you can use the MERGE command to add the second program safely. Check the results by using LIST.

Remember that for identical line numbers, the line in memory is replaced with the "merged" line. Otherwise, the "merged" line is inserted into the correct sequence. MERGE closes all files which may still be open.

REM

```
REM or '
```

You may have noticed the ' character in previous examples. This character allows you to place a remark (REMark), or a comment, in a program line. Either the ' character or REM must appear before the remark. Anything that follows the REM, including statements and commands, are considered by PC-BASIC as a remark. For example:

```
10 CLS:KEY OFF 'clear display screen, keys off
20 PRINT "Bomanns is ": 'what ?: PRINT "..."
```

In line 20 only the first "PRINT" is executed; the "PRINT" following the REM or the ' character isn't executed.

In Chapter 2 we learned that the colon can be used not only to separate statements but also as the only character in a line. A REM statement or the ' character significantly improves the structure and appearance of a program:

```
10 CLS:KEY OFF
20 .....
30 .....
40 GOSUB 1010 'keyboard-query
50 .....
60 .....
1000 :
1001 '----- keyboard-query -----
1002 :
1010 X$= INKEY$:IF X$="" THEN 1010
1020 RETURN
```

A subroutine and REM statement are identified quicker in the listing when they're between lines containing a colon. It's a matter of personal preference to use either a colon or the ' character.

EDIT

```
EDIT [<line-number>] [.]
```

We've already discovered that PC-BASIC operates in screen orientation. In simple terms this means that PC-BASIC has the EDIT command. With EDIT, the desired line is displayed on the screen and can be changed. EDIT also accepts the period (.) as a parameter for the last line processed or the current error line. EDIT clears all variable content. If necessary, check the variables before using the command.

TRON and TROFF

```
TRON
TROFF
```

You'll need the TRON/TROFF command to test complex program executions. TRON switches TRACE (program testing) on and TROFF turns it off. During the program execution, the line number of the currently executing line is displayed. However, in some cases, TRACE cannot be used because the display of the line numbers fills the screen. The screen display becomes disorganized after a short time and input tests from the display memory (see SCREEN command, Chapter 4) are no longer possible.

Disk Operations

After the call of PC-BASIC, all disk accesses are made to the current drive or the current subdirectory.

If, for example, you started the interpreter from the hard disk "C:" in the subdirectory "BASIC", all programs are loaded and started from that point. The input:

```
SAVE "TEST"
```

saves the program on the hard disk "C:" in subdirectory "BASIC". If you want to load or save a program from another drive or directory, enter this directly in the name. Using the example of hard disk "C:" and directory "BASIC", suppose that you want to store the program on drive "A:" in the directory "OLD_PRG". This requires the following input:

```
SAVE "A:\OLD_PRG\TEST"
```

PC-BASIC automatically attaches the .BAS extension.

If you want to permanently change the drive or subdirectory, PC-BASIC also offers appropriate commands. Refer to Chapter 7 for a list and explanations of these commands.

Use the <Alt> key shortcuts

At some time you may write programs with 100 or more lines. When this happens you'll find that continually entering the same commands or the same functions is a nuisance. So that you can concentrate on the essentials of your program, PC-BASIC has shortcut keys for the most important commands and functions that you're likely to use. For example, hold down the <Alt> key and press the <D> key. The DELETE command appears on the screen. In the Appendix you'll find commands and functions that can be entered this way. Remember there may be some differences in the version you're using.

3.6   PC-BASIC Variables

During program execution, values and text are stored in variables for additional processing. We assume that you're familiar with variables and why they're significant. In this section we'll concentrate on describing the different variable types. PC-BASIC provides variables for storing numeric and alphanumeric data.

Numeric variable

Numbers used for calculations. For example:

```
12.80
```

represents a numeric variable consisting of numeric data.

Alphanumeric variable

Alphanumeric data can consist of the complete character set and usually is enclosed in quote marks (""). This data is also called *character strings* or *strings*. For example:

```
"Good Morning, the price is $56.99"
```

represents a character string of alphanumeric data.

There are several ways to assign a value to variables:

1.   Assigning variables is accomplished using the LET command. For example:

```
LET INAME$="Hugo"

LET NUMBER%=15.
```

However, you can omit LET since the equal sign already informs PC-BASIC what to do. Therefore, INAME$="Hugo" or NUMBER%=15 is also permissible.

2.   You can also read in values from the keyboard. This is done while operating inside the program with variable data. Details of this method are in Chapter 4.

3.   It's also possible to read the values from a file. Since all data in RAM disappears when the computer is switched off, you'll need to save your data in files on the disk or hard disk for permanent storage. We'll explain this in Chapter 4.

Variable Names

In order to store data or to process the data stored in them, variables must be addressed from the program. Therefore, the variables can have a name using A-Z or 0-9 or combinations up to 40 characters. The first character, however, must be a letter:

```
Right:              Wrong:           Reason the variable is incorrect:

NAME1$              1NAME$           the name starts with the number "1"
ADDRESS2$           ADDRESS_2$       the name uses the character "_"
```

Use a period (.) as a separator in variable names instead of the "_" character:

```
PAY.HOUR%
PAY.WEEK%
PAY.MONTH%
PAY.YEAR%
```

This makes identifying variables, especially in larger programs, much easier.

Remember that keywords cannot be used as variable names. PC-BASIC would try to interpret this as a command or function. For example, the variable "POS$" produces a syntax error because POS is a function.

3.6.1 Character String Variables (Strings)

Since character strings are often called strings, we can use the term *string variables* when we are referring to variables that can store an individual character or character strings.

String variables are declared with a dollar sign ($), called the type-declaration character, at the end of the name. For example, the INAME$ variable is a string variable. If we tried to assign a numeric value to this variable, such as (INAME$=12.80), PC-BASIC responds with a "Type mismatch" error message. The assignment INAME$="12.80", however, prevents an error message since quotation marks (") can be assigned to a character string.

A string variable can be empty (i.e., INAME$=""), a single character (INAME$="A") or an entire sentence (INAME$="Today the weather is especially nice"). Spaces are considered characters. A string variable can accept a maximum of 255 characters. The error message "String too long" appears when the string variable exceeds this limit.

3.6.2 Numeric Variables

Integer Variables

Integer variables can accept whole numbers between -32,768 and +32,767. These variables are declared with a percent character (%). So, the NUMBER% variable is an integer variable. If we make an incorrect assignment, PC-BASIC sends a "Type mismatch" error message. If we assign a fractional value, such as NUMBER%=12.80, to an integer variable, PC-BASIC rounds this value to NUMBER%=13. Use floating-point variables if you need to use fractions.

If you need to work outside the range of the regular integer variables, use a long integer variable for whole numbers between -2,147,483,648 and 2,147,483,647. These variables are declared with an ampersand character (&) at the end of the name. For example, GAMEATTENDANCE&=45,000.

Floating-point Variables

You can use two types of floating-point variables. The first are single-precision variables. They can be assigned any value between -1.701412E38 and +1.701412E38. These variables are declared with an exclamation mark (!) at the end of the name. If you attempt to assign a string, the message "Type mismatch" is displayed. Otherwise, the values listed above present no problems.

The second type of floating-point variables are double-precision variables. These variables can have a value between -1.701411834604692E38 and +1.701411834604692E38. They're declared by the number character (#) at the end of the name. These variables have the same assignment requirements as the single precision variables.

General Comments on Variables

If the symbols mentioned above (%, # and !) are used for the numeric variables, they will be treated by PC-BASIC as single precision variables. During the value assignment, the value can be indicated in decimal (xxxx), hexadecimal (&Hxxxx) or octal (&Oxxxx). Integer variables are stored in 2 bytes. Single precision variables are stored in 4 bytes and double precision variables in 8 bytes. For faster comparisons and access, variable names are stored by their first two letters followed by a byte containing the number of characters to follow. You should be certain that the first two letters are different when selecting a name.

Global Type Definition

PC-BASIC is capable of making type definitions global. This means they're made valid for the entire program. This can be done in any desired location, at the beginning or during the course of the program. All variables without a *type designation* will be defined.

DEFINT A-D

Defines all variables with letters beginning from A to D as integer variables.

DEFSNG H-L

Defines all variables with letters beginning from H and L as single precision variables.

DEFDBL A-Z

Defines all variables of the program as double precision variables.

DEFSTR B-D

Defines all variables with letters beginning from B and D as string variables.

If the variables were already defined with a DEF, this takes precedence over the global definition. This can lead to errors in recognizing the variable. So, be careful in using DEF statements.

SWAP

In some applications, for example sort routines, variable contents must be swapped. To simplify this process, PC-BASIC provides the SWAP command:

```
SWAP <Variable 1>,<Variable 2>
```

This command exchanges the contents of the variables 1 and 2. The variables must be the same type. So, the swap between a single precision variable and an integer variable isn't possible. If you tried it anyway, the familiar message, "Type mismatch" appears. The SWAP command can also be used with arrays.

3.6.3 Matrix Variables (Arrays)

Besides the previously mentioned variable types there are also the matrix variables. These variables are also known as matrixes, fields and dimensional variables. Although each of these terms is acceptable, to use each in a book is confusing. Therefore, we'll use *arrays*, which is the term used in most programming languages. Data can be stored multidimensionally (i.e., indexed) in arrays. These arrays consist of one of the described variable types. The name can be selected according to the description in Section 3.6.

Until now we have dealt with variables which can store a single value:

```
STREET$="61000"
INAME$="Hugo"
NUMBER%= 12
```

These variables are also designated as *simple variables*. An array, however, is a variable which is composed of several single variables of the same type. For this reason we also call them *dimensional variables*. We can compare this with a drawer that is subdivided into several compartments. Each compartment has a number and the drawer has a name. If we indicate the name and the number, we can get data from the compartment or store it there. The name of an array doesn't differ from the name of a normal variable. The number of the compartment which we want to access depends on the structure of the array. This is called *indexing*. First let's examine a one-dimensional array in which we can store 7 values. DAY$(<number>) appears as follows:

1	2	3	4	5	6	7

Fig. 5: 1-D-Array

The individual "compartments" can be indexed with their number:

```
DAY$(1)="Monday":DAY$(7)="Sunday"
```

As you can see, this array starts with compartment 1. From now on we shall call these compartments by their correct name, *element*. The array starts with element number 1. This means that the indexing starts with 1.

OPTION BASE

Depending on the requirements, the lower limits for the start of the indexing of the arrays used in a program can be changed:

```
OPTION BASE 0 | 1
```

This command helps us determine whether our arrays should start with element 0 or 1. For PC-BASIC this means that memory space must be reserved. You'll save space by starting the indexing with 1. For example, let's assume we have created an array for the name of a month. Since a month 0 doesn't exist, we can determine that the indexing should begin with 1 by using OPTION BASE. Remember that the lower limit, which is set with OPTION BASE, is valid for all arrays of the program. If you set indexing to begin with 1 and attempt to address element 0, PC-BASIC displays the message, "Subscript out of range".

Multi-Dimensional Arrays

You can define arrays with a maximum of 255 dimensions using PC-BASIC. We'll concentrate on two dimensional arrays since they're used in 99% of all applications. Think of two dimensional arrays as a table. The indexing occurs through the line and the column of the table. A two dimensional array for storing addresses could appear as follows:

```
ADDRESS$(<line>,<column>)
```

	1	2	3	4	5	6
1	Name	First Name	Street	Cty	St	Phone
2						
3						
4						
5						
6						
7						

Fig. 6: 2-D Array

The following indicates the street of the 5 address:

```
PRINT ADDRESS$(5,3)
```

The 5 refers to the 5th line in the table and the 3 to the 3rd column in this line. The assignment of a value is:

```
ADDRESS$(5,3)="15 Main Street"
```

DIM

If an array doesn't contain more than 10 elements per dimension, PC-BASIC automatically reserves memory space. Since we need more than 10 elements (lines) for our address control, we must inform PC-BASIC to reserve the correct amount of space:

```
DIM ADDRESS$(<lines>,<columns>)
```

For our example, the assignment would be DIM ADDRESS$(50,6). In this array we can now store 50 addresses having a maximum of 6 elements.

As already mentioned, an array can have a maximum of 255 dimensions. The indexing is limited to a maximum of 32,767. An attempt to create an array larger than the available memory space produces the error message "Out of Memory".

If you attempt to address an element which is outside the borders, which were set with DIM, the "Subscript out of range" message will appear. The DIM command can only be used once with each array. The message "Duplicate definition" indicates any additional attempts.

Arrays with differing dimensions cannot have the same name. For example, X(4) prevents the use of X(7,8). The DIM command must be executed before the first access to the array. An organized programmer always places all DIM statements at the beginning of the program. Several arrays can be defined with one DIM command:

```
20 DIM ADDRESS$(50,6), INAME$(50,2), TABLE%(20,40)
```

After DIM, all elements of the numeric arrays have the value 0 and all elements of a string array have the value empty string ("").

ERASE

In certain applications, arrays are required only temporarily (i.e., to sort data). To release the memory that was reserved, with DIM, for an array, use the ERASE command:

```
ERASE<ARRAY-name...>
```

The array name is indicated without parentheses. ERASE can clear several arrays at once:

```
ERASE ADDRESS$,INAME$,TABLE%
```

ERASE also clears arrays which were automatically dimensioned (elements smaller than 11).

The ERASE command can also be used to change the size of arrays in the program:

```
100 DIM ADDRESS$(50,6)
.....
.....
240 ERASE ADDRESS$
250 DIM ADDRESS$(100,6)
```

Remember that DIM assigns the empty string ("") to the elements of the array. Before an access, a new assignment may be required, depending on the circumstances.

READ...DATA

In application programs, arrays receive data from a file, through the keyboard or from the program itself. The first two cases will be illustrated later with an example. At the moment we're interested in the third case: arrays to which we assign constant data directly from the program.

Suppose that the date is entered in the format 3-22-86 and you want to replace "03" with "March". With our current knowledge of arrays, the implementation appears as follows:

```
10 DIM MONTH$(12)
20 MONTH$(1)="January":MONTH$(2)="February"
30 MONTH$(3)="March" 'and so on .....
.....
.....
110 MONTH%=VAL(MID$(DATE$,3,2))
120 PRINT MONTH$(MONTH%)
```

Unfortunately, this solution requires a line for each month. However, it's possible to make the input mask more user-friendly by using DATA statements. The following solution is more efficient and saves you from extra typing:

```
10 DIM MONTH$(12)
20 RESTORE 60
30 FOR I=1 TO 12
40    READ MONTH$(I)
50 NEXT I
60 DATA "January","February","March","April","May","June"
70 DATA "July","August","September","October"
80 DATA "November","December"
```

In the above example we constructed a table, or list, inside the program which contains our constants. This data is identified through the preceding DATA. Because of this, PC-BASIC knows that the program line, at least to the next colon (:), contains data and no statements that can be interpreted. This data can be read with READ into an array. We do this with a loop corresponding to the size of the data to be read. For each element of the array we must have data, which is separated by commas (,), available with DATA. For string constants the text is enclosed in quotation marks ("). Numeric data is separated with commas. You can also write the string constants without quotation marks providing the program doesn't have to consider spaces. We recommend, for reasons of clarity, enclosing everything in quotation marks that is assigned to a string variable or a string array.

PC-BASIC internally administers a *data pointer* which is used for READ. This data pointer is reset at the start of the program. During the first READ command, this pointer is set to the first value after the first DATA in the program. With every READ, it's set to the next value. This occurs until the entire loop is completed. The data pointer remains behind the last value it read. During the next READ, PC-BASIC searches the program for the next DATA and sets the pointer to the first value.

Several arrays can be supplied with data through one READ command. Now we continue with the example of the input mask:

```
10 DIM YOURNAME$(6),FPOS%(6,2),FTYP$(6)
20 RESTORE 60
30 FOR I= 1 TO 6
40  READ YOURNAME$(I),FPOS%(I,1),FPOS%(I,2),FTYP$(I)
50 NEXT I
60 DATA "Name",5,5,"A","First-Name",6,5,"A"
70 DATA "Street",7,5,"A","CITY",8,5,"N"
80 and so on .....
```

FNAME$ contains the name of the field, FPOS% contains the line/column position of the field on the screen and FTYP$ provides information about the input. The input is alphanumeric "A" or numeric "N". Remember that in the data lines the values correspond to the variable types to prevent the message "Type mismatch".

The READ command doesn't necessarily have to be used in a loop:

```
10 READ FTYP$(1),FTYP$(2),FTYP$(3),FTYP$(4)
20 DATA "A","A","A","N"
```

If you provide less values in the data lines than the READ loop should read, PC-BASIC sends an "Out of data" message. If you provide more values, this isn't a big problem but, during the next READ, you'll be reading the wrong data.

You can attach additional statements to a data line with a colon (:) as a separator. However, you should avoid this since there is usually only data in a data line. During a quick scan of the program, there would probably be no one that would look at the end or the middle of a line.

RESTORE

If you use several READ...DATA commands in one program, it may be necessary to manipulate the data pointer. Perhaps you've created a table, which should be read into various arrays. After the first READ loop, the data pointer stands behind the last value read. Under some circumstances it must be set again to the beginning of the table. This can be accomplished with the RESTORE command:

```
RESTORE [<line-number>]
```

PC-BASIC sets the data pointer to the first value after the indicated line number in DATA. If a line number was omitted, PC-BASIC sets the data pointer to the first value after the first DATA in the program.

The RESTORE command enables you to read data from an entire table or after a certain line number. Be sure that the loop is changed when data is read from the middle of a table. This normally fills the entire array.

The data pointer is always set, with RESTORE, to the first value after the DATA. Use an empty READ if you need a value from the data line from another position:

```
10 FOR I=1 TO 5
20    READ X$
30 NEXT I
40 FOR I=1 TO 3
50    READ TEXT$(I)
60 NEXT I
70 DATA "x", "x", "x", "x" ,"x", "Text", "Text", "Text"
```

3.6.4 System Variables

PC-BASIC automatically defines some variables and functions which are reserved for certain data and which you can only slightly modify. Usually these variables serve the programmer as a source of information about the condition of the program or the program execution. In the following section we will briefly look at the names and significance of these variables. An exact explanation can be found in the descriptions of the task areas.

ERR

In this integer variable an error is recorded which occurred during the execution of a program (see Section 4.8.1).

ERL

This integer variable contains the line number of the error recorded in ERR (see Section 4.8.1).

DATE$

The date maintained by the PC is stored here (see Section 4.2.3).

TIME$

The time maintained by the PC is stored here (see Section 4.2.3).

3.6.5 The Stack

The *stack* is also a system variable of PC-BASIC. Data is temporarily stored in this variable. PC-BASIC automatically erases data it no longer requires.

For example, consider the call of a command. We have learned that, during the call, parameters must be passed. These parameters don't have to be stored permanently since they aren't needed after the command is executed. In other words, since they're only temporarily required, they're only temporarily stored.

PC-BASIC is organized in such a way that all parameters of a command or a function are passed to the stack. If you execute the command:

```
PRINT "Today's date is: ";DATE$
```

the parameters:

```
"Today's date is: "
```

and

```
DATE$
```

are stored on the stack. Then the routine for the PRINT command is called. This routine "looks" on the stack and knows, from the parameters stored there, what it has to do.

After completing its assignment, the PRINT routine erases the parameters which were passed from the stack. The stack is also used for many other purposes besides storing the passed parameters. We shall discuss these purposes in more detail in the next chapter.

So far, with only a few exceptions, we've discussed theories. Now we'll try some actual programming.

4. BASIC Statements, Commands and Functions

In this chapter we'll discuss the commands, statements, and functions that are needed for writing simple PC-BASIC programs. We've included these commands, statements and functions in several small programs which you can quickly enter, edit and execute.

Note: You may not yet be familiar with some of the commands, statements and functions that are used in the individual programs. Unfortunately, this is unavoidable because sometimes a program must use commands and functions that are discussed in other parts of the book. To find more information about a commands, statements and functions refer to the index, which will direct you to the proper chapter/section.

4.1 Screen Input/Output

Besides the keyboard, the most important communication tool for the user is the screen. Here the user can see what data has been entered and can obtain the desired results from queries, calculations and files. PC-BASIC offers many valuable commands, statements and functions for the screen input/output. In the following pages we'll discuss these commands, statements and functions.

Note: Remember that constants, function results or the contents of other variables can be used for the indicated parameter.

4.1.1 Screen Construction

In this section we're only interested in the text mode. This is the mode in which the complete ASCII character set can be displayed by the computer.

The ASCII character set

As you probably know, the keys on a typewriter's keyboard are always arranged in the same order. Therefore, you can use any typewriter regardless of the manufacturer because the keys are arranged in the same order. This is known as *standardization*.

This also applies to the character set of the PC. As you know, personal computers are designed by many different manufacturers. If these manufacturers didn't use a standardized character set, it's possible that the <A> key would produce an "A" on one computer and a "T" on another. Then it would be impossible to exchange programs or data. The ASCII character set represents the standard all PC manufacturers follow. ASCII is an acronym for the **A**merican **S**tandard **C**ode for **I**nformation **I**nterchange".

We'll now return to the text mode. Since this mode is usually separate from the installed video card, the program that you have developed will execute on (almost) all other PCs, without requiring any changes.

There is a difference between color and monochrome video cards. As its name implies, characters are displayed in various colors with a *color card*. These colors include, for example, red, green, blue or yellow. However, these characters contain *attributes* with a *monochrome card* instead of colors. This means that they can be displayed as normal, bold or underlined. If you developed a program on a PC with a color video card, you could display the text in blue. If this program is executed on a PC with a monochrome video card, instead of being displayed in blue, the character would be displayed in an attribute that corresponds to this color. In this case, this would be the underlined attribute.

A program which looks fine on one PC may look scrambled and disorganized on another because of the different representation. However, since there is a series of colors and attributes which can be used in either a color or monochrome card, the program can be used either way. We'll provide details on this when we discuss the commands/functions that are used for colors and attributes. The following program provides an overview of the characters that can be displayed by a PC.

```
10 'Character-Demo
20 :
30 CLS
40 FOR I=33 to 255
50 PRINT CHR$(I);" ";
60 NEXT I
```

As you can see, besides letters, numbers and other characters found on a typewriter, some interesting graphic characters can also be displayed. These enable you to construct interesting things, such as templates. There will be more information on this subject in Chapter 10.

How many characters per line?

The command:

```
WIDTH 40 | 80
```

determines how many characters should be displayed per line. After being switched on usually your computer is in the 80 character/25 lines mode. This means that 80 characters are displayed in each line and 25 lines are displayed on the screen. In the direct mode enter:

```
PRINT 80*25
```

The result (2000) shows the number of characters required to fill the screen. If you have problems reading the screen display, switch to the second display mode. This mode displays the characters twice as wide. However, you're only able to see 40 characters in one line but the 25 lines remain.

Enter:

```
WIDTH 40
```

to call the 40 character mode. Then query the computer for the number of characters that can be displayed:

```
PRINT 40*25.
```

Additional mathematical functions and calculations will be discussed later. The 80 character mode is set by entering:

```
WIDTH 80
```

You've probably also noticed that the WIDTH statement also clears the screen.

Note: If the PC you're using has a monochrome card, only the 80 character mode is available.

You must choose either 80 or 40 characters. If it's absolutely necessary, different characters can be displayed in graphics mode with some effort (see Chapter 6 and 17). Since the WIDTH statement will be used throughout the book, we'll provide more information on this statement later.

Note: In some interpreter/compiler versions, the WIDTH statement has the following syntax for screen output:

```
WIDTH <number_characters>,<number_lines>
```

Besides the number of characters to be displayed per line, you can also indicate how many lines should be represented. This is only possible if a video card is installed which supports more than 25 lines. These now include the EGA card with either 25 or 43 lines or the VGA card with up to 60 lines. You can determine whether one of these cards was installed by entering:

```
WIDTH 80,43 or WIDTH 80,60
```

Of course this depends on whether your version of PC-BASIC allows the WIDTH statement in this form. If the error message "Illegal Function Call" appears, it isn't possible to indicate how many lines should be represented. Otherwise, you'll see the results on the screen.

Colors and Attributes in the Text Mode

At the beginning of the chapter we mentioned that, depending on the video card, a character is displayed in a certain color or with certain attributes. In the following section we'll discuss the commands that can be used to do this.

| COLOR | display on a color monitor |

If you own a color video card and a color monitor, you can display up to 16 different character colors and 8 different background colors on the screen. PC-BASIC provides the following COLOR statement:

```
COLOR [<foreground>][,<background>]
```

The following program demonstrates the COLOR statement. Notice that adding the value 16 to the foreground color makes the character blink.

```
10 'COLOR-Test
20 :
25 CLS:KEY OFF
30 FOR I=0 TO 31
40 FOR K=0 TO 15
50 COLOR I,K
60 PRINT "COLOR";
70 NEXT K
80 PRINT
90 NEXT I
100 COLOR 7,0
110 PRINT:PRINT:PRINT
120 COLOR 31,0
130 PRINT "Strike any key....."
135 X$=INKEY$:IF X$="" THEN 135
140 COLOR 7,0
145 CLS
146 LOCATE 5,5
150 PRINT "The color of the frame can also be changed !"
160 FOR I=0 TO 15
170 OUT &H3D9,I
180 FOR K=1 TO 200:NEXT K
190 NEXT I
200 LOCATE 10,5
210 PRINT "We do nice work!"
215 PRINT
220 OUT &H3D9,0
230 COLOR 7,0
```

You've now learned a trick: the frame color can also be changed with PC-BASIC. This trick, usually not documented in PC-BASIC reference manuals is accomplished with the OUT statement, which writes directly into the *color-selection register* (Port 3D9H) of the 6845 video chip.

Note: Be very careful when using the OUT statement. Writing into the wrong port of the computer can cause your computer to freeze. Read Chapter 7 before experimenting.

It isn't possible with an EGA or VGA card installed to set the frame color in text mode. You'll have to use the black frame.

Foreground determines the color of the character and the *background* determines the color behind the character. If you analyze the program, you may wonder why only 8 background colors can be selected. This is because the color selection register for the background color in the text mode is only 3 bits wide. When expressed in binary terms, this is 1+2+4= 7 so only colors 0 to 7 can be selected as background color (see the following table). Larger values are simply converted into a valid parameter or result in an error message. You may only see the background for some values in the previous program. This is logical since, for example, a blue character on a blue background isn't visible.

Color-Value	Color
0	Black
1	Blue
2	Green
3	Turquoise/Cyan
4	Red
5	Purple/Magenta
6	Brown
7	Light Grey
8	Dark Grey
9	Light Blue
10	Light Green
11	Light Turquoise/Light Cyan
12	Bright Red
13	Bright Purple/Bright Magenta
14	Yellow
15	White

Try to limit the colors you use when selecting the screen color. Remember that too many colors may confuse the user.

Display on a Monochrome Monitor

On a monochrome monitor, instead of having colors, the characters are assigned attributes. You should still execute the "COLOR Test" program to observe the effect of the various colors on your screen. Generally, the following display settings are suitable for use on a monochrome monitor. They're also suitable for color monitors.

COLOR 7,0	Normal display
COLOR 0,7	Inverted display
COLOR 15,0	Double brightness
COLOR 31,0	Blinking display
COLOR 1,0	For monochrome cards "underlined", otherwise "blue"

Composite Monitors

A variation of the color monitor is the composite monitor. The color signals with this monitor are produced as a two color raster instead of as colors. Although composite monitors are cheaper than color monitors, with some colors the text cannot be read because of the raster. Execute the "COLOR Test" program to determine the best colors for your program on a composite monitor.

CLS   clear screen

This statement erases the screen. You should be familiar with this statement from previous examples.

```
CLS
```

Note: The CLS statement uses the colors which were set with the COLOR statement for the foreground and background. Enter the statement COLOR 15,4 if you want to create a program with white text on a red background. All output with PRINT and CLS will have this color throughout the program. At the end of the program you should set the colors to the normal value (COLOR 7,0), since some versions of PC-BASIC retain the set colors when they return to the operating system.

LOCATE

You may have noticed the LOCATE statement in the program for the COLOR statement. With this statement you can position the cursor in any desired line or column and determine if the cursor is switched on or off. You can also change the appearance of the cursor. Enter the following statement:

```
LOCATE [<line>] [,<column>] [,<on_off>] [,<from_line>] [,<to_line>]
```

Indicate the coordinates using <line> and <column>. For example, 1,1 is the top left corner and 80,25 is the right bottom corner. In the 40 character mode the coordinates must be adjusted accordingly.

For the <on_off> parameter: 0 = cursor off and 1 = cursor on. The following program shows the different cursor forms:

```
10 'LOCATE-Test
20 :
30 CLS:KEY OFF
40 FOR I=0 TO 31
50 FOR K=0 TO 31
60 LOCATE 23,2,0
70 COLOR 15,0
80 PRINT "Strike any key for next value"
90 COLOR 7,0
100 LOCATE 5,1
110 PRINT "from line: ";:PRINT USING "##";I        USE 15
120 PRINT "to line: ";:PRINT USING "##";K     USE 0 to 15
130 PRINT
140 PRINT "Cursor  : ";:LOCATE ,,1,I,K
150 X$=INKEY$:IF X$="" THEN 150
160 COLOR 7,0
170 NEXT K
180 NEXT I
190 COLOR 7,0
200 LOCATE ,,1,5,5
```

The <from/to_line> are raster lines or scan lines on the CRT instead of screen lines. Every screen line is composed of several raster lines. For compatibility reasons, on some monochrome/EGA cards, the loops I and K go up to 31, even though, usually after value 13, no reaction is visible for <to_line> and <from_line>.

In line 140 we use the comma (,) for missing parameters. The values from line 80 are accepted when you press a key. You may have to use <Ctrl><Break> to exit the program.

CRSLIN and POS   position cursor

With LOCATE we can position the cursor, switch it on and off and determine its appearance (80-45-90). In some applications we need the cursor's current line and column position in order to control it. PC-BASIC provides two functions for this:

```
CRSLIN (for the line)
```

and

```
POS(0) (for the column).
```

The following examples position the cursor in the top left corner after reaching the last screen position during output:

```
55 IF CRSLIN=25 AND POS(0)=80 THEN LOCATE 1,1
```

The result of this function can also be assigned to variables, which will be used later for additional processing.

```
55 LINE=CRSLIN:COLUMN=POS(0)
```

SCREEN   change page

Owners of a color graphic card are able to access, in text mode, 4 screen pages (80 character mode) or 8 screen pages (40 character mode). This means that you can display the first page and read it, while printing other text on the second page. Another application would be in the form of various input templates, which can be changed with the following statement:

```
SCREEN [<mode>] [,<color>] [,<output_page>] [,<display_page>]
```

The <mode> sets the graphic mode for graphic applications. We'll discuss this in more detail in Chapter 6. We're still describing text mode and <mode> is set to 0. The following program (not for monochrome cards) displays text on all 4 pages in 80 character mode and then switches the various pages.

```
10 ' SCREEN-Demo
20 :
30 CLS:KEY OFF
40 FOR DISPLYSCRN= 0 TO 3
50 SCREEN ,,DISPLYSCRN,0
60 CLS
70 FOR K=1 TO 10
80 LOCATE ,K
90 PRINT "This is display screen ";DISPLYSCRN
100 NEXT K
110 LOCATE 23,2
120 COLOR 15,0
130 PRINT "Next Page with <Return>, END with <Esc>"
140 COLOR 7,0
150 NEXT DISPLYSCRN
160 DISPLYSCRN= 0
170 SCREEN ,,DISPLYSCRN,DISPLYSCRN
180 X$=INKEY$:IF X$="" THEN 180
190 IF X$=CHR$(27) THEN CLS:END
200 IF X$<>CHR$(13) THEN BEEP:GOTO 180
210 DISPLYSCRN= DISPLYSCRN+1
220 IF DISPLYSCRN= 4 THEN DISPLYSCRN=0
230 GOTO 170
```

VIEW PRINT   limiting screen lines

In some applications it's not always necessary to clear the entire screen for new data. For example, you may want to keep the same text on the top and bottom of the screen. The VIEW PRINT statement allows you to limit the screen to a certain number of lines.

```
VIEW PRINT [<from_line>] TO [<to_line>]
```

Note: VIEW PRINT isn't implemented in some PC-BASIC versions and isn't available on a PC with a monochrome card.

With <from_line> you set the top line of the "newest" screen and with <to_line> you set the bottom line of the "new" screen. For example:

```
10 'VIEW PRINT-Demo
20 :
30 CLS:KEY OFF
40 COLOR 7,0
50 FOR I= 1 TO 25
60 PRINT STRING$(80,"*");
70 NEXT I
80 LOCATE 5,5
90 COLOR 0,7
100 PRINT " This part remains "
110 LOCATE 22,5
120 PRINT " This part also remains"
130 VIEW PRINT 10 TO 20
140 COLOR 15,0
150 FOR I= 1 TO 25
160 PRINT STRING$(80,"#");
170 NEXT I
180 LOCATE 14,5
190 COLOR 0,7
200 PRINT " This is the 'new' display screen "
210 COLOR 7,0
220 VIEW PRINT
```

If VIEW PRINT is entered without a parameter, the complete screen from line 1 to line 25 is active again. Remember that the commands CLS, LOCATE, PRINT and SCREEN follow the borders set with VIEW PRINT. For example, if you enter the statement, VIEW PRINT 15 TO 20, LOCATE 1,1 will move the cursor to column 1 of the 15th line instead of to the top left corner of the screen.

SCREEN   read character ASCII code

With the SCREEN function (not to be confused with the SCREEN statement) we can read, from the screen memory, the ASCII code or the attribute byte of a character.

```
SCREEN(<line>,<column>[,0 | 1])
```

Line and column are indicated as in the LOCATE statement. With another parameter you can indicate whether the ASCII code or the attribute byte should be read:

```
0= read ASCII-Code
1= read Attribute-Byte
```

Before experimenting, we need to discuss screen memory. Because of the design of the video chip, every character appearing on the screen consists of two bytes. These are stored in sequential memory locations in the screen memory. The first byte provides information about the ASCII code of the character and the second byte provides information about the attribute, which is the appearance of the character. The attribute represents the color on a color card and represents underlining, blinking, highlighting, etc. on a monochrome card.

The ASCII byte is stored in the screen memory in the even address (0, 2, 4, 6, 8...) and the attribute byte at the odd address (1, 3, 5, 7, 9...). This knowledge isn't crucial since the SCREEN function calculates the correction position itself. So far you've learned a lot about screen output and should be able to perform the following exercises.

Example: Using the COLOR statement, write various colored characters into the first line and determine, with the SCREEN function in direct mode, the character code and the attribute byte of the individual character.

PCOPY   copying permitted

If you're using graphic cards capable of supporting several screen pages (see SCREEN function), you can use PCOPY to copy screen display from one screen page to another.

```
PCOPY <from_page>,<to_page>
```

<from_page>

Indicates from which screen page the content should be copied (source).

<to_page>

Indicates to which page the content should be copied (destination).

For <from/to_page> you can set values between 0 and 7, depending on the graphic card:

```
CGA-card 80 character/line= 4 pages (0-3)
CGA-card 40 character/line= 8 pages (0-7)
EGA-card depending on model, up to 8 pages (0-7)
```

PCOPY can be used, for example, in a help function. You can load complete screen pages with the BLOAD command. One of these screen pages can contain help text, for example.

After the help, the preceding screen must be displayed again. However, this takes up a great deal of time.

This delay can be avoided by first storing the current screen with:

```
PCOPY 0,1 -> copy page 0 to 1
```

Then the help text is loaded:

```
DEF SEG= &HB800: BLOAD "HELP.TXT",0
```

After the help text is read, the previous screen is restored again:

```
PCOPY 1,0 -> copy page 1 to 0
```

Note: PCOPY isn't implemented in all versions of PC-BASIC.

4.1.2 Displaying Data on the Screen

In the last section we discussed the appearance of data and the screen construction. Now we'll present the commands and functions that enable you to display data on the screen.

We've already discussed PRINT, which is the most important command. This is a multifaceted command, which outputs all available data in the form of text, variables, results of computations, etc., on the screen:

```
PRINT [TAB(<column>)] [SPC(<number>)] [<expression>...] [;] [,]
```

The following can be used instead of <expression>:

PRINT "Testtext"

The text between the quotation marks (") can have a maximum length of 255 characters. You must consider the space required for quotation marks and the command as part of this length.

PRINT 5+3+5*2+(8-2)

The result of a calculation. Parentheses can be used to set priorities. Numeric variables can be used instead of numbers.

PRINT <Variable>

The content of variables. It doesn't matter whether these variables are numeric or string variables.

PRINT <Function>

The result of functions. An example is the DATE$ function previously introduced.

Several of the expressions can be combined in a PRINT command:

```
PRINT "Name: ";KNAME$;" Date: ";DATE$; " result: ";1+1
```

For this we use the semicolon (;), which causes the PRINT command to add expressions from one line to the preceding line. The semicolon suppresses the carriage return which PRINT performs after the <expression> is displayed. This allows multiple expressions to be printed on the same line.

Another parameter used with the PRINT command is the comma (,). For the PRINT command, all 14 character tabs are set. With the comma, the PRINT command is forced to jump to the next tab before the <expression> is displayed. Within certain limitations, this enables the screen output to be formatted in table form.

The following functions can also be used with PRINT:

TAB

While using the TAB function, the cursor is moved, before <expression> is displayed, to the column indicated by <column> in the current output line.

```
PRINT TAB(<column>)
```

If <column> is located to the left of the current cursor position, the cursor is moved to the <column> of the next line. If <column> is larger than the line width set by WIDTH, the right column is converted (column=<column> MOD WIDTH). The TAB function can appear more than once in a PRINT line:

```
PRINT TAB(10);"Hello, dear reader";TAB(60);"Test"
```

SPC

If this function is in a PRINT line, the spaces indicated by <number> are displayed before <expression> is displayed. SPC represents SPaCe.

```
PRINT SPC(<number>)
```

A conversion also occurs (space=<number> MOD WIDTH), in case <number> is larger than the line width set by WIDTH. Several SPCs can be used in one PRINT line:

```
PRINT SPC(15);"Good Day!";SPC(20);"Test"
```

The semicolon (;) doesn't necessarily have to be used with the TAB/SPC function because the output will be performed without a carriage return.

PRINT general

If <expression> is longer than the output line, the PRINT statement moves the output to the beginning of the next line. A space appears before and after numbers. The space in front of the number is reserved for the sign of the number. With a positive number the space remains empty. For a negative number, a minus sign (-) appears. PRINT, without an additional parameter, sets the cursor to the beginning of the next line, if the preceding output was made with a semicolon (;) or comma (,). Otherwise a blank line is displayed. While entering the PRINT statement you can use the question mark (?) as an acronym. PC-BASIC automatically converts it.

PRINT USING formatted output

A variation of the PRINT statement makes it possible to display formatted data. Normally the data is displayed starting at the current cursor position. To place numeric values in an orderly column, use the PRINT USING statement:

```
PRINT USING "<mask>"; <number> | <result> | <String>
```

The following program should demonstrate this:

```
10 'PRINT USING-Demo
20 :
30 CLS:KEY OFF
40 PRINT "The PRINT USING-command in action:"
50 PRINT:PRINT
60 LOCATE ,10
70 PRINT "only PRINT";
80 LOCATE ,40
90 PRINT "PRINT USING"
100 PRINT
110 PNUM1= 23.8:PNUM2= 9.45
120 FOR I= 1 TO 10
130 LOCATE ,10:PRINT PNUM1+PNUM2;
140 LOCATE ,40
150 PRINT USING "#####.##";PNUM1+PNUM2
160 PNUM1= PNUM1+109.45:PNUM2= PNUM2+102.89
170 NEXT I
```

Besides the output demonstrated here, various *masks* can be used to format any kind of data for output. The current *mask* should always be located in quotation marks.

Numeric data

PRINT USING "#####"

This mask is used to format integers. Every # represents a digit of the number to be displayed. Add another # character for a sign. Real numbers are rounded before they are displayed.

PRINT USING "#####.##"

This mask formats decimal numbers. PC-BASIC uses the period (.) to separate the digits before and after the decimal point. With the # character before and after the period, you can determine how many positions will be displayed before and after the decimal point. The value is rounded to the number of specified places if there aren't enough # characters for the digits following the decimal point.

PRINT USING "+#####.##" and PRINT USING "#####.##+"

A plus character (+) at the beginning or at the end of the mask displays the sign of the value at the beginning or at the end of the output.

PRINT USING "#####.##-"

The minus character (-) at the end of the mask causes a negative sign to appear at the end of the output. Positive values are displayed without a plus sign (+) character. The minus character must appear only at the end of the mask.

PRINT USING "#####.##^^^^"

This mask is required for the exponential notation of a value (scientific notation). The ^^^^ characters stand for E or D, the sign (+/-) and the two digits that represent the exponent to the power of 10.

*PRINT USING "**#####.##"*

If two asterisks (**) appear at the beginning of the mask, asterisks replace the spaces which are normally printed in the mask providing the value is smaller than the width of the mask.

PRINT USING "$$#####.##"

The dollar signs ($$) at the beginning of the mask place the dollar sign in front of every value. A combination with ^^^^ for the scientific notation isn't possible. For the combination with the ** mask, only one dollar sign should be indicated (**$###.##).

PRINT USING "#######,.##"

The comma (,) in the mask prints the digits in the mask in groups of three (1,254,267.80). For numbers containing four or more digits, this form should be used so that the numbers can be clearly displayed.

If the specified value is too large for the mask to format, PRINT USING indicates this condition by preceding the output with a percent sign (%). This can influence the complete screen construction. If the maximum number of digits to be output cannot be accurately predicted, it's better to select a larger mark, or to include a query on the size of the value in the application program.

Strings and Characters

The PRINT USING statement also offers some formatting capabilities for displaying strings:

"\\   \\"

This mask determines the number of characters to be displayed. The \\ character represents one character and the spaces between represent additional characters. If, for example, there are 5 spaces between the \\ characters, a total of 7 characters are displayed.

"&"

The ampersand character (&) causes the display of the unformatted output of the following string.

"!"

Only the first letter of the string is displayed using the exclamation mark.

"_"

If PRINT USING finds an underline character in the mask, the characters that follow it are printed without any formatting. This allows characters, which aren't usually permitted in the mask, to be included.

"#####.## <Text>"

The mask can include any desired character or text. Depending on its position in the mask, the text appears before or after the output: either "#####.## <Text>" or "<Text> #####.##".

PRINT USING   general

With PC-BASIC, PRINT USING can only be used a certain way. Don't try to assign a numeric value to a string mask, or vice versa, because the results would be a "Type mismatch" message. The mask for numeric data cannot contain more than 23 # characters for numbers before or after the decimal point. If you don't follow these rules, an "Illegal Function Call" message will appear. If you want another mask, you must use the string operations.

A single mask can display several values in a PRINT USING line:

```
PRINT USING "###.##"; 376.80, 12.46, 3.48, 59.00
```

It's also possible to include several masks and values in one PRINT USING line:

```
PRINT USING "##.##","###.##";12.80,301.78
```

If more masks than values are provided, the masks that aren't required are ignored:

Fig. 7: PRINT USING Example 1

If more values than masks are provided, the masks are processed from left to right. After the last mask, PRINT USING starts again with the first mask:

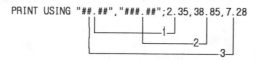

Fig. 8: PRINT USING Example 2

When there isn't sufficient space in the current output line, PRINT USING moves the output to the beginning of the next line. Unfortunately, it isn't easy to assign the formatted result to a variable. In an emergency you can use the output to the screen and input through the SCREEN function.

WRITE   output

PC-BASIC also offers the WRITE statement for displaying data on the screen. Since its syntax resembles the PRINT statement, we'll only discuss the differences:

•   All expressions are separated by commas (,) during output on the screen.

•   All expressions are enclosed in quotation marks (") during output on the screen.

•   Formatting with USING isn't possible.

•   The TAB function cannot be used with WRITE.

•   The semicolon (;) cannot be used to suppress the carriage return.

The screen as a file

Most likely, you'll read in your MS-DOS manual that connected peripherals (devices) can be addressed as files. For the screen, this is done as follows:

```
      OPEN "SCRN:" FOR OUTPUT AS #1
or
      OPEN "CONS:" FOR OUTPUT AS #1
```

The filenames SCRN: and/or CONS: are reserved by MS-DOS and cannot be used as names for your files. You'll receive incorrect results if you use them as disk file names. Most of the time this type of output to the screen is selected to make the input/output routines flexible, they could be used by the printer and the screen. Also, the ANSI Escape Sequences can be sent, which are then properly converted. This doesn't happen during the normal PRINT statement. Check the following example to see whether the ANSI driver is installed (see Chapter 3, if the ANSI.SYS driver is not installed the program will not operate correctly):

```
 10 ' OPEN "CONS:"-Demo
 20 :
 30 CLS:KEY OFF
 40 OPEN "CONS:" FOR OUTPUT AS #1
 50 PRINT#1,CHR$(27);"[J2":'clear display screen
 60 PRINT#1,"Testtext"
 70 PRINT#1,CHR$(27);"[1m";"Testtext";CHR$(27);"[0m"
 80 PRINT#1,CHR$(27);"[7m";"Testtext";CHR$(27);"[0m"
 90 PRINT#1,CHR$(27);"[5m";"Testtext";CHR$(27);"[0m"
100 CLOSE
```

Some commands of the file control, which are described in Section 4.6, have already been used. We had to include these commands because the screen as a file belongs in this section.

4.1.3 Input through the Keyboard

Although voice activated input/output is now possible, it's now too expensive for the common user. Therefore, communication between the user and the computer usually occurs through the keyboard.

For input of data through the keyboard, PC-BASIC offers various commands and functions, which we'll examine in detail.

Before a mathematical calculation or a string operation can be performed, all data to be processed is first stored in variables. This suggests that the commands/functions for data input through the keyboard must have been given one or more variable names. We know that PC-BASIC differentiates between the data types string and numeric. For the input of this data, different commands aren't used. PC-BASIC automatically recognizes the data type.

65

4.1.4 Input Strings (Character Strings)

To store and process the data, entered through the keyboard, as a string, you must provide a corresponding string variable as a parameter:

```
INPUT "character-string: ";CS$
```

With the dollar sign character ($) you can determine that the CS variable has the data type string. All characters, which the user enters through the keyboard, are easily stored in CS$ because this data type accepts every character.

4.1.5 Entering Numeric Data

Entering numeric data can sometimes be difficult because PC-BASIC checks the data types for accuracy and not all characters on the keyboard can be accepted as numbers. For this reason, you should be sure during the declaration of the variables that the expected input can be correctly stored. If, for example, a floating point number should be read in, the variable must be a single or double precision data type. The indication of an integer variable can lead to incorrect results because the fractional part will be cut by PC-BASIC without a message. Also, the error message "Overflow" can occur when the value input exceeds the limits of the indicated data type:

```
INPUT "INTEGER-number: ";NUMBER%
```

If, for example, you enter 45,738 at the "INTEGER-number:" prompt, the "Overflow" error message is displayed. An integer variable can store a value only to 32,767.

Another source of errors during the input of numbers are characters that cannot be interpreted as numbers:

```
INPUT "Annual-Salary: ";ASALARY#
```

If a letter is accidentally entered, the "?Redo from start" error message appears. A letter obviously isn't a number.

Here is a small routine which prevents the error message from ruining the input mask:

```
200 '
210 'Numeric input without "?Redo from start"
220 '
230 CLS:KEY OFF
240 TEST$="abcdefghijklmnopqrstuvwxyzABCDEFGHIJKLMNOPQRSTUVWXYZ"
250 :
260 LOCATE 10,5:COLOR 7,0
270 LINE INPUT "monthly earnings: ";MNTH.ERNING$
```

```
280 ERR. CODE= 0
290 FOR I= 1 TO LEN(TEST$)
300 IF INSTR(MNTH.ERNING$,MID$(TEST$,I,1))<> 0 THEN 330 ELSE NEXT
310 GOTO 380
320 :
330 'Invalid input
340 :
350 LOCATE 24,1:PRINT "Only numbers [0] to [9], or characters [.],[+] and [-] are
permitted!";SPACE$(81-POS(0));
360 BEEP:GOTO 260
370 :
380 'Valid input
390 :
400 LOCATE 24,1:PRINT VAL(MNTH.ERNING$);" Is a valid input!";SPACE$(81-POS(0));
410 IF INKEY$="" THEN 410 ELSE 260
```

The TEST$ variable depends on your own requirements. It is initialized according to the characters which should not be allowed. This routine can also be used for entering strings, in which, for example, numbers or graphic characters aren't allowed.

4.1.6 Commands for Keyboard Input

INPUT

The statement probably used most often for data input through the keyboard is the INPUT statement:

```
INPUT [;] [<"Comment">] [;|,] <Variables...>
```

With INPUT you can help the user by including a comment.

```
INPUT "Input your age: ";AGE$
```

On the screen your comment will be followed by a question mark (?). The question mark tells the user that an input is required. The input must be terminated with the <Return> key. The data that was entered is then assigned to the variables and a carriage return occurs.

After the word "INPUT", the first semicolon (;) is inserted when a carriage return shouldn't occur after the input. The semicolon should never be omitted after the input in the last screen line because the entire mask will be moved toward the top.

The comma (,) before the variables suppresses the question mark. If you don't want to display a "comment" and the question mark is suppressed with a comma, a blank string must be defined before the comma:

```
INPUT "",AGE$
```

In some versions, a carriage return occurs after the "comment" is displayed and the input is expected at the beginning of the next line. The carriage return can be suppressed by placing a second semicolon (;) before the variables. Several variables can be supplied with data through one INPUT statement:

```
INPUT "Name, age, salary: ";KNAME$,AGE1%, SALARY1!
```

To avoid a "?Redo from start" error, the variables must be separated with commas as the data is entered:

```
Smith,28,3.80 <Return>
```

Even if the variables do not require data, they must be separated with commas as the data is entered:

```
Smith,,3.80 <Return>
```

The various types must have the proper assignments. If this isn't true, the INPUT statement returns the message, "?Redo from start". The input must then be repeated for all indicated variables. If you answer the INPUT with:

```
3.80,Smith,28 <Return>
```

you'll receive a "?Redo from start" error. The assignment Smith cannot be sent to an integer variable. We explained how to prevent the "?Redo from start" error at the beginning of this section.

There is no problem of the input of 3.80 since a string variable accepts any character. The message you may receive is only a suggestion and not an error message. This does not affect the system variables ERR and ERL (see Section 4.8).

Unfortunately, during the INPUT statement, the maximum length of the input cannot be preset. So, a careless user could ruin your mask, for example, by holding down the <X> key. Try this yourself.

While data is being entered for a string variable, leading or trailing spaces are ignored by INPUT. Since the comma (,) is considered by INPUT as a separator, it cannot be easily used as an input character. To enter leading spaces, trailing spaces or a comma, they must be enclosed in quotation marks ("):

```
"   Smith, K.J.   ",28,3.80 <Return>
```

During the execution of the INPUT statement, the familiar edit keys are active. The input can be corrected with the <Ins> or <Del> key. The cursor can be moved in the input field with the control keys. Unfortunately, since the key combination <Ctrl><L> clears the screen, a careless user could also cause problems at this point.

System variables cannot be supplied with data through INPUT. In particular, these variables are DATE$, TIME$, ERR and ERL. DATE$ and TIME$ can be changed with the string operations (Section 4.2); basically ERR and ERL are administered only by PC-BASIC.

LINE INPUT

During the INPUT statement, certain characters cannot be entered. The following variant of the INPUT statement corrects this problem:

```
LINE INPUT [;] [<"comment">] [;] | [,] <StringVariable>
```

Since the syntax of LINE INPUT corresponds to the syntax of the INPUT statement, we'll only list the differences between the two commands:

• LINE INPUT only accepts string type variables.

• Multiple variables aren't permitted.

• Space, quotation marks ("), colon (:) and comma (,) are accepted.

The suggestions for the INPUT statement are also acceptable for this statement.

INPUT$

With the INPUT$ function, a limited number of characters can be read from the keyboard, a file or a data buffer:

```
INPUT$(<number_character>[,<#file-number>])
```

The following instruction waits, for example, until 5 characters have been entered through the keyboard:

```
X$=INPUT$(5)
```

All keys are considered characters. Some keys provide *extended codes*. The control keys, which consist of 2 bytes, can be recognized by the first byte as always being a 0. INPUT$ for control keys with the extended code only reads the first byte. You can determine that a control key was activated, but unfortunately you can't determine which control key it was. This will be further explained with the INKEY$ function below.

The characters read by the INPUT$ function aren't displayed on the screen. The input doesn't have to end with the <Return> key, since INPUT$ recognizes a <number_character> at the end of the input. The INPUT$ function can be terminated at any time with <Ctrl><C>.

The description of the INPUT$ function for files and data buffer can be found in Section 4.6. We're now only interested in keyboard input.

An interesting application of INPUT$ is, for example, reading passwords. Since the input characters aren't displayed, an observer cannot read the password, unless you type so slowly that the keys can be remembered. The following program demonstrates this application:

```
200 '
210 'Password-Routine
220 '
230 :
240 CLS:KEY OFF
250 PASSWORD$=""
260 LOCATE 10,5
270 PRINT "------";
280 LOCATE 10,5,1
290 X$=INPUT$(1):IF X$= CHR$(0) THEN 290
300 PRINT CHR$(254);
310 PASSWORD$= PASSWORD$+X$
320 IF LEN(PASSWORD$)=6 THEN 340
330 GOTO 290
340 IF PASSWORD$<>"abcdef" THEN BEEP:GOTO 240
350 .....
360 .....
```

The INKEY$ function couldn't be used here, since the activation of a function or control key would return a two byte code, which would have to be queried and ignored. In the program in line 290, you can see that the interception of the function and control keys is very simple. Each 0 byte is simply ignored.

INKEY$

The INKEY$ function returns a keyboard code which consists of a maximum of 2 bytes:

```
X$=INKEY$
```

If a key wasn't pressed, INKEY$ returns the space string ("") as the result. During the INPUT$ function we discovered that the control keys generate a 2 byte keyboard code. The first byte is usually a 0. The second byte reveals which control key was pressed. The following program will help illustrate this:

```
10 'INKEY$-Demo
20 :
30 CLS:KEY OFF:VIEW PRINT
40 COLOR 15,0
50 LOCATE 23,1
60 PRINT STRING$(80,"M")
70 LOCATE 24,2
80 PRINT "Strike any key or key combination,"
90 LOCATE 25,2
100 PRINT "interrupt program with <Ctrl> <C> or  <Ctrl> <Break> .....";
110 COLOR 7,0
120 VIEW PRINT 1 TO 21
130 LOCATE 1,1,1
140 X$=INKEY$:IF X$="" THEN 140
150 IF LEN(X$)=2 THEN 220
160 PRINT "Character: ";
170 COLOR 15,0:PRINT X$;:COLOR 7,0
180 PRINT " ASCII-Code: ";
190 COLOR 15,0:PRINT ASC(X$):COLOR 7,0
200 PRINT
210 GOTO 140
220 'control keys start here
230 PRINT "control key activated: ";
240 COLOR 15,0:PRINT ASC(RIGHT$(X$,1)):COLOR 7,0
250 PRINT
260 GOTO 140
```

Press on the function keys. The assignment of that function key may appear. For example, press <F1> and you may see the ASCII code for each of the L,I,S,T characters. If this happens, enter the following line in direct mode before executing the program:

```
FOR I=1 TO 10:KEY I,"":NEXT I
```

You'll receive the keyboard code, instead of the ASCII codes, of the assignment.

For some key combinations, the control characters are executed immediately. Don't be surprised by the way the program reacts. Once the program ends, activate the screen again with VIEW PRINT.

The keyboard as a file

During the screen output we noticed that the screen can be treated as a file. The same can be done with the keyboard:

```
OPEN "KYBD:" FOR INPUT AS #1
```

This form of input is used, for example, when the input doesn't always come from the keyboard, but is read from a file. Only the filename needs to be changed in order to read the data from the correct location. For example:

```
10 'OPEN "KYBD:"-Demo
20 :
30 CLS:KEY OFF
40 OPEN "KYBD:" FOR INPUT AS #1
50 X$=INPUT$(1,#1)
60 IF X$=CHR$(27) THEN CLOSE:CLS:END
70 PRINT X$
80 GOTO 50
```

We used a few commands from the file control. You'll find a description of these commands in Section 4.6.

In the next section we'll discuss commands and functions for the string operations.

4.2   String Operations

PC-BASIC provides many commands and functions for processing strings. We've already used some of these commands and functions in the programs. We'll discuss their significance in this section.

4.2.1 Similar Data Types

The string operations can generally be performed only with variables or constants of the string type. In the following section we'll see that, with the proper conversion, variables of other types can also be used.

4.2.2 Converting various Data Types

For special problem solutions we can rely on some of PC-BASIC's conversion functions, which allow converting numeric variables or constants into string variables.

HEX$

With this function we can convert decimal numbers into hexadecimal numbers and send the result to a string variable or with PRINT:

```
X$=HEX$(<number>)
```

Output a number that can have a value between -32768 and +65535. In the result string, a leading space, null (0) or the identification for hexadecimal values (&H) aren't displayed.

OCT$

Similar to the HEX$ function, a decimal value can be converted into an octal string:

```
X$=OCT$(<number>)
```

The same applies to the HEX$ function.

MKD$, MKI$, and MKS$

These functions are especially useful for storing numeric values in random files (see Section 4.6).

```
X$= MKI$
X$= MKS$
X$= MKD$
```

These functions convert numeric variables in string variables with a fixed length:

X$=MKI$(X)

This converts the integer variable X into a string 2 bytes in length.

X$=MKS$(X)

This converts the variable X with single precision into a string 4 bytes in length.

X$=MKD$(X)

This converts variable X with double precision to a string that is 8 bytes in length.

After the conversion, the values are assigned to the FIELD variables with LSET or RSET and are written with PUT. After the random file is read, the strings must be converted back with the functions CVI, CVS and CVD of the type named above. Details on this will be given in Sections 4.3 and 4.6.

It isn't possible to display the converted values with PRINT because data is stored internally as a bit pattern and not of printable ASCII characters.

STR$

This function closes the ring of conversion functions that PC-BASIC provides for the string variables. With the STR$ function, numeric variables are converted into a string. In contrast to MKI$, MKS$ and MKD$, the conversion is performed in ASCII numbers. Output with PRINT or a continuous processing with string operations is also possible:

```
<target-String>= STR$(<numeric_Variable>)
```

As in the output with PRINT, the first position of the target string is reserved for the sign of the number. A space doesn't follow the number.

Assign the numeric variable different values in direct mode using the STR$ function and verify the results with PRINT.

4.2.3 Pre-Defined Functions

Assignments to a String Variable

In Chapter 3 we discussed the assignments of data to string variables. The following is a short summary.

AGE$="12 years"
Assigns the string constants in quotation marks (") to the string variable.

TOD.DATE$=DATE$
Assigns the result from a function to the string variable.

AGE$=YEAR$
Assigns the content of one string variable to another string variable.

"Adding" Strings

Use the plus sign (+) to concatenate several string variables:

```
target_String= String+String+String...
```

Example:

```
ADDRESS$=KNAME$+STREET$+TOWN$
```

The ADDRESS$ variable contains the data of the individual variables INAME$, STREET$ and TOWN$. This can be verified in direct mode:

```
KNAME$="Louise Benzer "
STREET$="1234 Utopia Drive "
TOWN$="Richville, NY 19999 "
```

After you enter:

```
PRINT ADDRESS$
```

or

```
? ADDRESS$
```

you'll receive the following result:

```
Louise Benzer 1234 Utopia Drive Richville, NY 19999
```

It's often assumed that PC-BASIC automatically inserts a space between the variables. However, as you can see, that did not happen.

Thanks to Microsoft, not only variables, but also any character or result from functions can be combined with string variables using the plus sign:

```
ADDRESS$=KNAME$+" "+STREET$+" "+TOWN$
DATETIME$="Date: "+DATE$+" Time: "+TIME$
```

The "subtraction" of string variables is more difficult. We'll discuss this in more detail in the following pages.

Date and Time in Strings

Before discussing the "correct" string operations, we must explain the system variables DATE$ and TIME$, which were already mentioned in Section 3.6.4.

You know that the PC controls date and time automatically. Usually, after switching on the system, you enter the current values, which are automatically updated by the PC. You could also own a PC with a clock card or an AT. In this case, the date and time don't have to be entered because a battery keeps the clock running, even after the computer has been switched off.

DATE$ and TIME$ are commands and functions. This means that we can query the current values, or set new values. In various applications DATE$ and TIME$ are frequently used to display the date and time in the status line:

```
LOCATE 25,1
PRINT "date is: ";DATE$;
PRINT "time is: ";TIME$;
```

Here DATE$ and TIME$ are used as functions. They operate as commands in routines, which are used instead of the DOS commands DATE and TIME. Setting the date or time is handled like a normal assignment:

```
DATE$= "12.03.89"
TIME$= "12:30"
```

In Chapter 12 you will find an extensive routine for your own programs. Reading the date or time directly into the system variable isn't possible. The following attempt will cause the error message "Syntax error":

```
LINE INPUT "Date: ";DATE$
```

You must make a "detour" through a detour variable:

```
LINE INPUT "date: ";TOD.DATE$
DATE$= TOD.DATE$
```

Processing the partial content of a String Variable

Usually only a certain portion of a string variable is needed for further processing. PC-BASIC offers three functions and a statement, with which the partial content of string variables can be processed. Remember that variables can also be used for numeric parameters.

LEFT$

Through this function we obtain the left portion of a string variable:

```
<target-String>= LEFT$(<source-String>, <number_characters>)
```

For our example, TOWN$ contains "Richville, NY 19999". With:

```
CITY$=LEFT$(TOWN$,9)
```

the first 9 characters of the TOWN$ variable are assigned with CITY$. <number_characters> can have a value from 0 to 255.

With <number_characters=0>, the target string gets the empty string (""). If <number_characters> is larger than the length of source string, the complete source string is assigned to the target string.

MID$

With this function we can access the middle section of a string variable:

```
<target-String>= MID$(<source-String>, <first_character>
[,<number_characters>])
```

In our example, ADDRESS$ is displayed as "1234 Utopia Drive, Richville, NY 19999". When you use the function:

```
CITY$=MID$(ADDRESS$,22,9)
```

we assign the CITY$ variable 9 characters, starting at the 16th character of ADDRESS$:

22nd

```
"1234 Utopia Drive, Richville, NY 19999"
 12345678901234567890I234567 —> character position
     1          |2 |
                └──┴──> 9 characters = "Richville"
```

Fig. 9: MID$ function

<number_characters> must have a value between 0 and 255. If <number_characters> isn't indicated, the target string receives the rest of the source string, starting at <first_character>. If <first_character> is indicated larger than the length of the source string, the target string is assigned an empty string (""). If the source string contains, starting at <first_character>, fewer characters than indicated with <number_characters>, the remainder are assigned to the source string.

RIGHT$

Similar to the LEFT$ function, the right part of a string variable can be assigned:

```
<target-String>= RIGHT$(<source-String>, <number_characters>)
```

TOWN$ has the content "Richville, NY 19999". With the function:

```
ZIP$=RIGHT$(TOWN$,5)
```

The ZIP$ variable is assigned the last 5 characters of the TOWN$ string.

<number_characters> must again have a value between 0 and 255. If <number_characters> is larger than the length of the source string, the complete content is assigned to the target string. For <number_characters=0>, the space string ("") is assigned.

MID$

To assign a string variable a partially new content, we need the MID$ function:

```
MID$(<target-String>, <first_character> [,<number_characters>])= <source-
String>
```

TOWN$ has the content "Richville, NY 19999". To change the ZIP code we enter the following statement:

```
MID$(TOWN$,14)="19998"
```

If the parameter <number_characters> is omitted, the entire source string is used. The following statement clearly shows the difference:

```
MID$(TOWN$,14,1)="19998"
```

Even though a source string has 5 characters, only the first character is used for the assignment, since we indicated, with <number_characters>, that only one character would be exchanged.

<number_characters> must again have a value between 0 and 255. For <number_characters=0>, no assignment is made. <first_character> must be equal to or larger than 1, smaller than the total length of the target string, and must be long enough to accept the defined characters from the source string. With the MID$ statement the length of the target string cannot be shortened or lengthened. The source string will only accept as many characters as there is space available in the target string, even if <number_characters> indicated more. The source string can be a string constant ("19998"), another string variable (CITY$), or the result of a function (MID$(TOWN$,1,4)= LEFT$(CITY$,4)).

Suggestions for LEFT$, RIGHT$ and MID$

A target string can be used simultaneously as a source string:

```
CITY$=LEFT$(CITY$,4)
TOWN$=RIGHT$(TOWN$,7)
TOWN$=MID$(TOWN$,3,6)
```

Avoid performing too many operations in one line, because after a certain point you can loose track of them:

```
45 TEST$=MID$(CHAOS$,2,6)+LEFT$(MID$(CHAOS$,3,7),2)
```

LEN   determine the string length

In a few of the string operations we've described so far, the length of the string to be processed is important. PC-BASIC offers the following function for determining the length of a string:

```
X=LEN(<String-Variable>)
```

The LEN function returns the length of a string variable, including all spaces and control characters.

CHR$

On the screen output in Section 4.1 we noticed that the character set of our computer includes more characters than can be generated with the keyboard. These are primarily the *graphic characters*, whose ASCII codes are larger than 125. Because they're hidden while the keyboard is used, the only way to generate them is using the <Alt> key with a second key from the keyboard.

Instead of this method we can use the CHR$ function, which enables us to display any desired ASCII code on the screen, include it in string variables or use it for testing:

```
X$=CHR$(<ASCII-Code>)
```

Examples:

```
PRINT CHR$(185)
X$=INKEY$:IF X$<>CHR$(13) THEN xxxxx
A$= "Error! "+CHR$(7)
```

Any ASCII code value between 0 and 255 can be given. The ASCII codes, especially for the extended character set, may differ with different computer manufacturers. You should consult the reference manual for your computer system for a listing of the available ASCII characters. Remember that ASCII codes with a value smaller than 32 are partially control characters which clear the screen or move the cursor.

ASC

The ASC function is the opposite of the CHR$ function. It returns the decimal value of an ASCII character.

```
X=ASC(<expression>)
```

The expression can appear as follows:

X=ASC("H")
The ASCII function returns the ASCII code of the letter H (72).

X=ASC(<String>)
The ASCII function returns the ASCII code of the first character of a string.

X=ASC(<function>)
The ASCII function also processes the result of a function (X=ASC(DATE$)). The result is the ASCII code of the first character of the result of the DATE$ function.

Remember that the ASCII function can only be applied to a single character.

SPACE$

This function quickly displays a predetermined number of spaces or assigns them to a string variable:

```
X$= SPACE$(<number>)
```

A value between 0 and 255 can be set for <number>. In your applications you'll use the SPACE$ function mainly for erasing portions of the screen or for creating strings for operations in connection with file control:

```
LOCATE 24,1:PRINT SPACE$(160); -> erases line 24 and 25.
X$=SPACE$(80):LSET CITY$=X$     -> erases the FIELD-Variable CITY$.
```

STRING$

With the STRING$ function, PC-BASIC offers a helpful function for the screen output and string control:

```
X$= STRING$(<number>,<character>)
```

The STRING$ function creates a string of the length <number> with the content <character>. For <number>, a value between 0 and 255 can be used. For <character>, an ASCII code, a string constant (for example "=") or the result of a function (for example CHR$(34)) can be substituted. Of course the result of the STRING$ function can also be assigned to a string variable. The following program produces a border on the screen:

```
10 'STRING$-Demo
20 :
30 CLS:KEY OFF
40 PRINT CHR$(218);STRING$(78,196);CHR$(191)
50 FOR I=2 TO 21
60 LOCATE I, 1:PRINT CHR$(179)
70 LOCATE I,80:PRINT CHR$(179)
80 NEXT I
90 LOCATE 21,1:PRINT CHR$(192);STRING$(78,196);CHR$(217);
100 X$=INKEY$:IF X$="" THEN 100
```

INSTR

The INSTR function helps us search for a certain character in a string variable:

```
X= INSTR([<from_position>], <source-String>, <search-character>)
```

The result of the function is the position where the desired character is located in the source string. If INSTR returns the value 0, the character wasn't contained in the source string. With <from_position> we can indicate from which character in the source string the search should start. The normal value is position 1. Here are some examples:

```
CITY$="Chicago":PRINT INSTR(CITY$,"g")
```

The result is 6.

```
CITY$="Chicago":PRINT INSTR(CITY$,"w")
```

The result is 0.

```
CITY$="Chicago":PRINT INSTR(5,CITY$,"C")
```

The result is 1. (The result for a lowercase "c" is 4.)

INSTR is best used for dissecting a string into several pieces:

```
10 TOWN$="Richville, NY 19999"
20 X=INSTR(TOWN$," "):Y=LEN(TOWN$)
30 CITY$=LEFT$(TOWN$,X-1)
40 ZIP$=RIGHT$(TOWN$,Y-X)
```

4.2.4 User-Defined Functions

Until now, the functions we have discussed have all been defined by PC-BASIC. The programmer could change only the parameters and not the result.

PC-BASIC provides a user-defined function for special applications:

```
DEF FN<String>(<Parameter...>)= <function>
```

and for the call:

```
<target-String>= FN<String>(<Parameter...>)
```

The following example should demonstrate this:

```
10 'DEF FN-Demo
20 :
30 CLS:KEY OFF
40 LOCATE 24,1
50 PRINT STRING$(80,"=");
60 LOCATE 25,1
70 PRINT "Enter 99999 as ZIP code to end";
80 VIEW PRINT 1 TO 23
```

```
90 DEF FNX$(ZIP$,CTY$)=ZIP$+" "+CTY$
100 INPUT "ZIP code: ",ZIP$
110 IF ZIP$="99999" THEN 170
120 INPUT "city name: ",CTY$
130 TOWN$=FNX$(ZIP$,CTY$)
140 PRINT "result    : ";TOWN$
150 PRINT
160 GOTO 100
170 VIEW PRINT:CLS:END
```

Explanation:

```
90 DEF FNX$(CITY$,ZIP$)= CITY$+" "+ZIP$
              |   |                  |_____> function
              |   |___> Parameter
              |___> Name of the function X$

110 TOWN$= FNX$(CITY$,ZIP$)
       |     |    |_____> Parameter
       |     |___> Name of the function
       |___> result-String
```

Fig. 10: DEF FN/FN

Every DEF FN function must be defined before its first call. Otherwise, PC-BASIC sends the "Undefined User Function" error. Syntax errors are detected during the first call of the function. You should test all DEF FN functions during the test phase of your program. The parameters passed during the call must agree with the type, sequence and number of the parameter list in the definition. The DEF FN function cannot call itself (recursive call). Parameter variables provided during the definition, are the local variables and are used only in the function. During the program execution they have no defined value, but obtain them only through the call. The variables passed as parameters aren't changed, even when variables of the same name were mentioned in the definition as local variables (see example). A DEF FN function cannot be defined in the direct mode. The function cannot be longer than one program line.

Before moving to the next section, try one of the functions again. You can even completely switch off the computer.

4.3　Mathematical Functions/Calculations

PC-BASIC provides many mathematical functions for different calculations. You can also create user-defined functions, such as scientific formulas.

4.3.1 Similar Data Types

Mathematical operations and calculations can usually only be performed with variables or constants of the numeric type. Later we'll see that, with the proper conversions, other variables can be used.

4.3.2 Converting Various Data Types

For calculations, we can use integer variables and variables with single or double precision. For conversion of these types between each other and the conversion of a string into a numeric variable, PC-BASIC provides the following functions:

X=CINT(<expression>)

<expression>, which is converted to an integer value, can be a variable, the result of a calculation, a function or a number between -32768 and +32767.

X=CSNG(<expression>)

<expression>, which is converted into a single precision value, can be selected similar to CINT.

X=CDBL(<expression>)

<expression>, which is converted into a double precision value, can be selected similar to CINT.

CVI, CVS and CVD

In Section 4.2.2 we discussed the MKI$, MKS$ and MKD$ functions. These functions are required for storing random files. We'll need the CVI, CVS and CVD functions to convert the string variables back into numeric variables. The FIELD variable represents the string variable. This variable contains the string converted with the MKx$ function:

X=CVI(<FIELD variable>)

Conversion into an integer variable.

X=CVS(<FIELD variable>)

Conversion into a variable with single precision.

X=CVD(<FIELD variable>)

Conversion into a double precision variable.

An example for the MKI$, MKS$, MKD$, CVI, CVS and CVD functions is found in Section 4.6 with the description of the random files.

VAL	converts a string into a numeric variable

In Section 4.2 we used the STR$ function to convert a numeric variable into a string. Use the VAL function for the reverse operation:

```
<num_Variable>= VAL(<String-Variable>)
```

<num_variable> can be any numeric variable. String variables must contain a number sequence representing a numeric value:

```
NUMBER$= "12"
NUMBER%= VAL(NUMBER$)
```

The following conversion results in the value 0 since the first character isn't a number:

```
NUMBER$= "Richville, NY 19999"
NUMBER%= VAL(NUMBER$)
```

The VAL function ends when it encounters a character that isn't a number:

```
NUMBER$= "12.30 abcde 25.79"
NR!= VAL(NUMBER$)
```

The NR! variable receives the value 12.30, assigned by VAL.

Leading space, tab characters or CHR$(13) for the <Return> key, are ignored and the following numbers are correctly converted:

```
NUMBER$="     30"
NUMBER%= VAL(NUMBER$)
```

The correct value 30 is returned to NUMBER%.

4.3.3 Pre-Defined Functions for Arithmetic Calculations

We'll begin with the predefined functions for the basic arithmetic calculations provided by PC-BASIC:

Addition

Addition is performed with the plus sign (+):

```
RESULT= <expression_1> + <expression_2>
```

Subtraction

Subtraction is performed with the minus sign (-):

```
RESULT= <expression_1> - <expression_2>
```

Multiplication

For multiplication we use the asterisk (*):

```
RESULT= <expression_1> * <expression_2>
```

Division

Division is performed with the slash (/):

```
RESULT= <expression_1> / <expression_2>
```

For an integer division, or the division of whole number values, we can use the backslash (\):

```
RESULT= <expression_1> \ <expression_2>
```

Exponentiation

For exponentiation we use the caret (^):

```
RESULT= <expression_1> ^ <expression_2>
```

General information about basic calculation functions

The RESULT can be assigned:

```
X=2+3+4
```

can be output:

```
PRINT 2*3+4
```

or used for additional calculations:

```
X=2+3+(3*8)
```

Different calculations in a statement are possible:

```
RESULT=2+3-(3*8+(9/3))
```

Parentheses can be set according to requirements. The "Formula too complex" error message will be displayed if you include too many parentheses or the equation is too complicated for PC-BASIC. This also ends the program.

Additional messages warn of "Division by zero" and "Overflow" errors. These errors will not end or stop the program but the error message is displayed on the screen. You should test the values to be processed at any location where an error message is likely to be generated. Change or even delete this program section if necessary.

Enhanced functions

You can use the following functions, which PC-BASIC calculates internally, in your programs. Remember if PC-BASIC was called with the /D parameter that a double precision variable is required for the result.

X=ABS(<expression>)

Determines the absolute value of <expression>. The output is a positive value. The precision corresponds to the type specification for the variables used in <expression>.

X=ATN(<expression>)

The angle of the arctangent is calculated and returned (in radians) in single precision. If PC-BASIC was called with the /D parameter, the calculation will be performed in double precision.

X=COS(<expression>)

The cosine of <expression> is calculated and returned in radians in single precision. If PC-BASIC was called with the /D parameter, the calculation is performed in double precision.

X=EXP(<expression>)

The Eulers number e is raised to the power of <expression> and the result is calculated in single precision. If PC-BASIC was called with the /D parameter, the calculation is performed in double precision.

X=FIX(<expression>)

Determines the whole number value of <expression>. The fractional part is truncated and the result corresponds to the precision of the variable in <expression>. Both positive and negative values are processed.

X=INT(<expression>)

Determines the greatest integer function value for <expression>. The result corresponds to the variables in the expression. Both positive and negative values are allowed.

X=LOG(<expression>)

Determines the natural logarithm of the <expression> in single precision. If PC-BASIC was called with the /D parameter, the calculation is performed in double precision. <expression> must be greater than zero.

X=<number_1> MOD <number_2>

Determines the remainder of an integer division (Modulus).

X=SGN(<expression>)

Determines the sign of <expression>. SGN returns +1 if the sign was positive, -1 if it's negative and 0 if the <expression> is equal to zero.

X=SIN(<expression>)

The sine of <expression> in radians is calculated and returned (in radians) in single precision. If PC-BASIC was called with the /D parameter, the calculation is performed in double precision.

X=SQR(<expression>)

Returns the square root of <expression> in single precision. If PC-BASIC was called with the /D parameter, the calculation is performed in double precision. <expression> must be greater than or equal to zero.

X=TAN(<expression>)

The tangent of <expression> in radians is calculated and returned in single precision. If PC-BASIC was called with the /D parameter, the calculation is performed in double precision.

RND and RANDOMIZE — determine random numbers

PC-BASIC provides a statement and a function for determining random numbers. These are required, for example, in entertainment or animation sequences.

```
RANDOMIZE [<number>]; } statement
RND [(<number>)]; } function
```

If you use the RND function without a parameter to determine a random number, PC-BASIC generates the next random number in the sequence. A trained observer would be capable, for example in a game, to predict the outcome. With the RANDOMIZE statement you can determine the initial value and the sequence of the random numbers. Set <number> to a value between -32768 and +32767. PC-BASIC asks you to enter a number if you call RANDOMIZE without a number:

```
RANDOM NUMBER SEED (-32768 TO 32767) ?
```

Depending on your input, the beginning value and the sequence will be determined. You can also determine the beginning value and the sequence with the RND function in connection with the <number> parameter. The following program, which you can use to determine six lottery numbers (we cannot guarantee a winning combination), shows this:

```
10 'RND-Demo
20 :
30 CLS:KEY OFF
40 FOR I=1 TO 6
50 PRINT INT(RND*49)
60 NEXT I
```

4.3.4 User-Defined Functions for Scientific Calculations

The functions supplied by PC-BASIC may not be sufficient for scientific calculations. As in the string operations, user-defined functions can be created:

```
DEF FN<num_Variable>(<Parameter...>)= <function>
```

and for the call:

```
<result>= FN<num_Variable>(<Parameter...>)
```

The following program illustrates this:

```
10 'DEF FN-Demo
20 :
30 CLS:KEY OFF
40 LOCATE 24,1
50 PRINT STRING$(80,"=");
60 LOCATE 25,1
70 PRINT "Enter monthly salary of 0 to END";
80 VIEW PRINT 1 TO 23
90 DEF FNX(MNTHSAL)=MNTHSAL*12
100 INPUT "Monthly salary: ",MNTHSAL
110 IF MNTHSAL=0 THEN 160
120 ANNUALSALARY=FNX(MNTHSAL)
130 PRINT "Annual salary:";ANNUALSALARY
140 PRINT
150 GOTO 100
160 VIEW PRINT:CLS:END
```

And the explanation:

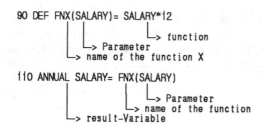

Fig. 11: DEF FN/FN

Refer to Section 4.2.4 for more information on DEF FN.

4.3.5 Logical Operators

We can use 6 *logical operators* for Boolean operations. These operators allow comprehensive bit manipulations. If you're not familiar with Boolean operations, you should read some introductory information about them. Unfortunately, a complete explanation would fill most of this book.

Logical operators are used for bit manipulation, comparing data and testing conditions.

X AND Y

During a logical operation with two values through AND, the bits are manipulated so that, in the result, the bit is false when it's false in X or Y. With AND, bits can be individually reset.

X OR Y

During a logical operation with two values with OR, the bits are manipulated so that, in the result, the bit is set if it was set in X or Y. With OR, bits can be set individually.

NOT X

NOT manipulates the bits so that, in the result, a set bit is reset and a reset bit is set.

X XOR Y

During the logical operation on two values with XOR, the bits are manipulated so that agreement between the bits in X and Y reset the bit in the result. Otherwise, the bit is set.

X EQV Y

During the logical operation on two values with EQV, the bits are manipulated so that, during agreement of the bits in X and Y, the bit in the result is set. Otherwise, the bit is reset.

X IMP Y

During the logical operation on two values with IMP, the bits are manipulated depending on the sequence of the values X and Y. So, during agreement of the bits in X and Y, the bit in the result is set. If a bit in X is set and in Y reset, it will be reset in the result. If a bit is reset in X and set in Y, it will be set in the result.

4.4 Comparing Data

Most problems cannot be solved without comparing data. The comparison of data during data input is important because this comparison with preset data may reveal an error in the input. In the following sections we'll present the capabilities offered by PC-BASIC for comparing data. You may remember the error message "Type mismatch", by which PC-BASIC informs the user of an incorrect type. Also, during data comparisons we must separate numeric and string variables. The comparison of data and the reaction, in the form of a branch to another program section, belong together. Therefore, we will begin with describing conditional branching.

4.4.1 Conditional Branching

The following syntax applies to the comparison of data and the resulting reaction of the program:

```
IF <condition> THEN <statement1> [ELSE <statement2>]
```

In <condition>, we test various values and, as a result, obtain the true or false condition. We can react in different ways in the program depending on this result. With IF, we start a comparison. The *statement* after the THEN is executed if the condition is true. If the <condition=false> then the <statement> after ELSE can be executed. IF..THEN..ELSE and the statements must be in one program line.

<statement> can contain commands, functions or the jump statements, GOTO and GOSUB. The jump statement GOTO directly after THEN or ELSE can be omitted. In some of the previous examples, we already used IF..THEN. The following program illustrates the ELSE branch of an IF query.

```
10 'ELSE-Demo
20 :
30 CLS:KEY OFF
40 X$=INKEY$:IF X$="" THEN 40
50 IF X$="1" THEN PRINT "key [1]" ELSE PRINT "key [";X$;"]"
60 IF X$=CHR$(27) THEN CLS:END
70 GOTO 40
```

4.4.2 Relational Operators

Data can be compared through various criteria. For example, they can be equal or not equal, because one value is larger or smaller. We'll use the *relational operators* to inform PC-BASIC of what criteria to use for the comparison.

An example of a keyboard query shows the effect of the various relational operators:

Relational operator = (equal)

```
10 X$=INKEY$:IF X$="" THEN 10
```

We test the condition *X$=""* in this line. This condition is true when a key isn't pressed. The relational operator is the equal sign (=). This line is processed until a key is pressed.

Relational operator < (less than)

```
10 X$=INKEY$:IF X$<CHR$(32) THEN 10
```

Tests the condition *X$<CHR$(32)*, which is true when the character in X$ is less than CHR$(32) (space). The relational operator is the open angle bracket (<). Our program doesn't allow the input of a character whose value is smaller than ASCII 32 (the space).

Relational operator > (greater than)

```
10 X$=INKEY$:IF X$>"Z" THEN 10
```

In this line we test the condition *X$>"Z"*, which is true when a key with a value greater than ASCII 90 is activated. The relational operator is the closed angle bracket (>). The program doesn't allow the input of a character that is greater than Z, for example a z. These relational operators can also be used in combinations:

Relational <= (less than or equal to)

```
10 X$=INKEY$:IF X$<="Z" THEN 10
```

This condition is true when the character entered is less than or equal to Z.

Relational >= (greater than or equal to)

```
10 X$=INKEY$:IF X$>="Z" THEN 10
```

The condition is true when the character entered is greater than or equal to Z.

Relational <> (unequal)

```
10 X$=INKEY$:IF X$<>"Z" THEN 10
```

The condition is true when the character entered is not Z.

Relational operator AND (and)

The logical operators AND, OR and NOT were discussed in Section 4.3.5. Now we'll learn how to use the relational operators AND and OR. These operators allow us to combine conditions:

```
10 X$=INKEY$:IF X$>"0" AND X$<"9" THEN 10
```

With AND, several conditions can be combined into one "big" combined condition. The result is true when all individual conditions are true. In our program line, the input of characters 1 to 8 is ignored.

Relational operator OR (or)

```
10 X$=INKEY$:IF X$="1" OR X$="0" THEN 10
```

Also, with OR, several conditions can be combined into one "big" condition. The result is true when one of the individual conditions is met. In our program line, for example, the <1> key or the <0> key is ignored.

Comparisons with AND and OR

Obviously, AND and OR can be combined:

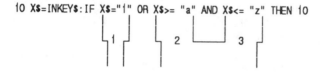

Fig. 12: AND/OR-relational

In this line, a test is made if the condition 1 or conditions 2 and 3, which are combined with an AND, are true. When the condition 1 is true, the conditions 2 and 3 aren't tested. If condition 1 is false, then conditions 2 and 3 must be true, so the statement after THEN can be executed. For the program, this means that the <1> key and all lowercase letters are ignored.

The NOT operator in comparisons

With NOT, the result of a condition is reversed:

```
10 X$=INKEY$:IF NOT(X$="1") THEN 10
```

If a key other than <1> is activated, the result of the condition *X$="1"* is false. Through NOT, the result becomes true and the statement after the THEN is executed. The program only continues when the <1> key is activated. We receive the same result with:

```
10 X$=INKEY$:IF X$<>"1" THEN 10
```

As you can see, you can achieve the same results in several ways. You can decide which query is more suitable for your needs.

4.4.3 Comparing Strings

In the previous section we discovered which operators allow the comparison of data. In this section we'll present special features for comparing strings.

As we know, strings can be variables and constants. In the previous examples we have compared string variables and string constants with each other on keyboard queries:

```
IF X$<>"1"
```

The content of the X$ variable is compared with the constant "1". In applications this is the most frequent comparison, with which, for example, input data or activated keys can be tested.

We use the comparison of two variables to determine if a certain input is already present in our file:

```
100 FOR I= 1 TO RECORD
110 IF KNAME$(I) = FIRSTNAME$ THEN 140
120 NEXT I
130 RETURN
140 PRINT "Name already exists ....."
```

As each record is entered the program jumps to the subroutine in 100 to determine if that record already exists in the file. If yes, an error message is displayed. Otherwise, we jump out of the subroutine back to the main program. The comparison of two strings is performed character by character from left to right. The value of the character depends on the ASCII codes. The following are some examples:

A$="ABCDEFG":B$="abcdefg"

In this case, A$ is less than B$, since the uppercase letters in the ASCII table occur before the lowercase letters.

A$="Smith ":B$="Smith"

In this example A$ is greater than B$, since it has one more character (the last character is a space).

For the comparison of strings, the results of functions can be used, in addition to variables and constants:

```
IF MID$(KNAME$,2,2)<>"ue"
```

You must convert numeric variables and strings to the other data type before you can compare them. Otherwise the message "Type mismatch" may appear.

4.4.4 Comparing Numeric Data

We differentiate between variables or constants (3+8*6) for numeric data. Values read, as in the example DEF FN Demo, are compared without problems:

```
IF SALARY=9999
```

Also, the results of functions can be used for the comparison:

```
IF ABS(DEGREES)>90
```

In order to compare variables, they must be the same type. For example, during a comparison of a single precision variable with a double precision variable, differences may appear in the results. The comparison of numeric variables with strings makes a preceding conversion of one of the two data types necessary.

4.5   Programming Techniques

So far we have learned many commands, statements and functions. These can be used, within certain limits, to write small programs. In this section we'll discuss how PC-BASIC solves certain problems.

4.5.1 Program Loops

A program loop can easily be implemented in PC-BASIC to have your program perform certain repetitive tasks in a very short time. A loop continues until either a predetermined condition has been met or the number of preset executions has been reached.

```
FOR...NEXT
```

The most important loop has already been used in many programs:

```
FOR <num_Variable> = <beginning> TO <end> [STEP <step>]
..............
NEXT [<num_Variable>]
```

FOR initiates the loop. The interpreter requires a <num_variable>. This variable is also designated as a counter variable and can be an integer variable or a single precision variable. You'll receive a "SYNTAX ERROR" error if you use an array as a counter variable. You'll receive a "Type mismatch" message if you use a double precision variable.

The size of the loop is determined with the values <beginning> TO <end>. NEXT marks the end of a loop. All statements between FOR and NEXT are executed.

In the following example, we want to display the text *"Hello, PC BASIC user"* 10 times. The following is one method of implementing this using the PRINT statement:

```
10 'FOR...NEXT-Demo 1
20 :
30 CLS:KEY OFF
40 PRINT "Hello, PC-BASIC user"
50 PRINT "Hello, PC-BASIC user"
60 PRINT "Hello, PC-BASIC user"
70 PRINT "Hello, PC-BASIC user"
80 PRINT "Hello, PC-BASIC user"
90 PRINT "Hello, PC-BASIC user"
100 PRINT "Hello, PC-BASIC user"
110 PRINT "Hello, PC-BASIC user"
120 PRINT "Hello, PC-BASIC user"
130 PRINT "Hello, PC-BASIC user"
```

The following method is better:

```
10 'FOR...NEXT-Demo 2
20 :
30 CLS:KEY OFF
40 FOR I=1 TO 10
50 PRINT "Hello, PC-BASIC user"
60 NEXT I
```

Although the result in both examples is identical, the first program requires 13 lines but the second program requires only 6 lines to execute. The FOR...NEXT loops in these programs count in ascending order (i.e. from a smaller value to a larger value).

There are situations when you'll want to count in descending order. The following program shows how this is done:

```
10 'FOR...NEXT-Demo 3
20 :
30 CLS:KEY OFF
40 FOR I=20 TO 10 STEP -1
50    LOCATE I,I
60    PRINT "Hello, PC-BASIC user"
70 NEXT I
```

The STEP parameter counts the steps in which the count proceeds. The example shows that with a negative STEP and a larger <beginning> to a smaller <end>, the count is backwards.

As its name suggests, STEP indicates the steps. Its value must be preceded with a minus sign (-) for a descending count. This value is omitted if the steps are one and the value is stated without a sign for an ascending count:

```
10 'FOR...NEXT-Demo 4
20 :
30 CLS:KEY OFF
40 FOR I=10 TO 20 STEP 2
50    PRINT "Hello, PC-BASIC user"
60 NEXT I
```

STEP can also be a number with a decimal point (for example, STEP 1.5). You should use an integer variable as a counter variable if the count is in whole numbers. This is so it can be quickly counted by the interpreter. For a simple loop with NEXT, the <num_variable> doesn't have to be indicated. This differs for nested FOR...NEXT loops:

```
10 'FOR...NEXT-Demo 5
20 :
30 CLS:KEY OFF
40 FOR I=1 TO 10
50    FOR K=1 TO 10
60       PRINT "Test";
70    NEXT K
80 NEXT I
```

Note: You can also use the following instead of the line 70 listed in this program:

```
70 NEXT K,I
```

You can improve the appearance of your program listing by indenting the lines. This also helps identify the content of every loop. However, you should avoid the solution presented in line 70.

As we can see, every FOR also requires a NEXT. Using NEXT to resolve the loop is very important:

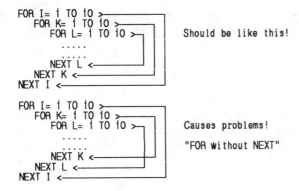

Fig. 13: FOR...NEXT

At the beginning of a loop, PC-BASIC searches for the NEXT relating to the FOR and notes its position in the program. The statement following NEXT is executed after the loop is processed. The counter variable can be used only once in nested loops.

Before executing the loop, PC-BASIC tests the parameters <beginning> TO <end> STEP. If it determines that <end> has been reached, the statements in the loop are no longer executed. So, the loop is terminated and the program continues after the NEXT. A FOR...NEXT loop is terminated by exiting the loop with GOTO or RETURN. This depends on the call of the program:

```
100 FOR I=1 TO 10
110    IF INPUT$(I)="end" THEN GOTO 500
120 NEXT I
130 .....
```

Avoid frequent "exits" from one or more FOR...NEXT loops. This seriously strains the stack of PC-BASIC. Each FOR...NEXT loop stores information about the beginning, end and counter variable of the loop. This data isn't deleted during the exit. It's better to set the counter variable to a value greater than the "end-value" of the loop and jump to the line with the NEXT statement:

```
100 FOR I=1 TO 10
110    IF INPUT$(I)="end" THEN I= 11:GOTO 130
120    PRINT INPUT$
130 NEXT I
```

For loops that run backwards (STEP -), the counter variable must be set to a smaller value. Unfortunately, PC-BASIC allows you to change the value of the counter variable inside the loop. This is dangerous because you may produce an infinite loop from which you cannot escape. So, be very careful when processing the values of the counter variable in the loop.

WHILE...WEND

An alternative to FOR...NEXT that PC-BASIC offers is the WHILE...WEND statement:

```
WHILE <condition>
<statements...>
WEND
```

If the <condition> is true, <statements> are executed. If the <condition> is false, <statements> after WEND are executed. Therefore, the loop executes as long as a given condition remains true. Unlike the FOR...NEXT loop, a condition instead of a counter variable is required. For example:

```
10 'WHILE...WEND-Demo
20 :
30 CLS:KEY OFF
40 KINPUT$=""
50 WHILE KINPUT$<>"99"
60     INPUT "Enter a letter or phrase: ";KINPUT$
70     PRINT "Your input was:";KINPUT$
80     PRINT
90 WEND
100 PRINT "That was it!"
```

In line 50 the condition "KINPUT$<>"99"" is tested. If the condition was met (i.e., "99" is entered in line 60), the program branches after the WEND to the statement in line 100. If the condition wasn't met, INPUT$ is displayed and the entire process repeats.

The WHILE...WEND loop is used in subroutines to execute several <statements>, depending on the value passed to <condition>. Since <condition> can be more flexible, the programmer has more alternatives with WHILE...WEND loops than with FOR...NEXT loops.

The WHILE...WEND loops can also be nested. It's also true that for every WHILE there must be a WEND otherwise a "WHILE without WEND" error message appears on the screen. Since WEND isn't tied to a counter variable, it's possible that the programs may be difficult to follow because of nested loops. Therefore, use the <Tab> key to indent WHILE and WEND statements. Also, a careful programmer sets the condition following WEND with a REM statement to obtain a complete overview:

```
100 WHILE X$<>CHR$(27) AND X$<>CHR$(13)
110     .....
120     .....
130     WHILE X$<>"1"
140         .....
150         .....
160     WEND:'X$<>"1"
170     .....
180 WEND:'X$<>CHR$(27) and X$<>CHR$(13)
```

As with a FOR...NEXT loop, you can prematurely exit or terminate a WHILE...WEND loop. However, this again seriously strains the stack of PC-BASIC. Also, this does not delete the stored information for WHILE...WEND. The <condition> for the WHILE...WEND loops should be carefully programmed. Otherwise, an endless loop could occur.

4.5.2 Subroutines

Although we have already mentioned *subroutines*, in this section we'll discuss them in detail.

GOSUB...RETURN

A PC-BASIC program may have several identical or similar program lines which are executed in different parts of the program. The best example of this is the keyboard query. Instead of writing the statements for every query in each section of the program, we can implement them as a subroutine. This not only saves available RAM but if changes are required, the entire program doesn't have to be revised. Only the subroutine containing the statements is changed. The following program is an example of how we can execute the subroutine on demand:

```
GOSUB <line-number>
.....
RETURN [<line-number>]
```

An example again:

```
10 'GOSUB...RETURN-Demo
20 :
30 CLS:KEY OFF
40 PRINT "--------- Menu ---------"
50 PRINT
60 PRINT "<1>.....input data"
70 PRINT "<2>.....display data"
```

101

```
 80 PRINT "<3>.....erase data"
 90 PRINT
100 PRINT "Please strike key <1>, <2>, <3> or <Esc> to END ..."
110 GOSUB 370:'keyboard query
120 IF X$="1" THEN 160
130 IF X$="2" THEN 230
140 IF X$="3" THEN 300
150 :
160 '----- data input
170 :
180 'This is the program part for data input
190 LOCATE 25,1:PRINT "More data input (Y/N)"
200 GOSUB 370:'keyboard query
210 IF X$="y" OR X$="Y" THEN 180 ELSE 30
220 :
230 '----- display data
240 :
250 'This is the program part for data display
260 LOCATE 25,1:PRINT "More data display (Y/N)"
270 GOSUB 370:'keyboard query
280 IF X$="y" OR X$="Y" THEN 250 ELSE 30
290 :
300 '----- erase data
310 :
320 'This is the program part to erase data
330 LOCATE 25,1:PRINT "erase more data (Y/N)"
340 GOSUB 370:'keyboard query
350 IF X$="y" OR X$="Y" THEN 320 ELSE 30
360 :
370 '----- subroutine - keyboard query
380 :
390 X$=INKEY$:IF X$="" THEN 390
400 IF X$=CHR$(27) THEN CLS:END
410 RETURN
```

Each time input is entered from the keyboard (line 110) the subroutine is executed with the GOSUB 370 statement. During the GOSUB statement, PC-BASIC remembers the current position in the program. After the subroutine executes, a jump is performed to the statement following GOSUB. In PC-BASIC, this is done with RETURN. You'll receive an "Undefined line number" error message if PC-BASIC cannot find the line number indicated with GOSUB.

In Chapter 3 we discussed the stack and discovered that it could be used for different purposes. One of these is to store the current line location during GOSUB. The current line location is stored on the stack when PC-BASIC encounters a GOSUB statement. This line location is deleted from the stack and is used as a return jump address during the next RETURN.

It's possible that after RETURN, instead of executing the statement following GOSUB, you would like to continue in an another section of the program (i.e. another line number).

To do this, simply add the appropriate line number to RETURN. PC-BASIC deletes the stored position for the normal return jump from the stack, finds this specified line indicated and continues the program from that line location. We could also ignore a subroutine. Although this would also be possible with GOTO, it would load the stack since it could delete the stored return jump location.

PC-BASIC permits the call of a subroutine from another subroutine. This can be done an infinite amount of times with a free stack. The following illustration demonstrates this:

```
      100 GOSUB 500 >┐
  ┌─> 110 .....     ┆
  ┆   120 END       ┆
  ┆                 ┆
  ┆   500 'subroutine 1 <────┘
  ┆   510 .....
  ┆   520 GOSUB 600 >┐
  ┌─> 530 .....      ┆
  └─< 540 RETURN    2┆
  ┆                  ┆
  ┆   600 'subroutine 2 <────┘
  2   610 .....
  ┆   620 .....
  ┆   630 GOSUB 700 >┐
  ┌─> 640 .....      ┆
  └─< 650 RETURN    3┆
  ┆                  ┆
  3   700 'subroutine 3 <────┘
  ┆   710 .....
  ┆   720 .....
  └─< 730 RETURN
```

Fig. 14: GOSUB/RETURN

With nested subroutines it's possible that, by using RETURN <line number>, the overview will be lost. So, use this return jump only when it cannot be avoided.

Also, the WHILE...WEND and FOR...NEXT loops, which are being processed, remain open. This may eventually lead to an error message. The recursive call of a subroutine (the call of the subroutine from itself) is possible:

```
500 :
510 '----- subroutine 1 -----
520 :
530 <statements>
540 GOSUB 510
550 <statements>
560 RETURN
```

Remember that this can become a trap in the form of an endless call. When the stack overruns and no RAM remains for storing return jump locations, You'll receive an "Out of Memory" error message when this occurs. In a subroutine, depending on the requirements, several RETURNs can be used instead of a condition:

```
100 GOSUB 200
110 .....
120 .....
200 'subroutine 1
210 X$=INKEY$:IF X$="" THEN 210
220 IF X$<"0" OR X$>"9" THEN 210
230 IF X$=CHR$(27) THEN RETURN
240 IF X$="1" THEN A=25+3
250 IF X$="2" THEN RETURN
260 IF X$="3" THEN B=25+3
270 IF X$="4" THEN RETURN
280 RETURN
```

Every RETURN uses the stored return jump position of the GOSUB from line 100.

Finally, PC-BASIC displays a "RETURN without GOSUB" error message when it encounters a RETURN without detecting a corresponding GOSUB in the program. For a RETURN, the next return jump position, which is available on the stack, is accepted as given. PC-BASIC doesn't test this if, for every GOSUB, a RETURN is available. However, this is dangerous because after a RETURN, a branch is made to a line, which wasn't intended.

4.5.3 Branching with ON X GOTO/GOSUB

To avoid comprehensive IF...THEN queries for branching, we can use the ON X statement from PC-BASIC:

```
ON <value> GOTO | GOSUB <line-number...>
```

After GOTO or GOSUB, enter a list of line numbers, depending on <value>, to which jumps are made. For example:

```
10 'ON X GOTO/GOSUB-Demo
20 :
30 CLS:KEY OFF
40 PRINT "---------- Menu ----------"
50 PRINT "<1>.....data input"
60 PRINT "<2>.....change data"
70 PRINT "<3>.....display data"
80 PRINT "<4>.....erase data"
90 PRINT "<5>.....sort data "
100 PRINT "<6>.....print data"
110 X$=INKEY$:IF X$="" THEN 110
120 IF X$<"1" OR X$>"6" THEN 110
130 VALUE=ASC(X$)-48
140 ON VALUE GOSUB 1000,2000,3000,4000,5000,6000
150 GOTO 30
```

The corresponding subroutines start with the line numbers 1000, 2000, 3000, 4000, 5000 and 6000. These lines correspond to the menu selection in lines 50, 60, 70, 80, 90 and 100. The value of the VALUE variable is processed with ON X. This is determined in line 130 by subtracting 48 from the ASCII code of the <1>...<6> key that was pressed. The <2> key, for example, contains the ASCII code 50. Subtracting 48 from 50 produces the value 2. So, the ON X branches to the second line number after GOTO/GOSUB. The following illustration demonstrates this:

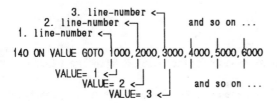

Fig. 15: ON X GOTO/GOSUB

The statements following ON X are executed when VALUE is 0 or is larger than the number of the indicated line numbers. After RETURN in a subroutine, the statements in the line following ON X line are executed. VALUE cannot be negative or larger than 255. Otherwise the "Illegal function call" error message is displayed. You'll receive an "Undefined line number" error message when a line number behind the GOTO/GOSUB cannot be found in the program.

4.5.4 Overlay Techniques and Data Transfer

In this section we'll show you what to do when your programs are too large to fit in available RAM. This happens, for example, when a multi-program application must be programmed. A simple example demonstrates how to use the overlay technique.

Suppose that you own a small business and want to use a PC to help with various tasks. First you must determine what tasks the PC will perform:

1.   Bookkeeping
2.   Loan and payroll calculations
3.   Word processing
4.   Customer file

The program should execute in such a way that these applications are called from a main menu. Each application will have its own menus from which individual programs are called. After a section of the program is completed, the higher level menu will be called again. This would appear as follows:

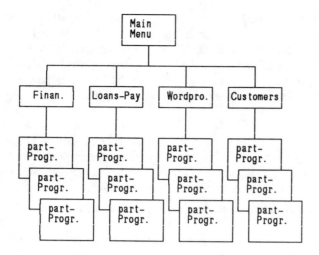

Fig. 16: Computer Algorithm

This would easily help you with your business. We can also make enhancements so that you can use addresses in the word processor for form letters, promotional flyers, etc.

You should be able to program the main menu. Refer to the programs we've discussed if you need examples. The application menus are loaded from the main menu as follows:

```
.....
.....:'the menu-program runs up to here
200 ON X GOTO 1000,2000,3000,4000
1000 LOAD "FINANCE.BAS",R
2000 LOAD "LOANS.BAS",R
3000 LOAD "WORDPRO.BAS",R
4000 LOAD "CLIENTS.BAS",R
```

This is an acceptable solution since variables aren't passed from the main menu to the application menus. You could use the RUN <filename> command instead of the LOAD command. For the return to the main menu, each applications menu ends with the statement:

```
LOAD "MAINMENU.BAS",R
```

The call of the individual program sections from the application menus is more complicated. You must pass variables with date, filenames or other information to the partial programs. This data could also be queried in the partial programs, but, under certain circumstances, this would produce double queries (i.e., for the date, for the bookkeeping as well as the loan and payroll calculations).

Overlays

Overlays are program sections which are either loaded over a program that is in RAM or are attached to it. In our example we'll attach the program sections to the application menus that are in memory.

Data Transmission

The data transmission between individual program sections occurs through a *COM area*. This is a protected area in which the variables, which are to be passed, are stored. This area must be arranged by the programmer. COM area is an acronym for *Common* and *area*. PC-BASIC protects this area to prevent overwriting by other data or programs.

CHAIN

We can use the CHAIN statement for merging overlays:

```
CHAIN      [MERGE]
  <file-spec.>
  [,<start-line>]
  [,ALL]
  [,DELETE <from_line>-<to_line>]
```

Don't be intimidated by all of these parameters. We'll discuss them in detail and discover how they function.

[MERGE]

We've already discussed the MERGE command for program input in Chapter 3. A second program is loaded (merged) into a program already in RAM. This means that the available lines are either replaced, inserted according to their number or attached to the existing program. Then either the new complete program or the section after the beginning line is executed.

<file spec>

Enter the file specification (i.e., drive, path, name and extension) of the program to be included.

<start line>

Enter the line corresponding to the line number in the called program. This is the line where CHAIN starts or executes the program. Execution starts at the first line if <start line> is omitted.

[ALL]

Use the ALL parameter so PC-BASIC retains all available variable values. If you do not use ALL, CHAIN erases all variables and releases the RAM space again. If only certain variables should be passed, use the COMMON statement (see below).

[DELETE <from_line> <to_line>

DELETE can only be used with MERGE. DELETE erases the lines indicated by *<from_line> <to_line>* before the program is merged with the program already in RAM.

Since there are so many parameters, there are obviously many requirements. For example, the program to be merged must be stored in ASCII format. This can be done with *SAVE <file spec.>,A* (see Chapter 3).

Because of the required conversion from ASCII to the program format or the merging with MERGE, CHAIN can take longer to execute. With very large programs, a normal PC may take 5 seconds to do this. You should inform your users that the program is still executing. Otherwise, they'll think that the program may have crashed.

If you use MERGE without ALL, all open files are closed, all variables are deleted and all open GOSUB...RETURN, FOR...NEXT and WHILE...WEND loops are closed. All files remain open if CHAIN is used without MERGE.

Any functions defined with DEF FN cannot be used in programs loaded with MERGE. These must be defined in the basic program. CHAIN performs a RESTORE before loading. Use READ...DATA in the program to be loaded to reset the data pointer, if necessary. The value determined with OPTION BASE for arrays, remains unchanged. RENUM has no effect on the start line. Remember that this must be corrected separately.

COMMON

This statement is used when only certain variables should be passed to the program to be merged:

```
COMMON <Variable...>
```

All available types, including arrays, can be indicated as variables. The COMMON statement can be used in the program at any location and as many times as necessary. A careful programmer places the COMMON statement at the beginning of the program. This allows the passed variables to be more visible.

A program to be merged must include the COMMON statement only if additional overlays, with data transmissions, will be made from there. A variable specified with COMMON must be supplied in the calling program with some content. If necessary, assign 0 or an empty string to it. During the passing of arrays remember that the DIM statement must occur before the COMMON statement.

An Application

Now we'll return to our example. A partial program will be called from the bookkeeping application menu and a variable will be passed:

```
10 'CHAIN and COMMON-Demo
20 :
30 CLS:KEY OFF
40 :
50 COMMON MONTH$
60 :
70 PRINT "---------- Financial Bookkeeping ----------"
80 PRINT
90 PRINT "<1>.....data input"
100 PRINT "<2>.....end of the month "
110 PRINT
120 PRINT "Please strike key <1>, <2> or <Exc> to END ....."
130 X$=INKEY$:IF X$="" THEN 130
140 IF X$="1" THEN 180
150 IF X$="2" THEN 200
160 IF X$<>CHR$(27) THEN 130
170 LOAD" MAINMENU.BAS",R:'End, back to main-menu
180 '---------- data input
190 LOAD"FINANCE.BAS",R
200 '---------- End of the Month
210 LOCATE 20,5
220 LINE INPUT "End of the Month [1 to 12]: ";MONTH
230 IF VAL(MONTH$)<1 OR VAL(MONTH$)>12 THEN BEEP:GOTO 210
240 CHAIN MERGE "FINANCE2.BAS",180,DELETE 180-240

180 '---------- This is all for the monthly program
190 CLS:KEY OFF
200 PRINT "You want to conclude the month ";MONTH$;"."
210 PRINT:PRINT:PRINT
220 PRINT "Strike any key to list the current program."
230 PRINT "This should show you the effect of the CHAIN-command."
240 IF INKEY$="" THEN 240
250 LIST
```

Copy the two programs as shown above. For the first program you can select any name, but the second must be called FINANCE2.BAS. This second program is attached to the application menu. This allows you to call the application menu immediately, without reloading it, after the partial program terminates.

Before reading the next sections, you should practice some of the material you've learned in this section. Eventually, you'll be able to handle overlays as easily as all the other statements, commands and functions.

4.5.5 The Function Keys

In Chapter 3 we discussed function keys and how they work with the editor. Now we'll discuss how function keys are used in programs. We already know that the text for the function keys can be used freely:

```
KEY <number>, "<text>" | <string> | <function>
```

With <number>, we indicate which function key should be assigned. The "<text>" can be a string constant, and/or a string variable and/or the result of a function. In programs, the function keys are generally used to support the user with help messages. With a keyboard query, the execution of a specific program section begins after a specific function key is pressed:

```
10 KEY 1,"HELP":KEY 2,"END":KEY 3,"PRINT"
.....
.....
100 X$=INKEY$:IF X$="" THEN 100
110 IF X$="H" THEN 1000:'<F1> activated
120 IF X$="E" THEN CLS:END:'<F2> activated
130 IF X$="D" THEN 2000:'<F3> activated
.....
.....
```

Unfortunately, the INKEY$ function doesn't return the extended keyboard codes when a function key was activated with KEY ON. Therefore, we must query the first letter. However, this query is dangerous because the program would also react if the uppercase H, E and D characters are entered. Also, we must include a routine in our program which reads the remaining characters from the keyboard buffer. A better solution is explained in Chapter 7.

A statement for providing an interesting but temporary variation on displaying the function keys is:

```
KEY LIST
```

This statement displays all 15 characters of the value for each function key. Using INPUT we can read the new text in a loop and assign keys.

4.6   File Control

You already know that all programs in RAM are lost after powering down the computer. Therefore, these programs must be permanently stored in files on a disk or a hard disk. In this chapter we'll discuss the two types of data storage which PC-BASIC supports.

What is a file?

A *file* is a collection of information. To illustrate this, think of a file as a card file. Cards containing addresses are stored in this card file. The addresses are the information and the card file stores all the information.

What is a record?

A file is composed of several *records*. To continue with our example, the card file is the file and the cards stored in it are the individual records.

What is a field?

A record consists of several *fields*. In our example, the file cards contain the addresses. These addresses are composed of name, street, ZIP code and city, which are the individual fields.

Summary

The smallest information unit in a file is the field. Several fields form a record, several records form a file.

4.6.1 Sequential Files

PC-BASIC differentiates between *sequential files* and *random files*. Using the card file example again, there are several methods that can be used to store the cards (records). They can be stored, for example, alphabetically.

In sequential files, the records are stored sequentially. Each field is the length of the information it contains. Every record ends with a marker that tells PC-BASIC that the record stops here and a new one starts. These markers consist of the decimal values 10 and 13. These values are designated as the CRLF sequence, which represent Carriage Return and Linefeed. This term corresponds to the output of a printer, where, after each line, the printhead is returned to the beginning of the line and a carriage return advances the paper to a new line.

The end of a file is marked with the decimal value 26. This mark is also designated as an EOF mark. The EOF is the acronym for End of File.

The length of the record in sequential files is limited to 255 characters. More characters cannot be stored in a string. Theoretically, it's possible to write several strings without separating them into a file. However, this data couldn't be read and processed as one unit.

Accessing a certain record isn't possible because of the different length of the records. So, the position of the data in the file cannot be determined. In order to be processed, the entire sequential file must be read into memory. A sequential file can be shown as follows:

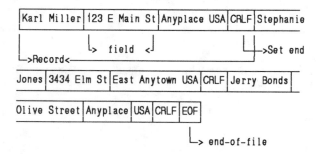

Fig. 17: Sequential File

This example shows that all data is separated by the CRLF and stored sequentially. Each field only occupies as much space as required by the information. The end of the file is the EOF mark.

We'll use an example to further illustrate this. Suppose that you collect stamps and bought a stamp album which is separated into various countries. You have a different number of stamps for each country. If each country represents a record, then each record has a different length because each country doesn't contain the same number of stamps. So, each country occupies a different number of pages in the album. Since you can't remember how many stamps of a certain country are stored on each page, you cannot access the stamps of a country on the basis of the page number. You must go through each page sequentially to access a specific country or a specific stamp.

The following program demonstrates how sequential files work. We're going to read some addresses from the keyboard, store them according to a field and then display them on the screen:

```
10 'Sequential File
20 :
30 CLS:KEY OFF
40 DIM ADDRESS$(10,6)
50 PRINT "---------- Entering the addresses ----------"
```

```
60 PRINT
70 PRINT "Enter END after 'Name' to terminate the input ....."
80 FOR I=1 TO 10
90 LOCATE 5,50
100 PRINT "Input record is:";:PRINT USING "##";I
110 VIEW PRINT 7 TO 20:CLS:VIEW PRINT
120 LOCATE 7,1
130 INPUT "Name: ";ADDRESS$(I,1)
140 IF ADDRESS$(I,1)="END" OR ADDRESS$(I,1)="end" THEN 250
150 INPUT "Address: ";ADDRESS$(I,2)
160 INPUT "City: ";ADDRESS$(I,3)
170 INPUT "State: ";ADDRESS$(I,4)
180 INPUT "Zip: ";ADDRESS$(I,5)
190 INPUT "Telephone: ";ADDRESS$(I,6)
200 LOCATE 20,1
210 PRINT "Input OK? (Y/N)"
220 X$=INKEY$:IF X$="" THEN 220
230 IF X$="n" OR X$="N" THEN 110
240 NEXT I
250 CLS
260 PRINT "----- Storing the addresses -----"
270 NUM.OF.RECRD=I-1
280 OPEN "address.dat" FOR OUTPUT AS #1
290 FOR I=1 TO NUM.OF.RECRD
300 LOCATE 5,50
310 PRINT "Storing record: ";:PRINT USING "##";I
320     FOR K=1 TO 6
330         PRINT#1,ADDRESS$(I,K)
340     NEXT K
350 NEXT I
360 CLOSE
370 CLS
380 PRINT "----- read and display the addresses -----"
390 OPEN "address.dat" FOR INPUT AS #1
400 I=1
410 WHILE NOT EOF(1)
420     LOCATE 5,50
430     PRINT "Reading/Displaying record: ";:PRINT USING "##";I
440     LOCATE 7,1
450       FOR K=1 TO 6
460           INPUT#1,ADDRESS$(I,K)
470           PRINT ADDRESS$(I,K);",";
480       NEXT K
490     LOCATE 20,1
500     PRINT "Strike any key to view next record"
510     IF INKEY$="" THEN 510
520     VIEW PRINT 6 TO 20:CLS:VIEW PRINT
530     I=I+1
540 WEND
550 CLOSE
560 CLS
570 PRINT "End of file....."
```

If you don't understand the commands, statements and functions used in this program, we'll discuss each of them in the next section.

4.6.2 Random Files (Direct Access Files)

The term *random* means *direct access*. This means that each record can be accessed directly.

This is possible because each record is a fixed length. This length is communicated to PC-BASIC while a file is created or read. All data records are numbered starting at zero in ascending order. This is the *record number*. With this system, PC-BASIC makes the data available immediately. In contrast to the sequential file, it doesn't have to be completely available in memory. So, there is more space for our program.

Handling a random file is more difficult than working with a sequential file. PC-BASIC makes the task easier through a series of statements, commands and functions. A typical random file appears as follows:

		Field 1	2	3
S	1	Miller, Karl	123 E Main St	Anyplace USA
a t	2	Stephanie Jones	3434 Elm St	East Anytown USA
z	3	Jerry Bonds	Olive Street	Anyplace USA

Fig. 18: Random File

Because the individual fields each has a fixed length, the record also has a fixed length. Therefore, you can calculate each record length in a random file. This allows you to access a random file more quickly than a sequential file. The example of the sequential file clearly illustrates this. If you need the fifth address from a sequential file, first the preceding four addresses must be read. But with random-access files we can directly access the fifth address.

For a clearer explanation let's return to our stamp collection example. This time let's assume that you only use one page for each country. One page has enough space for 80 stamps. To access a specific country, you only have to access its page number. Here's an example of a random file:

```
10 'Random File
20 :
30 CLS:KEY OFF
40 DIM ADDRESS$(10,6)
50 PRINT "---------- input of the addresses ----------"
60 PRINT
70 PRINT "Enter END after 'Name' to terminate the input ....."
80 FOR I=1 TO 10
90 LOCATE 5,50
```

```
100 PRINT "Input record is:";:PRINT USING "##";I
110 VIEW PRINT 7 TO 20:CLS:VIEW PRINT
120 LOCATE 7,1
130 INPUT "Name: ";ADDRESS$(I,1)
140 IF ADDRESS$(I,1)="END" OR ADDRESS$(I,1)="end" THEN 250
150 INPUT "Address: ";ADDRESS$(I,2)
160 INPUT "City: ";ADDRESS$(I,3)
170 INPUT "State: ";ADDRESS$(I,4)
180 INPUT "Zip: ";ADDRESS$(I,5)
190 INPUT "Telephone: ";ADDRESS$(I,6)
200 LOCATE 20,1
210 PRINT "Input OK? (Y/N)"
220 X$=INKEY$:IF X$="" THEN 220
230 IF X$="n" OR X$="N" THEN 110
240 NEXT I
250 CLS
260 PRINT "----- Storing the addresses-----"
270 NUM.OF.RECRDS=I-1
280 OPEN "R",#1,"address.dat",128
290 GOSUB 670:'FIELD-Definitions
300 FOR I=1 TO NUM.OF.RECRDS
310     LOCATE 5,50
320     PRINT "Storing record: ";:PRINT USING "##";I
330     LSET NME$=ADDRESS$(I,1)
340     LSET ADDR$=ADDRESS$(I,2)
350     LSET CTY$=ADDRESS$(I,3)
360     LSET ST$=ADDRESS$(I,4)
370     LSET ZIP$=ADDRESS$(I,5)
380     LSET TELEPHONE$=ADDRESS$(I,6)
390     PUT #1,I
400 NEXT I
410 CLOSE
420 CLS
430 PRINT "----- read and display the addresses -----"
440 PRINT
450 PRINT "Enter '99' as record number to terminate display ....."
460 OPEN "R",#1,"address.dat",128
470 GOSUB 670:'FIELD-Definitions
480 WHILE NOT EOF(1)
490 LOCATE 20,1
500 INPUT "Record number of the address: ";SET.NO$
510 IF SET.NO$="99" THEN 640
520 IF VAL(SET.NO$)<1 OR VAL(SET.NO$)>10 THEN BEEP:GOTO 490
530 LOCATE 5,50
540 PRINT "Reading/Displaying record: ";:PRINT USING "##";VAL(SET.NO$)
550 GET#1,VAL(SET.NO$)
560 LOCATE 7,1
570 PRINT NME$:PRINT ADDR$:PRINT CTY$;",";ST$;" ";ZIP$
580 PRINT TELEPHONE
590 LOCATE 20,1
600 PRINT "Strike any key to view next record"
610 IF INKEY$="" THEN 610
620 VIEW PRINT 5 TO 20:CLS:VIEW PRINT
```

115

```
630 WEND
640 CLOSE
650 CLS
660 PRINT "End of the example....."
670 '----- FIELD-Definitions -----
680 FIELD#1,30 AS NME$,30 AS ADDR$,30 AS CTY$,20 AS ST$,8 AS ZIP$,10 AS
    TELEPHONE$
690 RETURN
```

One disadvantage of random files is that the record number may not always be known. In some applications, this can be avoided. For example, if you're using the random file to keep track of customers, the customer's account number can be used as a record number. However, in other applications, in which the record number cannot be easily determined, it may be more difficult to find the record number.

The simplest solution is a combination of both files. In a sequential file we can store the name and the record number that applies. Since this will be a relatively small file, it can be easily stored in memory. With the random files, we store the entire record. To display an address, we search the sequential file for the name. After we obtain the record number through the name, we can display the record from the random file. This method of file control is called *index sequential* and will be explained in Chapter 14.

4.6.3 File Control Statements, Commands and Functions

In this section we'll discuss the statements, commands and functions in the order in which they are used in the program. Then we'll discuss the functions that PC-BASIC provides for file control.

OPEN

A file must be opened before you can work with it. This means that the operating system reserves a channel for the data transmission and provides a buffer to temporarily store the data. The data isn't read directly from the disk or hard disk. Actually, PC-BASIC requests the data from the operating system. This ensures that the data is read from the disk into a buffer and informs PC-BASIC where it can find the buffer. From there PC-BASIC obtains the data. The illustration on the following page demonstrates this:

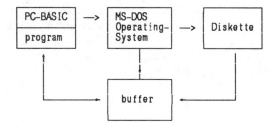

Fig. 19: Disk-Buffer

While reading the data, PC-BASIC requests it from the operating system, which reads the data block by block from the file and stores it in a buffer. From this buffer, PC-BASIC can obtain its data. This data is then written, by the operating system, block by block into the file.

If nothing else was determined during the call of PC-BASIC, a block will contain 128 bytes. The operating system controls a *data pointer* which indicates how many blocks of 128 bytes each were read (i.e., which is the current block or record in the file). Because of compatibility, the OPEN statement can be used in two ways:

```
OPEN <file-spec> FOR <mode> AS #<file-number> [,LEN=<set-length>]
```

If you're not familiar with <file spec>, refer to Section 3.4. You can tell PC-BASIC what is to be done with the file by using <mode>:

INPUT

The file opens to read data. The file pointer is set to the beginning of the file. PC-BASIC displays the message "File not found" error message if the file doesn't exist.

OUTPUT

The file is opened to write data into this file. The file pointer is set to the beginning of the file. If an existing file is opened, the existing data is overwritten. If the file doesn't exist, the operating system creates this file.

APPEND

The file is opened in OUTPUT mode to write data into this file. However, the file pointer is set to the end-of-file. This allows you to make the file larger (APPEND, also means attach). If PC-BASIC doesn't find the file, it will be created.

The INPUT, OUTPUT or APPEND modes can only be used for sequential files.

<file number> is assigned to <file spec>. For all input/output statements, only <file number> must be provided. <file number> can have a value between 1 and 15.

117

If you leave out the sequence, FOR <mode>, in the OPEN statement and work with LEN=<record length>, the file is opened as a random file. Remember that either/or is valid here. If you try to open a sequential file with LEN=, a SYNTAX ERROR will appear. If you omitted FOR <mode> and didn't indicate LEN=, this will also produce a SYNTAX ERROR. <record length> can have a value between 1 and 32,767.

The second way to use the OPEN statement appears as follows:

```
OPEN "<mode>", #<file-number>, <file-spec> [,<set-length>]
```

<file number> and <file spec> have the same significance as in the first variant of the OPEN statement. With <mode> you can determine what should be done with the file:

"I"

Represents INPUT. The statements for variant 1 apply.

"O"

Represents OUTPUT. The statements for variant 1 apply.

"A"

Represents APPEND. The statements for variant 1 apply.

In "I", "O" or "A" modes, record length shouldn't be indicated. Otherwise, you'll receive a "Syntax error" message.

"R"

Represents "R", a random file is opened. Although the record length must be given, LEN= isn't required.

During the OPEN statement, <mode> can be given with a string constant or string variables. Results of string functions aren't permitted:

Correct:

```
110 DNAME$="TEST"+"01+".DAT"
120 OPEN DNAME$ FOR OUTPUT AS #1
```

Incorrect:

```
120 OPEN MID$(INPUT$,5,3)+".DAT" FOR OUTPUT AS #1
```

Note: Several files may be opened and controlled simultaneously.

In the CONFIG.SYS file (see Chapter 3), the entry:

```
files= <number files>
```

must determine how many files must be simultaneously controlled by MS-DOS. Remember that, depending on the version, MS-DOS requires up to five files for itself. Also, depending on the version, the maximum number of files <number files> is limited. Generally, you can expect that 20 files are permitted. Set the switch /F during the call of PC-BASIC to determine how many files PC-BASIC should control.

```
GWBASIC /F:<number files>
```

Also, remember that PC-BASIC requires four files for internal control. If, for example, your program requires seven files, then CONFIG.SYS must have:

```
files= 16
```

This is five files for DOS, four files for PC-BASIC and seven files for your program. In other words, when files= 20 in CONFIG.SYS, you can use a maximum of 11 files. Again, this depends on the PC-BASIC version.

This limit shouldn't be exceeded because a large amount of programming is needed to control more than three files. For a "normal" program, almost no memory space remains free. It's also possible that, because of insufficient control, the program will be terminated without all the files being closed properly, which can lead to data loss.

PRINT#

To write data into a file, use the PRINT# statement. This is slightly different than the PRINT statement from Section 4.1:

```
PRINT#<file-number>, <Variables,...> [; | ,]
```

The difference exists only in the number character (#) and the file number, which is directly attached to the PRINT statement. The <file number> must agree with the file number used in the OPEN statement. Otherwise, it may access the wrong file or generate a "Bad file number" error message.

The PRINT# statement at the end of the output automatically writes the CRLF sequence (carriage return, line feed). The CRLF can be suppressed with the semicolon (;). The data is then written, without a separation mark, in the file. Be careful when using the semicolon. If it's incorrectly used it writes a useless or endless record which cannot be completely read.

As in a PRINT statement, the comma (,) tabs the data during the writing into the file. The tab is set every 14 characters. The area between these characters is filled with spaces.

PRINT# USING

Similar to PRINT USING for the screen, data can be written formatted into a file:

```
PRINT#<file-number> USING <"Mask">; <Variable,...>
```

There are no differences for "normal" PRINT USING except for the # character and the file number. Remember that the suggestions and explanations from the PRINT# statement are also valid for PRINT# USING.

WRITE#

This statement was also seen on the screen output. The only difference is the number character (#) and the file number located directly behind WRITE:

```
WRITE#<file-number>, <Variables,...>
```

It's not possible to suppress the automatically written CRLF sequence (carriage return, line feed with WRITE. Also, be sure that the file number is identical to the one in the OPEN statement.

Suggestions for PRINT#, PRINT# USING and WRITE#

As we already mentioned, all three statements are identical to those for the screen output, except for the number character (#) and the file number. You discovered that the data is read and written through a buffer during the OPEN statement. This buffer is only written to the disk or hard disk when it's full. Don't expect the disk or hard disk to move after every PRINT#, PRINT# USING or WRITE# statement.

All three statements use the CRLF sequence (carriage return, line feed) as a separator mark between the records. Additional separators are the quotation marks CHR$(34) (") and the comma CHR$(44) (,). These two characters must be between quotation marks if they're part of a string:

```
PRINT#1,CHR$(34);"Text";CHR$(34)
```

PRINT#, PRINT# USING and WRITE# can only be used with sequential files. For random files use the PUT#/GET# statements. We'll discuss these on the following pages.

INPUT#   read data

This statement is similar to the INPUT statement from Section 4.1:

```
INPUT#<file-number>, <Variable,...>
```

With this statement, the number character (#) and the file number used in the OPEN statement are placed after the INPUT to mark the reading from a file.

INPUT always reads complete records from the file and assigns them to <variable>. The CRLF sequence acts as a separator between records. If PRINT# was used to write the separators, quotation marks CHR$(34) (") or commas CHR$(44) (,) into the file, these are valid as separators for the next record and therefore cannot be part of a string. Use the LINE INPUT# statement instead. We recommend writing and reading records with a small test file before attempting a "real" program.

CHR$(32) is considered a separator while the numeric data is read. Remember this when using PRINT# USING. During INPUT# the message "Type mismatch" appears if you attempt to read data not corresponding to the variable types.

INPUT$

```
X$=INPUT$(<number_characters>,[#<file-number>])
```

With INPUT$, we can read a preset <number_characters> from the file opened with <file number>. INPUT$ reads everything that is sent to it. So any type of separator (except EOF, end of file) is returned as a result. With INPUT$ it's possible to save a damaged file, which couldn't be read with INPUT# OR LINE INPUT#. The file is read character by character and, from the individual characters, the new record is "constructed" and written into a second file.

LINE INPUT#

```
LINE INPUT#<file-number>, <Variable,...>
```

The difference between this statement and the INPUT# statement is that the LINE INPUT# statement only accepts the CRLF sequence as a separator between the records. So, we must include the quotation marks CHR$(34) (") and the comma CHR$(44) (,) as part of a string. For example, this statement can be used in a word processing application, since commas and quotation marks are frequently used in these applications. However, these problems rarely occur in file control.

121

Suggestions for INPUT#, INPUT$ and LINE INPUT#

These statements cannot assign data to the system variables ERR, ERL, DATE$ and TIME$. DATE$ and TIME$ can be assigned data but only PC-BASIC can assign data to ERR and ERL. Only a maximum of 255 characters can be read while writing into a string variable.

The INPUT#/LINE INPUT# statement or the INPUT$ function can also be applied to a random file after a GET# statement. The buffer variables, which were defined with FIELD, are assigned to the indicated variable. However with INPUT#/LINE INPUT#, it's possible that separators, which can easily be stored in random files, will produce incorrect results. We will discuss this in more detail later.

EOF

The EOF function represents *end-of-file*. The end of a sequential file is marked with the decimal value 26 (Hex 1A). If PC-BASIC encounters this mark while reading a file, another mark indicating that an EOF was reached during the reading is set internally:

```
EOF(<file-number>)
```

The file number must be identical to the file number provided in OPEN. As a result, 0 is returned when the end-of-file was not yet reached and -1 is returned when the end-of-file was reached. The result can be assigned or queried:

X=EOF(1):

The numeric variable X becomes 0 when the end-of-file hasn't been reached yet, or -1, when the end-of-file has been reached.

IF EOF(1) THEN

When the function returns the value -1, the end-of-file has been reached and the statements following THEN are executed.

WHILE NOT(EOF(1))

As long as the end-of-file hasn't been reached, the WHILE loop will be executed; otherwise a jump to WEND is made.

For random files, EOF returns the result -1 when a GET# is executed behind the last record of the file. The EOF mark in the file isn't required for this.

LOF

The LOF function represents *Length of File*. You can determine the size in bytes of a file using the LOF function:

```
LOF(<file-number>)
```

The file number must correspond to the one used in OPEN. LOF can be used with sequential and random files.

As a result, the function returns the number of bytes (characters) stored in the file, divided by the buffer size 128. For example, when a file on a disk or hard disk is listed in the directory with 12,598 bytes, LOF returns the value 99.

The result of the function can be assigned or queried. The query is used, for example, to determine if the file to be read is too large for an array:

```
10 DIM ARRAY(50,5)
.....
.....
110 IF LOF(1)>50 THEN CLOSE:PRINT "file too large"
```

LOC

By using the LOC function we can determine the current record number that was set to the last INPUT#, GET# or PUT# of the file pointer in random files.

```
110 RECORD=LOC(<file-number>)
```

The result is the number of blocks written or read for sequential files.

```
110 BYTES=LOC(<file-number>)*128
```

<file number> corresponds to the file number used with OPEN.

Special statements, commands and functions for random files

In Section 4.6.3 we mentioned that the control of random files requires more programming than sequential files. Now we'll discuss the statements, commands and functions specifically designed for controlling random files.

FIELD

As we discussed earlier, the advantage of direct access is the record length of the random files. You must define a buffer when transferring data. This buffer, which uses the fixed record length, is defined with the FIELD statement by determining a variable of a certain length for every field of the record into which data is read:

```
FIELD#<file-number>,<length> AS <Variable>...
```

For our addresses, the definitions could appear as follows:

```
230 FIELD#1,30 AS ANAME$,30 AS VNAME$, 30 AS
STREET$,4 AS CITY$,30 AS STATE$, 30 AS TELEPHONE$
```

The sum of the field length cannot exceed the record length indicated with OPEN; otherwise the "FIELD Overflow" error message appears. This error message doesn't appear when the sum of the field length is less than the record length indicated with OPEN. Only the data of the record, which has space in the FIELD variables, can be accessed.

After reading the data with GET#, the contents of the FIELD variables are either assigned to other variables, used by string functions or read with INPUT#/LINE INPUT#. It's not possible to assign values to the FIELD variables as we usually do. Instead, we must use the LSET and RSET statements. We'll discuss these shortly.

All FIELD variables must be of the string type. Immediately after the definition with FIELD, the variables have undefined contents. The data from the file are only transmitted with GET# into the FIELD variables. <file number> corresponds again with the OPEN statement for the corresponding file. You can use various FIELD definitions for a random file during the course of the program. An example of this is for a different record construction. Because of this, the FIELD definition can only have one program line. PC-BASIC accepts the last of the FIELD definitions as assigned by <file number>.

While programming a customer file, the following sequence causes errors:

```
110 FOR I=1 TO 5
115    FIELD#1,30 AS CLIENTS$(I)
120 NEXT I
```

This happened because, after the loop, CLIENTS$(5) was defined as a FIELD variable. So, the attempt to read something from CLIENTS$(1 to 4) didn't succeed. If you use random several times in a program, remember variables can't be defined twice in the FIELD statements.

GET#

After defining the buffer or variables for the data transfer with FIELD, we can read the record from the random file into the buffer by using GET# statement.

```
GET#<file-number>[,<set-number>]
```

GET# reads as many characters from the file as were indicated in <record length> during OPEN. Then GET# stores them in the variables that were defined with FIELD. If the sum of the field length is less than the record length, the extra characters are "swallowed".

Use <record number> to indicate the record from which you want to read. If you do not specify <record number>, GET# reads the record to which the file pointer is now pointing. A random file can be read sequentially using this method. The <record number> can theoretically have a value between 1 and 16,777,215. A file with a record length of 128 could contain a maximum of 2,147,483,520 bytes.

If you're reading a record using GET# which wasn't previously written with PUT#, the FIELD variables can have unexpected contents. For example, when you describe a tenth record in a new file using PUT#; nine records preceding the tenth record are automatically allocated. These nine records have an undefined content, since they aren't "officially" written yet. It's possible that a file or program was previously stored and deleted in the sectors of these records. After the file or program was deleted, these sectors were released by the operating system and, by chance, were assigned to your new file. Since, during the deletion of a file or during the assignment to a file, the content of the sectors wasn't deleted, the data is still available.

LSET and RSET

Before we can write data into the file with PUT#, we must assign the proper values to a FIELD variable. As we mentioned earlier, you can't assign values to a FIELD variable in the usual way because, during a normal assignment to a FIELD variable, this variable would be stored somewhere in memory. Obviously this wouldn't help because we need all FIELD variables which must be written into the file in one buffer. We must use special statements for the correct assignment. LSET left justifies the data and RSET right justifies the data.

These statements send an assignment directly into the buffer, from which the data is written into the file. If the assigning variable contains fewer characters than the FIELD variable can accept, spaces are automatically added to the left or right. If more than one character is available than the FIELD variable can accept, the excess characters are excluded.

```
LSET <FIELD-Variable>= <data-Variable>  —> left justified
```

```
┌──────────────────────────────────────────┬─────┐
│assigned with LSET                         │     │
└──────────────────────────────────────────┴─────┘
     FIELD-Variable
```

```
RSET <FIELD-Variable>= <data-Variable>  —> right justified
```

```
┌───────────────────────────────┬──────────────────┐
│                                │assigned with RSET│
└───────────────────────────────┴──────────────────┘
     FIELD-Variable
```

Fig. 20: LSET/RSET

String functions can be used for the assignment. You can also use LSET and RSET on normal variables:

```
LSET <Variable>=<Variable>
RSET <Variable>=<Variable>
```

Remember that the destination variable must first be assigned the correct length with the SPACE$ function. Otherwise, LSET and RSET act like assignments using the equal sign (=):

```
50 LNAME$="Miller, Freeman"
.....
.....
110 LSET ANAME$=LNAME$
```

result: "Miller, Freeman"

```
110 ANAME$=SPACE$(20)
120 LSET ANAME$=LNAME$
```

result: "Miller, Freeman   "

Storing Numeric Data in Random Files

As we know from the previous descriptions, all data stored in random files must be available in string format. Numeric variables must be converted into string variables. To do this we could use, for example, the STR$ function:

```
VALUE$=STR$(12456.89)
```

Including the sign, we should have a string that is nine characters long. Let's assume that, during each month of the year, a string of similar length appears in a household ledger. This means that we must process a string that is 108 characters long.

To solve this problem we can use the functions MKI$, MKS$, MKD$, CVI, CVS and CVD, which were designed for this.

```
10 DUMMY$=""
20 FOR I=1 TO 12
30    DUMMY$=DUMMY$+MKS$(MONTH!(I))
40 NEXT I
50 LSET YEAR$=DUMMY$
```

We stored the totals for a certain monthly expense in the MONTH!() array. In a loop we convert the 12 values with MKS$ into string format and attached it to a string variable. With LSET, we assign this variable to the FIELD variable. Since we use single precision variables, only MKS$ can be used for the conversion. MKS$ constructs a string four characters long. This is multiplied by 12, which results in 48. Therefore, this is less than half of the results with STR$.

As we learned in Section 4.2.2, the strings converted with MKx$ cannot be displayed because they contain the value in bit patterns instead of in ASCII numbers. So, the values must be changed into a form that can be displayed after the random file is read:

```
10 ANF=I:'Start/Position for MID$
20 FOR I=1 TO 12
30    MONTH!(I)=CVS(MID$(YEAR$,ANF,4))
40    ANF=ANF+4:'a sum corresponds to 4 Bytes
50 NEXT I
```

We must use CVS for the conversion because we are expecting values with single precision. For the MID$ function we need a pointer, which is increased depending on the length of the individual strings. Data converted with MKI$, MKS$ and MKD$ cannot be stored in sequential files because the bit pattern of a byte could correspond to a separator or an EOF marker.

PUT#

After the data has been given the proper format with MKI$, MKS$, MKD$, LSET and RSET, we can write them into the files. Use the PUT# statement to do this:

```
PUT#<file-number>[,<set-number>]
```

In the random file, PUT# writes as many characters from the buffer, defined with FIELD, as were specified by <record number> during the OPEN statement. The <file number> and the <record number> are the same as for the GET$ statement.

However, if the sum of the field length in the FIELD statement is smaller than the record length, the data located in the buffer, behind the last field, are also written to the file.

PC-BASIC follows the record length instead of following the sum of the field length in the FIELD definition.

CLOSE   close file

When you're finished working with any kind of file, it must be closed:

```
CLOSE[#<file-number...>]
```

The CLOSE statement writes data, which may still be available in the buffer, on the disk or hard disk and informs the operating system that the buffer and the file number are released. If you don't give a file number when using CLOSE, all the buffers are emptied sequentially, all files are closed and all file numbers and buffers are released.

After a file has been closed, any attempt to write into the file, read from a file or use a function produces the error message "Bad file number". Files are automatically closed through the following processes:

• Entering RUN or NEW;

• Editing a program line;

• Executing the following statements: END, CLEAR and CHAIN MERGE in the program.

KILL   deletes file

Deleting files should be familiar to you from the MS-DOS commands DEL and ERASE. Use the KILL command to delete files in PC-BASIC:

```
KILL <file-spec>
```

KILL can be used in either the direct mode or program mode. It has the same effect as the DEL and ERASE commands in MS-DOS.

The file specification must be enclosed in quotation marks (") if <filespec> is given as a constant. String variables are indicated without quotation marks. As in the OPEN statement, string functions cannot be used and <filespec> must be arranged as a string:

Correct:

```
10 DNAME$=DR$+PATH$+"TEST.BAS"
20 KILL DNAME$
```

Incorrect:

```
10 KILL DR$+PATH$+"TEST.BAS"
```

Insert a yes/no prompt before each KILL to prevent accidental deletion. If you try to delete an open file, PC-BASIC displays the "File already open" error message.

Note: The DOS wildcards, asterisk (*) and question mark (?) cannot be used with KILL. Each file must be individually deleted and an extension must be given. For example, if you want to delete a program called TEST.BAS, you must indicate the <filespec> as follows:

```
KILL "TEST.BAS"
```

NAME   rename file

Use the NAME command to rename a file:

```
NAME "<old_file-spec>" TO "<new_file-spec>"
```

The name of the file defined with <old_filespec> is replaced in the directory with the name in <new_filespec>. Constants must be enclosed in quotation marks (") if they're used for the file specification. String functions cannot be used. The string variable should already exist and be indicated without quotation marks. If the name indicated in <new_filespec> already exists, KILL terminates and the error message "File already exists" is displayed. The error message, "RENAME across disks" is sent when <filespec> indicates different drives. The message, "File already open" is sent if you try to rename a file that is open.

Also, remember that wildcards aren't permitted and an extension isn't automatically attached by PC-BASIC.

Additional Commands for File Control

Besides the commands and functions we have mentioned, you can also use the directory commands of PC-BASIC:

```
MKDIR
CHDIR
RMDIR
```

You may remember these commands from MS-DOS. In Chapter 7 we'll discuss them in detail.

```
┌────────────────────────────────────────────────────────┐
│ RESET                                                    │
└────────────────────────────────────────────────────────┘
```

There are times, for example during a fatal error, when every file must be simultaneously closed. Use the RESET command to do this:

```
RESET
```

You don't have to provide a file number because RESET is performed for all open files.

4.6.4 Files in a Network

In order to use PC-BASIC programs in networks (multi-user systems), special security features must be used to prevent simultaneous file and record processing. To do this, the OPEN statement will be enhanced and the LOCK and UNLOCK statements will be introduced.

Note: These capabilities are only available after Version 3.xx of PC-BASIC (or MS-DOS).

We'll use an example to show this. Suppose that several people want to use the same address file containing customers' names and addresses. This file, besides other uses, also contains billing information. A customer calls and informs user 1 of an address change. User 1 then makes the changes to the appropriate record. At the same time, user 2 wants to send a bill to the same customer. He calls the same record but the incorrect address remains stored there.

While user 1 is making the changes to the record, another user must be prevented from accessing the record. So, besides saving data, sometimes it's also necessary to lock an entire file.

Now, as an example, let's use a file that contains prices. If a price needs to be changed, the file must be locked so that it cannot be accessed. Otherwise, a price list containing both correct and incorrect prices will be printed.

To prevent access to files, use the statements that are explained on the following pages.

```
┌────────────────────────────────────────────────────────┐
│ OPEN                                        in the network│
└────────────────────────────────────────────────────────┘
        OPEN <file-spec> FOR <mode>
        [ACCESS <access>]
        [LOCK <mode> ]
        AS #<file-number>
        [LEN= <set-length>]
```

The OPEN statement was enhanced with the ACCESS and LOCK parameters. Since the other parameters didn't change, we will only discuss the new parameters. You can determine how the file should be treated using the <access> parameter:

ACCESS READ

This allows the file to be read-only. You cannot write to this type of file.

ACCESS WRITE

This allows the file to be write-only. You cannot read from this type of file.

ACCESS READ WRITE

This allows the file to be both read and write.

You determine, with ACCESS, what type of access the user has to a file. For example, depending on the number of users, it's possible that one file may be opened only for reading, while another file would be available in the READ/WRITE mode. In networks, data records can be locked to prevent simultaneous access. This is done with the LOCK parameter.

LOCK SHARED

Any user can open the file.

LOCK READ

The file can be opened in READ mode only the first time. Additional accesses are only permitted in WRITE mode.

LOCK WRITE

The file can be opened in WRITE mode only the first time. Additional accesses are only permitted in READ mode.

LOCK READ WRITE

The file can be opened only once (exclusive).

LOCK   lock data records

```
LOCK [#]<file-number>[, [<from-record>] [TO <to-record>]]
```

With LOCK, certain data records can be locked against simultaneous access in a network. This is necessary, for example, when several users can access the same file. Without LOCK, it's possible that user 1 will overwrite the changes made by user 2. The "Permission denied" error message is displayed if a user tries to access a locked file or record.

[#]<file number>

To avoid entering the complete filename each time a file is accessed, it's assigned a number during the OPEN statement. This number can be used for further accesses. Remember with LOCK, that the file is opened differently (refer to the OPEN statement).

<from record>

Indicate from which record the file should be protected against simultaneous access.

TO <to record>

Indicate up to which record the file should be protected against simultaneous access.

If LOCK #<file number> is indicated without any data records, the entire file is locked. If only <from record> is indicated, only the record that was specified is locked. If only <to record> is indicated, all data records from the first to the specified record are locked. Remember that a LOCK with the indication of the data records can only be used with random files. For a sequential file, the entire file is locked. For <record>, a value between 1 and 16,777,215 can be used.

Note: Remember that an error handling routine must provide the proper response for an orderly access to a locked file or a locked record. As we already know, the error message "access denied" is sent during access to a locked file or a locked record. Usually the error correction will try access in a loop, until the "access denied" error is no longer displayed. However, this may cause an endless loop, if, for example, the other user has forgotten to write the record or the file back again. In this case, the wait will be endless. It's better to use a counter so that after five access attempts, the user must clear the error condition.

UNLOCK   release records

```
UNLOCK [#]<file number>[, [<from record>] [TO <to record>]]
```

UNLOCK releases the records locked with the LOCK statement. The syntax of this statement is similar to the LOCK statement. UNLOCK must be executed with the same parameters for the indicated <records>. Otherwise, an error message is displayed. This can cause an endless loop in an error correction routine.

4.6.5 Error Messages

We've already discussed the most important error messages for the individual statements and functions of file control. There are also a series of error messages that correspond to disk drives or hard disks. You'll find a list of error messages, possible causes and tips on preventing them in the Appendix.

4.7 Printing Data

The ability of printing data is essential to almost every application. In PC-BASIC, printed data is usually in the form of lists and tables. Also, at times you may have to print graphics.

This section will help you with printing data. However, since there are several hundred different styles, types and manufacturers of printers, we can't provide information on each one you could use. Depending on the hardware, you can choose between the serial and the parallel interface. Most printers use the parallel interface and emulate the standards set by the IBM and Epson Corporations. If you use the printer on the serial interface, refer to Chapter 7, which contains some information about using the serial interface.

If you're not familiar with your printer's capabilities, keep the printer manual nearby so you can quickly refer to it.

4.7.1 Printing Program Listings

Most likely, the first thing you'll print with PC-BASIC is the program listing of your program. To do this, we'll use the LLIST statement:

```
LLIST [<from_line>][-][<to_line>]
```

The syntax of this statement corresponds to the LIST command presented in Chapter 3.

The "L" in front of the word "LIST" tells PC-BASIC that the listing should be printed. Remember that LLIST only operates on printers that are attached to the parallel interface.

The listing is reformatted and printed. If you use continuous sheets of paper and your printer is capable of performing the Skip over Perforation (SOP) command (usually ESC N), you should make the necessary preparations with LPRINT. For single sheet printing there are some problems. After the first page, PC-BASIC will send an "Out of paper" message. You should split the listing into manageable sections:

```
LLIST 10-150            insert new page
LLIST 160-300           insert new page
LLIST 310-450           insert new page and so on .....
```

It would be easier to store the program as an ASCII file and use a word processor to print it. LLIST doesn't change the status of your printer. You can easily preset the font, page length, number of lines, etc. with escape sequences.

LLIST assumes an output of 132 characters per line. For an 80 character per line printer, you may have to switch to smaller letters (Escape CHR$(15)=ON, CHR$(18)=OFF). The printer automatically inserts a carriage return/line feed after 80 characters.

4.7.2 Printing Data from the Program

The results of an application are usually printed in lists or tables. In this section we'll discuss the statements, commands and functions required for this.

LPRINT and LPRINT USING

We can create the LPRINT statement by adding an "L" to the beginning of "PRINT":

```
LPRINT [TAB(<column>)] [SPC(<number>)] [<expression...>] [;][,]
LPRINT USING "<mask>"; <number> | <result> | <String>
```

The only difference between PRINT/LPRINT is that LPRINT prints data on the printer, while PRINT displays data on the screen. The LPRINT USING statement formats output to the printer. Refer to Section 4.1 for a complete description of LPRINT.

WIDTH   for the printer

In Section 4.1 we discussed the WIDTH statement, which is used to set the number of characters per line for screen output. We can also use WIDTH to determine how many characters per line should be printed:

```
WIDTH LPRINT <number_characters>
```

or

```
WIDTH "LPT<x>:",<number_characters>
```

With <number_characters> we determine how many characters should be output on the printer before a CRLF (carriage return, line feed) sequence should be sent. <number_characters> can have a value between 0 and 255. With <x> you can indicate the number of the parallel interface through which the printer operates. Normally this is 1, but if you installed several interfaces, you can use a maximum of 3 for <x>.

After switching on the computer, the standard setting is for 80 characters/line for print output. An EPSON FX 80+, which we used to print 132 characters in a small font, still performed a CRLF after 80 characters, despite the proper setting. We found that the solution is the following statement:

```
WIDTH "LPT1:",255
```

134

LPOS

The data is first sent to a buffer before it is sent to the printer. Once this buffer is full, the output is sent to the printer. The buffer is controlled by the operating system through a buffer pointer. The position of this pointer in the buffer can be queried with the LPOS function:

```
X= LPOS(<printer_number>)
```

<Printer_number> can have a value between 1 and 3, depending on how many parallel interfaces are installed and which one should be addressed. Usually we use 1. It's possible that the print output could be sent without a CRLF sequence and, after a number of characters in the buffer, the CRLF would be added:

```
110 LPRINT PRINTOUTPUT$
120 IF LPOS(1)>= 40 THEN LPRINT CHR$(13);CHR$(10);
```

The printer as a file

From the MS-DOS reference manual, we know that interfaced devices can be treated as files. For the printer, this would appear as follows:

```
110 OPEN "LPT<x>:" FOR OUTPUT AS #1
120 PRINT#1,PRINTOUTPUT$
130 .....
140 .....
500 CLOSE
```

For <x> we indicate the number of the interface to which the output should be sent. The values 1 to 3 can be used. As commands for the output, all output commands for a sequential or a random file can be used (see Section 4.6). Remember that in random mode a CRLF isn't automatically sent. Logically, a print file cannot be opened as an input (INPUT) or append (APPEND) file.

4.7.3 Creating Hardcopy

A "copy" of the screen display is a *hardcopy* and can be output on the printer.

LCOPY

To print the current screen display to the printer, use the LCOPY statement. Even though this statement doesn't need an additional parameter, for compatibility reasons use the following syntax:

```
LCOPY(<number>)
```

<number> can be any value because PC-BASIC doesn't test this number. Remember that LCOPY only operates in text mode. A hardcopy of a graphic picture cannot be printed with LCOPY. Some PCs contain the GRAPHICS.COM program on the system disk. Once this program is called, you can output graphic hardcopy with <Shift><PrtSc>.

4.7.4 Graphics Mode

Almost every application is capable of presenting the results of an operation as a graphic on the screen or on the printer. In the preceding section we became familiar with the LCOPY statement to output the screen display as hardcopy on the printer. Since LCOPY only works in text mode, there are two possibilities for printing in graphics mode:

1.   Insert a special print routine in your program. Implementing such a routine isn't easy and is different for every printer. We'll discuss this in more detail in Chapter 17.

2.   Use the MS-DOS utility program GRAPHICS.COM. This program must be executed before calling PC-BASIC. After the graphic is displayed on the screen, a hardcopy can be obtained by pressing <Shift><PrtScr>.

We'll provide more information on graphics in Chapter 6.

4.7.5 Tips on Printing

In the previous sections, you've learned how to print data in PC-BASIC. However, the type of printer is very important to the printing process. With the proper control characters, most of the current printers are able to print in Pica and Elite and in normal, double wide, bold or small fonts. Many printers also offer horizontal and vertical tabs. The page length in lines or inches can also be selected. As we mentioned earlier, keep your printer manual handy so that you can use all of the capabilities of your printer.

On most printers you can set standard values through *DIP switches*. These are small rows of switches on or near the circuit board of the printer. These switches must be set to the proper values during the installation of the printer. Refer to your printer manual for specific instructions. Check the DIP switches if your printout is incorrect. Problems are usually caused by incorrect settings. Usually the control characters that were sent have a higher priority than the DIP switches setting. So, before setting the carriage return to 1/8 inch, you must first transmit the control characters for a 1/6 inch advance.

4.8   Correcting Errors

While working with PC-BASIC, you've become familiar with some of its error messages. You also know that after an error message, the program is terminated. The error messages are received in both the direct mode and program mode. With error messages, PC-BASIC protects you from incorrectly processing certain data, warns you of missing data or tells you that something is wrong with the hardware. As long as the error message is sent in direct mode or during the test phase of your programming, there shouldn't be a problem. However, imagine how an inexperienced user feels when receiving the following message:

```
Illegal function call in 120
ok
```

The worst case scenario is working for hours, not saving frequently and not knowing what to do next.

4.8.1 Error Messages

PC-BASIC usually displays error messages in normal text and indicates in which line the error occurred. For the "Syntax Error in xxx" error message, the defective line is also displayed so that the user can make corrections. With other error messages, displaying the defective line can be confusing. For example, an error in line XXX can originate from an incorrect calculation in line YYY. In these cases, PC-BASIC may not display the defective line.

The System Variables ERR and ERL

Similar to displaying error messages, PC-BASIC contains two system variables which contain the error number and the error line. These are the variables:

```
ERR       for the error-number and
ERL       for the error-line
```

Note: For an error in the direct mode, ERL is assigned the value 65,535 as line number.

In the following sections we'll demonstrate how these variables can be used by the program to prevent a situation, like the one described above. You can find complete listings of error messages in Appendix B and Appendix C.

4.8.2 Intercepting Errors in a Program

There are two ways to intercept errors in the program. First, the entered data can be checked:

```
120 INPUT "Input a number between 0 and 9:";NUMBER
130 IF NUMBER <0 OR NUMBER >9 THEN BEEP:GOTO 120
```

or

```
120 INPUT "filename (max. 8 characters):";FILENAME$
130 IF LEN(FILENAME$)=0 OR LEN(FILENAME$)>8 THEN BEEP:GOTO 130
```

In these examples the input is accepted only when it matches the value set by the programmer. However, there are some errors that cannot be predicted or tested. An example of this is a write protected disk. An attempt to write into a file on this disk produces the following error message:

```
Disk write protected
ok
```

ON ERROR GOTO

An error of this type can be intercepted in the program with the ON ERROR GOTO statement. Instead of an error message, the following appears:

```
ON ERROR GOTO <line-number>
```

<line number> indicates where the error correction routine begins in the program. Then we can query the system variables ERR and ERL and react accordingly. If 0 is indicated as <line number>, the error correction is switched off. The following program explains the ON ERROR GOTO statement:

```
10 'ON ERROR GOTO Demo
20 :
30 ON ERROR GOTO 130
40 CLS:KEY OFF
50 PRINT "An attempt is made to write into a file....."
60 PRINT
70 OPEN "A:TEST.DAT" FOR OUTPUT AS #1
80 PRINT#1,"Test-data"
90 CLOSE
100 PRINT "The data was written successfully ....."
110 END
120 :
130 'Here starts the error-correction routine
140 :
150 CLOSE
160 IF ERR=57 OR ERR=70 THEN 210:'process error
```

```
170 LOCATE 22,1:PRINT "System-Error ";ERR;" in line ";ERL
180 IF INKEY$="" THEN 180
190 END
200 :
210 'Error: Disk is write-protected or not inserted
220 :
230 LOCATE 22,1:PRINT "Diskette is write-protected or no diskette was inserted
!!!"
240 BEEP:PRINT "Check diskette and strike any key or <Esc> to quit"
250 X$=INKEY$:IF X$="" THEN 250
260 IF X$=CHR$(27) THEN CLS:END
270 RESUME 40
```

Note: You may have to change line 70 to read your current drive. For example, use this line if the current drive is C:

```
70 OPEN "C:TEST.DAT" FOR OUTPUT AS #1
```

Since there is only one line in which the error can occur, we don't have to query ERL. If several errors occur in one line or the same error occurs in several lines, both variables must be queried.

RESUME

The RESUME statement, which is important to the error correction, appears in line 270. This statement must be used as soon as the ON ERROR GOTO statement appears in the program. If PC-BASIC encounters a RESUME statement before executing an ON ERROR GOTO statement, the message "RESUME without error" appears. With RESUME, we indicate where the program should continue after the error correction. There are several possibilities:

RESUME<line number>

Specifies the line number at which the program execution should continue.

RESUME NEXT

The program continues at the statement immediately following the statement that caused the error.

RESUME [0]

The statement which caused the error is executed again. This is the same as specifying RESUME without parameters.

After RESUME, PC-BASIC sets ERR to the value 0. ERL retains the original value.

139

Suggestions for ERR, ERL, ON ERROR GOTO and RESUME

You should place ON ERROR GOTO at the beginning of the program. At the end of a program you should execute ON ERROR GOTO 0, which switches off the error correction. Otherwise, the error correction will continue to operate in direct mode. You can include several error corrections in the program and thereby activate various ON ERROR GOTOs. In most cases, a single error correction is sufficient.

An error correction should end with a message similar to the one in lines 170-190 in the previous example. These lines handle the errors that weren't intercepted.

If the indicated line numbers aren't available in the program, PC-BASIC displays the message, "Undefined line number". The query of the system variable ERL, in connection with the RENUM command, produces a strange effect:

```
20 IF 1230=ERL THEN...
```

RENUM doesn't accept the line number (1230) to the left of the equal sign (=).

```
20 IF ERL=1230 THEN...
```

With the above line, RENUM functions as usual. The messages used in error correction routines should be clear so that the user can easily understand them. For example, the message "Wrong key activated" confuses the user because there are approximately 90 available keys. So, any one of them could be the wrong key. A better message would be, "Only keys <x>, <y> and <z> are permitted".

ERROR

If you look at the list of error messages in Appendix B, you'll see that the errors aren't numbered sequentially from 1 to 255. Instead, some numbers are missing so that programmers can create their own error messages. The ERROR statement is used to do this:

```
ERROR <error-number>
```

With <error number>, you can indicate the error number you want to use and query it during error correction. Obviously, you shouldn't use an error number which is already being used by PC-BASIC. ERROR assigns the error number and the line number, in which the ERROR statement was issued, to the ERR and ERL variables.

If it's used in the direct mode, ERROR displays the message "Unprintable error" for an undefined error number.

4.8.3 Extended Error Functions

PC-BASIC provides three functions for the extended error correction which display the values administered by MS-DOS or PC-BASIC.

ERDEV

```
X= ERDEV
```

The ERDEV function returns a 16-bit integer value, which is supplied by the operating system MS-DOS and contains the following information:

LowByte

In LowByte, MS-DOS provides an error code of the defective device. A detailed explanation can be found in Appendix C.

HighByte

In HighByte, MS-DOS provides information about the driver, which belongs to the device causing the error. This is a bit sequence from the "Device header block" which allows the identification of the driver. For a detailed explanation, refer to Chapter 7.

We use the terms Low and HighByte because a 16-bit value, which consists of two 8-bit values, forms 2 bytes. To differentiate between these two bytes, one is designated "LowByte", which contains the less significant part of the number, and the other is designated "HighByte", which stores the more significant part of the number. The final value can be calculated with the formula:

```
value= (LowByte+(256*HighByte))
```

ERDEV$

This function returns the name of the device that is causing the errors:

```
X$= ERDEV$
```

During write/read errors with disks or with a hard disk, the name of the drive designation is followed by a colon (:) in the output:

```
PRINT ERDEV$
A:
```

EXTERR

```
X= EXTERR(<expression>)
```

MS-DOS and PC-DOS provide extended error codes which make it easier to identify an error. These codes are divided into four categories. These are specified with the <expression> parameter:

0   Requests the extended error code.

1   Requests the error class. The result permits identification of the error.

2   Requests the error correction expected from the operating system. The result indicates how to react to an error.

3   Requests the error localization. The result indicates where the error occurred in the system.

Note: Depending on the <expression>, the function EXTERR returns approximately 100 different results. You'll find a detailed description in Appendix C.

4.8.4 Detecting Errors

Very few programs execute without errors when they're first tested. It may take a programmer many days to discover the source of an error. In this section we'll provide some tips on error detection.

Even with good planning, an error can sneak into your program which can't be detected. It may be a syntax or logical error. The frequency of these errors can be predicted as follows:

Syntax Error

Usually a variable name, which is also a statement, is used:

```
10 IF POS= 24 THEN CLS:GOTO 50 'When line 24 has been reached, clear screen,
display next page
```

Number or Letter Reversals

These can be the worst errors, especially in variable names that don't appear in the same line:

```
10 ENTRY$=INKEY$:IF ENRTY$="" THEN 10
```

This error is fairly easy to detect.

```
10 INPUT#1, LASTNAME$
...
...
...
510 IF LASTNMAE$="END" THEN CLOSE#1
```

This error would be more difficult to find since there are several screen pages in the listing, comparing two lines isn't possible. Since PC-BASIC cannot send an error message, the result of a calculation or a query could be incorrect.

Logical Error

These errors usually appear in IF...THEN...ELSE or WHILE...WEND statements. For example, a variable, whose content can only be 0, may be tested because it was previously assigned this value. This variable may also be tested when a condition was never met because the variable was never assigned a concrete value. Using incorrect or similar variable names often causes errors also.

```
100 LAST.LINE= 23
110 LAST.SCR.LINE= 25
.....
.....
.....
500 IF CSRLIN= LAST.LINE THEN CLS
```

The LAST.SCR.LINE variable should be queried. During the error detection, regarding different variable names, save the program as an ASCII file:

```
SAVE <Program-name>,A
```

This allows the program to be loaded into a word processing program. With the SEARCH statement, each variable can be detected:

Search for:		
$	-->	Strings
%	-->	Integers
!	-->	Simple Real numbers
#	-->	Double Real numbers

Of course all variables must be marked individually instead of globally, with DEFINT, DEFSTR, DEFDBL or DEFSNG. Any deviation from this can be identified quickly and easily.

You'll most likely overlook an error if you spend a long time looking for it. Having someone else read the program listing for you may help.

5. Programming Sound

While working with your PC you've probably noticed that it can communicate both visually and audibly. Usually the PC emits a beep to indicate incorrect input or to warn you of a certain condition. The peripheral components (8253/8255) and a small built-in speaker produce this sound. We'll discuss how these tones are used in PC-BASIC in this chapter. However, you should remember that the tone can only be generated on one channel.

5.1   Sound as a Message

BEEP

BEEP produces a tone at a frequency of 800 Hz for one fourth of a second. It's used to indicate an error during input or to warn you of special conditions.

BEEP may also be performed using the following statement:

```
PRINT CHR$(7)
```

After pressing <Return> you'll hear the BEEP tone. The ASCII value for seven is called the BEL function and when printed activates the BEEP.

Both statements produce the same sound.

SOUND

The SOUND statement enables you to select the frequency and duration of the tone:

```
SOUND <frequency>,<duration>
```

Although the BEEP discussed above is used in many applications, other programs require more sophisticated sounds. PC-BASIC uses the SOUND statement to generate these different tones and sounds. Theoretically you can use values between 37 and 32,767 for <frequency>. However, because of the small PC speaker, the sound that's produced cannot be compared to that produced by a stereo system.

You can indicate how long the tone should continue by using <duration>. This value is specified in clock ticks. These occur every 18.2 seconds. The <duration> can have a value between 1 and 65,535. If you need to switch the current sound off use <duration=0>.

Here is a small program using the SOUND statement:

```
10 CLS
20 FOR I=100 TO 3500 STEP 100:SOUND I,1:NEXT I
30 FOR I=3500 TO 100 STEP -100:SOUND I,1:NEXT I
```

The frequency in this program quickly ascends and descends from 100 Hz to 3500 Hz in 100 Hz steps.

The following program allows you to enter a specific frequency from the keyboard:

```
10 'SOUND-Demo
20 :
30 CLS:KEY OFF
40 INPUT "Frequency (99999= end):";FREQUENZ
50 IF FREQUENZ=99999 THEN CLS:END
60 SOUND FREQUENZ,1
70 GOTO 40
```

Note: Some PCs contain a *Piezo Element* instead of a speaker. This is used to reproduce the tone. This element is a crystal that is put into oscillation by applying a voltage. With extremely high or low frequencies, only a crackling sound may be heard because the crystal is overextended.

5.2   Programming Tone Sequences

With a READ...DATA loop it's possible to use the SOUND statement to program tone sequences, such as songs. In this section we'll present some easier ways to do this.

PLAY

Although the SOUND statement produces many useful tones, the PLAY statement is more versatile and easier to program in producing musical notes and tunes. PC-BASIC simplifies the programming of longer tone sequences with the PLAY statement:

```
PLAY <String>
```

PLAY requires one or more strings, which provide exact specifications about the tone sequences. These specifications are:

MF (modeforeground)

Generates tones in the foreground. A new PLAY statement executes only when the current one is completed.

MB (modebackground)

Generates tone in the background and the program execution is continued. These notes are placed in a buffer and processed by the computer interrupts. A maximum of 32 characters can be passed for the tone generation.

MN (modenormal)

Generates tone of normal length (7/8 of the length specified by *L*).

ML (modelegato)

Generates *legato* (smooth) tones. Each note sounds for the full length of the note length as specified in the <string> by *L*.

MS (modestaccato)

Generates *staccato* (short) tones. Each note sounds for 3/4 of the length specified with *L*.

Ox (Octave)

Specifies the desired octave with *x*. The value for *x* ranges from 0 to 6. Middle C (just below A_440) begins with the third octave. Each octave number starts with C and continues through B. The default is the fourth octave when no octave is specified.

147

> (greater than symbol)

Use this symbol to raise the tone by one octave (to a maximum of 6).

< (less than symbol)

Use this symbol to lower the tone by one octave (to a minimum of 0).

A to G [-][+][#]

This represents the musical notes A to G. Sharps are indicated by a number/pound sign (#) or plus sign (+) following the note. Flats are indicated by a minus sign (-) following the note.

Note: Sharps and flats are legal only if they are not equal to another note value. For example, C flat is not legal because it's equal to B.

N<note_number>

This allows you to specify the specific note to be played without the need to separately specify the octave. Sounds one of the 84 possible notes within the seven available octaves. Values can range from 0 to 84 with 0 producing a rest.

P<note_length>

Produces a rest. The length of the rest corresponds to the <note_length>, which can have a value from 1 to 64. The parameter <note_length>=4> produces a quarter-note rest.

L<note_length>

Sets the duration of the subsequent notes. The <note_length> is specified in the range 1 to 64 and produces a note length of 1/n. If *L* with a parameter follows a note, *L* applies to this note only. A length of 1 equals a full note and a length of 32 equals one thirty-second note.

T<tempo>

Sets the *tempo* for the tone generation, which is the number of quarter notes per minute. <tempo> can have a value from 32 to 255.

<.> (Period)

The period causes the tone generation to run one and a half times longer (3/2) than the values set by *L* and *T*. Several successive periods increase the value correspondingly.

X<string_variable>

Executes *<string_variable>*. This is similar to a "musical subroutine". The PLAY statement requires quotation marks around the name of the string followed by a semicolon. To play the following string:

```
SONG$="ABCGDAB"
```

the correct syntax is:

```
PLAY "XSONG$;"
```

Variables can also be used for numeric parameters. In a string this appears as follows:

```
"T=Tempo; ......"
```

Remember an equal sign (=) and not *X*, must be used. The following program plays a small tone sequence:

```
10 'PLAY-Demo
20 :
30 CLS:KEY OFF
40 PRINT "Please relax....."
50 OCTAVE$="O2 "
60 TON$=OCTAVE$+"T190 P2 L8 ABCCDDEEEEDEEEEDCCCCBBDDDDAGGGDGGDE"
70 PLAY TON$
```

Note that the MF or MB parameters must be at the beginning of the first string of the PLAY statement. They're ignored at any other location. The MB parameter is responsible for having the tone generation execute in the background so that the program can continue to execute in the foreground. This makes it possible, for example with games, to program a continuous musical background. To do this we must use interrupt programming, which is discussed in Section 7.3.

The following program uses both the PLAY and SOUND statements. It also shows how you may store a song in strings:

```
10 'Bugs Plays Piano Demo
20 BUG1$=T20003L8F#EL4D.L8EDP8L4DF#AGB>D#D#P1"
30 BUG2$=T20003L8F#EL4D.L8EDP8L4DF#AGB>C#C#P2L4D#D#P1
40 BUGSRIGHT$="T20003L8F#EL4D.L8EDP8L4DF#AGB>DD"
50 PLAY "XBUG1$;"
60 PLAY "XBUG2$;"
70 PLAY "XBUGSRIGHT$;"
75 SOUND 37,10
80 END
```

6. Programming Graphics

With some applications, it's better to use graphics instead of a spreadsheet to display data. For example, graphics would be helpful in an application in which large number columns are displayed on the screen or the printer. By using a pie chart or a bar chart, data can be clearly displayed and understood.

In this chapter we'll discuss the many commands, statements and functions PC-BASIC provides for working with graphics.

Suggestions on working with Graphics

Graphics is a very complex subject. It requires a knowledge of mathematics and PC hardware. However, neither of these subjects can be adequately discussed in this book. We're only able to provide the syntax and the effect of the individual commands.

For this reason, you may give up because you don't completely understand graphics. However, we know from personal experience that you can learn a lot about a subject by simply practicing and experimenting.

Graphic Cards

There are numerous graphic cards, from various manufacturers, which can be installed in your PC. Also, if you work extensively with graphics, you may need a special monitor. In the following pages, we assume that you own a color graphics card that conforms to the IBM standard (CGA/EGA). The acronyms CGA and EGA represent Color Graphics Adapter and Extended Graphics Adapter respectively.

You can skip this chapter if a normal monochrome card (MDA) is installed in your system. Unfortunately, your PC will not respond to any graphic commands. These cards aren't equipped for displaying graphics. You'll receive the "Illegal function call" error message if you try using these commands.

The problem is more complicated if you own a Hercules graphic card. Although the Hercules card is designed to produce graphics, this capability is actually cancelled by the PC-BASIC's architecture, which was developed exclusively for operations with a CGA card. If you try executing a program with graphic commands, PC-BASIC sends the "Illegal function call" error message because a CGA card isn't installed in your PC.

Because of this, many CGA compatible cards have appeared on the market. These compatible cards have emulation modes which make PC-BASIC believe that, instead of the

HGC card, a CGA card is installed. If you don't have such a program, run the utility program in Chapter 17. However, it's possible that this program may not operate properly.

If you have a monochrome graphic card and CGA emulation, black-white, green or amber monitors, or a CGA/EGA card that uses a composite monitor, you may have to experiment with the colors if a difference between the colors cannot be detected on the monitor or the colors are presented as dot patterns with various resolutions.

6.1   Graphics Mode

In Chapter 4 we discussed how text mode relates to the screen output. As its name implies, this mode is only responsible for displaying text. The graphic card also contains a *graphics mode*, which we'll discuss in this section.

In the chapter on text mode we learned that a maximum of 80 characters per line can be displayed in 25 lines. A character (or letter) is composed of several dots, called *pixels*:

```
   000
 0000000
 00    00
 00    00
 0000000
 00    00
 00    00
 00    00
```

We can use the term *character matrix* to describe this illustration. In text mode, a single pixel in this matrix cannot be addressed. The character can only be displayed, for example, with PRINT "A". However, in graphics mode every pixel on the screen can be addressed. While these characters are being addressed, *coordinates*, instead of columns or lines, are used.

6.1.1 Resolution

We can determine the maximum number of pixels that can be displayed on the screen by its *resolution*. The resolution in text mode is 80*25 pixels. The resolution in graphics mode is 80*8= 640 pixels horizontally and 25*8=200 pixels vertically since a character on a CGA card is composed of 8*8 pixels. With the LOCATE statement we can indicate a column of a line. The cursor can be moved anywhere on the screen and a character can be displayed at that location. So, column and line are also addressed.

These values are indicated for the X axis (from left to right) and for the Y axis (from top to bottom). As with text mode, we can use lines (in the Y direction) and columns (in the X direction). The numbering for the Y axis begins at the top with 0 and for the X axis, at the left with 0:

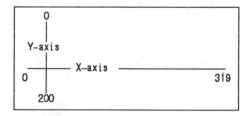

Fig. 21: Resolution

Resolution of the CGA card

Graphics are used on the CGA card in two resolutions:

•   resolution 1 with 320*200 pixels in 4 colors or black and white

•   resolution 2 with 640*200 pixels only in black and white

Resolution of the EGA card

The EGA card provides more capabilities than the CGA card. As graphic applications became more important, the low resolution of the CGA card no longer met the requirements of programmers and users. So, the EGA card, featuring a higher resolution with more colors, was developed. An additional popular feature for the development of the EGA card is that it was compatible with existing monitors or available programs.

As a result, the EGA card offers more colors with higher resolution, is fully compatible with the CGA card and can be operated in a monochrome mode. To achieve the highest resolution with all colors, a special monitor (Enhanced Graphics Display) is needed. A color monitor (Color Graphics Display) can only be used in CGA mode.

A CGA or composite monitor results in the following:

•   resolution 1 with 320*200 pixels in 4 colors or black and white

•   resolution 2 with 640*200 pixels only in black and white

The following resolutions, in addition to the CGA resolution, are available if you're using an EGA monitor:

•   resolution 3 with 320*200 pixels in 16 colors

•   resolution 4 with 640*200 pixels in 16 colors

•   resolution 5 with 640*350 pixels in 16 colors

In monochrome mode, a normal monochrome monitor can be connected to the EGA card. Unfortunately, the Hercules card wasn't considered, but the EGA card's basic resolution of 640*350 pixels remains. However, programs that were written for this graphics mode only run with an EGA card and the programs that were written for the HGC card only run in this EGA mode.

SCREEN

Before graphics can be created, we must tell PC-BASIC which resolution we need. In Chapter 4 we learned the statement used for screen output:

```
SCREEN [<mode>][,<color>][,<output_page>] [,<display_page>]
```

With <mode> we can select one of the following graphics modes:

0   text mode

1   graphics mode 320*200 pixels, 4 colors

2   graphics mode 640*200 pixels, black/white

3-n special mode for special color graphic cards

Remember that the <mode> parameter depends on the installed graphic card. For the CGA card, you can indicate a maximum of 2 for a resolution of 640*200, as shown above. For the EGA card the following values can be selected for <mode>:

0-2 same as CGA

7   graphics mode 320*200 pixels, 16 colors

8   graphics mode 640*200 pixels, 16 colors

9   graphics mode 640*350 pixels, 16 colors

10   graphics mode 640*350 pixels, monochrome

In the graphics mode, the CGA card only has one screen page and the <output_page> and <display_page> parameters aren't used. For the EGA card, depending on the resolution and options of the card, up to 8 pages can be addressed. The desired <output_page> and <display_page> are indicated with a value between 0 and 7:

```
EGA with 64K   320*200 pixels -> 2 pages
EGA with 128K  320*200 pixels -> 4 pages
EGA with 256K  320*200 pixels -> 8 pages

EGA with 64K   640*200 pixels -> 1 page
EGA with 128K  640*200 pixels -> 2 pages
EGA with 256K  640*200 pixels -> 4 pages

EGA with 256K  640*350 pixels -> 2 pages

EGA with 256K monochrome-mode -> 2 pages
```

If, during the call of the SCREEN statement, <color=1>, then the current colors remain, the standard colors for the graphics mode (black background and white foreground color) are set for the current mode with <color=0>.

When PC-BASIC hasn't been adapted to the card installed in a PC, it's possible to enter for <mode> a value which cannot be used with this particular graphic card. Under some circumstances this can causes strange reactions in the graphic card. For example, random graphics may appear on the monitor. However, this is very dangerous because these are errors in addressing the graphic card. With some PCs, these errors can actually cause the destruction of the graphic chips.

So while you're experimenting, be prepared to switch off the computer quickly. Usually when a chip is in danger, you can hear a high-pitched whistle that increases in frequency. If you immediately switch off the computer you may be able to prevent the worst damage. However, if you hear a short bang the chip is probably already destroyed.

Since the CGA card was the only graphic card for the PC for a long time, *HiRes* and *MidRes* were accepted as the two resolution modes. HiRes is an abbreviation of High Resolution (640*200 pixels) and MidRes is an abbreviation of Middle Resolution (320*200 pixels).

You're probably wondering if there is a LowRes (Low Resolution) mode. This resolution of 160*200 pixels does exist but it isn't supported by PC-BASIC. The card must be set to this mode through a direct register/port access. Also, some graphic routines for addressing the pixels must be developed. Unfortunately, it's always possible that the card will be destroyed because it doesn't support this mode.

6.1.2 Background and Foreground Colors

Once the resolution is set, PC-BASIC must know what colors will be used to create the graphic. The color selection depends on the graphic card.

CGA colors in the Graphics Mode

In the graphics mode, the CGA card displays a maximum of 4 colors with a resolution of 320*200 pixels. It displays 2 colors (black and white) with a resolution of 640*200 pixels. From the text mode we know that the CGA card can display a total of 16 colors. So, you may be wondering why the CGA card is limited to 4 colors in the graphics mode.

We know that in the graphics mode each pixel can be addressed individually. A pixel is either switched on or off. The pixel is off if it's displayed in the background color. A red dot on a red background isn't visible. The pixel is on when it's displayed in the foreground color. For example, a green pixel is on against a red background because it's visible.

Also, from the text mode we know that the color of a character is defined through a special attribute byte. In the same way we must also define the color of a pixel with an attribute byte. This means that 640*200 bytes (one byte for each pixel) is needed for a maximum resolution of 640*200 pixels. This is a total of 128,000 bytes. The PC, however, doesn't provide that much memory. So, the color information is stored as a bit instead of as a complete byte. For the half resolution of 320*200 pixels, two bits are available for each pixel and in two bits 4 values or 4 colors can be stored:

```
00    background-color 0 (1. color)
01    foreground-color 1 (2. color)
10    foreground-color 2 (3. color)
11    foreground-color 3 (4. color)
```

Zero indicates that the bit isn't set and 1 indicates that the bit is set. Now you know why the CGA card can only display 4 colors in the graphics mode.

EGA colors in the Graphics Mode

The EGA card differs from the CGA card because it contains its own memory. Depending on the requirements, this memory can be extended from 64,000 to 256,000 bytes. Actually, the memory consists of four individual memories. Each one of the basic colors, red, green and blue has its own memory. A fourth memory stores information about the color being displayed in normal or double intensity. Therefore, the color information for a pixel is stored in four bits:

```
0000   background-color       0   (1. color)
0001   foreground-color       1   (2. color)
0010   foreground-color       2   (3. color)
0011   foreground-color       3   (4. color)
0100   foreground-color       4   (5. color)
0101   foreground-color       5   (6. color)
0110   foreground-color       6   (7. color)
0111   foreground-color       7   (8. color)
```

```
1000   foreground-color      8   (9. color)
1001   foreground-color      9  (10. color)
1010   foreground-color     10  (11. color)
1011   foreground-color     11  (12. color)
1100   foreground-color     12  (13. color)
1101   foreground-color     13  (14. color)
1110   foreground-color     14  (15. color)
1111   foreground-color     15  (16. color)
```

This allows 16 colors to be displayed.

COLOR   for HiRes

As in the text mode, the colors in the graphics mode are also set with the COLOR statement. For HiRes (640*200 or 640*350 with EGA), the following syntax results:

```
COLOR [<foreground>][,<background>]
```

For the CGA card (SCREEN 2), all parameters are indicated with 0 for black or 1 for white. If you omit one of the parameters (only the comma (,) is given), the current value remains. If an incorrect value is given, PC-BASIC sends an "Illegal function call" message. Graphic commands that contain the <color> parameter refer to the values, determined by COLOR, for <foreground> and <background>. A conversion is made since only the values 0 to 3 can be used for <color>:

value 0 black

value 1 white

value 2 black

value 3 white

As the following example demonstrates, there is a trick for adding color:

```
10 'COLOR-Demo, 640*200 pixels
20 :
30 CLS:KEY OFF
40 SCREEN 2
50 OUTCOL=1
60 COLOR 1,1
70 OUT &H3D9,OUTCOL
80 CLS
90 CIRCLE (50,50),30,1
100 FOR I= 1 TO 4
110 CIRCLE STEP (20,0),30,1
```

```
120 NEXT I
130 LOCATE 12,1
140 PRINT "<Z> color for drawing:";:PRINT USING "##";OUTCOL
150 PRINT "<Esc> END"
160 X$=INKEY$:IF X$="" THEN 160
170 IF X$=CHR$(27) THEN 220
180 IF X$="z" THEN OUTCOL=OUTCOL+1
190 IF OUTCOL=8 THEN OUTCOL=9
200 IF OUTCOL=16 THEN OUTCOL=1
210 GOTO 70
220 SCREEN 0:WIDTH 80
```

Although we're using the COLOR statement, we're actually accessing the OUT statement to display the available colors on the screen.

Note: Some earlier versions of PC-BASIC send an "Illegal Function Call" message during the COLOR statement in the 640*200 pixel (SCREEN 2) resolution. This happens because a black background and white foreground color are set as a default and cannot be changed. Current versions allow a "reversal" with COLOR for black graphics on a white background.

With the EGA card (SCREEN 7 to 9) there is a total of 16 available colors. These are set accordingly using the COLOR statement. For <foreground> and <background> the values between 0 and 15 can be used where text output, with the PRINT statement, occurs in the current <foreground color>.

COLOR for MidRes

With the MidRes (SCREEN 1) everything appears on the screen in color:

```
COLOR[<foreground>][,<Palette>]
COLOR[<background>][,<Palette>][,<Graph_Bck_Grd>]
[,<Graph_For_Grd>][,<text-color>]
```

Two syntaxes can be used with the COLOR statement. The first syntax is used in the newer versions of PC-BASIC and the second one is used for the older versions. However some of the newer versions support both syntaxes. <foreground> sets the current drawing color; the values 0 to 3 can be used.

With <palette> we indicate which palette's colors will be used for the drawing color of the graphic commands:

Palette 0   color 0 = background color

              color 1 = green

color 2 = red

color 3 = yellow

Palette 1   color 0 = background color

color 1 = Cyan

color 2 = Magenta

color 3 = white

<background> sets the color for the background and the frame. The <Graph_Bck_Grd> and <Graph_For_Grd> parameters determine, with the palette, the standard values for the <drawing color> of the graphic command. <text color> indicates in which color of the palette the text will be displayed. Remember that color 0 for <text color> isn't allowed. PC-BASIC will send the "Illegal function call" message when it receives incorrect values. For omitted parameters (only the comma (,) is indicated), the current values remain active.

Unfortunately, PC-BASIC cannot display the colors of the palettes in double intensity. The OUT statement isn't capable of this either. So, with some graphic cards in palette 0 you can't detect a difference between colors 2 (red) and 3 (yellow). For example:

```
10 'COLOR2-Demo, 320*200 pixels
15 'This program uses the old format of the color command,
16 'and will not run on all versions of PC-BASIC.
20 :
30 CLS:KEY OFF
40 SCREEN 1
50 BKGRD=0:PALET=0:GRAF.FORGRD=1:GRAF.BKGRD=0:TXTCOLR=1
60 COLOR BKGRD,PALET,GRAF.FORGRD,GRAF.BKGRD,TXTCOLR
70 CIRCLE (50,50),30,1
80 FOR I= 1 TO 4
90 CIRCLE STEP (20,0),30,I
100 NEXT I
110 LOCATE 12,1
120 PRINT "<B> background:";:PRINT USING "##";BKGRD
130 PRINT "<P> Palette    :";:PRINT USING "##";PALET
140 PRINT "<F> graphic-foreground:";:PRINT USING "##";GRAF.FORGRD
150 PRINT "<H> graphic-background:";:PRINT USING "##";GRAF.BKGRD
160 PRINT "<T> Text-color :";:PRINT USING "##";TXTCOLR
170 PRINT "<Esc> END"
180 X$=INKEY$:IF X$="" THEN 180
190 IF X$=CHR$(27) THEN 260
200 IF X$="b" OR X$="B" THEN BKGRD=BKGRD+1:IF BKGRD=16 THEN BKGRD=0
210 IF X$="p" OR X$="P" THEN IF PALET=1 THEN PALET=0 ELSE PALET=1
220 IF X$="f" OR X$="F"THEN GRAF.FORGRD=GRAF.FORGRD+1:IF GRAF.FORGRD=4 THEN
    GRAF.FORGRD=0
230 IF X$="k" OR X$="K" THEN GRAF.BKGRD=GRAF.BKGRD+1:IF GRAF.BKGRD=4 THEN
    GRAF.BKGRD=0
240 IF X$="t" OR X$="T" THEN TXTCOLR=TXTCOLR+1:IF TXTCOLR=4 THEN TXTCOLR=1
250 GOTO 60
260 SCREEN 0:WIDTH 80
```

Suggestions for the COLOR statement

PCs often crash when a user is experimenting in graphics mode 1 or 2 with the COLOR statement. This usually happens when PC-BASIC accepts the commands but won't execute them. When this happens, a RESET from the keyboard must be performed. One reason for the crash is that, under certain circumstances, PC-BASIC becomes unsynchronized when a parameter is omitted from the COLOR statement and instead only commas are used. So, you should save your programs before executing the RUN command.

PALETTE   for EGA card

Unlike the CGA card, the EGA card can display a total of 16 colors. With the CGA card we can select the 4 colors. These colors are set and cannot be changed.

However, with the EGA card, a palette consists of 16 colors, which aren't set and can be selected from 64 colors. This is done with the statement:

```
PALETTE [<OldColor>,<NewColor>]
```

As we previously mentioned, with the COLOR statement we can indicate values between 0 and 15 for the <foreground> and <background> parameters. Each of these values can be assigned to one of the 64 colors. For <OldColor> the number must be between 0 and 15 and for <NewColor> the number must be between 0 and 63. If a value of -1 is given for <NewColor>, the current color assignment remains. The following program sequentially assigns the background color 0 to all the available 64 colors.

Note: The following program only works on a PC with an EGA card and version 3.xx of PC-BASIC:

```
10 'PALETTE-Demo EGA-card
20 :
30 CLS:KEY OFF
40 SCREEN 9 'resolution 640*350, 16 colors of 64
50 FOR COLR= 0 TO 63
60    PALETTE 0,COLR 'HG-color "0"= new color
70    LOCATE 25,1
80    PRINT USING "color is:## -> Strike any key or <Esc> to end";COLR;
90    X$= INKEY$:IF X$="" THEN 90
100   IF X$= CHR$(27) THEN 120 'ESC= End
110 NEXT COLR
120 PALETTE 0,0 'set old value again
130 SCREEN 0 'back to text-mode
```

PALETTE USING for EGA card

A color from 0 to 15 can be assigned a new color from 0 to 63 by using the PALETTE statement. However, when all 16 colors are assigned, 16 PALETTE statements are required. Usually in large programs this occupies a lot of space. Therefore, PC-BASIC provides an additional statement for assigning colors:

```
PALETTE USING [<ARRAY>(Index)]
```

All 16 colors can be assigned new values simultaneously when you use this statement. The new colors are read into an integer array. This can be done either with a direct assignment (ARRAY(1)= 5) or simply with a READ...DATA statement. Besides the name of the array, the PALETTE USING statement receives an index to this array as a parameter. This means that the next 16 values will be assigned, starting with the index, if an array with 50 fields is dimensioned. With the PALETTE USING ARRAY(10) statement, the following assignment is made:

```
color 0= value from field 10
color 1= value from field 11
color 2= value from field 12
color 3= value from field 13
color 4= value from field 14
color 5= value from field 15
and so on...
color 15= value from field 24
```

This means that several color assignments can be stored in an array. By simply changing the Index parameter with the PALETTE USING statement, new colors can be brought to the screen. The array can be dimensioned in any size, depending on the available storage. A one dimensional integer array should be used. The following program first draws 16 boxes in the standard palette and assigns new values sequentially from the PAL.AR%() array.

Note: The following program only executes on a PC with an EGA card and version 3.xx of PC-BASIC:

```
10 'PALETTE USING Demo EGA-card
20 :
30 CLS:KEY OFF
40 DIM PAL.AR%(63)
50 SCREEN 9 'resolution 640*350, 16 colors from 64
60 FOR I= 0 TO 63:PAL.AR%(I)= I:NEXT I 'initialize Array
70 FOR I= 0 TO 15
80   LINE (I*15,I*15)-(I*30,I*20),I,BF
90 NEXT I
100 FOR PAL= 0 TO 48
110   PALETTE USING PAL.AR%(PAL)
```

```
120 LOCATE 25,1
130 PRINT "Press any key to continue or press <Esc> to quit";
140   X$= INKEY$:IF X$="" THEN 140
150   IF X$= CHR$(27) THEN 170
160 NEXT PAL
170 PALETTE 'set old value again
180 SCREEN 0 'back to text-mode
```

6.1.3 Coordinates

As we learned in Section 6.1.1, in the graphics mode, the screen output is constructed with pixels. In programming, these pixels must be switched on or off according to need. This means that we must tell the graphic chip whether a pixel should be displayed. In order to do this we must know how to address the individual pixels. We have an X axis, which corresponds to a column on a page and the Y axis, which represents the lines. Together they are designated as coordinates. As with the LOCATE statement, the pixels can be addressed individually.

X-axis

Y	0,0	1,0	2,0	....	317,0	318,0	319,0
a	0,1	1,1	2,199	....	317,1	318,1	319,1
x	0,2	1,2	2,199	....	317,2	318,2	319,4
i s	0,3	1,3	2,199	....	317,3	318,3	319,5
	....	....	....	....	....	....	....
	0,196	1,196	2,196	....	317,196	318,196	319,196
	0,197	1,197	2,197	....	317,197	318,197	319,197
	0,198	1,198	2,198	....	317,198	318,198	319,198
	0,199	1,199	2,199	....	317,199	318,199	319,199

Fig. 22: Coordinates

We use the following format for the coordinates with all the graphic commands:

```
X,Y      (column,line)
```

Remember that, depending on the selected resolution and card, the X coordinates can have a maximum of 319 or 639 and the Y coordinates can have a maximum of 199 or 349.

6.2 Graphic Commands

In this section we'll discuss the graphic commands PC-BASIC provides. However, because of the interpreter's slow speed, don't expect to create the types of graphics that Open Access® or Lotus Symphony ® produce.

```
STEP                                              as parameter
```

STEP can be indicated as a parameter with all the graphic commands. We'll discuss this parameter now so that its description doesn't have to be repeated for each individual command. If we use the commands without STEP, the indicated coordinates (X,Y) relate to the actual (absolute) position of the pixel on the screen:

PSET (50,50),1

PSET places the pixel, which was calculated with the indicated coordinates X=50 and Y=50, on the screen. If STEP is also given, the values indicated as coordinates are calculated relative to the last position:

PSET STEP (10,5),1

PC-BASIC stores the coordinates of the last command. With STEP, the indicated coordinates (10,5) are added to the stored value. So, in this example, the actual position where the next pixel will be placed is X=60 and Y=55.

You'll find an example of this in the COLOR demo program for the CIRCLE statement.

Drawing Color

The color in which graphics appear on the screen is indicated the same way for all statements. A value between 0 and 3 can be used. The value 0 represents the background color, which means that an existing graphic can be "erased" by the new graphic if it overlaps. Actually "erase" isn't an accurate term. The color of the pixel is set to the same color as the background color making the pixel "invisible". Depending on the selected palette, the graphic is displayed in the color that corresponds to the value in the palette:

Palette 1:   color 0 = background color;   drawing color=0

   color 1 = Cyan;   drawing color=1

   color 2 = Magenta;   drawing color=2

   color 3 = white;   drawing color=3

If you don't indicate *drawing color*, the default value used in the COLOR statement will be inserted.

6.2.1 Pixels set/delete

The basic part of a graphic is the individual pixel. PC-BASIC provides two statements for accessing each pixel.

```
PSET
```

With the PSET statement we can set or erase each pixel of the graphic display:

```
PSET [STEP] (X,Y) [,<drawing color>]
```

If you use PSET without STEP, (X,Y) are the absolute coordinates. With STEP, (X,Y) indicates the position relative to the last position addressed. If the drawing color is missing, the value indicated by the COLOR statement for Graph_For_Grd or foreground is used.

This program draws multi-colored lines and erases the middle line.

```
10 'PSET-Demo
20 :
30 CLS:KEY OFF
40 SCREEN 1
50 A=1:B=2:C=3
60 FOR K=1 TO 10
70 FOR I=50 TO 150
80 PSET (I,I),A
90 PSET (I+1,I),A
100 PSET (I+3,I),B
110 PSET (I+4,I),B
120 PSET (I+6,I),C
130 PSET (I+7,I),C
140 NEXT I
150 IF A=1 THEN A=2:B=3:C=1:GOTO 180
160 IF A=2 THEN A=3:B=1:C=2:GOTO 180
170 IF A=3 THEN A=1:B=2:C=3
180 NEXT K
190 LOCATE 24,1:PRINT "Strike any key to continue";
200 IF INKEY$="" THEN 200
210 FOR I=50 TO 150
220 PSET (I+3,I),0
230 PSET (I+4,I),0
240 NEXT I
250 LOCATE 24,1:PRINT "Strike any key to continue";
260 IF INKEY$="" THEN 260
270 SCREEN 0:WIDTH 80
```

PRESET

The PRESET statement can be used to delete individual pixels:

```
PRESET [STEP] (X,Y) [,<drawing color>]
```

As you can see, the syntax of this statement is identical to the PSET statement. The result is also identical to the PSET statement. The only difference is that the pixel is deleted for a missing <drawing color>.

6.2.2 Drawing Lines and Rectangles

Theoretically, it's possible to create all conceivable graphics by using the PSET/PRESET statements. However, in order to make programming easier, PC-BASIC has grouped frequently used routines into statements.

LINE   draw lines

We've seen how to draw lines with the PSET statement. However, it's easier and faster to draw lines with the LINE statement:

```
LINE [STEP] [(from_X,from_Y)] - [STEP] (to_X,to_Y) [,<drawing
color>] [,B[F]] [,<Raster>]
```

If the coordinates (from_X,from_Y) are omitted, the coordinates of the previous statement apply. But (to_X,to_Y) must always be provided. The [STEP] has already been discussed. The <drawing color> and the parameters [,B[F]] aren't relevant at the moment. With <raster> we can determine the appearance of the line. The LINE statement converts coordinates, which are outside the maximum resolution defined with SCREEN, into the possible values without interrupting the program with an error message.

Draw Rectangles

PC-BASIC doesn't provide a special statement for drawing rectangles. The LINE statement can perform this task by using the [,B[F]] parameters. In this case, the (from_X,from_Y) and (to_X,to_Y) coordinates are used to determine the lower left and the upper right corner of the rectangle.

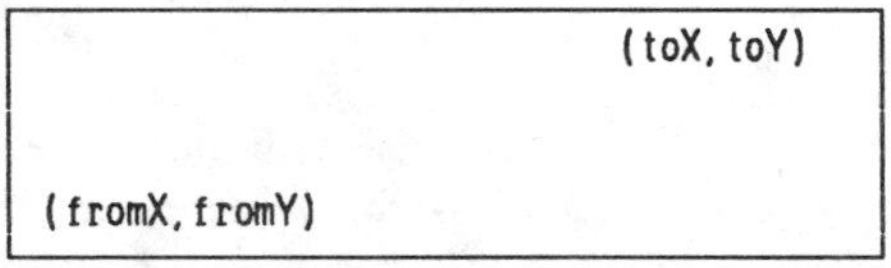

```
                              (toX, toY)


(fromX, fromY)
```

Fig. 23: Coordinates LINE

This statement presents a challenge for many programmers because for most of the graphic commands in other programming languages, the coordinates must be indicated for the upper left and the lower right corner. Since the opposite is required with the LINE statement, programmers must reverse their thinking. This can become very confusing while controlling windows. We'll discuss this in more detail later.

Fill Rectangles with Color

The parameter [F], which follows [B], indicates that the rectangle that was drawn should be filled with color. A special color cannot be specified for the shading. Instead, the <drawing color> (i.e., the default value) is used. The PAINT statement offers another option, which we'll discuss later. The following program demonstrates the capabilities of the LINE statement:

```
10 'LINE-Demo
20 :
30 CLS:KEY OFF
40 SCREEN 1
50 PRINT "Simple line"
60 LINE (10,10)-(150,150),2
70 LOCATE 24,1:PRINT "Strike any key to continue";
80 IF INKEY$="" THEN 80
90 CLS
100 PRINT "Simple rectangles"
110 A=5:B=5:C=20:D=20:COLR=1
120 FOR I= 50 TO 150 STEP 3
130 LINE (A+I,B+I)-(C+I,D+I),COLR,B
140 COLR=COLR+1:IF COLR=4 THEN COLR=1
150 NEXT I
160 LOCATE 24,1:PRINT "Strike any key to continue";
170 IF INKEY$="" THEN 170
180 CLS
190 PRINT "Colored rectangles"
200 FOR I= 50 TO 150 STEP 3
210 LINE (A+I,B+I)-(C+I,D+I),COLR,BF
220 COLR=COLR+1:IF COLR=4 THEN COLR=1
230 NEXT I
240 LOCATE 24,1:PRINT "Strike any key to continue";
250 IF INKEY$="" THEN 250
260 SCREEN 0:WIDTH 80
```

167

Line Type

During the LINE statement the appearance of the line can be determined with the <raster> parameter. Usually the line is simply drawn. We can indicate a 16-bit mask maximum for <raster>. The LINE statement "looks" at this mask for every pixel. If the bit is set so is the pixel. If the bit isn't set neither is the pixel set. This enables lines and rectangles to be drawn with different rasters. The following program draws a straight line and, depending on the mask, a second rastered line to clearly show the difference. You need to change your monitor's colors:

```
10 'LINE1-Demo
20 :
30 CLS:KEY OFF
40 SCREEN 1
50 PRINT "Different line types"
60 FOR I=1 TO 32767
70 LINE (10,10)-(150,150),1
80 LINE (10,10)-(150,150),2,,I
90 LOCATE 22,1:PRINT I;"  &H";HEX$(I)
100 LOCATE 24,1:PRINT "Strike a key to continue <Esc> to quit";
110 X$=INKEY$:IF X$="" THEN 110
120 IF X$=CHR$(27) THEN 150
130 LINE (10,10)-(150,150),0
140 NEXT I
150 SCREEN 0:WIDTH 80
```

6.2.3 Drawing Circles and Ellipses

Interesting visual graphics can be created with circles and ellipses. PC-BASIC provides a versatile statement for this task.

CIRCLE

We've already seen CIRCLE in some programs:

```
CIRCLE [STEP] (centerX,centerY), <radius> [,<drawing color>]
[,angle_start,angle_end] [,aspect]
```

Don't be intimated by these parameters; we'll explain each one separately and discuss its effect in the program.

(centerX,centerY) indicates the center point around which the circle or the ellipse should be drawn. With <radius> we indicate the radius, as measured along the major axis of the ellipse, in pixels. If <radius> produces values that are beyond the resolution determined by

SCREEN, only the part that is visible on the screen is drawn. PC-BASIC doesn't produce an error message and continues to execute the program.

For drawing circle/ellipse segments, <angle_start,angle_end> determines the segment to be drawn. The value describes the angle in the radians. Values from -2*PI to +2*PI are valid. For negative values the center point is connected with the circle-/ellipse radius. With some clever programming this can be used to create pie charts.

If any of you are mathematics experts, you probably laughed at the way we explained the difference between circles and ellipses. However, it's correct to say that a circle is simply an ellipse, in which the relationship of the X axis and the Y axis is 1:1. If we change this relationship, we obtain a "correct" ellipse. Now we know how the <aspect> parameter will be used. We'll explain this as follows: Depending on whether the <aspect> is larger or smaller than 1, the "dents" of the ellipse are drawn to the right or left, top or bottom. We apologize to the mathematicians for using such an unscientific explanation. Here is an example:

```
10 'CIRCLE-Demo
20 :
30 CLS:KEY OFF
40 SCREEN 1
50 PRINT "Circles  Ellipses  Angles"
60 FOR I=20 TO 120 STEP 3
70 CIRCLE (I,I),10,COLR
80 CIRCLE (I+70,I),10,COLR,,,4
90 CIRCLE (I+150,I),10,COLR,2,0
100 COLR=COLR+1:IF COLR=4 THEN COLR=1
110 NEXT I
120 LOCATE 24,1:PRINT "Strike any key to quit";
130 IF INKEY$="" THEN 130
140 SCREEN 0:WIDTH 80
```

6.2.4 Using Color or Patterns

After creating graphics with PSET, LINE or CIRCLE, you may want to fill portions of this graphic with certain colors or patterns.

PAINT

We can fill defined areas of our graphics with a certain color or pattern using the PAINT statement:

```
PAINT [STEP] (X,Y) [,<mode>][,<border attribute>]
```

The area we want to fill must be surrounded by a solid line and/or circle. The color of this border is indicated with 0 to 3, as border <attribute>, so that PAINT will know when the area is completely filled. Notice that, even if only one pixel of the border isn't set, the color or pattern bleeds through this gap and may fill the entire screen.

With <mode> we indicate whether the area should be filled with a color or a pattern. If <mode> has a value between 0 and 3, the *drawing color* will be used. Otherwise we can provide a mask, which is 8 bits wide and 64 bytes high, as a pattern. This pattern is then drawn in the color specified by COLOR. The pattern is defined with CHR$.

```
pattern:

76543210 --> Bit-value 128-64-32-16-8-4-2-1

x x x x    = CHR$(170)
  x x x x  = CHR$(85)
x x x x    = CHR$(170)
```

Fig. 24: Pattern with PAINT

If the corresponding bit=1 a pixel is set according to the patten during execution. The pixel isn't set if the bit=0. Look at the following program:

```
10 'PAINT-Demo
20 :
30 CLS:KEY OFF
40 SCREEN 1
50 PRINT "Figures filled with colors and patterns"
60 CIRCLE (50,50),20,2
70 PAINT (50,50),1,2
80 CIRCLE (130,50),20,2
90 PAINT (130,50),CHR$(90)+CHR$(90)+CHR$(90),2
100 LINE (50,100)-(100,160),2,B
110 PAINT (51,151),CHR$(12)+CHR$(12)+CHR$(15)+CHR$(90),2
120 PAINT (50,50),0,2
130 PAINT (50,50),3,2
140 PAINT (50,50),1,2
150 LOCATE 24,1:PRINT "Strike any key to continue";
160 IF INKEY$="" THEN 120
170 SCREEN 0:WIDTH 80
```

As you can see, this statement presents endless possibilities. You should know that the stack will be used extensively during the execution of the PAINT statement. For larger surfaces, under some circumstances, an "Out of memory" message may appear. This will only happen if, earlier in the program, you left many loops (FOR...NEXT, WHILE...WEND) or some GOSUBs unresolved so that the stack is still loaded with some of this data.

6.2.5 Drawing on the Screen

So far we've examined graphic commands that strictly execute their functions. PC-BASIC offers an additional command for more flexible applications.

```
DRAW
```

The function of the DRAW statement can be compared to the turtle used in LOGO or to a pencil. With different parameters, we can use the pencil in various ways. Similar to the PLAY statement, the DRAW statement obtains its parameters from strings and performs certain actions as a response.

```
DRAW <String>
```

<String> can be a constant, variable or an allowable logical connection (with the plus sign (+)) of both types, called a *string expression*. The current position, where DRAW begins, is either the center of the screen, immediately after the SCREEN statement, or the last position used by another graphic command. Other positions must be set with PSET, for example, before DRAW is executed. The following options/parameters can be part of the string:

U<number>

Draws <number> points up.

D<number>

Draws <number> points down.

L<number>

Draws <number> points to the left.

R<number>

Draws <number> points to the right.

E<number>

Draws <number> points diagonally to the upper right.

H<number>

Draws <number> points diagonally to the upper left.

F<number>

Draws <number> points diagonally to the lower right.

G<number>

Draws <number> points diagonally to the lower left.

If you want to specify <number> as a variable, you must first convert the numeric value into the string format. Otherwise DRAW must be told that you're using a variable. To signify this, place an equal sign (=) in front and a semicolon (;) after the variable:

```
DRAW "U=UP;"
```

B<direction>

Moves the "pencil" by one pixel in the given <direction> without drawing any points.

N<direction>

Moves the "pencil" one pixel in the given <direction>, setting that point. <direction> uses the characters: U, D, L, R, E, F, G or H.

M <X,Y>

If <X,Y> aren't preceded by a plus (+) or minus (-) sign, then a line is drawn from the current point to the point specified by <X,Y>. If <X,Y> are preceded by a sign (+/-), then <X,Y> are considered relative coordinates and the absolute position is calculated accordingly.

C<color>

Determines the drawing color based on the available palettes 0 to 3.

P<paint>,<border attribute>

Fills a figure, enclosed by <border attribute>, with <paint>. Both values can be between 0 and 3. The "pencil" must be positioned inside the border. Since *P* doesn't work with default values, both parameters must be provided. Otherwise PC-BASIC will terminate with the message "Missing operand".

A<angle>

Determines the angle for the subsequent movement. Possible values: 0=0 degrees, 1=90 degrees, 2=180 degrees and 3=270 degrees. This specification takes precedence over the direction of movement. For example, if you indicate A3, then *L* goes to the right instead of the left.

TA<angle>

Determines the angle for the subsequent movement. Unlike *A*, the angle can be freely selected. Possible values range from -360 to +360.

S<factor>

Determines the value according to the formula *factor*/4, by which all numeric parameters of the subsequent movements are multiplied. This allows figures to be drawn in different sizes. With *M*, *S* has only a relative coordinate effect. Possible values are 0 to 255.

X<String-Var>

The commands contained in <String-Var> are inserted into the current position and executed. So, you can exclude repetitive processes and, on demand, include them. Remember to include the semicolon (;) after the variables.

The following is an example of the DRAW statement:

```
10 'DRAW-Demo
20 :
30 CLS:KEY OFF
40 SCREEN 1
50 COLR=1:FILLP=2
60 C$="U10 L20"
70 PSET(290,190),0
80 FOR I=10 TO 100 STEP 5
90 FILLP$=RIGHT$(STR$(FILLP),1)
100 A$=STR$(I):A$=RIGHT$(A$,LEN(A$)-1)+" "
110 B$="C=COLR;"+" U"+A$+"L"+A$+"D"+A$+"R"+A$
120 B$=B$+"BH P"+FILLP$+","+CLR$+" X C$;"
130 DRAW B$
140 COLR=COLR+1:IF COLR=4 THEN COLR=1
150 FILLP=FILLP+1:IF FILLP=4 THEN FILLP=1
160 NEXT I
170 LOCATE 23,1:PRINT "Strike any";
180 LOCATE 24,1:PRINT "key to quit";
190 IF INKEY$="" THEN 70
200 SCREEN 0:WIDTH 80
```

We've now learned about the most flexible graphic command. Before beginning the next section, you should experiment and become familiar with the graphic statements and commands. Soon they'll be very easy to use.

6.2.6 Determining Pixel Color

PC-BASIC provides the POINT function for producing a graphic hardcopy or for setting pixels according to an existing pixel color.

POINT

POINT returns the color value of a pixel:

```
POINT(X,Y)
```

X and Y are the coordinates of the point to be examined. The result is between 0 and 3 and indicates the color, which was passed in the COLOR statement with <palette>.

6.3 Window Technique

You've probably worked with an application using windows. The screen is divided into smaller sections, or windows, which simultaneously display different data. This technique is usually used for HELP functions. For example, when you're working with a word processor in the large window, you can display a HELP screen when needed in a smaller window. However, these windows have little in common with those of PC-BASIC. The windows in PC-BASIC relate only to graphics. Although it's possible to display text in the window, it's easy to write over its frame into the next window because no borders are set for the window. However, with clever programming you can achieve the same results.

6.3.1 Creating a Window

The window must be defined before it can display any data. This means you must inform PC-BASIC of the location and dimensions for the window.

```
VIEW
```

PC-BASIC considers the entire screen as a window following a SCREEN statement. Except for the indicated size, the VIEW statement is used to define a window:

```
VIEW [SCREEN] (X1,Y1)-(X2,Y2) [,<Background_color>][,<border_color>]
```

The coordinates (X1,Y1)-(X2,Y2) specify the lower left and the upper right corner of the screen:

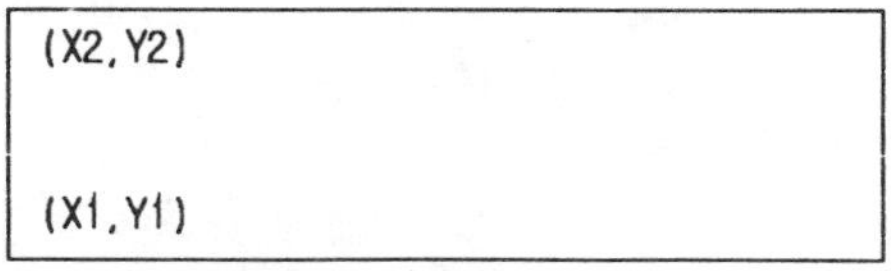

```
(X2,Y2)




(X1,Y1)
```

Fig. 25: VIEW coordinates

With <Background_color> we determine the background color of the window and with <border_color> we determine the color of the frame, which is formed around the window by a series of pixels. Remember that this is only drawn where space is available. If you place the window into a corner, it's possible that only the pages on the inside of the screen will be framed. If you don't need a frame or if the window should appear in the background color specified in the COLOR statement, simply omit the <border_color> and/or <Background_color>.

175

After VIEW all coordinates of the graphic commands, relative to the borders of the window, are valid. This means that for coordinates (10,10,), 10 is added to the right border and 10 is added to the top border of the window. If you want to work with absolute coordinates inside the window, you must indicate VIEW with the SCREEN option. The upper right corner of the window would then have the coordinates (0,0). You can define any number of windows. The current output window is always the last window defined with VIEW. All output which now occur in the window are drawn inside the window. This means that the graphic will be cut off at the border of the window if it is larger than the window.

WINDOW

So far we've become familiar with relative or absolute coordinates. It's possible that in some applications you cannot use these coordinates. For example, you may want to show a voltage curve with positive and/or negative current flow. In these instances, you can set your own coordinates with the WINDOW statement:

```
WINDOW [SCREEN] (X1,Y1)-(X2,Y2)
```

(X1,Y1)-(X2,Y2) again relate to the lower left and the upper right corner of the window. This can be changed with the SCREEN option. (X1,Y1) then relates to the upper left corner and (X2,Y2) to the lower right corner of the window. For the representation of the curve, we would use the WINDOW statement as follows:

```
WINDOW SCREEN (-10,10)-(10,-10)
```

On the screen the coordinates are as follows:

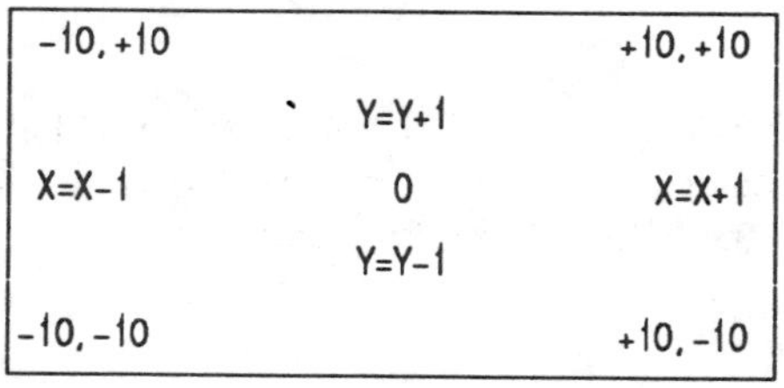

-10,+10		+10,+10
	Y=Y+1	
X=X-1	0	X=X+1
	Y=Y-1	
-10,-10		+10,-10

Fig. 26: New Coordinates through WINDOW

Although working with these commands may be difficult if you don't have any experience with graphics, they will become easier to use and understand once you've had some practice.

PMAP

The PMAP functions are used with the WINDOW statement. We can convert coordinates with these functions:

```
X= PMAP (<coordinates>),<mode>
```

<coordinates> is either an X or a Y coordinate converted according to <mode>:

mode=0

The indicated coordinate is considered an X coordinate that is set with WINDOW and converted to an absolute coordinate.

mode=1

The indicated coordinate is considered a Y coordinate that is set with WINDOW and converted to an absolute coordinate.

mode=2

The indicated coordinate is considered an absolute X coordinate, converted to the coordinate axes set in WINDOW.

mode=3

The indicated coordinate is considered an absolute Y coordinate, converted to the coordinate axes set with WINDOW.

6.3.2 Displaying Data in Windows

As we already mentioned, usually graphics are displayed in windows. Since the borders of a window don't apply to text output, some complicated programming may be required. The following is an example of how to use the VIEW and WINDOW statements:

```
10 'VIEW-Demo
20 :
30 CLS:KEY OFF
40 SCREEN 1
50 VIEW (150,50)-(50,150),1,2
60 FOR I= 32 TO 150 STEP 5:CIRCLE (I,I),30,3:NEXT I
70 VIEW (120,20)-(20,120),3,1
80 FOR I= 22 TO 120 STEP 5:CIRCLE (I,I),30,2:NEXT I
90 VIEW (180,80)-(80,180),2,3
100 FOR I= 50 TO 180 STEP 5:CIRCLE (I,I),30,1:NEXT I
110 LOCATE 24,1:PRINT "Strike any key to continue";
120 IF INKEY$="" THEN 120
```

177

```
130 LOCATE 24,1:PRINT SPACE$(39);
140 VIEW (180,80)-(80,180),2,3
150 WINDOW (80,180)-(180,80)
160 FOR I= 50 TO 180 STEP 5:CIRCLE (I,I),30,1:NEXT I
170 LOCATE 24,1:PRINT "Strike any key to quit";
180 IF INKEY$="" THEN 180
190 SCREEN 0:WIDTH 80
```

6.3.3 Moving Graphics in Windows

In this section we'll learn the PC capabilities for saving complete or partial graphics, moving them across the screen and placing them in a different location.

GET

With the GET statement, complete or partial graphics can be read into an array for storage:

```
GET [STEP] (X1,Y1)- [STEP] (X2,Y2),<ARRAY>
```

The coordinates (X1,Y1) and (X2,Y2) again refer to the lower left and the upper right corner. For <ARRAY> we indicate the name, without parentheses, of the array in which the graphic should be stored.

This array must have been previously dimensioned, with DIM, to the proper size. If the array is too small for storing the graphic, PC-BASIC returns the message "Parameter out of range". The dimensioning is calculated with the following formula:

```
X= 4+ INT(PixelsX * B +7) /8) * PixelsY
 |   |        |       |            L-> heights of the graphic
 |   |        |       |                in pixels
 |   |        |       L-> B= 1 for HiRes/ 2 colors
 |   |        |          B= 2 for MidRes/ 4 colors
 |   |        |          B= 4 for EGA/16 colors
 |   |        L-> width of the graphic in pixels
 |   L-> 4 Bytes in Array reserved for X/Y-dimension
 L-> size of the Array in Bytes
```

Fig. 27: Computing Array Size

You need to consider the number of bytes per element during the dimensioning. This number depends on the type:

Integer	2 bytes
Single precision	4 bytes
Double precision	8 bytes

The X dimension is stored in the first element (0) of the array and the Y dimension is stored in the second element (1). If the base of <ARRAY> is set to 1 with OPTION BASE 1, then the first element is 1 and the second element is 2. Following this is the bit map for the graphic. The bit map is read and stored line by line along the X axis. If the last points read from the graphic don't fill a byte, the rest of the element is filled with 0 bits. You should use an integer array for storing the graphic because data stored in such an array can be easily manipulated. One possible manipulation consists of reading the data from one array and storing them in a second array after the graphic has been rotated or reversed.

Before using the GET statement, the coordinate field for GET must be defined with WINDOW. You'll receive an "Illegal function call" error message if this isn't done.

PUT

Use the PUT statement to display a graphic stored with GET:

```
PUT (X,Y),<ARRAY>[,<mode>]
```

(X,Y) designates the upper left corner of the graphic to be transferred:

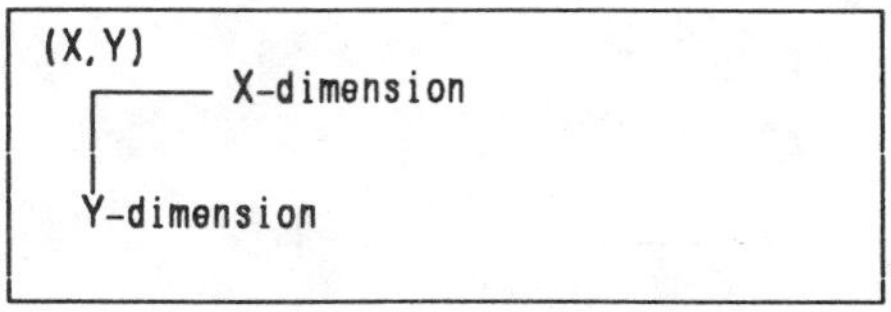

Fig. 28: PUT coordinates

<ARRAY> is the array containing the graphic to be output. With <mode> we indicate how to display the stored graphic:

PSET

The graphic is displayed exactly as it was read.

PRESET

The graphic is inverted, which means that the points stored as set are displayed as cleared and the points stored as cleared are set on the screen.

XOR

The graphic is XORed point by point with the area where it's displayed.

AND

The graphic is ANDed point by point with the area where it's displayed.

OR

The graphic is ORed point by point with the area where it's displayed.

The first program demonstrates the effect of the GET and PUT statements on storing and displaying a graphic. The second program demonstrates moving a graphic over the screen:

```
10 'GET/PUT-Demo
20 :
30 CLS:KEY OFF
40 DIM MOVEARRAY%(50,50)
50 SCREEN 1
60 VIEW (50,150)-(150,50),1,2
70 FOR I= 32 TO 150 STEP 5:CIRCLE (I,I),30,3:NEXT I
80 VIEW (20,120)-(120,20),3,1
90 FOR I= 22 TO 120 STEP 5:CIRCLE (I,I),30,2:NEXT I
100 LOCATE 8,4:PRINT " Stored with "
110 LOCATE 9,4:PRINT " GET  "
120 WINDOW (20,120)-(120,20)
130 GET(20,120)-(120,20),MOVEARRAY%
140 VIEW (80,180)-(180,80),2,3
150 FOR I= 50 TO 180 STEP 5:CIRCLE (I,I),30,1:NEXT I
160 LOCATE 24,1:PRINT "Strike any key to continue";
170 IF INKEY$="" THEN 170
180 VIEW (0,190)-(190,0),2,3
190 PUT(30,30),MOVEARRAY%,PSET
200 LOCATE 21,4:PRINT " Restored "
210 LOCATE 22,4:PRINT " with PUT "
220 IF INKEY$="" THEN 220
230 SCREEN 0:WIDTH 80


10 'GET/PUT1-Demo
20 :
30 CLS:KEY OFF
40 DIM MOVEARRAY%(50,50)
50 SCREEN 1
60 VIEW (0,199)-(199,0),1,2
70 WINDOW (0,199)-(199,0)
80 LINE (10,10)-(45,45),0,BF
90 LOCATE 22,3:PRINT "HJB"
100 GET(9,46)-(46,9),MOVEARRAY%
110 LOCATE 5,1:PRINT "Strike any key";
120 IF INKEY$="" THEN 120
130 VIEW (0,199)-(199,0),1,2
140 FOR I= 150 TO 50 STEP -5
150 VIEW (0,199)-(199,0),1,2
160 PUT (I-40,I-40),MOVEARRAY%,XOR
170 NEXT I
180 LOCATE 5,1:PRINT "Strike any key";
190 IF INKEY$="" THEN 190
200 SCREEN 0:WIDTH 80
```

180

7. Special Statements, Commands and Functions

In the previous chapters we have encountered statements, commands and functions that are the foundation for programming in PC-BASIC. In this chapter we'll present statements, commands and functions which are used in programs solving certain problems. We'll also discuss special topics such as the serial interface and assembler routines. However, these are discussed only as they relate to PC-BASIC. You should refer to other sources for more detailed information on these topics.

Even if you feel you'll never use some of the information found in this chapter, you should read this chapter for a better understanding of PC-BASIC programming.

7.1 Interfaces

Interfaces enable you to connect *peripheral devices* to your PC. If you look at the back of your PC, you'll see several different ports. Your monitor and keyboard are connected to two of these ports. Two additional ports are provided for your printer, an acoustic coupler or modem, and other peripheral devices. In certain cases you'll also see an additional port for a joystick or mouse. The number and type of cards that have been added to the expansion slot are important.

In the next section we'll discuss the serial and the parallel interface and their application under PC-BASIC. When data is sent through a serial interface, the bits are sent sequentially to the peripheral device. Although this transfer is somewhat slower than the parallel transfer, it requires fewer cables, which makes data transmission over telephone lines possible. For parallel data transfer a complete byte (8 bits) is sent to the peripheral device at one time. This type of data transmission is faster than a serial interface.

7.1.1 Serial Interface

The serial interface (also called the RS232 interface) is required for connecting a printer, a plotter, an acoustic coupler or modem or other peripheral devices that operate with serial data transfer. In order to operate the printer on the MS-DOS level, the interface must be initialized with the MODE statement as follows:

```
MODE COM1:9600,N,8,1
MODE COM1:=LPT1
```

The first command line determines the baud rate, the type of parity, the word length and the number of the stop bits. The second line redirects all output from the parallel to the serial interface. For example, the PrtScr routine can be used for the output of text hardcopy. If you have any problems, consult your MS-DOS reference manual for information on the MODE statement and your printer manual for information on the interface operation.

OPEN COM

In PC-BASIC we operate the serial interface like a normal file. You should have an understanding of the RS232 interface to completely understand the following operations.

```
OPEN "COM<channel>:
      [<Baud-Rate>]
      [,<parity>]
      [,<word-length>]
      [,<Stop-Bits>]
      [,RS]
      [,CS[<time>]] [,DS[<time>]] [,CD[<time>]]
      [,BIN] [,ASC] [,LF]"
      [FOR <mode>] AS #[<file-number>]
      [,LEN=<number>]
```

<channel>

Specifies the interface number. This is usually 1 since there is generally only one serial interface available on your PC.

<Baud-Rate>

Determines the number of bits per second for the data transfer. This value must match the baud rate of the device through which you're trying to communicate. The baud rate defaults to 300 if the specification is omitted. Possible values are: 75, 110, 150, 300, 600, 1200, 1800, 2400, 4800 and 9600.

<parity>

Determines the parity for data transfer. This value must match the setting on the peripheral device that was addressed. The parity is set to N if the specification is omitted. The following specifications can be used:

N   no parity

E   even parity

U   odd parity

S   space

M   mark

<word-length>

Determines the number of bits per character. For an omitted specification, 7 bits per character are set. Other possible values are 5, 6 and 8 bits per character.

<Stop-Bits>

Determines the number of stop bits that are sent after each character. This value must match the setting of the corresponding peripheral device that was addressed. If there is no specification, 2 stop bits are sent for baud rates that are less than/equal to 110. For all other baud rates, 1 stop bit is sent. Another possible value is 1.5.

R S

RS suppresses the RTS (Request To Send) signal during transmission.

CS<time>

Expects the CTS (Clear To Send) signal from the peripheral device. <time> sets the maximum waiting time in milliseconds. After this length of time, a *Device timeout* is signaled.

DS<time>

Waits for the DSR (Data Set Ready) signal from the peripheral device. <time> again determines the maximum waiting period in milliseconds. A *Device timeout* is signaled after this length of time.

CD<time>

Waits for the CD (Carrier Detect) signal from the peripheral device. <time> sets the maximum wait time in milliseconds. After this length of time, a *Device timeout* is signaled.

BIN

Specifies that the data received should be treated as binary data. All characters are processed unchanged. CR or LF isn't interpreted as the end of a line. The EOF character ($1A) is also ignored.

ASC

Handles the received data as ASCII data. The tab character (CHR$(9)) is converted to spaces (CHR$(32)). CR or LF are interpreted as end of a line. The transfer ends when the EOF character ($1A) is received.

LF

Specifies that an LF ($0A, !10) should be sent after every CR ($0D, !13). This option is used mainly for the output to the printer, which doesn't automatically perform a carriage return after CR.

183

<mode>

Sets the transfer mode. INPUT=receive, OUTPUT=send. If the *FOR <mode>* isn't indicated, the transfer is performed in random mode, which means that simultaneous input/output are possible.

<file-number>

Specifies the file number for input/output. Possible values range from 1 to 15.

<number>

Specifies the record length for data transfer. The default values are 256 bytes for INPUT and 128 bytes for OUTPUT. If you called PC-BASIC with the /C parameter, the record length cannot be longer than the values indicated during the call.

Suggestions for OPEN COM

If the values indicated in OPEN COM are different than the values you set with the MODE command, you must set the values again once the program is completed. Remember that some of the parameters must agree with the values set on the addressed peripheral devices. Any differences will cause errors in the data transfer. The <baud rate>, <parity>, <word-length> and <stop bits> parameters must be specified in the previous sequence. All other parameters and options can be in any order. Using BIN and LF together doesn't make sense because CR and LF are ignored when BIN is active. The transfer is terminated with *CLOSE #<file-number>*.

WIDTH	for serial interface

WIDTH sets the number of characters sent before a CR occurs:

```
WIDTH "COM<channel>:",<number_characters>
```

WIDTH ensures that during the output, a CR ($0D, !13) is automatically output after <number_characters>. The <channel> parameter corresponds to the OPEN COM statement.

GET	for serial interface

All input/output through the serial interface are handled by PC-BASIC through a buffer. From this buffer, the data that was read can be passed to variables. It uses the statements from the sequential file management. The GET statement is used as follows:

```
GET #<file-number>,<number_character>
```

<file-number> refers to the file number that was used in OPEN COM for the data transfer. <number_character> indicates how many characters should be read, from the interface, into the buffer. The number of characters cannot be larger than the record given in OPEN COM.

```
100 .....
110 OPEN "COM1:9600,N,8,1" AS #1
120 GET#1,128
130 X$=INPUT$(128,#1)
140 .....
```

PUT   for serial interface

After the data is written into the buffer with the statements used for sequential file control, PUT sends it to the serial interface:

```
PUT #<file-number>,<number_character>
```

The parameters correspond to those of the GET statement. <number_character> cannot be larger than the record length indicated in OPEN COM.

LOC and LOF   for serial interface

We can use the LOC and LOF functions on the buffer. They should be familiar to you from the file control:

```
X=LOC(<file-number>)
```

LOC returns the number of characters, in the buffer, that haven't been read yet.

```
X=LOF(<file-number>)
```

LOF returns the number of free characters in the buffer.

7.1.2 Parallel Interface

The parallel interface (also called the Centronics interface) is mainly used to connect a computer and a printer. It's the most popular method of transmitting data to a dot matrix printer because it's the fastest method. The Centronics interface is the standard for parallel printers and MS-DOS and PC-BASIC have both favored this interface for printer output. You don't need any special attachments or boards to transmit the data; only the parallel cable is required. All routines for the print output address this interface. We've previously discussed the PC-BASIC commands and statements for printer output. Details on the printer output from MS-DOS can be found in the MS-DOS reference manual.

7.1.3 Accessing Ports

We can understand the address registers, through which we can control the peripheral controllers of the CPU, by using ports. These ports are different than the interface ports we've discussed so far because a connection isn't made through a cable, etc. Instead, these ports are an interface between the software and hardware of the PC.

We already encountered a port in Chapters 4 and 6. This was the &H3D9 port, through which we have direct access to the graphic card. It can be used, for example, to change the border attribute. Since there are theoretically 65,535 available ports, we'll only discuss the commands and statements that can be accessed from PC-BASIC. Refer to your hardware manual for details on the ports to your PC. Use extreme caution if you experiment with the ports because sometimes important values can be changed. This may result in a system crash. So, be sure you thoroughly understand ports before working with them.

```
OUT
```

We can write a value into a port using the OUT statement:

```
OUT <Port-address>,<value>
```

<Port-address> indicates the port to which the data is written. The values 0 to 255 can be used since the ports can accept a value that is 8 bits wide.

```
INP
```

We can read a value from a port using INP:

```
X=INP(<Port-address>)
```

<Port-address> can be indicated with a value between 0 and 65,535.

Suggestions on OUT and INP

As we previously mentioned, you should be careful when experimenting with OUT and INP. A read access may change the content of a port, or it may return the wrong value if the port wasn't initialized for the read access. In the worst case, your system will crash. So, you'll have to perform a RESET.

WAIT

The WAIT statement suspends the execution of the program until a bit pattern is read from a port:

```
WAIT <Port-address>,<mask_1>,<mask_2>
```

A value between 0 and 65,535 can be used for <Port-address>. The value read from the port is XORed (exclusive OR) with <mask_1> and ANDed (logical AND) with <mask_2> as follows:

```
<value_read> XOR <mask_1> AND <mask_2>
```

If the result is 0, the port is read until the result does not equal 0. The bit pattern which is calculated is then available for further processing and the program continues executing. WAIT can create an infinite loop that cannot be terminated with <Ctrl> <C> or <Ctrl> <Break>.

7.2   Accessing Memory Areas

For some applications you must access memory areas directly. In this section we'll present some statements and functions that PC-BASIC provides for this purpose. You should be familiar with the terms *segment* and *offset*. Refer to your MS-DOS reference manual if you have questions about basic memory control.

DEF SEG

Because the memory addresses are divided into segments and offsets, some preparations must be made before accessing the memory areas. We must indicate which segment of the memory we want to access. This is done with the DEF SEG statement:

```
DEF SEG = <Segment_address>
```

indicates to which segment the subsequent statements and functions refer. Possible values range from 0 to 65,535. If you don't specify this parameter, the data segment (DS), which is currently occupied by PC-BASIC, is set as the default segment. PC-BASIC doesn't check if the selected segment is occupied with itself or other programs/data. This may lead to some problems. The computer crashes if you incorrectly define the segment and conflict with MS-DOS. You should be careful even while experimenting with PC-BASIC in its own data area. An incorrect POKE statement could lose your entire program.

7.2.1 Saving and Loading Areas

PC-BASIC provides two statements for saving and loading entire areas of RAM. These statements are mainly used for saving or loading screen contents or completed assembler routines.

BSAVE

We can store a defined area of memory on a diskette or hard disk using the BSAVE command:

```
BSAVE <filename>,<Offset>,<number_Bytes>
```

<filename> provides a name, for the file that is created, which corresponds to MS-DOS conventions (drive, path, filename). <Offset> specifies the address of the data to be saved,

set by DEF SEG. <number_Bytes> indicates how many bytes should be stored, starting at address <offset>.

You must use the DEF SEG statement to set the segment address to the start of the screen buffer. If you want to save the entire 16K screen buffer use an offset of 0 and 16384 for the number of bytes.

BLOAD

The BLOAD command loads a file from diskette or hard disk into a defined memory area:

```
BLOAD <filename>,<Offset>
```

<filename> is the specification for the file to be loaded. <Offset> specifies the address of the last segment, set by DEF SEG, into which the file is loaded. The data are read from the file and stored in RAM until the EOF character ($1A) is recognized.

Suggestions for BSAVE/BLOAD

Note: If you're using a EGA card in your PC, you cannot use BLOAD/BSAVE. The screen memory is organized differently than in the CGA card.

As we previously mentioned, any computer can react negatively if you enter the wrong data for the segment. So you should be very careful. The following example demonstrates how to use BSAVE and BLOAD:

```
10 'BLOAD/BSAVE-Demo
20 :
30 CLS:KEY OFF
40 PRINT "Do you have a <C>olor or a <M>onochrome monitor? --> ";
50 LOCATE ,,1,0,31
60 MONITOR$=INKEY$:IF MONITOR$="" THEN 60
70 IF MONITOR$<>"c" AND MONITOR$<>"m" THEN BEEP:GOTO 30
80 IF MONITOR$="c" THEN SEGMENT=&HB800 ELSE SEGMENT=&HB000
90 SEGMENT=SEGMENT+65536!
100 IF MONITOR$="c" THEN MONITOR$="color " ELSE MONITOR$="monochrome "
110 PRINT:PRINT:PRINT
120 PRINT "You're using a ";MONITOR$;"monitor. The video memory for it"
130 PRINT "is in segment: &H";HEX$(SEGMENT);" DEC";SEGMENT
140 PRINT:PRINT:PRINT
150 PRINT "We'll save the screen to diskette and"
160 PRINT "reload it."
170 GOSUB 310
180 :
190 DEF SEG=SEGMENT
200 BSAVE "a:bsave.scr",0,4000
```

```
210 CLS
220 PRINT "The screen is now empty"
230 GOSUB 310
240 :
250 BLOAD "a:bsave.scr"
260 LOCATE 23,1:COLOR 31,0
270 PRINT "Works well, doesn't it?"
280 COLOR 7,0
290 GOSUB 310
300 CLS:END
310 LOCATE 25,1:COLOR 0,7
320 PRINT "Strike any key to continue";
330 COLOR 7,0
340 IF INKEY$="" THEN 340
350 RETURN
```

7.2.2 Changing Memory Locations

You're able to read or write to any individual memory location of RAM using PC-BASIC.

PEEK

The PEEK function returns the content of a memory address:

```
PEEK(<Offset>)
```

We can determine from which segment the content of a memory address should be read using DEF SEG. If a DEF SEG wasn't executed earlier, PC-BASIC uses the current data segment (DS) as the segment. <Offset> provides the address within this segment.

POKE

We can write a value into any memory location in the current segment using the POKE statement:

```
POKE <Offset>,<value>
```

<Offset> indicates the address of the memory location in the current segment. <value> specifies the value to be written to the memory location. You can use values between 0 and 255.

The following is an example:

```
10 'PEEK/POKE-Demo
20 :
30 CLS:KEY OFF
40 PRINT "Do you have a <C>olor or a <M>onochrome monitor? --> ";
50 LOCATE ,,1,0,31
60 MONITOR$=INKEY$:IF MONITOR$="" THEN 60
70 IF MONITOR$<>"c" AND MONITOR$<>"m" THEN BEEP:GOTO 30
80 IF MONITOR$="c" THEN SEGMENT=&HB800 ELSE SEGMENT=&HB000
90 SEGMENT=SEGMENT+65536!
100 IF MONITOR$="c" THEN MONITOR$="color " ELSE MONITOR$="monochrome"
110 PRINT:PRINT:PRINT
120 PRINT "You're using a ";MONITOR$;"monitor. The video memory for it "
130 PRINT "is in segment: &H";HEX$(SEGMENT);" DEC";SEGMENT
140 PRINT:PRINT:PRINT
150 LOCATE 20,1 : PRINT "An example of using POKE statements to access individual
    memory locations."
160 DEF SEG=SEGMENT
170 LOCATE ,,0
180 :
190 FOR K=1 TO 255
200 FOR I=0 TO 1599
210 POKE(I),K
220 NEXT I
230 LOCATE 23,1:PRINT "Character: ASCII";PEEK(0)
240 NEXT K
```

7.2.3 Accessing Variable Memory

In order to include assembler routines, you must know which address the content of variables is stored in RAM. PC-BASIC provides two functions for this:

VARPTR

The result of this function is the address of the first byte in a variable:

```
VARPTR(<Variable>) or (#<file-number>)
```

Any variable types supported by PC-BASIC, including arrays, can be used for <Variable>. If the variable wasn't previously defined, PC-BASIC displays an "Illegal function call" error message.

The second variant of the VARPTR function returns the address of the first byte of the FCB (File Control Block) for sequential files. For random-access files, the address of the first byte of the FIELD buffer is returned. <file-number> corresponds to the file number used in the OPEN statement for the file.

VARPTR$

This function returns a 3-byte string containing information about variable type and address:

```
VARPTR$(<Variable>)
```

Any of the variable types supported by PC-BASIC, including the arrays, can be used as <Variable>. If the variable wasn't defined earlier, PC-BASIC displays an "Illegal function call" message. VARPTR$ cannot be used on FCBs or random-access buffers. The first byte of the result string contains information about the type of variable:

```
CHR$(2) = Integer          CHR$(3) = String
CHR$(4) = Single precision  CHR$(8) = Double precision
```

The second and third byte contain the address of the first byte of the variable in the format *LowByte/HighByte*:

```
address=LowByte+256*HighByte
```

Another example:

```
10 'VARPTR/VARPT$-Demo
20 :
30 :
40 CLS:KEY OFF
50 DEF SEG
60 A$="BASIC Programming Inside & Out"
70 PRINT "a$=";CHR$(34);"BASIC Programming Inside & Out";CHR$(34)
80 :
90 PRINT:PRINT "VARPTR:":PRINT
100 PRINT "The variable <A$> is stored at address: ";VARPTR(A$)
110 :
120 PRINT:PRINT "VARPTR$:":PRINT
130 X$=VARPTR$(A$)
140 PRINT "The variable <A$> has the format  :";ASC(X$)
150 PRINT "The variable <A$> is stored at address:
    ";ASC(MID$(X$,2,1))+256*ASC(RIGHT$(X$,1))
```

Suggestions for VARPTR/VARPTR$

The addresses returned by the two functions are offsets in the PC-BASIC data segment (DS). The DEF SEG statement doesn't have an effect on either function. The variables should have received a value before this function is used. Otherwise an error message will appear. Remember that variable addresses are changed with the "garbage collection". The result of one of these functions cannot be used throughout the entire program. Instead, it must be determined each time.

7.3 Interrupt Programming

PC-BASIC enables you to include the query of certain conditions, such as the keyboard or the interfaces, in the interrupt. The interrupt is called several times per second, depending on the clock frequency of the PC. The previously defined query is performed each time. Depending on the result, PC-BASIC executes a subroutine and then continues in the main program.

We can then create an event trap line number for a specified event. These events include accessing serial port communications, pressing function and other control keys, using the light pen or joysticks.

7.3.1 Timer

A *timer* in the PC controls the performance of all executions. We can control this timer using the ON TIMER(n) statement for time dependent applications:

```
ON TIMER (<seconds>) GOSUB <line-number>
TIMER ON|OFF|STOP
```

The <seconds> indicate in what intervals the subroutine executes starting at <line-number>. A value between 1 and 86,400 must be used for <seconds> otherwise you'll receive an "Illegal function call" error. With *TIMER ON*, the query is included in the interrupt. *TIMER OFF* terminates the query and *TIMER STOP* interrupts the query until the next *TIMER ON*.

7.3.2 Serial Port

Whether a byte is available at the COM port can be queried through the ON COM(n) statement. Depending on the outcome, this performs a subroutine:

```
ON COM<channel> GOSUB <line-number>
COM<channel> ON|OFF|STOP
```

We determine the number of the COM port with <channel>. The values are 1 or 2, depending on the installed peripherals. The <line-number> indicates where the subroutine begins in the program if a byte appears at the interface.

With *COM<channel> ON*, the query is included in the interrupt. *COM<channel> OFF* terminates the query in the interrupt and *COM<channel> STOP* stops the query until the next *COM<channel> ON*. While using several COMs, you should provide an interrupt routine for each COM because, after a successful branch, the source and, therefore, the channel of the interface can no longer be determined.

Note: Since a byte rarely appears alone, you should program the subroutine so that subsequent bytes are read until the transmission terminates. At high baud rates the reading and trapping of a single byte may cause the COM interrupt buffer to overflow and lose bytes.

7.3.3 Function Keys

Depending on the outcome of the query, certain keys are queried and a subroutine can be performed through the trap:

```
ON KEY(<key-number>) GOSUB <line-number>
KEY(x) ON|OFF|STOP
```

You can use the following values for <key-number>:

Key	Value
<F1> to <F10>	1 - 10
<Cursor Up>	11
<Cursor Left>	12
<Cursor Right>	13
<Cursor Down>	14

You can also define your own keys for the query. We'll present more information on this shortly. You can determine where the subroutine for a particular key begins in the main program with the <line-number> parameter.

With *KEY(<key-number>) ON* the query is included in the interrupt. *KEY(<key-number>) OFF* terminates the query in the interrupt and *KEY(<key-number>) STOP* interrupts the query until the next *KEY(<key-number>) ON*. Remember the keyboard buffer is empty after a completed trap for a defined key. So, a repeat query, for example with INKEY$, is impossible.

Defining keys for trapping

You can define your own keys for query in the interrupt by using the <Ctrl>, <Alt>, <NumLock> and <Shift> keys. These keys can contain the values 15 to 20:

```
KEY<key-number>,CHR$(<hexcode>)+ CHR$(<ScanCode>)
```

<key-number> can be from 15 to 20. For <hexcode> you can use the following values:

<Shift Right> activated   01 or &H01

<Shift Left> activated   02 or &H02

<Ctrl> activated   04 or &H04

<Alt> activated   08 or &H08

<NumLock> active   32 or &H20

<CapsLock> active   64 or &H40

There's no effect if you set scan codes as 59-68, 72, 75, 77 or 80 because function keys 1-14 are already defined.

7.3.4 Background Music

In Chapter 5 we discussed the PLAY statement. This statement allows you to program tone sequences. We can enable the tone sequences to execute continuously in the background using the interrupt capabilities with the PLAY statement and its MB parameter:

```
ON PLAY(<number_notes> GOSUB <line-number>
PLAY ON|OFF|STOP
```

This tests the notes which are still in the PLAY buffer. A branch occurs to the subroutine if the notes in the buffer are less than or equal to the <number_notes> parameter. This starts at <line-number>. PLAY can be initialized again so that continuous music can be played in the background. With *PLAY ON* the query is included in the interrupt. *PLAY OFF* terminates the query in the interrupt and *PLAY STOP* interrupts the query until the next *PLAY ON* occurs.

7.3.5 Light Pen

If a *light pen* is attached to your PC, you can control its action with interrupt programming:

```
ON PEN GOSUB <line-number>
PEN ON|OFF|STOP
```

As soon as the button on the light pen is depressed, the routine indicated by <line-number> is called and you can perform the evaluation. PC-BASIC provides the following function:

X = PEN(<mode>)

As a result, this function returns information about the status of the light pen. With <mode> you can indicate which status should be queried:

PEN(0)

The result is -1 if light pen has been polled since the last call of this function; otherwise it's 0.

PEN(1)

Returns the X coordinates that were recorded when the pen was last activated. The values must range from 0 to 319 for medium resolution and 0 to 639 for high resolution.

PEN(2)

Returns the Y coordinates that were recorded during the last activation of the button on the light pen. The value must range from 0 to 199.

PEN(3)

Returns the result -1 if down or 0 if up when the light pen switch is activated.

PEN(4)

Returns the last stored X coordinates. This is independent of the current light pen status. The values must range from 0 to 319 for medium resolution and 0 to 639 for high resolution.

PEN(5)

Returns the last stored Y coordinates. This is independent of the current light pen status. The value must range from 0 to 199.

PEN(6)

Returns the line (1-24) where the light pen was located when the button was last activated.

PEN(7)

Returns the column (1-80/1-40 depending on the screen width), in which the light pen was located when the button was last activated.

PEN(8)

Returns the last stored line (1-24) independent of the current light pen status.

PEN(9)

Returns the last stored column (1-80/1-40 depending on the screen width) independent of the current light pen status.

The X and Y coordinates that are returned as a result are in the following area, depending on the graphic card/SCREEN mode:

```
resolution 320*200: X= 0-319, Y= 0-199
resolution 640*200: X= 0-639, Y= 0-199
resolution 640*350: X= 0-639, Y= 0-349 (EGA)
```

To receive the current column or line in text mode, divide by 8 and add 1, as shown below:

```
line= (Y\8)+1
column= (X\8)+1
```

You must add 1 because the graphic coordinates for X and Y begin with 0. When the cursor is located in the first line, for example, the result is 8. After dividing by 8, a 1 must be added so that the LOCATE statement won't produce an error. This will happen because line 0 doesn't exist for this statement.

7.3.6 Joystick

You can enable or disable the trapping of the *joystick* buttons. Time can be saved, especially in games, because special routines don't have to be programmed for querying the joystick:

```
ON STRIG(<action>) GOSUB <line-number>
STRIG ON|OFF|STOP
```

With <action> you can indicate during which action the subroutine should be called:

```
0/2= buttons joystick 1
4/6= buttons joystick 2
```

As soon as one of the buttons on the joystick is activated, the routine indicated by the <line-number> is called and you can perform the evaluation there. PC-BASIC provides these functions:

```
X= STICK(<number>)
X= STRIG(<number>)
```

The STICK function returns the X/Y coordinates of two joysticks with <number>:

STICK(0)

Returns the X coordinates of joystick 1. Also stores x and y values for the two joysticks for the following three function calls:

STICK(1)

Returns the Y coordinates of joystick 1.

STICK(2)

Returns the X coordinates of joystick 2.

STICK(3)

Returns the Y coordinates of joystick 2.

The X and Y coordinates returned as a result depend on the graphic card/screen mode:

```
resolution 320*200: X= 0-319, Y= 0-199
resolution 640*200: X= 0-639, Y= 0-199
resolution 640*350: X= 0-639, Y= 0-349 (EGA)
```

In text mode you can obtain the current column or line by dividing by 8 and adding 1, as shown below:

```
line= (Y\8)+1
column= (X\8)+1
```

You must add 1 because the graphic coordinates for X and Y begin with 0. Therefore, if the cursor is located in the first line, the result is 8. This must be done; otherwise the LOCATE statement will produce an error. The line 0 doesn't exist there. As a result, the STRIG function returns the status of the joystick key specified by <number>:

STRIG(0)

Returns the result -1 if button 1 of joystick 1 has been pressed since the last call of this function; otherwise it returns 0.

STRIG(1)

Returns the result -1 if button 1 of joystick 1 has been pressed; otherwise it returns 0.

STRIG(2)

Returns the result -1 if button 1 of joystick 2 has been pressed since the last call of this function; otherwise it returns 0.

STRIG(3)

Returns the result -1 when button 1 of joystick 2 has been pressed; otherwise it returns 0.

STRIG(4,5,6,7)

As above, for button 2 of the joysticks.

General Comments on Trap Programming

While using the STOP option, a branch to the subroutine doesn't occur after the condition has been met during the query. PC-BASIC places a flag before the next ON parameter to indicate that the condition was met. Because of this flag, a branch occurs during the next ON. Therefore, a trap cannot occur when the specific event is stopped.

After the branch to a subroutine, an automatic STOP is set for the corresponding query in order to prevent an endless loop through a new call. The RETURN, at the end of the routine, causes an automatic ON for the query. This also applies to the error correction with ON ERROR GOTO. A STOP is also set during the branch into the routine, but for all queries. The RESUME causes an ON for all queries. The automatic ON, through RETURN or RESUME, can be suppressed in the routine with an OFF for the query.

Note: Be careful when you end an interrupt subroutine with *RETURN <line-number>*. Under some circumstances, a FOR...NEXT or WHILE...WEND loop could be executed in the main program and you'll receive an error message because this loop wasn't finished correctly.

Trapping cannot take place when PC-BASIC isn't executing a program. You should not use too many traps and subroutines requiring long execution time. Otherwise, it takes too long to process the main program. For example, for ON PLAY it's possible that the PLAY statement would require too much time for gathering the string data. The following is an example of interrupt programming:

```
10 'ON KEY/ON TIMER-Demo
20 :
30 CLS:KEY OFF
40 FOR I=1 TO 10:KEY I,"":NEXT I
50 PRINT "##########"
60 PRINT "#        #"
70 PRINT "##########"
80 :
90 ON TIMER (1) GOSUB 270
100 TIMER ON
110 :
120 ON KEY(1) GOSUB 330
130 KEY(1) ON
140 ON KEY(2) GOSUB 370
150 KEY(2) ON
160 ON KEY(3) GOSUB 410
170 KEY(3) ON
180 FOR I=1 TO 15
190 FOR K=1 TO 15
200 COLOR I,K
210 LOCATE 15,15:PRINT "                              "
220 LOCATE 16,15:PRINT "   main-program is executing .....   "
230 IF INKEY$<>"" THEN COLOR 7,0:CLS:END
240 LOCATE 17,15:PRINT "                              "
250 NEXT K,I
```

```
260 GOTO 180
270 'Routine ON TIMER
280 ROWNO=CSRLIN:COLMNO=POS(0):'save Cursor
290 COLOR 15,0:LOCATE 2,2
300 PRINT TIME$
310 LOCATE ROWNO,COLMNO:'Cursor back again
320 RETURN
330 'Routine ON KEY <1>
340 COLOR 31,0:LOCATE 23,1
350 BEEP:PRINT "key <F1> activated .....";:BEEP
360 RETURN
370 'Routine ON KEY <2>
380 COLOR 31,0:LOCATE 23,1
390 BEEP:PRINT "key <F2> activated.....";:BEEP
400 RETURN
410 'Routine ON KEY <3>
420 COLOR 31,0:LOCATE 23,1
430 BEEP:PRINT "key <F3> activated.....";:BEEP
440 RETURN
```

7.4   PC-BASIC and MS-DOS

PC-BASIC and MS-DOS work together extremely well since both derive from the same source. In this section we'll examine this relationship in detail.

7.4.1 Executing other Programs

Although PC-BASIC contains a large supply of statements and functions sometimes you may need a statement or function unavailable in PC-BASIC to solve a particular problem. In these cases you may need to use another program to solve this problem. For example, suppose that you want to format diskettes while still in PC-BASIC.

PC-BASIC provides the SHELL statement to solve such problems:

SHELL

The responsibility of the SHELL statement is to load and execute other programs, applications or batch files. After this program is finished executing, control is returned to PC-BASIC at the location of the statement following the SHELL statement.

```
SHELL <filename>
```

With <filename> we specify the program that we want to execute. This specification must be enclosed in quotation marks and appear exactly as if you were entering it in MS-DOS. The term *child process* refers to a program that's controlled by PC-BASIC. Although you can use string variables after SHELL, no string operations are allowed:

Incorrect:

```
SHELL DRIVE$+"FORMAT "+DRIVE$+PARAMETER$
```

Correct:

```
110 FILE$=DRIVE$+"FORMAT "+DRIVE$ +PARAMETER$
120 SHELL FILE$
```

Be sure that COMMAND.COM is available on the diskette currently in the disk drive when accessing SHELL. MS-DOS needs this file for all SHELL activity. If COMMAND.COM isn't on the diskette, you'll receive a "File not found" error message and you'll remain in PC-BASIC. In contrast, PC-BASIC won't send an error message when the program, called through SHELL, wasn't found.

You can call COMMAND.COM with SHELL and work as usual in MS-DOS. You can enter commands using SHELL which are usually entered through the command interpreter COMMAND.COM. For example, COPY, DIR, FORMAT and others are available in SHELL.

You can execute all programs using SHELL which have .COM, .EXE and .BAT extensions. After entering EXIT you'll return to PC-BASIC.

Note: You shouldn't use COMMAND.COM as <filename> because, for a missing file specification, the COMMAND is automatically executed.

Also, don't execute PC-BASIC a second time through SHELL. Although possible in some versions, in other versions you'll receive either a "Can't run BASIC as a child from BASIC" or "You cannot SHELL to BASIC" error message.

7.4.2 Accessing the Directory

From MS-DOS you're familiar with the MKDIR, CHDIR and RMDIR statements for creating, changing and removing a directory. These statements are also available from PC-BASIC:

```
MKDIR "<Directory-Name>"
CHDIR "<Directory-Name>"
RMDIR "<Directory-Name>"
```

Unlike MS-DOS, constants must be enclosed in quotation marks (") and string variables are allowed. After the statement, string operations cannot be performed:

Incorrect:

```
MKDIR "TEST"+MID$(X$,3,4)
```

Correct:

```
110 DIR$="TEST"+MID$(X$,3,4)
120 MKDIR DIR$
```

The MS-DOS terms MD, CD and RD aren't permitted under PC-BASIC.

7.4.3 Program Environment

You've probably heard about the MS-DOS environment. You deal with the MS-DOS environment every time you work with your computer even if you're not aware of it. Simple statements, such as PROMPT or PATH, deal directly with this environment. In this section we'll discover what makes up this environment and how to work with it from PC-BASIC.

ENVIRON

MS-DOS stores information about the system environment (PATH, SET, PROMPT, COMSPEC, etc.) in an *environment table* that can be accessed from PC-BASIC:

```
ENVIRON <entry=assignment>
```

<entry> must be a legal variable entry, such as PATH or COMSPEC, or a parameter specified by SET. <assignment> is the new parameter, which should be assigned to the <entry>:

```
ENVIRON "PATH= C:\WORDSTAR"
ENVIRON "PROMPT= $p$_$n:"
```

Remember that the new assignment cannot have more characters than the current entry. Otherwise PC-BASIC sends an "Out of memory" message.

ENVIRON$

The current assignments in the environment table can be determined with the ENVIRON$ function:

```
ENVIRON$ ("<entry>") or (<number>)
```

<entry> must be a legal variable entry, such as PATH, PROMPT, COMSPEC, etc. ENVIRON$ returns the current assignment of this entry:

```
PRINT ENVIRON$ ("PATH")
C:\WORDSTAR
```

ENVIRON$ can also be used to access a certain entry by its number in the table:

```
PRINT ENVIRON$(1)
C:\COMMAND.COM
```

For <number> you can indicate a value between 1 and 255. The following is an example for ENVIRON/ENVIRON$:

```
10 'ENVIRON/ENVIRON$-Demo
20 :
30 CLS:KEY OFF
40 GOSUB 140:'display current Environment
50 :
60 PRINT:PRINT
70 INPUT "New PATH: ";PATH$
80 PRINT:PRINT
90 PATH$="PATH="+PATH$
100 ENVIRON PATH$
110 GOSUB 140:'display changed Environment
120 END
130 :
140 'display Environment
150 FOR I=1 TO 5
160 PRINT ENVIRON$(I)
170 NEXT I
180 RETURN
```

7.4.4 PC-BASIC and Device Drivers

Similar to the environment table, the drivers controlling peripherals are items which are unfamiliar to most users, even though they use them daily. For example, you know that the ANSI.SYS file must be included in the configuration file CONFIG.SYS. Otherwise some programs won't run properly. Since the ANSI.SYS is a device driver for the screen and keyboard, few users know about it. For example, if you want a hardcopy of the directory of a diskette you would use the PRN driver with the MS-DOS command:

```
DIR > PRN
```

PRN ensures that the characters passed by DIR are sent to the printer. Since information on device drivers could fill an entire book, we cannot discuss them in detail here. Refer to a book on the "internals" of MS-DOS if you need additional information about device drivers.

IOCTL

Some device drivers allow the use of *control data strings* through which certain activities are initiated. For example, they can be used to pass format data or initialization values. From PC-BASIC you can use the IOCTL statement:

```
IOCTL #<file-number>,<control-string>
```

The device driver must have been previously opened, through OPEN, with a <file-number>. Then the <control-string> can be sent with the IOCTL. <control-string> can contain a maximum of 255 characters. Remember that the drivers normally used with MS-DOS won't accept IOCTL strings. You'll receive an "Illegal function call" error message if you try this.

IOCTL$

With this function you can receive control data strings from a device driver that was specifically adapted for it.

```
IOCTL$ (#<file-number>)
```

The device driver must be opened with OPEN and <file-number> before using IOCTL$. The result depends on the previously sent control data string and the response of the device driver. So, no universally valid indications can be provided. To obtain the baud rate from a special COM driver, enter:

```
IOCTL #1, "BAUD-RATE"
PRINT IOCTL$(#1)
9600
```

7.4.5 Time and the PC

In a previous chapter we discussed the most often used function for determining the system time: the TIME$ statement and variable. PC-BASIC also offers another function to directly access the time in your PC.

TIMER

This function returns, in the format seconds:hundredths, the time elapsed since 00:00 hours (midnight). The result can be queried with the TIMER function:

```
PRINT TIMER
1230.45
```

In some applications this is used for time measurement, since calculations with the TIME$ function are very complicated and inaccurate. Also, a conversion from string into the numeric format (and numeric into string) must be performed. The following program demonstrates how to use TIMER to measure reaction time.

```
10 'TIMER-Demo
20 :
30 CLS:KEY OFF
40 PRINT "Strike any key as fast as possible after hearing the tone"
45 PRINT:PRINT "Press <Return> to begin"
50 PRINT:PRINT
60 INPUT "Ready";X$
70 FOR I= 1 TO RND(TIMER)*10000:NEXT I
```

```
80 BEEP
90 A= TIMER
100 WHILE INKEY$= "":WEND
110 B= TIMER
120 PRINT:PRINT
130 PRINT USING "Your reaction time: ######.###";B-A
140 :PRINT:PRINT
```

7.5   Assembler Routines

For solving time-critical problems or for using special functions, routines in assembler (machine language) can be included and executed under PC-BASIC. At the moment, we'll only examine the statements that PC-BASIC provides and explain some basic ideas. Detailed information can be found in the reference manual for your assembler/compiler or in Chapter 8.

The assembler routines are loaded into a protected area of working memory and executed there. The protection of this area occurs during the call of PC-BASIC with the /M switch. The stack required for the routines should be made available inside the routine to ensure the intermediate storage of the current stack, so that PC-BASIC can continue to execute properly after leaving the routine.

7.5.1 Include Routines

After you've created an executable routine with an assembler or compiler and stored the file on a diskette, you can load this routine, with the BLOAD command (see Section 7.2.1), into working memory. Another possibility is to poke the routine, with a READ...DATA statement, through a FOR...NEXT loop into memory (see POKE in Section 7.2.2). Don't forget that with POKE and BLOAD you must define the segment with DEF SEG.

7.5.2 Calling Routines

For the call of the assembler routines, PC-BASIC provides two statements and a function.

CALL

An assembler routine is called with the CALL statement. At this time data can be passed to the routine for additional processing:

```
CALL <Offset-Variable>[,<data-variable,...>]
```

Before CALL, the segment in which the routine is stored must be defined with LEF SEG. The offset to the start address of the routine in this segment is assigned to a numeric variable, which is processed by CALL as the first parameter <Offset-Variable>. All numeric variable types, except for an array, can be used.

The data or values to be processed by the routine are indicated by a list of <data-variables>. With a variable, a 2-byte offset pointer to the data content of the variable, in the format *LowByte/HighByte*, is loaded on the stack and can be further processed.

```
10 'CALL-Demo
20 :
30 CLS:KEY OFF
40 PRINT "This program demonstrates the CALL statement."
50 PRINT
60 PRINT "The routine called is the system internal routine for booting the"
70 PRINT "system."
80 PRINT
90 PRINT "For diskette operation please insert a System Diskette"
100 PRINT "Drive A:"
110 LOCATE 23,1:COLOR 31,0
120 PRINT "Strike any key when you're ready"
130 COLOR 7,0
140 IF INKEY$="" THEN 140
150 DEF SEG = &HF000
160 RESETADDRESS=&HFFF0
170 CALL RESETADDRESS
```

CALLS

This is a variation of the CALL statement. For <data-variable> the current segment is loaded on the stack in the format *LowByte/HighByte*, before the 2-byte offset pointer to the data content of the variable. This segmented address is needed by special compilers. Refer to the documentation for these compilers for additional instructions.

USR

For compatibility with other BASIC versions, PC-BASIC provides the USR function to call an assembler routine:

```
USR <number> [,<data-variable>]
```

In contrast with CALL/CALLS, an offset variable isn't passed. Before the call, only the offset is determined with the statement DEF USR:

```
DEF USR <number> = <Offset>
```

<number> can have a value between 0 and 9. The last definition is the only valid one so that, for example, 3 different routines can be called. During USR <number>, the routine, whose offset was previously defined with DEF USR <number>, is called. Before the call of USR, the segment, in which the routine will be stored, must be determined with DEF SEG. If you don't provide a number with USR, PC-BASIC will use 0.

Another difference from CALL/CALLS is that only one <data-variable> can be passed to the routine. This transfer isn't made through the stack, but the CPU registers are loaded with the values:

AL

contains: &H02, if integer variable.
&H03, if string.
&H04, if single precision variable.
&H08, if double precision variable.

BX

For numeric variables, it contains an offset pointer to the FAC, in which the value is stored.

DX

For string variables it contains an offset pointer to a 3-byte area. The first byte contains the length of the string and the two subsequent bytes contain the offset address, in the format *LowByte/HighByte*, to the data content of the string.

8.   The Assembler is Required

If you examine BASIC programs developed by professionals, you'll find that they rarely operate without an assembler routine. These routines enable you to achieve a higher execution speed and to use some PC features that cannot be used by PC-BASIC.

Some people believe that using the assembler with PC-BASIC is too complicated. If you share this belief, this chapter should convince you otherwise. You don't have to be an assembler expert for your programs to run faster and be more user-friendly with assembler routines. A little basic knowledge about the assembler is all that's required.

8.1   Why Assembler Routines?

As we already mentioned, speed and PC capabilities are the two most important reasons for using assembler routines. The following is an explanation of each of these capabilities:

Speed Execution

Probably the most important task for assembler routines is the speed it executes the input/output. This isn't surprising since PC-BASIC is an interpreter and, therefore, takes a long time to execute some application programs. The screen output is a good example of this. For example, you have probably had to wait while screen templates were being constructed. This is very different from a professional program, in which the complete template quickly appears on the screen. However, this effect can be achieved with PC-BASIC by using a few bytes of assembler code. To see how this is done, refer to Chapter 11.

Using PC Capabilities

Even though PC-BASIC, which has more than 200 commands, statements and functions, uses many PC features, some capabilities are missing. One example is the file selection, which is included in many professional programs. PC-BASIC's FILES command isn't very helpful. So, in order to use such a feature, it must occur outside PC-BASIC. This is only possible with several assembler routines. Besides speed execution and the use of all PC capabilities, assembler routines also allocate memory better.

Assembler Routines Save Space

String functions require large amounts of temporary memory and cause short interruptions with the "garbage collection". As an example, let's consider converting the complete string content from lowercase letters to uppercase letters. Until now we've done this in the following way:

```
100 .....
110 FOR I= 1 TO LEN(TEXT$)
120    IF MID$(TEXT$,I,1)< "a" OR MID$(TEXT$I,1)> "z" THEN 140
130    MID$(TEXT$,I,1)= ASC(MID$(TEXT$,I,1))-32
140 NEXT I
150 .....
```

This algorithm not only requires time and space in the program, but it also burdens the string memory by using the MID$ function. The garbage collection eventually causes extensive periods of time.

This is an excellent example of when an assembler routine should be used. Throughout this chapter we'll develop this routine and use it as an example for the following sections. First we'll present some general comments about programming in assembler language.

8.2   General Information

The main reason people fear assembler programming of the 8088 or 8086 is that, while addressing the RAM, different rules apply than for programming an 8-bit CPU, such as the 6502 or the Z80. With an 8-bit CPU, the RAM area can be addressed in one piece. However, this isn't possible with the 8088 or 8086 processors because the internal structure of the CPU requires that segments up to 64K be used. The CPU can simultaneously access 4 different segments of 64K each. These segments are designated as follows:

Code-Segment (CS)

This segment contains the opcodes of the program that the CPU executes.

Data-Segment (DS)

This segment contains the data to be processed (variables, constants or tables).

Stack-Segment (SS)

This segment is required, by the CPU, for the stack. The stack is a memory area in which the return addresses are stored while the CPU executes a subroutine.

Extra-Segment (ES)

This segment is usually required for string operations but can also be "misused" for other tasks.

In order to access these segments, the CPU contains four 16-bit registers. Their designation always appears in parentheses. The content of each register points to the beginning address of the particular segment, therefore address 0000 is in the 64K block. These registers are designated as *segment registers*. To access an address inside the segment, other registers, whose content is the offset to the address, are required. These registers, which are also 16 bits wide, are called *pointer registers*.

For the code segment this is the Instruction Pointer (IP) register. This register points to the next opcode to be executed by the CPU. The CPU obtains the next opcode with the CS:IP register after a command is executed.

For the data and extra segment, the Source (SI) and Destination Index (DI) registers are available. These registers are loaded with addresses, depending on the statement that the CPU should execute. For example, when data should be transmitted from the data segment into the extra segment, the segment address of the data is in DS, the segment address of the extra segment is in ES, the offset of the data source is in SI and the offset of the data destination is in DI. The stack segment operates with the Stack Pointer (SP) or the Base Pointer (BP). The segment address is in SS, and the offset, for example for a return-jump address, is in SP or BP.

Besides the pointer registers, the *data registers*, which can have various significance and content depending on the statement, also exist. These registers can be used as 16 or 8-bit registers. They have the designation AX, BX, CX or DX if they have a 16-bit content. They are designated as AH, AL, BH, BL, CH, CL, DH or DL if they have an 8-bit content. The higher valued byte is in the registers with the ending "H" for "high", and the lower valued byte is in the registers with the ending "L" for "low".

The last 16-bit register is the *flag register*. In this register certain conditions are documented on the basis of individual bits. The flags are either set or reset with the operations of the program (bit = 0 or 1). Since these flags are the basis for comparisons and branching, it's very important to know their significance:

Bit 1 - CF: Carry Flag

This flag will be set if, during a mathematical operation, a carry from the operand was required.

Bits 2 - PF: Parity Flag

This flag indicates whether the result of an operation represents an even (bit = 1) or an odd (bit = 0) number of bits.

Bit 4 - AF: Auxiliary Flag (BCD)

An auxiliary flag is used, for example, for processing packed decimal values (bit = 1 carry from bit 3 of the operand).

Bit 6 - ZF: Zero Flag

If the result of an operation is 0, this is set to 0; otherwise it's 1.

Bit 7 - SF: Sign Flag

Provides information, during the processing of signed numbers, about the sign (bit = 1 negative, bit = 0 positive).

Bit 8 - TF: Trap/Singlestep Flag

This puts the CPU into the single-step mode (bit = 1 yes, bit = 0 no) for tests purposes.

Bit 9 - IF: Interrupt Flag

Through this flag the CPU recognizes whether interrupts from other system components are permitted (bit = 1 yes, bit = 0 no).

Bit 10 - DF: Direction Flag

This is needed for data transfer commands in order to determine the direction of the transfer (bit = 0 forward, bit = 1 backward).

Bit 11 - OF: Overflow Flag

Indicates if, for example during arithmetic operations, an overflow of a register occurred (bit = 1 yes, bit = 0 no).

The bits 1, 3, 5, 12, 13 14 and 15 have no significance. The following graphic representation of the register illustrates this:

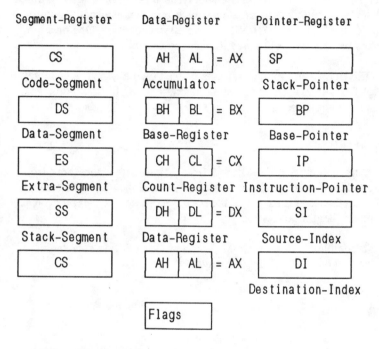

Fig. 29: Registers of the 8088/8086/80286

Unfortunately, since a discussion of the command set of the 8088 or 8086 CPU (about 130 mnemonics) would take up too much space in this book, we cannot discuss the details. Consult other sources if you need more information on this subject.

8.3 Creating Assembler Routines

There are two ways to create an assembler routine:

1.   You may already own an assembler. This program translates source code into machine language. The best known and most widely used assembler is the Macro Assembler from Microsoft. In this case, create a source program as usual. Assemble and link it; then process it with EXE2BIN to create an executable COM program. This is the easiest and usually the fastest way to make an assembler routine.

2.   You can also use DEBUG. Even though everyone doesn't own a Macro Assembler, everyone has a DEBUG.COM on the system diskette. You'll find additional instructions for this in the next section.

8.3.1 Using an Assembler

If you own an assembler, most likely it's the MASM from Microsoft or the same from IBM. We won't discuss how these assemblers operate since you have the reference manual. We're only interested in the method that is used. For the source program you can proceed as you normally would, but remember the following:

1.   The result must be a completely normal COM program. Don't define data segment, extra segment or stack segment. The "simple" way:

```
PCBASIC SEGMENT 'CODE'
        ASSUME CS: PCBASIC
        ORG 0100h

PCBASIC ENDS
```

is sufficient. ASSUME is only used for CS because DS, ES and SS are properly set by PC-BASIC during a CALL. You can enter any desired value for ORG. Since COM programs always start at 0100h and this value isn't important for later use in PC-BASIC, we'll leave it as is.

2.   The result must be completely relocatable. Don't use jumps beyond segment borders (FAR JUMPS or CALLS) or references to fixed addresses.

3.   The code is later stored in the PC-BASIC data segment and cannot be larger than this one segment. Because of this, subroutines shouldn't be declared as FAR. The adjustment to a compiler version doesn't require as much work. We'll discuss this shortly.

4. The internal stack of PC-BASIC is sufficient for small assembler routines. If you want to use larger routines with high stack requirements, you should either create a stack in the routine or set the stack area to a higher value by using CLEAR.

Using a Compiler at a Later Time

Disregard what we just discussed if you intend to use the assembler routines later in a program to be compiled. However, remember the following:

1. The compiler expects the assembler routine as an OBJ file. The source program can only be sent "through" the assembler.

2. The names of all the routines to be called must be declared as PUBLIC. Any references to variables of the main program or another OBJ module must be declared as EXTRN.

3. All routines or subroutines must be declared as FAR because it cannot be assumed that, during the later linking, all OBJ modules will be stored in the same code segment.

After you enter the source program, it's assembled, linked and converted using EXE2BIN into a COM program. During the linking, the message "No stack segment" is displayed. However, this message can be ignored because the stack is administered by PC-BASIC during the execution.

Let's return to the assembler routine for the lowercase and uppercase conversion that was mentioned earlier. A source program to implement this task could, for example, appear as follows:

```
PCBASIC SEGMENT BYTE PUBLIC

        ASSUME CS:PCBASIC

        PUBLIC UpCase ;conversion of a String lower-case-> upper-case

;------ EQUates -----------------------
;------ UpCase$ ----- CALL UPCASE(Text$)
UC_Str          equ word ptr [BP+6]  ;address of the String

;---------------------------------------
;CALL UPCASE(Text$)
;
;Converts all letters of the
;String into upper-case letters
;---------------------------------------
UPCASE          PROC        FAR
        push        bp
```

```
            mov      bp,sp              ;BP= SP for Parameter access
            push     ds                 ;store DS and ES
            push     es

            mov      si,UC_Str          ;load address of the String
            mov      cl,[si]            ;Length-Byte to CL
            xor      ch,ch              ;CH= 0
            jcxz     UC_Ende            ;if space-String, then End
            mov      di,[si+1]          ;ES:DI is destination, DI= Offset
            mov      si,[si+1]          ;DS:SI is source, SI= Offset
            push     ds
            pop      es                 ;source and destination equal
                                        ;Segment
UC_Loop:
            lodsb                       ;character from String
            cmp      al,'a'             ;character lower-case 'a'?
            jb       UC_Store           ;if yes, no action
UC_3:  cmp      al,'z'             ;character larger than 'z'?
            ja       UC_Store           ;if yes, no action
            sub      al,32              ;convert to upper-case letter
UC_Store:
            stosb                       ;after conversion, store again
            loop     UC_Loop            ;next character, until CX= 0
UC_Ende:
            pop      es                 ;restore ES
            pop      ds                 ;restore DS
            pop      bp                 ;restore BP
            ret      2                  ;remove 1 WORD from Stack
UPCASE           ENDP
;----------------------------------------
PCBASIC ENDS
            END
```

Refer to Section 8.3.3 to include this routine in a PC-BASIC program. This concludes creating a COM program with the assembler. Now it can be processed as a routine. We'll present more information on this in Section 8.3.4.

8.3.2 Smaller Routines with DEBUG

If you don't own a Macro Assembler, you can create smaller routines using the DEBUG.COM utility program on your system diskette. DEBUG contains a small line assembler, through which you can input mnemonics which are then assembled directly into memory. Refer to your MS-DOS reference manual for a description of DEBUG. It's suitable for your first attempts with assembler routines.

If you want to create larger routines or write professional level software, we recommend that you use a more complete assembler. A more complete assembler is easier to use and editing is faster. Also, since DEBUG cannot handle labels (for jumps), manual patching is required later. This not only makes the program difficult to follow, but also requires extra time. Therefore, you should use the following methods:

1.   Call DEBUG from the system level.

2.   Input the command "a 0100", which calls the assembler. The program will be stored at offset address &H0100.

3.   Input the mnemonics. Jumps must first be entered with any desired value. In our example you would first indicate the value for LOOP UC_Loop as 0100. After the complete routine was entered, determine the actual addresses with the DEBUG command "u". Note and correct the statements. Be sure that the corrections are actually made since a jump may end at an address which doesn't exist. The input is terminated by pressing the <Return> key immediately after the address (without mnemonics). Remember the last offset address that is used. You'll need it again in step 5.

4.   Determine the names through the command "n <program-name>".

5.   Determine the number of bytes to be stored with the command "r cx" (see step 3). Subtract this from the offset 0100h (256d) (see step 2).

6.   Write the program to diskette/hard disk with the command <w>.

7.   Exit DEBUG with <q>.

COM is now ready to execute the program <program> on the diskette or hard disk.

8.3.3 Including Assembler Routines

Including one or more assembler routines in PC-BASIC programs is usually accomplished without problems. However, you should know the following information. PC-BASIC needs a complete segment of 64K for its data. For a PC with less than 128K of RAM, this may be less. While PC-BASIC is being loaded, you'll be informed of this with the message, "xxxxx Bytes free".

This area is used for, among other things, variables. The variables are stored where there is available space. This space must be shared by assembler routines and variables. To prevent PC-BASIC from overwriting the assembler routines with data, you must indicate the presence of assembler routines. This is done, for example, during the call of PC-BASIC by using the switch /M, which determines the data area available. PC-BASIC administers some pointers; two of these contain the lowest and highest address of the space available for variables.

If the switch /M isn't indicated, PC-BASIC occupies the entire storage space for data in the data segment. With /M, the indicated address is set as the highest address for the variable storage. Everything that is stored after this address cannot be overwritten and is used as a space for assembler routines. The address for /M is calculated as follows:

```
NEW

HIGHEST.ADDRESS= FRE(0)

M.ADDRESS= HIGHEST.ADDRESS-LENGTH.OF.ROUTINE
```

You should add a few extra bytes for additional space, if needed. We recommend creating a small BATCH file, named AGW.BAT (AGW= Assembler-GW), which includes the following :

```
ECHO OFF

CLS

GW /M:54000 %1
```

This automatically reserves space for assembler routines after the indicated address. It then calls a program (%1) passed as a parameter.

Note: Be sure that enough space is reserved for the following experiments. You can do this either with a BATCH file or manually. All the programs assume that PC-BASIC was called with the switch /M:54000. You'll encounter many problems if this isn't the case.

Loading Assembler Routines with BLOAD

The assembler routines can be loaded in various ways. BLOAD can be used to load the routine to the location intended for it:

```
10 '------------------------------------------
20 'UPCASE2.BAS, Demo for Assembler-Routine
30 '------------------------------------------
40 :
50 CLS:KEY OFF
60 MP.START= &HE000
70 GOSUB 170 'initialize MP
80 UPCASE= MP.START
90 :
100 LOCATE 5,5
110 INPUT "Enter some characters: ",A$(5)
120 LOCATE 11,5:PRINT "Before....:";A$(5)
130 DEF SEG: CALL UPCASE(A$(5))
140 LOCATE 13,5:PRINT "After...:";A$(5)
150 :PRINT:PRINT:END
160 :
170 'upcase$.bld load
180 :
190 DEF SEG
200 BLOAD "8upcase.bld",MP.START
210 RETURN
```

BLOAD requires that the assembler routine have a header that indicates the address and length of the routine. This header is constructed as follows:

```
Byte 0        = mark &HFD

Byte 1 and 2 = Segment-address

Byte 3 and 4 = Offset-address

Byte 5 and 6 = length of the file
```

This header is usually written by BSAVE before the actual data. In an upcoming section you'll find a program (MK_BLOAD.BAS) for converting a COM file into this file format. This method of including a routine is not only fast but once it's created, it can be included in all programs. So, it's possible to create a library of assembler routines.

However, there is a disadvantage to this method. Besides the BASIC program, the file containing the assembler routine will always be needed. When you share or distribute your program, it's possible that the assembler routine will be modified with DEBUG and the program no longer executes.

Poking an Assembler Routine into Memory

Another method is to poke the assembler routine into memory by using a loop.

```
10 '------------------------------------
20 'UPCASE1.BAS, Demo for Assembler-Routine
30 '------------------------------------
40 :
50 CLS:KEY OFF
60 MP.START= &HE000
70 GOSUB 170 'initialize MP
80 UPCASE= MP.START
90 :
100 LOCATE 5,5
110 INPUT  "Enter some characters: ",A$(5)
120 LOCATE 11,5:PRINT "Before ....:";A$(5)
130 DEF SEG: CALL UPCASE(A$(5))
140 LOCATE 13,5:PRINT "After ...:";A$(5)
150 :PRINT:PRINT:END
160 :
170 'Data-lines from COM-file: upcase$.com
180 :
190 RESTORE 210
200 DEF SEG:FOR I=1 TO   66:READ X:POKE MP.START+I-1,X: NEXT I
210 DATA   85,139,236, 30,  6,139,118,  6,138, 12, 50
220 DATA  237,227, 46,139,124,  1,139,116,  1, 30,  7
230 DATA  172, 60, 97,114, 30, 60,132,117,  4,176,142
240 DATA  235, 22, 60,148,117,  4,176,153,235, 14, 60
250 DATA  129,117,  4,176,154,235,  6, 60,122,119,  2
260 DATA   44, 32,170,226,218,  7, 31, 93,202,  2,  0
270 RETURN
```

We believe this method is better than using BLOAD to load assembler routines. Even though, depending on the size of the routine, this method may require more time and memory, the program is self-contained so the assembler routine cannot be easily changed. It's also possible to construct a library because a converted assembler routine can be merged into any program. A program for converting a COM program in this type of data loader can be found in Section 8.3.6.

Executing an Assembler Routine in the String

This method can be used for assembler routines that can be stored in a string and contain a maximum of 255 bytes. The assembler routine is written, with the data loader, into a string whose beginning address is passed to the CALL statement.

With this method, memory space doesn't have to be reserved for assembler routines and the program is self-contained. The construction of a library is also possible once the routine has been converted. However, because of the garbage collection, the string is constantly moved within memory. So, the start address of the string must be determined before every CALL. If this is omitted, the computer can crash. This danger can be prevented with an appropriate subroutine. For example:

```
10 '----------------------------------------
20 'UPCASE3.BAS, Demo for Assembler-Routine
30 '----------------------------------------
40 :
50 CLS:KEY OFF
60 GOSUB 160 'initialize MP
70 :
80 LOCATE 5,5
90 INPUT  "Enter some characters: ",A$(5)
100 LOCATE 11,5:PRINT "Before....:";A$(5)
110 UPCASE= (PEEK(VARPTR(X$)+2)*256) + PEEK(VARPTR(X$)+1)
120 DEF SEG: CALL UPCASE(A$(5))
130 LOCATE 13,5:PRINT "After...:";A$(5)
140 :PRINT:PRINT:END
150 :
160 'Data-lines from COM-file: upcase$.com
170 :
180 RESTORE 210
190 X$=""
200 FOR I=1 TO   66:READ X:X$=X$+CHR$(X): NEXT I
210 DATA  85,139,236, 30,  6,139,118,  6,138, 12, 50
220 DATA 237,227, 46,139,124,  1,139,116,  1, 30,  7
230 DATA 172, 60, 97,114, 30, 60,132,117,  4,176,142
240 DATA 235, 22, 60,148,117,  4,176,153,235, 14, 60
250 DATA 129,117,  4,176,154,235,  6, 60,122,119,  2
260 DATA  44, 32,170,226,218,  7, 31, 93,202,  2,  0
270 RETURN
```

You'll also find a conversion program (MK_STRING.BAS) for this in Section 8.3.6.

8.3.4 Calling Assembler Routines

In Chapter 7 we presented descriptions of the statements PC-BASIC provides for the call. In this section we'll discuss the CALL statement in detail. You may recall the following:

```
DEF SEG
CALL <num_Variable>(<Para_Variables,...>)
```

With DEF SEG without a parameter, the data segment is declared as a current segment for additional accesses.

Note: You should never forget this before a CALL; otherwise it's possible that CALL will be at the correct offset but in the wrong segment. This could cause serious problems. We once spent several hours working on an assembler routine because we had forgotten this. The program, using

BSAVE, saved the screen display on a diskette. In addition, the segment of the video RAM was set with DEF SEG &HB8000. Obviously, CALL couldn't execute an assembler routine. Since then, whether it's necessary, we place a DEF SEG before every CALL.

<num_Variable> is a numeric variable which receives the offset address of the routine in the assigned data segment. This happens regardless of how the routine was stored in memory:

with POKE

The address corresponds to the offset, from which the routine was poked into memory.

with BLOAD

The address corresponds to the offset, which was indicated during the BLOAD command.

in the String

The address corresponds to the start address of the strings in memory. To find this address, use the VARPTR function:

```
ADDRESS= (PEEK(VARPTR(ASSM$)+2*256)) + PEEK(VARPTR(ASSM$)+1)
```

A conversion from the Low/High-Byte to the actual offset is necessary here. <Para_Variables> are one or more variables of any data type, whose content should be processed by the routine.

The exact number of parameters, which the routine expects and evaluates, must always be passed. If a parameter is missing, or there are too many, the assembler routine may react unpredictably during the return jump, which causes the computer to crash. This depends mainly on how you develop this routine. Usually problems occur with the RET command through stack cleaning. For example, if you wrote RET24 but only passed 11 parameters, one word of the return jump address is removed from the stack. This causes a system crash.

8.3.5 Passing Parameters to Assembler Routines

When PC-BASIC executes the CALL statement, a return jump address, consisting of segment and offset, is pushed onto the stack. Then the indicated <Para_Variables> are pushed onto the stack. The last variables are moved first:

```
CALL ASSM.ROUT(A%,B%,C%,D%)
                │  │  │  └> 1. PUSH
                │  │  └> 2. PUSH
                │  └> 3. PUSH
                └> 4. PUSH
```

Fig. 30: Parameter Passing CALL

The first variable is located on the top in the stack. Passing variables are performed "by reference".

by reference:

An address pointer is pushed on the stack, which points to the data (first byte) of the variables.

by value:

The data are completely pushed on the stack: an integer as two bytes, a string, with its complete content and Reals, as Exponent/Mantissa with 4 or 8 bytes. Since this type of parameter passing strains the stack, especially for strings, PC-BASIC always uses "by reference".

After CALL the stack has the following appearance:

		data
pointer A%	SP+12	
		data
pointer B%	SP+10	
		data
pointer C%	SP+8	
		data
pointer D%	SP+6	
Segment	SP+4	
		return-jump-address
Offset	SP+2	

Fig. 31: The stack during the CALL statement

It's easy to see what happens if, for example, you use RET 10 instead of RET 8. This would remove the segment address of the return jump address from the stack and insert the offset. This causes a *stack underflow* because SP has the value 0. If you don't request enough stack cleaning with RET, one or more of the data pointers are inserted as a return jump address. This would also cause a system crash.

Addressing the Variables on the Stack

After a CALL, the pointers to the data in the stack are ready for further processing. SP points, with a value of 0, to the beginning of the stack (top of the stack). The best way to perform the addressing is through the BP register after the following initialization:

```
AssmRoutine PROC    FAR
            push    bp
            mov     bp,sp          ;initialization

            mov     si,[bp+10]     ;from here on the Routine
            mov     ax,[si]
            .....
            and so on
```

In our example, the pointer to the B% variable, after MOV SI,[BP+10], is in SI. The statement MOV AX,[SI] brings the content of the B% variable to AX and can be further processed. Accessing the stack can be simplified by using EQUates. This is demonstrated in the following example:

```
Adr_A equ word ptr [BP+12]

Adr_B equ word ptr [BP+10]

Adr_C equ word ptr [BP+8]

Adr_D equ word ptr [BP+6]
.....


.....

mov   si,Adr_A
mov   ax,[si]
.....
```

While accessing strings, remember that instead of pointing to the first data byte, the pointer points to the length byte of the string. For example, to initialize CX for a LOOP, the following construction is required:

```
       . . . . .

       mov   si,Str_Adr       ;address of the String to SI

       mov   cl,[si]          ;length Byte of the String to CL

       xor   ch,ch            ;CH= 0
       . . . . .
```

Then there is the first actual address, which is loaded as follows:

```
       . . . . .

       mov   si,Str_Adr       ;address of the String to SI

       mov   cl,[si]          ;length Byte of the String to CL

       xor   ch,ch            ;CH= 0

       mov   di,[si+1]        ;pointer to data to DI

       . . . . .
```

8.3.6 Converting to PC-BASIC Format

The completed assembler routine appears as a COM program on the hard disk or diskette. There are two ways to make this routine accessible to PC-BASIC. Either it's POKEd into memory or loaded into memory using BLOAD.

Conversion for POKE

The COM program must be changed in order to use POKE. Use the following program to perform this task:

```
10 '------------------------------------
20 'MK_POKE.BAS   1986 (C) H.J.Bomanns
30 '------------------------------------
40 :
50 CLS:KEY OFF
60 PRINT STRING$(80,"=")
70 PRINT "This program creates a .BAS-Module from a COM-file consisting of data-"
80 PRINT "lines which can be included with MERGE in a program.
90 PRINT STRING$(80,"=")
100 :
110 LOCATE 7,5:LINE INPUT "Name of the COM-file: ";COM.DAT$
120 IF INSTR(COM.DAT$,".")= 0 THEN COM.DAT$= COM.DAT$+".com"
130 LOCATE 8,5:LINE INPUT "Name of the .BAS-file: ";BAS.DAT$
140 IF INSTR(BAS.DAT$,".")= 0 THEN BAS.DAT$= BAS.DAT$+".bas"
```

```
150 LOCATE 9,5:LINE INPUT "First line-number : ";ROWNO$
160 LOCATE 20,5,0:PRINT "time for coffee .....";
170 :
180 ROWNO= VAL(ROWNO$) 'line-numbering
190 DL= 10                'counter for DATA per line
200 :
210 OPEN "R",#1,COM.DAT$,1
220 FIELD#1,1 AS X$
230 OPEN BAS.DAT$ FOR OUTPUT AS #2
240 START=1:ENDE= LOF(1)
250 :
260 PRINT #2, USING "#####";ROWNO;:PRINT #2," 'Data-lines from COM-file:
    ";COM.DAT$:GOSUB 490 'lines-Nr.
270 PRINT #2, USING "#####";ROWNO;:PRINT #2,":":GOSUB 490 'lines-Nr.
280 PRINT #2, USING "##### RESTORE #####";ROWNO;ROWNO+2:GOSUB 490 'lines-Nr.
290 PRINT #2, USING "##### DEF SEG:FOR I=1 TO ####:";ROWNO;ENDE;:PRINT #2, "READ
    X:POKE MP.START+I-1,X: NEXT I"
300 :
310 FOR I= START TO ENDE
320 IF DL= 10 THEN GOSUB 410 'New data-line
330 GET #1,I
340 PRINT #2, USING ",###";ASC(X$);
350 DL= DL+1
360 NEXT I
370 GOSUB 490 'lines-Nr.
380 PRINT #2,
390 PRINT #2, USING "##### RETURN";ROWNO
400 CLOSE:CLS:END
410 '----- New Data-Line
420 PRINT #2,
430 GOSUB 490 'lines-Nr.
440 PRINT #2, USING "##### DATA ";ROWNO;
450 GET #1,I
460 PRINT #2,USING "###";ASC(X$);
470 DL= 0 'Counter for DATA per line
480 RETURN 360
490 '----- line-number + 1
500 ROWNO= ROWNO+1
510 RETURN
```

After the program begins, the filenames for the input and output files are queried from line 110 to line 150. If necessary, a COM or BAS extension is attached (line 120 and 140). Indicate the line number where the newly created subroutine should start.

How much data should be stored in one line is determined in line 190. During changes, line 320, in which the query of this variable occurs, must also be changed. Starting at line 210, the files are opened and the variables are initialized for the loop. The name of the COM file and a loop for poking are written (starting at line 290) in front of the data lines.

Beginning at line 310, the input file is read and converted into data lines. One byte from the input file, which was opened as a random file, is read (line 330) and formatted, with PRINT USING, for output to the output file (line 380). The* DL counter is then incremented by one (line 350).

The subroutine found in line 410 is activated after the correct number of DATAs has been written into a line (query in 350). At line 490, in the subroutine, the line number is incremented by one. In line 440 the output file is written after the formatting is complete. Then the next byte is read, formatted, and written (line 450/460). The DL counter is initialized (line 470) and the main program continues with the RETURN 360.

Finally a RETURN is written into the output file and both files are closed. The module that was created can be merged into your program with MERGE.

Converting for Call in a String

The conversion for the call in a string is almost identical to the conversion for poking in memory:

```
10 '-----------------------------------
20 'MK_STRNG.BAS  1986 (C) H.J.Bomanns
30 '-----------------------------------
40 :
50 CLS:KEY OFF
60 PRINT STRING$(80,"=")
70 PRINT "This program creates a STR-Module from a COM-file consisting of Data-"
80 PRINT "lines which can be merged into a program with MERGE.
90 PRINT STRING$(80,"=")
100 :
110 LOCATE 7,5:LINE INPUT "Name of the COM-file: ";COM.DAT$
120 IF INSTR(COM.DAT$,".")= 0 THEN COM.DAT$= COM.DAT$+".com"
130 LOCATE 8,5:LINE INPUT "Name of the STR-file: ";STR.DAT$
140 IF INSTR(STR.DAT$,".")= 0 THEN STR.DAT$= STR.DAT$+".str"
150 LOCATE 9,5:LINE INPUT "first line-number : ";ROWNO$
160 LOCATE 10,5:LINE INPUT "String-Variable    : ";VARNAME$
170 LOCATE 20,5,0:PRINT "time for coffee .....";
180 :
190 ROWNO= VAL(ROWNO$) 'line-numbering
200 DL= 10              'counter for DATAs per line
210 :
220 OPEN "R",#1,COM.DAT$,1
230 FIELD#1,1 AS X$
240 OPEN STR.DAT$ FOR OUTPUT AS #2
250 START=1:ENDE= LOF(1)
260 :
270 PRINT #2, USING "#####";ROWNO;:PRINT #2," 'Data-lines from COM-file:
    ";COM.DAT$:GOSUB 520 'lines-Nr.
280 PRINT #2, USING "#####";ROWNO;:PRINT #2,":":GOSUB 520 'line-number
290 PRINT #2, USING "##### RESTORE #####";ROWNO;ROWNO+3:GOSUB 520 'lines-Nr.
```

```
300 PRINT #2, USING "##### &";ROWNO;VARNAME$+"="+CHR$(34)+CHR$(34):GOSUB 520
    'line-number
310 PRINT #2, USING "##### FOR I=1 TO ####:";ROWNO;ENDE;
320 PRINT #2, "READ X:";VARNAME$;"=";VARNAME$;"+CHR$(X): NEXT I"
330 :
340 FOR I= START TO ENDE
350 IF DL= 10 THEN GOSUB 440 'new Data-line
360 GET #1,I
370 PRINT #2, USING ",###";ASC(X$);
380 DL= DL+1
390 NEXT I
400 GOSUB 520 'line-number
410 PRINT #2,
420 PRINT #2, USING "##### RETURN";ROWNO
430 CLOSE:CLS:END
440 '----- new Data-line
450 PRINT #2,
460 GOSUB 520 'line-number
470 PRINT #2, USING "##### DATA ";ROWNO;
480 GET #1,I
490 PRINT #2,USING "###";ASC(X$);
500 DL= 0 'counter for DATAs per line
510 RETURN 390
520 '----- line-number + 1
530 ROWNO= ROWNO+1
540 RETURN
```

The only difference is that in the FOR...NEXT loop no poking occurs, but the indicated string is initialized.

Conversion for BLOAD

Although a true conversion isn't required here, you must remember that a BLOAD file must have a header of 7 bytes. Otherwise the first seven bytes of the assembler routine will be considered as the header. The header has the following construction:

```
Byte 0        = mark &HFD
Byte 1 and 2 = Segment-address
Byte 3 and 4 = Offset-address
Byte 5 and 6 = length of the file
```

The following program simply places 5 bytes before the assembler routine as a "Dummy Header" and sets the length of the routine in bytes 5 and 6. Also the file receives the BLD extension to indicate that it's a BLOAD file:

```
10 '---------------------------------------
20 'MK_BLOAD.BAS   1986 (C) H.J.Bomanns
30 '---------------------------------------
40 :
50 CLS:KEY OFF
60 PRINT STRING$(80,"=")
70 PRINT "This program creates a BLD module from a COM file,"
80 PRINT "which can be loaded in memory using BLOAD."
90 PRINT STRING$(80,"=")
100 :
110 LOCATE 7,5:LINE INPUT "Name of the COM file: ";COM.FIL$
120 IF INSTR(COM.FIL$,".")= 0 THEN COM.FIL$= COM.FIL$+".com"
130 BLD.FIL$= LEFT$(COM.FIL$,INSTR(COM.FIL$,".")-1)+".bld"
140 LOCATE 9,5:PRINT "Name of BLD file: ";BLD.FIL$
150 LOCATE 20,5,0:PRINT "time for coffee";
160 :
170 OPEN "R",#1,COM.FIL$,1
180 FIELD#1,1 AS X$
190 OPEN BLD.FIL$ FOR OUTPUT AS #2
200 START=1:ENDE%= LOF(1)
210 :
220 PRINT #2, CHR$(&HFD)+"     "; 'BLOAD-KZ and 4 Dummy-Bytes for Header
230 PRINT #2, MKI$(ENDE%);        '2 Bytes length for Header
240 :
250 FOR I= START TO ENDE%
260    GET #1,I       'read 1 Byte to X$
270    PRINT #2,X$;   'write 1 Byte from X$ into destination-file
280 NEXT I
290 CLOSE:CLS:END
```

While loading with BLOAD, indicate the offset according to the start address for the assembler routine as follows:

```
BLOAD "ASSMROUT.BLD",&HE000
```

231

8.4   Interface for MS-DOS and for BIOS

Probably most of the problems that you'll want to solve with assembler routines won't be unique. If you think about the tasks of the operating system, for example, you'll find that the same actions occur there as in your programs. For example, consider the DIR statement from DOS and how it appears on the screen. The individual entries of the directory are output as strings. So, a routine, which performs this task, must exist somewhere. Naturally, this makes us wonder if this or any other routine can be used for our own purposes. The Microsoft Corporation has made it possible to do just that. With the interrupts, the operating system or the BIOS can perform certain tasks for us.

The interrupts, which are numbered sequentially, have various assignments. Some interrupts permit access through the BIOS to the hardware. Others permit direct access to the operating system. Usually these interrupts are addressed by loading the registers of the CPU with certain values, which differ according to the interrupt. The result of the interrupts are returned in these registers in order to permit additional processing on the basis of their reactions. Initializing the registers for an interrupt is possible either through an assembler, such as MASM, or through special provisions of the higher level language. Unfortunately, PC-BASIC or BASICA doesn't support this.

The interrupts cannot be called directly from PC-BASIC/BASICA. Again the support of an assembler routine is required. As we already mentioned, the design is simple. The CPU registers are loaded with certain values, which define the task and provide the necessary parameters. The results are returned, with INTs, into the registers. The output of a string occurs through an assembler as follows:

```
MOV AH,9                    ;9= function "Print String"

MOV DX,offset STRING        ;Offset of the String in the data-segment
(DS)

INT 21h                     ;INT 21h= MS-DOS function call
```

The first instruction is MOV AH,9 and defines the task for the operating system. In this case, the task is "Print String". In order to perform this task, MS-DOS must know where to find the string. The second instruction, MOV DX,offset STRING, supplies the DX register with the memory address where the string begins. With the last instruction, INT 21h, MS-DOS is called. MS-DOS tests the function number in AH and reacts accordingly. In this case, the designated string is output. In order for PC-BASIC to get the operating system or the BIOS to perform certain tasks, it must be possible to load the CPU registers with the correct values for the desired function.

The following assembler routine makes the connection between GW-BASIC or BASICA to MS-DOS or BIOS. The CPU registers are represented by BASIC variables of the same name. After the call of the routine, the contents of the variables are transmitted to the individual registers and then INT is called. After the call of INT, the results are transmitted from the registers to the variables and can be processed by GW-BASIC or BASICA. First let's look at the assembler listing for this:

```
;-------------------------------------------------------
; interface PC-BASIC to MS-DOS for Function- and
; BIOS-Calls
;-------------------------------------------------------
;CALL:
;-------
;CALL BAS_DOS(AH%,AL%,BH%,BL%,CH%,CL%,DH%,DL%,ES%,SI%,DI%,FLAGS%)
;
;The addresses of the Variables are moved during the call through CALL
;on the Stack as follows:
;
;    FLAGS%   SP+ 6        DI%   SP+ 8
;    SI%      SP+10        ES%   SP+12
;    DL%      SP+14        DH%   SP+16
;    CL%      SP+18        CH%   SP+20
;    BL%      SP+22        BH%   SP+24
;    AL%      SP+26        AH%   SP+28
;
;Then the values of the Variables must be transferred into the
;Registers. After the call of the INT, the
;Register contents are written as return into the Variables.
;
program  segment para 'CODE'
bas_dos  proc    far
         assume cs:program

         cli                  ;Please do not disturb
         push   bp            ;store base-pointer from GW
         mov    bp,sp         ;Stack-pointer --> Base-pointer
         push   ds            ;store call-DS
         push   es            ;store call-ES
         mov    si,[bp+6]     ;FLAGS% --> SI
         mov    ax,[si]       ;SI --> AX
         push   ax            ;on the Stack
         popf                 ;from there into the Flags
         mov    si,[bp+14]    ;Stack-Position DL%
         mov    dl,[si]       ;value in Register DL
         mov    si,[bp+16]    ;Stack-Position DH%
         mov    dh,[si]       ;value in Register DH
         mov    si,[bp+18]    ;Stack-Position CL%
         mov    cl,[si]       ;value in Register CL
         mov    si,[bp+20]    ;Stack-Position CH%
         mov    ch,[si]       ;value in Register CH
         mov    si,[bp+22]    ;Stack-Position BL%
         mov    bl,[si]       ;value in Register BL
         mov    si,[bp+24]    ;Stack-Position BH%
         mov    bh,[si]       ;value in Register BH
         mov    si,[bp+26]    ;Stack-Position AL%
```

```
        mov    al,[si]          ;value in Register AL
        mov    si,[bp+28]       ;Stack-Position AH%
        mov    ah,[si]          ;value in Register AH
        mov    si,[bp+8]        ;Stack-Position DI%
        mov    di,[si]          ;value in Register DI
        push   ax               ;to the Stack temporarily
                                ;for the following action
        mov    si,[bp+12]       ;Stack-Position ES%
        mov    ax,[si]          ;ES through AX
        mov    es,ax            ;value in Register ES
        pop    ax               ;AX from the Stack
        mov    si,[bp+10]       ;Stack-Position SI%
        mov    si,[si]          ;value in Register SI
        push   bp               ;store Base-pointer
        sti                     ;interrupts permitted again
        ;
        int    21h              ;DOS-/BIOS-calls
        ;
        cli                     ;please do not disturb
        pop    bp               ;return Base-pointer
        push   si               ;store Source-Index
        pushf                   ;store Flags
        mov    si,[bp+28]       ;Stack-Position AH%
        mov    [si],ah          ;Register content in AH%
        mov    si,[bp+26]       ;Stack-Position AL%
        mov    [si],al          ;register content in AL%
        mov    si,[bp+24]       ;Stack-Position BH%
        mov    [si],bh          ;register content in BH%
        mov    si,[bp+22]       ;Stack-Position BL%
        mov    [si],bl          ;register content in BL%
        mov    si,[bp+20]       ;Stack-Position CH%
        mov    [si],ch          ;register content in CH%
        mov    si,[bp+18]       ;Stack-Position CL%
        mov    [si],cl          ;register content in CL%
        mov    si,[bp+16]       ;Stack-Position DH%
        mov    [si],dh          ;register content in DH%
        mov    si,[bp+14]       ;Stack-Position DL%
        mov    [si],dl          ;register content in DL%
        pop    ax               ;get original Flag-values
                                ;back
        mov    si,[bp+6]        ;Stack-Position Flags%
        mov    [si],ax          ;write into FLAGS%
        pop    ax               ;return original SI
        mov    si,[bp+10]       ;Stack-Position SI%
        mov    [si],ax          ;and write in SI%
        mov    ax,es            ;Register ES to AX
        mov    si,[bp+12]       ;Stack-Position ES%
        mov    [si],ax          ;and write in ES%
        mov    si,[bp+8]        ;Stack-Position DI%
        mov    [si],di          ;and write in DI%
        pop    es               ;call-ES from Stack
        pop    ds               ;call-DS from Stack
        pop    bp               ;call-BP from Stack
```

```
        sti                         ;please do not disturb
        ret     24                  ;back to PC-BASIC,
                                    ;clean Stack
bas_dos endp
        program ends
        end
```

In the first part, the BP, ES and DS registers are stored on the stack because, under certain circumstances, they could change. They must retain their original value for the return jump and the continued processing with GW-BASIC or BASICA. Then the passed variables from the stack are transmitted into the individual registers or flags.

After all the registers have been initialized, the MS-DOS or the BIOS interrupts are called. In the assembler listing it's not obvious that this routine is intended for both. GW-BASIC or BASICA changes the number of the interrupt, in this case 21h, accordingly. There will be more information on this in the program. In the last part of the routine, the values that are available after the interrupt in the registers are written back into the variables. This is done to allow additional processing of the results by GW-BASIC or BASICA.

Then the BP, ES and DS registers are restored and the return jump to GW-BASIC or BASICA occurs. This routine can be used, as already indicated, for function calls of the operating system and BIOS calls. The following program illustrates this:

```
10 '----------------------------------------------------------------
20 'DOS_SN.BAS                                      1986 (C) H.J.Bomanns
30 '----------------------------------------------------------------
40 :
50 'DOS-SN is an interface from PC-BASIC to MS-DOS.  Through it
60 'all functions of the INT 21h or all BIOS-calls can be programmed
70 'and tested.  After the call of INT xxh the results are ouput in
80 'DEC und HEX.
90 '
100 CLS:KEY OFF
110 LOCATE 5,5:PRINT "Initialize machine-program....."
120 MP.START= &HE000
130 GOSUB 670 'Poke MP into memory
140 MP.ENDE= MP.START+I-1
150 LOCATE 5,5:PRINT SPACE$(80-POS(0)):PRINT
160 :
170 'In the following loop the address of the Interrupt-number is determined.
180 'The BIOS -/DOS Interrupt number can be poked at this address.
190 :
200 FOR I= MP.START TO MP.ENDE:IF PEEK(I)= 205 THEN INT.ADR= I+1 ELSE NEXT
210 :
220 A$="This is Test Text.....$"
230 :
240 DOS.SN= MP.START
250 AL%=0:AH%=0:BL%=0:BH%=0:CL%=0:CH%=0:DL%=0:DH%=0:ES%=0:SI%=0:DI%=0:FLAGS%=0
260 :
270 AH%=9:INT.NR%= &H21              'for example output of a string
280 DL%=PEEK(VARPTR(A$)+1):DH%=PEEK(VARPTR(A$)+2)  'Through INT 21h, function 9
290 :
300 'INT.NR%= &H11              'Or BIOS-Call 11h/Equipment
310 :
320 A.AH%=AH%:A.AL%=AL%:A.BH%=BH%:A.BL%=BL%:A.CH%=CH%:A.CL%=CL%:A.DH%=DH%:A.DL%=DL%
330 A.ES%=ES%:A.SI%=SI%:A.FLAGS%=FLASGS%
```

```
340 DEF SEG:POKE INT.ADR, INT.NR%
350 DEF SEG:CALL DOS.SN(AH%,AL%,BH%,BL%,CH%,CL%,DH%,DL%,ES%,SI%,DI%,FLAGS%)
360 :
370 LOCATE 25,1:PRINT "Strike any key.....";
380 IF INKEY$="" THEN 380
390 CLS
400 PRINT "INT-Number: ";INT.NR%;" - $";HEX$(INT.NR%):PRINT
410 PRINT "       before the call:            after the call:"
420 PRINT "                                                            "
430 PRINT "DEC  AH AL  BH BL  CH CL  DH DL  DEC  AH AL  BH BL  CH CL  DH DL  "
440 PRINT "                                                            "
450 PRINT "Regs ";USING "###|";A.AH%;A.AL%;A.BH%;A.BL%;A.CH%;A.CL%;A.DH%;A.DL%;
460 PRINT " Regs |";USING "###|";AH%;AL%;BH%;BL%;CH%;CL%;DH%;DL%
470 PRINT "                                                            "
480 PRINT "     AX     BX     CX     DX        AX     BX     CX     DX  "
490 PRINT "                                                            "
500 PRINT "Regs ";USING "
#####|";A.AL%+256*A.AH%;A.BL%+256*A.BH%;A.CL%+256*A.CH%;A.DL%+256*A.DH%;
510 PRINT " Regs |";USING "  #####|";AL%+256*AH%;BL%+256*BH%;CL%+256*CH%;DL%+256*DH%
520 PRINT "                                                            "
530 PRINT "                                                            "
540 PRINT "HEX  AH AL  BH BL  CH CL  DH DL  HEX  AH AL  BH BL  CH CL  DH DL  "
550 PRINT "                                                            "
560 PRINT "Regs ";USING
"$\\|";HEX$(A.AH%);HEX$(A.AL%);HEX$(A.BH%);HEX$(A.BL%);HEX$(A.CH%);HEX$(A.CL%);HEX$(A.DH%)
;HEX$(A.DL%);
570 PRINT " Regs |";USING
"$\\|";HEX$(AH%);HEX$(AL%);HEX$(BH%);HEX$(BL%);HEX$(CH%);HEX$(CL%);HEX$(DH%);HEX$(DL%)
580 PRINT "                                                            "
590 PRINT "     AX     BX     CX     DX        AX     BX     CX     DX  "
600 PRINT "                                                            "
610 PRINT "Regs ";USING "$ \  \
|";HEX$(A.AL%+256*A.AH%);HEX$(A.BL%+256*A.BH%);HEX$(A.CL%+256*A.CH%);HEX$(A.DL%+256*A.DH%)
620 PRINT " Regs |";USING "$ \  \
|";HEX$(AL%+256*AH%);HEX$(BL%+256*BH%);HEX$(CL%+256*CH%);HEX$(DL%+256*DH%)
630 PRINT "                                                            "
640 IF INKEY$="" THEN 640
650 END
660 :
670 'DATA-Lines from .COM-File: dos_sn.com
680 :
690 RESTORE 710
700 DEF SEG:FOR I=1 TO  151:READ X:POKE MP.START+I-1,X: NEXT I
710 DATA 250,  85,139,236,  30,   6,139,118,   6,139,   4
720 DATA  80,157,139,118,  14,138,  20,139,118,  16,138
730 DATA  52,139,118,  18,138,  12,139,118,  20,138,  44
740 DATA 139,118,  22,138,  28,139,118,  24,138,  60,139
750 DATA 118,  26,138,   4,139,118,  28,138,  36,139,118
760 DATA   8,139,  60,  80,139,118,  12,139,   4,142,192
770 DATA  88,139,118,  10,139,  52,  85,251,205,  33,250
780 DATA  93,  86,156,139,118,  28,136,  36,139,118,  26
790 DATA 136,   4,139,118,  24,136,  60,139,118,  22,136
800 DATA  28,139,118,  20,136,  44,139,118,  18,136,  12
810 DATA 139,118,  16,136,  52,139,118,  14,136,  20,  88
820 DATA 139,118,   6,137,   4,  88,139,118,  10,137,   4
830 DATA 140,192,139,118,  12,137,   4,139,118,   8,137
840 DATA  60,   7,  31,  93,251,202,  24,   0
850 RETURN
```

This program tests different operating systems or BIOS functions. After the call, the machine language program is initialized (line 100 to 150). As we already mentioned, the assembler routine can be used for operating systems and for BIOS functions. The number of the correct interrupt must replace the default INT 21h. This is done by having GW-BASIC or BASICA search for the value 205 from inside the assembler routine in memory (line

200). The value 205 represents the opcode for the INT instruction. At the next address (I+1) is the number of the interrupt, which can then be changed with POKE.

In line 220 a string, which is required for demonstrating DOS function 9, is initialized. The dollar sign character ($) at the end of the string acts as the end character in the function 9. The lines 270 and 280 execute additional initializations for the demonstration. The interrupt number is set to &H21 through the INT.NR% variable and function 9 is loaded into the AH register. In line 280, the DX register, which contains DH% and DL%, is given the address where the string begins. This address must be known for function 9. Line 300 points to another application and is switched off through REM (').

The program permits the comparison of the register contents before and after the call. For this the contents are stored in additional variables in line 320/330. The "A." indicates "old content". The call of the assembler routine occurs in the lines 340/350. First the interrupt number is set in line 340, which in line 350 calls the routine.

After line 370, the comparison of the register content occurs. In the development phase, this step is very helpful for test purposes. In the first line the number of the interrupt is displayed. The values before the call, on the left page, and the values after the call, on the right page, are presented in both hexadecimal and decimal representation. The data loader for the machine program, which starts at line 670, is located at the end of the program.

Remember that if, for example, functions that manipulate the memory are called, the computer can easily crash while DOS or BIOS functions are being tested. Before executing RUN, ensure that the correct values are used and that all required parameters are indicated. In Appendix F you'll find an overview of the DOS and BIOS functions. There will be more information on this subject in the next section.

8.5 MS-DOS and BIOS in Applications

In the Appendix you'll find an overview of the most important BIOS or MS-DOS interrupts and functions. Some of these functions are also implemented in PC-BASIC.

The use of the interrupts in PC-BASIC occurs through the DOS_SN.BAS interface, which was described earlier. This is done by loading the values indicated under CALL: with the register variables. The result is returned in the same variables.

Remember that all indications are in hexadecimal form. The designation ASCIZ represents a string which is terminated with a null byte (CHR$(0)). This null byte must be included because the functions use it to recognize the end of a character sequence. Some functions also require data areas for transferring path names, data sets or directory entries. This is the FCB (File Control Block) and the DTA (Disk Transfer Area or Disk Transfer Address). The FCB's structure is described in the following section. If, instead of following this specification, a function stores data differently, this will be explained in the description of the function.

FCB and Extended FCB

The File Control Block, as the name implies, is needed by MS-DOS to control the file operations. Besides the filenames, the FCB contains information about file size and file creation, as well as pointers to data records or blocks. The extended FCB is required by some functions for special operations, such as accessing volume ID or directory entries.

Construction of a normal FCB (offset is indicated in hexadecimal/decimal):

Offset	Length	Significance
00/00	1	Drive number
		1= A:, 2= B: etc.
01/01	8	Filename
09/09	3	File extension
0C/12	2	Current block, a block has 128 records
0E/14	2	Number (Low/High-Byte)
10/16	4	File size (Low/High-Word)

14/20	2	Date of last access
16/22	2	Time of last access
18/24	8	Not used
20/32	1	Current record in the block where the current record is stored
21/33	4	Current record in the file, relative record number since start of the file Start (Low/High-Word)
	37	

Construction of the extended FCB:

The extended FCB corresponds to the normal FCB. Only the following information precedes the FCB:

Offset	Length	Significance
00/00	1	Mark FF for the extended FCB
01/01	5	Unused
06/06	1	File attribute byte
07/07	1	Drive number 1= A:, 2= B: etc.
08/08	8	Filename
10/16	3	File extension
13/19	2	Current block, a block has 128 records
15/21	2	Number (Low/High-Byte)
17/23	4	File size (Low/High-Word)
1B/27	2	Date of last access
1D/29	2	Time of last access
1F/31	8	Unused

27/39	1	Current record in the block, in which the current record is stored.
28/40	4	Current record in the file, relative record number from file start (Low/High-Word)
	44	

DTA for DOS Calls

The DTA is a data area, whose beginning address is set through the function 1Ah of the interrupt 21h. This area is constructed differently, depending on the function, and can have a maximum size of 64K (theoretically). Usually the programmer must set the DTA according to the requirements of the function to be performed. The normal DTA is in PSP, starting at offset CS:80h. Since the parameters which were passed through the statement line by MS-DOS are stored at the same address, this data must be saved before the normal DTA is used for the first time. The current address of the DTA can be determined through the function 2Fh of the interrupt 21h.

File Attribute

Under MS-DOS the files and programs can be assigned attributes, which indicate special handling of the files through the operating system. An attribute byte, which is stored in the directory entry, has the following significance:

Byte = 00
Normal file.

Byte = 01
"Read only", the file can only be read.

Byte = 02
"Hidden", the file isn't displayed by the DIR command.

Byte = 04
"System", the file belongs to the operating system and isn't displayed by the DIR command.

Byte = 08
"Volume", the name of the diskette or hard disk.

Byte = 10
"Subdirectory", name of a subdirectory.

Byte = 20

"Archive", is set when a file was changed. This mark is queried by the BACKUP command.

A file can have several attributes at the same time.

Format for Date and Time

Date and time are stored in the directory as 16-bit values and transmitted, by some functions, in this format to the CB or DTA. The individual bits have the following meanings:

Date

```
15 14 13 12 11 10 9 8 7 6 5 4 3 2 1 0
<       year       > <month> <  day  >
```

Time

```
15 14 13 12 11 10 9 8 7 6 5 4 3 2 1 0
<  hour   > <  minute  > <second>
```

The following is an example for the rather complicated conversion of date and time into usable strings. This is based on the PDV.BAS program from Chapter 14.

```
7980 .....
7990 CLOCK.LO = ASC(MID$(DTA$,&H17,1)):CLOCK.HI= ASC(MID$(DTA$,&H18,1))
8000 Y= 0:MINUTE= 0
8010 FOR I= 5 TO 7
8020    IF (CLOCK.LO AND 2^I)<> 0 THEN MINUTE= MINUTE+ 2^Y 'Bit 5-7 minute
8030 Y= Y+1
8040 NEXT I
8050 FOR I= 0 TO 2
8060    IF (CLOCK.HI AND 2^I)<> 0 THEN MINUTE= MINUTE+ 2^Y 'Bit 8-10 minute
8070 Y= Y+1
8080 NEXT I
8090 Y= 0:HOUR= 0
8100 FOR I= 3 TO 7
8110    IF (CLOCK.HI AND 2^I)<> 0 THEN HOUR= HOUR+ 2^Y 'Bit 11-15 hour
8120 Y= Y+1
8130 NEXT I
8140 X$= STR$(HOUR):IF LEN(X$)= 2 THEN X$= "0"+RIGHT$(X$,1) ELSE X$= MID$(X$,2)
8150 MID$(DUMMY$,26,2)= X$
8160 X$= STR$(MINUTE):IF LEN(X$)= 2 THEN X$= "0"+RIGHT$(X$,1) ELSE X$= MID$(X$,2)
8170 MID$(DUMMY$,28,2)= X$
8180 CALENDAR.LO= ASC(MID$(DTA$,&H19,1)):CALENDAR.HI= ASC(MID$(DTA$,&H1A,1))
     'date
8190 Y= 0:DAY= 0
```

```
8200 FOR I= 0 TO 4
8210   IF (CALENDAR.LO AND 2^I)<> 0 THEN DAY=DAY+ 2^Y 'Bit 0-4 day
8220 Y= Y+1
8230 NEXT I
8240 Y= 0: MONTH= 0
8250 FOR I= 5 TO 7
8260   IF (CALENDAR.LO AND 2^I)<> 0 THEN MONTH= MONTH+ 2^Y 'Bit 5-7 month
8270   Y=Y+1
8280 NEXT I
8290 IF (CALENDAR.HI AND 2^0)<> 0 THEN MONTH= MONTH+ 2^Y 'last Bit of month
8300 Y= 0:YEAR= 0
8310 FOR I=1 TO 7
8320   IF (CALENDAR.HI AND 2^I)<> 0 THEN YEAR= YEAR+ 2^Y 'Bit 11-15 year
8330   Y=Y +1
8340 NEXT I
8350 YEAR= YEAR+80 'result= 0 bis 119, add (19)80 to this
8360 X$= STR$(TAG):IF LEN(X$)= 2 THEN X$= "0"+RIGHT$(X$,1) ELSE X$= MID$(X$,2)
8370 MID$(DUMMY$,20,2)= X$
8380 X$= STR$(MONTH):IF LEN(X$)= 2 THEN X$= "0"+RIGHT$(X$,1) ELSE X$= MID$(X$,2)
8390 MID$(DUMMY$,22,2)= X$
8400 X$= STR$(YEAR):IF LEN(X$)= 2 THEN X$= "0"+RIGHT$(X$,1) ELSE X$= MID$(X$,2)
8410 MID$(DUMMY$,24,2)= X$
8420 .....
```

Note: Depending on the compatibility of the PC, interrupts or functions, which are especially hardware sensitive, can produce results that differ from those described in the Appendix.

Error Messages

For an incorrect parameter or a wrong call, the functions return an error number in the AX register. Usually an error is signaled with a set carry flag. The following is a listing of error numbers and error messages:

01	Invalid function code
02	File not found
03	Path not found
04	Too many open files
05	Access denied
06	Invalid handle
07	Memory control block destroyed
08	Insufficient memory
09	Invalid memory block address
0A	Invalid environment
0B	Invalid format
0C	Invalid access code
0D	Invalid data
0E	Reserved

0F	Invalid drive
10	Attempt to remove current directory
11	Not same device
12	No more files
13	Disk is write-protected
14	Bad disk drive
15	Drive not ready
16	Invalid disk command
17	CRC error
18	Invalid length
19	Seek error
1A	Not a MS-DOS disk
1B	Sector not found
1C	Out of paper
1D	Write fault
1E	Read fault
1F	General failure
22	Wrong disk
23	File Control Block (FCB) unavailable

Again, remember that before every RUN make sure all the values are correct. Save your programs before execution and after major changes or additions. Don't forget that you are operating on the lowest level of programming. A syntax error or illegal function call will rarely be sent by DOS or the BIOS.

8.5.1 User-Friendly File Selection

This section will demonstrate how a program can become user-friendly through assembler routines and access to MS-DOS or the BIOS.

You have probably noticed that you don't have to memorize all the files from a diskette or hard disk because of the excellent file selection capabilities found in professional programs. Usually all available files can be displayed by pressing a key and files can be selected with the cursor keys. The following program, which you can use in all your programs, creates this type of file selection:

```
10 '---------------------------------
20 'DIRECTOR.BAS   1986 (C) H.J.Bomanns
30 '---------------------------------
40 '
50 COLOR 7,0:CLS:OUT &H3D9,0:KEY OFF:ON ERROR GOTO 3300
60 PRINT "Initialization";CHR$(254);::LOCATE ,POS(0)-1,1,0,8
70 GOTO 450 'Skip Subroutines
80 '
90 '----- Subroutines -----
```

```
100 '
110 '----- Display Bottom-Line -----
120 COLOR FONTFORGRD, FONTBAKGRD
130 LOCATE 25,2,0:PRINT FOOT$;SPACE$(80-POS(0));
140 RETURN
150 '----- Display Headline -----
160 COLOR NOTEFORGRD,NOTEBAKGRD
170 LOCATE 1,1,0:PRINT HEAD$;
180 COLOR FONTFORGRD,FONTBAKGRD
190 PRINT SPACE$(80-POS(0));
200 RETURN
210 '----- Erase Window -----
220 LOCATE CSRLIN,POS(0),0
230 COLOR FONTFORGRD,FONTBAKGRD:VIEW PRINT 2 TO 24:CLS:VIEW PRINT
240 RETURN
250 '----- Store Screen Display -----
260 BUFFER.OFS%= VARPTR(BUFFER%(0))
270 DEF SEG: CALL SAVESCRN(BUFFER.OFS%)
280 RETURN
290 '----- Restore Screen Display -----
300 BUFFER.OFS%= VARPTR(BUFFER%(0))
310 DEF SEG: CALL RESTSCRN(BUFFER.OFS%)
320 RETURN
330 '----- Erase Current Line -----
340 LOCATE CSRLIN,1:COLOR FONTFORGRD,FONTBAKGRD
350 PRINT SPACE$(79);
360 RETURN
370 '----- Output Prompt and Wait For Key -----
380 LOCATE 25,1:COLOR NOTEFORGRD,NOTEBAKGRD
390 PRINT MESSAGE$;" ";CHR$(254);" ";:LOCATE CSRLIN,POS(0)-2,1,0,31:BEEP
400 X$=INKEY$:IF X$= "" THEN 400
410 LOCATE 25,1:COLOR FONTFORGRD,FONTBAKGRD
420 PRINT SPACE$(LEN(MESSAGE$)+3);
430 RETURN
440 '
450 '----- Initialize Variables and Arrays -----
460 '
470 DIM BUFFER%(2000) 'Saving Screen Display
480 FOR I=1 TO 10: KEY I,"":NEXT I'erase function-key assignment
490 DIM HEAD$(3),FOOT$(3),DIR$(512)
500 DRV$= "C:": PATH$="\": FIL.MASK$= "*.*"
510 '
520 '----- Initialize Machine-Program  -----
530 '
540 'data-lines from COM-file: \masm\bas_asm\dos_sn.com
550 :
560 MP.START= &HE000
570 RESTORE 590
580 DEF SEG:FOR I=1 TO  151:READ X:POKE MP.START+I-1,X: NEXT I
590 DATA 250, 85,139,236, 30,  6,139,118,  6,139,   4
600 DATA  80,157,139,118, 14,138, 20,139,118, 16,138
610 DATA  52,139,118, 18,138, 12,139,118, 20,138, 44
620 DATA 139,118, 22,138, 28,139,118, 24,138, 60,139
```

```
630 DATA 118, 26,138,  4,139,118, 28,138, 36,139,118
640 DATA   8,139, 60, 80,139,118, 12,139,  4,142,192
650 DATA  88,139,118, 10,139, 52, 85,251,205, 33,250
660 DATA  93, 86,156,139,118, 28,136, 36,139,118, 26
670 DATA 136,  4,139,118, 24,136, 60,139,118, 22,136
680 DATA  28,139,118, 20,136, 44,139,118, 18,136, 12
690 DATA 139,118, 16,136, 52,139,118, 14,136, 20, 88
700 DATA 139,118,  6,137,  4, 88,139,118, 10,137,  4
710 DATA 140,192,139,118, 12,137,  4,139,118,  8,137
720 DATA  60,  7, 31, 93,251,202, 24,  0
730 DOS.SN= MP.START
740 :
750 'data-lines from COM-file: \masm\bas_asm\fs_color.com
760 :
770 MP.START= MP.START+I
780 RESTORE 800
790 DEF SEG:FOR I=1 TO    82:READ X:POKE MP.START+I-1,X: NEXT I
800 DATA  85,139,236, 30,  6,139,118, 12,138, 28,176
810 DATA 160,246,227, 45,160,  0, 80,139,118, 10,138
820 DATA  28,176,  2,246,227, 91,  3,195, 72, 72, 80
830 DATA 139,118,  8,138, 36,139,118,  6,138, 12,181
840 DATA   0,139,116,  1,191,  0,184,142,199, 91,139
850 DATA 251,186,218,  3,252,236,208,216,114,251,250
860 DATA 236,208,216,115,251,172,251,171,226,240,  7
870 DATA  31, 93,202,  8,  0
880 FASTSCRN= MP.START
890 :
900 'data-lines from COM-file: \masm\bas_asm\sr_scrnc.com
910 :
920 MP.START= MP.START+I
930 RESTORE 950
940 DEF SEG:FOR I=1 TO    75:READ X:POKE MP.START+I-1,X: NEXT I
950 DATA 235, 23,144, 85,139,236, 30,  6,139,118,  6
960 DATA 139,  4,139,240,191,  0,184,142,199, 51,255
970 DATA 235, 22,144, 85,139,236, 30,  6,139,118,  6
980 DATA 139,  4,139,248, 30,  7,190,  0,184,142,222
990 DATA  51,246,185,208,  7,186,218,  3,252,236,208
1000 DATA 216,114,251,250,236,208,216,115,251,173,251
1010 DATA 171,226,240,  7, 31, 93,202,  2,  0
1020 SAVESCRN= MP.START
1030 RESTSCRN= MP.START+3
1040 '
1050 '----- Which Monitor? -----
1060 '
1070 DEF SEG=0:IF (PEEK(&H410) AND &H30)= &H30 THEN GOTO 1200
1080 '
1090 '---- Determine Colors for Color-Monitor ----
1100 '
1110 MONITOR$="C": MONITOR.ADR= &HB800
1120 HG        = 1              'blue background
1130 FONTFORGRD= 7:FONTBAKGRD= BG 'grey letters on black background
1140 NOTEFORGRD= 15:NOTEBAKGRD=  4 'white letters, red background
1150 INPTFORGRD= 15:INPTBAKGRD=  2 'white letters, green background
```

245

```
1160 WNDOW.ATTR= 79               'white on red
1170 TXTENTR.ATTR= 47             'white on green
1180 GOTO 1290                    'continue in the program
1190 '
1200 '----- Determine Colors for Mono-Monitor -----
1210 '
1220 MONITOR$="M": MONITOR.ADR= &HB000
1230 BG        = 0 'black background
1240 FONTFORGRD=  7 :FONTBAKGRD= BG 'light-grey letters, black background
1250 NOTEFORGRD=  0 :NOTEFORGRD=  7 'light-grey reverse-video
1260 INPTFORGRD= 15 :INPTFORGRD= BG 'white letters, black background
1270 WNDOW.ATTR= 112 'black on light-grey
1280 TXTENTR.ATTR= 112 'black on light-grey
1290 CLS
1300 GOSUB 1320:COLOR 7,0:CLS:END
1310 '
1320 '----- Find File, Display and Select -----
1330 '
1340 GOSUB 210 'clear window
1350 HEAD$= " File Selection ":GOSUB 150
1360 LOCATE 3,3:COLOR NOTEFORGRD,NOTEBAKGRD
1370 PRINT " Mask: "
1380 INSTRING$= DRV$+PATH$+"*.*":TXT.LNGTH= -1:ROWNO= 3:COLMNO= 11:LNGTH=
     64:GOSUB 3370 'read subroutine
1390 IF X$= CHR$(27) THEN RETURN
1400 FOOT$="Reading Directory .....":GOSUB 110
1410 MASK$= INSTRING$:EXTENDED= 0 'transmit only file-name
1420 GOSUB 1910 'search files according to MASK$
1430 IF ENTRY<> 0 THEN 1510 'display files and select
1440 '
1450 FOOT$= "key <Y> or <N>":GOSUB 110
1460 MESSAGE$= " Found no file entries according to mask. New input? (Y/N)":GOSUB
     370 'wait for key
1470 IF X$="y" OR X$="Y" THEN GOSUB 330:GOTO 1380 'try again
1480 IF X$<>"n" AND X$<>"N" THEN BEEP:GOTO 1460
1490 RETURN
1500 '
1510 LOCATE 3,1:COLOR FONTFORGRD,FONTBAKGRD:PRINT SPACE$(80);
1520 COLOR FONTFORGRD,FONTBAKGRD
1530 LOCATE 3,1
1540 FOR I= 0 TO ENTRY-1
1550   PRINT DIR$(I),
1560 NEXT
1570 COLMNO(1)= 1:COLMNO(2)= 15: COLMNO(3)= 29: COLMNO(4)= 43: COLMNO(5)= 57
1580 FOOT$= "Select file with <"+CHR$(24)+">, <"+CHR$(25)+">, <"+CHR$(26)+"> and
     <"+CHR$(27)+">    <Return> for Ok or <Esc> to quit ":GOSUB 110
1590 COLMNO= 1:ENTR= 0:ROWNO= 3
1600 GOSUB 1800 'Bar On
1610 X$= INKEY$:IF X$="" THEN 1610
1620 IF X$= CHR$(27) THEN RETURN 'terminate
1630 IF X$=CHR$(13) THEN 1720 'file selected
1640 IF LEN(X$)<> 2 THEN BEEP:GOTO 1610
1650 ONKEY= ASC(RIGHT$(X$,1))
```

```
1660 IF ONKEY= 72 AND ROWNO> 3 THEN GOSUB 1850:ROWNO= ROWNO-1:ENTR= ENTR-5:GOTO
     1600
1670 IF ONKEY= 80 AND SCREEN(CSRLIN+1,COLMNO(COLMNO))<> 32 THEN GOSUB 1850:ROWNO=
     ROWNO+1:ENTR= ENTR+5:GOTO 1600
1680 IF ONKEY= 75 AND COLMNO> 1 THEN GOSUB 1850:COLMNO= COLMNO-1:ENTR= ENTR-
     1:GOTO 1600
1690 IF ONKEY= 77 AND COLMNO< 5 THEN IF SCREEN(CSRLIN,COLMNO(COLMNO+1))<> 32 THEN
     GOSUB 1850:COLMNO= COLMNO+1:ENTR= ENTR+1:GOTO 1600
1700 BEEP:GOTO 1610 'Only Cursor-up, down, left and right permitted
1710 '
1720 FIL.NAM$= DIR$(ENTR)
1730 IF MID$(MASK$,2,1)= ":" THEN DRV$= LEFT$(MASK$,2):MASK$= MID$(MASK$,3) 'find
     drive and remove from MASK$
1740 IF INSTR(MASK$,"\")= 0 THEN 1790 'no path indicated
1750 FOR I= LEN(MASK$) TO 1 STEP -1
1760   IF MID$(MASK$,I,1)= "\" THEN 1780 'end of the Path found
1770 NEXT I
1780 PATH$= LEFT$(MASK$,I)
1790 RETURN
1800 '----- Bar On -----
1810 LOCATE ROWNO,COLMNO(COLMNO)
1820 COLOR NOTEFORGRD,NOTEBAKGRD
1830 PRINT DIR$(ENTR);
1840 RETURN
1850 '----- Bar From -----
1860 LOCATE ROWNO,COLMNO(COLMNO)
1870 COLOR FONTFORGRD,FONTBAKGRD
1880 PRINT DIR$(ENTR);
1890 RETURN
1900 '
1910 '----- Search Files According To MASK$ -----
1920 '
1930 ENTRY= 0 'counter for DIR$()
1940 MAX.ENTRY= 80:IF EXTENDED THEN MAX.ENTRY= 512
1950 MASK$= MASK$+CHR$(0)
1960 AL%=0:AH%=0:BL%=0:BH%=0:CL%=0:CH%=0:DL%=0:DH%=0:ES%=0:SI%=0:DI%=0:FLAGS%=0
1970 INT.NR%= &H21:DEF SEG:POKE INT.ADR,INT.NR%
1980 :
1990 DTA$= SPACE$(64) 'area for result from FN 4Eh and 4Fh
2000 DL%=PEEK(VARPTR(DTA$)+1):DH%=PEEK(VARPTR(DTA$)+2) 'Pointer to DTA$
2010 AH%= &H1A 'FN Set DTA (disk transfer address)
2020 DEF SEG:CALL DOS.SN(AH%,AL%,BH%,BL%,CH%,CL%,DH%,DL%,ES%,SI%,DI%,FLAGS%)
2030 :
2040 DL%=PEEK(VARPTR(MASK$)+1):DH%=PEEK(VARPTR(MASK$)+2) 'Pointer - MASK$
2050 AH%= &H4E 'FN find first file
2060 CH%= &HFF:CL%= &HFF 'Attribute
2070 DEF SEG:CALL DOS.SN(AH%,AL%,BH%,BL%,CH%,CL%,DH%,DL%,ES%,SI%,DI%,FLAGS%)
2080 :
2090 IF (FLAGS% AND 1)= 0 THEN 2110 'Everything O.K., continue.....
2100 RETURN 'no files, ENTRY= 0
2110 GOSUB 2210 'transmit data from DTA into Array
2120 AH%= &H4F 'find next file
2130 DEF SEG:CALL DOS.SN(AH%,AL%,BH%,BL%,CH%,CL%,DH%,DL%,ES%,SI%,DI%,FLAGS%)
```

```
2140 :
2150 WHILE (FLAGS% AND 1)= 0 AND (ENTRY< MAX.ENTRY)
2160   GOSUB 2210 'transmit data from DTA into Array
2170   AH%= &H4F 'FN find next file
2180   DEF SEG:CALL DOS.SN(AH%,AL%,BH%,BL%,CH%,CL%,DH%,DL%,ES%,SI%,DI%,FLAGS%)
2190 WEND 'until FN 4Fh reports that no additional entries are available
2200 RETURN
2210 '
2220 '----- Transmit Data From DTA Into DIR$() ----
2230 '
2240 IF (ASC(MID$(DTA$,&H16,1)) AND &H10)= &H10 THEN RETURN 'no DIRs
2250 IF (ASC(MID$(DTA$,&H16,1)) AND &H8)= &H8 THEN RETURN 'no Volume-ID
2260 I= INSTR(&H1F,DTA$,CHR$(0))
2270 DIR$(ENTRY)= MID$(DTA$,&H1F,I-&H1F)
2280 IF NOT EXTENDED THEN 2870 'transmit only file-names
2290 '
2300 COLOR NOTEFORGRD,NOTEBAKGRD
2310 DUMMY$= SPACE$(105) 'duration of all infos
2320 LSET DUMMY$= DIR$(ENTRY) 'transmit name
2330 MID$(DUMMY$,30,1)= MID$(DTA$,&H16,1) 'Attribute from DTA
2340 CLOCK.LO = ASC(MID$(DTA$,&H17,1)):CLOCK.HI= ASC(MID$(DTA$,&H18,1))
2350 Y= 0:MINUTE= 0
2360 FOR I= 5 TO 7
2370   IF (CLOCK.LO AND 2^I) <> 0 THEN MINUTE= MINUTE+ 2^Y 'Bit 5-7 minute
2380 Y= Y+1
2390 NEXT I
2400 FOR I= 0 TO 2
2410   IF (CLOCK.HI AND 2^I) <> 0 THEN MINUTE= MINUTE+ 2^Y 'Bit 8-10 minute
2420 Y= Y+1
2430 NEXT I
2440 Y= 0:HOUR= 0
2450 FOR I= 3 TO 7
2460   IF (CLOCK.HI AND 2^I) <> 0 THEN HOUR= HOUR+ 2^Y 'Bit 11-15 hour
2470 Y= Y+1
2480 NEXT I
2490 X$= STR$(HOUR):IF LEN(X$)= 2 THEN X$= "0"+RIGHT$(X$,1) ELSE X$= MID$(X$,2)
2500 MID$(DUMMY$,26,2)= X$
2510 X$= STR$(MINUTE):IF LEN(X$)= 2 THEN X$= "0"+RIGHT$(X$,1) ELSE X$= MID$(X$,2)
2520 MID$(DUMMY$,28,2)= X$
2530 CLNDR.LO= ASC(MID$(DTA$,&H19,1)):CLNDR.HI= ASC(MID$(DTA$,&H1A,1)) 'Dat.
2540 Y= 0:DAY= 0
2550 FOR I= 0 TO 4
2560   IF (CLNDR.LO AND 2^I) <> 0 THEN DAY=DAY+ 2^Y 'Bit 0-4 day
2570 Y= Y+1
2580 NEXT I
2590 Y= 0: MONTH= 0
2600 FOR I= 5 TO 7
2610   IF (CLNDR.LO AND 2^I) <> 0 THEN MONTH= MONTH+ 2^Y 'Bit 5-7 month
2620   Y=Y+1
2630 NEXT I
2640 IF (CLNDR.HI AND 2^0) <> 0 THEN MONTH= MONTH+ 2^Y 'Last Bit of month
2650 Y= 0:YEAR= 0
2660 FOR I=1 TO 7
```

```
2670    IF (CLNDR.HI AND 2^I)<> 0 THEN YEAR= YEAR+ 2^Y 'Bit 11-15 year
2680    Y=Y +1
2690 NEXT I
2700 YEAR= YEAR+80 'result= 0 to 119, add to it (19)80
2710 X$= STR$(DAY):IF LEN(X$)= 2 THEN X$= "0"+RIGHT$(X$,1) ELSE X$= MID$(X$,2)
2720 MID$(DUMMY$,20,2)= X$
2730 X$= STR$(MONTH):IF LEN(X$)= 2 THEN X$= "0"+RIGHT$(X$,1) ELSE X$= MID$(X$,2)
2740 MID$(DUMMY$,22,2)= X$
2750 X$= STR$(YEAR):IF LEN(X$)= 2 THEN X$= "0"+RIGHT$(X$,1) ELSE X$= MID$(X$,2)
2760 MID$(DUMMY$,24,2)= X$
2770 SIZE.LO= ASC(MID$(DTA$,&H1B,1))+ 256* ASC(MID$(DTA$,&H1C,1))
2780 SIZE.HI= ASC(MID$(DTA$,&H1D,1))+ 256* ASC(MID$(DTA$,&H1E,1))
2790 IF SIZE.LO>= 0 THEN SIZE=65536!*SIZE.HI+SIZE.LO ELSE SIZE=
     65536!*SIZE.HI+65536!+SIZE.LO
2800 X$= STR$(SIZE):Y$= SPACE$(7):RSET Y$= MID$(X$,2)
2810 MID$(DUMMY$,13,7)= Y$ 'size of the file
2820 MID$(DUMMY$,31,11)= VOLUME.ID$ 'Diskette name
2830 MID$(DUMMY$,42,64)= FROM.DRV$+FROM.PATH$ 'Drive and Path
2840 DIR$(ENTRY)= DUMMY$
2850 LOCATE 23,18: PRINT USING "###";ENTRY
2860 '
2870 ENTRY= ENTRY+1
2880 RETURN
2890 '
2900 MESSAGE$="(Diskettes-) Error during reading of directories. Strike any key.
     ":GOSUB 370:RETURN 'Terminate and return to calling Routine
2910 '
2920 '----- Find Volume-ID -----
2930 '
2940 FOOT$="Reading VOLUME-ID.....":GOSUB 110
2950 MASK$= FROM.DRV$+"\*.*"+CHR$(0):VOLUME.ID$="???          "
2960 AL%=0:AH%=0:BL%=0:BH%=0:CL%=0:CH%=0:DL%=0:DH%=0:ES%=0:SI%=0:DI%=0:FLAGS%=0
2970 INT.NR%= &H21:DEF SEG:POKE INT.ADR, INT.NR%
2980 :
2990 DTA$= SPACE$(64) 'area for result from FN 4Eh and 4Fh
3000 DL%=PEEK(VARPTR(DTA$)+1):DH%=PEEK(VARPTR(DTA$)+2) 'Pointer to DTA$
3010 AH%= &H1A 'FN Set DTA (Disk Transfer Address)
3020 DEF SEG:CALL DOS.SN(AH%,AL%,BH%,BL%,CH%,CL%,DH%,DL%,ES%,SI%,DI%,FLAGS%)
3030 :
3040 DL%=PEEK(VARPTR(MASK$)+1):DH%=PEEK(VARPTR(MASK$)+2) 'Pointer - MASK$
3050 CL%= 255:CH%= 255 'Attribute
3060 AH%= &H4E 'FN find first file
3070 DEF SEG:CALL DOS.SN(AH%,AL%,BH%,BL%,CH%,CL%,DH%,DL%,ES%,SI%,DI%,FLAGS%)
3080 :
3090 IF (FLAGS% AND 1)= 0 THEN 3110 'Everything OK, continue.....
3100 RETURN 'error
3110 IF (ASC(MID$(DTA$,&H16,1)) AND 8)= 8 THEN GOSUB 3220:RETURN 'transmit name
     from DTA in VOLUME.ID$
3120 AH%= &H4F 'find next file
3130 DEF SEG:CALL DOS.SN(AH%,AL%,BH%,BL%,CH%,CL%,DH%,DL%,ES%,SI%,DI%,FLAGS%)
3140 :
3150 WHILE (FLAGS% AND 1)= 0
```

```
3160 IF (ASC(MID$(DTA$,&H16,1)) AND 8)= 8 THEN GOSUB 3220:RETURN 'transmit name
     from DTA into VOLUME.ID$
3170   AH%= &H4F 'FN find next file
3180   DEF SEG:CALL DOS.SN(AH%,AL%,BH%,BL%,CH%,CL%,DH%,DL%,ES%,SI%,DI%,FLAGS%)
3190 WEND 'until FN 4Fh reports that no additional entries are available
3200 RETURN
3210 '
3220 '-- Transmit Name From DTA To VOLUME.ID$ --
3230 '
3240 I= INSTR(&H1F,DTA$,CHR$(0))
3250 VOLUME.ID$= MID$(DTA$,&H1F,I-&H1F)
3260 RETURN
3270 '
3280 MESSAGE$="(Diskettes-) Error during reading of VOLUME-ID. Strike any key.
     ":GOSUB 370:RETURN 4960 'Terminate and return to calling Routine
3290 '
3300 '----- ERROR-ROUTINE -----
3310 '
3320 LOCATE 25,1,0:COLOR NOTEFORGRD,NOTEBAKGRD
3330 PRINT "Error: ";ERR;" in line: ";ERL;:BEEP
3340 IF INKEY$="" THEN 3340
3350 COLOR 7,0:CLS:END
3360 '
3370 '----- Read Subroutine -----
3380 '
3390 X$="":ONKEY= 0
3400 LOCATE ROWNO,COLMNO,0:COLOR INPTFORGRD,INPTBAKGRD:PRINT
     INSTRING$;SPACE$(LNGTH-LEN(INSTRING$));
3410 LOCATE ROWNO,COLMNO,1,0,8:CRSR.POS= 1
3420 X$= INKEY$:IF X$="" THEN 3420
3430 IF X$= CHR$(8) AND POS(0)> COLMNO THEN GOSUB 3560:GOTO 3420 'keys-Routine
3440 IF X$= CHR$(27) THEN ANYCHANGE= 0:RETURN
3450 IF X$=CHR$(13) THEN RETURN
3460 IF LEN(X$)= 2 THEN 3740 'control- and function-keys
3470 '
3480 IF X$< " " THEN BEEP:GOTO 3420 'character smaller than BLANK, omit
3490 IF TXT.LNGTH THEN IF X$>= "a" AND X$<= "z" THEN X$= CHR$(ASC(X$)-32)
3500 PRINT X$;:ANYCHANGE= -1
3510 IF CRSR.POS<= LEN(INSTRING$) THEN MID$(INSTRING$,CRSR.POS,1)= X$ ELSE
     INSTRING$= INSTRING$+X$
3520 CRSR.POS= CRSR.POS+1
3530 IF POS(0)> COLMNO+LNGTH-1 THEN BEEP:LOCATE ROWNO,COLMNO:CRSR.POS= 1:GOTO
     3420
3540 GOTO 3420
3550 '
3560 '----- BACKSPACE and DEL Keys -----
3570 '
3580 IF X$=CHR$(8) THEN INSTRING$= LEFT$(INSTRING$,CRSR.POS-
     2)+MID$(INSTRING$,CRSR.POS)
3590 IF ONKEY= 83  THEN INSTRING$= LEFT$(INSTRING$,CRSR.POS-
     1)+MID$(INSTRING$,CRSR.POS+1)
3600 LOCATE ROWNO,COLMNO:PRINT INSTRING$;" ";
3610 IF X$=CHR$(8) THEN CRSR.POS= CRSR.POS-1
```

```
3620 LOCATE CSRLIN,COLMNO+CRSR.POS-1
3630 ONKEY= 0: X$="":ANYCHANGE= -1
3640 RETURN
3650 '
3660 '----- Ins Key  -----
3670 '
3680 INSTRING$= LEFT$(INSTRING$,CRSR.POS-1)+" "+MID$(INSTRING$,CRSR.POS)
3690 PRINT " ";MID$(INSTRING$,CRSR.POS+1);
3700 LOCATE CSRLIN,COLMNO+CRSR.POS-1
3710 ANYCHANGE= -1
3720 RETURN
3730 '
3740 '----- Control- and Function-Keys -----
3750 '
3760 ONKEY= ASC(RIGHT$(X$,1))
3770 IF ONKEY= 63 THEN RETURN '[F5]= Selection
3780 IF ONKEY= 68 THEN RETURN '[F10]= input OK
3790 IF ONKEY= 72 OR ONKEY= 80 THEN RETURN 'Cursor up or down
3800 IF ONKEY= 73 OR ONKEY= 81 THEN RETURN 'PgUp and PgDn
3810 IF ONKEY= 75 AND POS(0)> COLMNO THEN LOCATE CSRLIN,POS(0)-1:CRSR.POS=
     CRSR.POS-1:GOTO 3420 'CRSR <--
3820 IF ONKEY= 77 AND POS(0)< COLMNO+LNGTH-1 THEN IF CRSR.POS<= LEN(INSTRING$)
     THEN LOCATE CSRLIN,POS(0)+1:CRSR.POS= CRSR.POS+1:GOTO 3420 'CRSR -->
3830 IF ONKEY= 83 AND CRSR.POS <= LEN(INSTRING$) THEN GOSUB 3560:GOTO 3420 'DEL
     treated similar to BACKSPACE
3840 IF ONKEY= 71 THEN LOCATE ROWNO,COLMNO:GOTO 3420 'Home, start of field
3850 IF ONKEY= 79 THEN LOCATE CSRLIN,COLMNO+LEN(INSTRING$)-1:CRSR.POS=
     LEN(INSTRING$):GOTO 3420 'End, set to last character
3860 IF ONKEY= 117 THEN INSTRING$= LEFT$(INSTRING$,CRSR.POS-1):PRINT
     SPACE$(LNGTH-CRSR.POS);:LOCATE CSRLIN,COLMNO+CRSR.POS-1:ANYCHANGE= -1:GOTO
     3420 'Ctrl-End, erase to end of field
3870 IF ONKEY= 82 AND CRSR.POS<= LEN(INSTRING$) AND LEN(INSTRING$)< LNGTH THEN
     GOSUB 3660:GOTO 3420 'Ins
3880 BEEP:GOTO 3420
```

The routines for fast screen output and storing and restoring the screen content are described in Chapter 11. Although we have tried to keep descriptions and explanations for a specific topic together, it may be necessary to place information in various locations. Therefore, a program listing sometimes precedes the complete explanation to avoid repeating the same information.

9. Using the Editor

The PC-BASIC internal editor contains, with a few exceptions, all the features that are needed for the user-friendly input of a program. Unfortunately, PC-BASIC doesn't offer its own commands or functions for search and/or replace. But it does enable you to store a program as an ASCII file:

```
SAVE <program-name>,A
```

This ASCII file can be called with any word processor and easily modified by using the word processor's functions. For example, it's quick and easy to rename a variable. Usually the word processor can even be called with the SHELL command, so that you don't have to leave PC-BASIC. However, remember that later the word processor can again store the program as an ASCII file. Control or formatting codes cannot be stored in this file.

The function key assignment during the call can present some problems. For example, some versions have assigned the SYSTEM sequence, with the CHR$(13), to the <F10> key. Many times we have forgotten to reassign this key before the input. As a result, we once lost a complicated algorithm that we had been working on for almost two hours. The corner of a book accidentally hit the <F10> key and before we knew what had happened, we saw the system prompt of the screen. Since then we keep books a safe distance from the keyboard and regularly save programs during the development phase. Although this incident caused us much grief, it motivated us to find a way to the change the keyboard assignment.

9.1 Modified Function Key Assignments

When calling PC-BASIC you can also give the name of a program to be executed immediately after the interpreter is loaded. We can easily solve our function key assignment problem using this information by specifying a program which changes the assignment of the function keys during the call of PC-BASIC:

```
GWBASIC FUNCKEY
```

The following is only one way that the FUNCKEY.BAS program could appear:

```
10 '-------------------------------------------
20 'FUNCKEY.BAS     1986 (C) H.J. Bomanns
30 '-------------------------------------------
40 :
50 CLS
60 :
70 KEY  1,CHR$(27)+"RUN"+CHR$(13) 'command RUN with immediate execution
80 KEY  2,CHR$(27)+"LIST " 'command LIST, then Parameter input
```

253

```
90 KEY   3,CHR$(27)+"LOAD"+CHR$(34) 'command LOAD, then program-name input
100 KEY   4,CHR$(27)+"SAVE "+CHR$(34) 'command SAVE, then program-name input
110 KEY   5,CHR$(27)+"CONT"+CHR$(13) 'command CONT with immediate execution
120 KEY   6,CHR$(27)+"RENUM " 'command RENUM, then Parameter input
130 KEY   7,CHR$(27)+"LIST ."+CHR$(13) 'command LIST, list current line
140 KEY   8,CHR$(27)+"MERGE " 'command MERGE, then program-name/Parameter input
150 KEY   9,CHR$(27)+"LLIST " 'command LLIST, then Parameter input
160 KEY  10,CHR$(27)+"GOTO " 'command GOTO, then line-number input
170 :
180 'CHR$(27) before each sequence ensures that the current line is
190 'erased. This avoids the "SYNTAX ERROR" message.
200 'You can also use CHR$(26), which erases the rest of the display screen page.
210 'CHR$(12) erases the complete display-screen.
```

The answer to the problem is so simple that it may have eluded you. You can change the program listing to correspond to the function key assignment you would like to use. Not only text can be used but also control characters.

Note: In some versions of PC-BASIC you can scroll the listing using <Ctrl><Y> and <Ctrl><X> toward the top or bottom. This can easily be accomplished by assigning the correct CHR$ values to two function keys:

```
KEY 1,CHR$(24) 'CTRL-X
KEY 2,CHR$(25) 'CTRL-Y
```

Patching the Program File

Another way to reassign the function keys is a more permanent solution. The GWBASIC.EXE program is *patched*, which means that the changes are made directly in the program file with the help of DEBUG or a utility program.

Note: If you own an original IBM-PC you can skip this section. Unfortunately, it's impossible to change the assignment permanently. You may know that, in the IBM-PC, parts of the interpreter are stored in ROM, a non-changeable section of the main memory. Since the function key assignment is located in ROM, changes cannot be made because the software can't access it. If you're using an EPROM programmer, you can read the IBM-BASIC ROM, starting at address F600:0000, change it and use your EPROM instead of the original EPROM.

In the following sections we'll present two ways to patch PC-BASIC. If you don't want to enter the utility program, you can use DEBUG, which is an assembler tool which appears as DEBUG.COM on your system diskette.

Fundamentals

In the program file, PC-BASIC reserves an area in which the function key assignment is stored. Sixteen bytes are available for each function key. The last byte (16th) must be $00 because PC-BASIC recognizes the end of the assignment during the output of text. Besides this one requirement, you can store everything, that you would normally input through the keyboard, in the remaining 15 bytes.

DEBUG	patching

You can skip to the next paragraph if you own a version of PC-BASIC with a .COM extension. If you don't, you must rename the file so that it doesn't have an .EXE extension before loading PC-BASIC into DEBUG. For example, use "GW.XXX" and call DEBUG with the name of the file as a parameter:

```
DEBUG GW.XXX
```

With the DEBUG command R (for Register), display the register, segment and offset values. If the length of the file, which is indicated in BX CX, is larger than $FFFF (5 places, BX <>$0000), you must add $1000 to the value in CS. Usually the table for the assignment is at the end of the file (offset $0500). If you don't find it there, search for it with the DEBUG command D (for Dump).

When you find the table, you can enter the new values by using the DEBUG command E (for Enter). These values must be entered in hexadecimal. In the Appendix you'll find a conversion table for this. Remember that excess characters must be filled with $00.

The DEBUG command W (for Write) writes the change back onto the diskette or hard disk. You can exit DEBUG with Q (for Quit). After renaming the file to its original name, you can call PC-BASIC with the modified assignment. You should make any changes in a copy of the program. Often the computer will crash during this procedure. The following is the hardcopy:

```
C:\BASIC
C:debug gw.xxx
-r ;display Register
AX=0000  BX=0001  CX=0E00  DX=0000  SP=CE2E  BP=0000  SI=0000  DI=0000
DS=4397  ES=4397  SS=4397  CS=4397  IP=0100    NV UP DI PL NZ NA PO NC
4397:0100 4D            DEC        BP
-d 5397:05e0 ;DUMP the affected area
5397:05E0  00 00 00 00 00 9B 03 4C-49 53 54 20 00 00 00 00   .......LIST ....
5397:05F0  00 00 00 00 00 00 00 00-52 55 4E 0D 00 00 00 00   .......RUN......
5397:0600  00 00 00 00 00 00 00 00-4C 4F 41 44 22 00 00 00   .......LOAD"....
5397:0610  00 00 00 00 00 00 00 00-53 41 56 45 22 00 00 00   .......SAVE"....
5397:0620  00 00 00 00 00 00 00 00-43 4F 4E 54 0D 00 00 00   .......CONT.....
```

255

```
5397:0630  00 00 00 00 00 00 00 2C-22 4C 50 54 31 3A 22 0D    .......,"LPT1:".
5397:0640  00 00 00 00 00 00 00 54-52 4F 4E 0D 00 00 00 00    .......TRON.....
5397:0650  00 00 00 00 00 00 00 54-52 4F 46 46 0D 00 00 00    .......TROFF....
-e 5397:0637 ;input of the new assignment
5397:0637  2C.4d
5397:0638  22.45   4C.52   50.47   54.45   31.20   3A.22   22.00   0D.00
5397:0640  00.
-w ;store on disk
Writing 10E00 bytes
-d 5397:05e0 ;check again for added security.....
5397:05E0  00 00 00 00 00 9B 03 4C-49 53 54 20 00 00 00 00    .......LIST ....
5397:05F0  00 00 00 00 00 00 00 52-55 4E 0D 00 00 00 00 00    .......RUN......
5397:0600  00 00 00 00 00 00 00 4C-4F 41 44 22 00 00 00 00    .......LOAD"....
5397:0610  00 00 00 00 00 00 00 53-41 56 45 22 00 00 00 00    .......SAVE"....
5397:0620  00 00 00 00 00 00 00 43-4F 4E 54 0D 00 00 00 00    .......CONT.....
5397:0630  00 00 00 00 00 00 00 4D-45 52 47 45 20 22 00 00    .......MERGE "..
5397:0640  00 00 00 00 00 00 00 54-52 4F 4E 0D 00 00 00 00    .......TRON.....
5397:0650  00 00 00 00 00 00 00 54-52 4F 46 46 0D 00 00 00    .......TROFF....
-q ;everything OK
```

Depending on the PC-BASIC version and the assignments in the main memory, the segment and offset addresses can be different in your system. Therefore, the semicolon (;), followed by comments, have been added to the text for clarity.

Utility Program for Patching

If DEBUG is too difficult to use or if changes must be made several times, the following program can be helpful.

As we already mentioned, the function key assignment is stored in the program file. The purpose of this program is to search the program file for this area. The best search criterion seems to be the assignment of the first function key, <F1>. After this area has been found, the changes can easily be written because every assignment is 16 bytes long.

Implementation

From the DOS level create a copy of the program file:

```
COPY GWBASIC.EXE GW1.EXE
```

Call the copy with the program:

```
GW1 PATCH_FN
```

This ensures that the function key assignment can be properly used for the search. After the start of the program, the current function key assignment is read directly from the 25th line and stored in a string array for the search. Enter the name of the program file in which the change should be made.

The current assignment for the function keys appears on the screen. You can then enter the necessary reassignments. The sequence CHR$(13) must receive special treatment because it's stored in the assignment as a "left arrow" or CHR$(27). In the program this is done by inserting the control character CHR$(27) after pressing the <Tab> key at the current cursor position. During later searches or saves of the new assignment, this control character is again converted to CHR$(13). All other control characters are entered with <Ctrl> and a second key (from <A> to <Z>) and are stored unchanged. We'll present an overview of the control characters and their functions following this section.

Press <End> after you complete the necessary changes. The program file opens as a random file with a record length of 120 bytes. To search for the patch area, two records are read into two variables and combined into a search variable. This is used to search for the original assignment.

If the search is unsuccessful, the record number is incremented by one and another two records are read. Because of this, the second record is now where the first record was in the search variable. If the assignment to be found was only partially present in the second record, it's now completely present in the search variable. The following graphic illustrates this:

```
search-criterion is "LIST":

record-number 122        record-number 123

 ....................  │  .................LI│

The search criterion will not be found here.

The record-number is increased by one and
the next two records are read:

record-number 123        record-number 124

 .................LI│ │ST................ │

Here the search-criterion is found and
exchanged.
```

Fig. 32: Search in data records

When the change has been made in the search variable, the two records are written back into the random file. For safety reasons, a search is performed for the next assignment that is in agreement (<F2>, <F3>, etc.). This ensures that the program file wasn't accidentally changed. To change this, write all 10 changed assignments, after the agreement, on the first assignment. However, by doing this you'll only save a small amount of time and, if you patched the wrong program file, you would have to start the whole process over from the beginning.

After all the changes have been made correctly, the program will inform you of this and terminate. Under certain conditions, such as the program file isn't complete or the patch area couldn't be found, you'll receive an appropriate error message and the program begins again.

Note: If you're using a monochrome card, you must change the segment address in line 230 for the program to function properly.

The following is the program listing:

```
10 '-------------------------------------------------
20 ' PATCH_FN.BAS            1986 (C) H.J.Bomanns
30 '-------------------------------------------------
40 :
50 COLOR 7,0:CLS:KEY ON:ON ERROR GOTO 1760
60 '
70 INPTFORGRD= 15:INPTBAKGRD= 0 'double bright
80 FONTFORGRD=  7:FONTBAKGRD= 0 'normal
90 NOTEFORGRD= 0:NOTEBAKGRD= 7 'reversed
100 PRG.FIL$= "GWBAK.EXE"
110 '
120 PRINT "<<< WARNING >>>  PATCH_FN.BAS changes the function-key assignment by
    patching"
130 PRINT "the program-file. USE A COPY OF THE PROGRAM-FILE."
140 PRINT STRING$(80,"="):PRINT
150 '
160 'read current assignment from 25th line:
170 :
180 'the detour through PEEK is necessary since the SCREEN-function cannot
    address the 25th line,
190 'as long as the assignment is being displayed.
200 'the changed assignment is stored in FUN.KEY$()
210 'for the comparison with the program-file in O.KEY$().
220 '
230 DEF SEG= &HB800 'for Monochrome: def seg= &HB000
240 OFFSET= (24*160)+2 'Offset for reading of status-line
250 FOR F.KEY=1 TO 10 '10 function-keys
260    FOR CHAR= 0 TO 11 STEP 2 '6 characters per key in the display
270       IF PEEK(CHAR+OFFSET)= 32 THEN 290 'no blanks !!!
280       FUN.KEY$(F.KEY)= FUN.KEY$(F.KEY)+CHR$(PEEK(CHAR+OFFSET))
290    NEXT CHAR
300    O.KEY$(F.KEY)= FUN.KEY$(F.KEY)
310    OFFSET= OFFSET+16
320 NEXT F.KEY
330 '
340 LOCATE 5,5:COLOR FONTFORGRD,FONTBAKGRD
350 PRINT "Name of the program-file...........: ";
360 COLOR INPTFORGRD,INPTBAKGRD
370 PRINT PRG.FIL$
```

```
380 '
390 MESSAGE$=" Confirm input with <Return> or quit with <Esc> ":GOSUB 1920
400 INSTRING$= PRG.FIL$:TXT.LNGTH= -1
410 ROWNO= 5: COLMNO= 41: LNGTH= 12: GOSUB 1250 'read subroutine
420 IF X$= CHR$(27) THEN COLOR FONTFORGRD,FONTBAKGRD:CLS:END
430 IF INSTRING$="" THEN BEEP:GOTO 680 ELSE PRG.FIL$= INSTRING$
440 '
450 OPEN PRG.FIL$ FOR INPUT AS #1:CLOSE#1 'file available ?
460 GOSUB 1980 'delete message line
470 '
480 '----- display of current assignment -----
490 '
500 ROWNO= 6
510 FOR I= 1 TO 10
520    LOCATE ROWNO+I,5
530    COLOR FONTFORGRD,FONTBAKGRD
540    PRINT USING "function-key ##.....: ";I;
550    COLOR INPTFORGRD,INPTBAKGRD
560    PRINT FUN.KEY$(I)
570 NEXT I
580 LOCATE 22,1:COLOR NOTEFORGRD,NOTEBAKGRD
590 PRINT " <Tab>= CHR$(13) insert, ";
600 PRINT " <Ctrl>+<A> thru <Z>= other control-characters ";SPACE$(81-POS(0));
610 '
620 '----- read the new assignment -----
630 '
640 INPT.ROWNO= 1:TXT.LNGTH= -1
650 MESSAGE$=" Terminate input of the changes with <End> or <Esc> to quit":GOSUB
    1920
660 '
670 WHILE F.KEY<> 79 'until <End> is activated
680    INSTRING$= FUN.KEY$(INPT.ROWNO)
690    ROWNO= INPT.ROWNO+6: COLMNO= 27: LNGTH= 15: GOSUB 1250 'read subroutine
700    IF X$= CHR$(27) THEN COLOR FONTFORGRD,FONTBAKGRD:CLS:END
710    FUN.KEY$(INPT.ROWNO)= INSTRING$
720    KEY INPT.ROWNO, INSTRING$
730    IF F.KEY= 72 THEN INPT.ROWNO= INPT.ROWNO-1
740    IF F.KEY= 80 OR X$=CHR$(13) THEN INPT.ROWNO= INPT.ROWNO+1
750    IF INPT.ROWNO< 1 THEN INPT.ROWNO= 10
760    IF INPT.ROWNO> 10 THEN INPT.ROWNO= 1
770 WEND
780 '
790 LOCATE 22,1:COLOR FONTFORGRD,FONTBAKGRD:PRINT SPACE$(80);
800 GOSUB 1980 'erase message line
810 MESSAGE$=" Please wait, program-file is being patched..... ":GOSUB
1920:LOCATE
    CSRLIN,POS(0),0
820 '
830 '--- search for patch-area in the program-file ---
840 '
850 OPEN "R",#1,PRG.FIL$,120
860 FIELD#1, 120 AS R.FIL$
870 REC.NUM= 1:MAX.REC= INT(LOF(1)/120):F.KEY= 1
```

```
880 '
890 IF F.KEY> 10 THEN 1170 'see above
900 IF REC.NUM> MAX.REC THEN ERROR 99 'patch area not localized
910 GET#1,REC.NUM
920 FIL1$= R.FIL$
930 GET#1,REC.NUM+1
940 FIL2$= R.FIL$
950 FIL$= FIL1$+FIL2$
960 SRCH.POS= INSTR(O.KEY$(F.KEY),CHR$(27)) 'mark for CHR$(13)
970 IF SRCH.POS= 0 THEN 990
980 MID$(O.KEY$(F.KEY),SRCH.POS)= CHR$(13):GOTO 960 'another mark ?
990 SRCH.POS= INSTR(FIL$,O.KEY$(F.KEY))
1000 IF SRCH.POS= 0 THEN REC.NUM= REC.NUM+1:GOTO 890 'continue search
1010 '
1020 '--- found patch-area for FUN.KEY$(F.KEY) -----
1030 '
1040 SRCH.POS= INSTR(FUN.KEY$(F.KEY),CHR$(27)) 'mark for CHR$(13)
1050 IF SRCH.POS= 0 THEN 1070
1060 MID$(FUN.KEY$(F.KEY),SRCH.POS)= CHR$(13):GOTO 1040 'another mark ?
1070 SRCH.POS= INSTR(FIL$,O.KEY$(F.KEY))
1080 IF LEN(FUN.KEY$(F.KEY))< 16 THEN FUN.KEY$(F.KEY)=
     FUN.KEY$(F.KEY)+CHR$(0):GOTO 1080
1090 MID$(FIL$,SRCH.POS)= FUN.KEY$(F.KEY) 'write in patch-area
1100 FIL1$=LEFT$(FIL$,120):LSET R.FIL$= FIL1$
1110 PUT #1,REC.NUM
1120 FIL2$=RIGHT$(FIL$,120):LSET R.FIL$= FIL2$
1130 PUT#1,REC.NUM+1
1140 F.KEY= F.KEY+1 'search for next key-assignment
1150 GOTO 890
1160 '
1170 '--- patching completed successfully (or perhaps not) ---
1180 '
1190 CLOSE
1200 MESSAGE$=" Patching of the function-key assignment completed, strike any key
     --> "+CHR$(254)+" ":GOSUB 1920
1210 LOCATE 23,73,1,0,31
1220 IF INKEY$="" THEN 1220
1230 COLOR FONTFORGRD,FONTBAKGRD:CLS:END
1240 '
1250 '----- read subroutine -----
1260 '
1270 X$="":F.KEY= 0
1280 LOCATE ROWNO,COLMNO,0:COLOR INPTFORGRD,INPTBAKGRD
1290 PRINT INSTRING$;
1300 PRINT SPACE$(LNGTH-LEN(INSTRING$));
1310 LOCATE ROWNO,COLMNO,1,0,31:CRSR.POS= 1
1320 X$= INKEY$:IF X$="" THEN 1320
1330 IF X$= CHR$(8) AND POS(0)> COLMNO THEN GOSUB 1460:GOTO 1320 'key-routine
1340 IF X$= CHR$(9) THEN X$=CHR$(27):GOTO 1390 'insert CR
1350 IF X$= CHR$(27) THEN ANYCHANGE= 0:RETURN
1360 IF X$= CHR$(13) THEN RETURN
1370 IF LEN(X$)= 2 THEN 1640 'control and function-keys
1380 '
```

```
1390 IF TXT.LNGTH THEN IF X$>= "a" AND X$<= "z" THEN X$= CHR$(ASC(X$)-32)
1400 PRINT X$;:ANYCHANGE= -1
1410 IF CRSR.POS<= LEN(INSTRING$) THEN MID$(INSTRING$,CRSR.POS,1)= X$ ELSE
     INSTRING$= INSTRING$+X$
1420 CRSR.POS= CRSR.POS+1
1430 IF POS(0)> COLMNO+LNGTH-1 THEN BEEP:LOCATE ROWNO,COLMNO:CRSR.POS= 1:GOTO
     1320
1440 GOTO 1320
1450 '
1460 '----- BACKSPACE and DEL keys -----
1470 '
1480 IF X$=CHR$(8) THEN INSTRING$= LEFT$(INSTRING$,CRSR.POS-
     2)+MID$(INSTRING$,CRSR.POS)
1490 IF F.KEY= 83  THEN INSTRING$= LEFT$(INSTRING$,CRSR.POS-
     1)+MID$(INSTRING$,CRSR.POS+1)
1500 LOCATE ROWNO,COLMNO:PRINT INSTRING$;" ";
1510 IF X$=CHR$(8) THEN CRSR.POS= CRSR.POS-1
1520 LOCATE CSRLIN,COLMNO+CRSR.POS-1
1530 F.KEY= 0: X$="":ANYCHANGE= -1
1540 RETURN
1550 '
1560 '----- INS key -----
1570 '
1580 INSTRING$= LEFT$(INSTRING$,CRSR.POS-1)+" "+MID$(INSTRING$,CRSR.POS)
1590 PRINT " ";MID$(INSTRING$,CRSR.POS+1);
1600 LOCATE CSRLIN,COLMNO+CRSR.POS-1
1610 ANYCHANGE= -1
1620 RETURN
1630 '
1640 '----- control and function keys -----
1650 '
1660 F.KEY= ASC(RIGHT$(X$,1))
1670 IF F.KEY= 79 OR F.KEY= 72 OR F.KEY= 80 THEN RETURN '<End>, Cursor up/down
1680 IF F.KEY= 75 AND POS(0)> COLMNO THEN LOCATE CSRLIN,POS(0)-1:CRSR.POS=
     CRSR.POS-1:GOTO 1320 'Cursor <--
1690 IF F.KEY= 77 AND POS(0)< COLMNO+LNGTH-1 THEN IF CRSR.POS<= LEN(INSTRING$)
     THEN LOCATE CSRLIN,POS(0)+1:CRSR.POS= CRSR.POS+1:GOTO 1320 'Cursor -->
1700 IF F.KEY= 83 AND CRSR.POS <= LEN(INSTRING$) THEN GOSUB 1460:GOTO 1320 '<Del>
     handled similar to <Backspace>
1710 IF F.KEY= 71 THEN LOCATE ROWNP,COLMNO:GOTO 1320 '<Home>, start of field
1720 IF F.KEY= 117 THEN INSTRING$= LEFT$(INSTRING$,CRSR.POS-1):PRINT
     SPACE$(LNGTH-CRSR.POS);:LOCATE CSRLIN,COLMNO+CRSR.POS-1:ANYCHANGE= -1:GOTO
     1320 '<Ctrl> <End>, erase to end of field
1730 IF F.KEY= 82 AND CRSR.POS<= LEN(INSTRING$) AND LEN(INSTRING$)< LNGTH THEN
     GOSUB 1560:GOTO 1320 '<Ins>
1740 BEEP:GOTO 1320
1750 '
1760 '----- ERROR-Routine -----
1770 '
1780 CLOSE
1790 IF ERL= 900 THEN ERRMSG$=" No patch-area found":GOSUB 1850:CLS:RESUME 10
     'start from the beginning
```

```
1800 IF ERL= 450 THEN ERRMSG$=" Error during opening of the program-file":GOSUB
1850:RESUME 400 'input again
1810 LOCATE 23,1:PRINT "Error: ";ERR;" in line: ";ERL;", strike any key -->
     ";CHR$(254);" ";:LOCATE CSRLIN,POS(0)-2,1,0,31:BEEP
1820 IF INKEY$="" THEN 1820
1830 RESUME
1840 '
1850 '----- display error text -----
1860 LOCATE 23,1:COLOR NOTEFORGRD,NOTEBAKGRD
1870 PRINT ERRMSG$;". Strike any key --> ";CHR$(254);" ";:LOCATE CSRLIN,POS(0)-
     2,1,0,31:BEEP
1880 IF INKEY$="" THEN 1880
1890 LOCATE 23,1:COLOR FONTFORGRD,FONTBAKGRD:PRINT SPACE$(80);
1900 RETURN
1910 '
1920 '----- display of a message in line 23 -----
1930 '
1940 LOCATE 23,1:COLOR NOTEFORGRD,NOTEBAKGRD
1950 PRINT MESSAGE$;SPACE$(81-POS(0));
1960 RETURN
1970 '
1980 '----- erase message-line -----
1990 '
2000 LOCATE 23,1:COLOR FONTFORGRD,FONTBAKGRD
2010 PRINT SPACE$(80);
2020 RETURN
```

Also, besides the edit commands, you can assign other text to the function keys. Some PC-BASIC statements can be called with the key combination <Alt> and <Letter> (see Appendix). If you're missing something, simply assign it to a function key. Also, the input of the frequently used variable names or statement sequences can be simplified in the following way:

```
KEY 3," file-name$ "
KEY 1,"FOR I=1 TO "
KEY 2,"STEP -1"
KEY 1,"X$=INKEY$:"
KEY 2,"IF X$="" THEN
```

When the assignment must be changed frequently, a program, which can be loaded with MERGE at the end of the current program, can be very helpful. The program executes its task after GOTO 65000 or RUN 65000 and then deletes itself:

```
65000 '-------------------------------------------------
65001 'FN1.BAS              1986 (C) H.J. Bomanns
65002 '-------------------------------------------------
65003 :
65004 RESTORE 65007
65005 FOR I=1 TO 10:READ A$:KEY I,A$:NEXT I
65006 DELETE 65000-
65007 DATA " F1", " F2", " F3", " F4", " F5", " F6", " F7", " F8", " F9", " F10"
```

By creating several of these small programs, the function key assignment can be made flexible. It's also possible to assign PC special characters to the function keys so that you don't have to use <Alt><Character Code> (see Appendix A).

9.2   Display Line, Column and Keyboard Status

We were once hired by a client in the metal working business to write a program to calculate material costs. Among other things, the program had to calculate the price per square foot for sheet metals of various alloys, in various thickness, size and weight. A table displaying the data also had to be generated.

Since it's impossible to use the interpreter directly to determine the current cursor position, we spent a lot of time counting columns while writing this program.

However, there is a solution. It should be possible to write a small program to determine the current cursor position and display it on the screen in a location that doesn't interfere with the coded program.

Despite several attempts, we were unable to implement this under PC-BASIC. Although this worked in program mode, through ON TIMER GOSUB, the display should occur in input mode, not program mode. Since we couldn't find a solution using PC-BASIC, we wondered how the operating system or the BIOS of the PC could be used with a small assembler routine.

Theoretically you should be able to use the PC's system clock in such a way that each clock cycle calls an interrupt routine that performs the required job. After some research, we discovered that the operating system provides an interrupt, for such purposes, that is called 18 times per second. Since this interrupt isn't normally used, it can be used for a special routine. Within this routine the cursor position is determined and displayed. This can only occur in text mode since no text is needed in graphics mode.

The following is the result as an assembler listing. After the listing we'll look at the routine in detail:

```
;----------------------------------------
; BAS_RC.ASM/COM
; This program displays through the BASIC
; interpreter the current line and
; column in the right upper corner.
; Also the status of the ins, caps, num
; and scroll-lock keys is displayed.
;----------------------------------------
Program         segment 'CODE'
                assume cs:Program,ds:Program
                org 0100h
Start:          jmp SetUp
;----------------------------------------
; Variables, Data etc.
;----------------------------------------
Inst_Flag       db 'RC'                       ;Flag that Prg. is installed
```

```
Org_Ofs         dw ?                    ;Original-Offset INT 1Ch
Org_Seg         dw ?                    ;Original-Segment INT 1Ch
BS_Address      dw 0                    ;Address Video-RAM
Line            db 0                    ;Line and Column from INT10h/FN 03
Column          db 0                     ;for display
Attribut        db 112                  ;Reverse Monochrome, black/cyan
Active          db 0                    ;Flag Routine active
Pause           db 0                    ;Flag for display off
Deleted         db 0                    ;Flag for message erased
Keys            db 0                    ;Keyboard-Status
Display         db ' R:    C:    ICNS '
BS_Position     dw 120                  ;Line 1, Column 61
;----------------------------------------
; INT 1Ch misused for our own purposes:
;----------------------------------------
BAS_RC              proc    near
                cli                     ;Interrupts off
                push    ax              ;store important Registers
                push    bx
                push    cx
                push    dx
                push    di
                push    si
                push    ds
                push    es
                push    cs
                pop     ds              ;DS is also CS
                cmp     [Active],1      ;test if in action
                jne     Action_1        ;no, execute
                jmp     No_Action       ;no, no action
;----------------------------------------
; Test if Display in Graphic-Mode
;----------------------------------------
Action_1:       mov     [Active],1      ;no, set Flag
                mov     ah,2            ;Get Shift Status
                int     16h
                cli
                mov     [Keys],al       ;store for later evaluation
                test    [Keys],4        ;CTRL activated ???
                je      Action_2        ;no, continue normally
                test    [Keys],1        ;SHIFT-right pushed ???
                je      Action_2        ;no, continue normally
                xor     [Pause],0FFh    ;Toggle display On/Off
                je      Action_1A       ;if 0, normal action
                jmp     Init_Display    ;else, erase display
Action_1A:      mov     [Deleted],0     ;Display not erase
Action_2:       xor     al,al
                mov     ah,15           ;Get Screen Status
                int     10h             ;BIOS-Call
                cli
                cmp     al,3            ;1,2 and 3 = Text Mode
                jbe     Action_3        ;4,5 and 6 = Graphic, if smaller, ok
                cmp     al,7            ;7= Monochrome
```

```
                  je      Action_3            ;also ok
                  jmp     No_Action           ;no display if Graphic
;-------------------------------------------------
; Display is in Text Mode, therefore Action
;-------------------------------------------------
Action_3:         mov     ah,3                ;Get Cursor Position
                  xor     bh,bh               ;Display-Page 0
                  int     10h                 ;BIOS-Call
                  cli
                  inc     dh                  ;Line = 0-24, incr. +1
                  inc     dl                  ;Column = 0-79, incr. +1
                  mov     [Line],dh           ;current Line and Column
                  mov     [Column],dl         ;retain for output
;-------------------------------------------------
; Erase Display field and initialize again
;
;-------------------------------------------------
Init_Display:     push    cs
                  pop     ds
                  mov     bx,offset Display   ;whole field 'Display'
                  mov     cx,17               ;17 characters
                  mov     al,' '              ;erase
LP:               mov     [bx],al
                  inc     bx
                  loop    LP
                  cmp     [Pause],0           ;no display ???
                  je      Display_full        ;continue normally
                  call    Output              ;erase display
                  mov     [Deleted],1         ;Display Flag is erased
                  jmp     No_Action           ;and back
Display_Full:     mov     Display[1],'R'      ;and initialize again
                  mov     Display[2],':'      ;this is faster than
                  mov     Display[7],'C'      ;erasing both fields for
                  mov     Display[8],':'      ;Z+S individually
;-------------------------------------------------
; Bring Line, Column and Keyboard-Status
; to the Display Field
;-------------------------------------------------
                  xor     ax,ax
                  mov     al,[Line]
                  mov     bx,offset Display[4]  ;Display Field 'R:'
                  call    BIN_ASCII             ;Line --> ASCII
                  xor     ax,ax
                  mov     al,[Column]
                  mov     bx,offset Display[10] ;Display Field 'S:'
                  call    BIN_ASCII             ;Column --> ASCII
;-------------------------------------------------
; Set Display according to Keyboard-Status
;-------------------------------------------------
                  test    [Keys],128          ;Insert active ???
                  je      Caps                ;no
                  mov     Display[13],'I'     ;Write 'I', Insert active
Caps:             test    [Keys],64           ;CapsLock active ???
```

```
                je      Num                 ;no
                mov     Display[14],'C'     ;Write 'C', CapsLock active
Num:            test    [Keys],32           ;NumLock active ???
                je      Scroll              ;no
                mov     Display[15],'N'     ;Write 'N', NumLock active
Scroll:         test    [Keys],16           ;ScrollLock active ???
                je      Done                ;no, display all
                mov     Display[16],'S'     ;Write 'S', ScrollLock active
Done:           Call    Output              ;and write direct to Screen
;----------------------------------------
; End of Action, Restore Registers
;----------------------------------------
No_Action:      cli
                pop     es                  ;Restore Registers
                pop     ds
                pop     si
                pop     di
                pop     dx
                pop     cx
                pop     bx
                pop     ax
                mov     cs:[Active],0       ;not active
                jmp     dword ptr cs:[Org_Ofs] ;Call original INT
                iret                        ;and return
BAS_RC          endp
;----------------------------------------
; Conversion of a Word/Byte to ASCII
;----------------------------------------
BIN_ASCII       proc    near
                cmp     ax,0009h            ;small 10 ???
                ja      BIN_ASCII_1         ;no, normal continue
                inc     bx                  ;jump decimal position
BIN_ASCII_1:    mov     dx,0
                mov     cx,10               ;decimal number
                div     cx
                push    dx
                or      ax,ax
                jz      BIN_ASCII_2
                call    BIN_ASCII_1
BIN_ASCII_2:    pop     ax
                add     al,30h              ; --> ASCII
                mov     [bx],al             ;Write to 'Display'
                inc     bx                  ;next character
                ret
BIN_ASCII       endp
;----------------------------------------
; Output 'Display' synchronized
;----------------------------------------
Output:         proc    near
                push    cs
                pop     ds                  ;CRT is also CS
                cmp     [Deleted],1         ;if Pause, already erased ???
                je      No_output           ;yes, return
```

```
                mov      di,[BS_Address]        ;Video-RAM
                mov      es,di                  ;for STOSW in ES
                mov      di,[BS_Position]       ;Default: 120 for Column 61
                mov      si,offset Display
                mov      dx,03DAh               ;6845-Control-Port
                cld                             ;forward
                mov      cx,18                  ;18 Bytes from 'Display'
                mov      ah,[Attribut]          ;REVERS for Mono
                cmp      [Pause],0              ;erase display ???
                je       Wait1                  ;no, continue
                mov      ah,0                   ;else Attribute 0= Erase
;----------------------------------------
; Synchronization for flickerfree output
;----------------------------------------
Wait1:          in       al,dx                  ;read Status 6845
                rcr      al,1                   ;check RETRACE
                jb       Wait1                 ;wait if necessary
Wait2:          in       al,dx
                rcr      al,1
                jnb      Wait2
                cli
                lodsb                           ;load Character from 'Display'in AL
                stosw                           ;and write on screen
                loop     Wait1                 ;until CX= 0
No_output:      ret
Output          endp
;----------------------------------------
; Install Program
;----------------------------------------
SetUp           proc     near
                call     Check                  ;already installed ???
                call     Get_BS_Address         ;which Video-Board ???
                call     Save_INT               ;Save Original-Vector
                call     Set_INT                ;Set new Vector
                call     Make_Resident          ;Make Prg. resident End
SetUp           endp
;----------------------------------------
; Test if already installed
;----------------------------------------
Check           proc     near
                mov      ah,35h                 ;Get Interrupt Vector
                mov      al,1Ch                 ;Nr. of INT
                int      21h                    ;DOS-Function call
                mov      ax,word ptr es:[Inst_Flag]
                mov      dx,word ptr cs:[Inst_Flag]
                                                ;Flag for 'Program ;installed'
                cmp      ax,dx                  ;agree ???
                jne      Not_Installed          ;no, do not install
                push     es                     ;secure Segment for DOS-Function 49h
;----------------------------------------
; If installed, then remove
;----------------------------------------
                cli                             ;no Interrupts
```

```
                mov      di,word ptr es:[Org_Seg]
                mov      ds,di
                mov      dx,word ptr es:[Org_Ofs]
                mov      ah,25h               ;Set Interrupt Vector
                mov      al,1Ch               ;Nr. of Interrupts
                int      21h                  ;DOS-Function call
                pop      es                   ;Segment to free
                mov      ah,49h               ;Free allocated memory
                int      21h                  ;
                push     cs
                pop      ds                   ;Display is DS again
                jnc      OK                   ;if no errors, all clear
                mov      dx,offset Free_Err   ;otherwise output error message
Check_End:      mov      ah,09                ;DOS-Function 'Print String'
                int      21h
                mov      ah,4Ch               ;DOS-Function 'End Process'
                int      21h
OK:             mov      dx,offset Free_Msg   ;Message 'all clear '
                jmp      Check_End
Not_Installed: ret                           ;return and install
Check          endp
Free_Err db 27,'[2J',13,10,10
         db 'BAS_ZS: Storage can not be cleared '
         db 'restart PC .....',7,13,10,10,'$'
Free_Msg db 27,'[2J',13,10,10
         db 'BAS_ZS: Deinstalled Storage cleared .....'
         db 7,13,10,10,'$'
;----------------------------------------
; Which Video-Board is installed ???
;----------------------------------------
Get_BS_Address proc     near
                mov      [BS_Address],0B000h  ;Video-RAM Monochrome
                int      11h                  ;Get Equipment
                and      ax,30h               ;Bit 4+5= CRT-Mode
                cmp      ax,30h               ;both Bits set = Mono-CRT
                je       Mono_BS
                add      [BS_Address],0800h   ;plus 800h= Video-RAM Color
                mov      Attribut,48          ;black on cyan
Mono_BS:        ret
Get_BS_Address endp
;----------------------------------------
; Save Original-Vector of INT 1Ch
;----------------------------------------
Save_INT        proc     near
                mov      ah,35h               ;Get Interrupt Vector
                mov      al,1Ch               ;Nr. of INT
                int      21h                  ;DOS-Function call
                mov      cs:[Org_Ofs],bx      ;Offset INT 1C
                mov      cs:[Org_Seg],es      ;Segment INT 1C
                ret
Save_INT        endp
;----------------------------------------
; Set new INT 1Ch-Vector
;----------------------------------------
```

269

```
Set_INT          proc    near
                 cli                             ;no Interrupts
                 push    cs
                 pop     ds
                 mov     dx,offset cs:BAS_RC;Start of Routine
                 mov     ah,25h                  ;Set Interrupt Vector
                 mov     al,1Ch                  ;Nr. of Interrupt
                 int     21h                     ;DOS-Function call
                 ret
Set_INT          endp
;----------------------------------------
; Make Routine resident and end Program
;
;----------------------------------------
Make_Resident    proc    near
                 mov     dx,offset SetUp_Msg
                 mov     ah,9                    ;DOS-Function 'Print String'
                 int     21h
                 mov     dx,offset cs:SetUp
                 sti                             ;Interrupts on again
                 int     27h                     ;Terminate but stay resident
Make_Resident    endp
SetUp_Msg db 27,'[2J',13,10,10
                 db 'BAS_RC: installed .....',7,13,10,10
                 db 'Switch display on/off with <Ctrl>-<Shift right>',13,10
                 db 'deinstall with call of BAS_RC.',13,10,10,'$'
;----------------------------------------
Program          ends
                 end     Start
```

A detailed look

The operating system calls interrupt 1Ch up to 18 times per second. This interrupt can be used for a routine which can be executed as many times as needed. This routine must be resident (i.e., part of the operating system). Since the display is usually only required in the interpreter, the routine must be capable of being switched off. In the program this is done by testing a flag during the call if the program is already installed (Proc Check). This is done through MS-DOS function 35h, which delivers the segment in which the interrupt routine runs in register ES. The flag RC is in this segment. If it's set, the program is removed, the old interrupt vector is set again, and the memory is released through function 49h of MS-DOS.

If the routine isn't installed, the current vector is determined through function 35h and retained when the program is removed (Proc Save_INT). The video board is checked for the output routine through interrupt 11h. The video RAM address is calculated accordingly and the display attribute is set (Proc Get_BS_Address). Once this is done the vector is set to its own routine (Proc Set_INT). Finally, the program section required for the interrupt is resident through function 31h of MS-DOS, which completes the installation (Proc

Make_Resident). This function reserves the memory required by the program and cannot be overwritten.

The routine is then called 18 times per second. A flag determines if the routine is already active. The call is terminated if the routine is active. If this isn't done, only the routine could run. Otherwise the flag is set in the active routine.

The first task will be to sense the status of the switches, through function 2 of interrupt 16h, and retain the value. Then a check is made to see if the display should be temporarily switched off. The key combination <Ctrl><Right Shift> is used for this. A flag is set or reset every time this key combination is activated. The flag controls further work in the routine. If the flag is set, the display is cleared and the interpreter appears. Otherwise function 15 of interrupt 10h senses whether the display is in graphics mode. If this is the case, a display doesn't appear; otherwise a display appears.

The current cursor position is sensed with function 3 of interrupt 10h, the display field is initialized and the values which were found are written with a conversion routine. Finally, the status of the <NumLock>, <ScrollLock>, <CapsLock> and <Insert> keys is checked on the basis of the stored value and, depending on their status, a character is written into the display as a flag.

The actual output occurs with a routine that writes directly into the display area. The 6845 video chips are synchronized to suppress the flickering that occurs when the 8088/8086 CPU and the 6845 graphic chip simultaneously access the data bus.

After the output, the active flag is cleared and the routine is terminated. If other routines are tied to interrupt 1Ch, they are executed through JMP. Otherwise JMP goes to an IRET, which completely terminates the interrupt.

Operation

The program must be available and called as a .COM file. The .COM file can be created either with DEBUG, an assembler or with the DATA loader we'll soon present. During the first program call, the routine is installed and begins to work. A further program call removes the routine again. To switch off the display temporarily, hold down the <Ctrl> key and press the right <Shift> key. Since it acts as a toggle switch, this key combination can be pressed again to switch on the display.

Although this program was actually developed for the BASIC interpreter, it can be used with other programs or under DOS. Owners of an original IBM PC should appreciate the display of the keyboard status since the keyboard has no LEDs for display. In programs that control the <Insert> key themselves, it's possible that an "I" for Insert is displayed, even though the insert mode is active (for example, in the TURBO Pascal editor). Also, the column indication display may not be accurate if the display is being scrolled to the left by the program. In this case, the current cursor column is always displayed.

Note: There may be problems with certain compatible PCs (for example Siemens PC-D) which don't use interrupts according to the IBM standard or use an incompatible BIOS. Even some original IBM-PCs may have problems. The computer wouldn't accept any input after installing this routine. We were unable to completely determine what happened. We suspect, however, that older versions of BIOS aren't compatible with newer operating systems (since 2.xx).

This program cannot be installed or removed with the SHELL command because this command disrupts the memory assignment. The interpreter may send the message, "Can't continue after SHELL" and return you to DOS or the system may crash. The following is the DATA loader for the program:

```
10  '----------------------------------------------------
20  'BAS_RC.BAS Data-Loader     1986 (C) H.J.Bomanns
30  '----------------------------------------------------
40  :
50  CLS:KEY OFF
60  PRINT "One moment please,.COM file being created .....";
70  :
80  OPEN "R",#1,"BAS_RC.COM",1
90  FIELD#1,1 AS X$
100 :
110 RESTORE 330
120 FOR I=1 TO   805
130    READ X
140    LSET X$= CHR$(X)
150    PUT#1 'record-number is incremented automatically
160 NEXT I
170 CLOSE
180 :
190 PRINT:PRINT:PRINT
200 PRINT "You have a program named BAS_RC.COM on your diskette or hard disk
    ":PRINT
210 PRINT "During the call of the program, the display of the row/column and the
    keyboard-"
220 PRINT "status is initialized. You will see it in the upper right corner
    of the screen.":PRINT
230 PRINT "The display is removed when you call the program again.":PRINT
240 PRINT "You can temporarily switch the display off by holding the <Ctrl> key
    down"
250 PRINT "while pressing the right <Shift> key. Repeat this combination"
260 PRINT "to switch the display on again."
270 LOCATE 25,1:PRINT "Strike any key to continue";
280 IF INKEY$="" THEN 280
290 CLS:END
300 :
```

```
310 'Data-lines from COM-file: \masm\BAS_RC.com
320 :
330 DATA 233,113,  1, 90, 83,  0,  0,  0,  0,  0,  0
340 DATA   0,  0,112,  0,  0,  0,  0, 32, 90, 58, 32
350 DATA  32, 32, 32, 83, 58, 32, 32, 32, 32, 73, 67
360 DATA  78, 83, 32,120,  0,250, 80, 83, 81, 82, 87
370 DATA  86, 30,  6, 14, 31,128, 62, 14,  1,  1,117
380 DATA   3,233,205,  0,198,  6, 14,  1,  1,180,  2
390 DATA 205, 22,250,162, 17,  1,246,  6, 17,  1,  4
400 DATA 116, 22,246,  6, 17,  1,  1,116, 15,128, 54
410 DATA  15,  1,255,116,  3,235, 43,144,198,  6, 16
420 DATA   1,  0, 50,192,180, 15,205, 16,250, 60,  3
430 DATA 118,  7, 60,  7,116,  3,233,145,  0,180,  3
440 DATA  50,255,205, 16,250,254,198,254,194,136, 54
450 DATA  11,  1,136, 22, 12,  1, 14, 31,187, 18,  1
460 DATA 185, 17,  0,176, 32,136,  7, 67,226,251,128
470 DATA  62, 15,  1,  0,116, 11,232,151,  0,198,  6
480 DATA  16,  1,  1,235, 94,144,198,  6, 19,  1, 82
490 DATA 198,  6, 20,  1, 58,198,  6, 25,  1, 67,198
500 DATA   6, 26,  1, 58, 51,192,160, 11,  1,187, 22
510 DATA   1,232, 83,  0, 51,192,160, 12,  1,187, 28
520 DATA   1,232, 72,  0,246,  6, 17,  1,128,116,  5
530 DATA 198,  6, 31,  1, 73,246,  6, 17,  1, 64,116
540 DATA   5,198,  6, 32,  1, 67,246,  6, 17,  1, 32
550 DATA 116,  5,198,  6, 33,  1, 78,246,  6, 17,  1
560 DATA  16,116,  5,198,  6, 34,  1, 83,232, 50,  0
570 DATA 250,  7, 31, 94, 95, 90, 89, 91, 88, 46,198
580 DATA   6, 14,  1,  0, 46,255, 46,  5,  1,207, 61
590 DATA   9,  0,119,  1, 67,186,  0,  0,185, 10,  0
600 DATA 247,241, 82, 11,192,116,  3,232,240,255, 88
610 DATA   4, 48,136,  7, 67,195, 14, 31,128, 62, 16
620 DATA   1,  1,116, 48,139, 62,  9,  1,142,199,139
630 DATA  62, 36,  1,190, 18,  1,186,218,  3,252,185
640 DATA  18,  0,138, 38, 13,  1,128, 62, 15,  1,  0
650 DATA 116,  2,180,  0,236,208,216,114,251,236,208
660 DATA 216,115,251,250,172,171,226,241,195,232, 12
670 DATA   0,232,215,  0,232,240,  0,232,254,  0,232
680 DATA   8,  1,180, 53,176, 28,205, 33, 38,161,  3
690 DATA   1, 46,139, 22,  3,  1, 59,194,117, 45,  6
700 DATA 250, 38,139, 62,  7,  1,142,223, 38,139, 22
710 DATA   5,  1,180, 37,176, 28,205, 33,  7,180, 73
720 DATA 205, 33, 14, 31,115, 11,186,196,  2,180,  9
730 DATA 205, 33,180, 76,205, 33,186, 18,  3,235,243
740 DATA 195, 27, 91, 50, 74, 13, 10, 10, 66, 65, 83
750 DATA  95, 82, 67, 58, 32, 67, 97,110,110,111,116
760 DATA  32, 82,101,108,101, 97,115,101, 44, 32, 82
770 DATA  69, 66, 79, 79, 84, 32, 80, 67, 46, 46, 46
780 DATA  46, 46,  0,  0,  0,  0,  0,  0,  0,  0,  0
790 DATA   0,  0,  0,  0,  0,  0,  0,  0,  0,  0,  0
800 DATA   0,  0,  0,  0,  0,  0,  0,  0,  7, 13, 10
810 DATA  10, 36, 27, 91, 50, 74, 13, 10, 10, 66, 65
820 DATA  83, 95, 82, 67, 58, 32, 68,101,105,110,115
830 DATA 116, 97,108,108,101,100, 32, 97,110,100, 32
```

273

```
 840 DATA 109,101,109,111,114,121, 32,102,114,101,101
 850 DATA 100, 46, 46, 46, 46, 46,  0,  0,  0,  0,  0
 860 DATA   0,  0,  0,  0,  0,  7, 13, 10, 10, 36,199
 870 DATA   6,  9,  1,  0,176,205, 17, 37, 48,  0, 61
 880 DATA  48,  0,116, 11,129,  6,  9,  1,  0,  8,198
 890 DATA   6, 13,  1, 48,195,180, 53,176, 28,205, 33
 900 DATA  46,137, 30,  5,  1, 46,140,  6,  7,  1,195
 910 DATA 250, 14, 31,186, 38,  1,180, 37,176, 28,205
 920 DATA  33,195,186,152,  3,180,  9,205, 33,186,116
 930 DATA   2,251,205, 39, 27, 91, 50, 74, 13, 10, 10
 940 DATA  66, 65, 83, 95, 82, 67, 58, 32,105,110,115
 950 DATA 116, 97,108,108,105,110,103, 46, 46, 46, 46
 960 DATA  46, 46,  7, 13, 10, 10, 84,111,103,103,108
 970 DATA 101, 32,116,104,101, 32,100,105,115,112,108
 980 DATA  97,121, 32, 98,121, 32,112,114,101,115,115
 990 DATA 105,110,103, 32, 60, 67, 84, 82, 76, 62, 60
1000 DATA  82,105,103,104,116, 32, 83, 72, 73, 70, 84
1010 DATA  62, 44, 13, 10,100,101,105,110,115,116, 97
1020 DATA 108,108, 32, 98,121, 32,101,110,116,101,114
1030 DATA 105,110,103, 32, 66, 65, 83, 95, 82, 67, 32
1040 DATA  97,103, 97,105,110, 32, 97,116, 32,116,104
1050 DATA 101, 32,112,114,111,109,112,116, 46, 13, 10
1060 DATA  10, 36
```

Remember that while switching the display on and off, the routine is called 18 times per second. Pressing the right <Shift> key too long causes the display to flicker. So you should press this key briefly to avoid the flickering.

9.3   Saving Protected Programs

A program can be saved as a "protected" program in PC-BASIC by adding the ",P" parameter after the SAVE command. After a protected program is loaded, attempting to edit it or list it causes the interpreter to display the "Illegal function call" error message. This function is used by programmers so that users cannot change the program.

However, as the programmer, you must keep two versions of the program with different names. You'll save one version normally and the other version with the ,P parameter. There is also the danger of the protected version overwriting the unprotected version, which would destroy the changeable source program. This could be a disaster with long programs.

You may think that this will never happen to you. However, you should be prepared since it's probably inevitable. One thing you should do is make daily backup copies. Before we discuss this, we'll explain how the interpreter saves a program.

The interpreter distinguishes between three methods of saving a program:

1.   Normal save:

      SAVE "<Program Name>"

      This method stores the program in tokenized form. This means that the commands, functions and statements aren't saved as words, such as PRINT, LOCATE or OPEN, but as 1 byte codes called *tokens*. The variables and constants are stored in the same way they're stored in memory. Every statement is assigned to its own fixed token byte which can, for example, be converted to real text. The variables are stored so that the first two bytes correspond to the first two characters of the name. Then information about the rest of the name, or the type and contents of the variable, follows. This method, when compared to saving this data as actual text, uses less space on the diskette or hard disk. Also, the program is stored in memory in token mode. This enables fast transmission since a conversion is unnecessary.

2.   Saving in ASCII format:

      SAVE "<Program Name>",A

      With this method, all tokens, variables and constants are stored in ASCII text format. This enables the file to be loaded into a word processor or into another BASIC editor for further processing. In addition, a compiler accepts BASIC source code only in ASCII format.

3.　　Saving as a protected program:

SAVE "<Program name>",P

In this method various versions must be recognized. The first byte of a program file is located at &HFF when it's stored in the normal mode. This shows the interpreter that the program file is in token mode, and therefore must be loaded 1:1. Older versions contain a first program file byte of &HFE instead of &HFF. During loading, an internal flag based on this first byte is set. This flag is tested for LIST or similar commands that change the program or make it visible. This may result in an "Illegal function call" error message. To make the program accessible again, set the byte to &HFF.

In newer versions, the program is also encoded according to a certain algorithm, so that the change from &HFE to &HFF fails, which can force the interpreter to crash under certain circumstances. Two options are available:

Original IBM PC owners:

The internal "protected/unprotected" flag in BASICA is normally stored in the standard segment at offset 1124. To confirm this, read this memory location for a protected and an unprotected program by using PEEK:

```
10 'any program
20 :
30 DEF SEG 'Segment in default
40 PRINT PEEK(1124)
50 END
```

Continue reading if you receive a "1" for "protected" and a "0" for "unprotected". Otherwise, you're using an interpreter called "BASICA" which doesn't correspond to the original IBM BASICA. Therefore, read the section on compatible PCs on the following page.

Since the internal flag can be changed, the program file doesn't have to be changed. PEEK and POKE usually send an "Illegal function call". But since BLOAD won't be read, the two commands can be used.

Input NEW. The memory location 1124 contains a "0". For safety reasons you can POKE a "0" into it:

```
DEF SEG:POKE 1124,0
```

With BSAVE, the internal flag is now saved as a file:

```
BSAVE "UNPRTCT.DAT",1124,1
```

This statement creates a file that is one byte long. The byte has the value "0", which will be needed later. You can also store "0" at any other memory location and save it with BSAVE. Make sure that no DATA or program sections are changed with POKE. Load the protected program and get the internal flag back with BLOAD:

```
BLOAD "UNPRTCT.DAT"
```

The program can then be listed and edited.

Compatible PC Owners

You should first temporarily change &HFE to &HFF. This is quickly accomplished with DEBUG:

```
debug <programname> <Return>
-e 0100 <Return>
fe.ff <Return>
-w <Return>
Writing xxxxx Bytes
-q <Return>
```

First call DEBUG, using the applicable program name for the parameter. Then <Return> indicates that the <Return> key must be pressed. DEBUG loads the file into the offset address 0100h. You may not understand why this happens. An explanation of this would exceed the scope of this book.

Unfortunately, you must enter the following program because it's impossible to load with BLOAD. We tried to use BLOAD with various versions but the internal flag isn't always at the same location and, even with BLOAD, an "Illegal function call" is reported.

This program simply reverses the protection provided by the interpreter:

```
10 '---------------------------------------------------------------
20 'UNPRTCT.BAS                         1985 (C) H.J. Bomanns
30 '---------------------------------------------------------------
40 :'
50 COLOR 7,0:CLS:KEY OFF
60 FONTFORGRD= 7: FONTBAKGRD= 0
70 INPTFORGRD=15: INPTBAKGRD= 0
80 NOTEFORGRD= 0: NOTEBAKGRD= 7
90 DIM FILPASSWRD1(13),FILPASSWRD2(13)
100 RESTORE 110:FOR I=1 TO 13:READ FILPASSWRD1(I), FILPASSWRD2(I): NEXT I
110 DATA &H9A,&H7C, &HF7,&H88, &H19,&H59, &H83,&H74, &H24,&HE0, &H63,&H97
120 DATA &H43,&H26, &H83,&H77, &H75,&HC4, &HCD,&H1D, &H8D,&H1E, &H84,0, &HA9,0
130 '
140 GOTO 680 'Jump over  Upros
150 '
160 '----- Read in Subroutine -----
```

277

```
170 '
180 X$="":USKEY= 0
190 LOCATE ROWNO,COLMNO,0:COLOR INPTFORGRD,INPTBAKGRD:PRINT
    INSTRING$;SPACE$(STRLNG-LEN(INSTRING$));
200 LOCATE ROWNO,COLMNO,1,0,31:CRSR.POS= 1
210 X$= INKEY$:IF X$="" THEN 210
220 IF X$= CHR$(8) AND POS(0)> COLMNO THEN GOSUB 350:GOTO 210 'Key-Routine
230 IF X$= CHR$(27) THEN ANYCHANGE= 0:RETURN
240 IF X$=CHR$(13) THEN RETURN
250 IF LEN(X$)= 2 THEN 530 'Control and Function keys
260 '
270 IF X$< " " THEN BEEP:GOTO 210 'erase BLANK character
280 IF TXTLNGTHS THEN IF X$>= "a" AND X$<= "z" THEN X$= CHR$(ASC(X$)-32)
290 PRINT X$;:ANYCHANGE= -1
300 IF CRSR.POS<= LEN(INSTRING$) THEN MID$(INSTRING$,CRSR.POS,1)= X$ ELSE
    INSTRING$= INSTRING$+X$
310 CRSR.POS= CRSR.POS+1
320 IF POS(0)> COLMNO+STRLNG-1 THEN BEEP:LOCATE ROWNO,COLMNO:CRSR.POS= 1:GOTO 210
330 GOTO 210
340 '
350 '----- BACKSPACE and DEL Keys  -----
360 '
370 IF X$=CHR$(8) THEN INSTRING$= LEFT$(INSTRING$,CRSR.POS-
    2)+MID$(INSTRING$,CRSR.POS)
380 IF USKEY= 83  THEN INSTRING$= LEFT$(INSTRING$,CRSR.POS-
    1)+MID$(INSTRING$,CRSR.POS+1)
390 LOCATE ROWNO,COLMNO:PRINT INSTRING$;" ";
400 IF X$=CHR$(8) THEN CRSR.POS= CRSR.POS-1
410 LOCATE CSRLIN,COLMNO+CRSR.POS-1
420 USKEY= 0: X$="":ANYCHANGE= -1
430 RETURN
440 '
450 '----- INS key -----
460 '
470 INSTRING$= LEFT$(INSTRING$,CRSR.POS-1)+" "+MID$(INSTRING$,CRSR.POS)
480 PRINT " ";MID$(INSTRING$,CRSR.POS+1);
490 LOCATE CSRLIN,COLMNO+CRSR.POS-1
500 ANYCHANGE=-1
510 RETURN
520 '
530 '----- Control and Function Keys -----
540 '
550 USKEY= ASC(RIGHT$(X$,1))
560 IF USKEY= 63 THEN RETURN '[F5]= Selection
570 IF USKEY= 68 THEN RETURN '[F10]= Input o.k.
580 IF USKEY= 72 OR USKEY= 80 THEN RETURN 'Cursor up and down
590 IF USKEY= 73 OR USKEY= 81 THEN RETURN '<PgUp> and <PgDn>
600 IF USKEY= 75 AND POS(0)> COLMNO THEN LOCATE CSRLIN,POS(0)-1:CRSR.POS=
    CRSR.POS-1:GOTO 210 'Cursor <--
610 IF USKEY= 77 AND POS(0)< COLMNO+STRLNG-1 THEN IF CRSR.POS<= LEN(INSTRING$)
    THEN LOCATE CSRLIN,POS(0)+1:CRSR.POS= CRSR.POS+1:GOTO 210 'Cursor -->
620 IF USKEY= 83 AND CRSR.POS <= LEN(INSTRING$) THEN GOSUB 350:GOTO 210 '<Del>
    handled similar to <Backspace>
```

```
630 IF USKEY= 71 THEN LOCATE ROWNO,COLMNO:GOTO 210 '<Home>, Field start
640 IF USKEY= 79 THEN LOCATE CSRLIN,COLMNO+LEN(INSTRING$)-1:CRSR.POS=
    LEN(INSTRING$):GOTO 210 '<End>, set to last character
650 IF USKEY= 117 THEN INSTRING$= LEFT$(INSTRING$,CRSR.POS-1):PRINT
    SPACE$(STRLNG-CRSR.POS);:LOCATE CSRLIN,COLMNO+CRSR.POS-1:ANYCHANGE= -1:GOTO
    210 '<Ctrl> <End>, erase to end of field
660 IF USKEY= 82 AND CRSR.POS<= LEN(INSTRING$) AND LEN(INSTRING$)< STRLNG THEN
    GOSUB 450:GOTO 210 '<Ins>
670 BEEP:GOTO 210
680 '
690 '----- Input of File Names  ------
700 '
710 PRINT "UNPRTCT.BAS                                  1986 (C) H.J. Bomanns"
720 PRINT STRING$(80,"="):PRINT
730 PRINT "This program unprotects a program stored with the ',P'option"
740 PRINT "and makes the source code accessible again."
750 LOCATE 10,5:COLOR FONTFORGRD,FONTBAKGRD
760 PRINT "Input-File:            [',P'-File]"
770 LOCATE 12,5
780 PRINT "Output-File:            [for source text]"
790 INSTRING$= INPTFILNAM$:ROWNO= 10: COLMNO= 20:STRLNG= 12
800 GOSUB 160 'Read in Subroutine
810 IF X$= CHR$(27) THEN CLS:END '<Esc> activated
820 INPTFILNAM$= INSTRING$
830 INSTRING$= OTPTFILNAM$:ROWNO= 12: COLMNO= 20:STRLNG= 12
840 GOSUB 160 'Read in Subroutine
850 IF USKEY= 72 THEN 790 'Cursor up
860 IF X$= CHR$(27) THEN CLS:END '<Esc> activated
870 OTPTFILNAM$= INSTRING$
880 '
890 '----- Open Files -----
900 '
910 OPEN "R",#1,INPTFILNAM$,1
920 FIELD#1,1 AS IPT$
930 OPEN "R",#2,OTPTFILNAM$,1
940 FIELD#2,1 AS OPT$
950 '
960 PNTR1= 13:PNTR2= 11 'Pointer in Array
970 MAX.BYTES= LOF(1)-2 'Number of Byte to be decoded
980                     'less EOF and KZ-Byte &HFF/&HFE
990 '
1000 GET#1                     'first Byte = &HFE, &HFF
1010 IF ASC(IPT$)= &HFE THEN 1060 'File protected, go on
1020 PRINT:PRINT
1030 PRINT "File not protected ....."
1040 PRINT:PRINT
1050 END
1060 LSET OPT$= CHR$(&HFF) 'first Byte in unprotected Program
1070 PUT#2                 'write first Byte
1080 '
1090 '----- Decode Bytes starting here -----
1100 '
1110 LOCATE 20,5:COLOR FONTFORGRD,FONTBAKGRD
```

```
1120 PRINT USING "File (###### Bytes) being decoded:";MAX.BYTES
1130 COLOR NOTEFORGRD,NOTEBAKGRD
1140 '
1150 FOR I= 1 TO MAX.BYTES
1160   GET#1 'without record number = read sequentially
1170   LOCATE 20,46,0:PRINT USING "######";I;
1180   BYTE= ASC(IPT$)
1190   BYTE= BYTE -PNTR2
1200   BYTE= FILPASSWRD1(PNTR1) XOR BYTE
1210   BYTE= FILPASSWRD2(PNTR2) XOR BYTE
1220   BYTE= BYTE +PNTR1
1230   IF BYTE>= 256 THEN BYTE= BYTE-256
1240   IF BYTE<0 THEN BYTE= BYTE+256
1250   LSET OPT$= CHR$(BYTE)
1260   PUT#2 'without record number = write sequentially
1270   PNTR1= PNTR1 -1
1280   IF PNTR1= 0 THEN PNTR1= 13
1290   PNTR2= PNTR2 -1
1300   IF PNTR2= 0 THEN PNTR2= 11
1310 NEXT I 'read next Byte decipher and write
1320 '
1330 CLOSE 'close all Files
1340 '
1350 COLOR FONTFORGRD,FONTBAKGRD:CLS
1360 PRINT "File ";INPTFILNAM$;" is decoded in ";OTPTFILNAM$;"
1370 PRINT:PRINT:END
```

Development

We spent many hours finding and decoding the encryption algorithm in the interpreter. The interpreter encodes the data on the basis of two different code tables, according to a simple algorithm (see listing, lines 1190-1220). For decoding, the program file and the target file are opened as random access files with a record length of 1 (lines 910-940). In one loop a single byte is read "in reverse", according to the algorithm, and written to the target file (lines 1150-1310). After loading the decoded file you can work with it as usual.

Note: It's not guaranteed that the encoding algorithm and the values of the keys are used in the same way in all versions and implementations. If a program treated with UNPRTCT doesn't execute as desired, your interpreter probably uses another algorithm or other keys. In this case, you must use DEBUG and search for it in the program file. After finding it, make the required changes according to the listing above.

UNPRTCT is Faster

We have used the program UNPRTCT.BAS on the PDV.BAS program, which is presented in Chapter 14. After saving with the ",P" parameter this program occupies slightly more than 38K. On an AT computer, running at 10 MHz and equipped with a very fast hard disk (average access 28 milliseconds (ms)), UNPRTCT.BAS requires just under 15 minutes for the encoding. You can imagine how much time would be required on a "normal" PC. Assuming that an AT is 3 to 5 times faster than a PC, the encoding would take at least 45 minutes.

However, this process doesn't need to take up so much time. In Chapter 8 we mentioned that the speed execution is one of the most important tasks of an assembler routine. So, we created the UNPRTCT.BAS program as an assembler program. As a result, the encoding of the same program on the same computer, under the same conditions, took exactly 2 seconds. This is an impressive demonstration of the advantages of an assembler. The following is the assembler listing of UNPRTCT.ASM. Since this program is long, we've added some comments to the listing:

```
;-------------------------------------------
; UNPROTCT.COM is a program to make
; programs which were stored protected
; under GW-BASIC with the switch ",P"
; legible again.
; You must set Device=Ansi.sys in your
; Config.sys file for correct screen output.
;-------------------------------------------
Program     segment
            assume cs:Program,ds:Program
            org     0100h

Start:      jmp  Begin

Logo        db 80 dup (205)
            db ' UnProtct V1.00',43 dup(' '), '1986 (C) H.J. Bomanns '
            db 80 dup (205)
Display     db 27,'[0m'
            db 27,'[5;5f input-file:',55 dup(177)
            db 27,'[7;5f output-file:',55 dup(177)
            db 27,'[1m$'                    ;input light intensity
```

The cursor is positioned and the colors for the screen output are set through ANSI-ESC sequences. Be sure that the configuration file CONFIG.SYS contains the entry:

```
device= ansi.sys
```

If it doesn't, you may receive strange results.

```
;-------------------------------------------
; Error-Reports and Messages
;-------------------------------------------
Err_Inp     db ' error during opening of the input-file'
Err_Inp2    db ' input-file not found$'
Err_Inp3    db ' wrong path for input-file$'
Err_InpL    db ' input-file is empty$'
Err_Out     db ' error during opening of the output-file$'
```

```
Err_Inp4    db ' file-name must be input$'
key         db ', [ESC]= termination, strike any key: ',7,27,'[D$'
Query       db ' output-file exists, overwrite (Y/N): ',7
            db 27,'[D$'

Again       db 27,'[0m',27,'[20;5f decode additional file (Y/N): ',7
            db 27,'[D$'

Abbr_Msg    db 27,'[0m',27,'[15;5f'
            db ' UnPrtct terminated .....',7,13,10,10,'$'

Read_Msg    db 27,'[0m',13,10
            db 27,'[C input-file is read.....',13,10,'$'
Decode_Msg  db 27,'[C data being decoded.....',13,10,'$'
Write_Msg   db 27,'[C output-file is being written .....',13,10,'$'
OK_Msg      db 27,'[C encoding successfully terminated.....',13,10,10
            db 27,'[0m','$'
Err_Attr    db 27,'[7m',27,'[10;5f','$'
ClrLine     db 27,'[0m',27,'[10;5f',75 dup(177),27,'[1m','$'

Pwd1        db      000h,09ah,0f7h,019h,083h
            db      024h,063h,043h,083h,075h
            db      0cdh,08dh,084h,0a9h

Pwd2        db      000h,07ch,088h,059h,074h
            db      0e0h,097h,026h,077h,0c4h
            db      01dh,01eh
```

Here are the two tables with the keys that correspond to the FPASSWORD.1 and FPASSWORD.2 arrays in the BASIC program.

```
Bytes       dw      0

E_Handle    dw      0                           ;Nr. of the input-Handle
A_Handle    dw      0                           ;Nr. of the output-Handle

Scrn_address dw     0

E_Buffer    db      0                           ;input-buffer for FN 0Ah
E_lngth     db      0,50 dup(' ')

MaxBuffer   dw      60000d
BufferOffs  dw      offset buffer               ;data area at end of program
Buffersize  dw      MaxBuffer-BufferOffs ;buffer size for read/write
;------------------------------------------
; Determine which Monitor
;------------------------------------------
Begin:      push    ds                          ;which Monitor?
            push    si
            mov     si,0000                     ;Segment= 0000
            mov     ds,si
            mov     al,ds:[410h]                ;display-screen-Flag DOS
```

```
                    pop     si
                    pop     ds
                    and     al,30h
                    cmp     al,30h
                    jz      Mono_scrn       ;if 0, then Monochrome
                    mov     scrn_address,47104   ;B800h
                    jmp     Init_Prg
Mono_scrn:          mov     scrn_address,45056   ;B000h
```

In the BIOS data segment (0000h:0400h or 0040h:0000) at offset 410h or 10h is the
equipment flag, which stores the hardware configuration of the computer. Bits 4 and 5
represent the installed video card. If both bits are set, a monochrome card is installed.
Otherwise, a color card is set.

```
;---------------------------------------
; Initialize Program and Variables
;---------------------------------------
Init_Prg:       call    Init_scrn       ;display-screen and Logo
SetUp:          mov     dx,offset Display   ;input-text
                mov     ah,09
                int     21h
                mov     [E_lngth],0         ;no input
;---------------------------------------
; Read input-file
;---------------------------------------
L1:             mov     dh,4            ;line
                mov     dl,20           ;column
                mov     ah,2            ;Function Set Cursor Position
                int     10h

                mov     [E_Buffer],50
                mov     dx,offset E_Buffer   ;input-buffer
                mov     ah,0ah          ;Buffered Keyboard Input
                int     21h
                xor     ax,ax
                mov     al,[E_lngth]    ;length of the input
                cmp     al,0            ;length= 0?
                jnz     L1A             ;input o.k.
                mov     dx,offset Err_Inp4   ;file-name not input
                call    Error
                jmp     L1
L1A:            mov     bx,ax
                add     bx,1
                mov     [E_lngth+bx],0000h   ;fabricate ASCII-String
                mov     ah,3dh          ;Open File
                mov     dx,offset E_lngth+1  ;name from here on
                mov     al,0            ;open file before reading
                int     21h
                jnc     Inp_OK          ;if OK, continue
                cmp     ax,2            ;error "File not found"
                jnz     L1B
                mov     dx,offset Err_Inp2   ;error "file not found"
```

```
                    call    Error
                    jmp     SetUp                   ;and again
        L1B:        cmp     ax,3                    ;error "Path not found"
                    jnz     L1C
                    mov     dx,offset Err_Inp3      ;error "False path..."
                    call    Error
                    jmp     SetUp                   ;and again
        L1C:        mov     dx,offset Err_Inp       ;general error
                    call    Error
                    jmp     SetUp
        Inp_OK:     mov     [E_Handle],ax           ;store number of the Handle
```

Through the function 0Ah of the interrupt 21h, the two required filenames are read. The names are read into a buffer and then passed to the functions for opening or creating files. An error during the file access is reported, by the operating system, through the carry flag. If the bit is set, there is an error. If the bit isn't set, no errors exist.

```
;-------------------------------------------
; Read Name output-file
;-------------------------------------------
L2:                 mov     dh,6                    ;line
                    mov     dl,20                   ;column
                    mov     ah,2                    ;Function Set Cursor Position
                    int     10h

                    mov     [E_Buffer],50
                    mov     dx,offset E_Buffer      ;input-buffer
                    mov     ah,0ah                  ;Buffered Keyboard Input
                    int     21h
                    xor     ax,ax
                    mov     al,[E_lngth]            ;length of the input
                    cmp     al,0                    ;length= 0?
                    jnz     L2A                     ;input o.k.
                    mov     dx,offset Err_Inp4      ;file-name not input
                    call    Error
                    jmp     L2
;-------------------------------------------
; open output-file
;-------------------------------------------
L2A:                mov     bx,ax
                    add     bx,1
                    mov     [E_lngth+bx],0000h      ;fabricate ASCII-String
                    mov     ah,3dh                  ;Open File
                    mov     dx,offset E_lngth+1     ;name from here on
                    mov     al,1                    ;open file for writing
                    int     21h
                    push    ax                      ;store Handle
                    jnc     Chk                     ;if OK, file is present
                                                    ;else, create file
;-------------------------------------------
; create output-file
;-------------------------------------------
```

```
                pop     ax                      ;clean Stack
                mov     ah,3ch                  ;create File
                mov     cx,20h                  ;Attribute archive
                mov     dx,offset E_lngth+1     ;name starts here
                int     21h
                jnc     Out_OK                  ;if OK, go
                mov     dx,offset Err_Out       ;general error
                call    Error
                mov     ah,3eh                  ;close file
                mov     bx,E_Handle             ;close input-file again
                int     21h
                jmp     SetUp                   ;and again
;-----------------------------------------
; output-file exists, overwrite?
;-----------------------------------------
Chk:            mov     dx,offset Err_Attr      ;reverse for question
                mov     ah,09
                int     21h
                mov     dx,offset Query         ;overwrite (Y/N)
                mov     ah,09
                int     21h
                mov     ah,0
                int     16h                     ;wait for key
                cmp     al,'j'
                jz      Out_OK1
                cmp     al,'J'
                jz      Out_OK1
                cmp     al,'n'
                jz      Return
                cmp     al,'N'
                jz      Return
                jmp     Chk
Return:         pop     ax
                mov     dx,offset ClrLine
                mov     ah,09
                int     21h
                jmp     SetUp
;-----------------------------------------
; output-file is open
;-----------------------------------------
Out_OK1:        pop     ax              ;restore AX after 'Query'
Out_OK:         mov     [A_Handle],ax      ;store Handle number
                mov     dx,offset ClrLine
                mov     ah,09
                int     21h
;-----------------------------------------
; read data from input-file into buffer
;-----------------------------------------
                mov     dx,offset Read_Msg
                mov     ah,09
                int     21h
                mov     dx,offset Buffer        ;buffer-address
                mov     cx,Buffersize           ;buffer-size
```

```
              mov       bx,E_Handle
              mov       ah,3fh              ;read from file
              int       21h
              or        ax,ax               ;was data read?
              jnz       Decode              ;yes, decode
              mov       dx,offset Err_InpL  ;no, error-message
              call      Error
              mov       ah,3eh              ;close file
              mov       bx,E_Handle         ;close input-file
              int       21h
              mov       ah,3eh
              mov       bx,A_Handle         ;close output-file
              int       21h
              jmp       SetUp               ;jump forward
;-------------------------------------------
; decode data in the buffer
;-------------------------------------------
Decode:       push      ax
              mov       dx,offset Decode_Msg
              mov       ah,09
              int       21h
              pop       ax
              mov       Bytes,ax            ;number of Bytes read
              mov       cx,ax               ;number to CX
              dec       cx                  ;deduct 2 for EOF/flag-Byte
              dec       cx
              inc       Buffer              ;skip first Byte FEh/FFh
              jnz       Not_pwd             ;was already FFh
              dec       Buffer              ;set to FEh again
              dec       Buffer
Not_pwd:      mov       dh,13               ;number Password1
              mov       dl,11               ;number Password2
              mov       si,offset Buffer+1
              mov       di,si
              cld
Loop1:        mov       bx,offset Pwd1
              mov       al,dh               ;pointer to key tables
              xor       ah,ah
              add       bx,ax
              lodsb                         ;read Byte from the buffer
              sub       al,dl
              xor       al,[bx]             ;change Byte
              push      ax                  ;store characters
              mov       bx,offset pwd2
              mov       al,dl               ;pointer tp key tables
              xor       ah,ah
              add       bx,ax
              pop       ax                  ;restore characters
              xor       al,[bx]             ;change Byte
              add       al,dh
              stosb                         ;write Byte into buffer
              dec       dl                  ;decrement Password2
              jnz       No1                 ;to 1
```

```
                    mov     dl,11            ;number Password2
No1:                dec     dh               ;decrement Password1
                    jnz     No2              ;down to 1
                    mov     dh,13            ;number Password1
No2:                loop    Loop1
```

In this LOOP the individual bytes of the input file are decoded directly in the buffer. The CX counter is initialized with the number of bytes actually read. As a result, the number of bytes is returned to the AX register during the call of the function 3Fh.

```
;-------------------------------------------
; write decoded data back
;-------------------------------------------
Write:              mov     dx,offset Write_Msg
                    mov     ah,09
                    int     21h
                    mov     dx,offset Buffer;write data from the buffer
                    mov     cx,Bytes         ;number of Bytes
                    mov     bx,A_Handle
                    mov     ah,40h           ;write to file
                    int     21h
                    mov     dx,offset OK_Msg
;-------------------------------------------
; terminate program with message or
; another run
;-------------------------------------------
Exit:               mov     ah,09
                    int     21h
                    mov     ah,3eh           ;close file
                    mov     bx,E_Handle      ;close input-file
                    int     21h
                    mov     ah,3eh
                    mov     bx,A_Handle      ;close output-file
                    int     21h

Again1:             mov     dx,offset Again
                    mov     ah,09
                    int     21h
                    mov     ah,0
                    int     16h              ;wait for key
                    cmp     al,'y'
                    jz      Over
                    cmp     al,'Y'
                    jz      Over
                    cmp     al,'n'
                    jz      End_Prg
                    cmp     al,'N'
                    jz      End_Prg
                    jmp     Again1
End_Prg:            mov     ch,3             ;window of current line
                    mov     cl,0             ;column 0
                    mov     al,22            ;22 delete lines
```

```
              mov     dh,24                ;window to line 24
              mov     dl,79                ;column 79
              mov     bh,7                 ;Attribute for deletion
              mov     ah,7                 ;scroll down
              int     10h                  ;scroll window
              mov     ah,02                ;set Cursor position
              mov     dh,5                 ;line
              mov     dl,0                 ;column
              xor     bh,bh                ;display-screen page 0
              int     10h
              mov     ah,4ch               ;end of program
              int     21h

Over:         jmp     Init_Prg
;----------------------------------------
; fill display-screen with '', output Logo
;----------------------------------------
Init_scrn     proc    near
              PUSH    CX
              PUSH    AX
              PUSH    DI
              PUSH    SI
              PUSH    ES
              MOV     CX,240               ;the first three lines
              MOV     DI,[scrn_address]     ;start-address disp-scrn
              MOV     ES,DI                ;target-Segment
              XOR     DI,DI                ;target-Offset= 0
              MOV     SI,offset Logo       ;Offset for characters from Logo
              MOV     AH,112               ;display Logo reversed
L_0:          LODSB                        ;read characters sequentially
              STOSW
              LOOP    L_0

              MOV     CX,1760              ;rest of the display-screen
              MOV     DI,[scrn_address]    ;start-address disp-scrn
              MOV     ES,DI                ;target-Segment
              MOV     DI,480               ;target-Offset= 4th.line, 1st. char
              MOV     AH,7                 ;Attribute Normal
              MOV     AL,'±'
L_1:          STOSW
              LOOP    L_1

              POP     ES
              POP     SI
              POP     DI
              POP     AX
              POP     CX
              RET
Init_scrn     endp
```

This routine initializes the screen. In order to display the logo, the first three lines are set to inverse video. The rest of the screen is filled with the ▓ character.

```
;------------------------------------------
;file-name not input
;------------------------------------------
Error          proc    near
               push    dx               ;Offset of the message
               mov     dx,offset Err_Attr ;position CRSR, reverse
               mov     ah,09
               int     21h
               pop     dx
               mov     ah,09
               int     21h              ;output error-message
               mov     dx,offset key
               mov     ah,09
               int     21h              ;message 'strike any key'
               mov     ah,0
               int     16h              ;wait for key
               cmp     al,27            ;ESC activated ?
               jnz     Wdth              ;no
               mov     dx,offset Abbr_Msg
               jmp     Exit

WDTH:          mov     dx,offset ClrLine ;delete line again
               mov     ah,09            ;Attribute of input
               int     21h
               ret
Error          endp
;------------------------------------------
; starting here are the data read
;------------------------------------------
buffer                 db      0

Program        ends
               end     Start
```

9.4   Mask Generator

One of the most frustrating tasks for a programmer is creating a mask or menu. To help you, we created a small menu/mask generator. The listing of the program begins on the next page.

Operation

Don't panic after calling the program. The screen is supposed to be empty. This is where you can create your masks or menu. As usual, the cursor is moved with the cursor keys. In the line you can jump to a tab stop every 5 characters by using the <Tab> key. This enables you to create tables easily. To create the mask or the menu, you can use all the characters that are available through the keyboard or the combination of <Alt> and <Character Code>. Remember that, during printing with <F3>, characters smaller than CHR$(32) cannot be interpreted as control characters by the printer.

Once you've created your design, you can store the mask or menu either as a listing with <F1> or as a file for BLOAD with <F2>. You can also print the mask, in sequential order, by using <F3>. This enables LOCATE to find a specific number quickly and easily.

Save as Listing

First a header for the program is written in the file that switches off the display of the function key assignment, sets the colors for the display and frame and clears the screen (line 650-690). Then the screen is read line by line and the characters are stored in a variable (line 710-800). Before the data is written into the file, this variable is searched, from back to front, for the first character that isn't equal to CHR$(32), the space (line 760-780). In this way, only the characters that are actually in a line are written into the file; trailing spaces are eliminated. Then the variable is written after a line number and a PRINT into the file (line 770). After all 25 lines have been read, the file is closed and a message is displayed (line 810/820).

Save for BLOAD

Depending on the address of the video RAM, which is determined during the start of the program (line 100/110), the memory of 4,000 bytes (80*25= 2,000 plus an attribute byte for each character = 4,000) is performed by BSAVE (line 860/870). Then another message is displayed (line 880). In Chapter 3 you'll find detailed information about the current video RAM or the attached monitor.

Scaled Hardcopy

The actual mask is equipped on the top, bottom, left and right with numbers, which makes counting much easier. Since more than 80 characters per line are needed (line 920/930), the printer is set for the Elite font.

Draw Frame

If you enter an "E" at position 1,1 on the screen and press <Alt><R>, a border (line 400/410) is drawn around the screen. Entering a "D" at the same location produces a double frame. The PC's semi-graphic characters are used (line 470-600).

Repeat Characters

With the <Alt><L> keys, the last character that was entered can be repeated. This can be used for graphics and special characters, which are created with <Alt> and a character code.

Since the program was written for internal use, it lacks a user interface and error correction. Also, it may not be as user-friendly as you would like. However, the program should serve as a guide for your own development:

```
10 '-------------------------------------------------
20 'MM_GEN.BAS             1986 (C) H.J. Bomanns
30 '-------------------------------------------------
40 :
50 KEY OFF:FOR I=1 TO 10:KEY I,"":NEXT I
60 DRWING.COLR= 7:TEXT.COLR= 7: BG.COLR= 0
70 OUT &H3D9,DRWING.COLR
80 COLOR TEXT.COLR,BG.COLR:CLS
90 :
100 MONITOR$="C":MONITOR.ADR= &HB800
110 DEF SEG= 0:IF (PEEK(&H410) AND &H30)= &H30 THEN MONITOR$="M":
    MONITOR.ADR=&HB000
120 :
130 LOCATE CSRLIN,POS(0),1,0,31
140 X$=INKEY$:IF X$="" THEN 140
150 IF LEN(X$)= 2 THEN 230 'Function key or cursor key activated
160 IF X$= CHR$(9) AND POS(0)+5< 81 THEN LOCATE CSRLIN,POS(0)+5: GOTO 130 'TAB
170 IF X$=CHR$(8) AND POS(0)> 1 THEN LOCATE CSRLIN,POS(0)-1:PRINT " ";:LOCATE
    CSRLIN,POS(0)-1:GOTO 130
180 IF X$=CHR$(8) AND POS(0)= 1 THEN BEEP:GOTO 130
190 IF CSRLIN= 25 AND POS(0)= 80 THEN PRINT X$;:LOCATE 1,1:GOTO 130
200 PRINT X$;:LAST.KEY$= X$
210 GOTO 130
220 :
230 '----- FN or Cursor-key -----
240 :
250 ONKEY= ASC(RIGHT$(X$,1))
260 IF ONKEY= 80 AND CSRLIN< 25 THEN LOCATE CSRLIN+1,POS(0):GOTO 140 'Cursor down
```

```
270 IF ONKEY= 80 AND CSRLIN= 25 THEN LOCATE 1,POS(0):GOTO 140 'Cursor down
280 IF ONKEY= 72 AND CSRLIN>  1 THEN LOCATE CSRLIN-1,POS(0):GOTO 140 'Cursor up
290 IF ONKEY= 72 AND CSRLIN=  1 THEN LOCATE 25,POS(0):GOTO 140 'Cursor up
300 IF ONKEY= 77 AND POS(0)< 80 THEN LOCATE CSRLIN,POS(0)+1:GOTO 140 'Cursor
    right
310 IF ONKEY= 77 AND POS(0)= 80 AND CSRLIN= 25 THEN LOCATE 1,1:GOTO 140
320 IF ONKEY= 77 AND POS(0)= 80 THEN LOCATE CSRLIN+1,1:GOTO 140
330 IF ONKEY= 75 AND POS(0)> 1 THEN LOCATE CSRLIN,POS(0)-1:GOTO 140 'Cursor left
340 IF ONKEY= 75 AND POS(0)= 1 AND CSRLIN= 1 THEN LOCATE 25,80:GOTO 140 'Cursor
    left
350 IF ONKEY= 75 AND POS(0)= 1 THEN LOCATE CSRLIN-1,80:GOTO 140 'Cursor left
360 IF ONKEY= 71 THEN LOCATE 1,1:GOTO 130 '<Home>
370 IF ONKEY= 79 THEN LOCATE 25,80:GOTO 130 '<End>
380 IF ONKEY= 15 AND POS(0)-5> 0 THEN LOCATE CSRLIN,POS(0)-5:GOTO 130 '<Shift>
    <TAB>
390 IF ONKEY= 38 THEN X$= LAST.KEY$:GOTO 190 '<Alt> <L>
400 IF ONKEY= 19 AND (SCREEN(1,1) OR 32)= ASC("e") THEN 470 '<Alt> <R>, simple
    frame
410 IF ONKEY= 19 AND (SCREEN(1,1) OR 32)= ASC("d") THEN 540 '<Alt> <R>, double
    frame
420 IF ONKEY= 59 THEN 620 '<F1>, store as listing
430 IF ONKEY= 60 THEN 840 '<F2>, store for BLOAD
440 IF ONKEY= 61 THEN 900 '<F3>, Hardcopy with scaling
450 PRINT ONKEY
460 GOTO 130
470 '----- simple frame -----
480 :
490 LOCATE 1,1
500 PRINT CHR$(218);STRING$(78,CHR$(196));CHR$(191)
510 FOR I= 2 TO 24:LOCATE I,1:PRINT CHR$(179);:LOCATE I,80:PRINT CHR$(179);:NEXT
    I
520 LOCATE 25,1:PRINT CHR$(192);STRING$(78,CHR$(196));CHR$(217);:LOCATE 1,1
530 GOTO 130
540 '-----double frame------
550 :
560 LOCATE 1,1
570 PRINT CHR$(201);STRING$(78,CHR$(205));CHR$(187)
580 FOR I= 2 TO 24:LOCATE I,1:PRINT CHR$(186);:LOCATE I,80:PRINT CHR$(186);:NEXT
    I
590 LOCATE 25,1:PRINT CHR$(200);STRING$(78,CHR$(205));CHR$(188);:LOCATE 1,1
600 GOTO 130
610 :
620 '----- Listing -----
630 :
640 OPEN "mm_gen.dat" FOR OUTPUT AS #1
650 PRINT #1,"10 KEY OFF:FOR I=1 TO 10:KEY I,";CHR$(34);CHR$(34);":NEXT I"
660 A$="20 color "+STR$(TEXT.COLR)+","+STR$(BG.COLR)
670 PRINT #1,A$
680 PRINT #1,"30 OUT &H3D9,";:PRINT #1,USING "##";DRWING.COLR
690 PRINT #1,"40 CLS"
700 ROWNO= 50
710 FOR I=1 TO 25
720    A$=""
```

```
730    FOR K=1 TO 80
740      A$=A$+CHR$(SCREEN(I,K))
750    NEXT K
760    FOR K= 80 TO 1 STEP -1
770      IF MID$(A$,K,1)<> " " THEN PRINT #1,USING "#### PRINT ";ROWNO;:PRINT
         #1,CHR$(34);LEFT$(A$,K);CHR$(34);CHR$(59):GOTO 790
780    NEXT K
790    ROWNO= ROWNO+10
800  NEXT I
810  CLOSE #1
820  CLS:PRINT "stored as file MM_GEN.DAT/ listing .....":PRINT:END
830  :
840  '----- BLOAD -----
850  :
860  DEF SEG= MONITOR.ADR
870  BSAVE "mm_gen.bld",0,4000
880  CLS:PRINT "stored as file MM_GEN.BLD/ for BLOAD .....":PRINT:END
890  :
900  '----- Hardcopy -----
910  :
920  LPRINT CHR$(27);"@";CHR$(27);"P";CHR$(18);CHR$(27);"M"; 'printer-reset to
     Elite
930  WIDTH "LPT1:",255
940  LPRINT
950  LPRINT "   ";:FOR I=1 TO 8:LPRINT "123456789.";:NEXT I:LPRINT
960  LPRINT "   ";:FOR I=1 TO 8:LPRINT "         |";:NEXT I:LPRINT
970  FOR I=1 TO 25
980    A$=""
990    FOR K=1 TO 80
1000     A$=A$+CHR$(SCREEN(I,K))
1010   NEXT K
1020 LPRINT USING "##_";I;:LPRINT A$;:LPRINT USING "_##";I
1030 NEXT I
1040 LPRINT "   ";:FOR I=1 TO 8:LPRINT "         |";:NEXT I:LPRINT
1050 LPRINT "   ";:FOR I=1 TO 8:LPRINT "123456789.";:NEXT I:LPRINT:LPRINT
1060 GOTO 130
```

10. Organization and Development

10.1 Problem to Solution

The root of all programming is either a problem that must be solved with the PC or a manual process that must be automated with the PC. This problem can usually be described in a few sentences or even a few words. In this way, a goal is defined. How this goal is achieved depends on the programmer.

Some programmers sit down at their computers and start to program. They actually formulate the program while entering statements. This method is well-suited for small projects. But for larger projects, this method isn't effective. For example, after days or weeks the programmer may find that another routine must be squeezed in during every RENUM, a special condition must be intercepted with an IF...THEN...GOTO...ELSE...GOTO construction and, in another location, there are 15 statements crowded into one program line. Finally, the scattered REMs are cleared to make more space for the program. Although the program may execute and perform its task, after two months the programmer must try to reconstruct the program logic and determine where something can be patched or changed without causing additional problems. Because of this disorganization, only fragmented documentation can be created. Obviously this isn't effective programming.

As you can see, organization is an important part of good programming. The time invested for organization actually saves the programmer time that would be spent making changes and/or additions.

Basically, the organization of a program (also called a project) is divided into various steps. First we define our goal. The next steps can be illustrated with an example. Over time, a programmer can collect numerous diskettes. It would be impossible to keep track of all the programs on these diskettes. A solution to this problem would be to create a program that oversees all the programs stored on the diskettes. The following information is needed:

On which diskette is the program stored?

What kind of program is it?

In what programming language was it written?

Does the program belong to a package?

Is the source code available?

How large is the program?

When was the program last changed?

Depending on your needs, this list can be extended. The program should be easy to use. The manual work, such as entering data, should be automated as much as possible. Besides the program name, it should also be possible to search for information with other criteria. Finally, the program must print out its data.

Once the programmer has created this list, he/she can begin the programming assignment. It's best to start a file folder or chart which can be used to keep track of all the papers and documentation. We'll call our project "Diskette Administration".

10.2   Organization

The actual organization is divided into six steps:

Step 1   Overall organization

Step 2   Detailed organization

Step 3   Programming

Step 4   Documentation

Step 5   Introduction/Training

Step 6   Changes/Additions

Step 1:   Overall Organization

In this step the requirements, from the viewpoint of the programmer, are written down and a test is performed to determine whether the project can be implemented. To do this, the following questions must be answered:

Is the hardware suitable for the project or is it too small?

Is a solution already available on the market?

Are cost factors reasonable?

Can the time requirements be met?

At the end of step 1, a proposal, which contains the answers to the above questions, is created. This proposal is submitted to the client for approval. The client decides whether the project should be continued. Changes or enhancements may also be suggested at this time.

Step 2:   Detailed Organization

In this step, the proposal is adjusted to meet the client's needs. Details, such as the following, are defined for the program's users:

Mask construction

List construction

Demands on the user interface

Composition of the information

The programmer produces a *quantity requirement* which contains information such as the number of data records and the number of fields. This information simplifies the decision of what kind of file administration should be used. The programmer determines what programming should be used and creates a new program flow chart. While creating the flow chart, the IPO should be used as a guideline. IPO is an acronym for:

Input

Processing

Output

This signifies that the programmer first plans the input, then the processing and finally the output.

At the end of this step, another document, which should include the following, is created:

Description of the specific requirements

Masks

Pattern lists

Data descriptions

User interface/Help functions

Overview of costs and schedules

Program execution plan

On the basis of this information, the client decides whether the programmer should continue the project.

Step 3:   Programming

In this step, the objectives set in step 2 are implemented. Since mask and file construction, user interface and program execution have already been determined, the programmer must decide the following:

Subroutine development

Variables used

Programming style

Interception of erroneous inputs

Prevention of serious damage caused by a system crash

After the programming is complete, the program is tested. To do this, a set of test data must be created. Besides the normal program functions, extreme situations are also tested. For example, what happens when nonsense input is entered or the diskette is removed from the drive during saving or loading. The client should be included in this step.

Step 4:   Documentation

The documentation includes:

Program documentation

User documentation

The *program documentation* contains, for example, a description of the program functions, mask design, list construction, file descriptions, variable and subroutine overview, program flow charts and the programming language used. All the information, which is needed in order to change or enhance the program, is included. Most of the documentation is already available from step 2.

The *user documentation* is the actual reference manual for the program. It contains information on how to load the program, how to enter data, make changes to or delete input, how to print lists, how to call help and what to do when the system crashes. Eventually, the data record description can become part of this documentation. For example, this can occur when the saved data should be processed by external programs.

Step 5:   Introduction and Training

In this step the user will become familiar with the program's functions and operation. Example data or *test data* will be used. Some lists are printed and the user's questions are answered.

Step 6:   Changes/Additions

This step basically covers the entire project. Usually clients will still want changes or replacements at this point.

The purpose of this step is to obtain changes or replacements from the user once the program has been in use for some time. These changes weren't considered in the previous steps.

This concludes our discussion of the various steps a programmer must follow in order to create a program. However, this is only an overview of the required steps. You should use this as a guideline for your own work.

10.3　The User

If you're not writing a program for yourself, the most important consideration during programming should be for the end user. This begins with the template design. Don't crowd too much information or too many input fields on one screen page. Distribute the information or input fields over two or more templates. The mask should be well-structured and easy to read.

Incorrect:

```
┌──────────────────────────────────────────────────────┐
│ Last Name:_____ First Name:_____ Address:_____ │
│ City:_____ Telephone:_____ Age:_____ │
│ Computer:_____ printer:_____ Monitor:_____ │
└──────────────────────────────────────────────────────┘
```

Correct:

```
┌──────────────────────────────────────────────────────┐
│                                                        │
│  Last Name:_____  First Name:_____    │
│                                                        │
│  Address:_____  City:_____       │
│                                                        │
│  Telephone:_____  age:_____      │
│                                                        │
│  Computer:_____  printer:_____        │
│                                                        │
│  Monitor:_____                              │
└──────────────────────────────────────────────────────┘
```

Fig. 33: Template Construction

You should also carefully design the menu. Using more than ten menu points could confuse the user. Use IPO as a guideline and create separate menus for input, processing and output.

While formulating a program, which should run on a color monitor, you should choose your colors carefully. Even though 16 different colors are available, all of them don't have to be used simultaneously. The following selections are the most user-friendly:

　　color for normal letters

　　color for input and error messages

　　color for the actual input

　　color for framing

　　color for menu/selection bar

In the next chapter you'll find detailed information on the screen display. Pay close attention to error messages. It's very frustrating for the user when a "beep" is sounded when a key is pressed and the message "wrong key activated" appears. The user must guess which of the more than 80 (with combinations more than 200) keys can be pressed. In Chapter 16 you'll find complete messages, an error correction routine and help functions.

10.4   Organizational Aides

A typical programmer's desk is usually a mess. Most likely there are piles of scrap paper containing notes and handwritten messages. Eventually, the programmer will forget where an important note is located.

This disorganization results in undocumented programs and incomplete operating instructions that, after a few months, even the programmer can't operate. In this section we'll discuss how programming and documentation can be simplified by using *organizational aides*.

10.4.1 Program Flow Charts (PFCs)

Usually a beginner has problems tracing the program logic and program execution in languages such as BASIC or Assembler. Critics claim that this occurs because these languages are "unstructured" since data, variables and program lines can be mixed in any sequence. Also, uncontrolled jumping is permitted with GOTO or JMP.

An inexperienced programmer can easily write a BASIC or Assembler program that cannot be analyzed or understood. However, there are BASIC and Assembler programs that, through their structure, resemble a program written in a "structured" programming language.

Other structured programming languages, such as Pascal, Modula 2 or COBOL, don't permit such disorganization. In these programs, data, variables, subroutines and the main program must be separated. The program logic and the program execution can quickly be seen by looking at the definition or declaration parts of the program. Usually a program's logic is obvious, so writing it down isn't necessary. For example, the purpose of a program that organizes addresses is evident. So, additional documentation isn't needed.

However, a flow chart (PFC) is required for program execution. You should use standard symbols so that anyone familiar with these symbols can analyze the program execution. Before examining a small flow chart, we'll present the most important symbols that are used in a PFC:

PFC Symbols

Symbol 1

This symbol marks both the start and the end of the program. The word "Start" or "End" is written inside the symbol.

Symbol 2

This symbol indicates all data processing (i.e., calculations, changes, deletions or searches).

Symbol 3

Subroutines with return jump (GOSUB...RETURN) are identified with this symbol. For larger PFCs, all subroutines are stored on a separate page and identified with a branch symbol.

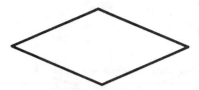

Symbol 4

Decisions followed by a branch (IF...THEN...ELSE) are identified. If possible, all yes and all no jumps should always be shown on the same side of the page (either left or right).

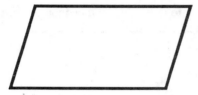

Symbol 5

The hardware access to a peripheral device or a file is marked by this symbol. When a file is read or written, this symbol is used.

Symbol 6

This symbol identifies every input through the keyboard. It also must be used for simple queries (Y/N), menu etc. If an output occurs at the same time, use the following symbol.

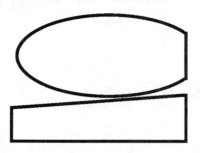

Symbol 7

This symbol is used for output to the screen and/or input through the keyboard. If only a display results, the lower part of the symbol is omitted.

Symbol 8

This symbol, which represents a document, indicates all output on the printer.

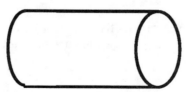

Symbol 9

A file of any type is marked by this symbol. If the name is known, it should be added for clarity. Also the type of file should be identified.

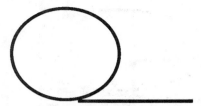

Symbol 10

This symbol probably won't be used with the PC because tape drives or cassette recorders aren't used. If such a device is present, it's usually a tape-streamer for data archiving.

Symbol 11

This symbol is usually found in larger PFCs, which are several pages long. It marks the source of a branch. In the circle, a sequential number, which is identical with the number in the symbol for the target of the branch, appears.

Symbol 12

This symbol, which marks the target of a branch, is the counterpart to the above symbol. The number of the source branch is in the circle.

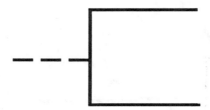

Symbol 13

If a symbol requires special comments or messages that don't fit inside the symbol, this symbol can be used. It's connected to the appropriate symbol. The height of the square bracket depends on the size of the comment.

Symbol 14

Data that leave the PC through a transmission line or modem are marked with this symbol.

Symbol 15

Every sort procedure, regardless of the criteria, is identified with this symbol. For clarity, details about the sort should be added. A plastic template enabling you to draw these symbols quickly and neatly, can be purchased at a computer or office supply store.

You may be wondering why all this effort is necessary. For very small programs, these flowcharts can be omitted. However, if you create larger programs, which will be used by others, you should use a PFC because it will simplify your work.

You'll find that it's beneficial to document every detail of a program with, at least, a program flow chart. For example, you may remember programming a certain routine, but to find out whether it can also be used in other programs, you must analyze the structure. You can quickly examine the available PFC. The following illustration demonstrates a simple program execution plan:

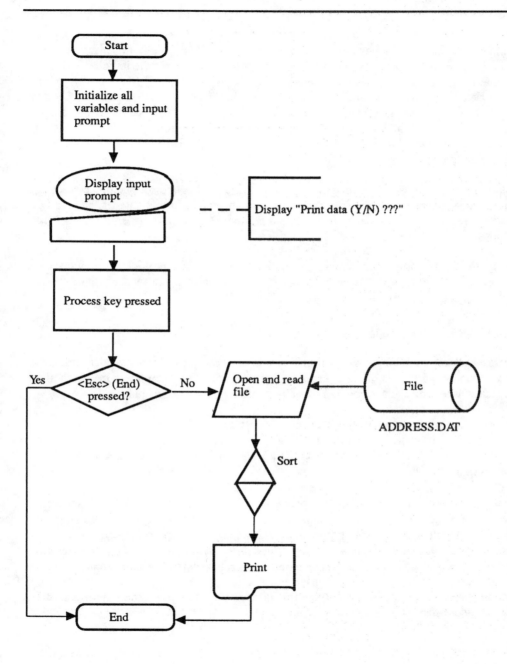

Fig. 34: Program Execution Plan

309

First the start of the routine is signified with the box that has rounded corners. For an application, you would enter the name of the routine and for a program start, you would enter the name of the program. The following processing box marks the initialization of the routine or the program. All assignments, READ...DATA loops or file accesses should occur here for the one-time initialization. In our example, the routine queries whether data should be printed. The next symbol identifies the output of the query on the screen and the subsequent query of the keyboard. The processing box with the following decision symbol, represents the evaluation of the activated key. Here an IF...THEN...ELSE construction is usually programmed.

If the <Esc> key was activated, a jump results to the end of the routine. Otherwise, the following input/output symbol clearly shows that an access, in this case of the data file, results. After the access, the data is sorted and printed. The jump to the "End" symbol then follows.

Analyzing this routine with the PFC requires about 15 seconds, depending on your experience with reading flowcharts. Obviously it would take much longer to analyze this routine by using the program listing.

10.4.2 Template Design

Designing templates may take several hours or several days. Properly positioning the output can be very complicated, especially for combination templates, in which field designations as well as data from a file or a previous input must be displayed.

In these cases, a *template design sheet* can help. On this sheet, the template is first created by hand. This is done by creating a facsimile of the screen on ruled paper. Lines and columns are indicated on the top and to the left. During programming, proceed along the line or column to identify the correct coordinates for the LOCATE command.

Again you may be wondering why all this work is necessary. A template design sheet isn't needed for simple displays or the continuous output of text with a PRINT command. However, if you're programming a template with many input and output fields and each position needs the LOCATE command, a design sheet should definitely be used. A small test will quickly convince you. Try programming a template with and without using a design sheet. The results will surprise you. A design sheet can also improve your documentation. The following is an example of a template design sheet for a program that manages addresses:

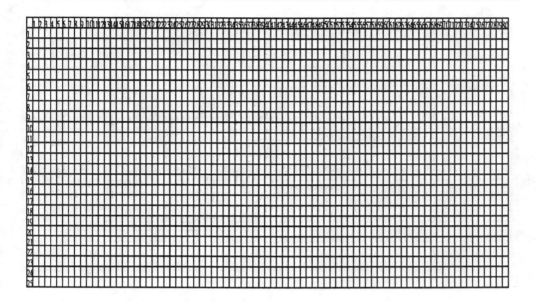

Fig. 35: Template Design Sheet

10.4.3 Designing the Printed Output

With a few changes, the template design sheet can also be used for designing the printout. You can use regular graph paper or design your own (be certain to have 80 columns and 25 rows). Make 3 copies of this design sheet, cut the individual pieces and paste them together. Cut off the last three lines on the last sheet so that there are only sixty-six lines.

On the last two sheets, enter the correct line numbers (26-66) in the left column. This design sheet represents the printer paper. Paste or tape additional copies on the right hand side if the printout will be wider than 80 characters. If you don't want to create your own paper, you can also purchase ruled paper at an office- or art supply store.

10.4.4 File Record Description

The last organizational aide is the *file record description*, which simplifies file administration and string handling.

The file record description was originally intended for use with structured files (random or ISAM files). This is appropriate since these files are a fixed length. Before examining the file record description in detail, let's look at an example:

311

Program:_____   Date:_____._____._____

Variable/File#:	Offset:	Record File Description:						
		1	2	3	4	5	6	7	8	9	0	1 2	3	4	5	6	7	8	9	0	1 2	3	4	5	6	7	8	9	0	1 2	3	4	5	6	7	8	9	0	1 2	3	4	5	6	7	8	9	0	1 2	3	4	5	6	7	8	9	0	1 2	3	4	5	6	7	8	9	0	1 2	3	4	5	6	7	8	9	0							

Variable/File#:	Offset:	Record File Description:						
		1	2	3	4	5	6	7	8	9	0	1 2	3	4	5	6	7	8	9	0	1 2	3	4	5	6	7	8	9	0	1 2	3	4	5	6	7	8	9	0	1 2	3	4	5	6	7	8	9	0	1 2	3	4	5	6	7	8	9	0	1 2	3	4	5	6	7	8	9	0	1 2	3	4	5	6	7	8	9	0							

Variable/File#:	Offset:	Record File Description:						
		1	2	3	4	5	6	7	8	9	0	1 2	3	4	5	6	7	8	9	0	1 2	3	4	5	6	7	8	9	0	1 2	3	4	5	6	7	8	9	0	1 2	3	4	5	6	7	8	9	0	1 2	3	4	5	6	7	8	9	0	1 2	3	4	5	6	7	8	9	0	1 2	3	4	5	6	7	8	9	0							

Variable/File#:	Offset:	Record File Description:						
		1	2	3	4	5	6	7	8	9	0	1 2	3	4	5	6	7	8	9	0	1 2	3	4	5	6	7	8	9	0	1 2	3	4	5	6	7	8	9	0	1 2	3	4	5	6	7	8	9	0	1 2	3	4	5	6	7	8	9	0	1 2	3	4	5	6	7	8	9	0	1 2	3	4	5	6	7	8	9	0							

Variable/File#:	Offset:	Record File Description:						
		1	2	3	4	5	6	7	8	9	0	1 2	3	4	5	6	7	8	9	0	1 2	3	4	5	6	7	8	9	0	1 2	3	4	5	6	7	8	9	0	1 2	3	4	5	6	7	8	9	0	1 2	3	4	5	6	7	8	9	0	1 2	3	4	5	6	7	8	9	0	1 2	3	4	5	6	7	8	9	0							

Fig. 36: File Record Description

This is a record description for the address management program, for which we created a template design sheet in Section 10.4.2. In the header we record the program and the date that the record description was created. You should always enter the date because it's very important for future changes. By doing this, the most recent record description can easily be identified.

Below this are seven boxes, in which the actual record description appears. In the "Variable/file#" field, enter either the variable names, for which the description is intended, or the number of the file that was assigned during the OPEN command. We'll discuss the variable description shortly. The file number is important for quickly finding information. For example, the following entry in the listing is meaningless because the current content of FILENAME$ isn't provided:

```
OPEN FILENAME$ FOR RANDOM AS #3
```

The file number is the only identification for the record description. The number of the FIELD indication is also entered in this field. Following this are the variable names, which are indicated in the FIELD assignment.

In our example there are two FIELD assignments. The first FIELD contains the actual address and personal data and the second FIELD contains comments. This is done so that the FIELD doesn't become too long and data can easily be accessed.

In the "Offset" field, we enter the position that's currently in this box. For each box there are 80 columns/characters available for the description. In the second box, under Offset, we

312

would have 0/1, as in the example. This information is later used to access the individual data fields through the MID$ functions. To read for the access to the "Birthday" field, the following command is needed:

```
BIR$= MID$(ADAT$,115,8)
```

As you can see, the record description can also be used for the description of string content. If, for example, only a portion of the address file is read into an array, the file record description can provide additional details and simplify access:

```
100 .....
110 FOR I= 1 TO RECORD.SIZE
120   GET#3,I
130   PRINT$(I)= LEFT$(ADAT$,20)+MID$(ADAT$,71,44)
140 NEXT I
150 .....
```

Here the fields Last name, Zip Code, City and Telephone are read into an array in order to print, for example, an address listing. In order to format the list, you should know where the fields are located in the array. Create a record description that shows the start of the individual fields in the array. Formatting with MID$ or PRINT USING shouldn't present any problems.

10.4.5 Large Programs

Programming large programs isn't much different than working with small programs. Organizational aides should be used for both of them.

Usually large projects aren't implemented as a single program. Instead, they utilize a construction, with CHAIN or RUN, which loads the individual program sections through a main menu. Each program section can almost be treated as a separate program.

During the design it's important to consider passing data between the various program sections. For example, if you want to pass addresses to the word processor for form letters, an interface must be provided in both programs.

This can be done in the form of a file, in which the address module writes the data, and from which the word processor reads the data. Here a file record description is very important, because it's possible that different FIELD assignments will exist in the two programs.

Another way to transmit data is through the COMMON area. You must ensure that in all program sections the same variable definitions are used. Otherwise, variables will be assigned the wrong content, overwritten or erased. We treated the COMMON area as an individual program section and numbered the lines from 10 to 90. The other program sections are numbered, beginning at line 100. When changes or additions are needed, they only occur on one location in the COMMON section. Then, after a DELETE -90, the COMMON section is merged into every program section that is affected by the change.

10.4.6 Module Programming

After you've been programming in PC-BASIC, you'll realize that many routines can be used, with almost no changes, in many other programs. Since this is possible we can also create a library from which the routines can be placed, with MERGE, into a new program. This process can be compared to a word processor, which can place various pieces of text into a single letter.

However, there is one difference; pieces of text don't have line numbers. This is the problem with the MERGE command. If the line numbers are identical, MERGE replaces the program lines with the additional lines and inserts all other lines into the existing ones. Obviously this can lead to complete disorder. Also, GOTOs cannot be used in these lines or line numbers.

The best way to solve these problems is to program all the routines which are to be used later as subroutines ending with a RETURN. The line numbering should be as high as possible. For example, from 50,000 and up. All routines should include sufficient REM lines, which explain what this routine does and indicate which variables are required or must be changed. If a GOTO cannot be avoided, the destination should only be within the current routine.

Note: Don't rely on the RENUM command too much. Although it reports an error if a line is missing at the location where a GOTO jumped, it's very difficult to reorganize after the completed RENUM. All errors must be noted and the program completely re-tested to ensure that a line wasn't forgotten. Don't assume that an error will be detected during the additional programming. Your users will find most of the errors.

Combining the routines is fairly simple. First construct a program header similar to the following:

```
10 '-------------------------------------
20 'ADDRESS.BAS Address Management
30 '-------------------------------------
40 :
50 CLS:KEY OFF
60 :
70 'GOTO xxxx 'skip subroutines
```

The first routine is loaded using MERGE. Then the complete program is renumbered with RENUM. The next routine with MERGE and another RENUM follows. This continues until all the routines are in the program.

Next change line 70 by erasing the first REM characters and jump to the next line after the last loaded routine. This could be done as follows:

```
10 '------------------------------------------------
20 'program/file-administration 1986 (C) H.J.Bomanns
30 '------------------------------------------------
40 '
50 COLOR 7,0:CLS:OUT &H3D9,0:KEY OFF:ON ERROR GOTO 8950
60 PRINT "Initialization ";CHR$(254);:LOCATE ,POS(0)-1,1,0,31
70 GOTO 1040 'skip subroutines
80 '
90 '----- subroutines -----
100 '
110 '----- display bottom line -----
120 COLOR TXT.FORGRD, TXT.BAKGRD
130 LOCATE 23,3,0:PRINT FOOTER$;SPACE$(80-POS(0));
140 RETURN
150 '----- display head line -----
160 COLOR MSSG.FORGRD,MSSG.BAKGRD
170 LOCATE 2,16,0:PRINT HEADER$;
180 COLOR TXT.FORGRD,TXT.BAKGRD
190 PRINT SPACE$(58-POS(0));
200 RETURN
210 '----- clear window -----
220 LOCATE CSRLIN,POS(0),0
230 COLOR TXT.FORGRD,TXT.BAKGRD:VIEW PRINT 4 TO 21:CLS:VIEW PRINT
240 RETURN
250 '----- store display-screen -----
260 BUFFER.OFS%= VARPTR(BUFFER%(0))
270 DEF SEG: CALL SAVESCRN(BUFFER.OFS%)
280 RETURN
290 '----- restore display-screen -----
300 BUFFER.OFS%= VARPTR(BUFFER%(0))
310 DEF SEG: CALL RESTSCRN(BUFFER.OFS%)
320 RETURN
330 '----- erase current line -----
340 LOCATE CSRLIN,1:COLOR TXT.FORGRD,TXT.BAKGRD
350 PRINT SPACE$(79);
360 RETURN
370 '----- output note and wait for key -----
380 LOCATE 25,1:COLOR MSSG.FORGRD,MSSG.BAKGRD
390 PRINT MSSG$;" ";CHR$(254);" ";:LOCATE CSRLIN,POS(0)-2,1,0,31:BEEP
400 X$=INKEY$:IF X$= "" THEN 400
410 LOCATE 25,1:COLOR TXT.FORGRD,TXT.BAKGRD
420 PRINT SPACE$(LEN(MSSG$)+3);
430 RETURN
440 '----- output template -----
450 DEF SEG= MONITOR.ADR:ATTR%= PEEK(1):COLMNO%= 1
460 FOR I= 4 TO 21
470   ROWNO%= I
480   DEF SEG: CALL FASTSCRN(ROWNO%,COLMNO%,ATTR%,MASK$(I-3))
490 NEXT I
500 RETURN
510 '.....
520 ADDITIONAL SUBROUTINES
530 '.....
1040 '----- initialize Variables and Arrays -----
```

11. Professional Screen Display Construction

Slow screen display construction is one of PC-BASIC's weakest features. There are two reasons for this: PC-BASIC is an interpreter and the operating system is slow in creating screen output. You can use assembler routines or use BLOAD to read complete templates to speed up this process. We'll discuss both of these solutions in this chapter.

11.1 What Video Card is Installed?

An important aspect of program development is the program's ability to operate on PCs with different video cards or monitors. Providing individual versions of the program is only practical if the routines can be universally inserted into the individual versions with the MERGE command. In this section we'll examine this problem.

As we previously mentioned, screen attribute representation varies among monochrome monitors and color composite monitors. So the programmer must ensure that the program can operate with all of these monitors. A composite monitor should be treated like a color monitor because some cards that are used with this monitor display the colors as raster instead of as grey scale. It's possible to determine whether a color graphic card is installed, but it's more difficult to determine whether a color or a composite monitor is attached. Although the user could input this information, most users wouldn't know if the colors on a composite monitor are displayed as grey scale or as raster. You could provide some sample choices from which the user could choose. However, going through this procedure each time the program is called would be very tiresome. Therefore, the colors should be represented as raster so only the colors that can be displayed without problems will be selected.

Determining Display Mode through the Equipment Flag

How do we determine, using PC-BASIC, which card is installed in the PC? After PC-BASIC is booted, the operating system sets a flag, which provides information about the installed card. This flag, also called the equipment flag, is at address &H0000:0410 or &H0040:&H0010 and can be queried with PEEK. In the following pages you'll find two routines which read the equipment flag and then set the colors attribute, depending on the result:

```
270 '---------- Which Monitor? -------------------------WMON_01.BAS
280 :
290 DEF SEG=0:IF (PEEK(&H410) AND &H30)= &H30 THEN GOTO 490 'A monochrome-card is
    installed
300 :
310 '---- determine colors for color-display ----
320 :
330 MONITOR$="C": MONITOR.ADR= &HB800
340 :
350 CLS:KEY OFF
360 PRINT "Do you have a color monitor attached? (Y/N)";
370 X$=INKEY$:IF X$="" THEN 370
380 X$= CHR$(ASC(X$) OR 32) 'BIG -->small
390 IF X$<>"y" AND X$<>"n" THEN BEEP:GOTO 370
400 IF X$="n" THEN 520 'colors for composite-monitor same as for monochrome
410 :
420 BKGRD  =  1 'blue background
430 TXT    = 15 'white letters
440 MSSAGE = 12 'bright red for error-/input messages
450 INPT   = 14 'yellow for the input
460 :
470 GOTO 580 'continue in the program
480 :
490 '-- determine colors for mono-display ------
500 :
510 MONITOR$="M": MONITOR.ADR= &HB000
520 BKGRD  =  0 'black background
530 TXT    =  7 'light grey letters
540 MSSAGE = 15 'white for error-/input-messages
550 INPT   = 15 'white for the input
560 :
570 '-------------------------------------------------------------
580 'continue in the program
```

How this routine works

In line 290 of the routine, PEEK reads the value of the memory location at offset address &H0410. The segment &H0000 is determined with DEF SEG. At this memory location, the operating system stores information that specifies whether a color or monochrome card was detected during the test routines that are performed during the booting process. Bits 4 and 5 of this value provide information about the installed card:

both bits set   monochrome card

bit 4 set   color card 40*25

bit 5 set   color card 80*25

Whether both bits are set will be determined through a logical AND with the value in &H30/48. If they are set, the result is &H30/48; so a monochrome card is installed and the corresponding colors are set, starting at line 490. Otherwise, a color card is installed whether it's 40*25 characters per line or 80*25 characters per line. The colors are set starting at line 310. The routine also checks, with the color card that was detected, whether a composite monitor is attached. If it's a composite monitor, the colors are set according to monochrome card defaults in order to prevent the color display as raster.

In this routine the color assignment is based on the application area. Each time an input is read in, a color is immediately assigned:

```
255 COLOR TXT.COLR,0
260 PRINT "Monthly Pay: ";
265 COLOR INPT.COLR,0
270 INPUT "";MNTH.PAY
```

Using a program is much easier because of these uniform color assignments. The user will soon realize that bright red indicates an error or input message, light green indicates an input, or that the normal template is displayed in yellow.

Theoretically, the second routine works the same way. Use this routine when the colors should or must be individually set. An assignment to fixed applications areas doesn't exist:

```
270 '---------- What Monitor? --------------------------WMON_02.BAS
280 :
290 DEF SEG=0:IF (PEEK(&H410) AND &H30)= &H30 THEN GOTO 610
300 :
310 '----- determine colors for color-display ----
320 :
330 MONITOR$="C": MONITOR.ADR= &HB800
340 :
350 CLS:KEY OFF
360 PRINT "Do you have a color-monitor attached (Y/N)?";
370 X$=INKEY$:IF X$="" THEN 370
380 X$= CHR$(ASC(X$) OR 32) 'BIG -->small
390 IF X$<>"y" AND X$<>"n" THEN BEEP:GOTO 370
400 IF X$="n" THEN 650 'colors for composite-monitor as for monochrome
410 :
420 BLACK  = 0
430 BLUE =   1
440 GREEN=   2
450 CYAN=    3
460 RED=     4
470 MAGENTA= 5
480 BROWN=   6
490 WHITE=   7
500 GRAY =   8
510 LBLUE=   9
520 LGREEN=  10
530 LCYAN=   11
540 LRED=    12
550 LMAGENTA=13
560 YELLOW=  14
```

```
570 BRIT.WHT=15
580 :
590 GOTO 830 'continue in the program
600 :
610 '---- determine colors for mono-display ------
620 :
630 MONITOR$="M": MONITOR.ADR= &HB000
640 :
650 BLACK=    0
660 BLUE=     1
670 GREEN=    2
680 CYAN=     3
690 RED=      4
700 MAGENTA=  5
710 BROWN=    6          '} here are the colors you selected
720 WHITE=    7
730 GRAY =    8
740 LBLUE=    9
750 LGREEN=  10
760 LCYAN=   11
770 LRED=    12
780 LMAGENTA=13
790 YELLOW=  14
800 BRIT.WHT=15
810 :
820 '------------------------------------------------------------
830 'continue in the program
```

A disadvantage of this routine is that too many colors may be used. The color can change with every input since there is not a default for an input color. This can confuse the user.

Besides the methods we've already described, there are two other ways to determine which video card is installed and which monitor is being used. To do this, we'll use the BIOS (Basic Input/Output System) of the PC. Although the BIOS is usually considered software, we can also consider it as hardware since most of the BIOS assignments are related to hardware control. The BIOS is partially located in ROM (Read Only Memory), on the main circuit board of your PC. Another part, which is loaded into the RAM (Random Access Memory) of the PC during booting, executes its assignment with the BIOS located in ROM. Some assignments, which cannot be executed through PC-BASIC, can be transferred to the BIOS. Unlike other programming languages, PC-BASIC doesn't offer a BIOS interface of its own, so an assembler routine must be used in order to use this interface.

Since BIOS access (i.e., the MS-DOS function calls) is impossible from PC-BASIC, a machine language routine, which PC-BASIC gets through CALL, is needed. Since this routine can be used universally and wasn't developed specifically for this problem, we've included a detailed description of it in Chapter 8. The following are the basics you'll need to know:

Values are passed to this routine through variables that roughly correspond to the register structure of the CPU and the result of a call is returned through them. This routine must store the contents of important registers and handle the variables. The important registers are stored through PUSH in the beginning of the routine. Corresponding POPs, at the end of the routine, restore the original contents. With CALL, the variables are passed through the stack to the routine. However, their values must be read out of the stack and into the CPU registers after execution by the CPU registers is re-established.

The assignment of the BIOS interrupts &H10 and &H11 are important. The first provides information on available PC equipment. The second provides information and handles everything connected with the display. In Appendix F you'll find descriptions of both of these BIOS interrupts.

For example, function 15 of INT 10h indicates that the display mode is currently being used. Since PC-BASIC switches to basic mode after being called, we can determine which video card is installed.

Note: To execute the following programs correctly, PC-BASIC must be called with the /M switch as follows:

```
GWBASIC /M:54000
```

Determining Screen Mode through INT 10h

The following program uses BIOS interrupt 10h to determine in which mode the video card is currently set:

```
10 '-------------------------------------------------
20 'Display_MODE.BAS          1986 (C) H.J.Bomanns
30 '-------------------------------------------------
40 :
50 'this program determines through DOS_SN and the INT 10h the current display
60 'mode.
70 :
80 CLS:KEY OFF
90 LOCATE 5,5:PRINT "initialize machine-program ....."
100 MP.START= &HE000
110 GOSUB 520 'poke machine-program into memory
120 MP.END= MP.START+I-1
130 LOCATE 5,5:PRINT SPACE$(80-POS(0)):PRINT
140 :
150 'in the following loop the address of the interrupt-number is determined.
160 'the BIOS-/DOS interrupt-number can be poked to this address.
170 :
180 FOR I= MP.START TO MP.END:IF PEEK(I)= 205 THEN INT.ADR= I+1 ELSE NEXT
190 :
200 DOS.SN= MP.START
210 AL%=0: AH%=0: BL%=0: BH%=0: CL%=0: CH%=0: DL%=0: DH%=0: ES%=0: SI%=0: DI%=0:
    FLAGS%=0
220 :
```

```
230 AH%= 15:INT.NR%= &H10 'BIOS-Call display-screen functions
240 :
250 DEF SEG:POKE INT.ADR,INT.NR%
260 DEF SEG:CALL DOS.SN(AH%, AL%, BH%, BL%, CH%, CL%, DH%, DL%, ES%, SI%, DI%,
    FLAGS%)
270 :
280 'The result in Register AX contains the following INFOs:
290 '
300 'AX  | AH                      | AL                        |
310 '&H10 : BIOS-Call display-screen functions
320 '
330 '      number of columns:      current mode:
340 '      80 or                   AL= 0: text black/white 40*25
350 '      40                      AL= 1: text color 40*25
360 '                              AL= 2: text black/white 80*25
370 '                              AL= 3: text color 80*25
380 '                              AL= 4: graphic 320*200 color
390 '                              AL= 5: graphic 320*200 S/W
400 '                              AL= 6: graphic 640*200 S/W
410 '                              AL= 7: MONOCHROME-card 80*25
420 :
430 RESTORE 440:FOR I=0 TO 7:READ MODE$(I):NEXT I
440 DATA "text 40*25 S/W","text 40*25 color","text 80*25 S/W","text 80*25
    color","graphic 320*200 color","graphic 320*200 S/W","graphic 640*200
    S/W","monochrome-card"
450 :
460 PRINT "Following display mode is reported by INT $10: ":PRINT
470 PRINT MODE$(AL%)
480 LOCATE 25,1,0:PRINT "strike any key....."
490 IF INKEY$="" THEN 490
500 CLS:END
510 :
520 'data-lines from the COM-file: dos_sn.com
530 :
540 RESTORE 560
550 DEF SEG:FOR I=1 TO 151:READ X:POKE MP.START+I-1,X: NEXT I
560 DATA 250, 85,139,236, 30,  6,139,118,  6,139,  4
570 DATA  80,157,139,118, 14,138, 20,139,118, 16,138
580 DATA  52,139,118, 18,138, 12,139,118, 20,138, 44
590 DATA 139,118, 22,138, 28,139,118, 24,138, 60,139
600 DATA 118, 26,138,  4,139,118, 28,138, 36,139,118
610 DATA   8,139, 60, 80,139,118, 12,139,  4,142,192
620 DATA  88,139,118, 10,139, 52, 85,251,205, 33,250
630 DATA  93, 86,156,139,118, 28,136, 36,139,118, 26
640 DATA 136,  4,139,118, 24,136, 60,139,118, 22,136
650 DATA  28,139,118, 20,136, 44,139,118, 18,136, 12
660 DATA 139,118, 16,136, 52,139,118, 14,136, 20, 88
670 DATA 139,118,  6,137,  4, 88,139,118, 10,137,  4
680 DATA 140,192,139,118, 12,137,  4,139,118,  8,137
690 DATA  60,  7, 31, 93,251,202, 24,  0
700 RETURN
```

How this routine works

After the program begins, a subroutine (line 520) POKEs an assembler routine, representing the BIOS interface, into memory. This assembler routine can be used for BIOS and MS-DOS calls. For this reason, the memory location of the interrupt number is determined within the routine at line 180. This is based on the value 205, which represents the opcode for the INT instruction.

The next memory location contains the interrupt number. The BIOS interrupt number (lines 230-250) is POKEd here. The variables to be passed are initialized in lines 210-230. The routine call occurs in line 260. In lines 280-410 of the listing, you can determine the significance of the information that was passed by function 15 of INT 10h through the AH% or AL% variable, which sets the color accordingly.

Determining Display Mode through INT 11h

We use INT 11h to find information about the video card and the remaining equipment, such as the number of disk drives, the number of serial and parallel ports and whether a game port is connected. Theoretically, this program works the same way as the previous one except that INT 11h is called. The result is also delivered in the AL% and AH% variables. In the listing you'll discover the significance of the information that is returned in lines 280-490. What is available in and on the PC is determined through a logical AND combined with the values that are passed.

```
10 '-------------------------------------------------
20 'EQUIPMNT.BAS            1986 (C) H.J.Bomanns
30 '-------------------------------------------------
40 :
50 'This is a program which through DOS_SN provides information about the
60 'equipment in and on the PC.
70 :
80 CLS:KEY OFF
90 LOCATE 5,5:PRINT "initialize machine-program....."
100 MP.START= &HE000
110 GOSUB 850 'poke machine-program into memory
120 MP.END= MP.START+I-1
130 LOCATE 5,5:PRINT SPACE$(80-POS(0)):PRINT
140 :
150 'in the following loop the address of the interrupt-number is sensed.
160 'the BIOS-/DOS-Interrupt-number can be poked to this address.
170 :
180 FOR I= MP.START TO MP.ENDE:IF PEEK(I)= 205 THEN INT.ADR= I+1 ELSE NEXT
190 :
200 DOS.SN= MP.START
210 AL%=0: AH%=0: BL%=0: BH%=0: CL%=0: CH%=0: DL%=0: DH%=0: ES%=0: SI%=0: DI%=0:
    FLAGS%=0
220 :
230 INT.NR%= &H11 'BIOS-Call 11h/equipment
```

```
240 :
250 DEF SEG:POKE INT.ADR,INT.NR%
260 DEF SEG:CALL DOS.SN(AH%, AL%, BH%, BL%, CH%, CL%, DH%, DL%, ES%, SI%, DI%,
    FLAGS%)
270 :
280 'the result in Register AX contains the following INFO:
290 'AL (bits 00-07)
295 '    00 - Diskettes
300 '    01 - Free
305 '    02, 03 - RAM Banks  (1
310 '    04, 05 - Display Screen Mode  (2
315 '    06, 07 - Number of Diskettes  (3
325 '
330 'AH (bits 08-15)
335 '    08 - Free
340 '    09, 10, 11 - Number of RS232-C Interfaces  (4
345 '    12 - Joystick Adapter Available
350 '    13 - Free
355 '    14,15 - Number of Centronics Interfaces  (5
440 '
450 '(1 00= 1, 01= 2, 10= 3, 11= 4 RAM-Banks
460 '(2 01= COLOR 40*25, 10= COLOR 80*25, 11= MONOCHROME 80*25
470 '(3 00= 1, 01= 2, 10= 3, 11= 4 drives (only if Bit 0= 1
480 '(4 000= none, 001= 1, 010= 2, 100= 3 etc. V.24/RS232C-interfaces
490 '(5 00= none, 01= 1, 10= 2, 11= 3 CENTRONICS-interfaces
500 :
510 PRINT "INT $11 reports the following equipment: ":PRINT
520 PRINT "Number of disk drives:..... ";
530 IF AL% AND 1= 0 THEN PRINT "none":GOTO 580
540 IF (AL% AND 192)= 0 THEN PRINT "one"
550 IF (AL% AND 192)= 64 THEN PRINT "two"
560 IF (AL% AND 192)= 128 THEN PRINT "three"
570 IF (AL% AND 192)= 192 THEN PRINT "four"
580 PRINT "RAM-Banks.................: ";
590 IF (AL% AND 12)= 0 THEN PRINT "one"
600 IF (AL% AND 12)= 4 THEN PRINT "two"
610 IF (AL% AND 12)= 8 THEN PRINT "three"
620 IF (AL% AND 12)= 12 THEN PRINT "four"
630 PRINT "Monitor...................: ";
640 IF (AL% AND 48) = 0 THEN PRINT "not identifiable"
650 IF (AL% AND 48) = 16 THEN PRINT "COLOR 40*25"
660 IF (AL% AND 48) = 32 THEN PRINT "COLOR 80*25"
670 IF (AL% AND 48) = 48 THEN PRINT "MONOCHROME 80*25"
680 PRINT "number of RS232C.ports....: ";
690 IF (AH% AND 14)= 0 THEN PRINT "none"
700 IF (AH% AND 14)= 2 THEN PRINT "one"
710 IF (AH% AND 14)= 4 THEN PRINT "two"
720 IF (AH% AND 14)= 8 THEN PRINT "three"
730 PRINT "Number of Centronics ports: ";
740 IF (AH% AND 192)= 0 THEN PRINT "none"
750 IF (AH% AND 192)= 64 THEN PRINT "one"
760 IF (AH% AND 192)= 128 THEN PRINT "two"
770 IF (AH% AND 192)= 192 THEN PRINT "three"
```

```
780 :PRINT:PRINT
790 PRINT "a game adapter is ";:IF (AH% AND 12)= 0 THEN PRINT "not ";
800 PRINT "interfaced"
810 LOCATE 25,1,0:PRINT "Strike any key....."
820 IF INKEY$="" THEN 820
830 CLS:END
840 :
850 'data-lines from COM-file: dos_sn.com
860 :
870 RESTORE 890
880 DEF SEG:FOR I=1 TO  151:READ X:POKE MP.START+I-1,X: NEXT I
890 DATA 250, 85,139,236, 30,  6,139,118,  6,139,  4
900 DATA  80,157,139,118, 14,138, 20,139,118, 16,138
910 DATA  52,139,118, 18,138, 12,139,118, 20,138, 44
920 DATA 139,118, 22,138, 28,139,118, 24,138, 60,139
930 DATA 118, 26,138,  4,139,118, 28,138, 36,139,118
940 DATA   8,139, 60, 80,139,118, 12,139,  4,142,192
950 DATA  88,139,118, 10,139, 52, 85,251,205, 33,250
960 DATA  93, 86,156,139,118, 28,136, 36,139,118, 26
970 DATA 136,  4,139,118, 24,136, 60,139,118, 22,136
980 DATA  28,139,118, 20,136, 44,139,118, 18,136, 12
990 DATA 139,118, 16,136, 52,139,118, 14,136, 20, 88
1000 DATA 139,118,  6,137,  4, 88,139,118, 10,137,  4
1010 DATA 140,192,139,118, 12,137,  4,139,118,  8,137
1020 DATA  60,  7, 31, 93,251,202, 24,  0
1030 RETURN
```

As we already mentioned, in Chapter 8 you'll find a detailed description of the interface to DOS or BIOS. If you're not familiar with the assembler, you should read Chapter 8 to increase your understanding of this subject.

Note: Although directly reading the equipment flags to determine screen mode is easier than using INT 10h or INT 11h, if the flag address is modified (i.e., through a new BIOS), your program would no longer be compatible. So, it's better to use INT 11h, which simply reads the equipment flag and returns the result in AX. If the flag address is modified, this interrupt is also adjusted so that the compatibility of a program that uses this INT is always guaranteed.

11.1.1 Special Circumstances

So far we've learned how to determine whether a monochrome or color card is installed. This usually works for programs that operate in text mode. However, with graphic programs, additional information is needed. Not only the various resolutions, but also the maximum number of available colors must be considered. Based on the current hardware, the following information must be considered:

```
monochrome graphic     720*348 pixels, 2 colors
EGA graphic,           640*350 pixels, monochrome
CGA graphic,           320*200 pixels, 4 colors
CGA graphic,           640*200 pixels, 2 colors
EGA graphic,           640*350 pixels, 16 colors
```

Monochrome Cards

The methods we've described so far determine whether a monochrome card is installed, but they don't indicate whether it is:

1. a "normal" monochrome card (i.e. doesn't support graphics)
2. a Hercules card with 720*348 pixels
3. an EGA card in monochrome mode with 640*350 pixels

How can we determine which video card is used? Let's begin with the simplest case: the EGA card. In the BIOS data segment, at address &H0040:&H0088, there is a monitor flag that is only used by EGA cards (and the recent VGA card). When the computer is switched on, the EGA card tests which monitor is interfaced and stores the result in this flag. The monitors have the following values:

```
&H0040:0088= F9h: EGA- or MultiSync-monitor
&H0040:0088= F8h: CGA-monitor
&H0040:0088= FBh: monochrome-monitor
```

Since the other cards aren't able to determine which monitor is connected, the flag remains at 0 for them. The only thing you can do is test the flag for a value that doesn't equal 0. At zero it can be assumed that an EGA card isn't installed; it's only possible that an MDA or Hercules card is installed. If the flag is FBh, an EGA card in monochrome mode is installed and the resolution should be set for 640*350 pixels.

Differentiating between an MDA and Hercules card

Now the process becomes more complicated. Since MDA and Hercules cards are compatible, it's difficult to differentiate between them. The only difference on the bit level can be found in the status register &H03BA. The seventh bit isn't used by the MDA card. The Hercules card, however, always sets this bit to 0 when the vertical synchronization signal occurs (the cursor returns to the top of the screen after the last screen line is reached). So, periodically, it must be determined whether the seventh bit of the status register contains a value of 0 or 1.

If it does, a Hercules card is interfaced and the resolution is set to 720*348. Otherwise, an MDA card, which doesn't support graphics, is installed. In this case, an error message will appear.

The following program tests the seventh bit of the status register. This is done repeatedly, in a loop, because on a single access the seventh bit could contain a 0 by coincidence. The HGC variable is first set to 0. In the loop the status register is read and the seventh bit is tested. If it's determined that it's set, the HGC variable is set to 1. If the seventh bit was never set, the HGC variable remains 0:

```
10 '------------------------------------------
20 'MDA_HGC.BAS          1988 (c) H.J. Bomanns
30 '------------------------------------------
40 :
50 CLS:KEY OFF
60 PRINT "test MDA <-> Hercules executing ..."
70 HGC= 0
80 FOR I=1 TO 1000
90   X= INP(&H3BA)
100    IF (X AND &H80) <> 0 THEN HGC= 1
110 NEXT I
120 :
130 IF HGC= 1 THEN PRINT "HGC is installed " ELSE PRINT "no HGC found "
140 :PRINT:PRINT
```

Color Card

If it's determined, through interrupt 10h/11H or with the equipment flag, that a color card is installed, you still must determine whether a CGA or EGA card is used. Again we can use the monitor flags at address &H0040:&H0088. As we learned earlier, the value &HF9 is stored there for an EGA Multisync monitor or &HF8 for a normal CGA monitor.

Now this flag must be tested. If the values 0 or &HF8 are stored there, it can be assumed that either a CGA card is installed, or that a normal CGA monitor is interfaced to the installed EGA card. The resolution or the colors are set accordingly to 320*200 pixels with 4 colors or 640*200 pixels with 2 colors.

If the value &HF9 appears in this flag, an EGA card is installed and an EGA MultiSync monitor is interfaced. Resolution and colors are set according to the desired mode.

11.2   Fast Screen Display Construction

As we mentioned at the beginning of this chapter, PC-BASIC's screen construction is very slow. In this section we'll present ways to increase this speed.

You may be wondering why PC-BASIC is slow. Since PC-BASIC is an interpreter, every program line must be processed from beginning to end and the statements must be executed in the sequence in which they occur. For example, the execution of the following command:

```
PRINT A$(I)
```

requires the following steps:

1. Search a table for the PRINT statement.
2. Branch to the PRINT routine.
3. Call a parameter selection subroutine for selecting the parameter.
4. Determine the address of I and the value of I.
5. Determine the address of A$(I).
6. Determine the length of A$(I).
7. Loop for the output of the individual characters from A$(I).

Obviously, from these seven steps you can understand why PC-BASIC works at its slow pace, even for a simple command or statement.

A Faster Method

The only way to speed up this procedure is by using an assembler routine, called by CALL, that handles the output. First PRINT and then the DOS output routine must be bypassed. This can be achieved by sending the output directly into video RAM. However, remember that when using a color graphics card, video RAM access creates a flickering on the screen that should be prevented. The assignment of the routine can be described as follows:

> Display the string contents, at a certain position and with a certain display attribute, directly into video RAM. Ensure that flickering doesn't occur during this process.

This means that the routine must first calculate the position in video RAM on the basis of the line and column passed. Then it must calculate the length and address of the string and write the individual characters from the string, with the display attributes, into video RAM. The flickering always occurs when the 8088/8086 CPU and the 6845 graphic chip simultaneously operate in RAM. Let's look at the assembler listing:

```
;-------------------------------------------------------
; FASTSCRN.ASM
;-------------------------------------------------------
; Assembler-Routine for fast output of a String
; through direct writing into the display-storage.
; To prevent flickering synchronization is used.
;-------------------------------------------------------
;
;CALL:
;-------
;
;   CALL FASTSCRN(LINE%,ROW%,ATTR%,STRING$)
;
;The addresses of the Variables are stored on the Stack during CALL as follows:
;
;   STRING$ SP+6,   ATTR% SP+8,   ROW% SP+10,   LINE%  SP+12
;
;
program   segment para 'CODE'
          assume cs:program

fastscrn  proc   far
          push   bp               ;store Basepointer of GW
          mov    bp,sp            ;Stackpointer --> Basepointer
          push   ds               ;store call-DS
          push   es               ;store call-ES

          mov    si,[bp+12]       ;storage-address LINE%
          mov    bl,[si]          ;value to BL, multiply current line
          mov    al,160d          ;by 160
          mul    bl               ;line*160
          sub    ax,160d          ;deduct 160
          push   ax               ;store result in AX
          mov    si,[bp+10]       ;storage-address ROW%
          mov    bl,[si]          ;value to BL, current column
          mov    al,2             ;multiply by 2
          mul    bl               ;column*2, result in AX
          pop    bx               ;restore result line*160
          add    ax,bx            ;add
          dec    ax
          dec    ax               ;deduct 2
          push   ax               ;store for later

          mov    si,[bp+8]        ;storage-address ATTR%
          mov    ah,[si]          ;for STOSW in AH

          mov    si,[bp+6]        ;storage-address String-Descriptor
          mov    cl,[si]          ;length of the string
          mov    ch,0             ;for LOOP in CX
          mov    si,[si+1]        ;address of the String
                                  ;remains for LODSB in SI
```

(handwritten annotations in margin, left column:)
8₇
139-236
30
6
139-118-12
138-28
176-160
246-227
45-160
0   80
139-118-10
138-28
176-2
296
229
92-3
196-12
72
80
139-118-8
138-36
139-118-6
138-12
81-0
139-116-1

(handwritten, bottom:) 80   push AX   store for later

```
            80 push    ax              ;retain for later
191-0 -176     mov     di,0B000h       ;Segment-address Video-RAM Mono
179-0          mov     bl,0            ;Flag for Synchro-no
205            int     11h             ;get Equipment-Flag
17-37          and     ax,30h          ;test Bit 4 and 5
               cmp     ax,30h          ;monochrome-card ?
               je      Mono            ;if yes, is B000h OK
               add     di,0800h        ;else add 0800h for Color-RAM
               mov     bl,1            ;Flag for Synchro-yes
Mono:          mov     es,di           ;Segment-address must be in ES for STOSW
               pop     ax              ;restore AX with Attribute
               pop     di              ;restore value from (line*160)+(column*2)-2
                                       ;as Offset in the display-storage for output
               cld                     ;DIRECTION= forward
               mov     dx,03DAh        ;6845 Status-Port

Wait1:         cmp     bl,0            ;output on monochrome?
               je      WithoutSynchro  ;if yes, no Synchro required
               in      al,dx           ;else: read status of 6845
               rcr     al,1            ;check RETRACE
               jb      Wait1          ;wait if necessary
               cli
Wait2:         in      al,dx           ;as above
               rcr     al,1
               jnb     Wait2
WithoutSynchro:
               lodsb                   ;load individual character from String in AL
               sti
               stosw                   ;and write in display
               loop    Wait1           ;continue until CX= 0

            81 pop     es              ;call-ES from Stack
            93 pop     ds              ;call-DS from Stack
           202 pop     bp              ;call-BP from Stack
             8 ret     8               ;clean Stack and return
                                       ;to GW-BASIC

 0   fastscrn  endp
               program ends
               end
```

During the call, all the important registers are first saved to the stack with PUSH. In PC-BASIC the call and variable passing are performed with the CALL command. The interpreter routine passes the variables in such a way that, for each variable, a pointer (offset address) to the memory address, in which the value is stored, is brought to the stack. Then, on the basis of these pointers, the contents of the passed variables are read from the stack and processed.

This is really the calculation of the address, in video RAM, from which the output should be made. This occurs on the basis of the ROW% and COL% variables. Since a character in video RAM is composed of the ASCII code and an attribute byte, a complete line is 160 characters long. So, in order to calculate the column position, multiply by 2.

330

After the address has been calculated, the output can begin. The address of the string descriptors, which had been stored there during CALL, is read from the stack. The first byte of the descriptor, which contains the string length, is loaded into the CL register for terminating the loop. The following bytes of the descriptor represent the offset, within the data segment, for the characters of the string and are loaded, for addressing, into the source register SI. The destination register DI is loaded with the result of the line/column calculation.

Through interrupt 11h, the equipment flag is obtained and bits 4 and 5 are tested. If it's determined that a color card is installed, the value &H0800 is added to the value of &HB000 in the DI register in order to correctly address the video RAM. The result is then loaded into the segment register ES and DI is loaded, with POP, with the result of the line/column calculation.

The output is performed with a loop containing the LODSB and STOSW commands. LODSB loads a single character from the memory location, indicated by register DS:SI, into the AL register. The AH register always contains the attribute, which was read from the stack out of the ATTR% variable. STOSW writes the character attribute, in the AX register, to the memory location addressed with register ES:DI.

A test is performed if BL = 0. If it is, a monochrome card is installed and a synchronization isn't required. If BL = 1, a synchronization is performed.

Synchronization for CGA

To prevent flickering during color adapter output in video RAM, *synchronization* is needed. This flickering always occurs when both the 8088/86 CPU and the 6845 video chip try to access the data bus at the same time. Synchronization simply waits until the video chip doesn't access the data bus. Exactly at that moment, data is written directly into video RAM. After completing the loop, the saved registers are read from the stack and the normal program returns. The stack must be corrected on the basis of the existing variable pointers. The parameter to be passed to the RET instruction can be calculated according to the following formula:

```
Number of variables*2
```

This parameter is added to the stack pointer SP before the return jump. Because of this, the SP points to the correct return jump address.

In a monochrome card, flickering doesn't occur during direct writing into video RAM. However, we couldn't find out why this happens. According to the descriptions, the operation of the 6845 is the same on both cards. So, a monochrome card doesn't require synchronization.

Note: To be able to execute the following program correctly, PC-BASIC must be called with the parameter /M as follows:

```
GWBASIC /M:54000
```

The program first POKEs the assembler routine into a memory range PC-BASIC reserves thus preventing overwriting files, etc. A normal PC-BASIC output appears first with the time required for the display to execute. After striking a key you'll see the FASTSCRN output execute. Although the time may differ, depending on computer type, clock speed and CPU, you can see that the assembler routine is about 100 times faster than normal.

11 FASTSCN. BAS

```
10 '--------------------------------------------------------------
20 'FASTSCRN.BAS program for fast display-output    1986 (C) H.J.Bomanns
30 '--------------------------------------------------------------
40 :
50 'Outputs a String at the position indicated (line,column) with the
60 'indicated Attributes. For output on a COLOR-monitor, a
70 'synchronization to prevent flickering is included.
80 :
90 CLS:KEY OFF:DIM A$(25)
100 LOCATE 5,5:PRINT "initialize machine-program ....."
110 MP.START= &HE000
120 GOSUB 310 'poke machine language routine into memory
130 MP.ENDE= MP.START+I-1
140 FASTSCRN= MP.START
150 :
160 FOR I=1 TO 24:A$(I)= STRING$(80,64+I):NEXT
170 :
180 CLS:A1= TIMER
190 FOR I=1 TO 24:PRINT A$(I);:NEXT I
200 A2= TIMER:LOCATE 25,1:PRINT USING "normal output: ##.## seconds    Strike any
    key to view FASTSCRN display";A2-A1;
210 IF INKEY$="" THEN 210
220 :
230 CLS:A1= TIMER
240 FOR I= 1 TO 24:ROWNO%=I:COLMNO%=1:ATTR%= 11
250 DEF SEG:CALL FASTSCRN(ROWNO%,COLMNO%,ATTR%,A$(I))
260 NEXT I
270 A2= TIMER:LOCATE 25,1:PRINT USING "output with FASTSCRN: ##.## seconds";A2-
    A1;
280 IF INKEY$="" THEN 280
290 CLS:END
300 :
310 'data-lines from COM-file: fastscrn.com
320 :
330 RESTORE 350
340 DEF SEG:FOR I=1 TO 105:READ X:POKE MP.START+I-1,X: NEXT I
350 DATA  85,139,236, 30,  6,139,118, 12,138, 28,176
360 DATA 160,246,227, 45,160,  0, 80,139,118, 10,138
370 DATA  28,176,  2,246,227, 91,  3,195, 72, 72, 80
380 DATA 139,118,  8,138, 36,139,118,  6,138, 12,181
```

```
390 DATA    0,139,116,   1, 80,191,   0,176,179,   0,205
400 DATA   17, 37, 48,   0, 61, 48,   0,116,   6,129,199
410 DATA    0,  8,179,   1,142,199, 88, 95,252,186,218
420 DATA    3,128,251,   0,116, 11,236,208,216,114,246
430 DATA  250,236,208,216,115,251,172,251,171,226,235
440 DATA    7, 31, 93,202,  8,  0
450 RETURN
```

To use this routine in your own programs, you need the DATA loader, starting at line 310. Before calling this loader, the MP.START variable must receive the address, from which the routine will execute later. Remember that important data areas of MS-DOS will be overwritten and the system may crash. Also, the FASTSCRN variable, which is required for CALL, must have the same assigned address. If this isn't done, the starting address of the routine will be assumed as address "0". This can also cause MS-DOS data areas to be overwritten and a system crash. Finally, the call variables must be initialized. Only integer variables can be used for numeric values.

Screen Display Construction through BLOAD

If you still don't want to work with assembler routines, you could use BLOAD. However, you will only be able to speed up the construction of templates and/or menus. Other data will be sent to the display at the usual speed.

BLOAD loads a file into a reserved area of main memory:

```
DEF SEG= &HB000
BLOAD "MAIN.MNU",0
```

This file could, for example, be the contents of the display. Chapter 9 contains a simple template/menu generator, which can be used to create such a file. We'll use an example to demonstrate this. Suppose that you have an application with four templates the generator creates: one for the menu; one for data input and output; one for printing the listing; and one for deleting. Within the program, call a subroutine that loads a template with BLOAD. The template name is derived from the menu choice and the main menu is at the beginning.

In a PC with a monochrome card (MDA), you must load the four templates individually as needed. The monochrome card only has enough memory for one display page. A color graphics card offers a total of four display pages at a time. You can load all four templates at the start of the program:

```
10 DEF SEG= &HB800: BLOAD "MAINMNU.MSK",0
20 DEF SEG= &HB900: BLOAD "IN_OUT.MSK",0
30 DEF SEG= &HBA00: BLOAD "LIST.MSK",0
40 DEF SEG= &HBB00: BLOAD "DELETE.MSK",0
```

In the program you can easily switch between the templates by using the SCREEN command:

```
55 SCREEN ,,0 'main-menu
...
160 SCREEN ,,1 'input-output
etc.
```

or the following:

```
10 MAIN.MENU= 0
11 IN.OUT= 1
12 LIST= 2
13 DELETE= 3
...
...
55 SCREEN,,MAIN.MENU
...
160 SCREEN ,,IN.OUT
```

However, problems can occur. Once we tried to develop a similar program where four templates were loaded at the beginning of the program. Everything worked fine providing the individual templates were called immediately after the start of the program. Once the program was running (i.e., data was being input, processed and output) the problem occurred and, after switching, only empty displays were visible. Sometimes only the last display was visible and at other times it was the last two or three displays. But the first, which was the main display, was never visible. So, be sure to thoroughly test your program before calling it complete.

11.3   Saving/Restoring the Screen Display

While using professional programs you have probably noticed how error or other messages appear in separate windows and then the previous display is restored. You can use this capability in your own programs for error messages, input prompts or help text.

As usual, when speed is important, an assembler routine must be used. In Section 11.2 we presented a routine for fast screen display construction. However, we still need a routine that stores the current screen contents and, after the message or prompt has been displayed, restores the screen contents.

The biggest problem is where to save the current screen contents. On a PC with a color graphics card, one of the available screen pages can be used. However, if you're using several screen pages, one of these must always be used for memory. Since only one screen page is available, this method can't be used on a PC with a monochrome card. While developing the assembler routine, we made sure that the screen contents were stored in a normal integer array.

Unlike the color card, using an array to store screen contents enables you to store several screens at once. This type of array can be saved on a diskette or the hard disk and read at any time.

First we'll examine the assembler routine in detail and then the demo program. Then we'll present some general explanations. The following is the assembler listing:

```
;-----------------------------------------------------
; BS_STORE.ASM
; Assembler-Routine for storing the current
; display in an intermediate-buffer or the restoration
; of the display from there.
;-----------------------------------------------------
;
;CALL:
;-------
;
;   CALL SAVESCRN(BUFFER%)
;
program   segment para 'CODE'
          assume cs:program

          jmp    Savescrn

Restscrn  proc   far

          push   bp              ;store Basepointer of GW
          mov    bp,sp           ;Stackpointer --> Basepointer
          push   ds              ;store call-DS
```

```
                push    es              ;store call-ES
                ;
                mov     si,[bp+6]       ;storage-address BUFFER%
                mov     ax,[si]         ;value in AX
                mov     si,ax           ;for LODSW in SI, Segment is DS
                ;
                mov     di,0B000h       ;Segment Video-RAM Mono
                mov     bl,0            ;Flag for Synchro-No
                int     11h             ;get Equipment-Flag
                and     ax,30h          ;test Bit 4 and 5
                cmp     ax,30h          ;Is it a monochrome-card?
                je      Mono            ;if yes, default-values OK
                add     di,0800h        ;Video-RAM Color is B800h
                mov     bl,1            ;Flag for Synchro-Yes
Mono:
                mov     es,di           ;For STOSW in ES
                xor     di,di
                ;
                jmp     S_1             ;continue at Savescrn
Restscrn        endp

Savescrn        proc    far

                push    bp              ;store Basepointer of GW
                mov     bp,sp           ;Stackpointer --> Basepointer
                push    ds              ;store call-DS
                push    es              ;store call-ES
                ;
                mov     si,[bp+6]       ;storage-address BUFFER%
                mov     ax,[si]         ;value in AX
                mov     di,ax           ;for STOSW in DI
                push    ds
                pop     es              ;data segment BUFFER% in ES
                ;
                mov     si,0B000h       ;Segment Video-RAM Mono
                mov     bl,0            ;Flag for Synchro-No
                int     11h             ;get Equipment-Flag
                and     ax,30h          ;test Bit 4 and 5
                cmp     ax,30h          ;Is it a monochrome-card?
                je      Mono1           ;if yes, default-values OK
                add     si,0800h        ;Video-RAM Color is B800h
                mov     bl,1            ;Flag for Synchro-Yes
Mono1:
                mov     ds,si           ;for LODSW in DS
                xor     si,si

S_1:            mov     cx,2000         ;2000 characters/Attribute
                cld                     ;DIRECTION= forward
                mov     dx,03DAh        ;6845 Status-Port

Wait1:
                cmp     bl,0            ;is it a monochrome-card?
                je      WithoutSynchro  ;if yes, no Synchro required
```

```
                in      al,dx          ;else, read Status of the 6845
                rcr     al,1           ;check RETRACE
                jb      Wait1          ;wait if necessary
                cli
Wait2:          in      al,dx          ;as above
                rcr     al,1
                jnb     Wait2
WithoutSynchro:
                lodsw                  ;load characters and Attribute in AX
                sti
                stosw                  ;and write into buffer
                loop    Wait1          ;until CX= 0

                pop     es             ;call-ES from Stack
                pop     ds             ;call-DS from Stack
                pop.    bp             ;call-BP from Stack
                ret     2              ;back to GW-BASIC,
                                       ;clean Stack
Savescrn        endp

                program   ends
                end
```

How this routine works

The assembler routine consists of two parts. In the SAVESCRN part, the current screen contents are stored in an array. The RESTSCRN part displays, on the screen, the contents of the buffer variable. Within the PROCs, the registers BP, ES and DS are first saved on the stack because they are partially altered or must have their original contents after completion. Then the offset of the buffer variable is loaded from the stack into the destination or source register DI or SI. The segment registers DS and ES, which are needed for the data transfer, are initialized. For this the equipment flag is read through interrupt 11h. If the test reveals that a color card is installed, 0800h is added to B000h and the BL flag is set to 1 for the synchronization.

For SAVESCRN the source segment must correspond to the video RAM segment. The current value is loaded into the DS register. The destination segment corresponds to the data segment of PC-BASIC/BASICA and is initialized by pushing DS in ES.

For RESTSCRN the opposite is needed. Here the destination segment is initialized with the segment of the video RAM and the current value is loaded into the ES register. The source segment corresponds to the data segment of PC-BASIC/BASICA. Therefore, the DS register remains unchanged. Then a jump occurs to the PROC SAVESCRN because the transmission of data from the buffer to the screen can occur through the same synchronization or output routine.

Through this routine, the characters or attributes are transmitted from the video RAM to the buffer variable, or from there to the screen. Since this was already explained in Section 11.2, we won't discuss it again. After all characters or attributes have been transmitted, the

BP, ES and DS registers are returned from the stack again and the routine is terminated through RET.

The following is the demo program:

Note: To execute the following program correctly, call PC-BASIC with the /M switch as follows:

```
GWBASIC /M:54000
```

```
10 '-------------------------------------------------
20 'BS_STORE.BAS                    1986 (C) H.J.Bomanns
30 '-------------------------------------------------
40 :
50 'SAVESCRN stores the current display in a buffer. Then
60 'messages etc. can be output in a window. Afterwards the display
70 'can be restored again with RESTSCRN.
80 :
90 CLS:KEY OFF:DIM A$(25),BUFFER%(2000)
100 LOCATE 5,5:PRINT "initialize machine-program ....."
110 MP.START= &HE000
120 GOSUB 410
130 SAVESCRN= MP.START
140 RESTSCRN= MP.START+3
150 :
160 FOR I=1 TO 24: A$(I)= STRING$(80,64+I):NEXT I
170 :
180 CLS
190 COLOR 11,0:FOR I= 1 TO 24:PRINT A$(I);:NEXT I:COLOR 12,0
200 :
210 DEF SEG:BUFFER.OFS%= VARPTR(BUFFER%(0)):CALL SAVESCRN(BUFFER.OFS%)
220 :
230 CLS
240 LOCATE 12,1
250 PRINT "The preceding screen was stored. This is a test message...."
260 PRINT
270 PRINT "Strike any key to make the previous display reappear....."
280 :
290 IF INKEY$="" THEN 290
300 :
310 DEF SEG:BUFFER.OFS%= VARPTR(BUFFER%(0)):CALL RESTSCRN(BUFFER.OFS%)
320 :
330 LOCATE 12,1
340 PRINT "This is the previous screen....."
350 PRINT
360 PRINT "Strike any key to quit....."
370 :
380 IF INKEY$="" THEN 380
390 COLOR 7,0:CLS:END
400 :
410 'data-lines from COM-file: bs_store.com
```

```
420 :
430 RESTORE 450
440 DEF SEG:FOR I=1 TO  116:READ X:POKE MP.START+I-1,X: NEXT I
450 DATA 235, 41,144, 85,139,236, 30,  6,139,118,  6
460 DATA 139,  4,139,240,191,  0,176,179,  0,205, 17
470 DATA  37, 48,  0, 61, 48,  0,116,  6,129,199,  0
480 DATA   8,179,  1,142,199, 51,255,235, 40,144, 85
490 DATA 139,236, 30,  6,139,118,  6,139,  4,139,248
500 DATA  30,  7,190,  0,176,179,  0,205, 17, 37, 48
510 DATA   0, 61, 48,  0,116,  6,129,198,  0,  8,179
520 DATA   1,142,222, 51,246,185,208,  7,252,186,218
530 DATA   3,128,251,  0,116, 11,236,208,216,114,246
540 DATA 250,236,208,216,115,251,173,251,171,226,235
550 DATA   7, 31, 93,202,  2,  0
560 RETURN
```

This program demonstrates how the SAVE and RESTSCRN routines are used. Once the program begins, the machine program is POKEd into memory (line 100 to 140, subroutine starting at line 410). After line 160, a test screen is constructed and stored in line 210. After this screen is cleared in the lines 230-290 and some text is displayed, the original screen is output again in line 310. After line 330, a termination message is displayed and the program ends.

To include this in your own program, you need the data loader in lines 110 to 140 and the subroutine that starts at line 410. You must also dimension an integer array BUFFER% with at least 2,000 elements. In an integer array, every element can store 2 bytes. We need space for 2,000 characters and their attributes - a total of 4,000 characters in memory. As demonstrated in line 210 or 310, the call of the two routines can occur at any location in your program.

Saving or Restoring Several Screen Displays

In the previous example program, only one screen content was saved and restored again. Depending on the available space, you can also save and restore several screen displays.

As we already mentioned, an area of 4,000 bytes or 2,000 integers is required for each screen. In most applications usually no more than four screens must be saved. For most programs you should first save the main menu, after a menu option is selected. The menu doesn't have to be constructed again once the function is complete. Then save a screen for the display of a selection. For example, if a filename should be entered in a field, the template is saved and various files are displayed. Once a file is selected, the template is quickly restored and the input can continue. The third screen must be saved when help is requested during a selection. In the array there are three screens for the main menu, the input template and the selection window. The fourth screen display is used as a reserve or in case an error message needs to be displayed inside the help feature.

A read error could occur at this time. In this case, the current display is saved in the fourth screen and the error message is displayed. The following is a demo program that generates four screens, saves them and then restores them again sequentially.

Note: To execute the following program correctly, you must call PC-BASIC with the /M switch as follows:

```
GWBASIC /M:54000
```

```
10 '-------------------------------------------------
20 'BS_STOR1.BAS              1986 (C) H.J.Bomanns
30 '-------------------------------------------------
40 :
50 'SAVESCRN stores the current display-screen in a buffer. Then
60 'messages etc. can be output in a window. Afterwards the display-
70 'content can be restored with RESTSCRN. This program demonstrates
80 'the control of several display-screens.
90 :
100 CLS:KEY OFF:DIM A$(25),BUFFER%(2000*4)
110 LOCATE 5,5:PRINT "initialize machine-program ....."
120 MP.START= &HE000
130 GOSUB 390
140 SAVESCRN= MP.START
150 RESTSCRN= MP.START+3
160 :
170 FOR BS= 0 TO 3
180    CLS
190    FOR I=1 TO 24
200      A$(I)= "display-screen number: "+STR$(BS+1)+STRING$(50,"x")
210      PRINT A$(I);
220    NEXT I
230    DEF SEG:BUFFER.OFS%= VARPTR(BUFFER%(BS*2000)):CALL SAVESCRN(BUFFER.OFS%)
240 NEXT BS
250 :
260 CLS:COLOR 15,6: PRINT " ... Strike any key for restoration ... "
270 IF INKEY$="" THEN 270
280 :
290 FOR BS= 3 TO 0 STEP -1
300    DEF SEG:BUFFER.OFS%= VARPTR(BUFFER%(BS*2000)):CALL RESTSCRN(BUFFER.OFS%)
310    LOCATE 5,17:PRINT "... strike any key for next display ..."
320    IF INKEY$= "" THEN 320
330 NEXT BS
340 :
350 LOCATE 15,21:PRINT "... strike any key for END ....."
360 IF INKEY$="" THEN 360
370 COLOR 7,0:CLS:END
380 :
390 'data-lines from COM-file: bs_store.com
400 :
410 RESTORE 430
420 DEF SEG:FOR I=1 TO  116:READ X:POKE MP.START+I-1,X: NEXT I
```

```
430 DATA 235, 41,144, 85,139,236, 30,  6,139,118,  6
440 DATA 139,  4,139,240,191,  0,176,179,  0,205, 17
450 DATA  37, 48,  0, 61, 48,  0,116,  6,129,199,  0
460 DATA   8,179,  1,142,199, 51,255,235, 40,144, 85
470 DATA 139,236, 30,  6,139,118,  6,139,  4,139,248
480 DATA  30,  7,190,  0,176,179,  0,205, 17, 37, 48
490 DATA   0, 61, 48,  0,116,  6,129,198,  0,  8,179
500 DATA   1,142,222, 51,246,185,208,  7,252,186,218
510 DATA   3,128,251,  0,116, 11,236,208,216,114,246
520 DATA 250,236,208,216,115,251,173,251,171,226,235
530 DATA   7, 31, 93,202,  2,  0
540 RETURN
```

This program works similar to the previous demo program, BS_STORE.BAS. In this program, four screens are generated, saved and restored in a loop.

It's best to use subroutines to control the SAVESCRN and RESTSCRN routines, which save (SAVESCRN) and restore (RESTSCRN) the current display on the basis of a counter:

```
50 DIM BUFFER%(8000)
110 CUR.SCRN= 0    'current display-screen
120 MAX.SCRN= 3    'maximum number of screens (0-3= 4) to be stored
500 '----- store current display-screen -----
510 :
520 DEF SEG:BUFFER.OFS%= VARPTR(BUFFER%(CUR.SCRN*2000)): CALL
    SAVESCRN(BUFFER.OFS%)
530 CUR.SCRN= CUR.SCRN+1 'current counter plus one for next SAVE
540 RETURN
550 :
560 '----- restore last display-screen -----
570 :
580 IF CUR.SCRN= 0 THEN RETURN 'last display is already displayed
590 CUR.SCRN= CUR.SCRN-1 'reset to last display-screen
600 DEF SEG:BUFFER.OFS%= VARPTR(BUFFER%(CUR.SCRN*2000)): CALL
    RESTSCRN(BUFFER.OFS%)
610 RETURN
620 .....
```

11.4   The Screen Manager

In this section we'll discuss how to use the routines for fast screen output and the routines for saving and restoring screens.

To do this the assembler routines were combined into one program, called SCREEN.ASM. The routines don't have to be loaded separately. Let's look at the assembler program. It isn't much different than the routines described in the previous sections. However, there is an important item concerning combining assembler routines, which we'll discuss shortly. The following is the listing:

```
;----------------------------------------------------
; SCREEN.ASM
;----------------------------------------------------
; combination routine for fast output of a String
; by direct writing into the display screen storage and the
; storing or restoring of display screens. Synchronization is
; used to prevent flickering,
;----------------------------------------------------
;
;CALL:
;-------
;   CALL FASTSCRN(LINE%,ROW%,ATTR%,STRING$)
;
;The addresses of the Variables are stored on the Stack
; as follows during the CALL:
;
;   STRING$ SP+6,   ATTR% SP+8,   ROW% SP+10,   LINE% SP+12
;
;CALL:
;--------
;   CALL SAVESCRN(BUFFER%)
;   CALL RESTSCRN(BUFFER%)
;
;The addresses of the Variables are stored on the Stack
;as  follows during the CALL:
;
;   BUFFER% SP+6
;----------------------------
program   segment para 'CODE'
          assume cs:program

          jmp     Half_Distance
          jmp     RestScrn
;----------------------------
FastScrn  proc    far

          push    bp              ;store Basepointer from GW
          mov     bp,sp           ;Stackpointer --> Basepointer
          push    ds              ;store call-DS
```

```
          push    es                  ;store call-ES

          mov     si,[bp+12]          ;storage-address LINE%
          mov     bl,[si]             ;value to BL, current line
          mov     al,160d             ;multiply with 160
          mul     bl                  ;line*160
          sub     ax,160d             ;subtract 160
          push    ax                  ;store result in AX
          mov     si,[bp+10]          ;storage-address ROW%
          mov     bl,[si]             ;value to BL, current column
          mov     al,2                ;multiply by 2
          mul     bl                  ;column*2, result in AX
          pop     bx                  ;restore result line*160
          add     ax,bx               ;Add
          dec     ax
          dec     ax                  ;subtract 2
          push    ax                  ;store for later

          mov     si,[bp+8]           ;storage-address ATTR%
          mov     ah,[si]             ;occurs before STOSW in AH

          mov     si,[bp+6]           ;storage-address String-Descriptor
          mov     cl,[si]             ;length of the String
          mov     ch,0                ;for LOOP in CX
          mov     si,[si+1]           ;address of the String
                                      ;remains for LODSB in SI

          push    ax                  ;retain for later
          mov     di,0B000h           ;Segment-address Video-RAM Mono
          mov     bl,0                ;Flag for Synchro-No
          int     11h                 ;get Equipment-Flag
          and     ax,30h              ;test Bit 4 and 5
          cmp     ax,30h              ;monochrome-card present ?
          je      Mono0               ;if yes, is B000h OK
          add     di,0800h            ;else add 0800h for Color-RAM
          mov     bl,1                ;Flag for Synchro-Yes
Mono0:    mov     es,di               ;Segment-address must be for STOSW in ES
          pop     ax                  ;restore AX with Attribute
          pop     di                  ;restore value of (line*160)+(column*2)-2
                                      ;as Offset into the display-storage for output
          cld                         ;DIRECTION= forward
          mov     dx,03DAh            ;6845 Status-Port
Wait0a:   cmp     bl,0                ;output on monochrome?
          je      WithoutSynchro0     ;if yes, no synchro required
          in      al,dx               ;else, read Status of the 6845
          rcr     al,1                ;check RETRACE
          jb      Wait0a              ;wait if necessary
          cli
Wait0b:   in      al,dx               ;as above
          rcr     al,1
          jnb     Wait0b
WithoutSynchro0:
          lodsb                       ;load single characters from the String into AL
```

```
                sti
                stosw             ;and write into display
                loop    Wait0a    ;until CX= 0
                pop     es        ;call-ES from Stack
                pop     ds        ;call-DS from Stack
                pop     bp        ;call-BP from Stack
                ret     8         ;return to GW-BASIC,
                                  ;and clean Stack

FastScrn  endp
;-----------------------------
Half_Distance:  jmp SaveScrn
;-----------------------------
RestScrn  proc    far

                push    bp        ;store Basepointer from GW
                mov     bp,sp     ;Stackpointer --> Basepointer
                push    ds        ;store call-DS
                push    es        ;store call-ES
                ;
                mov     si,[bp+6] ;storage-address BUFFER%
                mov     ax,[si]   ;value in AX
                mov     si,ax     ;for LODSW in SI, Segment is DS
                ;
                mov     di,0B000h ;Segment Video-RAM Mono
                mov     bl,0      ;Flag for Synchro-No
                int     11h       ;get Equipment-Flag
                and     ax,30h    ;test Bit 4 and 5
                cmp     ax,30h    ;is it a monochrome-card?
                je      Mono1     ;if yes, default-values OK
                add     di,0800h  ;Video-RAM Color is B800h
                mov     bl,1      ;Flag for Synchro-Yes
Mono1:
                mov     es,di     ;for STOSW in ES
                xor     di,di
                jmp     S_1       ;continue at Savescrn

RestScrn  endp
;-----------------------------
SaveScrn  proc    far

                push    bp        ;store Basepointer from GW
                mov     bp,sp     ;Stackpointer --> Basepointer
                push    ds        ;store call-DS
                push    es        ;store call-ES
                ;
                mov     si,[bp+6] ;storage-address BUFFER%
                mov     ax,[si]   ;value in AX
                mov     di,ax     ;for STOSW in DI
                push    ds
                pop     es        ;data segment BUFFER% in ES
                ;
                mov     si,0B000h ;Segment Video-RAM Mono
```

```
                mov     bl,0              ;Flag for Synchro-No
                int     11h               ;get Equipment-Flag
                and     ax,30h            ;test Bit 4 and 5
                cmp     ax,30h            ;is it a monochrome-card?
                je      Mono2             ;if yes, default-values OK
                add     si,0800h          ;Video-RAM Color   B800h
                mov     bl,1              ;Flag for Synchro-Yes
Mono2:
                mov     ds,si             ;for LODSW in DS
                xor     si,si

S_1:            mov     cx,2000           ;2000 characters/Attribute
                cld                       ;DIRECTION= forward
                mov     dx,03DAh          ;6845 Status-Port

Wait1a:         cmp     bl,0              ;is it a monochrome-card?
                je      WithoutSynchro1   ;if yes, no synchro required
                in      al,dx             ;else, read status of the 6845
                rcr     al,1              ;check RETRACE
                jb      Wait1a            ;wait if necessary
                cli
Wait1b:         in      al,dx             ;as above
                rcr     al,1
                jnb     Wait1b
WithoutSynchro1:
                lodsw                     ;load characters and Attributes in AX
                sti
                stosw                     ;and write in buffer
                loop    Wait1a            ;until CX= 0

                pop     es                ;call-ES from Stack
                pop     ds                ;call-DS from Stack
                pop     bp                ;call-BP from Stack
                ret     2                 ;return to GW-BASIC and
                                          ;clean Stack

SaveScrn  endp
;----------------------------
program  ends
         end
```

You've probably noticed a small difference in this routine. At the beginning you see the following:

```
JMP Half_Distance
```

Then at this label you see:

```
JMP SaveScrn
```

We know that an assembler routine must exist without direct jumps (FAR JUMPs) and without direct references to variables. Otherwise the routine cannot properly execute in the PC-BASIC memory. Only short jumps (NEAR JUMPs) can be used because they indicate, for the JUMP, the distance, in bytes, of the command to which the jump should be made, instead of its direct address. So this routine can be located at any place in memory. The distance isn't changed by a different start address.

The distance from the current command to the destination command can only be within a certain area. This distance is 128 bytes after or 127 before the current command. Otherwise a FAR JUMP, which isn't possible under PC-BASIC, is required. This area is used because only one byte is available for the "distance measurement". The processor doesn't provide more memory for this. In this byte, the seventh bit is used as a direction indicator. If this bit is set, the jump is in the direction of the program start. If the bit isn't set, the jump will be in the direction of the program end.

If too many routines (or large routines) are stored between the start point and the routine, to which the jump will be made, a NEAR JUMP cannot be executed. A trick must be used to "hopscotch" one or more "half_distances", which aren't more than the permitted 127 or 128 bytes apart. In this way, the NEAR JUMPs reach the desired routine.

We need to discuss one thing before concluding our discussion of combining assembler routines. As you may know, by adding SHORT, jumps can be forced by the assembler as a two byte code. Without SHORT the assembler always generates three bytes: one for the opcode of JMP, one for the distance and one for a NOP. So FAR JUMPs can occur in the current segment or from the current segment into another segment. A JUMP in the segment only needs 2 bytes, since the segment is only 64 Kbytes. If the assembler determines that the jump occurs inside the segment and the distance is less than 128 or 127 bytes, it generates a pseudo short jump. The highbyte of the destination address is replaced by the NOP. In a "real" SHORT, only the opcode and the distance are translated into code. This is important for assigning the jump addresses to the variables for CALL:

```
80 SAVESCRN= MP.START
90 RESTSCRN= MP.START+3
100 FASTSCRN= MP.START+6
```

Notice that in line 90 and 100 three bytes per JUMP are always considered. If you indicated a SHORT before the JMPs in the assembler program, only two bytes must be considered. It should appear as follows:

```
80 SAVESCRN= MP.START
90 RESTSCRN= MP.START+2
100 FASTSCRN= MP.START+4
```

All the routines in an application

This screen manager can be used in an application, as demonstrated in the following program:

```
10 '-----------------------------------------------------------------
20 'SCREEN.BAS Demonstration of the combination of the routines FastScrn,
   SaveScrn, RestScrn
30 '-----------------------------------------------------------------
40 :
50 CLS:KEY OFF:FOR I=1 TO 10:KEY I,"":NEXT I
60 MP.START= &HE000
70 GOSUB 990 'initialize MP
80 SAVESCRN= MP.START
90 RESTSCRN= MP.START+3
100 FASTSCRN= MP.START+6
110 MAX.SCRN= 3
120 DIM BUFFER%(2000*MAX.SCRN)
130 CUR.SCRN= 0
140 CLS
150 :
160 M$(1)="  _____  "
170 M$(2)="|                         |"
180 M$(3)="|  [I]= input data        |"
190 M$(4)="|  [C]= display/change    |"
200 M$(5)="|  [P]= print list        |"
210 M$(6)="|  [X]= exit              |"
220 M$(7)="|_____|"
230 M$(8)="                           "
240 :
250 COLMNO%= 5: COLR%= 7
260 FOR I%= 5 TO 12
270   DEF SEG:CALL FASTSCRN(I%,COLMNO%,COLR%,M$(I%-4))
280 NEXT I%
290 :
300 LOCATE 25,1:PRINT "Strike [I] for 'input data ' or [X] for 'exit'...";SPACE$(80-
    POS(0));
310 LOCATE 12,20,1
320 X$= INKEY$:IF X$="" THEN 320
330 IF X$= "x" OR X$= "X" THEN COLOR 7,0:CLS:END
340 IF X$= "i" OR X$= "I" THEN GOSUB 370:GOTO 300 'input data, query menu again
350 BEEP: GOTO 310
360 :
370 '----- Example Routine -----
380 :
390 GOSUB 840 'store screen
400 M$(1)="  _____  "
410 M$(2)="|                         |"
420 M$(3)="|  Name:                  |"
430 M$(4)="|  First Name:            |"
440 M$(5)="|  Street:                |"
450 M$(6)="|  City:                  |"
460 M$(7)="|                         |"
470 M$(8)="|_____|"
480 :
```

```
490 COLMNO%= 15: COLR%= 112
500 FOR I%= 7 TO 14
510   DEF SEG:CALL FASTSCRN(I%,COLMNO%,COLR%,M$(I%-6))
520 NEXT I%
530 :
540 LOCATE 25,1:PRINT "Strike <F1> for 'Help' or <Esc> for 'back'...";SPACE$(80-POS(0));
550 LOCATE 9,25,1
560 X$= INKEY$:IF X$="" THEN 560
570 IF X$= CHR$(27) THEN GOSUB 910:RETURN 'restore display and call menu again
580 IF ASC(RIGHT$(X$,1))= 59 THEN GOSUB 610:GOTO 550 'display Help, continue with input
590 BEEP:GOTO 550
600 :
610 '----- Example for Help -----
620 :
630 GOSUB 840 'store display
640 M$(1)="  _____  "
650 M$(2)=" |                    | "
660 M$(3)=" | Indicate here the  | "
670 M$(4)=" | name of the client | "
680 M$(5)=" | This field must    | "
690 M$(6)=" | have some content. | "
700 M$(7)=" |                    | "
710 M$(8)=" |_____| "
720 :
730 COLMNO%= 20: COLR%= 15
740 FOR I%= 3 TO 10
750   DEF SEG:CALL FASTSCRN(I%,COLMNO%,COLR%,M$(I%-2))
760 NEXT I%
770 :
780 LOCATE 25,1:PRINT "Strike <Esc> for 'back'...";SPACE$(80-POS(0));
790 LOCATE ,,0
800 X$= INKEY$:IF X$="" THEN 800
810 IF X$= CHR$(27) THEN GOSUB 910:RETURN
820 BEEP:GOTO 790
830 :
840 '----- store current display-screen -----
850 :
860 IF CUR.SCRN= MAX.SCRN THEN BEEP:RETURN
870 DEF SEG:BUFFER.OFS%= VARPTR(BUFFER%(CUR.SCRN*2000)):CALL SAVESCRN(BUFFER.OFS%)
880 CUR.SCRN= CUR.SCRN+1
890 RETURN
900 :
910 '----- restore last display-screen -----
920 :
930 IF CUR.SCRN= 0 THEN BEEP:RETURN
940 CUR.SCRN= CUR.SCRN-1
950 DEF SEG:BUFFER.OFS%= VARPTR(BUFFER%(CUR.SCRN*2000)):CALL RESTSCRN(BUFFER.OFS%)
960 RETURN
970 :
980 :
990 'data-lines from COM-file: screen.com
1000 :
1010 RESTORE 1030
1020 DEF SEG:FOR I=1 TO  227:READ X:POKE MP.START+I-1,X: NEXT I
```

```
1030 DATA 235,109,144,235,109,144, 85,139,236, 30,  6
1040 DATA 139,118, 12,138, 28,176,160,246,227, 45,160
1050 DATA   0, 80,139,118, 10,138, 28,176,  2,246,227
1060 DATA  91,  3,195, 72, 72, 80,139,118,  8,138, 36
1070 DATA 139,118,  6,138, 12,181,  0,139,116,  1, 80
1080 DATA 191,  0,176,179,  0,205, 17, 37, 48,  0, 61
1090 DATA  48,  0,116,  6,129,199,  0,  8,179,  1,142
1100 DATA 199, 88, 95,252,186,218,  3,128,251,  0,116
1110 DATA  11,236,208,216,114,246,250,236,208,216,115
1120 DATA 251,172,251,171,226,235,  7, 31, 93,202,  8
1130 DATA   0,235, 41,144, 85,139,236, 30,  6,139,118
1140 DATA   6,139,  4,139,240,191,  0,176,179,  0,205
1150 DATA  17, 37, 48,  0, 61, 48,  0,116,  6,129,199
1160 DATA   0,  8,179,  1,142,199, 51,255,235, 40,144
1170 DATA  85,139,236, 30,  6,139,118,  6,139,  4,139
1180 DATA 248, 30,  7,190,  0,176,179,  0,205, 17, 37
1190 DATA  48,  0, 61, 48,  0,116,  6,129,198,  0,  8
1200 DATA 179,  1,142,222, 51,246,185,208,  7,252,186
1210 DATA 218,  3,128,251,  0,116, 11,236,208,216,114
1220 DATA 246,250,236,208,216,115,251,173,251,171,226
1230 DATA 235,  7, 31, 93,202,  2,  0
1240 RETURN
```

First the program constructs a main menu. After one of the assigned function keys is activated, the program saves the current display and constructs the input template. By restoring the saved display, after the input is complete, the menu doesn't have to be reconstructed repeatedly.

In the input template, users can call HELP with <F1> or a return to the main menu can be made with <Esc>. If <Esc> is activated, the saved display is restored and the menu is queried again. After <F1> is activated, the current screen is saved and then help is displayed. The main menu and the input template are located in the BUFFER% array. If help is terminated with <Esc>, the last screen display, in this case the input template, is restored and the input continues.

A test is performed to determine whether the central counter CUR.SCRN is within the permitted limits. If it isn't, a warning tone is sounded and the routine isn't executed. If this test isn't performed and incorrect values are entered during program development, it's possible that data areas before or after BUFFER%() would be overwritten by SAVESCRN or that incorrect screen displays would be restored by RESTSCRN. When the program executes without problems, this query could be removed. A few bytes aren't significant in most cases. As you can see, with an assembler and some subroutines, it's not difficult or time consuming to create professional looking programs.

11.5   Windows: Simple but Effective

Most of today's PC programs use user-friendly *window technology*. However, there are differing opinions on this subject. Sometimes it seems like the software manufacturers are competing to see whose software can produce the most windows simultaneously. For example, on a color monitor a different color could be used for each window. Obviously this could confuse the user.

We believe that windows are only effective when they're used for a specific purpose. For example, you can use a basic template over which a window can be superimposed for a search string. Help messages and input instructions are partly performed with windows, but in such a way that the user can see, on the basic template, where the help or input instructions apply. Although window technology has worked well until now and has received much praise from users, whether to use windows is the programmer's decision.

Since implementing window technology is a very complicated subject, it would take an entire book to discuss it thoroughly. Assembler routines must be used in order to use windows in PC-BASIC. We briefly discussed windows in the previous section, although they weren't very user-friendly.

Now we'll discuss how we can produce a window by using a small assembler routine from PC-BASIC. The simplest way to create windows is using the VIEW PRINT command to define an area of the screen as a window. This line includes the first column of the first line to the last column of the last line:

```
VIEW PRINT 5 to 15
```

This statement defines a window from column 1, line 5 to column 80, line 15. The interpreter is forced to accept this area as the actual screen display for every subsequent output with PRINT. The areas above and below this are no longer accessible. Even using CLS to clear the screen doesn't work.

You should use this feature in programs which require a header and footer line to always be displayed while other areas on the screen display are changed. The execution time for the header and footer are no longer needed. Since there is less to erase, CLS executes somewhat faster since there is less area to clear on the screen. The background of the window can be highlighted in color to distinguish it from the rest of the screen:

```
10 KEY OFF
20 COLOR 7,0 'grey letters on black background
30 CLS
40 :
50 VIEW PRINT 5 TO 15
60 COLOR 15,4 'white letters on red background
70 CLS
...
...
```

If you're using a color monitor, this short program using VIEW PRINT can be used as an interesting start for programming games:

```
10 '--------------------------------------------------------------
20 'VP.BAS, Doodle for Color-Monitor       1986 (C) H.J. Bomanns
30 '--------------------------------------------------------------
40 CLS:KEY OFF
50 COLR= 0
60 FIRST.ROWNO= 1:LAST.ROWNO= 24
70 :
80 VIEW PRINT FIRST.ROWNO TO LAST.ROWNO
90 COLOR ,COLR
100 CLS
110 FIRST.ROWNO= FIRST.ROWNO+1:IF FIRST.ROWNO= 13 THEN 160
120 LAST.ROWNO= LAST.ROWNO -1
130 COLR= COLR+1:IF COLR= 8 THEN COLR= 0
135 X$ = INKEY$:IF X$ = CHR$(27) THEN 250   '<Esc> to exit
140 GOTO 80
150 :
160 VIEW PRINT FIRST.ROWNO TO LAST.ROWNO
170 COLOR ,COLR
180 CLS
190 FIRST.ROWNO= FIRST.ROWNO-1:IF FIRST.ROWNO= 1 THEN 60
200 LAST.ROWNO= LAST.ROWNO +1
210 COLR= COLR+1:IF COLR= 8 THEN COLR= 0
215 X$ = INKEY$:IF X$ = CHR$(27) THEN 250   '<Esc> to exit
220 GOTO 160
230 :
240 '---exit routine ---
250 VIEW PRINT 1 TO 24
260 SCREEN 0
270 CLS
280 END
```

Additionally, a limited number of windows can be created and highlighted in color using VIEW PRINT. Other window construction capabilities are possible with a color graphics card (CGA/EGA) or with a CGA emulator for HGC cards. In the following example we'll use the window technology offered by PC-BASIC in the graphics mode:

```
10 '------------------------------------------------------------
20 ' VW.BAS, Window in Graphics Mode        1986 (C) H.J.Bomanns
30 '------------------------------------------------------------
40 :
50 CLS:KEY OFF
60 SCREEN 1
70 VIEW (150,50)-(50,150),1,2
80 LOCATE 8,8:PRINT "Window 1"
90 GOSUB 170
100 VIEW (180,80)-(80,180),2,3
110 LOCATE 13,12:PRINT "Window 2"
120 GOSUB 170
130 VIEW (190,30)-(30,150),3,2
140 LOCATE 7,7:PRINT "Window 3"
150 GOSUB 170
160 SCREEN 0:WIDTH 80:END
170 LOCATE 24,1:PRINT "Strike any key.....";
180 IF INKEY$="" THEN 180
190 RETURN
```

The VIEW statement, which defines a window in the graphics mode, controls this program. In this window, output appears as normal text using PRINT. The colors are limited to the three colors from the current palette. These were set by the COLOR parameter in the VIEW statements. However, all output commands must change as a window moves. This can only be avoided by using a very complicated procedure.

Window through Interrupt 10h

In this section we'll demonstrate how the BIOS is used to create windows. The DOS interface, which was previously used, will help access the BIOS. As we already mentioned, the detailed description of this routine can be found in Chapter 8. The task for the BASIC routine is creating a window of any size and at any location. Also, a frame should automatically appear around the window.

To do this, use interrupt 10h of the BIOS. This interrupt controls everything connected to the screen display and graphics. An overview of all the functions of interrupt 10h can be found in Appendix F. In our example, function 6 is significant. This function is normally used for scrolling the screen display toward the top. Function 6 of interrupt 10h expects various parameters. These parameters define the area and the number of lines to be scrolled. Also an attribute can be indicated for the blank lines which are created. If 0 is indicated as the number of lines to be scrolled, the window defined with this attribute is cleared. We pass the parameters to the interrupt through the DOS interface. The following program creates various windows with different colors and a frame:

```
10 '----------------------------------------------------------------
20 'MAKE_WND.BAS, window through INT 10h      1986 (C) H.J.Bomanns
30 '----------------------------------------------------------------
40 :
50 COLOR 7,0:CLS:KEY OFF
60 PRINT "Initialization.....";
70 DIM WNDOW(5,5) 'x,y,x,y,color
80 RESTORE 100
90 FOR I=1 TO 5:FOR K=1 TO 5:READ WNDOW(I,K):NEXT K:NEXT I
100 DATA 5,5,10,35,64,  8,40,13,75,16,  15,20,20,50,112, 3,3,7,45,80,
    20,15,22,45,32
110 GOSUB 640 'poke machine language routine in memory
120 :
130 DOS.SN= MP.START
140 INT.NR%= &H10:POKE INT.ADR,INT.NR%
150 :
160 '----- create screen display-----
170 :
180 CLS:FOR I=1 TO 24:PRINT STRING$(80,CHR$(178));:NEXT I
190 :
200 '----- create colored window -----
210 :
220 FOR I=1 TO 5
230    FROM.ROWNO%= WNDOW(I,1):FROM.COLMNO%= WNDOW(I,2)
240    TO.ROWNO%= WNDOW(I,3):TO.COLMNO%= WNDOW(I,4)
250    COLR%= WNDOW(I,5):NUM.OF.LINES%= 0
260    GOSUB 540 'create window
270 NEXT I
280 GOSUB 470 'wait for key
290 :
300 '----- create window with frame -----
310 :
320 FOR I=1 TO 5
330    FROM.ROWNO%= WNDOW(I,1)-1:FROM.COLMNO%= WNDOW(I,2)-1
340    TO.ROWNO%= WNDOW(I,3)+1:TO.COLMNO%= WNDOW(I,4)+1
350    COLR%= WNDOW(I,5):NUM.OF.LINES%= 0
360    GOSUB 540 'create window
370    FROM.ROWNO%= WNDOW(I,1):FROM.COLMNO%= WNDOW(I,2)
380    TO.ROWNO%= WNDOW(I,3):TO.COLMNO%= WNDOW(I,4)
390    COLR%= 0:NUM.OF.LINES%= 0
400    GOSUB 540 'create window
410 NEXT I
420 GOSUB 470
430 GOTO 180
440 :
450 '----- query keyboard -----
460 :
470 LOCATE 23,50:PRINT " <Return> to continue or <Esc> to End ";
480 X$= INKEY$:IF X$="" THEN 480
490 IF X$<>CHR$(27) THEN RETURN
500 CLS:END
510 :
520 '----- window-routine -----
```

```
530 :
540 AH%= 6
550 AL%= NUM.OF.LINES%
560 CH%= FROM.ROWNO%-1:CL%= FROM.COLMNO%-1
570 DH%= TO.ROWNO%-1:DL%= TO.COLMNO%-1
580 BH%= COLR%
590 DEF SEG:CALL DOS.SN(AH%, AL%, BH%, BL%, CH%, CL%, DH%, DL%, ES%, DI%, SI%,
    FLAGS%)
600 RETURN
610 :
620 'data-lines from COM-file: dos_sn.com
630 :
640 MP.START= &HE000
650 RESTORE 670
660 DEF SEG:FOR I=1 TO  151:READ X:POKE MP.START+I-1,X: NEXT I
670 DATA 250, 85,139,236, 30,  6,139,118,  6,139,  4
680 DATA  80,157,139,118, 14,138, 20,139,118, 16,138
690 DATA  52,139,118, 18,138, 12,139,118, 20,138, 44
700 DATA 139,118, 22,138, 28,139,118, 24,138, 60,139
710 DATA 118, 26,138,  4,139,118, 28,138, 36,139,118
720 DATA   8,139, 60, 80,139,118, 12,139,  4,142,192
730 DATA  88,139,118, 10,139, 52, 85,251,205, 33,250
740 DATA  93, 86,156,139,118, 28,136, 36,139,118, 26
750 DATA 136,  4,139,118, 24,136, 60,139,118, 22,136
760 DATA  28,139,118, 20,136, 44,139,118, 18,136, 12
770 DATA 139,118, 16,136, 52,139,118, 14,136, 20, 88
780 DATA 139,118,  6,137,  4, 88,139,118, 10,137,  4
790 DATA 140,192,139,118, 12,137,  4,139,118,  8,137
800 DATA  60,  7, 31, 93,251,202, 24,  0
810 MP.END= MP.START+I-1
820 FOR I= MP.START TO MP.END:IF PEEK(I)= 205 THEN INT.ADR= I+1 ELSE NEXT
830 RETURN
```

After the start of the program, the machine program for the DOS interface is POKEd into memory starting at line 620 with a subroutine. Then the variables are initialized. This program creates five windows in different locations and colors in the first part. The subroutine in line 520 starts the actual work. Here the values of the variables are prepared. This is necessary because the BIOS counts the lines from 0-24 and the columns from 0-79. To avoid coordinate confusion, the positions can be indicated as in the LOCATE statement.

In the second part, starting at line 300, the same window is created with a frame. To create the frame, a line is drawn around a window with the proper attribute. This attribute is one line and one column larger than the window. Then the actual window is created, with attribute 0, inside the recently created window.

To use this routine in your programs, you need the data loader, which starts at line 620. It initializes the machine program and the routine (starting at line 520) that passes the parameters through the DOS interface to interrupt 10h. The lines 130/140, in which the variable for CALL is initialized and the number of the interrupt to be addressed is poked, is important. The parameter variables FROM.ROWNO%, FROM.COLMNO%,

TO.ROWNO%, TO.COLMNO%, COLR% and NUM.OF.LINES% are initialized, depending on the requirements. There are two ways to determine the attributes.

You can query them in direct mode:

```
COLOR <foreground>,<background>
CLS
DEF SEG= &HB800 'for monochrome DEF SEG= &HB000
? PEEK(1)
```

Or you can use the following program. It presents an example of the output and the selected attributes:

```
10  '-------------------------------------------------------------
20  ' COLORS.BAS, determine Attributes        1986 (C) H.J.Bomanns
30  '-------------------------------------------------------------
40 :
50 CLS:KEY OFF:DIM COLRS$(15)
60 RESTORE 80
70 FOR I=0 TO 15:READ COLRS$(I):NEXT I
80 DATA black, blue, green, cyan, red, magenta, brown, LGrey, DGrey, LBlue,
   LGreen, LCyan, LRed, LMagenta, yellow, white
90 FG= 7:BG= 0
100 CHAR$="":FOR I= 32 TO 255:CHAR$=CHAR$+CHR$(I):NEXT I 'ASCII char set
110 :
120 COLOR FG,BG:VIEW PRINT:CLS:OUT &H3D9,HG
130 FOR I=1 TO 3:PRINT CHAR$:NEXT   'print ASCII set 3 times
140 PRINT STRING$(79,"-")
145 PRINT "DON'T PANIC - THIS IS THE ASCII CHARACTER SET"
150 PRINT STRING$(79,"-")
160 COLOR 7,0
170 VIEW PRINT 20 TO 24:CLS
180 LOCATE 21,1
190 PRINT "Foreground: ";FG;"/";COLRS$(FG);"     Background:
    ";BG;"/";COLRS$(BG);"      Attribute: ";:DEF SEG= &HB800:PRINT PEEK(1);
200 LOCATE 23,1,1,0,31
210 PRINT "<F>oreground, <B>ackground or <Esc> --> ";
220 :
230 X$=INKEY$:IF X$="" THEN 230
240 IF X$="b" OR X$="B" THEN 310 'background
250 IF X$="f" OR X$="F" THEN 430 'foreground
260 IF X$= CHR$(27) THEN COLOR 7,0:VIEW PRINT:CLS:END
270 BEEP:GOTO 230
280 :
290 '----- background -----
300 :
310 LOCATE 23,1:PRINT "Background <+>, <->, number or <Esc>  --> ";
320 Y$= INKEY$:IF Y$="" THEN 320
330 IF Y$= CHR$(27) THEN 200
340 IF Y$="+" THEN BG= BG+1
350 IF Y$="-" THEN BG= BG-1
```

```
360 IF Y$>="0" AND Y$<="9" THEN LOCATE 25,1:INPUT "Value:";BG
370 IF BG= 8 THEN BG= 0
380 IF BG< 0 THEN BG= 7
390 GOTO 120
400 :
410 '----- foreground -----
420 :
430 LOCATE 23,1:PRINT "Foreground <+>, <->, number or <Esc>    --> ";
440 Y$= INKEY$:IF Y$="" THEN 440
450 IF Y$= CHR$(27) THEN 200
460 IF Y$="+" THEN FG= FG+1
470 IF Y$>="0" AND Y$<="9" THEN LOCATE 25,1:INPUT "Value:";FG
480 IF Y$="-" THEN FG= FG-1
490 IF FG= 16 THEN FG= 0
500 IF FG< 0 THEN FG= 15
510 GOTO 120
```

The program displays the PC character set in the current foreground or background color. To modify the foreground color use the <F> key and to modify the background color use the <B> key. <Esc> terminates the program. After activating the <F> or <B> keys, you can increase or decrease the color by one with the <+> and <-> keys. A color code can be entered directly with INPUT by entering a number. If you're using a PC with a monochrome card, change line 190 to appear as follows:

```
190 PRINT "Foreground: ";FG;"/";COLRS$(FG);"    Background:
    ";BG;"/";COLRS$(BG);"       Attribute: ";:DEF SEG= &HB000:PRINT PEEK(1);
```

11.5.1 Universal Window Routine

In the previous sections we presented examples for creating simple windows. You can also create professionally appearing programs for more complex applications. This section demonstrates how a universal and fast window routine can be created with the help of the screen display manager presented in Section 11.4. We'll also briefly discuss background development.

Background Development

In most professional programs, menus, templates and messages aren't displayed on a "naked" screen. Instead, a *background* is filled with one of the PC graphic characters. This not only makes the program visually appealing but also preserves compatibility with existing applications. For example, if the user calls your program with GEM from Digital Research, you can provide the same background as GEM. If a different user interface appears each time a program is changed, a user can become very irritated. A good example of compatibility is the APPLE computer, which has a uniform user interface. It doesn't matter which program is called, the background appearance of the screen and the window control are almost identical.

The previous background implementation was always affected by the slow screen display output of PC-BASIC. This can be fixed with the FASTSCRN routine from Section 11.2. It's important that first the characters to be used are selected. There are four suitable characters in the PC character set:

While developing the background routine, we assumed that the entire screen display wouldn't continuously need reconstruction but that only portions of the screen may require new construction. The routine must work with the proper parameters. These parameters must determine which area of the screen display must be filled with which characters and with what attribute. Usually this is combined with the window routine. This saves variables and doesn't require new considerations during the assignment of the parameters.

Background and Windows in Applications

The following program demonstrates the routine for the background development and the universal window routine:

```
10  '---------------------------------------------------
20  'WINDOWS.BAS    Demonstration of Window Techniques
30  '---------------------------------------------------
40  :
50  DEFINT A-Z
60  CLS:KEY OFF:FOR I=1 TO 10:KEY I,"":NEXT I
70  MP.START= &HE000
80  GOSUB 1010 'initialize MP
90  SAVESCRN= MP.START
100 RESTSCRN= MP.START+3
110 FASTSCRN= MP.START+6
120 FALSE= 0: TRUE= NOT FALSE
130 MAX.SCRN= 3
140 DIM BUFFER%(2000*MAX.SCRN)
150 CUR.SCRN= 0
160 WNDW.BKG= 112: MESSG.BKG= 127: HDFT.TXT= 7
```

Line 160 determines the attributes for the window. We selected black on grey for normal display, white on grey for messages and grey on black for the bar.

```
170 CLS
180 :
190 BKG.CHAR$= CHR$(177): BKGCOLR= 15
```

Line 190 determines the characters and the attribute for the background.

```
200 WD.ROW= 1: WD.COLM= 1: WD.LGTH= 80: WD.HGT= 25
210 GOSUB 520 'initialize background
```

The WD.ROW, WD.COLM, WD.LGTH and WD.HGT parameters define the area that will be filled with the background. In this case, the entire screen display from line 1, column 1 to a width of 80 characters and a height of 25 lines, is initialized.

```
220 GOSUB 870 'store screen display
230 RW=2: CL=5: X$= "A simple and quick background. Strike any key ... "
240 CALL FASTSCRN(RW,CL,MESSG.BKG,X$)
250 IF INKEY$= "" THEN 250
260 :
270 WD.ROW= 5:WD.COLM= 5:WD.LGTH= 50: WD.HGT= 10: WD.SHADOW= FALSE
280 HEAD$= "Window technique...": FOOT$= "<Esc>= back"
290 GOSUB 600 'display window
```

The parameters for a window are set in the lines 270 to 280. The variables for determining the area are the same as those for the background. The HEAD$ and FOOT$ variables in line 280 are new. The content of these variables is displayed at the top and bottom window border. The display appears in the attribute bar, which highlights it from the rest of the window. HEAD$ contains a message about the current function, for example "copy file:" or "search for data:". In FOOT$, an input message is displayed, for example "<F1>= Help" or "<Esc>= back". Use the WD.SHADOW parameter for a drop shadow to appear behind the window. Your programs may have a more pleasing and interesting appearance when using this technique. However, using drop shadows is a question of personal taste.

```
300 RW= WD.ROW+5: CL= WD.COLM+5:X$= "Strike any key..."
310 CALL FASTSCRN(RW,CL,MESSG.BKG,X$)
320 K$ = INKEY$:IF K$= "" THEN 320
321 IF K$ = CHR$(27) THEN GOSUB 930 ELSE 330
323 CUR.SCRN = CUR.SCRN + 1
325 GOTO 230
330 GOSUB 870 'store display
340 :
350 WD.ROW= 10:WD.COLM= 10:WD.LGTH= 50: WD.HGT= 10: WD.SHADOW= TRUE
360 HEAD$= "Window technique with drop shadow...": FOOT$= "<Esc>= back "
370 GOSUB 600 'display window
```

In line 350 to 370, a window with a shadow is demonstrated.

```
380 RW= WD.ROW+5: CL= WD.COLM+5:X$= "Strike any key..."
390 CALL FASTSCRN(RW,CL,MESSG.BKG,X$)
400 IF INKEY$= "" THEN 400
410 :
420 GOSUB 930 'display back
430 IF INKEY$= "" THEN 430
440 GOSUB 930 'display back
450 RW=10:CL=10:X$= " Strike any key... "
460 CALL FASTSCRN(RW,CL,MESSG.BKG,X$)
470 IF INKEY$= "" THEN 470
480 :
490 COLOR 7,0:CLS:END
```

```
500 :
510 '----- background initialize -----
520 :
530 X$= STRING$(WD.LGTH,BKG.CHAR$)
540 FOR RW= WD.ROW TO WD.ROW+WD.HGT
550   CALL FASTSCRN(RW,WD.COLM,BKGCOLR,X$)
560 NEXT RW
570 RETURN
580 :
```

This is the routine for the background. First X$ is loaded with the width, of the background to be initialized, with the background character BKG.CHAR (line 530). Then X$ is output in a loop, which corresponds to the height of the area with the BKG.COLR attribute.

```
590 '----- universal-routine for window -----
600 :
610 X$= CHR$(218)+STRING$(WD.LGTH%,CHR$(196))+CHR$(191)
620 DEF SEG:CALL FASTSCRN(WD.ROW,WD.COLM,WNDW.BKG,X$)
630 X$= CHR$(179)+STRING$(WD.LGTH%," ")+CHR$(179)
640 IF WD.SHADOW THEN X$= X$+CHR$(178)+CHR$(178)
650 FOR RW= WD.ROW+1 TO WD.ROW+WD.HGT
660   DEF SEG:CALL FASTSCRN(RW,WD.COLM,WNDW.BKG,X$)
670 NEXT RW
680 X$= CHR$(192)+STRING$(WD.LGTH%,CHR$(196))+CHR$(217)
690 IF WD.SHADOW THEN X$= X$+CHR$(178)+CHR$(178)
700 RW= WD.ROW+WD.HGT+1
710 DEF SEG:CALL FASTSCRN(RW,WD.COLM,WNDW.BKG,X$)
720 IF HEAD$= "" THEN 760 'continue with footing
730   X$= " "+HEAD$+" "
740   CL= WD.COLM+3
750   CALL FASTSCRN(WD.ROW,CL,HDFT.TXT,X$)
760 IF FOOT$= "" THEN 800 'continue with shadow
770   X$= " "+FOOT$+" "
780   RW= WD.ROW+WD.HGT+1:CL= WD.COLM+3
790   CALL FASTSCRN(RW,CL,HDFT.TXT,X$)
800 IF NOT WD.SHADOW THEN 840 'back
810   X$= STRING$(WD.LGTH+2,CHR$(178))
820   RW= WD.ROW+WD.HGT+2:CL= WD.COLM+2
830   CALL FASTSCRN(RW,CL,WNDW.BKG,X$)
840 RETURN
850 :
```

This is the routine for the window. Unfortunately string or mathematical operations cannot be performed in a CALL command. So the path through X$ or the escape variables RW and CL is required. Without these detours, the routine would only be half its size. The routine consists of four parts. In the first part (line 610/620), the first line of the window is generated according to the width that was set. The second part, starting at line 630, generates the middle (the actual window), according to the indicated height. In the third part (starting at line 680), the lowest line is generated in relation to the top line. The last part tests whether something should be displayed on the top or bottom and if a shadow should be attached to the bottom window border.

Note: The WD.LGTH and WD.HGT parameters always refer to the actual window, without frame and shadow. The size of the window can be calculated from WD.LGTH plus 2 or WD.HGT plus 2 or, if a shadow should be displayed, the same plus 4.

The remainder of the program was previously discussed in Section 11.4.

```
860 '----- store current display-screen -----
870 :
880 IF CUR.SCRN= MAX.SCRN THEN BEEP:RETURN
890 DEF SEG:BUFFER.OFS%= VARPTR(BUFFER%(CUR.SCRN*2000)):CALL
    SAVESCRN(BUFFER.OFS%)
900 CUR.SCRN= CUR.SCRN+1
910 RETURN
920 :
930 '----- restore last display-screen -----
940 :
950 IF CUR.SCRN= 0 THEN BEEP:RETURN
960 CUR.SCRN= CUR.SCRN-1
970 DEF SEG:BUFFER.OFS%= VARPTR(BUFFER%(CUR.SCRN*2000)):CALL
    RESTSCRN(BUFFER.OFS%)
980 RETURN
990 :
1000 'data-lines from COM-file: screen.com
1010 :
1020 RESTORE 1040
1030 DEF SEG:FOR I=1 TO  227:READ X:POKE MP.START+I-1,X: NEXT I
1040 DATA 235,109,144,235,109,144, 85,139,236, 30,  6
1050 DATA 139,118, 12,138, 28,176,160,246,227, 45,160
1060 DATA   0, 80,139,118, 10,138, 28,176,  2,246,227
1070 DATA  91,  3,195, 72, 72, 80,139,118,  8,138, 36
1080 DATA 139,118,  6,138, 12,181,  0,139,116,  1, 80
1090 DATA 191,  0,176,179,  0,205, 17, 37, 48,  0, 61
1100 DATA  48,  0,116,  6,129,199,  0,  8,179,  1,142
1110 DATA 199, 88, 95,252,186,218,  3,128,251,  0,116
1120 DATA  11,236,208,216,114,246,250,236,208,216,115
1130 DATA 251,172,251,171,226,235,  7, 31, 93,202,  8
1140 DATA   0,235, 41,144, 85,139,236, 30,  6,139,118
1150 DATA   6,139,  4,139,240,191,  0,176,179,  0,205
1160 DATA  17, 37, 48,  0, 61, 48,  0,116,  6,129,199
1170 DATA   0,  8,179,  1,142,199, 51,255,235, 40,144
1180 DATA  85,139,236, 30,  6,139,118,  6,139,  4,139
1190 DATA 248, 30,  7,190,  0,176,179,  0,205, 17, 37
1200 DATA  48,  0, 61, 48,  0,116,  6,129,198,  0,  8
1210 DATA 179,  1,142,222, 51,246,185,208,  7,252,186
1220 DATA 218,  3,128,251,  0,116, 11,236,208,216,114
1230 DATA 246,250,236,208,216,115,251,173,251,171,226
1240 DATA 235,  7, 31, 93,202,  2,  0
1250 RETURN
```

The demonstration program generates a background, saves it and displays a window without a shadow. Next, this screen display is also saved and a window with a shadow is displayed. Then all the saved screen displays are restored sequentially. As you can see, it's easy to generate a user interface by using an assembler and two brief subroutines.

However, this program could be greatly enhanced. For example, the window attributes could be switched according to application areas. In your programs you could provide separate attributes for "NORMAL", "INPUTS", "ERRORS and MESSAGES", "HELP" and "MENUS". Therefore, the user can recognize, through the colors, whether a menu or an input template is being displayed.

11.6   User-Friendly Menus

The background and window technique are not the only consideration for developing professional user-friendly programs. The menus are also important. In this section we'll present the three most important menu methods.

11.6.1 Selection Menus

The simplest way to create a menu is to display the available menu options and allow the user to press a corresponding key. The first PCs contained menus similar to the following:

```
[1]= input data
[2]= display/change data
[3]= search for data
[4]= delete data
[5]= print data

[9]= end program
```

Although these menus were easy to program, they were confusing to use. First the user had to find the desired function on the right and then he/she had to strike the correct key. Since there isn't a logical connection between the number and the function, it's difficult to remember the correct number.

This type of menu can also be used with letters, which indicate functions. The following program demonstrates this type of selection menu. It uses the screen manager and the routines, which were described in the previous section, for background and window:

```
10 '----------------------------------------------------
20 'A_MENU.BAS    demonstration of a selection-menu
30 '----------------------------------------------------
40 :
50 DEFINT A-Z
60 OPTION BASE 0
70 CLS:KEY OFF:FOR I=1 TO 10:KEY I,"":NEXT I
80 MP.START= &HE000
90 GOSUB 1310 'initialize MP
100 SAVESCRN= MP.START
110 RESTSCRN= MP.START+3
120 FASTSCRN= MP.START+6
130 FALSE= 0: TRUE= NOT FALSE
140 MAX.SCN= 3:DIM BUFFER%(2000*MAX.SCN)
150 MAX.MENU= 8: DIM MENU$(MAX.MENU)
160 CUR.SCN= 0
170 WNDW.BKG= 112: MESSG.BKG= 127: HDFT.TXT= 7
180 RESTORE 200
190 FOR I= 0 TO MAX.MENU:READ MENU$(I):NEXT I
200 DATA "<< Sorting >>"
```

```
210 DATA "Last Name "
220 DATA "First Name "
230 DATA "Street "
240 DATA "ZIP code "
250 DATA "City "
260 DATA "Telephone"
270 DATA "Hobby"
280 DATA "End"
290 :
```

The individual menu options are stored in a one dimensional string array.

```
300 BKG.CHAR$= CHR$(177): BKGCOLR= 15
310 WD.ROW= 1: WD.COLM= 1: WD.LGTH= 80: WD.HGT= 25
320 GOSUB 820 'background initialize
330 RW= 1: CL= 1: X$= " file administration V1.00 (C) 1987 H.-J. Bomanns "
340 DEF SEG: CALL FASTSCRN(RW,CL,MESSG.BKG,X$)
350 :
360 GOSUB 490 'menu-selection
370 IF MENU= 0 THEN 470 'clear screen and End
380 SORT.ART= MENU
390 :
```

The menu is called as a type of "function". One return message appears in the MENU variable. This is 0 if the user selected either the "End" button or the <Esc> key. Otherwise, MENU can be used for additional branching and for calling the current function.

```
400 WD.ROW= 15:WD.COLM= 40:WD.LGTH= 23: WD.HGT= 3:WD.SHADOW= TRUE
410 WD.HEAD$= "Sort according to:": WD.FOOT$= "<Esc> End "
420 GOSUB 900 'display window
430 RW= 17: CL= 44: X$= MENU$(MENU)+"..."
440 DEF SEG:CALL FASTSCRN(RW,CL,MESSG.BKG,X$)
450 :
460 IF INKEY$="" THEN 460
470 COLOR 7,0:CLS:PRINT "*** END ***":PRINT:END
480 :
490 '----- print menu and control selection -----
500 :
510 MAX.LGTH= 0
520 FOR I=0 TO MAX.MENU
530    IF LEN(MENU$(I)) > MAX.LGTH THEN MAX.LGTH= LEN(MENU$(I))
540 NEXT I
```

The longest entry must be determined before displaying the menu. The window is then dimensioned accordingly.

```
550 WD.ROW= 5: WD.COLM= 10: WD.SHADOW= FALSE
560 WD.LGTH= MAX.LGTH+6: WD.HGT= MAX.MENU+2
570 WD.HEAD$= MENU$(0):WD.FOOT$= "<F1> for Help"
580 GOSUB 900 'display window
590 CL= WD.COLM+3
600 FOR I= 1 TO MAX.MENU
610    RW= WD.ROW+I+1
620    DEF SEG:CALL FASTSCRN(RW,CL,WNDW.BKG,MENU$(I))
630    X$= LEFT$(MENU$(I),1)
640    DEF SEG:CALL FASTSCRN(RW,CL,MESSG.BKG,X$)
650 NEXT I
660 RW=25: CL= 1: X$= " Please strike letter key or <Esc> to quit": X$=
    X$+SPACE$(80-LEN(X$))
670 DEF SEG:CALL FASTSCRN(RW,CL,MESSG.BKG,X$)
680 LOCATE ,,0
690 WHILE ONKEY$<> CHR$(27) AND ONKEY$<> CHR$(13) AND ONKEY$<> CHR$(101)
700    ONKEY$= INKEY$:IF ONKEY$= "" THEN 700
710    IF ONKEY$= CHR$(27) OR ONKEY$= CHR$(101) OR ONKEY$= CHR$(69) THEN MENU=
       0:GOTO 770
720    IF LEN(ONKEY$)= 2 THEN 700 'kill special keys
730    IF ASC(ONKEY$) > 96 THEN ONKEY$= CHR$(ASC(ONKEY$)-32) 'change to upper case
740    FOR I= 1 TO MAX.MENU
750       IF LEFT$(MENU$(I),1)= ONKEY$ THEN MENU=I:ONKEY$= CHR$(13)
760    NEXT I
770 WEND
```

The keyboard is queried in the WHILE...WEND loop and evaluates the selected key. A test, beginning at line 740, is made to determine whether the selected letter key corresponds to one of the letters found on the menu buttons. If it does, the result variable MENU is initialized accordingly and the menu terminates. This is done by setting ONKEY$ to CHR$(13). This terminates the WHILE...WEND loop and the return jump occurs.

```
780 RW= 25: CL= 1: X$= SPACE$(80)
790 DEF SEG:CALL FASTSCRN(RW,CL,MESSG.BKG,X$) 'erase Status
800 RETURN
810 :
```

The remainder of the program should be familiar to you from the previous sections.

```
820 '----- initialize background -----
830 :
840 X$= STRING$(WD.LGTH,BKG.CHAR$)
850 FOR RW= WD.ROW TO WD.ROW+WD.HGT
860    CALL FASTSCRN(RW,WD.COLM,BKGCOLR,X$)
870 NEXT RW
880 RETURN
890 :
900 '----- universal-routine for window -----
910 :
920 X$= CHR$(218)+STRING$(WD.LGTH%,CHR$(196))+CHR$(191)
930 DEF SEG:CALL FASTSCRN(WD.ROW,WD.COLM,WNDW.BKG,X$)
```

```
940 X$= CHR$(179)+STRING$(WD.LGTH%," ")+CHR$(179)
950 IF WD.SHADOW THEN X$= X$+CHR$(178)+CHR$(178)
960 FOR RW= WD.ROW+1 TO WD.ROW+WD.HGT
970   DEF SEG:CALL FASTSCRN(RW,WD.COLM,WNDW.BKG,X$)
980 NEXT RW
990 X$= CHR$(192)+STRING$(WD.LGTH%,CHR$(196))+CHR$(217)
1000 IF WD.SHADOW THEN X$= X$+CHR$(178)+CHR$(178)
1010 RW= WD.ROW+WD.HGT+1
1020 DEF SEG:CALL FASTSCRN(RW,WD.COLM,WNDW.BKG,X$)
1030 IF WD.HEAD$= "" THEN 1070 'continue with footing
1040   X$= " "+WD.HEAD$+" "
1050   CL= WD.COLM+3
1060   CALL FASTSCRN(WD.ROW,CL,HDFT.TXT,X$)
1070 IF WD.FOOT$= "" THEN 1110 'continue with shadow
1080   X$= " "+WD.FOOT$+" "
1090   RW= WD.ROW+WD.HGT+1:CL= WD.COLM+3
1100   CALL FASTSCRN(RW,CL,HDFT.TXT,X$)
1110 IF NOT WD.SHADOW THEN 1150 'back
1120   X$= STRING$(WD.LGTH+2,CHR$(178))
1130   RW= WD.ROW+WD.HGT+2:CL= WD.COLM+2
1140   CALL FASTSCRN(RW,CL,WNDW.BKG,X$)
1150 RETURN
1160 :
1170 '----- store current display-screen -----
1180 :
1190 IF CUR.SCN= MAX.SCN THEN BEEP:RETURN
1200 DEF SEG:BUFFER.OFS%= VARPTR(BUFFER%(CUR.SCN*2000)):CALL
     SAVESCRN(BUFFER.OFS%)
1210 CUR.SCN= CUR.SCN+1
1220 RETURN
1230 :
1240 '----- restore last display-screen -----
1250 :
1260 IF CUR.SCN= 0 THEN BEEP:RETURN
1270 CUR.SCN= CUR.SCN-1
1280 DEF SEG:BUFFER.OFS%= VARPTR(BUFFER%(CUR.SCN*2000)):CALL
     RESTSCRN(BUFFER.OFS%)
1290 RETURN
1300 :
1310 'data-lines from COM-file: screen.com
1320 :
1330 RESTORE 1350
1340 DEF SEG:FOR I=1 TO  227:READ X:POKE MP.START+I-1,X: NEXT I
1350 DATA 235,109,144,235,109,144, 85,139,236, 30,  6
1360 DATA 139,118, 12,138, 28,176,160,246,227, 45,160
1370 DATA   0, 80,139,118, 10,138, 28,176,  2,246,227
1380 DATA  91,  3,195, 72, 72, 80,139,118,  8,138, 36
1390 DATA 139,118,  6,138, 12,181,  0,139,116,  1, 80
1400 DATA 191,  0,176,179,  0,205, 17, 37, 48,  0, 61
1410 DATA  48,  0,116,  6,129,199,  0,  8,179,  1,142
1420 DATA 199, 88, 95,252,186,218,  3,128,251,  0,116
1430 DATA  11,236,208,216,114,246,250,236,208,216,115
1440 DATA 251,172,251,171,226,235,  7, 31, 93,202,  8
```

```
1450 DATA    0,235, 41,144, 85,139,236, 30,  6,139,118
1460 DATA    6,139,  4,139,240,191,  0,176,179,  0,205
1470 DATA   17, 37, 48,  0, 61, 48,  0,116,  6,129,199
1480 DATA    0,  8,179,  1,142,199, 51,255,235, 40,144
1490 DATA   85,139,236, 30,  6,139,118,  6,139,  4,139
1500 DATA  248, 30,  7,190,  0,176,179,  0,205, 17, 37
1510 DATA   48,  0, 61, 48,  0,116,  6,129,198,  0,  8
1520 DATA  179,  1,142,222, 51,246,185,208,  7,252,186
1530 DATA  218,  3,128,251,  0,116, 11,236,208,216,114
1540 DATA  246,250,236,208,216,115,251,173,251,171,226
1550 DATA  235,  7, 31, 93,202,  2,  0
1560 RETURN
```

This program provides various sort criteria through options in the menu. The result is displayed in a window. These types of menus are practical for the user because a direct relationship can be established between the letters and their respective functions.

11.6.2 Bar Menus

This & Pull Down menu will overflow black on Repeated center

After selection menus, bar menus became popular. Apparently some programmers believed that activating two cursor keys and the <Return> key would be easier than pressing a single letter key. This is also a matter of personal preference; many users still prefer this type of menu.

Its implementation is similar to the selection menu. The control and bar display are more comprehensive. The following program illustrates this:

```
10 '----------------------------------------------------
20 'B_MENU.BAS    demonstration of bar-menu
30 '----------------------------------------------------
40 :
50 DEFINT A-Z
60 OPTION BASE 0
70 CLS:KEY OFF:FOR I=1 TO 10:KEY I,"":NEXT I
80 MP.START= &HE000
90 GOSUB 1540 'initialize MP
100 SAVESCRN= MP.START
110 RESTSCRN= MP.START+3
120 FASTSCRN= MP.START+6
130 FALSE= 0: TRUE= NOT FALSE
140 MAX.SCN= 3:DIM BUFFER%(2000*MAX.SCN)
150 MAX.MENU= 8: DIM MENU$(MAX.MENU)
160 CUR.SCN= 0
170 WNDW.BKG= 112: MESSG.BKG= 127: HDFT.TXT= 7    ← COLOR ATTRIBUTES SEE PAGE 645
180 RESTORE 200
190 FOR I= 0 TO MAX.MENU:READ MENU$(I):NEXT I
200 DATA " MAIN MENU "
210 DATA "prepare"
220 DATA "delete"
230 DATA "search"
```

ONE core both this.
40b F! = FRE(X$)

366

```
240 DATA "change"
250 DATA "list"
260 DATA "import"
270 DATA "export"
280 DATA "End"
290 :
300 BKG.CHAR$= CHR$(177): BKGCOLR= 15
310 WD.ROW= 1: WD.COLM= 1: WD.LGTH= 80: WD.HGT= 25
320 GOSUB 1050 'initialize background
330 RW= 1: CL= 1: X$= " File management V1.00 (C) 1987 H.J. Bomanns "
340 DEF SEG: CALL FASTSCRN(RW,CL,MESSG.BKG,X$)
350 :
360 GOSUB 690 'menu-selection
370 IF MENU= 0 THEN MENU = 8 'shift End
380 GOSUB 1400 'store screen
390 ON MENU GOSUB 430,450,470,580,600,620,640,660
400 GOSUB 1470 'restore screen
410 GOTO 360 'menu query again
420 :
430 '----- prepare -----
440 RETURN
450 '----- delete -----
460 RETURN
470 '----- search -----
480 WD.ROW= 8: WD.COLM= 30: WD.LGTH= 40: WD.HGT= 3:WD.SHADOW= TRUE
490 WD.HEAD$= MENU$(MENU): WD.FOOT$= "<F1> for Help"
500 GOSUB 1130 'display window
510 RW= WD.ROW+2: CL= WD.COLM+2: X$= "search criteria:"
520 DEF SEG:CALL FASTSCRN(RW,CL,WNDW.BKG,X$)
530 LOCATE WD.ROW+2,WD.COLM+18,1
540 RW=25: CL= 1: X$= " input search criteria, <Return> to search or <Esc> to
    End": X$= X$+SPACE$(80-LEN(X$))
550 DEF SEG:CALL FASTSCRN(RW,CL,MESSG.BKG,X$)
560 IF INKEY$= "" THEN 560
570 RETURN
580 '----- change -----
590 RETURN
600 '----- list -----
610 RETURN
620 '----- import -----
630 RETURN
640 '----- export -----
650 RETURN
660 '----- End -----
670 COLOR 7,0:CLS:PRINT "*** END ***":PRINT:END
680 :
690 '----- display menu and control selection -----
700 :
710 MAX.LGTH= 0
720 FOR I=0 TO MAX.MENU
730    IF LEN(MENU$(I)) > MAX.LGTH THEN MAX.LGTH= LEN(MENU$(I))
740 NEXT I
750 WD.ROW= 5: WD.COLM= 10: WD.SHADOW= FALSE
```

[handwritten annotations: "COLOR ATTRIBUTE — CHANGE TO 9 OR 17" pointing to line 300; "IN WINDOW" pointing to line 510; "BOTTOM OF SCREEN" pointing to line 540]

```
760 WD.LGTH= MAX.LGTH+6: WD.HGT= MAX.MENU+2
770 WD.HEAD$= MENU$(0):WD.FOOT$= "<F1> for help"
780 GOSUB 1130 'display window
790 CL= WD.COLM+3
800 FOR I= 1 TO MAX.MENU
810   RW= WD.ROW+I+1
820   DEF SEG:CALL FASTSCRN(RW,CL,WNDW.BKG,MENU$(I))
830 NEXT I
840 RW=25: CL= 1: X$= " Use <"+CHR$(24)+"> and <"+CHR$(25)+"> to select and
    <Enter> to execute or <Esc> to End": X$= X$+SPACE$(80-LEN(X$))
850 DEF SEG:CALL FASTSCRN(RW,CL,MESSG.BKG,X$)
860 HDFT.ROW= 1: CL= WD.COLM+1: ONKEY$= "": LOCATE ,,0
870 WHILE ONKEY$<> CHR$(27) AND ONKEY$<> CHR$(13)
880   RW= WD.ROW+HDFT.ROW+1
890   X$= "  "+MENU$(HDFT.ROW): X$= X$+SPACE$(MAX.LGTH+6-LEN(X$))
900   DEF SEG:CALL FASTSCRN(RW,CL,HDFT.TXT,X$)
910   ONKEY$= INKEY$:IF ONKEY$= "" THEN 910
920   DEF SEG:CALL FASTSCRN(RW,CL,WNDW.BKG,X$)
930   IF ONKEY$= CHR$(27) THEN MENU= 0
940   IF ONKEY$= CHR$(13) THEN MENU= HDFT.ROW
950   ONKEY= ASC(RIGHT$(ONKEY$,1))
960   IF ONKEY= 72 THEN HDFT.ROW= HDFT.ROW-1 'Cursor up
970   IF ONKEY= 80 THEN HDFT.ROW= HDFT.ROW+1 'Cursor down
980   IF ONKEY= 71 THEN HDFT.ROW= 1 '<Home>
990   IF ONKEY= 79 THEN HDFT.ROW= MAX.MENU
1000   IF HDFT.ROW < 1 THEN HDFT.ROW= MAX.MENU
1010   IF HDFT.ROW > MAX.MENU THEN HDFT.ROW= 1
1020 WEND
1030 RETURN
1040 :
```

The most important routine is the HDFT.ROW variable. It's used for positioning and displaying the bar menu. Before the query of the keyboard, the bar menu is set to the current menu option and displayed in inverse video (line 880-900). After the keyboard query, the menu option is returned to the normal representation (line 920). Depending on the key that was selected, the HDFT.ROW variable is activated (lines 960-990) and checked (lines 1000 and 1010).

```
1050 '----- initialize background -----
1060 :
1070 X$= STRING$(WD.LGTH,BKG.CHAR$)
1080 FOR RW= WD.ROW TO WD.ROW+WD.HGT
1090   CALL FASTSCRN(RW,WD.COLM,BKGCOLR,X$)
1100 NEXT RW
1110 RETURN
1120 :
1130 '----- universal-routine for window -----
1140 :
1150 X$= CHR$(218)+STRING$(WD.LGTH%,CHR$(196))+CHR$(191)
1160 DEF SEG:CALL FASTSCRN(WD.ROW,WD.COLM,WNDW.BKG,X$)
1170 X$= CHR$(179)+STRING$(WD.LGTH%," ")+CHR$(179)
```

```
1180 IF WD.SHADOW THEN X$= X$+CHR$(178)+CHR$(178)
1190 FOR RW= WD.ROW+1 TO WD.ROW+WD.HGT
1200   DEF SEG:CALL FASTSCRN(RW,WD.COLM,WNDW.BKG,X$)
1210 NEXT RW
1220 X$= CHR$(192)+STRING$(WD.LGTH%,CHR$(196))+CHR$(217)
1230 IF WD.SHADOW THEN X$= X$+CHR$(178)+CHR$(178)
1240 RW= WD.ROW+WD.HGT+1
1250 DEF SEG:CALL FASTSCRN(RW,WD.COLM,WNDW.BKG,X$)
1260 IF WD.HEAD$= "" THEN 1300 'continue with footing
1270   X$= " "+WD.HEAD$+" "
1280   CL= WD.COLM+3
1290   CALL FASTSCRN(WD.ROW,CL,HDFT.TXT,X$)
1300 IF WD.FOOT$= "" THEN 1340 'continue with shadow
1310   X$= " "+WD.FOOT$+" "
1320   RW= WD.ROW+WD.HGT+1:CL= WD.COLM+3
1330   CALL FASTSCRN(RW,CL,HDFT.TXT,X$)
1340 IF NOT WD.SHADOW THEN 1380 'Back
1350   X$= STRING$(WD.LGTH+2,CHR$(178))
1360   RW= WD.ROW+WD.HGT+2:CL= WD.COLM+2
1370   CALL FASTSCRN(RW,CL,WNDW.BKG,X$)
1380 RETURN
1390 :
1400 '----- store current screen display -----
1410 :
1420 IF CUR.SCN= MAX.SCN THEN BEEP:RETURN
1430 DEF SEG:BUFFER.OFS%= VARPTR(BUFFER%(CUR.SCN*2000)):CALL
     SAVESCRN(BUFFER.OFS%)
1440 CUR.SCN= CUR.SCN+1
1450 RETURN
1460 :
1470 '----- restore last screen display -----
1480 :
1490 IF CUR.SCN= 0 THEN BEEP:RETURN
1500 CUR.SCN= CUR.SCN-1
1510 DEF SEG:BUFFER.OFS%= VARPTR(BUFFER%(CUR.SCN*2000)):CALL
     RESTSCRN(BUFFER.OFS%)
1520 RETURN
1530 :
1540 'data-lines from COM-file: screen.com
1550 :
1560 RESTORE 1580
1570 DEF SEG:FOR I=1 TO  227:READ X:POKE MP.START+I-1,X: NEXT I
1580 DATA 235,109,144,235,109,144, 85,139,236, 30,  6
1590 DATA 139,118, 12,138, 28,176,160,246,227, 45,160
1600 DATA   0, 80,139,118, 10,138, 28,176,  2,246,227
1610 DATA  91,  3,195, 72, 72, 80,139,118,  8,138, 36
1620 DATA 139,118,  6,138, 12,181,  0,139,116,  1, 80
1630 DATA 191,  0,176,179,  0,205, 17, 37, 48,  0, 61
1640 DATA  48,  0,116,  6,129,199,  0,  8,179,  1,142
1650 DATA 199, 88, 95,252,186,218,  3,128,251,  0,116
1660 DATA  11,236,208,216,114,246,250,236,208,216,115
1670 DATA 251,172,251,171,226,235,  7, 31, 93,202,  8
1680 DATA   0,235, 41,144, 85,139,236, 30,  6,139,118
```

```
1690 DATA    6,139,   4,139,240,191,   0,176,179,   0,205
1700 DATA   17,  37,  48,   0,  61,  48,   0,116,   6,129,199
1710 DATA    0,   8,179,   1,142,199,  51,255,235,  40,144
1720 DATA   85,139,236,  30,   6,139,118,   6,139,   4,139
1730 DATA  248,  30,   7,190,   0,176,179,   0,205,  17,  37
1740 DATA   48,   0,  61,  48,   0,116,   6,129,198,   0,   8
1750 DATA  179,   1,142,222,  51,246,185,208,   7,252,186
1760 DATA  218,   3,128,251,   0,116,  11,236,208,216,114
1770 DATA  246,250,236,208,216,115,251,173,251,171,226
1780 DATA  235,   7,  31,  93,202,   2,   0
1790 RETURN
```

This program demonstrates the administration of a bar menu and, with an example routine (search), shows you how to use the screen manager for saving and restoring screen displays. You can see that the menu is only constructed once. Since the screen display was saved before the function call (line 380) and restored after the function call (line 400), this isn't necessary.

11.6.3 Pull-Down Menus

The newest type of menu is the pull-down menu. As the name indicates, the entire menu is "pulled down" once you select the first option in the main menu (usually located across the top line of the screen).

Implementing a pull-down menu is more complicated than the other menu types. The program must control both the main menu in the first line and the pull-down menu, which belongs to it, must be controlled. Because of this there are always two results: first the number of the menu option from the main menu and then the number of the menu option from the pull-down menu. Also, initializing the menu options that will be displayed is more difficult than in other menus.

In the following program you'll notice that the menu options aren't passed as individual elements of an array, as in other menus, but as strings which are separated by a special character. The element 0 is always the main menu and the elements 1 to n are the pull down menus.

This has several advantages. Assigning a complete menu is faster than working with individual elements. Also, this method requires less memory space than when each entry represents an element in an array. Finally, the menu structure is more visible during programming because several pages of assignments to individual array elements aren't needed.

However, there is also a disadvantage. Separating the individual strings requires a lot of time. Even using FASTSCRN, the display's slowness is obvious. However, mainly in large projects, in which more than one main menu exists and requires many assignments,

```
10 '-------------------------------------------------
20 'PD_MENU.BAS   demonstration of a Pull-Down menu
30 '-------------------------------------------------
40 :
50 DEFINT A-Z
60 OPTION BASE 0
70 CLS:KEY OFF:FOR I=1 TO 10:KEY I,"":NEXT I
80 MP.START= &HE000
85 GOSUB 2190 ' Initialize MP
90 SAVESCRN= MP.START
100 RESTSCRN= MP.START+3
110 FASTSCRN= MP.START+6
120 FALSE= 0: TRUE= NOT FALSE
130 MAX.SCN= 3:DIM BUFFER%(2000*MAX.SCN)
140 MAX.BARMENU= 6
150 DIM MENU$(MAX.BARMENU),BARMENU$(MAX.BARMENU),BARMENU.POS(MAX.BARMENU+1)
160 MAX.PDMENU= 10
170 DIM PDMENU$(MAX.PDMENU)
180 CUR.SCN= 0
190 WNDW.BKG= 112: MESSG.BKG= 127: HDFT.TXT= 7
200 BKG.CHAR$= CHR$(177): BKGCOLR= 15
210 :
220 WD.ROW= 1: WD.COLM= 1: WD.LGTH= 80: WD.HGT= 25
230 GOSUB 1700 'initialize background
240 :
250 MENU$(0)= "File|Process|Print|Options|Help|End|"
260 MENU$(1)= "load|save|erase|copy|rename|"
270 MENU$(2)= "edit|discard|new|"
280 MENU$(3)= "current file|other file|"
290 MENU$(4)= "colors|printer|"
300 MENU$(5)= "general|keyboard|mouse|"
310 MENU$(6)= "terminate program|"
```

In lines 250 to 310, the array for the pull-down menus is initialized. The individual menu options (or "suboptions") are separated by the | character. This character must be entered after the last option; otherwise an evaluation, through the control program, won't provide the desired result.

```
320 GOSUB 750 'menu-selection
330 IF BAR.ITEM<> 0 AND PD.ITEM<> 0 THEN 360 'call functions
```

Again the menu works as a type of function. The result is returned in the BAR.ITEM and PD.ITEM variables. BAR.ITEM is the selected option of the main menu and PD.ITEM is the menu point of the pull-down menu.

```
340 COLOR 7,0:CLS:PRINT "*** END ***":PRINT:END
350 :
360 '----- branch according to BAR.ITEM -----
370 :
380 ON BAR.ITEM GOSUB 430, 460, 490, 520, 550, 580
390 GOTO 320 'query menu again
400 :
410 '----- branch according to PD.ITEM -----
420 :
430 '----- BAR.Item= 1 -----
440 ON PD.ITEM GOSUB 620, 620, 620, 620
450 RETURN
460 '----- BAR.Item= 2 -----
470 ON PD.ITEM GOSUB 620, 620, 620
480 RETURN
490 '----- BAR.Item= 3 -----
500 ON PD.ITEM GOSUB 620, 620
510 RETURN
520 '----- BAR.Item= 4 -----
530 ON PD.ITEM GOSUB 620, 620
540 RETURN
550 '----- BAR.Item= 5 -----
560 ON PD.ITEM GOSUB 620, 620, 620
570 RETURN
580 '----- BAR.Item= 6 -----
590 ON PD.ITEM GOSUB 620
600 RETURN
610 :
```

Notice that the branch is more comprehensive than in other menus. However, it's very easy to understand.

```
620 '----- example-routine -----
630 :
640 GOSUB 2050 'save screen display
650 WD.ROW= 10: WD.COLM= 20: WD.LGTH= 50: WD.HGT= 5: WD.SHADOW= TRUE
660 WD.HEAD$= "example...":WD.FOOT$= "Strike <Esc> to exit"
670 GOSUB 1780 'display window
680 RW= WD.ROW+3: CL= WD.COLM+4
690 X$= BAR.CHOICE$+"/"+PD.CHOICE$
700 DEF SEG:CALL FASTSCRN(RW,CL,MESSG.BKG,X$)
710 IF INKEY$= "" THEN 710
720 GOSUB 2120 'restore screen
730 RETURN
740 :
```

This example routine demonstrates how, on the basis of the results from BAR.ITEM and PD.ITEM, branching can occur. The construction ON X GOSUB must be adjusted to the conditions of the actual program application.

```
750 '----- display main-menu and control selection -----
760 :
770 COUNTER= 1: BARMENU.POS(COUNTER)= 5: X$= MENU$(0)
780 WHILE INSTR(X$,"|")<> 0
790    BARMENU$(COUNTER)= LEFT$(X$,INSTR(X$,"|")-1)
800    BARMENU.POS(COUNTER+1)= BARMENU.POS(COUNTER)+LEN(BARMENU$(COUNTER))+2
810    COUNTER= COUNTER+1
820    X$= MID$(X$,INSTR(X$,"|")+1,99)
830 WEND
```

This loop constructs the main menu. At this time the current menu option, before the
separator, is transferred from the element 0 of the array to the second array BARMENU$().
Simultaneously, in the BARMENU.POS() array, a record is made in the column, of the
first line, in which the menu option should be displayed.

```
840 RW= 1:CL= 1: X$= SPACE$(80)
850 DEF SEG:CALL FASTSCRN(RW,CL,MESSG.BKG,X$)
860 FOR I= 1 TO MAX.BARMENU
870    CL= BARMENU.POS(I)
880    DEF SEG:CALL FASTSCRN(RW,CL,MESSG.BKG,BARMENU$(I))
890 NEXT I
900 RW= 25: CL= 1
910 X$= " Use <"+CHR$(27)+"> and <"+CHR$(26)+"> to select and <Return> to execute
    or <Esc> to End": X$= X$+SPACE$(80-LEN(X$))
920 DEF SEG:CALL FASTSCRN(RW,CL,MESSG.BKG,X$)
930 PD.FLAG= FALSE:BAR.ITEM= 1: ONKEY$= "": LOCATE ,,0
940 WHILE ONKEY$<> CHR$(27) AND ONKEY$<> CHR$(13)
950    IF PD.FLAG THEN 1020 'continue with next Pull-Down
960    RW= 1:CL= BARMENU.POS(BAR.ITEM)-1:X$= " "+BARMENU$(BAR.ITEM)+" "
970    DEF SEG:CALL FASTSCRN(RW,CL,HDFT.TXT,X$)
980    ONKEY$= INKEY$:IF ONKEY$= "" THEN 980
990    DEF SEG:CALL FASTSCRN(RW,CL,MESSG.BKG,X$)
1000   IF ONKEY$= CHR$(27) THEN BAR.ITEM= 0:PD.ITEM= 0:GOTO 1160 'End menu
1010   IF ONKEY$<> CHR$(13) THEN 1070 'test special-keys
1020      PD.FLAG= TRUE
1030   BAR.CHOICE$= BARMENU$(BAR.ITEM)
1040      GOSUB 1220 'display Pull-Down menu
1050      IF ONKEY$= CHR$(13) THEN 1160 'End, menu-point selected
1060      IF ONKEY$= CHR$(27) THEN 960 'Pull-Down interrupted, continue query
1070   IF LEN(ONKEY$)<> 2 THEN BEEP:GOTO 960 'wrong key, continue query
1080   ONKEY= ASC(RIGHT$(ONKEY$,1))
1090   IF ONKEY= 77 THEN BAR.ITEM= BAR.ITEM+1 'Cursor right
1100   IF ONKEY= 75 THEN BAR.ITEM= BAR.ITEM-1 'Cursor left
1110   IF ONKEY= 71 THEN BAR.ITEM= 1 '<Home> key
1120   IF ONKEY= 79 THEN BAR.ITEM= MAX.BARMENU '<End> key
1130   IF ONKEY= 80 THEN 1020 'display Pull-Down menu
1140   IF BAR.ITEM< 1 THEN BAR.ITEM= MAX.BARMENU
1150   IF BAR.ITEM> MAX.BARMENU THEN BAR.ITEM= 1
1160 WEND
```

The keyboard query and control take place in a larger WHILE...WEND loop. The bar is
positioned horizontally. If the <Return> or <Cursor Down> keys are activated, a subroutine

is called to display the pull-down menu (starting at line 1010 or 1130). The PD.FLAG variable controls the display of the pull-down menus. For the keys mentioned above, this is set to TRUE. If, in the control program for the pull-down menus, the <Cursor Right> or <Cursor Left> keys are activated, this variable remains TRUE. This allows selection during the display of the pull-down menu in the main menu and ensures a better overview during the selection. If, during the control of the pull-down menu, another key is activated, the variable is set to FALSE and a selection cannot be made.

```
1170 PD.FLAG= FALSE
1180 RW= 25: CL= 1: X$= SPACE$(80)
1190 DEF SEG:CALL FASTSCRN(RW,CL,MESSG.BKG,X$) 'erase Status
1200 RETURN
1210 :
1220 '----- control Pull-Down menu display and selection -----
1230 :
1240 GOSUB 2050 'save screen display
```

Before a pull-down menu is displayed, the current screen display is saved.

```
1250 COUNTER= 1: X$= MENU$(BAR.ITEM)
1260 WHILE INSTR(X$,"|")<> 0
1270    PDMENU$(COUNTER)= LEFT$(X$,INSTR(X$,"|")-1)
1280    COUNTER= COUNTER+1
1290    X$= MID$(X$,INSTR(X$,"|")+1,99)
1300 WEND
```

The way the individual options of the pull-down menu are prepared is similar to the main menu. Since the options are displayed vertically, the column positions don't have to be recorded. The individual options are transmitted into a second array, PDMENU$().

```
1310 MAX.PDITEMS= COUNTER-1 'number of entries in this pull-down menu
1320 MAX.LGTH= 0
1330 FOR I= 1 TO MAX.PDITEMS
1340    IF LEN(PDMENU$(I))> MAX.LGTH THEN MAX.LGTH= LEN(PDMENU$(I))
1350 NEXT I
```

In this loop, the widest menu option is determined. Depending on the results, the variables for the window are initialized (line 1370).

```
1360 WD.ROW= 2: WD.COLM= BARMENU.POS(BAR.ITEM):WD.SHADOW= FALSE
1370 WD.LGTH= MAX.LGTH+2:WD.HGT= MAX.PDITEMS: WD.HEAD$="": WD.FOOT$=""
1380 GOSUB 1780 'window display
1390 CL= WD.COLM+2
1400 FOR I= 1 TO MAX.PDITEMS
1410    RW= WD.ROW+I
1420    DEF SEG:CALL FASTSCRN(RW,CL,WNDW.BKG,PDMENU$(I))
1430 NEXT I
1440 RW=25: CL= 1
```

```
1450 X$= " Use <"+CHR$(24)+"> and <"+CHR$(25)+"> to select and <Return> to
     execute or <Esc> to exit this option ": X$= X$+SPACE$(80-LEN(X$))
1460 DEF SEG:CALL FASTSCRN(RW,CL,MESSG.BKG,X$)
1470 PD.ITEM= 1: CL= BARMENU.POS(BAR.ITEM)+1: ONKEY$= "": LOCATE ,,0
1480 PD.READY= FALSE
1490 WHILE NOT PD.READY
1500 PD.CHOICE$= PDMENU$(PD.ITEM)
1510    RW= PD.ITEM+2
1520    X$= " "+PDMENU$(PD.ITEM): X$= X$+SPACE$(MAX.LGTH+2-LEN(X$))
1530    DEF SEG:CALL FASTSCRN(RW,CL,HDFT.TXT,X$)
1540    ONKEY$= INKEY$:IF ONKEY$= "" THEN 1540
1550    DEF SEG:CALL FASTSCRN(RW,CL,WNDW.BKG,X$)
1560    IF ONKEY$= CHR$(27) THEN PD.ITEM= 0:PD.READY= TRUE:PD.FLAG= FALSE:GOTO
1660 'back
1570    IF ONKEY$= CHR$(13) THEN PD.READY= TRUE:GOTO 1660 'selected, back
1580    ONKEY= ASC(RIGHT$(ONKEY$,1))
1590    IF ONKEY= 72 THEN PD.ITEM= PD.ITEM-1 'Cursor up
1600    IF ONKEY= 80 THEN PD.ITEM= PD.ITEM+1 'Cursor down
1610    IF ONKEY= 71 THEN PD.ITEM= 1 '<Home> key
1620    IF ONKEY= 79 THEN PD.ITEM= MAX.PDITEMS
1630    IF ONKEY= 75 OR ONKEY= 77 THEN PD.READY= TRUE 'Cursor left/right
1640    IF PD.ITEM < 1 THEN PD.ITEM= MAX.PDITEMS
1650    IF PD.ITEM > MAX.PDITEMS THEN PD.ITEM= 1
1660 WEND
```

The keyboard query and control of the bar occurs in a WHILE...WEND loop. The positioning and display of the bar corresponds to the routine from the program B_MENU.BAS. If the <Esc> key is pressed, the pull-down menu is terminated. The PD.FLAG variable is set to FALSE, which prevents the "endless" display of this pull-down menu. Otherwise, a return jump is made in the control of the main-menu (line 950).

```
1670 GOSUB 2120 'restore display
```

The saved screen display is restored.

```
1680 RETURN
1690 :
```

The rest of the program should be familiar from the previous programs.

```
1700 '----- initialize background -----
1710 :
1720 X$= STRING$(WD.LGTH,BKG.CHAR$)
1730 FOR RW= WD.ROW TO WD.ROW+WD.HGT
1740    CALL FASTSCRN(RW,WD.COLM,BKGCOLR,X$)
1750 NEXT RW
1760 RETURN
1770 :
1780 '----- universal-routine for window -----
1790 :
```

```
1800 X$= CHR$(218)+STRING$(WD.LGTH%,CHR$(196))+CHR$(191)
1810 DEF SEG:CALL FASTSCRN(WD.ROW,WD.COLM,WNDW.BKG,X$)
1820 X$= CHR$(179)+STRING$(WD.LGTH%," ")+CHR$(179)
1830 IF WD.SHADOW THEN X$= X$+CHR$(178)+CHR$(178)
1840 FOR RW= WD.ROW+1 TO WD.ROW+WD.HGT
1850    DEF SEG:CALL FASTSCRN(RW,WD.COLM,WNDW.BKG,X$)
1860 NEXT RW
1870 X$= CHR$(192)+STRING$(WD.LGTH%,CHR$(196))+CHR$(217)
1880 IF WD.SHADOW THEN X$= X$+CHR$(178)+CHR$(178)
1890 RW= WD.ROW+WD.HGT+1
1900 DEF SEG:CALL FASTSCRN(RW,WD.COLM,WNDW.BKG,X$)
1910 IF WD.HEAD$= "" THEN 1950 'continue with footing
1920    X$= " "+WD.HEAD$+" "
1930    CL= WD.COLM+3
1940    CALL FASTSCRN(WD.ROW,CL,HDFT.TXT,X$)
1950 IF WD.FOOT$= "" THEN 1990 'continue with shadow
1960    X$= " "+WD.FOOT$+" "
1970    RW= WD.ROW+WD.HGT+1:CL= WD.COLM+3
1980    CALL FASTSCRN(RW,CL,HDFT.TXT,X$)
1990 IF NOT WD.SHADOW THEN 2030 'back
2000    X$= STRING$(WD.LGTH+2,CHR$(178))
2010    RW= WD.ROW+WD.HGT+2:CL= WD.COLM+2
2020    CALL FASTSCRN(RW,CL,WNDW.BKG,X$)
2030 RETURN
2040 :
2050 '----- save current screen display -----
2060 :
2070 IF CUR.SCN= MAX.SCN THEN BEEP:RETURN
2080 DEF SEG:BUFFER.OFS%= VARPTR(BUFFER%(CUR.SCN*2000)):CALL
     SAVESCRN(BUFFER.OFS%)
2090 CUR.SCN= CUR.SCN+1
2100 RETURN
2110 :
2120 '----- restore last display-screen -----
2130 :
2140 IF CUR.SCN= 0 THEN BEEP:RETURN
2150 CUR.SCN= CUR.SCN-1
2160 DEF SEG:BUFFER.OFS%= VARPTR(BUFFER%(CUR.SCN*2000)):CALL
     RESTSCRN(BUFFER.OFS%)
2170 RETURN
2180 :
2190 'data-lines from COM-file: screen.com
2200 :
2210 RESTORE 2230
2220 DEF SEG:FOR I=1 TO  227:READ X:POKE MP.START+I-1,X: NEXT I
2230 DATA 235,109,144,235,109,144, 85,139,236, 30,  6
2240 DATA 139,118, 12,138, 28,176,160,246,227, 45,160
2250 DATA   0, 80,139,118, 10,138, 28,176,  2,246,227
2260 DATA  91,  3,195, 72, 72, 80,139,118,  8,138, 36
2270 DATA 139,118,  6,138, 12,181,  0,139,116,  1, 80
2280 DATA 191,  0,176,179,  0,205, 17, 37, 48,  0, 61
2290 DATA  48,  0,116,  6,129,199,  0,  8,179,  1,142
2300 DATA 199, 88, 95,252,186,218,  3,128,251,  0,116
```

```
2310 DATA  11,236,208,216,114,246,250,236,208,216,115
2320 DATA 251,172,251,171,226,235,  7, 31, 93,202,  8
2330 DATA   0,235, 41,144, 85,139,236, 30,  6,139,118
2340 DATA   6,139,  4,139,240,191,  0,176,179,  0,205
2350 DATA  17, 37, 48,  0, 61, 48,  0,116,  6,129,199
2360 DATA   0,  8,179,  1,142,199, 51,255,235, 40,144
2370 DATA  85,139,236, 30,  6,139,118,  6,139,  4,139
2380 DATA 248, 30,  7,190,  0,176,179,  0,205, 17, 37
2390 DATA  48,  0, 61, 48,  0,116,  6,129,198,  0,  8
2400 DATA 179,  1,142,222, 51,246,185,208,  7,252,186
2410 DATA 218,  3,128,251,  0,116, 11,236,208,216,114
2420 DATA 246,250,236,208,216,115,251,173,251,171,226
2430 DATA 235,  7, 31, 93,202,  2,  0
2440 RETURN
```

Even though pull-down menus are more extensive than selection or bar menus, they're fairly easy to implement. One thing to keep in mind is that implementing the functions in a user-friendly manner doesn't leave much space for this type of menu. Using a simple menu usually is more effective. Also, remember that user-friendly error and help functions require a lot of space (refer to Chapter 16).

11.7   Scrolling Screen Areas

We mentioned in Section 11.5 that the BIOS screen areas (or window) can be scrolled up or down using interrupt 10h. During *scrolling*, the contents of a window are moved up or down a certain number of lines and a new output can appear in the cleared area.

Scrolling is normally used to display listings on the screen. For example, after displaying 15 lines of a listing, you can then display the preceding or subsequent 15 lines by pressing a key. However, it would be very difficult to compare two lines that appear on different screen pages. In these instances, scrolling line by line is needed. However, this would require too much time in PC-BASIC. By using the DOS interface, which has already been used, we can quickly solve this problem through the BIOS.

The task is assigned to interrupt 10h of the BIOS. Parameters must be passed over the DOS interface to the interrupt and the area to be scrolled must be defined with coordinates. An attribute must be provided for the empty lines that are created. First look at the following program, which demonstrates this:

```
 10 '-------------------------------------------------------------
 20 'SCROLL.BAS, scrolling of display areas     1986 (C) H.J.Bomanns
 30 '-------------------------------------------------------------
 40 :
 50 CLS:KEY OFF
 60 PRINT "Initialization .....";
 70 DIM WNDOW(3,4) 'x,y,x,y
 80 RESTORE 100
 90 FOR I=1 TO 3:FOR K=1 TO 4:READ WNDOW(I,K):NEXT K:NEXT I
100 DATA 5,5,10,35,   8,40,13,75,   15,20,20,50
110 DIM CHAR$(26)
120 FOR I=1 TO 26:CHAR$(I)= STRING$(60,CHR$(I+64)):NEXT I
130 GOSUB 1150 'poke machine program in memory
140 :
150 DOS.SN= MP.START
160 INT.NR%= &H10:POKE INT.ADR,INT.NR%
170 :
180 '----- construct display-screen -----
190 :
200 CLS:FOR I=1 TO 24:PRINT STRING$(80,CHR$(177));:NEXT I
210 :
220 '----- clear window -----
230 :
240 FOR I=1 TO 3
250    FROM.ROWNO%= WNDOW(I,1):FROM.COLMNO%= WNDOW(I,2)
260    TO.ROWNO%= WNDOW(I,3):TO.COLMNO%= WNDOW(I,4)
270    COLR%= 112:NUM.OF.LINES%= 0:SCROLL$= "up"
280    GOSUB 940 'clear window
290 NEXT I
300 :
```

```
310 '----- output window content -----
320 :
330 LOCATE 23,1:PRINT "<Return> to continue or <Esc> to end ";
340 GOSUB 1040
350 :
360 '----- scroll window  -----
370 :
380 IF SCROLL$="down" THEN SCROLL$="up" ELSE SCROLL$= "down"
390 FOR ROWNO= 1 TO 6
400    FOR I=1 TO 3
410       FROM.ROWNO%= WNDOW(I,1): FROM.COLMNO%= WNDOW(I,2)
420       TO.ROWNO%= WNDOW(I,3): TO.COLMNO%= WNDOW(I,4)
430       COLR%= 112:NUM.OF.LINES%= 1
440       GOSUB 940 'scroll window
450    NEXT I
460    FOR K=1 TO 600:NEXT K
470 NEXT ROWNO
480 FOR K=1 TO 600:NEXT K
490 IF INKEY$="" THEN 340 'scroll until key is activated
500 :
510 '----- scroll table up/down -----
520 :
530 CLS
540 FROM.ROWNO%= 4:FROM.COLMNO%= 5:TO.ROWNO%= 15:TO.COLMNO%= 70
550 COLR%= 112:NUM.OF.LINES%= 0
560 GOSUB 940 'clear window
570 LOCATE 5,1 'first line in the window
580 FOR I=1 TO 10
590    LOCATE ,8:PRINT CHAR$(I)
600 NEXT I
610 LOCATE 24,1:PRINT "[";CHR$(24);"] and [";CHR$(25);"] to scroll table or <Esc>
    to quit";
620 :
630 '----- keyboard-control -----
640 :
650 CURRENT.LINE= 1
660 X$=INKEY$:IF X$="" THEN 660
670 IF LEN(X$)= 2 THEN 690
680 IF X$= CHR$(27) THEN CLS:END
690 ONKEY= ASC(RIGHT$(X$,1))
700 IF ONKEY= 72 AND CURRENT.LINE >  1 THEN 760 'Cursor up
710 IF ONKEY= 80 AND CURRENT.LINE < 17 THEN 850 'Cursor down
720 BEEP:GOTO 660
730 :
740 '----- Cursor up -----
750 :
760 FROM.ROWNO%= 5:FROM.COLMNO%= 8:TO.ROWNO%= 14:TO.COLMNO%= 70
770 COLR%= 112:NUM.OF.LINES%= 1:SCROLL$= "down"
780 GOSUB 940
790 CURRENT.LINE= CURRENT.LINE-1
800 LOCATE 5,8:PRINT CHAR$(CURRENT.LINE)
810 GOTO 660
820 :
```

```
830 '----- Cursor down -----
840 :
850 FROM.ROWNO%= 5:FROM.COLMNO%= 8:TO.ROWNO%= 15:TO.COLMNO%= 70
860 COLR%= 112:NUM.OF.LINES%= 1:SCROLL$= "up"
870 GOSUB 940
880 LOCATE 14,8:PRINT CHAR$(CURRENT.LINE+10)
890 CURRENT.LINE= CURRENT.LINE+1
900 GOTO 660
910 :
920 '----- window-routine -----
930 :
940 IF SCROLL$="up" THEN AH%= 6 ELSE AH%= 7
950 AL%= NUM.OF.LINES%
960 CH%= FROM.ROWNO%-1:CL%= FROM.COLMNO%-1
970 DH%= TO.ROWNO%-1:DL%= TO.COLMNO%-1
980 BH%= COLR%
990 DEF SEG:CALL DOS.SN(AH%, AL%, BH%, BL%, CH%, CL%, DH%, DL%, ES%, DI%, SI%,
    FLAGS%)
1000 RETURN
1010 :
1020 '----- output window content -----
1030 :
1040 FOR I=1 TO 3
1050    LOCATE WNDOW(I,1)-1,WNDOW(I,2):PRINT " window";I
1060    FOR ROWNO= 0 TO 4
1070       LOCATE WNDOW(I,1)+ROWNO,WNDOW(I,2)
1080       PRINT "line";ROWNO+1;STRING$(20,"x");
1090    NEXT ROWNO
1100 NEXT I
1110 RETURN
1120 :
1130 'data-lines from COM-file: dos_sn.com
1140 :
1150 MP.START= &HE000
1160 RESTORE 1180
1170 DEF SEG:FOR I=1 TO  151:READ X:POKE MP.START+I-1,X: NEXT I
1180 DATA 250, 85,139,236, 30,  6,139,118,  6,139,  4
1190 DATA  80,157,139,118, 14,138, 20,139,118, 16,138
1200 DATA  52,139,118, 18,138, 12,139,118, 20,138, 44
1210 DATA 139,118, 22,138, 28,139,118, 24,138, 60,139
1220 DATA 118, 26,138,  4,139,118, 28,138, 36,139,118
1230 DATA   8,139, 60, 80,139,118, 12,139,  4,142,192
1240 DATA  88,139,118, 10,139, 52, 85,251,205, 33,250
1250 DATA  93, 86,156,139,118, 28,136, 36,139,118, 26
1260 DATA 136,  4,139,118, 24,136, 60,139,118, 22,136
1270 DATA  28,139,118, 20,136, 44,139,118, 18,136, 12
1280 DATA 139,118, 16,136, 52,139,118, 14,136, 20, 88
1290 DATA 139,118,  6,137,  4, 88,139,118, 10,137,  4
1300 DATA 140,192,139,118, 12,137,  4,139,118,  8,137
1310 DATA  60,  7, 31, 93,251,202, 24,  0
1320 MP.ENDE= MP.START+I-1
1330 FOR I= MP.START TO MP.ENDE:IF PEEK(I)= 205 THEN INT.ADR= I+1 ELSE NEXT
1340 RETURN
```

A GOSUB to line 1130 POKEs the machine language routine in memory. Then the variables for the window positions and the output texts are initialized. Starting at line 220, three different sized windows are created. As we explained in the previous section, the scroll function is also used here, by indicating 0 as the number of lines to be scrolled. The defined area, with the indicated attribute, is cleared.

The program portion from line 310 to 490 demonstrates the up and down scrolling of the text in the individual windows. To observe the function more clearly, time delay loops are provided in line 460 and 480. In the following program section, starting at line 510, a table is scrolled on a line by line basis with the cursor keys. The keyboard control occurs after line 630. The display is scrolled either one line up or down.

To include this in your programs, you need the subroutine, starting at line 1130, for initializing the assembler routine and the subroutine, starting at line 920, for passing parameters to the DOS interface. The lines 150/160, in which the variable for CALL is initialized and the number of the interrupts to be addressed is set, are important. Before the call of the subroutines, the parameter variables obtain their values according to need, starting at line 920.

12. Keyboard Input

The most important interaction between program, hardware and user is entering data through the keyboard. PC-BASIC provides, depending on the application being used, various commands, statements and functions for this interaction. A user-friendly input interface will make your program more impressive. In this chapter we'll examine what input capabilities should be used in certain situations. We'll also present the framework for a user-friendly input routine. Finally we'll discuss the advantages and disadvantages of using a mouse.

12.1   Input Statements

Let's review the input statements and functions:

```
INPUT [;] "<comment>" ,|; <Variable,...>
```

This is probably the most often used command for keyboard input. The input is terminated with the <Return> key. Then the program continues. The input can be stopped with <Ctrl><C> or <Ctrl><Break>.

```
LINE INPUT [;] "<comment>" ,|; <Variable>
```

This is similar to the INPUT statement but punctuation marks, such as commas (,) and semicolons (;), are allowed as input.

```
X$= INKEY$
```

This function delivers the ASCII code of a pressed key. A two byte code is given when a function key is pressed. If a key isn't pressed, the result is a null string ("") and the program isn't interrupted.

```
X$= INPUT$(<count>)
```

This function interrupts the program until the number of keys, indicated by <count>, have been pressed; the result is then given in a string. Function keys aren't recognized because only one byte code is transmitted. The input is stopped with <Ctrl><C> or <Ctrl><Break>.

You're probably already familiar with INPUT or LINE INPUT, as well as the error message, "Redo from start", which is displayed when an illegal code is entered for a numeric variable. The following is a routine that prevents this from happening:

```
200 '---------------------------------------------
210 'INPUT.BAS numeric input without "Redo from start"
220 '---------------------------------------------
230 CLS:KEY OFF
240 TEST$="abcdefghijklmnopqrstuvwxyzABCDEFGHIJKLMNOPQRSTUVWXYZ"
250 :
260 LOCATE 10,5:COLOR 7,0
270 LINE INPUT "Your monthly earnings: ";MNTH.EARNING$
280 ERR.MESG= 15
290 FOR I= 1 TO LEN(TEST$)
300 IF INSTR(MNTH.EARNING$,MID$(TEST$,I,1))<> 0 THEN 330 ELSE NEXT
310 GOTO 380
320 :
330 'invalid input
340 :
350 LOCATE 24,1:PRINT "Enter only numbers <0> to <9> and characters <.>,<+> and
    <->!";SPACE$(81-POS(0));
360 BEEP:GOTO 260
370 :
380 'valid input
390 :
400 LOCATE 24,1:PRINT VAL(MNTH.EARNING$);" is a valid input!";SPACE$(81-POS(0));
410 IF INKEY$="" THEN 410 ELSE 260
```

The TEST$ variable is initialized according to the invalid characters. You can use this routine to read strings which, for example, do not allow numbers or graphic characters. If you're familiar with assembler programming, you can use a routine to check this (see Chapter 8). This saves a lot of time with longer comparisons. If you do not want the characters (and therefore the password) to appear on the screen, use the INPUT$() function. The following is an example of a routine reading in a password:

```
200 '----------------
210 'Password Routine PASSWORD.BAS
220 '----------------
230 :
240 PASSWORD$=""
250 CLS:KEY OFF
260 LOCATE 10,5:PRINT "------";:LOCATE 10,5,1
270 X$=INPUT$(1):IF X$= CHR$(0) THEN 270
280 PRINT CHR$(254);
290 PASSWORD$= PASSWORD$+X$
300 IF LEN(PASSWORD$)=6 THEN 320
310 GOTO 270
320 IF PASSWORD$<>"abcdef" THEN BEEP:GOTO 240
```

The INKEY$ function isn't easy to use in this instance because a 2 byte code, which must be queried or ignored, is returned each time a function or control key is activated. In line 270 of the program you'll see that intercepting the function and control keys is simple.

12.2   User-Friendly Input Routine

When we began programming in PC-BASIC, we always used INPUT or LINE INPUT to enter data through the keyboard. However, even with small programs the memory requirements can be limited. But larger programs, in which complex problems must be solved and larger data quantities, in several arrays, must be administered, present more problems.

For example, help on an array level is impossible with the INPUT and LINE INPUT functions because help can only be offered by the program when it reacts to the key that's pressed. A reaction is possible for INPUT only after the <Return> key is pressed. But by the time the <Return> key is pressed, it's too late to receive input help because the input is already complete. There can also be problems with the input length because neither of these commands require that the maximum length be stated. Also, complicated display attributes must be used to highlight input.

We once worked on an inventory control program which required six templates. The smallest template had 17 input fields and the largest template had 74 input fields. Since many fields contained 1 byte flags, we had to find a way to display the available flags through a help key. Speed was essential since among other tasks, telephone inquiries were going to be answered with the help of the system.

The following program shows excerpts from this program. By using these ideas and the Help/Error routines found in Chapter 16, you can develop an excellent input interface.

```
10 '--------------------------
20 'user-friendly input-routine USER FRIENDLY.BAS
30 '--------------------------
40 :
50 CLS:KEY OFF:KEY 1,""
60 MAX.MASK= 2 'two templates for DEMO
70 DIM MAX.FIELD%(2) 'maximum count fields per template
80 MAX.FIELD%(1)= 5:MAX.FIELD%(2)= 5 '5 fields per template
90 DIM INPT$(2,5) 'input default or stored
100 DIM MASK%(2,5,3)
110 '          | | |
120 '          | | > line,column,length of the field
130 '          | > count max. fields per template (field-number)
140 '          > count templates (templates-number)
150 RESTORE 210
160 FOR M=1 TO 2
170    FOR F=1 TO 5
180       READ MASK%(M,F,1),MASK%(M,F,2),MASK%(M,F,3)
190    NEXT F
200 NEXT M
210 DATA 5,5,10 ,7,5,15  ,9,5,20 ,11,5,15 ,13,5,30 :'fields 1. template
220 DATA 6,8,15 ,8,8,23 ,10,8,13 ,12,8,17 ,14,8,45 :'fields 2. template
230 :
```

```
240 TXT.FORGRD= 7:INPT.FORGRD= 15 'determine colors
250 TXT.BAKGRD= 0:INPT.BAKGRD=  4
260 CURR.MASK= 1
270 OUTPT$="Test"
280 :
290 '--------- construction of the template ----------
300 '
310 'the template is usually read in with BLOAD or output with FASTSCRN.
320 'For demonstration with PRINT:
330 :
340 COLOR TXT.FORGRD,TXT.BAKGRD:CLS
350 IF CURR.MASK> MAX.MASK THEN CURR.MASK= 1
360 IF CURR.MASK< 1 THEN CURR.MASK= MAX.MASK
370 CURR.FIELD= 1 'new template always first field
380 PRINT USING "This is template number #";CURR.MASK
390 FOR F= 1 TO 5
400   LOCATE MASK%(CURR.MASK,F,1),1,0 '1. column for field designation, Cursor 0
410   PRINT USING "F #:";F
420 NEXT F
430 :
440 'The field content are normally read from a file, here
450 'by assignment for demonstration:
460 :
470 FOR I= 1 TO 5: INPT$(1,I)= "Test":INPT$(2,I)= "Test":NEXT I
480 COLOR INPT.FORGRD,INPT.BAKGRD
490 FOR F=1 TO 5
500   LOCATE MASK%(CURR.MASK,F,1),MASK%(CURR.MASK,F,2)
510   PRINT INPT$(CURR.MASK,F);SPACE$(MASK%(CURR.MASK,F,3)-
      LEN(INPT$(CURR.MASK,F)));
520 NEXT F
530 '---------- control of the input -----------
540 :
550 GOSUB 580 'call input-routine
560 COLOR TXT.FORGRD,TXT.BAKGRD:CLS:END
570 :
580 '---------- input-routine begins here ----------
590 :
600 IF CURR.FIELD> MAX.FIELD%(CURR.MASK) THEN CURR.FIELD= 1
610 IF CURR.FIELD< 1 THEN CURR.FIELD= MAX.FIELD%(CURR.MASK)
620 LOCATE MASK%(CURR.MASK,CURR.FIELD,1),MASK%(CURR.MASK,CURR.FIELD,2)
630 COLOR INPT.FORGRD,INPT.BAKGRD
640 INSTRING$= SPACE$(MASK%(CURR.MASK,CURR.FIELD,3)) 'create blank string
650 LSET INSTRING$= INPT$(CURR.MASK,CURR.FIELD) 'default field content
660 PRINT INSTRING$
670 :
680 ROWNO= MASK%(CURR.MASK,CURR.FIELD,1):COLMNO=
    MASK%(CURR.MASK,CURR.FIELD,2):LNGTH= MASK%(CURR.MASK,CURR.FIELD,3)
690 LOCATE ROWNO,COLMNO,1,0,31 'position Cursor for input
700 X$= INKEY$:IF X$="" THEN 700
710 IF X$=CHR$(27) THEN LAST.KEY= ESC:RETURN 'input interrupted
720 IF X$=CHR$(13) THEN GOSUB 1030:CURR.FIELD= CURR.FIELD+1:GOTO 600 'other field
730 IF X$=CHR$(8) AND POS(0)> COLMNO THEN LOCATE CSRLIN,POS(0)-1:PRINT "
    ";:LOCATE CSRLIN,POS(0)-1:GOTO 700
```

```
740 IF LEN(X$)= 2 THEN 790 'function- or control-key
750 IF X$<" " THEN BEEP:GOTO 700 'key less than space key ?
760 PRINT X$;:IF POS(0)>= COLMNO+LNGTH THEN 680 'field full, set to first column
    in the field
770 GOTO 700
780 :
790 '---------- function- or control-key ----------
800 :
810 ONKEY= ASC(RIGHT$(X$,1))
820 IF ONKEY= 72 THEN GOSUB 1030:CURR.FIELD= CURR.FIELD-1:GOTO 600 'Cursor up, 1
    field back
830 IF ONKEY= 80 THEN GOSUB 1030:CURR.FIELD= CURR.FIELD+1:GOTO 600 'Cursor down,
    1 field ahead
840 IF ONKEY= 75 AND POS(0)> COLMNO THEN LOCATE CSRLIN,POS(0)-1:GOTO 700 'Cursor
    left
850 IF ONKEY= 77 AND POS(0)< COLMNO+LNGTH-1 THEN LOCATE CSRLIN,POS(0)+1:GOTO 700
    'Cursor right
860 IF ONKEY= 71 THEN CURR.FIELD= 1:GOTO 600 '<Home>, first field
870 IF ONKEY= 79 THEN CURR.FIELD= MAX.FIELD%(MASK.NR):GOTO 600 '<End>, n. field
880 IF ONKEY= 73 THEN CURR.MASK= CURR.MASK-1:GOTO 290 '<PgUp>, template restored
890 IF ONKEY= 81 THEN CURR.MASK= CURR.MASK+1:GOTO 290 '<PgDn>, template ahead
900 IF ONKEY= 59 THEN GOSUB 930:GOTO 700 'Help display, continue in the text
910 BEEP:GOTO 700 'wrong key
920 :
930 '---------- HELP-routine ----------
940 :
950 'here you can include the HELP-routine from chapter 16
960 'as assignment for the help text use CURR.MASK and CURR.FIELD
970 'for larger help texts use a combination of
980 'SAVESCRN and BLOAD. With a color-card you can display the help
990 'on one of the free pages.
1000 :
1010 RETURN
1020 :
1030 '---------- store field content ----------
1040 :
1050 'during the change in field the content of the field is read
1060 'into the Variable INPT$():
1070 :
1080 LOCATE CSRLIN,POS(0),0 'Cursor out
1090 Y$=""
1100 FOR I= COLMNO TO COLMNO+LNGTH-1
1110    Y$= Y$+CHR$(SCREEN(CSRLIN,I))
1120 NEXT I
1130 INPT$(CURR.MASK,CURR.FIELD)= Y$
1140 RETURN
```

The purpose of this program is to capture a data record with a template. Sometimes a data record requires several templates. The input routine is the same for all templates. This means that help is available through <F1>, termination occurs with <Esc>, field movement with the cursor keys and switching templates with <PgDn> and <PgUp>. Saving the data depends on the application. For example, it's possible that saving will occur during the template change or during the change to the next data record. The input fields are highlighted with color so that the user can quickly find them. After leaving the input field, it can be set to the normal color of the template.

The type of help text that's displayed depends on the application. In some cases, brief explanations are sufficient for experienced users. Although you do not have to include every key on the help template, you should include the most important keys.

We divided help into three steps in one application. The first step included references to possible inputs, flags, etc. The second step produced basic advice on input and the third step displayed an overview of all keys and their functions.

The editing keys for the input are also important. In many applications the keys <Ins> and <Del> serve their normal purposes of insert and delete. These keys should always be available providing sufficient space and memory are available. Two other keys which you should include are <Ctrl><Home> so the field can be cleared and <Ctrl><End> so it's possible for the user to delete a line from the cursor position to the end.

12.3 Entering Date and Time

The following is a routine for entering date and time. This program can be added to another program, or called during initialization with AUTOEXEC.BAT:

```
10 '--------------
20 'date & time                 1985 (C) H.J.Bomanns =DATETIME.BAS
30 '--------------
40 '
50 CLS:KEY OFF
60 LOCATE 1,1,0,0,31
70 COLOR 15,0:PRINT CHR$(218);:COLOR 0,7:PRINT " Date & Time        1985 (C)
   H.J.BOMANNS ";:COLOR 15,0:PRINT CHR$(191)
80 PRINT CHR$(179);:LOCATE CSRLIN,42:PRINT CHR$(179)
90 PRINT CHR$(179);:LOCATE CSRLIN,42:PRINT CHR$(179)
100 PRINT CHR$(179);:LOCATE CSRLIN,42:PRINT CHR$(179)
110 PRINT CHR$(179);:LOCATE CSRLIN,42:PRINT CHR$(179)
120 PRINT CHR$(179);:LOCATE CSRLIN,42:PRINT CHR$(179)
130 PRINT CHR$(179);:LOCATE CSRLIN,42:PRINT CHR$(179)
140 PRINT CHR$(179);:LOCATE CSRLIN,42:PRINT CHR$(179)
150 PRINT CHR$(192);STRING$(40,CHR$(196));CHR$(217)
160 T$=TIME$
170 DT$=LEFT$(DATE$,2)+"-"+MID$(DATE$,4,2)+"-90"
180 REM----------------------------------------date & time----
190 COLOR 7,0
200 LOCATE  3, 5:PRINT "Please input today's date or"
210 LOCATE  4, 5:PRINT "accept the default date"
220 LOCATE  5, 5:PRINT "with <Return>"
230 LOCATE  7, 5:COLOR 7,0
240 PRINT "Date: ";:COLOR 15,0:PRINT DT$
250 MODE$="d":ROWNO=7:COLMNO=11:GOSUB 510
260 DT$="":FOR I=1 TO 8:DT$=DT$+CHR$(SCREEN(7,10+I)):NEXT I
270 IF MID$(DT$,1,2)<"01" OR MID$(DT$,1,2)>"12" THEN 320
280 IF MID$(DT$,4,2)<"01" OR MID$(DT$,4,2)>"31" THEN 320
290 IF MID$(DT$,7,2)<"80" THEN 320
300 IF DT$="01.01.80" THEN 320
310 GOTO 330
320 LOCATE  9,6:COLOR  0,7:PRINT " ERROR: Invalid Date";:SOUND 400,2:SOUND
800,2:SOUND 400,2:COLOR 15,0:GOTO 250
330 DATE$=LEFT$(DT$,2)+"-"+MID$(DT$,4,2)+"-"+RIGHT$(DT$,2)
340 LOCATE  9,6:COLOR  15,0:PRINT STRING$(21,CHR$(196));
350 COLOR 7,0
360 LOCATE  3, 5:PRINT "Please input current time, or "
370 LOCATE  4, 5:PRINT "accept the default time"
380 LOCATE  7, 5:COLOR 7,0
390 PRINT "Time: ";:COLOR 15,0:PRINT T$
400 MODE$="t":ROWNO=7:COLMNO=11:GOSUB 510:IF CHANGE=0 THEN 460
410 T$="":FOR I=1 TO 8:T$=T$+CHR$(SCREEN(7,10+I)):NEXT
420 IF MID$(T$,1,2)<"00" OR MID$(T$,1,2)>"23" THEN 500
430 IF MID$(T$,4,2)<"00" OR MID$(T$,4,2)>"59" THEN 500
440 IF MID$(T$,7,2)<"00" OR MID$(T$,7,2)>"59" THEN 500
```

```
450 TIME$=T$
460 COLOR 7,0
470 '****************************************************
480 CLS:END 'or RETURN
490 '****************************************************
500 LOCATE  9,6:COLOR  0,7:PRINT " ERROR: Invalid Time";:SOUND 400,2:SOUND
    800,2:SOUND 400,2:COLOR 15,0:GOTO 400
510 REM -----------Subroutine date & time-------
520 LOCATE ROWNO,COLMNO,1
530 X$=INKEY$:IF X$="" THEN 530
540 COLOR 15,0
550 IF LEN(X$)=2 THEN 630
560 IF X$=CHR$(13) THEN LOCATE 25,1,0:PRINT SPACE$(70);:RETURN
570 IF X$<"0" OR X$>"9" THEN BEEP:GOTO 530
580 COLOR 15,0:PRINT X$;:CHANGE=CHANGE+1
590 IF POS(0)=10 OR POS(0)=13 OR POS(0)=16 THEN LOCATE CSRLIN,POS(0)+1:GOTO 530
600 IF MODE$="d" THEN IF POS(0)=19 THEN 520
610 IF MODE$="t" THEN IF POS(0)=19 THEN 520
620 GOTO 530
630 ONKEY=ASC(RIGHT$(X$,1))
640 IF ONKEY=75 AND POS(0)>11 THEN LOCATE ,POS(0)-1:GOTO 680
650 IF ONKEY=77 AND MODE$="d" AND POS(0)<19 THEN LOCATE ,POS(0)+1
660 IF ONKEY=77 AND MODE$="t" AND POS(0)<19 THEN LOCATE ,POS(0)+1
670 GOTO 590
680 IF POS(0)=10 OR POS(0)=13 OR POS(0)=16 THEN LOCATE CSRLIN,POS(0)-1:GOTO 530
690 GOTO 530
```

This program was written so that the date and time wouldn't have to be entered with COMMAND.COM or the DOS commands DATE and TIME. The date is entered as month/day/year in North America but other countries, particularly in Europe, the date is entered as day/month/year. Usually date and time are entered after the PC has been switched on. By including this program in AUTOEXEC, your program will be more user-friendly. Simply add the following line to AUTOEXEC.BAT with EDLIN:

```
GWBASIC DATETIME
```

You should delete any DATE and TIME commands that are in the file. While the PC is being initialized, the interpreter followed by the program are loaded and executed. After the start of the program, lines 50 to 150 create a small window in the left upper corner of the screen. Date and time are then loaded into this window. The date is read in starting at line 180. The subroutine called in line 250 controls the input and the format which starts in line 510. For example, the periods are placed in the input field, so that the user only has to enter 6 numbers for the date and then press the <Enter> key. After the date is entered, it's verified in lines 270 to 300. The routine repeats if the input contains an invalid date.

The time input, starting at line 360, is done the same way. The time verification, in lines 420 to 440, also requires new input when the program detects an invalid entry.

12.4   Intercepting <Ctrl><Break>

A program that's executing can always be interrupted with the key combination <Ctrl><Break>. This is very helpful for the programmer during the testing phase. The computer doesn't have to be rebooted when the PC-BASIC program enters an endless loop. This is not the case with assembler programs.

After using this key combination, you'll see a "Break in XXXX" (referring to the line number) and an "Ok". However, sometimes using this key combination can have serious consequences. It's possible that you'll lose data which you'll have to reenter.

It's interesting to see how the PC and PC-BASIC handle this key combination. As you may know, these keys are not read by INKEY$ or INPUT$ because by pressing <Ctrl><Break> you can avoid the normal input routine. Some key codes aren't stored in the input buffer and cannot be detected. The keyboard control of the PC performs an interrupt 1Bh or 23h. These interrupts call their own routines for handling these key combinations. In DOS a running function is interrupted and you are again in the input level behind the (>) prompt.

In PC-BASIC, depending on the version, one of these interrupts is set to a routine in the interpreter. This routine stops the program execution and returns to direct mode. To avoid a termination, this routine must be switched off. Unfortunately, this isn't easy to do and isn't always possible. First, because of the different versions it's difficult to know which interrupt was flagged, and there are versions in which timer interrupt 8h replaces the flagged interrupt vector to ensure that an interrupt is always possible. This is far easier in PC-BASIC.

<Ctrl><Break> on the IBM-PC

With an IBM-PC, interrupt vector 1Bh is usually flagged. This can be changed by repositioning the vector. However, you must ensure that the vector points to assembler instructions that are executable; otherwise the computer will crash. Basically only one instruction, an IRET (Return from Interrupt), is required. This IRET causes the PC to continue, without further action, at the location from which it was called by interrupt 1Bh. This type of IRET can be found, for example, in BIOS-ROM at address &HF000:FF53. The following lines store the original address of interrupt 1Bh and set the vector to the IRET:

```
10 RESTORE 20:FOR I=1 TO 4:READ NEW.VECTOR%(I):NEXT I
20 DATA &H53,&HFF,&H0,&HF0
30 :
40 DEF SEG= &H0 'Segment of the Interrupt-Vectors
50 FOR I= &H6C TO &H6F
60 ORG.VECTOR%(I-&H6B)= PEEK(I)
```

```
 70 POKE I,NEW.VECTOR%(I-&H6B)
 80 NEXT I
 90 DEF SEG
100 :
490 :
500 DEF SEG= &H0
510 FOR I= &H6C TO &H6F
520    POKE I,ORG.VECTOR%(I-&H6B)
530 NEXT I
540 DEF SEG
```

<Ctrl><Break> on IBM and PC compatibles

Remember that before the end of the program the original vector must be set again. Otherwise DOS will no longer sense the <Ctrl><Break> key combination. If this routine has no effect, the version of BASIC you're using may be called BASICA but it isn't the IBM-BASICA. If this is the case, refer to the next section for more information.

Interrupt programming under PC-BASIC/BASICA allows you to call a program routine by pressing a certain key in the command sequence:

```
ON KEY(x) GOSUB xxxx:KEY (x) ON
```

Substitute a number for "x" which is assigned to a function or control key:

key	number
<F1> to <F10>	1 to 10
<Cursor Up>	11
<Cursor Left>	12
<Cursor Right>	13
<Cursor Down>	14

Other keys can also be defined for the numbers 15 to 20:

```
KEY <number>, CHR$(<Code1>)+ CHR$(<Code2>)
```

Use 15 to 20 for <number>. <Code1> and <Code2> define a key or keys which should cause some action when pressed. Code isn't the ASCII code of the key, but a scan code sent by the keyboard. We'll discuss this in more detail soon. First let's look at the following program:

```
10 '--------------------------------------------------------------
20 ' NO_BRK.BAS                    1986 (C) V. Sasse/H.J. Bomanns
30 '--------------------------------------------------------------
40 :
50 CLS:KEY OFF
60 TXT.FORGRD= 7:TXT.BAKGRD= 0
70 INPT.FORGRD= 15:INPT.BAKGRD= 0
```

```
80  MSSG.FORGRD=  0:MSSG.BAKGRD=  7
90  KEY 15, CHR$(4)+CHR$(70): KEY (15) ON: ON KEY (15) GOSUB 180
100 PRINT "This program cannot be interrupted with <Ctrl><Break>"
110 PRINT STRING$(80,"=")
120 LOCATE 10,5:COLOR TXT.FORGRD,TXT.BAKGRD
130 PRINT "This is a test input: "
140 INSTRING$="Testtext":ROWNO= 10: COLMNO= 32:LNGTH= 30
150 GOSUB 340 'read subroutine
160 GOTO 120
170 '
180 '--- here a <Ctrl>-<Break> is intercepted -----
190 '
200 CURR.ROWNO= CSRLIN:CURR.COLMNO= POS(0) 'store Cursor position
210 LOCATE 25,1
220 PRINT "Terminate program ? (Y/N) --> ";CHR$(254);" ";:LOCATE CSRLIN,POS(0)-
    2,1,0,31:SOUND 800,1:SOUND 1200,1:SOUND 800,1
230 Y$= INKEY$:IF Y$="" THEN 230
240 IF Y$="n" OR Y$="N" THEN 300
250 IF Y$<>"y" AND Y$<>"Y" THEN BEEP:GOTO 210
260 KEY (15) OFF:CLS:COLOR 7,0:END
270 '
280 '-- key <N> activated, back to the program ---
290 '
300 LOCATE 25,1:PRINT SPACE$(79);
310 LOCATE CURR.ROWNO,CURR.COLMNO
320 RETURN
330 '
340 '----- read subroutine -----
350 '
360 X$="":ONKEY= 0
370 LOCATE ROWNO,COLMNO,0:COLOR INPT.FORGRD,INPT.BAKGRD:PRINT
    INSTRING$;SPACE$(LNGTH-LEN(INSTRING$));
380 LOCATE ROWNO,COLMNO,1,0,31:CRSR.POS= 1
390 X$= INKEY$:IF X$="" THEN 390
400 IF X$= CHR$(8) AND POS(0)> COLMNO THEN GOSUB 530:GOTO 390 'key-routine
410 IF X$= CHR$(27) THEN ANYCHANGE= 0:RETURN
420 IF X$=CHR$(13) THEN RETURN
430 IF LEN(X$)= 2 THEN 710 'control- and function-keys
440 '
450 IF X$< " " THEN BEEP:GOTO 390 'kill characters smaller than BLANK
460 IF TXT.LNGTH THEN IF X$>= "a" AND X$<= "z" THEN X$= CHR$(ASC(X$)-32)
470 PRINT X$;:ANYCHANGE= -1
480 IF CRSR.POS<= LEN(INSTRING$) THEN MID$(INSTRING$,CRSR.POS,1)= X$ ELSE
    INSTRING$= INSTRING$+X$
490 CRSR.POS= CRSR.POS+1
500 IF POS(0)> COLMNO+LNGTH-1 THEN BEEP:LOCATE ROWNO,COLMNO:CRSR.POS= 1:GOTO 390
510 GOTO 390
520 '
530 '----- BACKSPACE and DEL keys -----
540 '
550 IF X$=CHR$(8) THEN INSTRING$= LEFT$(INSTRING$,CRSR.POS-
    2)+MID$(INSTRING$,CRSR.POS)
560 IF ONKEY= 83  THEN INSTRING$= LEFT$(INSTRING$,CRSR.POS-
    1)+MID$(INSTRING$,CRSR.POS+1)
570 LOCATE ROWNO,COLMNO:PRINT INSTRING$;" ";
580 IF X$=CHR$(8) THEN CRSR.POS= CRSR.POS-1
590 LOCATE CSRLIN,COLMNO+CRSR.POS-1
600 ONKEY= 0: X$="":ANYCHANGE= -1
```

```
610 RETURN
620 '
630 '----- INSERT key -----
640 '
650 INSTRING$= LEFT$(INSTRING$,CRSR.POS-1)+" "+MID$(INSTRING$,CRSR.POS)
660 PRINT " ";MID$(INSTRING$,CRSR.POS+1);
670 LOCATE CSRLIN,COLMNO+CRSR.POS-1
680 ANYCHANGE= -1
690 RETURN
700 '
710 '----- control- and function-keys -----
720 '
730 ONKEY= ASC(RIGHT$(X$,1))
740 IF ONKEY= 63 THEN RETURN '<F5>= selection
750 IF ONKEY= 68 THEN RETURN '<F10>= input OK
760 IF ONKEY= 72 OR ONKEY= 80 THEN RETURN 'Cursor up and down
770 IF ONKEY= 73 OR ONKEY= 81 THEN RETURN '<PgUp> and <PgDn>
780 IF ONKEY= 75 AND POS(0)> COLMNO THEN LOCATE CSRLIN,POS(0)-1:CRSR.POS=
    CRSR.POS-1:GOTO 390 'Cursor <--
790 IF ONKEY= 77 AND POS(0)< COLMNO+LNGTH-1 THEN IF CRSR.POS<= LEN(INSTRING$)
    THEN LOCATE CSRLIN,POS(0)+1:CRSR.POS= CRSR.POS+1:GOTO 390 'Cursor -->
800 IF ONKEY= 83 AND CRSR.POS <= LEN(INSTRING$) THEN GOSUB 530:GOTO 390 '<Del> is
    handled similar to <Backspace>
810 IF ONKEY= 71 THEN LOCATE ROWNO,COLMNO:GOTO 390 '<Home>, start of field
820 IF ONKEY= 79 THEN LOCATE CSRLIN,COLMNO+LEN(INSTRING$)-1:CRSR.POS=
    LEN(INSTRING$):GOTO 390 '<End>, set to last character
830 IF ONKEY= 117 THEN INSTRING$= LEFT$(INSTRING$,CRSR.POS-1):PRINT SPACE$(LNGTH-
    CRSR.POS);:LOCATE CSRLIN,COLMNO+CRSR.POS-1:ANYCHANGE= -1:GOTO 390
    '<Ctrl><End>, erase to end of field
840 IF ONKEY= 82 AND CRSR.POS<= LEN(INSTRING$) AND LEN(INSTRING$)< LNGTH THEN
    GOSUB 630:GOTO 390 '<Ins>
850 BEEP:GOTO 390
```

Line 90 is significant in this program. The key combination <Ctrl><Break> is assigned the number 15 for the following ON KEY (x) GOSUB xxx. CHR$(4) is the scan code of the <Ctrl> key, CHR$(70) is the scan code for the <Break> key. In the same line, the subroutine is defined, starting at line 180, for interrupt handling and switches on the sensing. Then a test input is requested, starting at line 120. If you press <Ctrl><Break>, you'll see that, instead of an interruption, a prompt appears (line 180) that must be answered either yes or no. Depending on the answer, the program continues or terminates after closing all files.

Note: Our attempts to safeguard the program against termination in this way have shown that this isn't always possible with all versions of PC-BASIC. Sometimes only the initial pressing of the key combination <Ctrl><Break> can be intercepted. If the program continues and the keys are pressed again, "BREAK IN XXXX" and "OK" appear. Unfortunately, we don't know why this happens. If you have a version that behaves this way, there's not much you can do.

In the Appendix you'll find an overview of the scan codes for the IBM and compatible keyboards. Then you can define your own keys.

12.5   Displaying the Status of Special Keys

In Chapter 9 you'll find two programs called BAS_RC: one in assembly language and one in BASIC. Both of these programs display the line/column position of the cursor and the status of the <Ins>, <Caps Lock>, <Num Lock> and <Scroll Lock> special keys. This program was designed to simplify the program input. In other words, it will be used in direct mode. The numeric keypad is used for entering numbers and for moving the cursor. The <Num Lock> key switches between these two modes. By pressing the <Num Lock> key once, you can enter numbers from the numeric keypad. By pressing this key again, you can use the cursor keys to move the cursor on the screen.

The IBM keyboard and some compatible keyboards do not have LEDs showing the status of these special keys. If the keyboard sends a signal that one of the special keys has been activated, the operating system sets a flag. On the basis of this flag it's determined whether to move the cursor, enter the numeric input, or display the characters in uppercase letters which were entered (<Caps Lock> active).

This flag can be read with PEEK and then evaluated. The address of the flag is &H0040:0017:

```
DEF SEG= &H0040
? PEEK(&H17)
```

As a result, we receive a byte whose individual bits reflect the status:

Bit 0	Right <Shift> key
Bit 1	Left <Shift> key
Bit 2	<Ctrl> key
Bit 3	<Alt> key
Bit 4	<Scroll Lock> key
Bit 5	<Num Lock> key
Bit 6	<Caps Lock> key
Bit 7	<Ins> key

If the bit is set (1), then the key assigned to it is active and the corresponding mode is switched on.

We'll examine two programs which display special key status on the screen. The first program accesses the flags just described, evaluates them and generates a display:

395

```
10 '---------------------------------------------------------------
20 ' T_STAT1.BAS                           1985 (C) H.J. Bomanns
30 '---------------------------------------------------------------
40 :
50 COLOR 7,0:CLS:KEY OFF
60 TXT.FORGRD=  7: TXT.BAKGRD=  0
70 INPT.FORGRD= 15: INPT.BAKGRD=  0
80 MESSG.FORGRD=  0: MESSG.BAKGRD=  7
90 DEF SEG= &H40: S= &H17 'Segment:Offset BIOS-Flag keyboard-Status
100 ON TIMER(1) GOSUB 220 'query status every second and display
110 TIMER ON
120 :
130 PRINT "This program displays the status of the <NumLock>, <CapsLock> and
    <ScrollLock > and"
140 PRINT "<Ins> keys at any location in an executing program."
150 PRINT STRING$(80,"=")
160 '
170 LOCATE 10,5:COLOR TXT.FORGRD,TXT.BAKGRD
180 PRINT "This is a test input:"
190 INSTRING$= "Testtext":ROWNO= 10: COLMNO= 33: LNGTH= 30
200 GOSUB 350:GOTO 190
210 '
220 '- query of the keyboard-status and display --
230 '
240 TIMER STOP
250 CURR.ROWNO= CSRLIN: CURR.COLMNO= POS(0)
260 LOCATE 25,1,0
270 IF (PEEK(S) AND 128)= 128 THEN PRINT "Insert ";
280 IF (PEEK(S) AND  64)=  64 THEN PRINT "Caps ";
290 IF (PEEK(S) AND  32)=  32 THEN PRINT "Num ";
300 IF (PEEK(S) AND  16)=  16 THEN PRINT "Scroll ";
310 PRINT SPACE$(81-POS(0));
320 LOCATE CURR.ROWNO,CURR.COLMNO,1
330 RETURN
340 '
350 '----- read subroutine -----
360 '
370 X$="":ONKEY= 0
380 LOCATE ROWNO,COLMNO,0:COLOR INPT.FORGRD,INPT.BAKGRD:PRINT
    INSTRING$;SPACE$(LNGTH-LEN(INSTRING$));
390 LOCATE ROWNO,COLMNO,1,0,31:CRSR.POS= 1
400 X$= INKEY$:IF X$="" THEN 400
410 IF X$= CHR$(8) AND POS(0)> COLMNO THEN GOSUB 540:GOTO 400 'key-routine
420 IF X$= CHR$(27) THEN COLOR 7,0:CLS:END '<Esc> to exit
430 IF X$=CHR$(13) THEN RETURN
440 IF LEN(X$)= 2 THEN 720 'control- and function-keys
450 '
460 IF X$< " " THEN BEEP:GOTO 400 'kill characters smaller than BLANK
470 IF TXT.LNGTH THEN IF X$>= "a" AND X$<= "z" THEN X$= CHR$(ASC(X$)-32)
480 PRINT X$;:ANYCHANGE= -1
490 IF CRSR.POS<= LEN(INSTRING$) THEN MID$(INSTRING$,CRSR.POS,1)= X$ ELSE
    INSTRING$= INSTRING$+X$
500 CRSR.POS= CRSR.POS+1
```

```
510 IF POS(0)> COLMNO+LNGTH-1 THEN BEEP:LOCATE ROWNO,COLMNO:CRSR.POS= 1:GOTO 400
520 GOTO 400
530 '
540 '----- BACKSPACE and DEL keys -----
550 '
560 IF X$=CHR$(8) THEN INSTRING$= LEFT$(INSTRING$,CRSR.POS-
    2)+MID$(INSTRING$,CRSR.POS)
570 IF ONKEY= 83  THEN INSTRING$= LEFT$(INSTRING$,CRSR.POS-
    1)+MID$(INSTRING$,CRSR.POS+1)
580 LOCATE ROWNO,COLMNO:PRINT INSTRING$;" ";
590 IF X$=CHR$(8) THEN CRSR.POS= CRSR.POS-1
600 LOCATE CSRLIN,COLMNO+CRSR.POS-1
610 ONKEY= 0: X$="":ANYCHANGE= -1
620 RETURN
630 '
640 '----- INS key----
650 '
660 INSTRING$= LEFT$(INSTRING$,CRSR.POS-1)+" "+MID$(INSTRING$,CRSR.POS)
670 PRINT " ";MID$(INSTRING$,CRSR.POS+1);
680 LOCATE CSRLIN,COLMNO+CRSR.POS-1
690 ANYCHANGE= -1
700 RETURN
710 '
720 '----- control- and function-keys -----
730 '
740 ONKEY= ASC(RIGHT$(X$,1))
750 IF ONKEY= 63 THEN RETURN '[F5]= selection
760 IF ONKEY= 68 THEN RETURN '[F10]= input OK
770 IF ONKEY= 72 OR ONKEY= 80 THEN RETURN 'Cursor up and down
780 IF ONKEY= 73 OR ONKEY= 81 THEN RETURN '<PgUp> and <PgDn>
790 IF ONKEY= 75 AND POS(0)> COLMNO THEN LOCATE CSRLIN,POS(0)-1:CRSR.POS=
    CRSR.POS-1:GOTO 400 'Cursor <--
800 IF ONKEY= 77 AND POS(0)< COLMNO+LNGTH-1 THEN IF CRSR.POS<= LEN(INSTRING$)
    THEN LOCATE CSRLIN,POS(0)+1:CRSR.POS= CRSR.POS+1:GOTO 400 'Cursor -->
810 IF ONKEY= 83 AND CRSR.POS <= LEN(INSTRING$) THEN GOSUB 540:GOTO 400 '<Del>
    handled similar to <Backspace>
820 IF ONKEY= 71 THEN LOCATE ROWNO,COLMNO:GOTO 400 '<Home>, start of field
830 IF ONKEY= 79 THEN LOCATE CSRLIN,COLMNO+LEN(INSTRING$)-1:CRSR.POS=
    LEN(INSTRING$):GOTO 400 '<End>, set to last character
840 IF ONKEY= 117 THEN INSTRING$= LEFT$(INSTRING$,CRSR.POS-1):PRINT SPACE$(LNGTH-
    CRSR.POS);:LOCATE CSRLIN,COLMNO+CRSR.POS-1:ANYCHANGE= -1:GOTO 400
    '<Ctrl><End>, erase to end of field
850 IF ONKEY= 82 AND CRSR.POS<= LEN(INSTRING$) AND LEN(INSTRING$)< LNGTH THEN
    GOSUB 640:GOTO 400 '<Ins>
860 BEEP:GOTO 400
```

The status is based on the ON TIMER (x) GOSUB xxxx construction. After the interrupt initializes (lines 100-110), the routine is called every second, starting at line 220, and displays the message. For demonstration purposes, a test input is requested starting at line 170. Enter something and activate one of the special keys. The status appears on the bottom line of the screen. You've probably noticed that the status display doesn't immediately appear. This happens because the update not only occurs once every second but time is also needed to generate the display.

We selected another path in the second program. The display is generated with an ON KEY (x) GOSUB xxxx construction:

```
10 '-----------------------------------------------------------
20 ' T_STAT2.BAS                          1985 (C) H.J. Bomanns
30 '-----------------------------------------------------------
40 :
50 COLOR 7,0:CLS:KEY OFF
60 TXT.FORGRD=  7: TXT.BAKGRD=  0
70 INPT.FORGRD= 15: INPT.BAKGRD=  0
80 MSSG.FORGRD=  0: MSSG.BAKGRD=  7
90 KEY 15, CHR$(0)+CHR$(69):ON KEY (15) GOSUB 250:KEY (15) ON '<NumLock>
100 KEY 16, CHR$(0)+CHR$(70):ON KEY (16) GOSUB 330:KEY (16) ON '<ScrollLock>
110 KEY 17, CHR$(0)+CHR$(58):ON KEY (17) GOSUB 410:KEY (17) ON '<CapsLock>
120 KEY 18, CHR$(0)+CHR$(82):ON KEY (18) GOSUB 490:KEY (18) ON '<Insert>
130 :
140 PRINT "This program displays the status of the <NumLock>, <CapsLock> and
    <ScrollLock > and"
150 PRINT "<Ins> keys at any location in an executing program."
160 PRINT STRING$(80,"=")
170 '
180 LOCATE 10,5:COLOR TXT.FORGRD,TXT.BAKGRD
190 PRINT "This is a test input:"
200 INSTRING$= "Testtext":ROWNO= 10: COLMNO= 33: LNGTH= 30
210 GOSUB 560:GOTO 200
220 '
230 '----- NumLock key -----
240 '
250 CURR.ROWNO= CSRLIN: CURR.COLMNO= POS(0)
260 LOCATE 25,1
270 NUMLOCK= NOT NUMLOCK:IF NUMLOCK THEN PRINT "Num"; ELSE PRINT "   ";
280 LOCATE CURR.ROWNO,CURR.COLMNO,1
290 RETURN
300 '
310 '----- ScrollLock key -----
320 '
330 CURR.ROWNO= CSRLIN: CURR.COLMNO= POS(0)
340 LOCATE 25,5
350 SCROLLLOCK= NOT SCROLLLOCK:IF SCROLLLOCK THEN PRINT "Scroll"; ELSE PRINT " ";
360 LOCATE CURR.ROWNO,CURR.COLMNO,1
370 RETURN
380 '
390 '----- CapsLock key -----
400 '
410 CURR.ROWNO= CSRLIN: CURR.COLMNO= POS(0)
420 LOCATE 25,12
430 CAPSLOCK= NOT CAPSLOCK:IF CAPSLOCK THEN PRINT "Caps"; ELSE PRINT "    ";
440 LOCATE CURR.ROWNO,CURR.COLMNO,1
450 RETURN
```

```
460 '
470 '----- Insert key -----
480 '
490 CURR.ROWNO= CSRLIN: CURR.COLMNO= POS(0)
500 LOCATE 25,17
510 INSERT= NOT INSERT:IF INSERT THEN PRINT "Ins"; ELSE PRINT "    ";
520 X$= CHR$(0)+CHR$(82) 'for INKEY$
530 LOCATE CURR.ROWNO,CURR.COLMNO,1
540 RETURN
550 '
560 '----- read subroutine -----
570 '
580 X$="":ONKEY= 0
590 LOCATE ROWNO,COLMNO,0:COLOR INPT.FORGRD,INPT.BAKGRD:PRINT
    INSTRING$;SPACE$(LNGTH-LEN(INSTRING$));
600 LOCATE ROWNO,COLMNO,1,0,31:CRSR.POS= 1
610 X$= INKEY$:IF X$="" THEN 610
620 IF X$= CHR$(8) AND POS(0)> COLMNO THEN GOSUB 750:GOTO 610 'key-routine
630 IF X$= CHR$(27) THEN COLOR 7,0:CLS:END    '<Esc> to exit
640 IF X$=CHR$(13) THEN RETURN
650 IF LEN(X$)= 2 THEN 930 'control- and function-keys
660 '
670 IF X$< " " THEN BEEP:GOTO 610 'kill characters smaller than BLANK
680 IF TXT.LNGTH THEN IF X$>= "a" AND X$<= "z" THEN X$= CHR$(ASC(X$)-32)
690 PRINT X$;:ANYCHANGE= -1
700 IF CRSR.POS<= LEN(INSTRING$) THEN MID$(INSTRING$,CRSR.POS,1)= X$ ELSE
    INSTRING$= INSTRING$+X$
710 CRSR.POS= CRSR.POS+1
720 IF POS(0)> COLMNO+LNGTH-1 THEN BEEP:LOCATE ROWNO,COLMNO:CRSR.POS= 1:GOTO 610
730 GOTO 610
740 '
750 '----- BACKSPACE and DEL key -----
760 '
770 IF X$=CHR$(8) THEN INSTRING$= LEFT$(INSTRING$,CRSR.POS-
    2)+MID$(INSTRING$,CRSR.POS)
780 IF ONKEY= 83  THEN INSTRING$= LEFT$(INSTRING$,CRSR.POS-
    1)+MID$(INSTRING$,CRSR.POS+1)
790 LOCATE ROWNO,COLMNO:PRINT INSTRING$;" ";
800 IF X$=CHR$(8) THEN CRSR.POS= CRSR.POS-1
810 LOCATE CSRLIN,COLMNO+CRSR.POS-1
820 ONKEY= 0: X$="":ANYCHANGE= -1
830 RETURN
840 '
850 '----- INS key -----
860 '
870 INSTRING$= LEFT$(INSTRING$,CRSR.POS-1)+" "+MID$(INSTRING$,CRSR.POS)
880 PRINT " ";MID$(INSTRING$,CRSR.POS+1);
890 LOCATE CSRLIN,COLMNO+CRSR.POS-1
900 ANYCHANGE= -1
910 RETURN
920 '
930 '----- control- and function-keys -----
940 '
```

```
 950 ONKEY= ASC(RIGHT$(X$,1))
 960 IF ONKEY= 63 THEN RETURN '<F5>= selection
 970 IF ONKEY= 68 THEN RETURN '<F10>= input OK
 980 IF ONKEY= 72 OR ONKEY= 80 THEN RETURN 'Cursor up and down
 990 IF ONKEY= 73 OR ONKEY= 81 THEN RETURN '<PgUp> and <PgDn>
1000 IF ONKEY= 75 AND POS(0)> COLMNO THEN LOCATE CSRLIN,POS(0)-1:CRSR.POS=
     CRSR.POS-1:GOTO 610 'Cursor <--
1010 IF ONKEY= 77 AND POS(0)< COLMNO+LNGTH-1 THEN IF CRSR.POS<= LEN(INSTRING$)
     THEN LOCATE CSRLIN,POS(0)+1:CRSR.POS= CRSR.POS+1:GOTO 610 'Cursor -->
1020 IF ONKEY= 83 AND CRSR.POS <= LEN(INSTRING$) THEN GOSUB 750:GOTO 610 '<Del>
     is handled similar to <Backspace>
1030 IF ONKEY= 71 THEN LOCATE ROWNO,COLMNO:GOTO 610 '<Home>, start of field
1040 IF ONKEY= 79 THEN LOCATE CSRLIN,COLMNO+LEN(INSTRING$)-1:CRSR.POS=
     LEN(INSTRING$):GOTO 610 '<End>, set to last character
1050 IF ONKEY= 117 THEN INSTRING$= LEFT$(INSTRING$,CRSR.POS-1):PRINT
     SPACE$(LNGTH-CRSR.POS);:LOCATE CSRLIN,COLMNO+CRSR.POS-1:ANYCHANGE= -1:GOTO
     610 '<Ctrl><End>, erase to end of field
1060 IF ONKEY= 82 AND CRSR.POS<= LEN(INSTRING$) AND LEN(INSTRING$)< LNGTH THEN
     GOSUB 850:GOTO 610 '<Ins>
1070 BEEP:GOTO 610
```

Lines 90 to 120 define the four special keys using KEY(x)= CHR$. The subroutines are announced and initialized. Starting at line 230 you see the individual subroutines (there is an individual routine for every special key). A test input is requested in line 180. Enter normal characters and press one of the special keys as you do this. The display will immediately appear. This happens because, under ON KEY (x) GOSUB xxxx, sensing the timer interrupt of the PC occurs 18 times per second.

On the basis of appearance, you might prefer to use the second method in your program. However, you must use the first method if you're going to use KEY (x)= CHR$... to handle other keys in addition to the special keys.

Remember that when sensing a key combination consisting of a switching key and another key, the scan code of the switching key uses a value other than the first CHR$(x), according to the following table:

> 1 = combination with <Shift> keys
> 4 = combination with <Ctrl> key
> 8 = combination with <Alt> key

The first CHR$(x) is always "0", if only one key without a switching key (<Ctrl>, <Alt> or <Shift>) is sensed.

12.6   Mouse vs. Keyboard

Since the Apple Macintosh was introduced, program control with a mouse has become popular. Now Microsoft also offers the graphic user interface Windows for the PC. Programs and functions are no longer called through the command line. Instead they're called through *icons* which appear on the screen. For example, a small typewriter icon represents a word processor and an easel and a palette icon represents a paint or drawing program. By moving the mouse on the desk, the user moves the pointer over the screen to the application to be executed. By *clicking*, or pressing, the mouse button, the user can call and execute the appropriate program located under the pointer.

Another way to activate programs and options is by using *pull-down* menus. A menu bar is displayed across the first line of the screen. The user executes a menu option using the mouse pointer to "click" on the specific option. This opens the menu belonging to this option. Since the mouse is so easy to use, it's an excellent way for beginners to become accustomed to the computer. Also, many applications would be almost impossible to use without the mouse. For example, trying to control the cursor of a CAD program using the cursor keys is almost impossible.

A mouse is available from several manufacturers for prices ranging from around $30 to $200. A lower priced mouse usually contains only minimum software and documentation. Other manufacturers may provide a painting program, a mouse control system for existing applications and several reference manuals.

The mouse is actually controlled through software. The functions for the control are called through a DOS interrupt. The Microsoft mouse has set a standard which most manufacturers use. In the following examples, we assumed that you're using a Microsoft or compatible mouse.

The mouse is usually connected through the RS232C interface. A control program queries this interface and passes the result to the calling program. This control program, also called a *mouse driver*, usually occurs through the CONFIG.SYS file:

```
device= mouse.sys
```

The mouse driver is also sometimes called a COM program, or it's in a ROM on a card in the PC.

Controlling the Mouse from the Program

A mouse must be interfaced during the call of the program in order to control the mouse from your program:

The control of the mouse is handled through interrupt &H33. After the PC boots, all unused interrupt vectors contain either the address 0000:0000 or the address of the instruction IRET (Return from Interrupt). During initialization, the mouse driver writes its segment:offset address in one of these vectors through which it's called.

After the test, the mouse can be initialized for the program. This is required because PC-BASIC alone doesn't search for a mouse. You can use the mouse in both text and graphics mode. The following program demonstrates how the mouse is used in text mode during menu selection:

```
10 '--------------------------------------
20 'mouse in text-mode Mouse_1.BAS;
25 'PC-Basic must be called with /M:60000
30 '--------------------------------------
40 :
50 CLS:KEY OFF:SCREEN 2
60 GOSUB 60000
70 INR% = &H33
150 :
160 '----- construct menu -----
170 :
180 PRINT "-------- menu-selection: --------"
190 LOCATE  5,10:PRINT "MENU-OPTION 1"
200 LOCATE  6,10:PRINT "MENU-OPTION 2"
210 LOCATE  7,10:PRINT "MENU-OPTION 3"
220 LOCATE  8,10:PRINT "MENU-OPTION 4"
230 LOCATE  9,10:PRINT "MENU-OPTION  5"
240 :
250 'Is the mouse-driver loaded and hardware OK?
260 :
270 FUNCTION%= 0:AH%=0:AL%=0:GOSUB 430 'check hardware
280 IF (AH%=0) AND (AL%=0) THEN CLS:PRINT "Error in the mouse-hardware.....":END
290 :
300 '----- menu-control -----
310 :
320 AH%=0:AL%= 10:BH%=0:BL%=0:CH%=0:CL%= &HFFFF:DH%=0:DL%= &H7700:GOSUB 430 'set
    text Cursor
330 AH%=0:AL%=4:CH%=0:CL%= 10:DH%=0:DL%= 10:GOSUB 430 'set Cursor position
340 AH%=0:AL%= 1:GOSUB 430 'show Cursor
350 LOCATE 17,1:PRINT "Set cursor to menu option  and then press mouse
    button....."
360 AH%=0:AL%= 3:GOSUB 430 'get position and Button status
370 ROWNO= (DL%\8)+1:COLMNO= (CL%\8)+1
380 '
```

(handwritten margin notes:)
TEST FUNC 0
INPUT FUNC 10
INPUT FUNC 4
INPUT FUNC 1
TEST FUNC 3

(handwritten bottom notes:)
BL%= BUTTON STATUS
LEFT   1
CENTER 3
RIGHT   2
NONE   0

```
390 IF ROWNO< 5 OR ROWNO> 9 OR COLMNO <10 OR COLMNO >21 THEN LOCATE 1,50:PRINT
    SPACE$(20);:GOTO 410 'outside the menu
400 IF (AL% AND 1) OR (AL% AND 2) THEN LOCATE 1,50: PRINT USING "menu-option
    #";(DL% \ 8)-3; <——
410 IF INKEY$="" THEN 360 ELSE CLS:END
420 :
430 '----- call mouse-function -----
440 :
450 CALL IA(INR%,AH%,AL%,BH%,BL%,CH%,CL%,DH%,DL%,DI%,SI%,ES%,FLAGS%)
460 RETURN
470 :
480 :
60000 '*********************************************************************'
60010 '* initialize the routine for the interrupt call              *'
60015 '* This routine taken from the Abacus title:  "PC System       *'
60016 '* Programming for Developers", by Michael Tischer.           *'
60020 '*----------------------------------------------------------*'
60030 '* Input : none                                               *'
60040 '* Output: IA is the Start address of the Interrupt routine    *'
60050 '*********************************************************************'
60060 '
60070 IA=60000!          'Start address of the routine in the BASIC segment
60080 DEF SEG                                  'set BASIC segment
60090 RESTORE 60130
60100 FOR I% = 0 TO 160 : READ X% : POKE IA+I%,X% : NEXT 'poke Routine
60110 RETURN                                       'back to caller
60120 '
60130 DATA  85,139,236, 30,  6,139,118, 30,139,  4,232,140,  0,139,118
60140 DATA  12,139, 60,139,118,  8,139,  4, 61,255,255,117,  2,140,216
60150 DATA 142,192,139,118, 28,138, 36,139,118, 26,138,  4,139,118, 24
60160 DATA 138, 60,139,118, 22,138, 28,139,118, 20,138, 44,139,118, 18
60170 DATA 138, 12,139,118, 16,138, 52,139,118, 14,138, 20,139,118, 10
60180 DATA 139, 52, 85,205, 33, 93, 86,156,139,118, 12,137, 60,139,118
60190 DATA  28,136, 36,139,118, 26,136,  4,139,118, 24,136, 60,139,118
60200 DATA  22,136, 28,139,118, 20,136, 44,139,118, 18,136, 12,139,118
60210 DATA  16,136, 52,139,118, 14,136, 20,139,118,  8,140,192,137,  4
60220 DATA  88,139,118,  6,137,  4, 88,139,118, 10,137,  4,  7, 31, 93
60230 DATA 202, 26,  0, 91, 46,136, 71, 66,233,108,255
```

After the program begins, a test is made in lines 250 to 290 to determine whether a mouse or a mouse driver is available. A message appears if a mouse isn't available and the program terminates. The program then displays a small demonstration menu for additional options.

The hardware condition is checked before performing the mouse control. This is done lines 270 and 280 through the mouse driver. It's possible that a mouse driver was loaded but a mouse wasn't correctly interfaced. This is done through a subroutine starting at line 430, which represents the interface to the mouse driver. You'll receive a message in case of an error and the program will end.

Otherwise, the control of the menu selection with the mouse starts at line 300. Also, the mouse driver is addressed again through the subroutine at line 430. The return message from the driver is evaluated in this control and the proper reaction occurs.

The basis is the current position of the mouse, which is returned in graphic coordinates with a resolution of 640*200 pixels. The values are converted in line 370. The letters are composed of an 8*8 matrix, so the position must be calculated as line/column coordinates.

Using a mouse doesn't produce problems. In this example, only the mouse is queried for the menu selection. To make everything more user-friendly in your programming, the keyboard should also be queried along with the mouse.

Mouse in Graphics Mode

The mouse can also be easily used in graphics mode. You can define the appearance of the mouse pointer in this mode. The initialization, inclusion and query of the mouse routine occur as described in the previous section. The coordinates only have to be converted if the mouse position is based on the line/column.

You'll find a listing of the functions to be called in the Appendix. Remember that the functions are only valid for a Microsoft or compatible mouse driver. The computer can crash under certain circumstances (i.e., when an interrupt other than &H33 is used or the functions perform differently) using other drivers. The functions can also return different results. If you're not sure, consult the user manual or other technical documentation for the mouse. You'll find information explaining the interrupt and the functions there.

13. Sorting Data

Since the invention of electronic data processing, the problem of *sorting* has perplexed programmers. Sorting involves, for example, printing or displaying data from an address file in alphabetic order or data from an inventory file in numeric order. Different sort criteria is used to do this. For example, an address file is usually sorted according to last name and ZIP code.

One of the most important aspects of a sort routine is speed. During the past years various sort algorithms have been developed to increase the speed of the sort routine. Today, however, only a handful of these algorithms remain in use. Bubble sort and quick sort are the most popular sort algorithms.

Which sort algorithm should you use?

Which algorithm you use depends on how you want to organize the data and the amount of data. Algorithms such as *quick sort* quickly determine whether data are already sorted. However, other algorithms, such as *bubble sort*, don't detect if data have already been sorted. These algorithms process the data without producing any noticeable changes.

The algorithms for bubble sort and quick sort are used in PC programming. In the following sections we'll examine these two algorithms and discuss their advantages and disadvantages.

13.1 Bubble Sort

Although this is a very slow sort algorithm, it's still used today because it's very simple, can be programmed with little effort and is easy to understand. Also, using a faster routine may not always be necessary since many applications need to sort only a small amount of data.

13.1.1 How does bubble sort work?

To explain how bubble sort works, let's use the last names in an address file. These names are stored in a one dimensional array. The bubble sort compares two neighboring elements. If one element is larger than the other, the two elements are switched. Through the exchange of elements, the larger element slowly "floats" or "bubbles up" to the top according to size. This can be compared to a rising air bubble in a glass of water.

13.1.2 Advantages and disadvantages of using bubble sort

As we already mentioned, the bubble sort can easily be programmed. In the following program you'll see that the algorithm occupies less than 10 program lines, which saves memory space. In the program we used a few extra lines for clarity. Another advantage is that a bubble sort is easy to recognize and understand when analyzing a program. This is especially helpful for beginners.

One disadvantage of the bubble sort is its slowness. With larger quantities of data, the sort requires much time. The second disadvantage is related to PC-BASIC. Since the bubble sort works well with string operations, the garbage collection is called frequently. So, besides the actual sort time, additional time is needed for garbage collection.

13.1.3 Using bubble sort

The bubble sort is used when small amounts of data must be sorted and/or when a fast processing time isn't important.

The amount of data that should be used with a bubble sort can be determined through experimentation. A bubble sort for 100 sets of addresses is acceptable on a fast AT computer, but on a PC perhaps a quick sort should be used.

The importance of processing time depends on the situation. If the address data must be displayed interactively, the time needed for sorting is very important. The situation is different when various sorted lists must be printed. With a PC, this can be done during a coffee break or lunch hour.

Now let's look at the program. Here a string array is filled with unsorted data and then sorted with a bubble sort. We have added comments to the listing so that you can clearly understand the program:

```
10 '-------------------------------------------
20 ' BSORT.BAS   demonstration-program for Bubble-Sort
30 '-------------------------------------------
40 :
50 CLS:KEY OFF:OPTION BASE 0
60 FALSE= 0: TRUE= NOT FALSE
70 MAX.SIZE= 25
80 DIM ALPHA$(MAX.SIZE)
90 RESTORE 110
100 FOR I= 0 TO MAX.SIZE READ ALPHA$(I):NEXT I
110 DATA ZEBRA,ABACUS,XYLOPHONE,BASIC,YELLOW,CREAM,WATCHDOG,DISKETTE
120 DATA Vacation, Example,Umpire,Frequency,Tourist,General,Sheri
130 DATA Helmet,Renaissance,Ice,Quality,Justice,Print,Key,Observation
140 DATA Locate,Numeric,Mathematics
150 :
```

The unsorted data is saved in data lines beginning with line 110. We selected elements beginning with different letters to demonstrate how the bubble sort works.

```
160 :
170 COLOR 15,0:PRINT "Unsorted Array:":COLOR 7,0
180 FOR I= 0 TO MAX.SIZE
190 PRINT ALPHA$(I);" ";
200 NEXT I
210 PRINT:PRINT
220 :
```

The unsorted data is displayed in the loop, starting after line 180.

```
230 START= TIMER
240 GOSUB 370 'sort data in ALPHA$ ...
250 FINISH= TIMER
260 :
```

The START and FINISH variables are initialized with the current value of the timer to determine the sort time. The actual sort occurs in a subroutine following line 370.

```
270 COLOR 15,0:PRINT "Sorted Array:":COLOR 7,0
280 FOR I= 0 TO MAX.SIZE
290   PRINT ALPHA$(I);" ";
300 NEXT I
310 :
320 LOCATE 25,1
330 PRINT USING "Sort time: ##.##      Strike any key...";FINISH-START;
340 IF INKEY$= "" THEN 340
350 CLS:END
```

After the sort, the data is output in the loop, starting with line 280. Then line 330 displays the time required for the sort.

```
360 '
370 '----- subroutine BubbleSort -----
380 '
390 UNSORTED= TRUE
400 LAST.ELEMENT= MAX.SIZE
410 WHILE UNSORTED
420   UNSORTED= FALSE
430   FOR ELEMENT= 0 TO LAST.ELEMENT-1
440     IF ALPHA$(ELEMENT) > ALPHA$(ELEMENT+1) THEN GOSUB 500
450   NEXT  ELEMENT
460   LAST.ELEMENT= UNSORTED
470 WEND
480 RETURN
```

A subroutine following line 370 sorts the data in a WHILE...WEND and FOR...NEXT loop. The WHILE loop executes until the sort is complete. The UNSORTED variable is responsible for keeping track of this. For the first run this variable must be set to TRUE (line 390). For every run of the FOR...NEXT loop the variable is set to FALSE. If an element was switched (line 440/subroutine after line 500), UNSORTED is initialized with the current "swap line" and stands at TRUE. If an element wasn't swapped, it remains FALSE and the WHILE loop is terminated (line 470). The bubble sort is performed quickly in this case because the LAST.ELEMENT variable is set to the line in which the last swap occurred (line 460). Because of this, only the unsorted part of the data is processed.

```
490 '
500 '----- swap elements -----
510 '
520 SWAP ALPHA$(ELEMENT),ALPHA$(ELEMENT+1)
530 UNSORTED= ELEMENT
540 RETURN
```

The subroutine performs the exchange of the elements and sets UNSORTED to the last processed element (line 530). In line 460 its content is passed to the LAST.ELEMENT variable to increase the speed of the process.

13.2 Quick Sort

As its name implies, the quick sort operates quicker than the bubble sort. Although requiring more programming, this sort routine can handle large amounts of data. Compare the sort time for both algorithms. The quick sort is about ten times faster than the bubble sort.

13.2.1 How does quick sort work?

With the bubble sort we saw that the data was processed from the first to the last (sorted) element. So, elements that were already sorted were compared again. However, because of its sophisticated algorithm, quick sort only compares unsorted elements. This is done as follows: First an element from the middle of the data is selected as a comparison element. The comparison with the other elements occurs from the middle toward the left and right (or to the top or bottom, depending on how you view the data). The larger element is pushed toward the middle. Similarly the smaller element is moved from the left toward the middle. Since the left and right limit of the data is newly set after every run and always moves in the direction of the middle of the data, there are fewer elements to compare.

13.2.2 Advantages and disadvantages of using quick sort

We've already mentioned that the advantage of using quick sort is its fast execution time. Quick sort is fast because it processes only unsorted elements instead of sorted elements, as in the bubble sort.

Despite its speed, quick sort also presents some disadvantages. One disadvantage is that the required programming is more complicated than the programming for bubble sort. The following program shows that about three or four times more program lines and memory space are required for quick sort. Also, for the beginner, the algorithm isn't as easy to understand as the bubble sort. The quick sort also relies heavily on the string administration and, therefore, the garbage collection of PC-BASIC.

13.2.3 Using quick sort

Quick sort is mainly used in "fast" applications where the data sort speed is important. It's also used with medium and large amounts of data, for which a bubble sort would be too slow. Professional programmers often use quick sort instead of bubble sort even with small amounts of data in order to achieve the maximum speed from their programs.

The following is a program for quick sort:

```
10 '-------------------------------------------
20 ' QSORT.BAS    demonstration-program for QuickSort
30 '-------------------------------------------
40 :
50 CLS:KEY OFF:OPTION BASE 0
60 MAX.SIZE= 25
70 DIM ALPHA$(MAX.SIZE)
80 RESTORE 100
90 FOR I= 0 TO MAX.SIZE:READ ALPHA$(I):NEXT I
100 DATA ZEBRA,ABACUS,XYLOPHONE,BASIC,YELLOW,CREAM,WATCHDOG,DISKETTE
110 DATA Vacation,Example,Umpire,Frequency,Tourist,General,Sheri
120 DATA Helmet,Renaissance,Ice,Quality,Justice,Print,Key,Observation
130 DATA Locate,Numeric,Mathematics
140 :
150 :
160 COLOR 15,0:PRINT "Unsorted Array:":COLOR 7,0
170 FOR I= 0 TO MAX.SIZE
180    PRINT ALPHA$(I);" ";
190 NEXT I
200 PRINT:PRINT
210 :
220 START= TIMER
230 GOSUB 360 'sort data in ALPHA$ ...
240 FINISH= TIMER
250 :
260 COLOR 15,0:PRINT "Sorted Array:":COLOR 7,0
270 FOR I= 0 TO MAX.SIZE
280    PRINT ALPHA$(I);" ";
290 NEXT I
300 :
310 LOCATE 25,1
320 PRINT USING "Sort time: ##.##     Strike any key...";FINISH-START;
330 IF INKEY$= "" THEN 330
340 CLS:END
```

Up to this point the quick sort program is similar to the bubble sort program. The following subroutine is responsible for further sorting.

```
350 '
360 '----- subroutine QuickSort -----
370 '
380 LEFT= 0
390 RIGHT= 1
400 TAB.START= 0
410 TAB.END= MAX.SIZE
420 PATH= 1
430 TAB.INDEX(1,LEFT)= TAB.START
440 TAB.INDEX(1,RIGHT)= TAB.FINISH
450 :
```

In line 380 to 440 the variables for the subroutine are initialized. LEFT and RIGHT (line 380/390) are constants which are used for indexing the TAB.INDEX array. TAB.START

410

and TAB.FINISH (line 400/410) specify the borders of the section of the table that must be sorted. The PATH variable is required for indexing the TAB.INDEX array and is also used as a flag which indicates "finished/not finished". As soon as PATH contains the value 0, the table is sorted and the subroutine is terminated (line 670/680).

```
460 TAB.START= TAB.INDEX(PATH,LEFT)
470 TAB.END= TAB.INDEX(PATH,RIGHT)
480 PATH= PATH-1
490 TEMP.LEFT= TAB.START
500 TEMP.RIGHT= TAB.END
510 X$= ALPHA$( (TAB.START+TAB.END) \ 2)
520 WHILE ALPHA$(TEMP.LEFT) < X$ : TEMP.LEFT= TEMP.LEFT+1  : WEND
530 WHILE X$ < ALPHA$(TEMP.RIGHT): TEMP.RIGHT= TEMP.RIGHT-1: WEND
540 IF TEMP.LEFT <= TEMP.RIGHT THEN GOSUB 700:GOTO 520
550 IF TEMP.RIGHT-TAB.START < TAB.END-TEMP.LEFT THEN 610
560 IF TAB.START >= TEMP.RIGHT THEN 600
570 PATH= PATH+1
580 TAB.INDEX(PATH,LEFT)= TAB.START
590 TAB.INDEX(PATH,RIGHT)= TEMP.RIGHT
600 TAB.START= TEMP.LEFT:GOTO 660
610 IF TEMP.LEFT >= TAB.END THEN 650
620 PATH= PATH+1
630 TAB.INDEX(PATH,LEFT)= TEMP.LEFT
640 TAB.INDEX(PATH,RIGHT)= TAB.END
650 TAB.END=TEMP.RIGHT
660 IF TAB.START < TAB.END THEN 490
670 IF PATH THEN 460
```

The actual sorting of the data and initializing the left/right border for the unsorted portion of the table occurs in lines 460 to 670. In line 510 a comparison element is selected from the middle of the unsorted table. In lines 520 and 530 the left and right border are tested with a WHILE loop. The counters TEMP.LEFT and TEMP.RIGHT are incremented or decremented until a larger/smaller element is found in comparison. Line 540 tests this and, if necessary, calls the subroutine (line 700) for swapping the elements. There the borders are reset (line 730/740). Various queries ensure that the borders of the unsorted part remain within logical values and, if necessary, initialize the limits again (line 550, 560, 610, 660).

```
680 RETURN
690 '
700 '----- swap elements -----
710 '
720 SWAP ALPHA$(TEMP.LEFT),ALPHA$(TEMP.RIGHT)
730 TEMP.LEFT= TEMP.LEFT+1
740 TEMP.RIGHT= TEMP.RIGHT-1
750 RETURN
```

The subroutine, after line 700, exchanges the affected elements and resets the borders for the unsorted part of the table.

13.3   Assembler Sort

The *assembler sort* is several hundred times faster than either the bubble or quick sort but is difficult to use. In certain applications, such as inventory control which use long numbers or address files that contain several hundred records, you'll find that using quick sort is too slow. You should use the assembler sort in these situations.

13.3.1 How does assembler sort work?

Although operating similar to the bubble sort, the assembler sort has two important differences. The complicated and time consuming "interpretation" is avoided since the operations are performed in machine language. Also, only the string descriptors, not the elements' contents, are exchanged. PC-BASIC stores arrays in such a way that a descriptor is created for each element. This descriptor consists of 3 bytes:

  Byte #1   Length of the string

  Byte #2   Low byte of the address of the string

  Byte #3   High byte of the address of the string

The second and third byte form the offset in the data segment and point to the address storing the content of the string.

The descriptors of a string array are sequentially spaced three bytes apart in memory. This is very important for assembler programming. So, within a sort routine only the length bytes and the pointers to the elements, not the content of the elements, are swapped. The listing in this section demonstrates this.

13.3.2 Advantages and disadvantages of using assembler sort

The speed of the assembler sort is its biggest advantage. As the demonstration program executes, you'll discover that a sort time of 0.0 is partly displayed. Instead of indicating that a sort wasn't performed, this only indicates that the PC-BASIC function TIMER was unable to determine the speed. Another advantage is that string operations don't occur; only pointers are swapped. Exchanging pointers is faster than exchanging entire string contents. Also the garbage collection isn't required. Finally, the sort routine in the assembler requires less memory space (only 172 bytes) than its counterpart in PC-BASIC.

A disadvantage of using assembler sort is that a sort routine first must be developed in assembler language. However, since we've already performed this task, you don't have to worry about it for the moment.

Many programmers avoid assembler programming. However, throughout this book we've seen several impressive examples of the capabilities of assembler routines in PC-BASIC. This should convince you to try assembler sort.

13.3.3 Using assembler sort

This routine should be used when data must be sorted quickly. For example, it can be used for applications, such as telephone inquiries, in which information must be provided quickly. Another reason to use the assembler sort is to conserve memory space. As we mentioned earlier, only 172 bytes are needed for this routine. It's important to save as much memory space as possible. This is especially true in large programs. Let's look at the assembler listing:

```
;----------------------------------------
; ASM_SORT.ASM
;
; Bubble-Sort in Assembler...
;----------------------------------------
PCBASIC SEGMENT BYTE PUBLIC
        ASSUME CS:PCBASIC, DS:PCBASIC
        PUBLIC AsmSort ;sorting a $-Arrays
;------ EQUates -----------------------
False= 0
True= NOT False
;------ AsmSort ----- CALL AsmSort(MAX.SIZE,ALPHA$(0),X,X,X,X,X,X,X)
AS_Cnt   equ word ptr [BP+22] ;number of elements
AS_Adr   equ word ptr [BP+20] ;address of the String
L_element  equ word ptr [BP+18]
Unsorted   equ word ptr [BP+16]
element    equ word ptr [BP+14]
address    equ word ptr [BP+12]
Adr1       equ word ptr [BP+10]
Adr2       equ word ptr [BP+8]
Cnt1       equ byte ptr [BP+7]
Cnt2       equ byte ptr [BP+6]
```

Here is the first difference between the assembler sort routine and other sort routines A sort routine cannot exist without its own variables for saving pointers or intermediate results. In this case, we provided a temporary area for the required variables on the STACK. The routine is called from PC-BASIC with a number of "dummy" parameters. A total of 14 bytes is required. With the call, which uses seven dummy integer variables (X, see above), these bytes are provided on the stack and reserved. The individual bytes or words are assigned to the variable names with EQU.

The assembler sort works exactly like its PC-BASIC bubble sort counterpart. For a better understanding, the following are the PC-BASIC lines:

```
;-----------------------------------------------------------------------
;
;CALL AsmSort(MAX.SIZE,ALPHA$(0),X,X,X,X,X,X,X)
;
;Sorts the Array starting at element (0) with 'MAX.SIZE' elements
;Algorithm= BUBBLE
;
;360 '
;370 '----- subroutine BubbleSort -----
;380 '
;390 UNSORTED= TRUE
;400 LAST.ELEMENT= MAX.SIZE
;410 WHILE UNSORTED
;420   UNSORTED= FALSE
;430   FOR ELEMENT= 0 TO LAST.ELEMENT-1
;440     IF ALPHA$(ELEMENT) > ALPHA$(ELEMENT+1) THEN GOSUB 500
;450   NEXT  ELEMENT
;460   LAST.ELEMENT= UNSORTED
;470 WEND
;480 RETURN
;490 '
;500 '----- swap elements -----
;510 '
;520 SWAP ALPHA$(ELEMENT),ALPHA$(ELEMENT+1)
;530 UNSORTED= ELEMENT
;540 RETURN
;-----------------------------------------------------------------------

START:
```

The assembler routine is read with BLOAD.

```
Start:

BLOAD_Hdr db 0FDh
BLOAD_Adr dw ?,?
BLOAD_Len dw End-Start
```

This assumes that a BLOAD header is available. This header is declared here. The first byte (BLOAD_Hdr, 0FDh) is the BLOAD flag. PC-BASIC recognizes that a BLOAD file exists here using this flag. The two subsequent words (BLOAD_Adr) aren't significant. After a BSAVE, the segment:offset of the memory area is located here. Since the routine should be loaded at any desired location (BLOAD <Name>,<address>), we don't consider the entry. The last word (BLOAD_Len) determines the length of the routine in bytes. We let the assembler calculate by setting the labels "Start" and "End" and entering the difference there.

```
BEGIN:
;--------------------------------------
AsmSort PROC      FAR
        push      bp                    ;store BP
        mov       bp,sp                 ;BP= SP for Parameter access
        push      ds                    ;store DS and ES
        push      es

        mov       si,AS_Cnt             ;address 'Number'
        mov       ax,[si]               ;load 'Number' to AX
        mov       L_element,ax          ;retain for loop
        mov       si,AS_Adr             ;address 1. element
        mov       ax,[si]               ;load to AX
        mov       address,ax            ;and hold
        mov       Unsorted,True         ;data is unsorted
        push      ds
        pop       es                    ;ES= DS
```

In this part the temporary variables are preset. "L_element" is the counter variable for the FOR...NEXT simulation after LABEL FOR_element. "address" is the offset to the first string descriptor of the array. "Unsorted" is the flag of the same name for the WHILE...WEND loop.

```
WHILE:
        ov        Unsorted,False        ;Default: everything sorted
        mov       element,0             ;start in front of Array

FOR_element:
        mov       ax,element            ;address current element
        mov       bx,3                  ;3 Bytes for each entry
        imul      bx                    ;AX*BX= pointer to Descriptor
        add       ax,address            ;AX= AX plus Array-Start
```

The loop counter "element" contains the current element. The address of the descriptors is calculated here by multiplying the content by three and then adding the offset to the descriptor table.

```
        mov       si,ax                 ;SI= first element for comparison
        mov       bl,byte ptr [si]      ;length-Byte first element to BL
        mov       Adr1,si               ;store for possible exchange
        mov       Cnt1,bl               ;same
        add       si,1                  ;points to String address
        mov       si,[si]               ;points to String content

        add       ax,3                  ;AX+3= 2. element for comparison
        mov       di,ax                 ;DI= 2. element for comparison
        mov       cl,byte ptr [di]      ;length-Byte second element to CL
        mov       Adr2,di               ;keep for eventual exchange
        mov       Cnt2,cl               ;same
        add       di,1                  ;points to String-address
        mov       di,[di]               ;points to String-content
```

SI is used as a pointer to the first element. First the length byte of the first element is read into BL and stored in "Cnt1" for an eventual exchange. Then the address of the descriptor is stored in "Adr1" for an eventual exchange. Then SI is incremented by one and points to the address bytes in the descriptor. The last statement loads SI with this address so that the content of the string can be addressed through SI. DI serves as a pointer to the second element. Three is simply added to AX because a descriptor is always 3 bytes long and two adjacent elements are always compared. Otherwise, proceed as in SI. The length byte of the second element is stored in CL.

```
        xor     ch,ch           ;CH= 0
        cmp     cl,bl           ;second element smaller than first?
        jbe     W1              ;if yes, continue
        xchg    cl,bl           ;else exchange, CL must be <= BL
W1:     cmpsb                   ;compare first and second element
        je      Next            ;if first = second, then next character
        ja      Swap            ;if first > second, then exchange
        jmp     W2              ;else, next run

Next:   loop    W1              ;until CX= 0
        jmp     W2              ;then next run
```

After the SI and DI pointers have been initialized, the byte by byte comparison of the string is performed. For the comparison, CX is used as a counter. For this it must be determined that CX is loaded with the smaller of the two length bytes (BL/CL). If the second element is shorter than the first element, bytes which aren't related to the second element are compared.

The comparison is made with CMPSB. This statement compares the bytes addressed with DS:SI and ES:DI. If both are equal (JE Next), the next byte is compared in a LOOP until one of the bytes is larger (JA Swap) or smaller (JMP W2) or CX= 0 (JMP W2).

```
swap:
        mov     si,Adr1         ;else, swap Descriptors ...
        mov     bl,Cnt1         ;length first element
        mov     di,Adr2
        mov     cl,Cnt2         ;length second element

        mov     byte ptr [si],cl  ;exchange length-Bytes
        mov     byte ptr [di],bl

        add     si,1            ;skip length-Bytes
        add     di,1

        mov     ax,[si]         ;address first element
        mov     bx,[di]         ;address second element
        mov     [si],bx         ;exchange addresses
        mov     [di],ax

        mov     ax,element      ;...and initialize loop again
        mov     Unsorted,ax
```

Here the two descriptors are exchanged if the first element was larger than the second element. For addressing, SI and DI or the length bytes BL and CL are used. Finally "Unsorted" is initialized with the value from "element".

```
W2:     mov     ax,element          ;next element
        inc     ax                  ;plus 1
        mov     element,ax          ;store for loop
                                    ;inc        ax
        cmp     ax,L_element        ;loop done ?
        jae     W3                  ;if yes, next run
        jmp     FOR_element         ;else, continue

W3:     mov     ax,Unsorted
        mov     L_element,ax        ;last element= current exchange
        cmp       Unsorted,False    ;Is everything sorted ?
        je      WEND                ;if yes, End
        jmp     WHILE               ;else, next run
```

In this part first a test is made to determine whether the current loop, terminated with "L_element", is already finished. If it is (JAE W3), the new loop is initialized. If it isn't, the next elements are compared (JMP FOR_element). In W3 a test is made if "Unsorted" is FALSE. If it is (JE WEND) the sorting is terminated; otherwise the next loop is executed (JMP WHILE).

```
WEND:
        pop     s                   ;restore ES
        pop     ds                  ;restore DS
        pop     bp                  ;restore BP
        ret     18                  ;remove 9 words from the Stack
```

The stored registers ES, DS and BP are restored and the stack is cleared, with RET 18, for the correct return jump to PC-BASIC.

```
AsmSort ENDP
Ende:
;----------------------------------------
PCBASIC ENDS
        END Start
```

Although this may seem complicated now, with some experience you'll be able to develop an assembler routine based on a PC-BASIC routine. Simply remember the peculiarities of the assembler and provide the proper constructions. The assembler even offers constructions that make the solution simpler than in BASIC or Pascal (see CMPSB or LOOP).

You're probably wondering how PC-BASIC uses the routine. As we saw in the listing, the routine should be loaded with BLOAD. In the program only the start address of the routine must be indicated for BLOAD and a call variable assigned for CALL. The following program illustrates this. Usually the program corresponds to the example presented in the bubble sort section. We'll include comments only when there are differences from the earlier example:

Note: To execute the following program correctly, call PC-BASIC with the /M switch as follows:

```
GWBASIC /M:54000
```

```
10 '------------------------------------------------
20 ' ASORT.BAS    demonstration-program for Assembler-Sort
30 '------------------------------------------------
40 :
50 CLS:KEY OFF:OPTION BASE 0:DEFINT A-Z
60 DEF SEG
70 BLOAD "ASMSRT.COM",&HE000
80 ASMSRT= &HE000
```

The assembler routine is loaded. Both the address &HE000 for BLOAD (line 70) and the assignment to the CALL variable "ASMSORT", which appears in line 80, are important.

```
90 FALSE= 0: TRUE= NOT FALSE
100 MAX.SIZE= 25: X= 0
```

The assignment of 0 to the X variable is also important. With the DEFINT A-Z statement (line 50) above, an assignment must occur during CALL. Otherwise, a syntax error will result because CALL won't consider the variable as an integer variable.

```
110 DIM ALPHA$(MAX.SIZE)
120 RESTORE 140
130 FOR I= 0 TO MAX.SIZE:READ ALPHA$(I):NEXT I
140 DATA Zebra,Abacus,Xylophone,Basic,Yellow,Cream,Watchdog,Diskette
150 DATA Vacation,Example,Umpire,Frequency,Tourist,General,Sheri
160 DATA Helmet,Renaissance,Ice,Quality,Justice,Print,Key,Observation
170 DATA Locate,Numeric,Mathematics
180 :
190 :
200 COLOR 15,0:PRINT "Unsorted Array:":COLOR 7,0
210 FOR I= 0 TO MAX.SIZE
220   PRINT ALPHA$(I);" ";
230 NEXT I
240 PRINT:PRINT
250 :
260 START#= TIMER
270 GOSUB 530 'sort data in ALPHA$ ...
280 ENDE#= TIMER
290 COLOR 15,0:PRINT "Sorted array (BubbleSort):":COLOR 7,0
300 FOR I= 0 TO MAX.SIZE
310   PRINT ALPHA$(I);" ";
320 NEXT I
```

```
330 PRINT:PRINT USING "sort-time: ##.####";ENDE#-START#:PRINT
340 :
350 RESTORE 140
360 FOR I= 0 TO MAX.SIZE:READ ALPHA$(I):NEXT I
370 :
380 START#= TIMER
390 ADDRESS= VARPTR(ALPHA$(0)):CALL ASMSRT(MAX.SIZE,ADDRESS,X,X,X,X,X,X,X)
400 ENDE#= TIMER
```

The assembler routine is called here. Don't forget the dummy variables. Otherwise, the assembler routine will write into an area of the stack that isn't reserved (i.e., the return jump with RET 18 won't work). Again, don't be surprised if a sort time of 0.0 is displayed. TIMER can no longer be used for such a short period of time.

```
410 :
420 COLOR 15,0:PRINT "sorted Array (AsmSort):":COLOR 7,0
430 FOR I= 0 TO MAX.SIZE
440    PRINT ALPHA$(I);" ";
450 NEXT I
460 PRINT:PRINT USING "sort-time: ##.####";ENDE#-START#;
470 :
480 LOCATE 25,1
490 PRINT "strike any key ...";
500 IF INKEY$= "" THEN 500
510 CLS:END
520 '
530 '----- subroutine BubbleSort -----
540 '
550 UNSORTED= TRUE
560 LAST.ELEMENT= MAX.SIZE
570 WHILE UNSORTED
580    UNSORTED= FALSE
590    FOR ELEMENT= 0 TO LAST.ELEMENT-1
600       IF ALPHA$(ELEMENT) > ALPHA$(ELEMENT+1) THEN GOSUB 660
610    NEXT  ELEMENT
620    LAST.ELEMENT= UNSORTED
630 WEND
640 RETURN
650 '
660 '----- exchange elements -----
670 '
680 SWAP ALPHA$(ELEMENT),ALPHA$(ELEMENT+1)
690 UNSORTED= ELEMENT
700 RETURN
```

Changing the assembler routine

The assembler routine is only designed for sorting string arrays, starting at element 0, for the number of elements in "Number". If you only want to sort a partial area of the array (which usually isn't done), the "element" variable, in the assembler listing, must be initialized accordingly. This can either be done as a constant when the array is basically sorted from another element or you can add a parameter which is placed into the "element" variable. However, this requires that another temporary variable be created on the stack and another dummy parameter be provided. The RET statement must also be changed accordingly.

It may also be necessary to compare partial strings. If you store a complete address in a structured string and want to search for the ZIP code, the offset into the string and the sorting length must be passed as a parameter. The usual offset is added to SI and DI and CL is then loaded into the sorting length. Other temporary variables must be created. Additional dummy parameters must be passed and the RET statement must also be changed. To conclude we need a small program that demonstrates the speed of the assembler sort with larger quantities of data. In the program PDV.BAS (on the companion diskette) 1,000 lines are read and then sorted:

Note: To be able to execute the following program correctly, you must call PC-BASIC with the switch /M as follows:

```
GWBASIC /M:54000
```

```
10 '-------------------------------------------
20 ' ASORT1.BAS   demonstration-program for Assembler-Sort
30 '-------------------------------------------
40 :
50 CLS:KEY OFF:OPTION BASE 0:DEFINT A-Z
60 DEF SEG
70 BLOAD "ASM_SORT.COM",&HE000
80 ASMSORT= &HE000
90 MAX.SIZE= 1000: X= 0
100 DIM ALPHA$(MAX.SIZE)
110 PRINT "One moment please. Initialize ALPHA$()..."
120 OPEN "PDV.BAS" FOR INPUT AS #1
130 I= 0
140 WHILE NOT EOF(1) AND I <= MAX.SIZE
150    LINE INPUT #1,ALPHA$(I)
160    I= I+1
170 WEND
180 CLOSE
190 :
200 START#= TIMER
210 ADDRESS= VARPTR(ALPHA$(0)):CALL ASMSORT(MAX.SIZE,ADDRESS,X,X,X,X,X,X,X)
220 ENDE#= TIMER
230 :
240 COLOR 15,0:PRINT "Sorted ALPHA$():"
250 FOR I=1 TO MAX.SIZE
260    PRINT ALPHA$(I);" ";
270 NEXT I
280 PRINT:PRINT USING "sort-time: ##.####";ENDE#-START#;
290 :
```

```
300 LOCATE 25,1
310 PRINT "strike any key...";
320 IF INKEY$= "" THEN 320
330 CLS:END
```

If you don't have the companion diskette that accompanies this book, simply save one of your own larger programs as an ASCII file by using the ",A" option. Then change line 120 according to the name of your program.

13.4   A Different Way to Sort

Almost every book about personal computers contains alternative ways to sort data. So, instead of presenting another routine, we'll discuss a different <u>method</u> for sorting.

As you know, with the SHELL command you can call every COM program, EXE program or a BAT file from PC-BASIC. Also, there is the SORT.EXE utility program on the system diskette which, as the name implies, is responsible for sorting.

If SHELL and SORT were combined and used in a program, only one line is needed instead of long sort routines. For example:

```
 10 '---------------------------------
 20 'SORT.BAS sorting - somewhat different
 30 '---------------------------------
 40 :
 50 CLS:KEY OFF
 60 :
 70 'write 100 records
 80 :
 90 PRINT "Write unsorted data into a file .....":PRINT:PRINT
100 :
110 OPEN "unsort.dat" FOR OUTPUT AS #1
120 FOR I= 1 TO 2
130   FOR K= 65 TO 127:A$= CHR$(K)+" test text"
140     PRINT#1, A$:PRINT A$
150   NEXT K
160 NEXT I
170 CLOSE
180 :
190 CLS
200 PRINT "Now the data is being sorted .....":PRINT:PRINT
210 :
220 SHELL "SORT <UNSORT.DAT >SORT.DAT"
230 :
240 CLS:PRINT "The data has been sorted:"
250 :
260 OPEN "sort.dat" FOR INPUT AS #1
270 WHILE NOT EOF(1)
280   INPUT #1,WORD$
290   PRINT WORD$
300 WEND
310 CLOSE
320 :
330 PRINT:PRINT "That's all there is....."
```

Compare these lines with the usual routines that are used for sorting. As you can see, this method requires fewer lines.

However, this method has its drawbacks. If the file is fairly large, and SORT.EXE requires too much memory space (maximum of 64 Kbytes), the computer may crash. This may be caused by the error handling of SORT.EXE which doesn't function properly through SHELL. Everything works correctly during the call from the DOS. Then you receive an "Insufficient memory" error message and are returned to the DOS prompt. In your program you must check the size of the file to be sorted and, if necessary, terminate the sorting. In order to do this you'll need to experiment in order to find the correct value, which depends on the size of the RAM , the system, utility programs (SideKick, etc.) or all of these.

The greater than (>) and less than (<) characters under DOS indicate a redirection of the input or output. In our case, we redirect the input from the keyboard to the UNSORT.DAT file and the output from the screen to the SORT.DAT file. The sort can be in ascending or descending order by using a parameter:

```
SORT <UNSORT.DAT >SORT.DAT /R
```

However, the sort is usually in ascending order. According to the ASCII table this means from 1 to 9 or from A to Z, or from a to z. If the /R parameter is indicated, the sequence is reversed to descending order: from 9 to 1, from Z to A and from z to a. You can also indicate from which position in the record the sorting should begin. For example, suppose you want to sort an addresses file according to the ZIP code. During the call, you would indicate the position of the ZIP code field as a parameter:

```
SORT <UNSORT.DAT >SORT.DAT /+41
```

The corresponding field would be starting at position 41 in the record. For most sorting this method is adequate. However, there are problems when records must be sorted according to several fields. In these instances, use the routine described above.

14. File Management

The problems involved with successfully managing files has received much attention over the years. This isn't surprising since there are various file management options and nearly all programs cannot function without successful file management. In this chapter we'll discuss the three most common methods of managing files.

14.1   Which file should be used?

Before selecting a type of file management, you must determine the structure of the data to be stored and the best way to access this data. How the programming language and the operating system support file management is also important. Some programming languages provide complete ISAM file controls. This decreases the work of the programmers. Unfortunately, PC-BASIC/BASICA isn't one of these programming languages. So using ISAM files in PC-BASIC requires some extra effort.

PC-BASIC/BASICA offers two easily programmed types of file management:

```
Sequential files
Random-access files (sometimes called direct access files)
```

Records of different lengths and structures are stored in *sequential files*. These records are separated by the ASCII character <RETURN> (CHR$(13)). The only limitation is the maximum length of a record, which is 255 characters; a string variable cannot accept more characters than this. In order for a file to be processed, it must be loaded into memory. Changes can only be made here. However, under PC-BASIC/BASICA, it's possible to attach records to a sequential file without having to load the file.

In a *random-access* file the records are stored with a fixed length and structure. You must enter the specific record number to access an individual record. A record to be edited or changed must first be loaded into memory. After the edit is complete, the record is written back to its original location in the file.

Now let's return to our original question: What file should be used for what data? Let's consider some example problems which must often be solved for file management.

Managing information

Often while reading books, magazines and newspapers you may find information that you would like to keep for future reference.

A sequential file is frequently used for this type of data. The data to be stored can easily fit into the available 255 bytes of a data record. A PC with 640K of memory can easily maintain up to 500 records in memory since usually records won't require 255 bytes. Also, you can easily search for data with a sequential file.

To ensure flexibility, various files are used. Each file is assigned a subject or application area:

> Software
> Hardware

or:

> PC
> Monitors
> Printers
> Mice
> Hard disks

At the beginning of the program the complete file is loaded into an array in memory. The best way to do this is with a loop whose counters provide information, after the file is loaded, about the number of available records.

```
190 .....
200 OPEN "MONITOR.DAT" FOR INPUT AS #1
210 SIZE= 1
220 WHILE NOT EOF(1)
230   LINE INPUT #1,RECORD$(SIZE):SIZE= SIZE+1
240   IF SIZE> 500 THEN CLOSE #1:ERROR 32 'file full
250 WEND
260 CLOSE #1
270 LAST.SIZE= SIZE-1:CURRENT.SIZE= 1
280 .....
```

The record's allocation could appear as follows:

```
Byte  1 to 15 -> keyword
Byte 15 to nn -> notes
```

After the file is loaded, the program automatically jumps to the change mode and expects a keyword to be entered. A search routine is used to determine whether any entries are available on this subject. If there are, these entries can be expanded, changed or deleted. Otherwise, a new record is constructed in the array:

```
290 .....
300 FOR I=1 TO LAST.SIZE
310   IF KEYWORD$= LEFT$(RECORD$(I),15) THEN 500 'display
320 NEXT I
330 IF I> 500 THEN ERROR 32 'file full
340 LAST.SIZE= LAST.SIZE+1
350 CURRENT.SIZE= LAST.SIZE:GOTO 600 'input
360 .....
```

When a record is deleted, the last record is placed at this location and the counter decreases by one:

```
690 .....
700 'CURRENT.SIZE is for example 157
710 LOCATE 24,1,1:COLOR 15,0
720 PRINT "delete record (Y/N)? --> ";
730 X$=INKEY$:IF X$="" THEN 730
740 IF X$="n" OR X$="N" THEN RETURN 'do not delete
750 IF X$<>"y" AND X$<>"Y" THEN BEEP:GOTO 730
760 RECORD$(CURRENT.SIZE) = RECORD$(LAST.SIZE)
770 LAST.SIZE= LAST.SIZE-1
780 .....
```

Once the program ends, the file is completely written back:

```
990 .....
1000 OPEN "MONITOR.DAT" FOR OUTPUT AS #1
1010 FOR I=1 TO LAST.SIZE
1020   PRINT #1,LAST$(I)
1030 NEXT I
1040 CLOSE #1
1050 RETURN
1060 .....
```

Since the complete file is in RAM, it's possible that a power failure or an accidental shutdown would cause you to lose any changes or additions entered since the last save. You can avoid this by writing the file back after every five changes or other specified amount of time. This is quick and easy if you're using a hard disk. However, this would take longer on a floppy disk drive.

Inventory control

All wholesale and retail businesses need to keep track of their inventory. An inventory control system must be used for a current overview of merchandise "onhand". Usually this is done by organizing the product numbers sequentially. A random-access file is required for this.

Each product is assigned a number which can also be used as a record number in the random file. For larger inventories, the products should be divided into groups. Each group is assigned its own file. The access can be organized as follows:

```
190 '.....
200 INPUT "product-group......: ";PG$
210 INPUT "product-number...:";PN$
220 FILNAM= "PG"+PG$
230 OPEN "R",#1,FILNAM$,700
240 FIELD#1,2 AS PG$,10 AS PN$,20 AS LABEL$.....
250 '.....
300 SIZE= VAL(PN$)
310 GET#1,SIZE
320 .....
```

It's easy to make changes or additions to a random file. A changed record is written to its old position in the file. A new record is attached to the end of the file according to its product number. This eventually creates empty records. For example, when the last record has product number 234 and the new record has product number 301, PC-BASIC automatically creates records 235 to 300. You must use either SPACE$ or STRING$ to create blank data records and fill the gap between records 235-300.

It's more difficult to delete a record. You shouldn't delete a record that is located in the middle of the file. Although possible, this would disrupt the order of the product numbers. For example, if you deleted product number 456 all subsequent records would be moved up one position (product number 457 becomes product number 456, etc.). As you can see, deleting several numbers would ruin how the file is organized.

Instead, every record has a field one byte long which stores a delete flag. The rest of the record remains unchanged. This flag is queried. During the output it sends the message "Record deleted" or "Record has delete flag". This indicates that the data contained in it shouldn't be considered during calculations or statistical operations. The user can remove this delete flag using a special menu option. When this is done, the previously deleted data remains unchanged during accidental deletions.

14.2 ISAM File Management

You may have already discovered that certain data cannot be organized numerically. Therefore it cannot be accessed using a record number. Also, the amount of information that must be stored may be too large for a sequential file or the length of the record may exceed 255 bytes.

In these cases you should use the ISAM file. ISAM is an acronym for Index Sequential Addressing Method.

14.2.1 Structure of an ISAM file

The word "Index" signifies a random file. A record number is actually an index into the file. The word "Sequential" signifies a sequential file. So, an ISAM is a combination of a random and sequential file.

We'll explain this by using an example. The term "ISAM file" isn't accurate because there are actually two files. The random file is designated as the *data file* and the sequential file as the *index file*. However, since "ISAM file" is always used, we'll also use this term.

We can describe the structure of an ISAM file as follows: the data are stored in a random file. The record length isn't important and can be defined according to the structure of the data. A field of the record is defined to access the data. The content of the field and the number of the record are stored in a sequential file. During the access, the sequential file is searched for the search criteria. The record number found during this search permits access to the random file. Although this may sound complicated at first, you'll soon see that it isn't very difficult.

14.2.2 Using ISAM file management

In Chapter 10 we described a problem that could be solved by using an ISAM file. You may recall that the problem was to organize the numerous programs and files which accumulate over time. Many users follow this procedure to locate a certain program or file:

1. Place all the diskettes which may contain the file in a big pile.

2. Place the first diskette into the drive. Use the DIR command to verify whether the file is located on the diskette.

3. If it isn't on this diskette, repeat step 2 for each of the remaining diskettes until the file is found.

As you can see, this method is very time consuming and can't even guarantee that you'll find the file. Instead of doing this, let your PC manage your diskettes.

In its original version, the program we developed for this purpose required 45K of memory. During program development, our main goal was the management of text files. These files contained translations, end user programs, documentation and manuscripts.

Other features, such as searching files for certain concepts or converting various formats, are also included. These features increased the size of the program. We have changed this program so that the diskette management can be used universally. After we discuss the theory behind the program, you'll find the complete listing, along with comments and explanations so that you can easily design this program according to your own needs.

First you must understand the construction of the random file and the structure of the records that are stored in it. This includes deciding the field, through which the access should occur.

14.2.3 Record Allocation in an ISAM file

The records could be allocated as follows:

```
Byte 01-12        program name
Byte 13-14        diskette number
Byte 15-54        brief program description
Byte 55-64        programming language
Byte 65-nn        additional information as needed
```

You can select the program name, for example, as the access field.

14.2.4 Data collection or input

Next you must determine how to collect the data. We decided to use an assembler routine to do this. The assembler routine reads the directory of the diskette into an array and then further processes the information. So, you don't have to type in the data. You'll find a program below. After some minor changes, this routine can be used, for example, to display a list of filenames that are located on a diskette. A more developed example for selecting files can be found in Chapter 8.

Note: To execute the following program correctly, you must call PC-BASIC/BASICA with the switch /M:

```
GWBASIC /M:54000
```

```
10 '----------------------------------------
20 'READ_DIR.BAS     1986 (C) H.J.Bomanns
30 '----------------------------------------
40 :
50 CLS:KEY OFF
60 DIM DIR$(500):ENTRY= 0
70 MP.START= &HE000
80 RESTORE 100
90 DEF SEG:FOR I=1 TO  151:READ X:POKE MP.START+I-1,X: NEXT I
100 DATA 250, 85,139,236, 30,  6,139,118,  6,139,  4
110 DATA  80,157,139,118, 14,138, 20,139,118, 16,138
120 DATA  52,139,118, 18,138, 12,139,118, 20,138, 44
130 DATA 139,118, 22,138, 28,139,118, 24,138, 60,139
140 DATA 118, 26,138,  4,139,118, 28,138, 36,139,118
150 DATA   8,139, 60, 80,139,118, 12,139,  4,142,192
160 DATA  88,139,118, 10,139, 52, 85,251,205, 33,250
170 DATA  93, 86,156,139,118, 28,136, 36,139,118, 26
180 DATA 136,  4,139,118, 24,136, 60,139,118, 22,136
190 DATA  28,139,118, 20,136, 44,139,118, 18,136, 12
200 DATA 139,118, 16,136, 52,139,118, 14,136, 20, 88
210 DATA 139,118,  6,137,  4, 88,139,118, 10,137,  4
220 DATA 140,192,139,118, 12,137,  4,139,118,  8,137
230 DATA  60,  7, 31, 93,251,202, 24,  0
240 MP.ENDE= MP.START+I-1
250 DOS.SN= MP.START
260 :
270 'In the following loop the address of the Interrupt-number is determined.
280 'The BIOS-/DOS-Interrupt-number can be poked to this address.
290 :
300 FOR I= MP.START TO MP.ENDE:IF PEEK(I)= 205 THEN INT.ADR= I+1 ELSE NEXT
310 :
320 AL%=0: AH%=0: BL%=0: BH%=0: CL%=0: CH%=0: DL%=0: DH%=0: ES%=0: SI%=0: DI%=0:
    FLAGS%=0
330 INT.NR%= &H21:DEF SEG:POKE INT.ADR,INT.NR%
340 :
350 DTA$= SPACE$(64) 'area for result from FN 4Eh and 4Fh
360 DL%=PEEK(VARPTR(DTA$)+1):DH%=PEEK(VARPTR(DTA$)+2) 'Pointer to DTA$
370 AH%= &H1A 'FN Set DTA (Disk Transfer Address)
380 DEF SEG: CALL DOS.SN(AH%, AL%, BH%, BL%, CH%, CL%, DH%, DL%, ES%, SI%, DI%,
    FLAGS%)
390 :
400 MASK$="*.BAS"+CHR$(0) 'search for all BASIC files
410 DL%=PEEK(VARPTR(MASK$)+1):DH%=PEEK(VARPTR(MASK$)+2) 'Pointer to MASK$
420 AH%= &H4E 'FN Search first file
430 DEF SEG: CALL DOS.SN(AH%, AL%, BH%, BL%, CH%, CL%, DH%, DL%, ES%, SI%, DI%,
    FLAGS%)
440 :
450 IF (FLAGS% AND 1)= 0 THEN 510 'Everything OK, continue.....
460 CLS
470 IF AL%=  2 THEN PRINT "invalid template indicated....."
480 IF AL%= 18 THEN PRINT "no entries found for ";MASK$;" ....."
485 PRINT "error: ";AL%
490 END
```

```
500 :
510 PRINT "Reading Directory.....":PRINT
520 GOSUB 670 'transmit data from DTA to the Array
530 AH%= &H4F 'Find next file
540 DEF SEG: CALL DOS.SN(AH%, AL%, BH%, BL%, CH%, CL%, DH%, DL%, ES%, SI%, DI%,
    FLAGS%)
550 GOSUB 670 'transmit data from DTA to the Array
560 :
570 WHILE (FLAGS% AND 1)= 0
580   AH%= &H4F 'FN find next file
590   DEF SEG: CALL DOS.SN(AH%, AL%, BH%, BL%, CH%, CL%,DH%, DL%, ES%, SI%, DI%,
    FLAGS%)
600   GOSUB 670 'transmit data from DTA to the Array
610 WEND 'until FN 4Fh reports that no additional entries are available
620 PRINT "Directory Listing.....":PRINT
630 :
640 FOR I=1 TO ENTRY:PRINT DIR$(I),:NEXT I
650 END
660 :
670 '--- transmit data from DTA to the Array -----
680 :
690 Y$="":I= 0
700 WHILE ASC(MID$(DTA$,&H1F+I,1))<> 0 'end of the name = 0-Byte
710   Y$= Y$+MID$(DTA$,&H1F+I,1)
720   I=I+1
730 WEND
740 DIR$(ENTRY)= Y$
750 ENTRY= ENTRY+1
760 RETURN
```

A detailed look

Starting at line 70 to 250, the machine program is POKEd into the area protected against BASIC/BASICA. This is the DOS interface which has already been used and explained in Chapter 8. Then the disk transfer area (DTA) is set with function &H1A, starting at line 350 through 380. This area is needed for passing data from the diskette or hard disk to the program during the subsequent calls.

The transmission occurs through the &H4E or &H4F functions. The &H4E function searches the current directory for the first filename that matches the sample passed to it (line 400 to 490). As a result, the data are transmitted in the DTA, or the carry flag is set as a flag for an error. In case of an error, an error number is passed in AL%. The &H4F function searches for additional entries that match the indicated extension and transmits the result to the DTA or sets the carry flag when additional entries aren't available (line 570 to 620). From the DTA, the data (in this case only the filename) is transmitted to an array for later processing (starting at line 670). Refer to the Appendix for more information on the 1Ah, 4Eh and 4Fh functions.

After reading a directory, the data is transmitted sequentially from the array into the input template. You can enter the missing information (i.e. the programming language or the diskette number) there.

14.2.5 Saving data in an ISAM file

Data is saved in an ISAM file as follows. First the sequential file is read:

```
290 .....
300 OPEN "IFM.SEQ" FOR INPUT AS #1
310 SIZE= 1
320 WHILE NOT EOF(1)
330   INPUT #1, PRG.NAME$(SIZE),CURR.SIZE%(SIZE)
340 WEND
350 CLOSE #1
360 LAST.SIZE= SIZE-1
370 '.....
```

Now in memory are all the program names saved so far and the record numbers of the records in which the information is stored in the random file. To verify this information, compare the program names with those in the DIR$() variable. DIR$() can also help you find duplicate data which should be deleted.

However, this is dangerous because programs or files with the same name can be stored on different diskettes. In this case, the corresponding record must be read from the random file and the significant data must be compared, before the deletion in DIR$(). Now we can store recently read data:

```
490 '.....
500 OPEN "R",#1,"IFM.DAT",450
510 FIELD #1, <SIZE_DESCRIPTION>
520 GET#1,1
530 RAND.SIZE= VAL(P.NAME$)
540 FOR I=0 TO ENTRY
550   LAST.SIZE= LAST.SIZE+1
560   PRG.NAME$(LAST.SIZE)= DIR$(I)
570   CURR.SIZE%(LAST.SIZE)= RAND.SIZE
580   LSET <DATA from DIR$()> = <Field>
590   LSET .....
600   LSET .....
610   PUT#1,RAND.SIZE
620   RAND.SIZE= RAND.SIZE+1
630 NEXT I
640 LSET P.NAME$= STR$(RAND.SIZE)
650 PUT #1,1
660 CLOSE #1
670 .....
```

A detailed look

The data of the sequential file is still in memory and the random file is opened. In line 510 the FIELD statement, corresponding to the data record, is indicated. In line 520 the first record of the random file is read. This record will be "misused" as a control record. The next record number to be written in the random file is stored in the first field of the record. After this is saved, the last record number is stored here (line 640/650).

In a loop the program name from DIR$() and the record number RAND.SIZE are transmitted into the arrays for the sequential file (PRG.NAME$() and SIZE.NR%()). At this time, the counter LAST.SIZE is incremented. Through LSET, the data are transmitted from DIR$() into the buffer for the random file and in line 610 are written into the file. The RAND.SIZE counter is also incremented. After record number 1 of the random file is completed to the last record number, the action terminates. The sequential file can also be saved and/or kept in memory for additional accesses.

14.2.6 Searching for data in an ISAM file

In order to search for data, the sequential file must be in memory. Usually this isn't a problem. However, with large amounts of data, you must read in parts of a sequential file by using a counter, for example. You would set a counter, which stores the number of the last record that was read. As the next part loads, all records up to this counter are skipped. The records following this counter are then read into the array.

The actual search process can be implemented as shown below. We assume that the random file is already open and the sequential file is in memory:

```
290 .....
300 INPUT "Name of the program, or file: ";SEARCH$
310 GOSUB 500 'search-routine
320 GOSUB 900 'display data
500 FOR I= 1 TO LAST.SIZE
510   IF SEARCH$= PRG.NAME$(I) THEN 540
520 NEXT I
530 PRINT "search-criteria not found"
540 RAND.SIZE= CURR.SIZE%(I)
550 GET#1, RAND.SIZE
560 NOT.FOUND= 0:RETURN
570 .....
```

14.2.7 Deleting data in an ISAM file

Deleting data is performed in two steps. As we mentioned earlier, every record has a field for the deletion flag. This flag is set to 1 during the deletion. During later accesses, the message "Record deleted" is displayed on the basis of this flag. The flag can also be set to 0 again. This reverses the deletion.

Occasionally, a file must be reorganized through a special program. Otherwise, you'll have unnecessarily large files which may contain more deletions than data records. This reorganization program simply reads the random file sequentially. Records with deletion flags are skipped. Current records are written into a second file of the same format. Simultaneously, the sequential file is newly constructed in memory. Once this is done, the old random file is deleted and the second one is renamed. The old sequential file can simply be overwritten by opening FOR OUTPUT and writing the arrays from memory.

You may be wondering whether you'll be able to search only for the program name. To do this, you can create additional sequential files, with a special program, in which the access could occur, for example, through the field "programming language". This program reads the random file again sequentially and transmits field contents and record number into the file to be created. During the search, the sequential file is loaded in order to search for the criteria. Problems can occur during changes, deletions or additions. All available sequential files must be updated. This not only increases execution time, but also the work involved. Finally, you must decide what is required and how user-friendly your program should be.

Another way to search for data that aren't captured through a sequential file consists of reading the random file sequentially and comparing every record with the search criteria. The execution time for this is also high, but you don't have to update the individual sequential files.

14.3 ISAM in Applications: Diskette Management

The following is the complete listing for the diskette management. We've included comments and explanations where necessary to help you rewrite the program according to your needs.

Note: To correctly execute this program, call PC-BASIC with the /M switch:

```
GWBASIC /m:61000/s:360
```

```
10 '------------------------------
20 'PDV.BAS    1986 (C) H.J.Bomanns
25 'BASIC must be called with /m:61000/s:360
30 '------------------------------
40 '
50 COLOR 7,0:CLS:OUT &H3D9,0:KEY OFF:ON ERROR GOTO 8950
60 PRINT "Initialization ";CHR$(254);:LOCATE ,POS(0)-1,1,0,31
70 GOTO 1040 'Skip Subroutines
```

Line 70 ignores or bypasses the subsequent subroutines. When the interpreter encounters a GOSUB, it searches through the program starting with the first line. This search takes time, especially if subroutines are scattered throughout the program. Therefore, placing the subroutines at the beginning of the program increases the speed of the program execution.

```
80 '
90 '----- Subroutines -----
100 '
110 '----- Display Footer -----
120 COLOR TXT.FORGRD, TXT.BAKGRD
130 LOCATE 23,3,0:PRINT FOOT$;SPACE$(80-POS(0));
140 RETURN
150 '----- Display Header -----
160 COLOR MSG.FORGRD,MSG.BAKGRD
170 LOCATE 2,16,0:PRINT HEAD$;
180 COLOR TXT.FORGRD,TXT.BAKGRD
190 PRINT SPACE$(58-POS(0));
200 RETURN
```

The display footer subroutine shows the control key assignment at the bottom of the screen. The display header subroutine shows current program information across the top of the screen.

```
210 '----- Erase Window -----
220 LOCATE CSRLIN,POS(0),0
230 COLOR TXT.FORGRD,TXT.BAKGRD:VIEW PRINT 4 TO 21:CLS:VIEW PRINT
240 RETURN
```

The Erase Window subroutine deletes the area between the header and footer of the template.

The following subroutines store or restore the current screen content. This is done with an assembler routine. Since it is an assembler routine, it performs the entire task in a fraction of a second. With a new construction of the template, the program is able to display messages without waiting for PRINT. The previous screen is simply restored. You can find more information on this type of routine in Chapter 7.

```
250 '----- Store Screen Display -----
260 BUFFER.OFS%= VARPTR(BUFFER%(0))
270 DEF SEG: CALL SAVESCRN(BUFFER.OFS%)
280 RETURN
290 '----- Restore Screen Display -----
300 BUFFER.OFS%= VARPTR(BUFFER%(0))
310 DEF SEG: CALL RESTSCRN(BUFFER.OFS%)
320 RETURN
330 '----- Erase current line -----
340 LOCATE CSRLIN,1:COLOR TXT.FORGRD,TXT.BAKGRD
350 PRINT SPACE$(79);
360 RETURN
```

The Output message subroutine displays a corresponding message. The user needs to press any key to respond to the message.

```
370 '----- Output message and wait for key -----
380 LOCATE 25,1:COLOR MSG.FORGRD,MSG.BAKGRD
390 PRINT MSG$;" ";CHR$(254);" ";:LOCATE CSRLIN,POS(0)-2,1,0,31:BEEP
400 X$=INKEY$:IF X$= "" THEN 400
410 LOCATE 25,1:COLOR TXT.FORGRD,TXT.BAKGRD
420 PRINT SPACE$(LEN(MSG$)+3);
430 RETURN
```

The routine for fast screen output from Chapter 11 is used to increase speed of displaying the output template. The appearance of the template is determined during the initialization through the MASK$ variable.

```
440 '----- Output template ----
450 DEF SEG= MONITOR.ADR:ATTR%= PEEK(1):COLMNO%= 1
460 FOR I= 4 TO 21
470    ROWNO%= I
480    DEF SEG: CALL FASTSCRN(ROWNO%,COLMNO%,ATTR%,MASK$(I-3))
490 NEXT I
500 RETURN
```

The next subroutine reads a single record from the random file and prepares it for the display.

```
510 '----- read current record and display -----
520 'RECNUM.RNDM= record number for random file
530 GET#2,RECNUM.RNDM:X$= R.FIL$
540 ATTR%= INPT.COLR
```

```
550 FOR I=1 TO 14 '14 fields in R.FIL$ or X$
560    TEXT$(I)= MID$(X$,PNTR(I,1),PNTR(I,2)) 'for display
570 NEXT I
580 TEXT$(4)= TEXT$(5)+"/"+TEXT$(4)+"/"+TEXT$(6) 'date
590 TEXT$(5)= TEXT$(7)+":"+TEXT$(8) 'Time
600 FOR I= 6 TO 11:TEXT$(I)= TEXT$(I+3):NEXT I
610 TEXT$(12)= R.WRITE1$:TEXT$(13)= R.WRITE2$:TEXT$(14)= R.WRITE3$
620 FOR I=1 TO 14
630    ROWNO%= FLD(I,1):COLMNO%= FLD(I,2)
640    X$= SPACE$(FLD(I,3)) 'length
650    LSET X$= TEXT$(I)
660    DEF SEG: CALL FASTSCRN(ROWNO%,COLMNO%,ATTR%,X$)
670 NEXT I
680 LOCATE 9,24,0:COLOR INP.FORGRD, INP.BAKGRD
690 ATTRIBUT= ASC(TEXT$(6))
700 FOR I= 0 TO 7
710    IF (ATTRIBUT AND 2^I)<>0 THEN PRINT ATTRIBUT$(I);",";
720 NEXT I
730 RETURN
```

The following subroutine controls the input into the individual fields. The parameter for the field positions is determined in the FELD(x,y) array during the initialization.

```
740 '----- read data for displayed record -----
750 BACK= 0:FLD= 7
760 WHILE NOT BACK 'until return conditions have been met
770    ROWNO= FLD(FLD,1):COLMNO= FLD(FLD,2):LNGTH= FLD(FLD,3)
780    INSTRING$= TEXT$(FLD)
790    GOSUB 9050 'read Subroutine
800    TEXT$(FELD)= INSTRING$
810    IF ONKEY= 72 THEN FLD= FLD-1:IF FLD=  6 THEN FLD= 14
820    IF ONKEY= 80 OR X$=CHR$(13) THEN FLD= FLD+1:IF FLD= 15 THEN FLD= 7
830    IF ONKEY= 68 OR ONKEY=73 OR ONKEY= 81 OR X$= CHR$(27) THEN BACK= -1
840    '<F10>, <PgUp>, <PgDn> and <Esc> keys terminate the subroutine
850 WEND
860 RETURN
```

The following subroutine stores the record currently on the screen if there were any changes to it

```
870 '----- store current record -----
880 IF NOT ANYCHANGE THEN RETURN
890 Y$= TEXT$(4): X$= TEXT$(5) 'are overwritten, therefore store
900 LSET R.WRITE1$= TEXT$(12)
910 LSET R.WRITE2$= TEXT$(13)
920 LSET R.WRITE3$= TEXT$(14)
930 FOR I= 14 TO 6 STEP-1:TEXT$(I)= TEXT$(I-3):NEXT
940 TEXT$(4)= LEFT$(Y$,2):TEXT$(5)= MID$(Y$,4,2):TEXT$(6)= RIGHT$(Y$,2) 'Date
950 TEXT$(7)= LEFT$(X$,2):TEXT$(8)= RIGHT$(X$,2) 'time
960 X$= SPACE$(142)
970 FOR I=1 TO 14
```

```
980    MID$(X$,PNTR(I,1),PNTR(I,2))= TEXT$(I)
990 NEXT I
1000 LSET R.FIL$= X$
1010 PUT#2,RECNUM.RNDM
1020 RETURN
```

The initialization of the program begins in line 1030. All the variables are assigned values and the machine language routine is placed in memory. Since parameters mostly control the program, several changes are possible in this section of the program.

```
1030 '
1040 '----- Variable and Array initialization -----
1050 '
1060 DIM BUFFER%(2000) 'for screen display
1070 DIM SRCH.REG(512) 'register of the record number for the search
1080 MAX.MENU= 3:MAX.MENU.ENTRY= 5
1090 DIM MENU.ENTRY(MAX.MENU)
1100 MENU.ENTRY(1)= 5: MENU.ENTRY(2)= 4: MENU.ENTRY(3)= 4
1110 FOR I=1 TO 10: KEY I,"":NEXT 'erase function key assignment
1120 DIM MENU$(MAX.MENU,MAX.MENU.ENTRY)
1130 DIM HEAD$(3),FOOT$(3),DIR$(512),INDEX$(512),MASK$(18)
1140 DIM TEXT$(14)' 14 Fields for the display
1150 DIM FLD(14,3) 'row,column,length
1160 RESTORE 1170:FOR I= 1 TO 14:READ FLD(I,1),FLD(I,2),FLD(I,3):NEXT I
1170 DATA 5,24,12, 5,56,11, 7,24,7, 7,56,8, 7,65,5, 9,24,50, 11,24,15, 11,56,20, 13,24,1,
     13,56,1, 15,8,64, 18,3,70, 19,3,70, 20,3,70
1180 DIM PNTR(14,2) 'pointers in R.FIL$ and length of field
1190 RESTORE 1200:FOR I=1 TO 14:READ PNTR(I,1),PNTR(I,2):NEXT I
1200 DATA 1,12, 31,11, 13,7, 20,2, 22,2, 24,2, 26,2, 28,2, 30,1, 106,15, 123,20, 121,1,
     122,1, 42,64
1210 DIM ATTRIBUT$(7)
1220 RESTORE 1230:FOR I=0 TO 7:READ ATTRIBUT$(I):NEXT
1230 DATA ReadOnly,Hidden,System,Volume,Directory,Archiv,?,?
1240 HEAD$(1)=
     "┌─────────────────────────────────────────────────────────────────────┐"
1250 HEAD$(2)= "| PDV V2.00                                      1985 (C) H.J.
     Bomanns |"
1260 HEAD$(3)=
     "└─────────────────────────────────────────────────────────────────────┘"
1270 MENU$(1,1)= "• Search for Entry/Process     •"
1280 MENU$(1,2)= "• Read New Data from Diskette •"
1290 MENU$(1,3)= "• Select Data File             •"
1300 MENU$(1,4)= "• Output Lists                 •"
1310 MENU$(1,5)= "• Terminate Program            •"
1320 MENU$(2,1)= "• Search for Program Name      •"
1330 MENU$(2,2)= "• After Matchcode              •"
1340 MENU$(2,3)= "• Sequential Display           •"
1350 MENU$(2,4)= "• Main Menu                    •"
1360 MENU$(3,1)= "• To Screen                  •"
1370 MENU$(3,2)= "• To Printer                   •"
1380 MENU$(3,3)= "• To File                      •"
1390 MENU$(3,4)= "• Main Menu                    •"
```

```
1400 FOOT$(1)=
     "                                                                    "
1410 FOOT$(2)= "| Select with <"+CHR$(24)+"> and <"+CHR$(25)+">   Press <Enter> to execute
                                             |"
1420 FOOT$(3)=
     "                                                                    "
1430 '
1440 MASK$(1)=
     "                                                                    "
1450 MASK$(2)= "| Program-Name......:  _____.___    Disk-ID.......: _____   Size:
     |"
1460 MASK$(3)= "|
     |"
1470 MASK$(4)= "| Size..............:  _____ Bytes   Date/Time.....: xx/xx/xx.xx:xx
     |"
1480 MASK$(5)= "|
     |"
1490 MASK$(6)= "| Attribute-Bytes....: _____
     |"
1500 MASK$(7)= "|
     |"
1510 MASK$(8)= "| Program Language...: _____ Program
     Package:_____    |"
1520 MASK$(9)= "|
     |"
1530 MASK$(10)= "| Source-Code........: _ (Y/N)       Object-Code...: _ (Y/N)
     |"
1540 MASK$(11)= "|
     |"
1550 MASK$(12)= "| From:_____
     |"
1560 MASK$(13)= "|
     |"
1570 MASK$(14)= "| Description:
     |"
1580 MASK$(15)= "| _____
     |"
1590 MASK$(16)= "| _____
     |"
1600 MASK$(17)= "| _____
     |"
1610 MASK$(18)=
     "                                                                    "
1620 '
1630 WORKING= 0 'no file in execution
1640 DR$= "C:": PATH$="\BASIC\": FIL.NAME$="PDV.SEQ"
1650 DIR.DR$= "A:": DIR.PATH$= "\": FIL.MASK$= "*.*"
1660 CURR.MENU= 1
```

The machine language routines are initialized here. They consist of the routines for the fast screen output (described in Chapter 4), the DOS interface (described in Chapter 9) and the routine for storing and restoring the screen content (described in Chapter 11).

```
1670 '
1680 '----- Initialize Machine Programs -----
1690 '
1700 'DATA-Lines from COM-File: \masm\bas_asm\dos_sn.com
1710 :
1720 MP.START= &HF000
1730 RESTORE 1750
1740 DEF SEG:FOR I=1 TO  151:READ X:POKE MP.START+I-1,X: NEXT I
1750 DATA 250, 85,139,236, 30,  6,139,118,  6,139,  4
1760 DATA  80,157,139,118, 14,138, 20,139,118, 16,138
1770 DATA  52,139,118, 18,138, 12,139,118, 20,138, 44
1780 DATA 139,118, 22,138, 28,139,118, 24,138, 60,139
1790 DATA 118, 26,138,  4,139,118, 28,138, 36,139,118
1800 DATA   8,139, 60, 80,139,118, 12,139,  4,142,192
1810 DATA  88,139,118, 10,139, 52, 85,251,205, 33,250
1820 DATA  93, 86,156,139,118, 28,136, 36,139,118, 26
1830 DATA 136,  4,139,118, 24,136, 60,139,118, 22,136
1840 DATA  28,139,118, 20,136, 44,139,118, 18,136, 12
1850 DATA 139,118, 16,136, 52,139,118, 14,136, 20, 88
1860 DATA 139,118,  6,137,  4, 88,139,118, 10,137,  4
1870 DATA 140,192,139,118, 12,137,  4,139,118,  8,137
1880 DATA  60,  7, 31, 93,251,202, 24,  0
1890 DOS.SN= MP.START
1900 :
1910 'DATA-Lines from  COM-File: fastscrn.com
1920 :
1930 MP.START= MP.START+I : RESTORE 1950
1940 DEF SEG:FOR I=1 TO  105:READ X:POKE MP.START+I-1,X: NEXT I
1950 DATA  85,139,236, 30,  6,139,118, 12,138, 28,176
1960 DATA 160,246,227, 45,160,  0, 80,139,118, 10,138
1970 DATA  28,176,  2,246,227, 91,  3,195, 72, 72, 80
1980 DATA 139,118,  8,138, 36,139,118,  6,138, 12,181
1990 DATA   0,139,116,  1, 80,191,  0,176,179,  0,205
2000 DATA  17, 37, 48,  0, 61, 48,  0,116,  6,129,199
2010 DATA   0,  8,179,  1,142,199, 88, 95,252,186,218
2020 DATA   3,128,251,  0,116, 11,236,208,216,114,246
2030 DATA 250,236,208,216,115,251,172,251,171,226,235
2040 DATA   7, 31, 93,202,  8,  0
2050 FASTSCRN= MP.START
2060 'DATA-Lines from COM-File: bs_store.com
2070 :
2080 MP.START= MP.START+I : RESTORE  2100
2090 DEF SEG:FOR I=1 TO  116:READ X:POKE MP.START+I-1,X: NEXT I
2100 DATA 235, 41,144, 85,139,236, 30,  6,139,118,  6,139,  4
2110 DATA 139,240,191,  0,176,179,  0,205, 17, 37, 48,  0, 61
2120 DATA  48,  0,116,  6,129,199,  0,  8,179,  1,142,199, 51
2130 DATA 255,235, 40,144, 85,139,236, 30,  6,139,118,  6,139
2140 DATA   4,139,248, 30,  7,190,  0,176,179,  0,205, 17, 37
2150 DATA  48,  0, 61, 48,  0,116,  6,129,198,  0,  8,179,  1
2160 DATA 142,222, 51,246,185,208,  7,252,186,218,  3,128,251
2170 DATA   0,116, 11,236,208,216,114,246,250,236,208,216,115
2180 DATA 251,173,251,171,226,235,  7, 31, 93,202,  2,  0
2190 SAVESCRN= MP.START : RESTSCRN= MP.START+3
```

The following subroutine determines whether you're using a color or a monochrome monitor. The colors are set depending on this query. Input always appears in the same color because the colors are set according to a "test area".

```
2200 '
2210 '----- Which Monitor ??? -----
2220 '
2230 DEF SEG=0:IF (PEEK(&H410) AND &H30)= &H30 THEN GOTO 2360
2240 '
2250 '----- Set Colors for Color-Monitor -----
2260 '
2270 MONITOR$="C": MONITOR.ADR= &HB800
2280 BG       = 1 'blue background
2290 TXT.FORGRD=  7:TXT.BAKGRD= BG 'Grey letters, blue background
2300 MSG.FORGRD= 15:MSG.BAKGRD= 4 'white letters, red background
2310 INP.FORGRD= 15: INP.BAKGRD= 2 'white letters, green background
2320 ERROR.COLR= 79 'white on red
2330 INPT.COLR= 47 'White on green
2340 GOTO 2460 'Continue in Program
2350 '
2360 '----- Set colors for Mono-Monitor -----
2370 '
2380 MONITOR$="M": MONITOR.ADR= &HB000
2390 BG       = 0 'Black Background
2400 TXT.FORGRD=  7 :TXT.BAKGRD= BG 'Light-grey letters, Black background
2410 MSG.FORGRD= 0 :MSG.BAKGRD=  7 'light grey reversed
2420 INP.FORGRD= 15 : INP.BAKGRD= BG 'white letters, black background
2430 ERROR.COLR= 112 'black on light grey
2440 INPT.COLR= 112 'black on light grey
```

Now the menu is displayed, the keyboard queried and the selected program portion is called. The menu is displayed through the routine for the fast screen output (from Chapter 4).

```
2450 '
2460 '----- Main Menu -----
2470 '
2480 LOCATE CSRLIN,POS(0),0
2490 COLOR TXT.FORGRD,TXT.BAKGRD:CLS 'initialize screen
2500 OUT &H3D9,BG 'background frame color
2510 DEF SEG= MONITOR.ADR:ATTR%= PEEK(1): COLMNO%= 1
2520 FOR I=1 TO 3:ROWNO%= I
2530   DEF SEG:CALL FASTSCRN(ROWNO%,COLMNO%,ATTR%,HEAD$(I))
2540 NEXT I
2550 HEAD$= " Main Menu ":GOSUB 150
2560 COLMNO%= 7:DISPLY.ROWNO= 5
2570 DEF SEG= MONITOR.ADR:ATTR%= PEEK(1) 'must be double
2580 FOR I=1 TO MENU.ENTRY(CURR.MENU):ROWNO%= DISPLY.ROWNO+I
2590   DEF SEG:CALL FASTSCRN(ROWNO%,COLMNO%,ATTR%,MENU$(CURR.MENU,I))
2600 NEXT I
2610 COLMNO%= 1
2620 FOR I=22 TO 24:ROWNO%= I
```

```
2630    DEF SEG:CALL FASTSCRN(ROWNO%,COLMNO%,ATTR%,FOOT$(I-21))
2640 NEXT I
2650 '
2660 '----- Menu Control -----
2670 '
2680 IF (CURR.MENU=1) AND (NOT WORKING) THEN ENTRY= 3:GOTO 2700 'pre-position
2690 ENTRY= 1 'line of menu entry
2700 GOSUB 3030 'bar on
2710 X$= INKEY$:IF X$="" THEN 2710
2720 IF X$=CHR$(27) AND CURR.MENU> 1 THEN CURR.MENU=1:GOSUB 210:GOTO 2510 'erase window,
     main menu
2730 IF X$=CHR$(13) THEN 2830 'Key <<⌐¹> activated
2740 IF LEN(X$)<> 2 THEN BEEP:GOTO 2710 'Only CR Permitted
2750 ONKEY= ASC(RIGHT$(X$,1))
2760 IF ONKEY<> 72 AND ONKEY<> 80 THEN BEEP:GOTO 2710 'only crsr up/down
2770 IF ONKEY= 72 THEN GOSUB 3100:ENTRY= ENTRY-1 'Bar off and up
2780 IF ONKEY= 80 THEN GOSUB 3100:ENTRY= ENTRY+1 'Bar off and down
2790 IF ONKEY< 1 THEN ONKEY= MENU.ENTRY(CURR.MENU)
2800 IF ENTRY> MENU.ENTRY(CURR.MENU) THEN ENTRY= 1
2810 GOTO 2700
2820 '
2830 GOSUB 3100 'Bar off
2840 COLOR TXT.FORGRD,TXT.BAKGRD
2850 ON CURR.MENU GOTO 2860,2880,2900 'Menu 1, 2 und 3
2860 ON ENTRY GOTO 2930,4760,5900,2940,6650
2870 '              search/process, read, select file, List, END
2880 ON ENTRY GOTO 4370,4190,4100,2960 'Menu " Search "
2890 '          Prg.-Name, Matchcode, seqential, Main-Menu
2900 ON ENTRY GOTO 3420,3310,3170,2960 'Menu "LIST "
2910 '          screen,printer,file,main menu
2920 '
2930 IF WORKING THEN CURR.MENU= 2:HEAD$=" Search / Process ":GOSUB 150:GOSUB 210:GOTO 2560
     ELSE 2980
2940 IF WORKING THEN CURR.MENU= 3:HEAD$=" Output List ":GOSUB 150:GOSUB 210:GOTO 2560 ELSE
2980
2950 '
2960 CURR.MENU= 1:GOSUB 210:GOTO 2550 'erase window
2970 '
2980 MSG$= "No Datafile selected. Strike any key ":GOSUB 370
2990 GOTO 2660 'continue with menu control
3000 MSG$= "Datafile is empty. Strike any key ":GOSUB 370
3010 GOTO 2660 'continue with menu control
3020 '
3030 '----- Bar On -----
3040 '
3050 LOCATE ENTRY+5,7,0
3060 COLOR MSG.FORGRD,MSG.BAKGRD
3070 PRINT MENU$(CURR.MENU,ENTRY);
3080 RETURN
3090 '
3100 '----- Bar Off -----
3110 '
3120 LOCATE ENTRY+5,7,0
```

```
3130 COLOR TXT.FORGRD, TXT.BAKGRD
3140 PRINT MENU$(CURR.MENU,ENTRY)
3150 RETURN
```

The following program lines include the output routines for screen display and accessing files and your printer.

```
3160 '
3170 '----- Output list to File -----
3180 '
3190 IF SEQ.SIZE= 0 THEN 3000 'Data-file empty
3200 HEAD$= " Output List to File "
3210 FIL.OUTPUT= -1:PRINTER= 0
3220 LOCATE 20,1:COLOR MSG.FORGRD,MSG.BAKGRD
3230 PRINT " Name of the File for List Output: "
3240 FOOT$="<Enter> if input is Ok or   <Esc> for Main Menu":GOSUB 110
3250 INSTRING$="PDV_LIST.TXT":ROWNO= 20:COLMNO=36:LNGTH=12:GOSUB 9050
3260 IF X$= CHR$(27) THEN GOSUB 210:GOTO 2940 'Clear Window, Menu
3270 OUPUT.FIL$= INSTRING$
3280 OPEN OUTPUT.FIL$ FOR OUTPUT AS #9
3290 GOTO 3470 'Sort and Output
3300 '
3310 '----- Output Listing to Printer -----
3320 '
3330 IF SEQ.SIZE= 0 THEN 3000 'data-file empty
3340 HEAD$=" Output Listing to Printer "
3350 PRINTER= -1:FIL.OUTPUT= 0
3360 MSG$="Adjust paper and strike any key when ready or <Esc> for Main Menu ":GOSUB 370
3370 IF X$= CHR$(27) THEN 3260 'Erase window, Menu
3380 LPRINT CHR$(27);"N";CHR$(5); '5 lines over perforation
3390 LPRINT "PDV V2.00":LPRINT STRING$(80,"="):LPRINT:LPRINT
3400 GOTO 3470 'Sort and output
3410 '
3420 '----- List to Screen -----
3430 '
3440 IF SEQ.SIZE= 0 THEN 3000 'Data-file is empty
3450 HEAD$= " List to display-screen "
3460 PRINTER= 0:FIL.OUTPUT= 0
3470 GOSUB 150 'output header
3480 FOOT$="Sorting Data:":GOSUB 110
3490 COLOR MSG.FORGRD,MSG.BAKGRD
3500 '
3510 LFT=0:RGHT=1:TAB.START=0:TAB.ENDE=SEQ.SIZE-
     1:GATE=1:TAB.INDEX(1,LFT)=TAB.START:TAB.INDEX(1,RGHT)=TAB.ENDE
3520 LOCATE 23,25:PRINT USING "###";GATE
3530 TAB.START=TAB.INDEX(GATE,LFT)
3540 TAB.ENDE=TAB.INDEX(GATE,RGHT)
3550 GATE=GATE-1
3560 C.LFT=TAB.START
3570 C.RGHT=TAB.ENDE
3580 X$= LEFT$(INDEX$((TAB.START+TAB.ENDE)\2),12) 'Element in the middle
3590 WHILE LEFT$(INDEX$(C.LFT),12)<X$: C.LFT=C.LFT+1: WEND
```

```
3600 WHILE X$<LEFT$(INDEX$(C.RGHT),12): C.RGHT=C.RGHT-1: WEND
3610 IF C.LFT<=C.RGHT THEN SWAP INDEX$(C.LFT),INDEX$(C.RGHT):C.LFT=C.LFT+1:C.RGHT=C.RGHT-
     1:GOTO 3590
3620 IF C.RGHT-TAB.START < TAB.ENDE-C.LFT THEN 3660
3630 IF TAB.START>=C.RGHT THEN 3650
3640 GATE=GATE+1:TAB.INDEX(GATE,LFT)=TAB.START:TAB.INDEX(GATE,RGHT)=C.RGHT
3650 TAB.START=C.LFT:GOTO 3690
3660 IF C.LFT>= TAB.ENDE THEN 3680
3670 GATE=GATE+1:TAB.INDEX(GATE,LFT)=C.LFT:TAB.INDEX(GATE,RGHT)=TAB.ENDE
3680 TAB.ENDE=C.RGHT
3690 IF TAB.START < TAB.ENDE THEN 3560
3700 IF GATE THEN 3520 'continue sort
3710 '
3720 FOOT$="Display List"
3730 IF PRINTER THEN FOOT$="Print List"
3740 IF FIL.OUTPUT THEN FOOT$="Output List to File"
3750 GOSUB 110 'Display footer
3760 '
3770 WHILE X$<>CHR$(27)
3780    GOSUB 210 'erase window
3790    LOCATE 5,1,0
3800    FOR DISPLY= 0 TO SEQ.SIZE-1
3810      X= VAL(MID$(INDEX$(DISPLY),13))
3820      GET#2,X:X$= R.FIL$
3830      FOR I=1 TO 14 '14 Fields in R.FIL$ or X$
3840        TEXT$(I)= MID$(X$,PNTR(I,1),PNTR(I,2)) 'for display
3850      NEXT I
3860      TEXT$(4)= TEXT$(5)+"/"+TEXT$(4)+"/"+TEXT$(6) 'date
3870      TEXT$(5)= TEXT$(7)+":"+TEXT$(8) 'time
3880      FOR I=6 TO 11:TEXT$(I)= TEXT$(I+3):NEXT I
3890      X$="":FOR I=1 TO 7:X$= X$+TEXT$(I)+"-":NEXT I
3900      Y$="":FOR I=8 TO 10:Y$= Y$+TEXT$(I)+"-":NEXT I
3910      IF PRINTER THEN 3940
3920      IF FIL.OUTPUT THEN 3950
3930      PRINT X$:PRINT Y$:PRINT TEXT$(11):PRINT STRING$(79,"-"):GOTO 3960
3940      LPRINT X$:LPRINT Y$:LPRINT TEXT$(11):LPRINT STRING$(79,"-"):GOTO 4000
3950      PRINT#9,X$:PRINT#9,Y$:PRINT#9,TEXT$(11):PRINT#9,STRING$(79,"-"):GOTO 4000
3960      IF CSRLIN< 20 THEN 4000
3970      MSG$= "Strike any key or <Esc> to end ":GOSUB 370
3980      IF X$=CHR$(27) THEN 4080 'End display
3990      GOSUB 210:LOCATE 5,1,0 'erase window
4000    NEXT DISPLY
4010    X$=" Dispaly"
4020    IF PRINTER THEN X$="Printer"
4030    IF FIL.OUTPUT THEN X$="File"
4040    MSG$= X$+": <Enter> to list again or <Esc> to end ":GOSUB 370
4050 WEND
4060 IF FIL.OUTPUT THEN CLOSE#9
4070 IF PRINTER THEN LPRINT CHR$(12) 'Advance page
4080 GOSUB 210:GOTO 2940 'erase window, Menu
```

You can display the captured data sequentially (i.e. in the sequence in which they were entered).

```
4090 '
4100 '----- sequential display -----
4110 '
4120 IF SEQ.SIZE= 0 THEN 3000 'Data-file is empty
4130 SRCH.REG= 0
4140 FOR I=2 TO RAN.SIZE-1
4150    SRCH.REG(SRCH.REG)= I:SRCH.REG= SRCH.REG+1
4160 NEXT I
4170 GOTO 4570 'display
```

During the search any character combination can be used. The records of the random file are read sequentially. When a match is made with the search criteria, the number of the record is retained in a marker (SRCH.REG). The later output occurs on the basis of SRCH.REG. This enables faster output because queries aren't required.

```
4180 '
4190 '----- Search for Matchcode -----
4200 '
4210 IF SEQ.SIZE= 0 THEN 3000 'Data-file is empty
4220 LOCATE 20,1:COLOR MSG.FORGRD,MSG.BAKGRD
4230 PRINT " Search for Matchcode: "
4240 FOOT$="Press <Enter> if input is Ok or <Esc> for Main Menu ":GOSUB 110
4250 INSTRING$="":ROWNO= 20:COLMNO=25:LNGTH= 12:GOSUB 9050
4260 IF INSTRING$="" OR X$=CHR$(27) THEN GOSUB 330:GOTO 2560 'continue in menu
4270 SRCH$= INSTRING$:SRCH.REG= 0
4280 FOOT$="Search: ":GOSUB 110
4290 COLOR MSG.FORGRD,MSG.BAKGRD
4300 FOR I=2 TO RAN.SIZE-1
4310    LOCATE 23,10:PRINT USING "###";I
4320    GET#2,I:X$= R.FIL$
4330    IF INSTR(X$,SRCH$)<>0 THEN SRCH.REG(SRCH.REG)= I:SRCH.REG= SRCH.REG+1
4340 NEXT I
4350 GOTO 4530 'test if found and display
```

During the search for the file or program name, the sequential file in memory is searched. Once a match occurs, the record numbers are again stored in a marker location.

```
4360 '
4370 '----- Search for program name -----
4380 '
4390 IF SEQ.SIZE= 0 THEN 3000 'Data-file is empty
4400 LOCATE 20,1:COLOR MSG.FORGRD,MSG.BAKGRD
4410 PRINT " Search for Program Name: "
4420 FOOT$="Strike <Enter> if input is Ok or  <Esc> for Main Menu":GOSUB 110
4430 INSTRING$="":ROWNO= 20:COLMNO=29:LNGTH= 12:GOSUB 9050
4440 IF INSTRING$="" OR X$=CHR$(27) THEN GOSUB 330:GOTO 2560 'continue in Menu
4450 SRCH$= INSTRING$:SRCH.REG= 0
```

```
4460 FOOT$="Search: ":GOSUB 110
4470 COLOR MSG.FORGRD,MSG.BAKGRD
4480 FOR I=0 TO SEQ.SIZE-1
4490    LOCATE 23,10:PRINT USING "###";I
4500     IF LEFT$(INDEX$(I),LEN(SRCH$))= SRCH$ THEN SRCH.REG(SRCH.REG)=
        VAL(MID$(INDEX$(I),13)):SRCH.REG= SRCH.REG+1
4510 NEXT I
4520 '
4530 IF SRCH.REG<> 0 THEN 4570
4540 MSG$= "Entry not Found, Strike any Key ":GOSUB 370
4550 LOCATE 20,1:X$=CHR$(27):GOTO 4440 'found nothing, back with a trick
4560 '
4570 MAX.SRCH.REG= SRCH.REG-1:SRCH.REG= 0
4580 HEAD$=" Process data ":GOSUB 150
4590 GOSUB 440 'display template
4600 FOOT$=" <"+CHR$(24)+"/"+CHR$(25)+">, <Enter> to select field <F10> to store <Esc>
        Main Menu ":GOSUB 110
4610 WHILE X$<> CHR$(27)
4620    RECNUM.RNDM= SRCH.REG(SRCH.REG)
4630    GOSUB 510 'dispaly current record
4640    LOCATE 5,75,0:COLOR MSG.FORGRD,MSG.BAKGRD:PRINT USING "###";RECNUM.RNDM
4650    ANYCHANGE= 0:GOSUB 740 'read data for display record
4660    IF ONKEY= 73 THEN GOSUB 870:SRCH.REG= SRCH.REG-1 'PgUp
4670    IF ONKEY= 81 OR ONKEY= 68 THEN GOSUB 870:SRCH.REG= SRCH.REG+1 'PgUp/F10
4680    'subroutine 820, store current record when changed
4690 IF ONKEY= 71 THEN SRCH.REG= 0 'Home
4700 IF ONKEY= 79 THEN SRCH.REG= MAX.SRCH.REG 'End
4710    IF SRCH.REG<0 THEN BEEP:SRCH.REG=0:GOTO 4650
4720    IF SRCH.REG> MAX.SRCH.REG THEN BEEP:SRCH.REG= MAX.SRCH.REG:GOTO 4650
4730 WEND
4740 GOSUB 210:GOTO 2930 'erase window, back to menu
```

The following program section is responsible for reading new data. You can indicate the drive, path and a file extension. The directory is read, evaluated and prepared for later additions with the DOS interface.

```
4750 '
4760 '----- Read Data from Diskette -----
4770 '
4780 IF WORKING THEN 4810 'data-file selected?
4790 MSG$= "No Datafile selected. Strike any key ":GOSUB 370
4800 GOTO 2660 'continue with menu control
4810 GOSUB 250 'Store screen
4820 GOSUB 210 'erase window
4830 HEAD$= " Read Data from Diskette ":GOSUB 150
4840 FOOT$=" <"+CHR$(24)+"/"+CHR$(25)+">   <Enter> to select field  <F10> Ok   <Esc> Main
        Menu":GOSUB 110
4850 LOCATE 10,1:COLOR MSG.FORGRD,MSG.BAKGRD
4860 PRINT " Drive.......:"
4870 PRINT " Path........:"
4880 PRINT " File-Mask...:":PRINT
4890 CL= 16
```

```
4900 TMP$(1)= DIR.DR$:TMP$(2)= DIR.PATH$:TMP$(3)= FIL.MASK$
4910 TMP(1) = 2  :TMP(2) = 64   :TMP(3) = 12
4920 COLOR INP.FORGRD,INP.BAKGRD
4930 FOR I=10 TO 13
4940   LOCATE I,CL,0:PRINT TMP$(I-9);SPACE$(TMP(I-9)-LEN(TMP$(I-9)));
4950 NEXT I
4960 RW= 10:CL= 16:MAK.CAPS= -1:X$= "":ONKEY= 0
4970 '
4980 WHILE (ONKEY <> 68) AND (X$ <> CHR$(27)) 'until <F10> or <Esc>
4990   INSTRING$= TMP$(RW-9):ROWNO= RW: COLMNO= CL:LNGTH= TMP(RW-9)
5000   GOSUB 9050:TMP$(RW-9)= INSTRING$ 'read subroutine
5010   IF ONKEY= 72 THEN RW= RW-1:IF RW=  9 THEN RW= 12 'Cursor up
5020   IF ONKEY= 80 OR X$= CHR$(13) THEN RW= RW+1:IF RW= 13 THEN RW= 10
5030 WEND
5040 '
5050 IF X$= CHR$(27) THEN GOSUB 290:GOTO 2660 'screen back,menu control
5060 DIR.DR$= TMP$(1): DIR.PATH$= TMP$(2): FIL.MASK$= TMP$(3)
5065 IF LEN(DIR.PATH$)=0 THEN DIR.PATH$="\":GOTO 5080
5066 TEST1$ = SPACE$(LEN(DIR.PATH$))
5067 TEST2$ = SPACE$(LEN(DIR.PATH$)-1)
5068 TEST3$ = MID$(DIR.PATH$,2,(LEN(DIR.PATH$)-1))
5069 IF (DIR.PATH$ = TEST1$) OR (TEST2$ = TEST3$) THEN DIR.PATH$ = "\"
5070 IF MID$(DIR.PATH$,LEN(DIR.PATH$),1)<>"\" THEN DIR.PATH$= DIR.PATH$+"\"
5080 IF RIGHT$(DIR.DR$,1)<>":" THEN MID$(DIR.DR$,2,1)= ":"
5090 IF FIL.MASK$= "" THEN FIL.MASK$="*.*"
5100 GOSUB 8570 'find volume ID
5110 MASK$= DIR.DR$+DIR.PATH$+FIL.MASK$:EXTENDED= -1 'read flag for DTA
5120 FOOT$= "Reading Directory: ":GOSUB 110
5130 X= INSTR(VOLUME.ID$,".")
5140 IF X<> 0 THEN VOLUME.ID$= LEFT$(VOLUME.ID$,X-1)+MID$(VOLUME.ID$,X+1)
5150 GOSUB 7560 'read Directory and move data to DIR$()
5160 IF ENT<> 0 THEN 5240 'Evaluate data read
5170 '
5180 FOOT$= "Key <N> or <Y>":GOSUB 110
5190 MSG$="No Files Found, new Input? (Y/N) ":GOSUB 370 'msg
5200 IF X$="Y" OR X$="y" THEN 4960 'new input
5210 IF X$<>"N" AND X$<>"n" THEN 5190
5220 GOSUB 290:GOTO 2660 'screen back, menu control
5230 '
5240 IF SEQ.SIZE+ENT-1 <= 512 THEN 5420 'space in INDEX ???
5250 '
5260 GOSUB 210 'erase window
5270 LOCATE 10,1:COLOR MSG.FORGRD,MSG.BAKGRD
5280 PRINT " No space in the datafile ":PRINT:BEEP
5290 PRINT " Free Records......: ";
5300 COLOR INP.FORGRD,INP.BAKGRD
5310 PRINT USING "####";512-SEQ.SIZE
5320 COLOR MSG.FORGRD,MSG.BAKGRD
5330 PRINT " Reading Records...: ";
5340 COLOR INP.FORGRD,INP.BAKGRD
5350 PRINT USING "####";ENT-1
5360 FOOT$= "Stike any Key.....":GOSUB 110
5370 LOCATE 20,1:COLOR MSG.FORGRD,MSG.BAKGRD
```

```
5380 PRINT " Select Another Data-file or Fewer files, Strike any Key ";CHR$(254);"
     ";:LOCATE CSRLIN,POS(0)-2,1,0,31
5390 IF INKEY$="" THEN 5390
5400 GOSUB 290:GOTO 2660 'screen back, menu control
5410 '
5420 FOOT$= "Processing data: ":GOSUB 110
5430 NEW.SIZE= SEQ.SIZE 'first new record
5440 COLOR MSG.FORGRD,MSG.BAKGRD
5450 FOR I= 0 TO ENT-1
5460    LOCATE 23,28: PRINT USING "###";RAN.SIZE
5470    INDEX$(SEQ.SIZE)= SPACE$(16) '12= Name, 4= recnum
5480    X$= LEFT$(DIR$(I),12) 'Prg.-Name for INDEX$()
5490    Y$= STR$(RAN.SIZE) 'recnum for INDEX$()
5500    LSET INDEX$(SEQ.SIZE)= X$ 'transmit Prg.-Name in INDEX$()
5510    MID$(INDEX$(SEQ.SIZE),13)= Y$ 'transmit record number in INDEX$()
5520    LSET R.FIL$= SPACE$(142) 'fill data partly with BLANK
5530    LSET R.FIL$= DIR$(I) 'transmit data from DiR$() to RANDOM-buffer
5540    LSET R.WRITE1$= SPACE$(70) 'first store space
5550    LSET R.WRITE2$= SPACE$(70)
5560    LSET R.WRITE3$= SPACE$(70)
5570    PUT#2,RAN.SIZE 'store data in random file
5580    SEQ.SIZE= SEQ.SIZE+1:RAN.SIZE= RAN.SIZE+1
5590 NEXT I
5600 GET#2,1
5610 LSET R.FIL$= STR$(RAN.SIZE) 'store next free record-number for additional records
5620 PUT#2,1
5630 '
5640 HEAD$= " Supplement Data Read in ":GOSUB 150
5650 RECNUM.SEQ= NEW.SIZE
5660 GOSUB 440 'display template
5670 FOOT$=" <"+CHR$(24)+"/"+CHR$(25)+">, <Enter> to select field <F10> to store <Esc>
     Main Menu ":GOSUB 110
5680 WHILE X$<> CHR$(27)
5690 RECNUM.RNDM= VAL(MID$(INDEX$(RECNUM.SEQ),13))
5700    GOSUB 510 'display current record
5710    LOCATE 5,75,0:COLOR MSH.FORGRD,MSG.BAKGRD:PRINT USING "###";RECNUM.RNDM
5720    ANYCHANGE= 0:GOSUB 740 'read data for displayed record
5730    IF ONKEY= 73 THEN GOSUB 870:RECNUM.SEQ= RECNUM.SEQ-1
5740    IF ONKEY= 81 OR ONKEY= 68 THEN GOSUB 870:RECNUM.SEQ= RECNUM.SEQ+1
5750    'Subroutine 820: store current record when changes
5760 IF ONKEY= 71 THEN RECNUM.SEQ= NEW.SIZE 'Home
5770 IF ONKEY= 79 THEN RECNUM.SEQ= SEQ.SIZE-1 'End
5780    IF RECNUM.SEQ< NEW.SIZE THEN BEEP:RECNUM.SIZE= NEW.SIZE:GOTO 5720
5790    IF RECNUM.SEQ>= SEQ.SIZE THEN BEEP:RECNUM.SEQ= SEQ.SIZE-1:GOTO 5720
5800 WEND
5810 FOOT$= "Storing files..... ":GOSUB 110
5820 CLOSE#1
5830 OPEN SEQ.FIL$ FOR OUTPUT AS #1
5840 FOR I= 0 TO SEQ.SIZE-1
5850    PRINT#1, INDEX$(I)
5860 NEXT I
5870 CLOSE#1
5880 GOSUB 290:GOTO 2660 'screen back, menu control
```

Since the program operates with several data files, it can be separated according to programming languages, etc. The data file must be selected after the program start. It's possible to change to another file at any time.

```
5890 '
5900 '----- Select Datafile -----
5910 '
5920 IF NOT WORKING THEN 6070 'no file selected
5930 '
5940 MSG$=" File in processing, select new file? (Y/N) ":GOSUB 370
5950 IF X$="n" OR X$="N" THEN 2550 'continue with menu
5960 IF X$<>"y" AND X$<>"Y" THEN BEEP:GOTO 5940
5970 GOSUB 250 'store screen
5980 FOOT$= "Storing files..... ":GOSUB 110
5990 CLOSE#1
6000 OPEN SEQ.FIL$ FOR OUTPUT AS #1
6010 FOR I= 0 TO SEQ.SIZE-1
6020   PRINT#1, INDEX$(I)
6030 NEXT I
6040 CLOSE
6050 GOTO 6080
6060 '
6070 GOSUB 250 'store screen
6080 GOSUB 210 'erase window
6090 HEAD$= " Select Datafile ":GOSUB 150
6100 LOCATE 10,1:COLOR MSG.FORGRD,MSG.BAKGRD
6110 PRINT " Drive.......:"
6120 PRINT " Path........:"
6130 PRINT " Filename...:":PRINT
6140 PRINT " <F5> to Select "
6150 CL= 16
6160 TMP$(1)= DR$:TMP$(2)= PATH$:TMP$(3)= FIL.NAME$
6170 TMP(1) = 2  :TMP(2) = 64   :TMP(3) = 12
6180 FOOT$=" <"+CHR$(24)+"/"+CHR$(25)+">   <Enter> to select field  <F10> Ok   <Esc> Main
     Menu":GOSUB 110
6190 COLOR INP.FORGRD, INP.BAKGRD
6200 FOR I=10 TO 13
6210   LOCATE I,CL,0:PRINT TMP$(I-9);SPACE$(TMP(I-9)-LEN(TMP$(I-9)));
6220 NEXT I
6230 RW= 10:CL= 16:MAK.CAPS= -1:X$= "":ONKEY= 0
6240 '
6250 WHILE (ONKEY <> 68) AND (X$ <> CHR$(27)) 'until <F10> or <Esc>
6260   INSTRING$= TMP$(RW-9):ROWNO= RW: COLMNO= CL:LNGTH= TMP(RW-9)
6270     GOSUB 9050:TMP$(RW-9)= INSTRING$ 'read subroutine
6280   IF ONKEY= 72 THEN RW= RW-1:IF RW=  9 THEN RW= 12 'Cursor up
6290   IF ONKEY= 80 OR X$= CHR$(13) THEN RW= RW+1:IF RW= 13 THEN RW= 10
6300   IF ONKEY= 63 THEN GOSUB 6970:GOTO 6080 '<F5>, selection, new display
6310 WEND
6320 '
6330 IF X$= CHR$(27) THEN GOSUB 290:GOTO 2660 'screen back, menu control
6340 DR$= TMP$(1): PATH$= TMP$(2): FIL.NAME$= TMP$(3)
6345 IF LEN(PATH$) = 0 THEN PATH$ ="\"
```

```
6346 TEST1$ = SPACE$(LEN(PATH$))
6347 TEST2$ = SPACE$(LEN(PATH$)-1)
6348 TEST3$ = MID$(PATH$,2,(LEN(PATH$)-1))
6349 IF (PATH$=TEST1$) OR (TEST2$=TEST3$) THEN PATH$="\"
6350 IF MID$(PATH$,LEN(PATH$),1)<>"\" THEN PATH$= PATH$+"\"
6360 IF RIGHT$(DR$,1)<>":" THEN MID$(DR$,2,1)= ":"
6370 IF FIL.NAME$= "" THEN MSG$="Filename missing. Strike any key ":GOSUB 370:GOTO 6230
     'does not work this way
6380 DAT.FIL$= DR$+PATH$+FIL.NAME$
6390 X= INSTR(DAT.FIL$,".") 'file with extension?
6400 IF X= 0 THEN SEQ.FIL$= DAT.FIL$+".seq":RAN.FIL$= DAT.FIL$+".dat" 'attach ".seq" and
     ".dat"
6410 IF X<>0 THEN SEQ.FIL$= LEFT$(DAT.FIL$,X-1)+".seq":RAN.FIL$= LEFT$(DAT.FIL$,X-
     1)+".dat" 'replace extension as precaution
6420 OPEN SEQ.FIL$ FOR INPUT AS #1:CLOSE#1 'Test if file is present
6430 GOTO 6490 'file available
6440 'with ON ERROR GOTO the following line is executed
6450 MSG$="Datafile not found. Create new file? (Y/N) ":GOSUB 370 'message
6460 IF X$="Y" OR X$="y" THEN GOSUB 6510:GOTO 6490 'create file and initialize
6470 IF X$<>"N" AND X$<>"n" THEN 6450
6480 GOTO 6230 'query again
6490 GOSUB 6800:GOSUB 290:GOTO 2660 'open files, screen back, menu control
```

You can create a new data file by entering a new filename during the selection of a data file. This part of the program creates the new files.

```
6500 '
6510 '----- Create New Files -----
6520 '
6530 LOCATE CSRLIN,POS(0),0
6540 OPEN SEQ.FIL$ FOR OUTPUT AS #1:CLOSE#1 'create seq. file
6550 OPEN "R",#1,RAN.FIL$,352
6560 FIELD#1, 142 AS R.FIL$,70 AS R.WRITE1$, 70 AS R.WRITE2$, 70 AS R.WRITE3$
6570 X$="2" 'first free record in random file
6580 LSET R.FIL$= X$
6590 LSET R.WRITE1$= "Control Record - Do Not Use For Storage          "
6600 LSET R.WRITE2$= "Control Record - Do Not Use For Storage          "
6610 LSET R.WRITE3$= "Control Record - Do Not Use For Storage          "
6620 PUT#1,1:CLOSE#1 'this also creates the random file
6630 RETURN
```

The following program portion terminates the program after an acknowledgement prompt. The sequential file in memory is written back and then the data and the sequential file are closed.

```
6640 '
6650 '----- Terminate Program -----
6660 '
6670 MSG$="Terminate Program? (Y/N) ":GOSUB 370
6680 IF X$="n" OR X$="N" THEN GOTO 2550 'continue with menu
6690 IF X$<>"y" AND X$<>"Y" THEN BEEP:GOTO 6670
```

```
6700 IF NOT WORKING THEN 6770 'no file open
6710 FOOT$="Storing files.....":GOSUB 110
6720 CLOSE#1
6730 OPEN SEQ.FIL$ FOR OUTPUT AS #1
6740 FOR I= 0 TO SEQ.SIZE-1
6750    PRINT#1,INDEX$(I)
6760 NEXT I
6770 CLOSE
6780 CLS:PRINT "PDV V2.00 Finished....":PRINT:PRINT:END
```

The following program portion opens the files, reads the sequential file into memory and initializes all pointers for new input.

```
6790 '
6800 '----- Initialize Files -----
6810 '
6820 OPEN SEQ.FIL$ FOR INPUT AS #1
6830 OPEN "R",#2,RAN.FIL$,352
6840 FIELD#2, 142 AS R.FIL$,70 AS R.WRITE1$, 70 AS R.WRITE2$, 70 AS R.WRITE3$
6850 SIZE= 0 'INDEX in sequential file
6860 WHILE NOT EOF(1)
6870    INPUT#1, INDEX$(SIZE) 'INDEX$= Table of prg. names and rec. number
6880    SIZE= SIZE+1
6890 WEND
6900 CLOSE#1
6910 SEQ.SIZE= SIZE 'SEQ.Size= pointers for new record in sequential file
6920 GET#2,1 'first rec. of random file is control record
6930 RAN.SIZE= VAL(R.FIL$) 'RAN.SIZE= pointers to new records in random file
6940 WORKING= -1 'flag for open files
6950 RETURN 'RANDOM-File remains open
```

To select the data file, you can call for a listing of available files by pressing the <F5> key. This program portion reads the directory on the basis of an extension that must be entered. After the display, one of the files can be selected with the cursor keys.

```
6960 '
6970 '----- find file, display and select -----
6980 '
6990 GOSUB 210 'erase window
7000 HEAD$= " File Selection ":GOSUB 150
7010 LOCATE 10,1:COLOR MSG.FORGRD,MSG.BAKGRD
7020 PRINT " Template: "
7030 INSTRING$= DR$+PATH$+"*.*":MAK.CAPS= -1:ROWNO= 10:COLMNO= 9:LNGTH= 64:GOSUB 9050
     'read subroutine
7040 IF X$= CHR$(27) THEN RETURN
7050 FOOT$="Reading directory.....":GOSUB 110
7060 MASK$= INSTRING$:EXTENDED= 0 'transmit only file name
7070 GOSUB 7560 'search for files according to mask
7080 IF ENT<> 0 THEN 7160 'display files and select
7090 '
7100 FOOT$= "Key <Y> or <N>":GOSUB 110
```

```
7110 MSG$= "No file entries found. New input? (Y/N)":GOSUB 370 'message and wait for key
7120 IF X$="y" OR X$="Y" THEN GOSUB 330:GOTO 7030 'try again
7130 IF X$<>"n" AND X$<>"N" THEN BEEP:GOTO 7110
7140 RETURN
7150 '
7160 LOCATE 10,1:COLOR TXT.FORGRD,TXT.BAKGRD:PRINT SPACE$(80);
7170 COLOR TXT.FORGRD,TXT.BAKGRD
7180 LOCATE 5,1
7190 FOR I= 0 TO ENT-1
7200   PRINT DIR$(I),
7210 NEXT
7220 COLMNO(1)= 1:COLMNO(2)= 15: COLMNO(3)= 29: COLMNO(4)= 43: COLMNO(5)= 57
7230 FOOT$= "Press <"+CHR$(24)+">,<"+CHR$(25)+">, <"+CHR$(26)+"> or <"+CHR$(27)+"> to
     select <Enter> to accept   <Esc> Main Menu":GOSUB 110
7240 COLMNO= 1:ENTRY= 0:ROWNO= 5
7250 GOSUB 7450 'Bar on
7260 X$= INKEY$:IF X$="" THEN 7260
7270 IF X$= CHR$(27) THEN RETURN 'termination
7280 IF X$=CHR$(13) THEN 7370 'file selected
7290 IF LEN(X$)<> 2 THEN BEEP:GOTO 7260
7300 ONKEY= ASC(RIGHT$(X$,1))
7310 IF ONKEY= 72 AND ROWNO> 5 THEN GOSUB 7500:ROWNO= ROWNO-1:ENTRY= ENTRY-5:GOTO 7250
7320 IF ONKEY= 80 AND SCREEN(CSRLIN+1,COLMNO(COLMNO))<> 32 THEN GOSUB 7500:ROWNO=
     ROWNO+1:ENTRY= ENTRY+5:GOTO 7250
7330 IF ONKEY= 75 AND COLMNO> 1 THEN GOSUB 7500:COLMNO= COLMNO-1:ENTRY= ENTRY-1:GOTO 7250
7340 IF ONKEY= 77 AND COLMNO< 5 THEN IF SCREEN(CSRLIN,COLMNO(COLMNO+1))<> 32 THEN GOSUB
     7500:COLMNO= COLMNO+1:ENTRY= ENTRY+1:GOTO 7250
7350 BEEP:GOTO 7260 'only cursor keys permitted
7360 '
7370 FIL.NAME$= DIR$(ENTRY)
7380 IF MID$(MASK$,2,1)= ":" THEN DR$= LEFT$(MASK$,2):MASK$= MID$(MASK$,3) 'find drive and
     remove from mask
7390 IF INSTR(MASK$,"\")= 0 THEN 7440 'no path indicated
7400 FOR I= LEN(MASK$) TO 1 STEP -1
7410   IF MID$(MASK$,I,1)= "\" THEN 7430 'End of path found
7420 NEXT I
7430 PATH$= LEFT$(MASK$,I)
7440 RETURN
7450 '----- Bar On -----
7460 LOCATE ROWNO,COLMNO(COLMNO)
7470 COLOR MSG.FORGRD,MSG.BAKGRD
7480 PRINT DIR$(ENTRY);
7490 RETURN
7500 '----- Bar Off -----
7510 LOCATE ROWNO,COLMNO(COLMNO)
7520 COLOR TXT.FORGRD,TXT.BAKGRD
7530 PRINT DIR$(ENTRY);
7540 RETURN
```

The following subroutine reads the directory from the diskette or hard disk on the basis of a default extension. The data transfer occurs through a special DTA.

```
7550 '
7560 '----- Search for files according to mask -----
7570 '
7580 ENT= 0 'counter for DIR$()
7590 MAX.ENTRY= 80:IF EXTENDED THEN MAX.ENTRY= 512
7600 MASK$= MASK$+CHR$(0)
7610 AL%=0:AH%=0:BL%=0:BH%=0:CL%=0:CH%=0:DL%=0:DH%=0:ES%=0:SI%=0:DI%=0:FLAGS%=0
7620 INT.NR%= &H21:DEF SEG:POKE INT.ADR,INT.NR%
7630 :
7640 DTA$= SPACE$(64) 'result of FN 4Eh und 4Fh
7650 DL%=PEEK(VARPTR(DTA$)+1):DH%=PEEK(VARPTR(DTA$)+2) 'Pointer to DTA$
7660 AH%= &H1A 'FN Set DTA (Disk transfer Adress)
7670 DEF SEG:CALL DOS.SN(AH%,AL%,BH%,BL%,CH%,CL%,DH%,DL%,ES%,SI%,DI%,FLAGS%)
7680 :
7690 DL%=PEEK(VARPTR(MASK$)+1):DH%=PEEK(VARPTR(MASK$)+2) Pointer to MASK$
7700 AH%= &H4E 'FN Find first file
7710 CH%= &HFF:CL%= &HFF 'Attribute
7720 DEF SEG:CALL DOS.SN(AH%,AL%,BH%,BL%,CH%,CL%,DH%,DL%,ES%,SI%,DI%,FLAGS%)
7730 :
7740 IF (FLAGS% AND 1)= 0 THEN 7760 'everything Ok, continue.....
7750 RETURN 'no files, ENTRY=0
7760 GOSUB 7860 'Move data from DTA to array
7770 AH%= &H4F 'Find next file
7780 DEF SEG:CALL DOS.SN(AH%,AL%,BH%,BL%,CH%,CL%,DH%,DL%,ES%,SI%,DI%,FLAGS%)
7790 :
7800 WHILE (FLAGS% AND 1)= 0 AND (ENT< MAX.ENTRY)
7810    GOSUB 7860 'move data from DTA to ARRAY
7820    AH%= &H4F 'FN Find next file
7830    DEF SEG:CALL DOS.SN(AH%,AL%,BH%,BL%,CH%,CL%,DH%,DL%,ES%,SI%,DI%,FLAGS%)
7840 WEND 'Until no more entries
7850 RETURN
```

This subroutine transfers the data from the DTA into the DIR$() array. The data in the DTA receives special treatment during this process. You should review DTA construction and the data transfer (refer to Chapter 8).

```
7860 '
7870 '----- Move data from DTA in DIR$() ----
7880 '
7890 IF (ASC(MID$(DTA$,&H16,1)) AND &H10)= &H10 THEN RETURN 'no DIRs
7900 IF (ASC(MID$(DTA$,&H16,1)) AND &H8)= &H8 THEN RETURN 'no Volume-ID
7910 I= INSTR(&H1F,DTA$,CHR$(0))
7920 DIR$(ENT)= MID$(DTA$,&H1F,I-&H1F)
7930 IF NOT EXTENDED THEN 8520 'move only file name
7940 '
7950 COLOR MSG.FORGRD,MSG.BAKGRD
7960 DUMMY$= SPACE$(105) 'length of information
7970 LSET DUMMY$= DIR$(ENT) 'move name
7980 MID$(DUMMY$,30,1)= MID$(DTA$,&H16,1) 'Attribut from DTA
7990 TIME.LO = ASC(MID$(DTA$,&H17,1)):TIME.HI= ASC(MID$(DTA$,&H18,1))
8000 Y= 0:MINUTE= 0
8010 FOR I= 5 TO 7
```

```
8020    IF (TIME.LO AND 2^I)<> 0 THEN MINUTE= MINUTE+ 2^Y 'Bit 5-7 Minute
8030 Y= Y+1
8040 NEXT I
8050 FOR I= 0 TO 2
8060    IF (TIME.HI AND 2^I)<> 0 THEN MINUTE= MINUTE+ 2^Y 'Bit 8-10 Minute
8070 Y= Y+1
8080 NEXT I
8090 Y= 0:HOUR= 0
8100 FOR I= 3 TO 7
8110    IF (TIME.HI AND 2^I)<> 0 THEN HOUR= HOUR+ 2^Y 'Bit 11-15 Hour
8120 Y= Y+1
8130 NEXT I
8140 X$= STR$(HOUR):IF LEN(X$)= 2 THEN X$= "0"+RIGHT$(X$,1) ELSE X$= MID$(X$,2)
8150 MID$(DUMMY$,26,2)= X$
8160 X$= STR$(MINUTE):IF LEN(X$)= 2 THEN X$= "0"+RIGHT$(X$,1) ELSE X$= MID$(X$,2)
8170 MID$(DUMMY$,28,2)= X$
8180 DATE.LO= ASC(MID$(DTA$,&H19,1)):DATE.HI= ASC(MID$(DTA$,&H1A,1)) 'Date
8190 Y= 0:DAY= 0
8200 FOR I= 0 TO 4
8210    IF (DATE.LO AND 2^I)<> 0 THEN DAY=DAY+ 2^Y 'Bit 0-4 day
8220 Y= Y+1
8230 NEXT I
8240 Y= 0: MONTH= 0
8250 FOR I= 5 TO 7
8260    IF (DATE.LO AND 2^I)<> 0 THEN MONTH= MONTH+ 2^Y 'Bit 5-7 Month
8270    Y=Y+1
8280 NEXT I
8290 IF (DATE.HI AND 2^0)<> 0 THEN MONTH= MONTH+ 2^Y 'last Bit Month
8300 Y= 0:YEAR= 0
8310 FOR I=1 TO 7
8320    IF (DATE.HI AND 2^I)<> 0 THEN YEAR= YEAR+ 2^Y 'Bit 11-15 year
8330    Y=Y +1
8340 NEXT I
8350 YEAR= YEAR+80
8360 X$= STR$(DAY):IF LEN(X$)= 2 THEN X$= "0"+RIGHT$(X$,1) ELSE X$= MID$(X$,2)
8370 MID$(DUMMY$,20,2)= X$
8380 X$= STR$(MONTH):IF LEN(X$)= 2 THEN X$= "0"+RIGHT$(X$,1) ELSE X$= MID$(X$,2)
8390 MID$(DUMMY$,22,2)= X$
8400 X$= STR$(YEAR):IF LEN(X$)= 2 THEN X$= "0"+RIGHT$(X$,1) ELSE X$= MID$(X$,2)
8410 MID$(DUMMY$,24,2)= X$
8420 FSIZE.LO= ASC(MID$(DTA$,&H1B,1))+ 256* ASC(MID$(DTA$,&H1C,1))
8430 FSIZE.HI= ASC(MID$(DTA$,&H1D,1))+ 256* ASC(MID$(DTA$,&H1E,1))
8440 IF FSIZE.LO>= 0 THEN FSIZE=65536!*FSIZE.HI+FSIZE.LO ELSE FSIZE=
     65536!*FSIZE.HI+65536!+FSIZE.LO
8450 X$= STR$(FSIZE):Y$= SPACE$(7):RSET Y$= MID$(X$,2)
8460 MID$(DUMMY$,13,7)= Y$ 'size of the file
8470 MID$(DUMMY$,31,11)= VOLUME.ID$ 'Name of the disk
8480 MID$(DUMMY$,42,64)= DIR.DR$+DIR.PATH$ 'drive and path
8490 DIR$(ENT)= DUMMY$
8500 LOCATE 23,18: PRINT USING "###";ENT
8510 '
8520 ENT= ENT+1
8530 RETURN
```

```
8540 '
8550 MSG$="(Diskette-) Error During Reading of Directory, Stike any Key ":GOSUB 370:RETURN
     'return to calling routine
```

The volume ID (or disk label) is read separately from the directory, on the basis of your file attribute. Details on the file attributes can be found in Chapter 8. Otherwise the reading is similar to the reading of normal files.

```
8560 '
8570 '----- Find Volume-ID -----
8580 '
8590 FOOT$="Read VOLUME-ID.....":GOSUB 110
8600 MASK$= DIR.DR$+"\*.*"+CHR$(0):VOLUME.ID$="???        "
8610 AL%=0:AH%=0:BL%=0:BH%=0:CL%=0:CH%=0:DL%=0:DH%=0:ES%=0:SI%=0:DI%=0:FLAGS%=0
8620 INT.NR%= &H21:DEF SEG:POKE INT.ADR,INT.NR%
8630 :
8640 DTA$= SPACE$(64) 'result of FN 4Eh und 4Fh
8650 DL%=PEEK(VARPTR(DTA$)+1):DH%=PEEK(VARPTR(DTA$)+2) 'Pointer to DTA$
8660 AH%= &H1A 'FN Set DTA (Disk transfer Adress)
8670 DEF SEG:CALL DOS.SN(AH%,AL%,BH%,BL%,CH%,CL%,DH%,DL%,ES%,SI%,DI%,FLAGS%)
8680 :
8690 DL%=PEEK(VARPTR(MASK$)+1):DH%=PEEK(VARPTR(MASK$)+2) 'Pointer to MASK$
8700 CL%= 255:CH%= 255 'Attribut
8710 AH%= &H4E 'FN Find first file
8720 DEF SEG:CALL DOS.SN(AH%,AL%,BH%,BL%,CH%,CL%,DH%,DL%,ES%,SI%,DI%,FLAGS%)
8730 :
8740 IF (FLAGS% AND 1)= 0 THEN 8760 'Everything Ok, continue....
8750 RETURN 'error
8760 IF (ASC(MID$(DTA$,&H16,1)) AND 8)= 8 THEN GOSUB 8870:RETURN 'move name from DTA in
     VOLUME.ID$
8770 AH%= &H4F 'Find next file
8780 DEF SEG:CALL DOS.SN(AH%,AL%,BH%,BL%,CH%,CL%,DH%,DL%,ES%,SI%,DI%,FLAGS%)
8790 :
8800 WHILE (FLAGS% AND 1)= 0
8810 IF (ASC(MID$(DTA$,&H16,1)) AND 8)= 8 THEN GOSUB 8870:RETURN
8820   AH%= &H4F 'FN Find next file
8830   DEF SEG:CALL DOS.SN(AH%,AL%,BH%,BL%,CH%,CL%,DH%,DL%,ES%,SI%,DI%,FLAGS%)
8840 WEND 'until no more entries
8850 RETURN
8860 '
8870 '----- move name from DTA to VOLUME.ID$ -----
8880 '
8890 I= INSTR(&H1F,DTA$,CHR$(0))
8900 VOLUME.ID$= MID$(DTA$,&H1F,I-&H1F)
8910 RETURN
8920 '
8930 MSG$="(Diskette-) Error While Reading VOLUME-ID, Strike any Key ":GOSUB 370:RETURN
     4960 'return to calling routine
```

The error routine only displays the most important errors. All other errors are displayed as error number or error line. Refer to Chapters 7 and 16 for informaiton on how to easily change these error numbers or lines.

```
8940 '
8950 '----- Error Routine -----
8960 '
8970 IF ERL= 6420 THEN RESUME 6450 'file not found
8980 IF ERL= 7720 THEN RESUME 8550 'error reading Directory
8990 IF ERL= 8720 THEN RESUME 8930 'errpr reading VOLUME-ID
9000 LOCATE 25,1,0:COLOR MSG.FORGRD,MSG.BAKGRD
9010 PRINT "ERROR: ";ERR;" in Line: ";ERL;:BEEP
9020 IF INKEY$="" THEN 9020
9030 GOTO 2460
```

All input is accepted by the following subroutine. This is a very user-friendly input routine, which uses the <Backspace>, <Del> and <Ins> keys.

```
9040 '
9050 '----- Read Subroutine ----
9060 '
9070 X$="":ONKEY= 0
9080 LOCATE ROWNO,COLMNO,0:COLOR INP.FORGRD,INP.BAKGRD:PRINT INSTRING$;SPACE$(LNGTH-
     LEN(INSTRING$));
9090 LOCATE ROWNO,COLMNO,1,0,31:CRSR.POS= 1
9100 X$= INKEY$:IF X$="" THEN 9100
9110 IF X$= CHR$(8) AND POS(0)> COLMNO THEN GOSUB 9240:GOTO 9100 'Keys routine
9120 IF X$= CHR$(27) THEN ANYCHANGE= 0:RETURN
9130 IF X$=CHR$(13) THEN RETURN
9140 IF LEN(X$)= 2 THEN 9420 'control and Function keys
9150 '
9160 IF X$< " " THEN BEEP:GOTO 9100 'kill char smaller than a blank
9170 IF MAK.CAPS THEN IF X$>= "a" AND X$<= "z" THEN X$= CHR$(ASC(X$)-32)
9180 PRINT X$;:ANYCHANGE= -1
9190 IF CRSR.POS<= LEN(INSTRING$) THEN MID$(INSTRING$,CRSR.POS,1)= X$ ELSE INSTRING$=
     INSTRING$+X$
9200 CRSR.POS= CRSR.POS+1
9210 IF POS(0)> COLMNO+LNGTH-1 THEN BEEP:LOCATE ROWNO,COLMNO:CRSR.POS= 1:GOTO 9100
9220 GOTO 9100
9230 '
9240 '----- BACKSPACE and DEL keys-----
9250 '
9260 IF X$=CHR$(8) THEN INSTRING$= LEFT$(INSTRING$,CRSR.POS-2)+MID$(INSTRING$,CRSR.POS)
9270 IF ONKEY= 83  THEN INSTRING$= LEFT$(INSTRING$,CRSR.POS-1)+MID$(INSTRING$,CRSR.POS+1)
9280 LOCATE ROWNO,COLMNO:PRINT INSTRING$;" ";
9290 IF X$=CHR$(8) THEN CRSR.POS= CRSR.POS-1
9300 LOCATE CSRLIN,COLMNO+CRSR.POS-1
9310 ONKEY= 0: X$="":ANYCHANGE= -1
9320 RETURN
9330 '
9340 '----- Ins Keys-----
```

```
9350 '
9360 INSTRING$= LEFT$(INSTRING$,CRSR.POS-1)+" "+MID$(INSTRING$,CRSR.POS)
9370 PRINT " ";MID$(INSTRING$,CRSR.POS+1);
9380 LOCATE CSRLIN,COLMNO+CRSR.POS-1
9390 ANYCHANGE= -1
9400 RETURN
9410 '
9420 '----- Control and Function Keys -----
9430 '
9440 ONKEY= ASC(RIGHT$(X$,1))
9450 IF ONKEY= 63 THEN RETURN '<F5>= Selection
9460 IF ONKEY= 68 THEN RETURN '<F10>= Input Ok
9470 IF ONKEY= 72 OR ONKEY= 80 THEN RETURN 'Cursor up and down
9480 IF ONKEY= 73 OR ONKEY= 81 THEN RETURN '<PgUp> and <PgDn>
9490 IF ONKEY= 75 AND POS(0)> COLMNO THEN LOCATE CSRLIN,POS(0)-1:CRSR.POS= CRSR.POS-1:GOTO
9100 'Cursor <--
9500 IF ONKEY= 77 AND POS(0)< COLMNO+LNGTH-1 THEN IF CRSR.POS<= LEN(INSTRING$) THEN LOCATE
CSRLIN,POS(0)+1:CRSR.POS= CRSR.POS+1:GOTO 9100 'Cursor -->
9510 IF ONKEY= 83 AND CRSR.POS <= LEN(INSTRING$) THEN GOSUB 9240:GOTO 9100 '<Del> handled
like <Backspace>
9520 IF ONKEY= 71 THEN LOCATE ROWNO,COLMNO:GOTO 9100 '<Home>, start of field
9530 IF ONKEY= 79 THEN LOCATE CSRLIN,COLMNO+LEN(INSTRING$)-1:CRSR.POS= LEN(INSTRING$):GOTO
9100 '<End>, set to last character
9540 IF ONKEY= 117 THEN INSTRING$= LEFT$(INSTRING$,CRSR.POS-1):PRINT SPACE$(LNGTH-
CRSR.POS);:LOCATE CSRLIN,COLMNO+CRSR.POS-1:ANYCHANGE= -1:GOTO 9100 '<Ctrl><End>, erase to
end of field
9550 IF ONKEY= 82 AND CRSR.POS<= LEN(INSTRING$) AND LEN(INSTRING$)< LNGTH THEN GOSUB
9340:GOTO 9100 '<Ins>
9560 BEEP:GOTO 9100
```

14.3.1 Suggestions for the PDV Program

Program Start

PC-BASIC/BASICA must be called with the /M:61000/s:360 switch. After the start of the program, the machine language routine, variables and flags are initialized.

General Information

All functions are called through the menu. The individual functions can be interrupted or terminated with <Esc>. You are always returned to the calling function. The header displays the current function. The footer displays the key assignment or the current activity (sorting, search, etc.). A single routine handles all input. The most important errors are intercepted through an ON ERROR GOTO or through flags. Errors, which don't include a correction, are displayed as error numbers or line numbers on the bottom of the screen. The program then continues in the main menu.

The data are always written into the random file after being read or changed. Only the index file remains in memory during the execution and until the end of the program. An exception to this is when new data is read. Then the index file is saved. If a program is accidentally interrupted and the index file isn't saved, you can try to save whatever is possible, in the direct mode, as follows:

```
FOR I=0 TO SEQ.SIZE-1: PRINT#1,INDEX$(I): NEXT: CLOSE
```

Obviously, a line or variable shouldn't be changed before executing this statement.

Data Files

A data file must be selected before reading or writing data. This file contains the random file (which stores all data) and the index file (which only stores the program name and record numbers). The required selection of the data file is signaled by setting the menu bar to this entry. The data file can have any desired name. The program uses .SEQ and .DAT extensions regardless of any extension that may be entered. By using several data files, the files remain small and organized. Existing data files can be displayed and selected through a selection function.

Read data from diskette

The data is read from the diskette or hard disk. The drive, path and extension (for example *.EXE) can be indicated. The directory entries are read and assigned through the DOS interface. Then the new data is displayed and can be enhanced.

Search/Processing

Data can be searched for a program name or for search criteria. The program name must be entered completely and correctly; wildcards aren't permitted. For search criteria any desired character sequence can be entered. Periods or colons cannot be used for date and time. The records that are found are saved so that they can be paged forward and backward.

Sequential Display

All data is displayed or processed according to the sequence of the input.

List Output

You can send a list to the screen, printer or a file.

Suggestions for Changes

The individual functions are clearly identified with REMarks. The most often called subroutines are placed at the beginning of the program to reduce the search time. The variables' names indicate their purpose. By dividing the program into individual modules (overlays), there is more space for enhancements.

15. Printing

Usually connecting a printer and a PC is accomplished quickly and easily using an appropriate printer driver. However, at times things can go wrong. For example, the output through DOS may work properly but when the word processor is called, the printer suddenly switches to graphics mode or advances page by page, without printing a single character on the paper. In the first part of this chapter you'll find information on how to design your programs so that they'll work with various printers.

We'll also discuss how to write programs for "printer control" in such a way that it won't matter whether a dot matrix, ink jet or laser printer is connected to your PC. We'll discuss programs for multi-column and sideways printing. We're also including a useful program for printing diskette labels in various formats.

15.1   Connecting various printers

Almost anything that's capable of producing a character on paper from a dot matrix printer to an old typewriter can be connected to a PC. The only requirement is that one of the PC interfaces agrees with the printer interface.

15.1.1 Daisy wheel printers

Eighty percent of all daisy wheel printers are connected through the serial interface (RS232C) of the PC. This is where most problems begin. If your daisy wheel printer operates on the parallel interface (Centronics), please continue with the next section.

Both the printer and PC must use the same transmission parameters. On the printer you can usually set these through the DIP switches. Unfortunately, these switches are different from one printer to another so we cannot provide a general description. The best source of information about the DIP switches is in the manual for the appropriate printer.

MS-DOS provides the utility program MODE.COM for the configuration of the serial interface. The syntax is as follows:

```
MODE COMx:    <baud rate>
              <,parity>
              <,data bits>
              <,stop bits>
              <,P>
```

For x, insert the number of the serial interface where the printer is connected. Usually this is the number 1. <baud rate>, <parity>, <data bits> and <stop bits> must agree with the values set in the printer. P indicates that special printer error messages are used.

MS-DOS displays all printer output on the LPT1: interface, which is the parallel (Centronics) interface. If necessary, you have to redirect the output to the printer interfaced to the serial interface:

```
MODE LPT1: = COMx:
```

For x insert the number of the serial interface to which the printer is connected and which was initialized, through MODE, with the proper transmission parameters. The printer will operate properly when everything is ready.

However, it's possible that problems will still occur. The cable is the source of most problems. Unfortunately, the pin assignments for the PC and printers often differ. Some PCs are delivered with a 25 pin cable and others with a 9 pin cable. Most printers have a 25 pin cable. Consult your manual for both devices; then see your computer dealer for the proper cable.

To convert a 9 pin cable to a 25 pin cable or vice versa, use the following table:

Pin number (9 pin)	Signal	Pin number (25 pin)
1	Carrier Detect	8
2	Receive Data	3
3	Transmit Data	2
4	Data Terminal Ready	20
5	Signal Ground	7
6	Data Set Ready	6
7	Request to Send	4
8	Clear to Send	5
9	Ring Indicator	22

If the cable isn't causing the problems, check the DIP switch and the MODE setting again.

The worst problems are caused by programs whose print output goes directly to the parallel interface or serial interface instead of through DOS. The redirection doesn't apply here. Unfortunately, since nothing can be done about this, we recommend not using these programs.

For daisy wheel printers with automatic single sheet feed, there can be a problem with the left margin. We once had some difficulty with a printer, which always started printing in column 1. So the beginning of the line was printed on the platen instead of the paper. In the printer manual we found that there was a DIP switch for "Set left margin". After the switch was set, the output begin at column 35, which is the first column of a single sheet of paper.

If your daisy wheel printer runs but doesn't print the proper characters, refer to the section on the printer drivers.

15.1.2 Dot matrix and ink jet printers

Installing these types of printers is fairly easy. For most printers the connection occurs through the parallel interface (Centronics). If your printer operates through the serial interface, refer to the previous section about daisy wheel printers.

A connecting cable is available for almost all of the printers. After connecting this cable, the printer should operate properly. Of course there still could be problems:

- The cable usually isn't responsible for the problems unless it's defective. Your dealer should be able to determine whether the cable is defective.

- Some printers can be interfaced either to the serial or the parallel interface. This must be reflected in the setting of the DIP switches. Check whether these switches are properly set.

- If the printer still doesn't print correctly, have your dealer or service center examine it.

- If the printer operates, but prints the wrong characters, refer to the section on the printer driver.

15.1.3 Plotter

Most plotters are connected to the serial interface. The plotter is controlled through the control sequences that are sent by a program. Usually these are CAD or drawing programs. The plotter must understand these control sequences; otherwise only scribbles appear on the paper. This indicates that a program must be adjusted to the plotter. For a printer it may be possible to output characters simply as ASCII code, but the control sequences differ from one plotter to another. Various applications indicate that, with a few exceptions, a program written for the Hewlett-Packard plotter usually work with other plotters.

15.2　Printer Driver and Configuration

If you work with foreign languages, you may have noticed that sometimes it's difficult to print certain characters. Although appearing correct on the screen, these characters appear as strange symbols on the hardcopy.

Usually the PC uses a character set that only partially adheres to the standard ASCII character set. If you have problems with your printer, try the following solutions:

1.　Check whether your printer has been properly installed in the word processor. Select the menu option "Install printer" or "Installation". A list of the printers that are supported by the program is displayed. Select your printer. If your printer isn't on the list, try others. Usually there is a printer that is very similar to yours. The driver for the Epson FX printer should work. If it doesn't, use a generic printer driver such as TTY.

2.　Most word processors have an internal conversion table that can be modified. This means that you can determine which character will be printed for the character displayed on the screen. Refer to your printer manual which has tables of characters and codes. Often there is a menu option, such as "Printer interfacing" or "Installation".

3.　A final solution is the *printer driver*. This is a program which is inserted between the program and the printer. Every character, which will be printed, is first intercepted by this program and checked against a conversion table. For example, in the table shows that the ([) square bracket character should be replaced with the "Umlaut" Ä. In some cases the character is simply replaced with another. A printer driver is a special program which is included with software or can be purchased separately.

In PC-BASIC programs you can create your own printer driver, within certain limits. All data that is sent to the printer must be routed through a special routine which converts the characters:

```
10 .....
20 FOR I=1 TO LEN(PRINTX$)
30   IF MID$(PRINTX$,I,1)= "a" THEN MID$(PRINTX$,I,1)= "{"
     ...
     ...
90 NEXT I
100 LPRINT PRINTX$
110 .....
```

In a loop the output string is searched for a character to be exchanged. Usually this type of conversion is needed if the printer only accepts the ASCII character set.

The following table demonstrates the conversion of the foreign character set on a printer using the ASCII character set:

```
screen   printer

  ä         {
  ö         |
  ü         }
  ß         ~
  Ä         [
  Ö         \
  Ü         ]
```

If one of the characters from the left side of the table appears in the string to be printed, the character on the right side of the table must be substituted.

15.3   Escape Codes

The newer printers have many capabilities for defining the printer output. Fonts such as Pica, Elite and Courier are available in most printers. Different styles and types such as bold, underline, italics and superscript or subscript are also available.

By using an *escape code*, the printer is told which fonts, sizes, etc. should be expected. This code contains an escape character that indicates that an escape code is being set.

This escape character (ESC) is CHR$(27). Various characters may follow, depending on the printer. These characters indicate further action. One of the biggest printer manufacturers set a standard that many other manufacturers follow. If you can't find your printer during the program installation, select the Epson FX-80, for example. The normal attributes, such as bold and underline, should work. The following table displays the most often used escape codes. These codes can be used on about 70% of all printers:

ESC Code	Action
ESC x(1|0)	switch NLQ on/off
ESC M	switch on Elite
ESC P	switch on Pica
ESC p(1|0)	switch Proportional on/off
ESC W(1|0)	switch expanded on/off
ESC E	switch on bold
ESC F	switch bold off
ESC -(1|0)	switch underline on/off
ESC S(1|0)	switch on Sub-/Superscript
ESC T	switch off Sub-/Superscript
ESC G	switch on double-strike
ESC H	switch off double-strike
ESC 4	switch on cursive
ESC @	printer-Reset

Control Characters without ESC	
CHR$(8)	button for one column back
CHR$(15)	small letters on
CHR$(18)	small letters off

The output of an ESC code to the printer is just as simple as the output of normal text:

```
240 .....
245 LPRINT "This is a test text"
250 LPRINT CHR$(27);"W";CHR$(1);"print elongated"
255 LPRINT CHR$(27);"W";CHR$(0)
260 .....
```

15.4   Universal Printer Installation

All well written programs are capable of working with many printers. These programs usually use an *installation program* to do this. This installation program allows users to select a specific printer from a selection menu of printers. A printer installation is essential for your program if it's to be used with a variety of printers.

There are various ways to do this under PC-BASIC. You can create individual files with the printer specific data. These files, depending on the user's selection, are read into an array which controls the output. A selection menu of the printers, for which files were created, is provided for the user.

Another method is to provide a larger array containing data for all of the printers. Again the user selects the printer from a menu and the specific data is then transmitted to a control array.

Finally, the user should be able to define his/her own printer. This means that the files or the array should be expanded with additional descriptions. However, this will cause problems with the second method because it's impossible to predict the size of the array.

We used the first method in our program. The advantage of this method is that a new file is created at any time for a new printer. Also, descriptions for older printers can easily be handled and the user can provide additional printer definitions.

Implementation

The simplest solution is to create an array into which all printer specific data is loaded during the call of the program. The array is one-dimensional and the following functions are assigned to the elements:

```
element 0          printer-Reset
element 1          bold on
element 2          bold off
element 3          underline on
element 4          underline off
...
...
...
element n          load single sheet
```

In the printer file, which has the name of the printer (for example EP_FX_80.PRT or NEC_P6.PRT), the special escape codes of the printer are stored for the individual functions. If the printer cannot perform a function, a null byte is provided in the file. In the program, the statement:

```
IF PRINTER$(3)<> CHR$(0) THEN LPRINT PRINTER$(3)
```

sends the correct escape code regardless of the attached printer.

In order for the user to define a printer, a table, in which the user can enter the proper escape codes (found in the printer manual), appears on the screen. When the conversion table is used, the characters to be converted are captured.

Conversion Tables

Conversion tables are easy to use with PC-BASIC. A one dimensional array is essential. Each element contains the character which should be output, instead of the character corresponding to the ASCII table. In the printer file the data is stored after the escape codes:

```
10 DIM PRINTER(39) '40 functions are possible (0-39)
20 DIM CONVERSION$(255) 'for every character one element
30 OPEN "PARAM.DAT" FOR INPUT AS #1
40 INPUT #1,PRINTER.NAME$
50 CLOSE #1
60 PRINTER.FILE$= PRINTER.NAME$+".PRT"
70 OPEN PRINTER.FILE$ FOR INPUT AS #1
80 FOR I= 0 TO 39
90   LINE INPUT #1,PRINTER$(I)
100 NEXT I
110 FOR I= 32 TO 255
120   LINE INPUT #1, CONVERSION$(I)
130 NEXT I
140 CLOSE
150 .....
890 .....
900 '----- printer output with conversion -----
910 FOR I= 1 TO LEN(PRINT$)
920   SYMBOL= ASC(MID$(PRINT$,I,1))
930   IF SYMBOL < 32 THEN LPRINT CHR$(SYMBOL) ELSE LPRINT CONVERSION$(SYMBOL)
940 NEXT I
950 RETURN
960 .....
```

Remember that the CONVERSION$() array is occupied only after element 32, the space. All the characters that appear before this array are control characters for the printer and cannot be changed.

15.5   Multi-Column Printing

You may have noticed that your printer uses only half of a page in certain situations, for example when printing a DOS directory. This also occurs when printing program listings. Using multi-column printing not only saves paper but is also a suitable format for various documents.

While developing a program to do this, first we had to ensure that words too large to fit on one line could be hyphenated. We also had to set right and left margins for justified text. A test is performed for the hyphenation to determine whether the last character of the line is equal to a space, a dash or a colon (for the listing). If the character isn't equal to any of these, a function is called which outputs the line. The character to be hyphenated is located with the cursor control. Details can be found in the following listing.

True justification isn't possible if you're using a printer not capable of proportional spacing. The space at the end of a line may vary depending on the last word.

Implementation

Note: To execute the multi-column printout program correctly, call PC-BASIC with the /M switch:

```
GWBASIC /M:54000
```

Also, you may have to use extensions when the program requests filenames.

The basis of the program is a three-dimensional array, TEXT$, into which the lines of the file are read. A maximum of three pages is possible with this demonstration program. After the call of the program, you're asked whether you want a printout of the file (line 110). After the file is formatted, it's possible to save it again for later or repeated processing. If such a file should be output, the program branches according to the FILE.NAME variable, reads the filename and then the file. Once you determine where to display the output (printer or screen (line 230)) it begins at line 1260.

If the program is processing a new file, you need to answer some questions concerning the format (line 170). These formats include the number of columns per page that should be printed, if there should be hyphenation and if the text should be justified. You can also enter a header, which is printed at the top center of each page. Finally indicate the name of the file and enter the output destination (printer or display). The OUTPUT.FILE$ variable is set either to LPT1: or SCRN: for the output. This avoids queries inside the program regarding the output destination and the reactions which may result:

```
245 IF OUTPUT$="Dd" THEN LPRINT <data> ELSE PRINT <data>
```

This type of query would have to occur during every output action and would increase the size of the program considerably. So updating such a program would become more complicated. Under some circumstances you would indicate the logical file KBRD: or CONS:, instead of SCRN:, for the output to the screen. This depends on the MS-DOS and PC-BASIC version being used. You should experiment if nothing appears on your screen.

The variables required for formatting the new file are calculated or the constants are determined starting at line 540. Line 560 calculates the width of the columns based on a line length of 80 characters. The columns are separated by three space characters. You can change this to fit your own requirements. For more than 80 characters per line, you must include the escape codes used for switching the printer into another font. In line 570 a variable, which is needed for formatting the individual lines (line 2070), is initialized. In line 580 the constants for PRNT.ROWNO and PAGE.LNGTH are determined. These values depend on the paper you're using in your printer. The values used in this example are based on standard fanfold paper. In line 590 the counters for the TEXT$ array are set to the initial value 1. Line 610 opens the file to be processed as a text file.

The file is read and the lines are processed starting at line 630. First a test is made to determine whether it's a blank line (line 640). If it is, it's accepted without any further action and the next line is read (line 680-700). Starting at line 740, the lines, which are smaller in length than the calculated width of a column, are processed. These lines are cleared of blank spaces at the beginning (line 760-780) and transmitted, without being justified, into the array.

Any lines which are longer than the calculated width are processed starting at line 830. The left part is accepted into the array. The hyphenation routine is skipped if the text is accepted without hyphenation. Then the rest of the line is processed. Otherwise, a test starts at line 870 of the last character of the line. The space, dash and colon characters are accepted as separators to terminate the hyphenation at this point. Every other character causes the execution of the hyphenation starting at line 900. The complete line is printed. The part of the line which can be accepted into the array is highlighted in bold type and the rest is shown in normal text. This makes it easier to see the complete line for the hyphenation.

Use the <Cursor Left> and <Cursor Right> keys to position the cursor before the character where the hyphenation should occur. Once the position is set, use the <-> key to insert a dash as a hyphen, the <Return> key to accept the line without hyphenation or the <Spacebar> to insert a space as a separator. The hyphenation can be terminated by striking the <Esc> key. This means that the rest of the file is accepted into the array. Starting at line 1130, the hyphenated line is accepted into the array and then the rest of the lines are processed.

Starting at line 1260, the formatted file is output on the basis of the constants PAGE.LNGTH and PRNT.ROWNO. Besides the header, a page number is also printed (line 1430). After the file has been displayed or printed, a query occurs after line 1480 to determine the next step. You can either end the program with <Esc>, save the file with <S> or repeat the output with <R>.

If necessary, the formatted file is stored starting at line 1570. Besides the array, the constants and variables are stored (line 1620-1640). A single line is read and its length is found in line 1760. First a test is made in line 1780 to determine whether the end of the file has been reached. In this case the subroutine is abandoned, through RETURN 1280, and the output is called starting at line 1280.

The subroutine, starting at line 1820, increments the variables and is responsible for justification. The query in line 1840 skips the justification routine, if necessary, and only causes the implementation of the PAGE, ROWNO, COLNO variables starting at line 2060. All spaces at the beginning and end of the line are removed (line 1890-1940) for the justification. An auxiliary variable X$ is used (line 1880) to make the queries and assignments shorter. In line 1950 a test is made to determine whether there should be spaces in the line. If there shouldn't, spaces don't have to be inserted for the justification and processing continues in line 2060.

The preparation for the justification occurs after line 1960 in a WHILE...WEND loop. The line is searched, from the beginning to the end, for a space. Any space that is found is doubled in line 1990. When the end of the line is reached (BLK.POS= 0), the line is searched again from the beginning (line 1980/1970). This continues until the line is as wide as the column. After this the variables are restored and the next line is read.

This is the listing for the multi-column printout program:

```
10 '-------------------------------------------------
20 ' MULTICOL.BAS          1985 (C) H.J. Bomanns
30 '-------------------------------------------------
40 :
50 CLS:KEY OFF
60 PRINT "This program outputs a multi-column ASCII text file to either"
70 PRINT "your printer or the screen."
80 PRINT STRING$(80,"-")
90 PRINT
100 :
110 PRINT "Output stored file? (Y/N) --> ";:LOCATE ,,1,0,31
120 X$= INKEY$:IF X$="" THEN 120
130 IF X$= CHR$(27) THEN CLS:END '<Esc>= End
140 IF X$="y" OR X$="Y" THEN OLD.FILE= -1:PRINT:PRINT:GOTO 210
150 IF X$<>"n" AND X$<>"N" THEN BEEP:GOTO 120
160 PRINT:PRINT
170 INPUT "Columns per page.........: ",COLM.PER.PAGE
180 INPUT "Text for header .......: ",HEAD.TXT$
190 INPUT "Use hyphenation? .(Y/N)...: ",S$:IF S$="y" OR S$="Y" THEN
    SEPARATE= -1 ELSE SEPARATE= 0
```

```
200 INPUT "Justified. (Y/N).............: ",J$:IF J$="y" OR J$="Y" THEN
    JUSTIFY= -1 ELSE JUSTIFY= 0
210 INPUT "Name of the ASCII-file.......: ",FIL.NAME$
220 PRINT
230 PRINT "Send output to <P>rinter or <D>isplay or <Esc> to end --> ";
240 X$=INKEY$:IF X$="" THEN 240
250 IF X$= CHR$(27) THEN CLS:END '<Esc>= End
260 IF X$="d" OR X$="D" THEN OUTPUT.FILE$= "SCRN:":GOTO 300
270 IF X$="p" OR X$="P" THEN OUTPUT.FILE$= "LPT1:":GOTO 300
280 BEEP:GOTO 240
290 :
300 VIEW PRINT 4 TO 15:CLS:VIEW PRINT
310 LOCATE 5,1,0:PRINT "File being processed. One moment please .....";
320 :
330 DIM TEXT$(3,COLM.PER.PAGE,72*3) 'for demo only three pages
340 :
350 IF NOT OLD.FILE THEN 560
360 :
370 '----- read existing file and display -----
380 :
390 OPEN FIL.NAME$ FOR INPUT AS #1
400 LINE INPUT#1, HEAD.TXT$
410 INPUT#1,PAGE: INPUT#1,LAST.ROWNO: INPUT#1, COLM.PER.PAGE
420 INPUT#1,PRNT.ROWNO: INPUT#1,PAGE.LNGTH
430 ERASE TEXT$:DIM TEXT$(3,COLM.PER.PAGE,72*3) 'for demonstration only
    three pages
440 FOR PAGES= 1 TO PAGE
450   FOR ROWS= 1 TO PRNT.ROWNO
460     FOR COLMS= 1 TO COLM.PER.PAGE
470       LINE INPUT#1,TEXT$(PAGES,COLMS,ROWS)
480     NEXT COLMS
490   NEXT ROWS
500 NEXT PAGES
510 CLOSE
520 GOTO 1290 'output
530 :
540 '----- initialize Variables for new file -----
550 :
560 WDTH= INT((80-((COLM.PER.PAGE-1)*3))/COLM.PER.PAGE)
570 BLANK$= SPACE$(WDTH+3)
580 PRNT.ROWNO= 63: PAGE.LNGTH= 72
590 COLMNO= 1: ROWNO= 1: PAGE= 1
600 :
610 OPEN FIL.NAME$ FOR INPUT AS #1
620 :
630 GOSUB 1780 'read a line from file
640 IF NUM.OF.CHARS= 2 THEN 680 ELSE 740 '2 character= $0D0A
650 :
660 '----- line is only $0D0A/ CRLF -----
670 :
680 TEXT$(PAGE,COLMNO,ROWNO)= DAT$
690 GOSUB 2060 'one line more, not justification - $0D0A
700 GOTO 630 'next line
```

```
710 :
720 '--- line is not blank and shorter than WDTH ---
730 :
740 IF NUM.OF.CHARS< WDTH THEN 750 ELSE 850
750 X$= DAT$
760 FOR I=1 TO LEN(X$) 'erase blanks at beginning
770    IF MID$(X$,I,1)=" " THEN 780 ELSE X$= MID$(X$,I):GOTO 790
780 NEXT I
790 TEXT$(PAGE,COLMNO,ROWNO)= X$
800 GOSUB 2060 'one more line, no justification if line is not complete
810 GOTO 630 'next line
820 :
830 '----- line is longer than WDTH -----
840 :
850 TEXT$(PAGE,COLMNO,ROWNO)= LEFT$(DAT$,WDTH)
860 IF NOT SEPARATE THEN 1210
870 SEP.CHAR$=RIGHT$(TEXT$(PAGE,COLMNO,ROWNO),1)
880 IF SEP.CHAR$<>"-" AND SEP.CHAR$<>" " AND SEP.CHAR$<>":" THEN 920 ELSE 1210
890 :
900 '----- hyphenate last word of the line -----
910 :
920 LOCATE 14,1,0:COLOR 15,0
930 PRINT STRING$(80,"-")
940 PRINT "Hyphenation occurs before the character under the cursor.
    Use <Cursor> key to set hyphenation:"
950 PRINT "<-> to separate with dash  <Spacebar> to separate without
    dash  <Return> for no hyphenation
960 PRINT "<Esc> to switch off hyphenation"
970 PRINT STRING$(80,"-")
980 LOCATE 20,1,0
990 PRINT TEXT$(PAGE,COLMNO,ROWNO);:P=POS(0):COLOR 7,0
1000 PRINT MID$(DAT$,P,80-P);SPACE$(80-POS(0));
1010 LOCATE 20,P-1,1
1020 X$= INKEY$:IF X$="" THEN 1020
1030 IF X$= CHR$(27) THEN SEPARATE= 0:VIEW PRINT 14 TO 25:CLS:VIEW PRINT:GOTO
1210 'starting here do not hyphenate
1040 IF X$= CHR$(13) THEN 1210 'do not hyphenate
1050 IF LEN(X$)= 2 THEN 1090
1060 IF X$=" " OR X$="-" THEN T.POS= POS(0):GOTO 1130 'hyphenate
1070 BEEP:GOTO 1020
1080 :
1090 IF ASC(RIGHT$(X$,1))= 77 AND POS(0)< LEN(TEXT$(PAGE,COLMNO,ROWNO)) THEN
     LOCATE ,POS(0)+1:GOTO 1020
1100 IF ASC(RIGHT$(X$,1))= 75 AND POS(0)> 1 THEN LOCATE ,POS(0)-1:GOTO 1020
1110 BEEP:GOTO 1020
1120 :
1130 TEXT$(PAGE,COLMNO,ROWNO)= MID$(DAT$,1,T.POS-1)+X$
1140 GOSUB 1840 'one more line
1150 DAT$= MID$(DAT$,T.POS)
1160 NUM.OF.CHARS= LEN(DAT$)
1170 GOTO 740 'process rest of the line
1180 :
1190 '----- process line without hyphenation -----
```

```
1200 :
1210 GOSUB 1840 'one more line with justification, since line is longer than WDTH
1220 DAT$= MID$(DAT$,WDTH+1)
1230 NUM.OF.CHARS= LEN(DAT$)
1240 GOTO 740 'process the rest of the line
1250 :
1260 '-- output Array on the printer or screen display --
1270 :
1280 CLOSE 'close data-file
1290 IF OUTPUT.FILE$="SCRN:" THEN CLS
1300 OPEN OUTPUT.FILE$ FOR OUTPUT AS #1 '"SCRN:" or "LPT1:"
1310 FOR OUTPUT.PAGE= 1 TO PAGE
1320   PRINT#1, :'first line free
1330   PRINT#1,TAB((80-LEN(HEAD.TXT$))/2);HEAD.TXT$ 'centered
1340   PRINT#1,STRING$(80,"-")
1350   FOR OUTPUT.ROWNO= 1 TO PRNT.ROWNO
1360     FOR OUTPUT.COLMNO= 1 TO COLM.PER.PAGE
1370       PRINT #1,TEXT$(OUTPUT.PAGE,OUTPUT.COLMNO,OUTPUT.ROWNO);
1380     NEXT OUTPUT.COLMNO
1390     PRINT#1,
1400   NEXT OUTPUT.ROWNO
1410   FOR I= OUTPUT.ROWNO+3 TO PAGE.LNGTH-3:PRINT#1,:NEXT I
1420   PRINT #1,
1430   PRINT #1,TAB(34);"page -";OUTPUT.PAGE;"-"
1440   PRINT#1,
1450 NEXT OUTPUT.PAGE
1460 CLOSE 'close output
1470 :
1480 '--- end of program, continue or store ? -----
1490 :
1500 LOCATE 25,1,1:PRINT "<S>tore  <R>epeat output  <Esc> to end  --> ";
1510 X$= INKEY$:IF X$="" THEN 1510
1520 IF X$="r" OR X$="R" THEN 1280
1530 IF X$="s" OR X$="S" THEN 1590
1540 IF X$<>CHR$(27) THEN BEEP:GOTO 1510
1550 CLS:END
1560 :
1570 '----- store Array and Variables -----
1580 :
1590 LOCATE 25,1:PRINT SPACE$(79);:LOCATE 25,1
1600 LINE INPUT;"store in file: ",FIL.NAME$
1610 OPEN FIL.NAME$ FOR OUTPUT AS #1
1620 PRINT#1, HEAD.TXT$
1630 PRINT#1,PAGE: PRINT#1,LAST.ROWNO: PRINT#1, COLM.PER.PAGE
1640 PRINT#1,PRNT.ROWNO: PRINT#1,PAGE.LNGTH
1650 FOR PAGES= 1 TO PAGE
1660   FOR ROWS= 1 TO PRNT.ROWNO
1670     FOR COLMS= 1 TO COLM.PER.PAGE
1680       PRINT#1,TEXT$(PAGES,COLMS,ROWS)
1690     NEXT COLMS
1700   NEXT ROWS
1710 NEXT PAGES
1720 CLOSE
```

```
1730 LOCATE 25,1:PRINT SPACE$(79);
1740 GOTO 1500
1750 :
1760 '----- read a line of file -----
1770 :
1780 IF EOF(1) THEN RETURN 1280
1790 LINE INPUT#1,DAT$ 'read a line of file
1800 NUM.OF.CHARS= LEN(DAT$) 'length of the line read
1810 RETURN
1820 '----- update justification Variables for ROWNO AND COLMNO -----
1830 :
1840 IF NOT JUSTIFY THEN 2060 'no justification
1850 :
1860 '----- prepare line for justification -----
1870 :
1880 X$= TEXT$(PAGE,COLMNO,ROWNO):JUST.POS= 1
1890 FOR I=1 TO LEN(X$) 'erase blanks at beginning
1900    IF MID$(X$,I,1)=" " THEN 1910 ELSE X$= MID$(X$,I):GOTO 1920
1910 NEXT I
1920 FOR I=LEN(X$) TO 1 STEP-1 'erase blanks at end
1930    IF MID$(X$,I,1)<> " " THEN 1940 ELSE NEXT I:GOTO 1950
1940 X$= LEFT$(X$,I)
1950 IF INSTR(X$," ")= 0 THEN 2060 'no blanks
1960 WHILE LEN(X$) < WDTH
1970    JUST.POS= INSTR(JUST.POS,X$," ")
1980    IF JUST.POS= 0 THEN JUST.POS= 1:GOTO 1970
1990    X$= LEFT$(X$,JUST.POS)+MID$(X$,JUST.POS)
2000    JUST.POS= JUST.POS+2
2010 WEND
2020 TEXT$(PAGE,COLMNO,ROWNO)= X$
2030 :
2040 '----- update Variables -----
2050 :
2060 IF COLMNO = COLM.PER.PAGE THEN 2090 'no space last column
2070 TEXT$(PAGE,COLMNO,ROWNO)= TEXT$(PAGE,COLMNO,ROWNO)+ LEFT$(BLANK$,
     (WDTH+3)-LEN(TEXT$(PAGE,COLMNO,ROWNO)))
2080 MID$(TEXT$(PAGE,COLMNO,ROWNO),LEN(TEXT$(PAGE,COLMNO,ROWNO))-1,1)= "|"
2090 ROWNO= ROWNO+1
2100 IF ROWNO > PRNT.ROWNO THEN COLMNO= COLMNO+1:ROWNO= 1
2110 IF COLMNO > COLM.PER.PAGE THEN PAGE= PAGE+1:COLMNO=1:ROWNO= 1
2120 IF PAGE> 3 THEN 1280 'output
2130 RETURN
```

Modifying this program shouldn't present a problem because of the extensive REMs. For example, it's possible to have an automatic hyphenation feature so that the cursor is set to the location where the hyphenation should occur. However, this requires a lot of programming and testing.

15.6   Printing Sideways

The idea for printing characters sideways occurred to us after acquiring a graphics printer. We tried to control individual pins in the printhead hoping for the capability of plotting function curves and for modifying the axes on the printer. Soon we were able to print characters, which had been turned 90 degrees, to modify the axes. After doing this, printing text sideways was easily accomplished.

Design

Basically, the text is read into an array and from there is used to control the printer. The characters are output on a bit-by-bit basis. So, the array must be read from the bottom to the top on a column basis and the characters, which are processed for output, are read from left to right.

We've inserted comments into the listing to explain the different algorithms. You'll find detailed instructions for controlling single pins on the printhead in Section 15.1.1. Let's look at the result:

```
10 '----------------------------------------------------------------
20 'PRT_QUER.BAS                        1985 (C) H.J.Bomanns
30 '----------------------------------------------------------------
40 :
50 CLS:KEY OFF
60 PRINT "This Program prints an ASCII file in sideways format on standard
   fanfold paper,"
70 PRINT
80 PRINT STRING$(80,"-"):PRINT:PRINT
90 CHAR.ROM.SEG= &HF000:CHAR.ROM.OFS= &HFA6E
```

The bit pattern of individual characters is read from the so-called "character ROM" of the PCs with PEEK. In this ROM 8 bytes are stored for every character. They're required for representing a character in the 8*8 dot matrix (8 bytes*8 bits). For the readout the segment address (for PEEK) as well as the offset address (for the calculation of the character position) must be set in line 90. Usually a change isn't needed here. You need only to provide the addresses (from your PC manual) if your PC deviates from the standard.

```
100 DIM TEXT$(72)              'line-Array for one Page
110 CHAR.HGT=10                   'Character height of Font 8*8 +2 Blank Lines
```

The distance between the individual lines is determined by CHAR.HGT. Usually a text line is 8 graphic lines high. If two graphic lines are added for the separation of lines, the height in CHAR equals 10. As the value changes, for example 8, the distance between lines becomes much smaller. So more lines will fit on a page but the readability decreases.

```
120 MAX.ROWS=INT(480/CHAR.HGT) 'maximum number of lines per page
```

The maximum number of lines that can be printed per page results from the maximum horizontal resolution of the printer. In this case, the printer can produce 480 individual pixels per graphic line. By dividing this by CHAR.HGT, you can calculate the number of printable lines per page.

```
130 RESOLUTION= 1              'Resolution "K"/"L"
```

Here you indicate the resolution of the graphic that your printer can handle. Most printers are at least capable of printing a graphic with *single density* (one pin per pixel) or *double density* (two pins per pixel).

```
140 :
150 LINE INPUT "File Name: ",FIL.NAME$
160 IF FIL.NAME$="" THEN CLS:END
170 OPEN FIL.NAME$ FOR INPUT AS #1
180 PRINT:PRINT:PRINT "Printout being processed, please wait ....."
190 WIDTH "LPT1:",255
200 LPRINT CHR$(27);"3";CHR$(24); 'Set line spacing for Graphic
```

In the graphics mode the individual pins of the printhead are controlled by a bit pattern in a byte. A linefeed occurs in some PCs after the 80th byte. This is inappropriate here because we determine that more than 80 characters will be sent in line 190.

In line 200 the line feed is adjusted to the graphics mode, since this deviates from the usual 6 lines per inch. The sequence CHR$(27);"3";CHR$(24) means that a line feed corresponding to 7.5 characters per inch should be used. Unfortunately you'll have to experiment to find this value. Smaller values cause the individual characters of the line to be close together or even overlap.

```
210 ROWNO= 0:MAX.LEN= 0
220 '
230 WHILE NOT EOF(1)
240   LINE INPUT #1,X$
250   IF LEN(X$)>MAX.LEN THEN MAX.LEN=LEN(X$)
260   TEXT$(ROWNO)= X$:ROWNO= ROWNO+1
270   IF ROWNO>=MAX.ROWS THEN GOSUB 350:ROWNO=0:MAX.LEN=0 'Print Page
280 WEND
290 CLOSE
300 IF ROWNO THEN GOSUB 350 'print last Page when necessary
310 LPRINT CHR$(27);"2";  'line feed again 6 lines/Inch
320 LPRINT CHR$(27);"@";  'reset printer
330 CLS:END
```

From lines 230 to 280 a page is read into the TEXT$ array, depending on the maximum number of lines which can be printed (line 120). Printing occurs (line 270) through the call for the subroutine, starting at line 350.

In line 300 a test is made to determine whether the last page is already printed as a complete page. If it isn't complete, it has less than MAX.ROWS lines. In this case, ROW isn't equal to "0" and the last page is printed.

The printer is set to the normal line feed (line 310) and a general printer reset is performed in line 330. This is necessary because some printers are reset from graphics mode to text mode although the line feed remains set.

```
340 '
350 FOR PRNT.COLMNO=1 TO MAX.LEN 'from top to bottom
360    LPRINT CHR$(27);CHR$(74+RESOLUTION); MKI$(MAX.ROWS* CHAR.HGT*
```

Line 360 switches the printer into the graphics mode where the resolution is set depending on RESOLUTION. The "74" in the second CHR$() indicates the letter "J", which, with RESOLUTION, results in "K" or "L". Through "K" and "L" either single density or double density is switched on. How many bytes constitute the bit pattern of a graphic line to be printed is indicated through MKI$().

```
370    FOR PRNT.ROWNO= MAX.ROWS-1 TO 0 STEP-1 'from left to right
380       CHAR=ASC( LEFT$( MID$( TEXT$( PRNT.ROWNO ), PRNT.COLMNO, 1)+ " ", 1))
390       FOR I=9 TO CHAR.HGT 'Space between lines
400          LPRINT STRING$(RESOLUTION,0); 'according to resolution
410       NEXT I
```

In line 380 a single character is read from the array. For shorter lines the MID$ function doesn't deliver a result but the null ("") string, in the ASC() function, causes an error message. To prevent this, a blank is attached to the character that was read via LEFT$. If a character isn't present, the blank can be used for further processing; otherwise it's ignored.

From line 390 to 410 the bit pattern "0", corresponding to RESOLUTION, is sent for the line spacing.

```
420       DEF SEG= CHAR.ROM.SEG
430       FOR BYTE=7 TO 0 STEP-1 'Bit pattern of the character from CHAR-ROM to
          printer
440          LPRINT STRING$ (RESOLUTION ,PEEK(CHAR.ROM.OFS +(CHAR*8) +BYTE));
450       NEXT BYTE
```

In lines 420 to 450 the 8 bytes are read out of the character ROM, which correspond to the ASCII code defined in line 380, and are sent, as bit pattern for the single pin control, to the printer. When printing from left to right, this occurs in a reversed loop (STEP -1) so that the bit pattern is composed from bottom to top. The first bit is assigned to the first pin in the printhead, the second to the second pin, etc. This causes the character to rotate 90 degrees.

```
460    NEXT PRNT.ROWNO
470    LPRINT
480 NEXT PRNT.COLMNO
490 LPRINT CHR$(12);  'Page advance
500 RETURN
```

Line 490 advances a page before printing the next page.

Remember that a single line shouldn't be longer than a page since the page advance may interfere with the page breaks. Depending on the printer, resolution and line spacing, the maximum line length can vary. So you will need to experiment with this.

15.7 Printing Diskette Labels

To conclude this chapter, we'll present a program for printing diskette labels. Various fonts (Pica, Elite and micro print) can be used. By using micro print, more information will fit on the label. The program was designed for NEC-Series P5, P6 and P7 printers but, by changing the escape codes slightly, it will run on any printer that can print the PC character set.

About the program

The assignment of the function keys is deleted in line 70 because the keys are needed as control keys in the program. Line 80 installs an error correction routine.

In line 120 the arrays required for printing output and the program control are initialized. From line 140 the constants and variables are assigned.

For a query of the function and control keys in later programs, the keyboard codes are assigned important constants starting at line 220.

The type of monitor connected to your PC (refer to Chapter 3) is determined from lines 270 to 440. The colors for the output are set separately.

The output of the template occurs at line 460. In line 500 the color of the frame is set according to the color of the background. You can delete this line if you're using a monochrome card. Once the template is printed, in lines 530 to 550, the control keys, assignment is displayed on the left side. Starting at line 760, the label strip is displayed on the right side of the template. The width of the display can vary since the program is capable of using various fonts. The area will not be erased before the output. Because of this, larger labels may partially overlap. We did this so that a size would be easier to select.

Instructions starting at line 970 control the input. A loop evaluates the activated keys, which, depending on the results, calls the routines assigned to them. The FIELD() array is used to position the cursor in the individual fields. Depending on the selected label, the position and length of the field are saved. If one of the elements is "0", no field exists but control must be continued at the next field (lines 1010 to 1030). On the basis of the activated key, it's decided whether the next or the preceding field should be activated. This procedure is necessary because the labels can be printed with or without the date.

From line 1090 to 1180, the keys that produce a normal ASCII code are processed. The program ends with <Esc>. Strike <Tab> to produce the output of other frames. Strike <Return> and <Ctrl><Return> to make any changes to the fields. All other ASCII codes are evaluated as input for the field, checked and then output.

Following line 1200, the listing provides information for the function and control keys. These keys deliver an extended keyboard code consisting of a 0 byte and a key code. Depending on the key, the assigned routine and the routine which will be described next are called.

Starting in line 1460, the change to the next field is prepared. First the current field content is read into the PRNT$() array. Then the index for the fields is incremented by one and checked to determine whether the valid limits have been maintained (lines 1520/1530). The same is valid for the program portion starting at line 1560. Here the change to the preceding field is prepared.

The subroutine, starting at line 1660, reads the current field content into the PRNT$() array. This occurs through the SCREEN function, which reads a character directly from the display memory. The position is derived from the content of the FIELD() array.

Starting at line 1790 the individual label frames are printed. This part of the program is called after the <Tab> or <Shift><Tab> keys are pressed. It first tests the FRAME variable, makes any necessary corrections (lines 1830/1840), provides the FIELD() with valid values (lines 1860 to 2010) and then branches, according to the value in FRAME, to a routine for constructing the proper frame on the basis of a ON X GOSUB construction (line 2020). After the output of the frame, the content of the PRNT$ array is output for the new label starting at line 2040. You can test a label without having to enter the content again. The program ends by displaying the font, characters per inch, etc.

Starting at line 2100, the individual frames are printed. Various combinations are available. A total of 14 different frames can be produced.

The subroutine starting at line 2580 displays the current values. Besides the number of the selected frame, the font and the characters per inch and the number of labels to be printed are also displayed.

The labels are printed during the program section that starts at line 2750. After the printer initialization in lines 2820 to 2870, the program prints the required number of labels. The printing can be stopped at any time. The individual characters of the label are read directly from the display memory through the SCREEN function. So the complicated formatting of the print strings is avoided.

The conclusion of the program is the error routine. This starts at line 3000. Only the error number and line are displayed since the program was written for internal use. Then the program restarts.

We're also providing comments and REM statements in the listing so you can easily adapt the program to your own needs.

```
10 '-----------------------------------------------------------------
20 'Disk-label printer Program          1986 (C) H.J. Bomanns
30 'Created: 9/13/86, last change: 1/14/87
40 'V2.00 for IBM  and compatible printers.
50 '-----------------------------------------------------------------
60 :
70 KEY OFF:FOR I=1 TO 10:KEY I,"":NEXT I
80 ON ERROR GOTO 3000
90 :
100 '---------- Dimensioning ----------------------------
110 :
120 DIM PRNT$(7),PRNT.CHAR(3),FONT$(3),FIELD.NUM(7,3)
130 :
140 '---------- Assignments ----------------------------------
150 :
160 COPYR$="1987 (C) H.J.Bomanns"
170 PRNT$(1)= "<< NAME >>":PRNT$(2)= "000": PRNT$(7)=
    LEFT$(DATE$,2)+"/"+MID$(DATE$,4,2)+"/"+RIGHT$(DATE$,2)
180 PRNT.CHAR(1)= 43:PRNT.CHAR(2)= 30:PRNT.CHAR(3)= 25
190 FONT$(1)="Micro/ 15": FONT$(2)="Elite/ 12": FONT$(3)= "Pica/ 10"
200 FONT= 1:NUMBER= 1:FRAME= 1
210 :
220 '---------- Keys ------------------------------------------
230 :
240 F1= 59: F2= 60: F3= 61: F4= 62: NTAB= 9: SHIFTTAB=15: ESC= 27: HOME= 71: ENDE= 79:
    CHOME= 119: CRSR.UP= 72: CRSR.DOWN= 80
250 SF2= 85: SF3= 86: SF4= 87: CRSR.RIGHT= 77: CRSR.LEFT= 75: CR= 13:CCR= 10: C.RIGHT=
    116: C.LEFT= 115
260 :
270 '---------- Which Monitor ??? ----------------------------
280 :
290 MONITOR$="C":DEF SEG=0:IF (PEEK(&H410) AND &H30)= &H30 THEN MONITOR$="M":GOTO 410
    'Determine colors for Mono-Display
300 :
310 '---------- Colors for Color-Display -------------------
320 :
330 BG    = 1 'blue
340 TEXT= 15 'white
350 MESSG= 12 'bright red
360 INPT= 14 'yellow
370 GOTO 500 'Color-Monitor connected
380 :
390 '---------- Determine Colors for Mono-Display --------------------
400 :
410 BG    = 0 'black
420 TEXT= 7 'light gray
430 MESSG= 15 'white
440 INPT= 15 'white
450 :
460 '-----------------------------------------------------------------
470 'Construct template
480 '-----------------------------------------------------------------
490 :
```

```
500 OUT &H3D9,BG 'background
510 COLOR TEXT,BG
520 CLS:LOCATE CSRLIN,POS(0),0
530 PRINT "┌";STRING$(78,"-");"┐";
540 PRINT "| DSKETK V2.00";SPC(44);COPYR$;" █";
550 PRINT "└";STRING$(78,"■");"█";
560 LOCATE 5,1,0
570 COLOR BG,TEXT:PRINT "<Tab>";:COLOR TEXT,BG:PRINT ".......frame +"
580 COLOR BG,TEXT:PRINT "s<Tab>";:COLOR TEXT,BG:PRINT "......frame -"
590 COLOR BG,TEXT:PRINT "<Esc>";:COLOR TEXT,BG:PRINT ".......End"
600 COLOR BG,TEXT:PRINT "<F1>";:COLOR TEXT,BG:PRINT "........Print "
610 COLOR BG,TEXT:PRINT "<F2>";:COLOR TEXT,BG:PRINT "........Font +"
620 COLOR BG,TEXT:PRINT "s<F2>";:COLOR TEXT,BG:PRINT ".......Font -"
630 COLOR BG,TEXT:PRINT "<F3>";:COLOR TEXT,BG:PRINT ".......Number +1"
640 COLOR BG,TEXT:PRINT "<sF3>";:COLOR TEXT,BG:PRINT "......Number +10"
650 COLOR BG,TEXT:PRINT "<F4>";:COLOR TEXT,BG:PRINT ".......Number -1"
660 COLOR BG,TEXT:PRINT "<sF4>";:COLOR TEXT,BG:PRINT "......Number -10"
670 COLOR BG,TEXT:PRINT "<Return";:COLOR TEXT,BG:PRINT ".... field forward "
680 COLOR BG,TEXT:PRINT "c<Return>";:COLOR TEXT,BG:PRINT "..field backwards "
690 COLOR BG,TEXT:PRINT "<Home>";:COLOR TEXT,BG:PRINT "....first field "
700 COLOR BG,TEXT:PRINT "<End>";:COLOR TEXT,BG:PRINT ".......last field "
710 COLOR BG,TEXT:PRINT "c<Home>";:COLOR TEXT,BG:PRINT "...erase field "
720 COLOR BG,TEXT:PRINT "c<LeftCurs>";:COLOR TEXT,BG:PRINT ".beginning of field "
730 COLOR BG,TEXT:PRINT "c<RghtCurs>";:COLOR TEXT,BG:PRINT ".end of field "
740 PRINT:PRINT "'s' = <shift> and  'c' = <Ctrl>"
750 :
760 '---------- Display label strip -----------------------
770 :
780 COLOR BG,TEXT:CL=31
790 LOCATE  7,CL:PRINT "|o|";SPC(PRNT.CHAR(FONT));"|o|"
800 LOCATE  8,CL:PRINT "|o|";SPC(PRNT.CHAR(FONT));"|o|"
810 LOCATE  9,CL:PRINT "|o|";STRING$(PRNT.CHAR(FONT),"-");"|o|"
820 LOCATE 10,CL:PRINT "|o|";SPC(PRNT.CHAR(FONT));"|o|"
830 LOCATE 11,CL:PRINT "|o|";SPC(PRNT.CHAR(FONT));"|o|"
840 LOCATE 12,CL:PRINT "|o|";SPC(PRNT.CHAR(FONT));"|o|"
850 LOCATE 13,CL:PRINT "|o|";SPC(PRNT.CHAR(FONT));"|o|"
860 LOCATE 14,CL:PRINT "|o|";SPC(PRNT.CHAR(FONT));"|o|"
870 LOCATE 15,CL:PRINT "|o|";SPC(PRNT.CHAR(FONT));"|o|"
880 LOCATE 16,CL:PRINT "|o|";SPC(PRNT.CHAR(FONT));"|o|"
890 LOCATE 17,CL:PRINT "|o|";SPC(PRNT.CHAR(FONT));"|o|"
900 LOCATE 18,CL:PRINT "|o|";STRING$(PRNT.CHAR(FONT),"-");"|o|"
910 LOCATE 19,CL:PRINT "|o|";SPC(PRNT.CHAR(FONT));"|o|"
920 LOCATE 20,CL:PRINT "|o|";SPC(PRNT.CHAR(FONT));"|o|"
930 LOCATE 21,CL:PRINT "|o|";SPC(PRNT.CHAR(FONT));"|o|"
940 LOCATE 22,CL:PRINT "|o|";SPC(PRNT.CHAR(FONT));"|o|"
950 COLOR TEXT,BG
960 :
970 '----- input control ------------------------------
980 :
990 GOSUB 1790 'Output label frame depending  on 'FRAME'
1000 FIELD.NUM= 1
1010 IF FIELD.NUM(FIELD.NUM,1)= 0 AND ONKEY= CR THEN 1140 'one field ahead
1020 IF FIELD.NUM(FIELD.NUM,1)= 0 AND ONKEY= CCR THEN 1150 'one field back
```

```
1030 IF FIELD.NUM(FIELD.NUM,1)= 0 THEN ONKEY= CR:GOTO 1140 'one field ahead
1040 LOCATE FIELD.NUM(FIELD.NUM,1),FIELD.NUM(FIELD.NUM,2),1,0,31:COLOR INPT,BG
1050 X$=INKEY$:IF X$="" THEN 1050
1060 'LOCATE 24,1:PRINT ASC(X$),ASC(RIGHT$(X$,1))
1070 if LEN(X$)= 2 then 1200
1080 :
1090 '---------- ASCII-keys ----------------------------------
1100 :
1110 ONKEY= ASC(X$)
1120 IF ONKEY= ESC THEN COLOR 7,0:OUT &H3D9,0:CLS:END
1130 IF ONKEY= NTAB THEN FRAME= FRAME+1:GOSUB 1790:GOTO 1010 'Output label frame
1140 IF ONKEY=  CR THEN GOSUB 1460:GOTO 1010 'Test field position, field +
1150 IF ONKEY= CCR THEN GOSUB 1560:GOTO 1010 'Test field position, field -
1160 IF ONKEY>= 32 AND ONKEY <256 THEN PRINT CHR$(ONKEY);
1170 IF POS(0)>= FIELD.NUM(FIELD.NUM,2)+FIELD.NUM(FIELD.NUM,3) THEN BEEP:ONKEY= CR:GOTO
     1140 'one field ahead, when field full
1180 GOTO 1050
1190 :
1200 '---------- control and function keys --------------------
1210 :
1220 ONKEY= ASC(RIGHT$(X$,1))
1230 IF ONKEY= SHIFTTAB THEN FRAME= FRAME-1:GOSUB 1790:GOTO 1010 'SH-TAB, label frame
1240 IF ONKEY= CRSR.UP    THEN ONKEY= CCR:GOTO 1150 'one field back
1250 IF ONKEY= CRSR.DOWN THEN ONKEY=  CR:GOTO 1140 'one field forward
1260 IF ONKEY= F1 THEN 2750 'Print
1270 IF ONKEY= F2 THEN GOSUB 1660:FONT= FONT+1:IF FONT> 3 THEN FONT=1
1280 IF ONKEY= SF2 THEN GOSUB 1660:FONT= FONT-1:IF FONT< 1 THEN FONT=3
1290 IF ONKEY= F2 OR ONKEY= SF2 THEN 760 'Construct Display with changed Font
1300 IF ONKEY= F3 AND NUMBER< 999 THEN NUMBER=NUMBER+1:GOSUB 2580
1310 IF ONKEY= F4 AND NUMBER>   1 THEN NUMBER=NUMBER-1:GOSUB 2580
1320 IF ONKEY= SF3 AND NUMBER+10< 999 THEN NUMBER=NUMBER+10:GOSUB 2580
1330 IF ONKEY= SF4 AND NUMBER-10>=  1 THEN NUMBER=NUMBER-10:GOSUB 2580
1340 IF ONKEY= CRSR.RIGHT AND POS(0)< FIELD.NUM(FIELD.NUM,2)+FIELD.NUM(FIELD.NUM,3)-1 THEN
     LOCATE CSRLIN,POS(0)+1
1350 IF ONKEY= CRSR.RIGHT AND POS(0)= FIELD.NUM(FIELD.NUM,2)+FIELD.NUM(FIELD.NUM,3)-1 THEN
     ONKEY= CR:GOTO 1140 'one field ahead
1360 IF ONKEY= CRSR.LEFT AND POS(0)> FIELD.NUM(FIELD.NUM,2) THEN LOCATE CSRLIN,POS(0)-1
1370 IF ONKEY= CRSR.LEFT AND POS(0)= FIELD.NUM(FIELD.NUM,2) THEN ONKEY= CCR: GOTO 1150
     'one field back
1380 IF ONKEY= HOME THEN GOSUB 1660:FIELD.NUM= 1:GOTO 1010
1390 IF ONKEY= ENDE AND FIELD.NUM(7,1)= 0 THEN GOSUB 1660:FIELD.NUM= 6:GOTO 1010
1400 IF ONKEY= ENDE THEN GOSUB 1660:FIELD.NUM= 7:GOTO 1010
1410 IF ONKEY= CHOME THEN LOCATE FIELD.NUM(FIELD.NUM,1),FIELD.NUM(FIELD.NUM,2),0:PRINT
     SPACE$(FIELD.NUM(FIELD.NUM,3));::PRNT$(FIELD.NUM)="":GOTO 1010
1420 IF ONKEY= C.RIGHT THEN LOCATE CSRLIN,FIELD.NUM(FIELD.NUM,2)+FIELD.NUM(FIELD.NUM,3)-
     1:GOTO 1050
1430 IF ONKEY= C.LEFT  THEN LOCATE CSRLIN,FIELD.NUM(FIELD.NUM,2):GOTO 1050
1440 GOTO 1050
1450 :
1460 '-----------------------------------------------------------
1470 'Test field positioning, field +
1480 '-----------------------------------------------------------
1490 :
```

```
1500 GOSUB 1660
1510 FIELD.NUM= FIELD.NUM+1
1520 IF FIELD.NUM= 7 AND FRAME< 8 THEN FIELD.NUM= 1:RETURN
1530 IF FIELD.NUM> 7 THEN FIELD.NUM= 1:RETURN
1540 RETURN
1550 :
1560 '---------------------------------------------------------------
1570 'Test field positioning, field -
1580 '---------------------------------------------------------------
1590 :
1600 GOSUB 1660
1610 FIELD.NUM= FIELD.NUM-1
1620 IF FIELD.NUM< 1 AND FRAME< 8 THEN FIELD.NUM= 6:RETURN
1630 IF FIELD.NUM< 1 AND FRAME> 7 THEN FIELD.NUM= 7:RETURN
1640 RETURN
1650 :
1660 '---------------------------------------------------------------
1670 'Read in field content in PRNT$(FIELD.NUM)
1680 '---------------------------------------------------------------
1690 :
1700 IF FIELD.NUM(FIELD.NUM,1)= 0 THEN RETURN
1710 PRNT$(FIELD.NUM)= ""
1720 LOCATE CSRLIN,POS(0),0
1730 FOR I= 0 TO FIELD.NUM(FIELD.NUM,3)-1
1740   PRNT$(FIELD.NUM)= PRNT$(FIELD.NUM)+ CHR$(SCREEN(CSRLIN,FIELD.NUM(FIELD.NUM,2)+I))
1750 NEXT I
1760 LOCATE CSRLIN,POS(0),1,0,31
1770 RETURN
1780 :
1790 '---------------------------------------------------------------
1800 'Output label frame
1810 '---------------------------------------------------------------
1820 :
1830 IF FRAME> 14 THEN FRAME= 1
1840 IF FRAME< 1 THEN FRAME= 14
1850 CL= 34:LOCATE CSRLIN,POS(0),0:COLOR TEXT,BG
1860 '----- Determine field position and length
1870 FIELD.NUM(1,1)= 11: FIELD.NUM(1,2)= 35                   'field 1
1880 FIELD.NUM(1,3)= PRNT.CHAR(FONT)-6
1890 FIELD.NUM(2,1)= 11: FIELD.NUM(2,2)= 34+PRNT.CHAR(FONT)-4 'field 2
1900 FIELD.NUM(2,3)= 3
1910 FIELD.NUM(3,1)= 13: FIELD.NUM(3,2)= 35                   'field 3
1920 FIELD.NUM(3,3)= PRNT.CHAR(FONT)-2
1930 FIELD.NUM(4,1)= 14: FIELD.NUM(4,2)= 35                   'field 4
1940 FIELD.NUM(4,3)= PRNT.CHAR(FONT)-2
1950 FIELD.NUM(5,1)= 15: FIELD.NUM(5,2)= 35                   'field 5
1960 FIELD.NUM(5,3)= PRNT.CHAR(FONT)-2
1970 FIELD.NUM(6,1)= 16: FIELD.NUM(6,2)= 35                   'field 6
1980 FIELD.NUM(6,3)= PRNT.CHAR(FONT)-2
1990 FIELD.NUM(7,1)= 17: FIELD.NUM(7,2)= 34+PRNT.CHAR(FONT)-10 'field 7
2000 FIELD.NUM(7,3)= 8
2010 IF FRAME< 8 THEN FIELD.NUM(7,1)= 0 'No Data field
```

```
2020 ON FRAME GOSUB 2100,2190,2280,2370,2430,2490,2530, 2100,2190,2280,2370,2430,2490,2530
     'output frame
2030 COLOR INPT,BG
2040 FOR I= 1 TO 7
2050   IF FIELD.NUM(I,1)<> 0 THEN LOCATE FIELD.NUM(I,1),FIELD.NUM(I,2):PRINT
       LEFT$(PRNT$(I),FIELD.NUM(I,3));
2060 NEXT I
2070 COLOR TEXT,BG
2080 GOSUB 2580 'Display Values set
2090 RETURN
2100 LOCATE 10,CL:PRINT "┌";STRING$(PRNT.CHAR(FONT)-6,"-");"┌────┐"
2110 LOCATE 11,CL:PRINT "|";STRING$(PRNT.CHAR(FONT)-6," ");"|    |"
2120 LOCATE 12,CL:PRINT "├";STRING$(PRNT.CHAR(FONT)-6,"-");"└────┘"
2130 LOCATE 13,CL:PRINT "|";SPC(PRNT.CHAR(FONT)-2);"|"
2140 LOCATE 14,CL:PRINT "|";SPC(PRNT.CHAR(FONT)-2);"|"
2150 LOCATE 15,CL:PRINT "|";SPC(PRNT.CHAR(FONT)-2);"|"
2160 LOCATE 16,CL:PRINT "|";SPC(PRNT.CHAR(FONT)-2);"|"
2170 LOCATE 17,CL:IF FRAME= 1 OR FRAME= 4 OR FRAME= 7 THEN PRINT
       "L";STRING$(PRNT.CHAR(FONT)-2,"-");"┘" ELSE PRINT "L";STRING$(PRNT.CHAR(FONT)-
       12,"-");"┤       |┘"
2180 RETURN
2190 LOCATE 10,CL:PRINT "╔";STRING$(PRNT.CHAR(FONT)-6,"=");"╔═══╗"
2200 LOCATE 11,CL:PRINT "‖";STRING$(PRNT.CHAR(FONT)-6," ");"‖   ‖"
2210 LOCATE 12,CL:PRINT "╠";STRING$(PRNT.CHAR(FONT)-6,"=");"╚═══╝"
2220 LOCATE 13,CL:PRINT "‖";SPC(PRNT.CHAR(FONT)-2);"‖"
2230 LOCATE 14,CL:PRINT "‖";SPC(PRNT.CHAR(FONT)-2);"‖"
2240 LOCATE 15,CL:PRINT "‖";SPC(PRNT.CHAR(FONT)-2);"‖"
2250 LOCATE 16,CL:PRINT "‖";SPC(PRNT.CHAR(FONT)-2);"‖"
2260 LOCATE 17,CL:IF FRAME= 2 OR FRAME= 5 OR FRAME= 6 THEN PRINT
       "╚";STRING$(PRNT.CHAR(FONT)-2,"=");"╝" ELSE PRINT "╚";STRING$(PRNT.CHAR(FONT)-
       12,"=");"┤       ╝"
2270 RETURN
2280 LOCATE 10,CL:PRINT "┌";STRING$(PRNT.CHAR(FONT)-6,"-");"┌────┐"
2290 LOCATE 11,CL:PRINT "|";STRING$(PRNT.CHAR(FONT)-6," ");"█   █"
2300 LOCATE 12,CL:PRINT "├";STRING$(PRNT.CHAR(FONT)-6,"■");"█████"
2310 LOCATE 13,CL:PRINT "|";SPC(PRNT.CHAR(FONT)-2);"█"
2320 LOCATE 14,CL:PRINT "|";SPC(PRNT.CHAR(FONT)-2);"█"
2330 LOCATE 15,CL:PRINT "|";SPC(PRNT.CHAR(FONT)-2);"█"
2340 LOCATE 16,CL:PRINT "|";SPC(PRNT.CHAR(FONT)-2);"█"
2350 LOCATE 17,CL:IF FRAME= 3 THEN PRINT "L";STRING$(PRNT.CHAR(FONT)-2,"■");"█" ELSE PRINT
       "L";STRING$(PRNT.CHAR(FONT)-12,"■");"┤       █"
2360 RETURN
2370 LOCATE 10,CL:PRINT "┌";STRING$(PRNT.CHAR(FONT)-6,"-");"┌────┐"
2380 LOCATE 11,CL:PRINT "|";STRING$(PRNT.CHAR(FONT)-6," ");"|   |"
2390 LOCATE 12,CL:PRINT "L";STRING$(PRNT.CHAR(FONT)-6,"-");"└────┘"
2400 LOCATE 13,CL:PRINT "┌";STRING$(PRNT.CHAR(FONT)-2,"-");"┐"
2410 FIELD.NUM(3,1)= 0
2420 GOTO 2140 'lower part of simple frame
2430 LOCATE 10,CL:PRINT "╔";STRING$(PRNT.CHAR(FONT)-6,"=");"╔═══╗"
2440 LOCATE 11,CL:PRINT "‖";STRING$(PRNT.CHAR(FONT)-6," ");"‖   ‖"
2450 LOCATE 12,CL:PRINT "╚";STRING$(PRNT.CHAR(FONT)-6,"=");"╚═══╝"
2460 LOCATE 13,CL:PRINT "╔";STRING$(PRNT.CHAR(FONT)-2,"=");"╗"
2470 FIELD.NUM(3,1)= 0
```

```
2480 GOTO 2230 'lower part of double frame
2490 LOCATE 10,CL:PRINT "┌";STRING$(PRNT.CHAR(FONT)-6,"-");"┬────────┐"
2500 LOCATE 11,CL:PRINT "|";STRING$(PRNT.CHAR(FONT)-6," ");"│        │"
2510 LOCATE 12,CL:PRINT "└";STRING$(PRNT.CHAR(FONT)-6,"-");"┴────────┘"
2520 GOTO 2460 'lower part of double frame
2530 LOCATE 10,CL:PRINT "╔";STRING$(PRNT.CHAR(FONT)-6,"=");"╦════════╗"
2540 LOCATE 11,CL:PRINT "║";STRING$(PRNT.CHAR(FONT)-6," ");"║        ║"
2550 LOCATE 12,CL:PRINT "╚";STRING$(PRNT.CHAR(FONT)-6,"=");"╩════════╝"
2560 GOTO 2400 'lower part. simple frame
2570 :
2580 '-------------------------------------------------------------
2590 'Display Values set
2600 '-------------------------------------------------------------
2610 :
2620 OLD.ROWNO= CSRLIN:OLD.COLMNO= POS(0)
2630 LOCATE CSRLIN,POS(0),0
2640 CL= 34
2650 COLOR BG,TEXT
2660 LOCATE 19,CL:PRINT USING "Frame: ##";FRAME;
2670 IF FRAME> 7 THEN PRINT "/ date" ELSE PRINT "      "
2680 LOCATE   ,CL:PRINT      "Font:   ";FONT$(FONT)
2690 LOCATE   ,CL:PRINT USING "Character: ##";PRNT.CHAR(FONT)-2
2700 LOCATE   ,CL:PRINT USING "Number: ###";NUMBER
2710 COLOR TEXT,BG
2720 LOCATE OLD.ROWNO,OLD.COLMNO,1,0,31
2730 RETURN
2740 :
2750 '-------------------------------------------------------------
2760 'Print label
2770 '-------------------------------------------------------------
2780 :
2790 LOCATE 25,1,1: COLOR MESSG,BG:PRINT "Adjust label, strike any key, return
     to program with <Esc> --> ";:BEEP
2800 X$=INKEY$: IF X$="" THEN 2800
2810 IF X$=CHR$(27) THEN 2980
2820 LPRINT CHR$(18);CHR$(27);"@";CHR$(27);"x0";CHR$(27);"P";'P15 off, reset, NLQ off,
     Pica on
2830 LOCATE 25,1,1: COLOR MESSG,BG:PRINT "Printing, strike any key to
     interrupt.....";SPACE$(79-POS(0));:COLOR TEXT,BG
2840 IF FONT= 1 THEN LPRINT CHR$(15);
2850 IF FONT= 2 THEN LPRINT CHR$(27);"M";
2860 IF FONT= 3 THEN LPRINT CHR$(27);"P";
2870 LPRINT CHR$(27);"p0";CHR$(27);"x1"; 'Proportional off, NLQ on
2880 LOCATE CSRLIN,POS(0),0
2890 FOR PRNT=1 TO NUMBER
2900   FOR ROWNO= 10 TO 17:IF INKEY$<>"" THEN 2970
2910     FOR COLMNO= 34 TO 33+PRNT.CHAR(FONT):IF INKEY$<>"" THEN 2970
2920       CHAR$= CHR$(SCREEN(ROWNO,COLMNO)): IF CHAR$>= " " THEN LPRINT CHAR$;
2930     NEXT COLMNO
2940     LPRINT
2950   NEXT ROWNO
2960 NEXT PRNT
2970 LPRINT CHR$(18);CHR$(27);"@";CHR$(27);"x0" 'P15 off, reset, NLQ off
```

16. Help Functions and Error Handling

In the beginning programmers weren't very interested in help functions and error handling. The only error messages likely to be displayed were "wrong input" if the user entered the wrong data or "wrong key was activated" when an incorrect key was pressed. As the individual input fields and the assignment of available keys increased, so did the user's confusion.

The same confusion also occurred with error handling. For example, the same "File error" message appeared if the diskette wasn't inserted properly, was full or was write-protected. Since this message doesn't indicate exactly what's wrong, the user had to search through manuals to discover how to correct the problem.

Now, however, the success of an applications program depends on the user-friendliness of the help function and the error handling. By studying some applications from the last five years we can see how both of these features have developed.

Programmers eventually began to give the user more specific information on incorrect input and file access errors. Messages such as "Input can only consist of numbers" or "Only keys <F1> to <F5> are permitted" give the user more information about the type of error. For error handling, suggestions, such as "Diskette is full, insert another diskette" or "Please remove the write-protect" simplify the user's search for the source of the error.

Then windows were introduced. This development affected almost all programs. Even though the first implementations weren't perfect (i.e., the complete screen display had to be reconstructed after the help window was displayed), the user finally received some help. The following are examples of the suggestions in these windows:

```
┌── Input-Error: ───────────┐
│                           │
│ In this field only the numbers
│ 0, 1, 2, 3, 4, 5, 6, 7, 8 and 9,
│ the characters "+", "-" and the period
│  "." may be input.        │
│                           │
└── return with <Esc> ──────┘
```

or

```
┌── File-Error: ────────────┐
│                           │
│ The diskette you're using is write
│ protected. Please remove the write
│ protect tab and then strike <Return>
│ to continue. Strike the <Esc> key to
│ interrupt the procedure.  │
│                           │
└───────────────────────────┘
```

This information provides enough information about the error(s) and allow the program to continue once the input is repeated or the error is corrected. You may be wondering why these features weren't available earlier. There are two reasons for this:

1.   In the early days of PC programming, programmers didn't have the documentation required to use these features. Over the years, programmers gained the information needed to write user-friendly programs. For example, it wasn't possible to determine whether a monochrome or a color graphic card was installed in the PC. This information is needed in selecting the colors and display attributes. Only when this information became available through the BIOS data segment (starting at address &H0040:&H000), could the equipment flag be read with PEEK and the type of the video card could be determined (Section 11.1). So, the BIOS and DOS interrupts could only be used effectively when information about these interrupts was available and suitable interfaces could be developed.

2.   The users were responsible for many of the developments that occurred. Over time users began to demand more user-friendly programs. So, programmers and software vendors had to respond to the users' demands; otherwise their products wouldn't last on the market. Today, programs that don't include a user-friendly help function and error handling routine aren't popular.

16.1   Manuals vs. Help Functions and Error Handling

You may be wondering why so much effort is put into creating help and error handling routines. Obviously there are reference manuals which contain the same information. However, remember that as application programs became more complex, so did their reference manuals. It's very time consuming to consult reference manuals when a problem occurs or when encountering unknown errors. First you need to know where to find the explanation in the reference manual (or manuals, if there are several). Unfortunately these manuals don't always have a complete index or even table of contents. So usually several locations must be checked before locating the proper explanation.

Referring to manuals also interrupts the user's work with his/her project. Each time the user has to look for something in the manual, his/her concentration is interrupted. This not only frustrates the user, but may also make the user dislike the program.

From the user's viewpoint, a help function is a major advantage because the desired information is immediately available; searching through manuals isn't required. Also, the user's work isn't interrupted. Developing a help function is usually more work for the programmer even though this isn't always true, as we shall see later. By creating a help function, the programmer can devote less time to the reference manual because it will be limited to topics such as the installation, configuration for the available hardware and general information about the program.

16.2   What help features are available?

In a program, there are several ways to provide help for the user. Which one is used depends on the target group of users for whom this program was intended. For example, if you're writing an accounting program, the users will obviously be familiar with this subject. So including a familiar accounting topic in the help function isn't very effective.

The situation is completely different for a word processing application. Most likely the users never worked with this type of program or they used a completely different program. For example, consider a secretary who has only worked with a typewriter. Since word processing on a PC is completely different than using a typewriter, the help function must cover a lot of material. So, functions, such as setting the right margin or page breaks, must be explained in detail.

16.2.1 General Help

In this section we'll discuss a help function that provides general information about the program: its capabilities, functions and, if necessary, some error handling. This style of help function displays one or more help screens after activating the help key. Each screen covers a specific subject. For example, the first screen could explain the program's purpose, the second screen could present the available functions, the third screen could provide information about key assignments and a fourth screen could give suggestions for correcting errors.

The number of screens needed depends on the program's complexity. Suppose that your program contains over thirty help screens. From the viewpoint of the user, this is similar to using the reference manuals and "paging" through each help screen until locating the desired information.

This type of help feature can easily be programmed. Activating the help key opens a sequential text file where text can be found by using a word processor or editor. A screen is displayed and then the program waits for another key to be pressed before displaying the next screen. This process is continued until the complete file has been displayed. Usually it isn't possible to page through the file backwards.

16.2.2 Context-Sensitive Help

Suppose you're working with a word processor program and are having difficulties defining addresses with form letters. Among other fields, there is a "country codes" field. Since you're not familiar with the term country code, you'll need to press the help key. After pressing the help key, a help screen appears providing information about the subject you're currently working on. For example, the following display shows this function of the "country codes":

```
 ┌── Country Codes: ──────────────────────────┐
 │                                            │
 │ For a correct address, the mail to a       │
 │ foreign customer must show the code        │
 │ for the country in the address field       │
 │ Please enter the proper code for the       │
 │ country as follows:                        │
 │                                            │
 │ D   - Germany                              │
 │ A   - Austria                              │
 │ USA - United States of America             │
 │ I   - Italy                                │
 │             ...                            │
 └── return with <Esc> ───────────────────────┘
```

The user can immediately continue working after the help message is displayed. Although this type of help function requires complex programming, it's not more complicated than other help functions. We'll describe context-sensitive help in detail in Section 16.3.

16.2.3 Automatic Help

So far we've discussed help functions that are only activated when the help key is pressed. There are some types of help screens which automatically appear on the screen providing necessary information on the selected application or option. Although perhaps more of an inconvenience to experienced users, this type of help function increases a program's user-friendliness for new users.

An example of automatic help is a help function displayed in the status line. Refer to Section 16.2.5 for more information.

16.2.4 Help in the Menu

In Chapter 11 we discussed the various kinds of menus. Usually menu options consist of one or more words which explain the functions behind it.

In these cases, a menu help should be used. For each menu option there is a brief explanation, which describes what is located behind it or what the function does. This menu help can contain up to three lines and appear at a specific location on the screen. This location in many programs is the bottom line.

The following program demonstrates how to use a menu help. The program's construction is similar to the B_MENU.BAS program, presented in Chapter 11, for implementing menu bars. Refer to Chapter 11 for a complete explanation. The functions that were added for the menu help are explained in the listing:

Note: In order to execute the following program correctly, you must call PC-BASIC with the /M switch as follows:

```
GWBASIC /M:54000
```

```
10  '---------------------------------------------------
20  'MENUHELP.BAS   Menu/Help Demonstration
30  '---------------------------------------------------
40  :
50  DEFINT A-Z
60  OPTION BASE 0
70  CLS:KEY OFF:FOR I=1 TO 10:KEY I,"":NEXT I
80  MP.START= &HE000
90  GOSUB 2050 'initialize MP
100 SAVESCRN= MP.START
110 RESTSCRN= MP.START+3
120 FASTSCRN= MP.START+6
130 FALSE= 0: TRUE= NOT FALSE
140 MAX.SCN= 3:DIM BUFFER%(2000*MAX.SCN)
150 MAX.MENU= 8: DIM MENU$(MAX.MENU),MENU.HELP$(MAX.MENU,3)
```

The text for the menu help is stored in the MENU.HELP$() array. This array is dimensioned in line 150. Three lines of menu help are available for each option.

```
160 CUR.SCN= 0
170 WNDW.BKG= 112: MESSG.BKG= 127: HDFT.TXT= 7: WDW.HELP= 112
```

The WDW.HELP variable determines the color and attribute display of the menu help.

```
180 BKG.CHAR$= CHR$(177): BKG.COLR= 15
190 :
200 RESTORE 220
210 FOR I= 0 TO MAX.MENU:READ MENU$(I):NEXT I
220 DATA " MAIN MENU "
230 DATA "Input mask"
240 DATA "Add records"
250 DATA "Search"
260 DATA "Change"
270 DATA "List"
280 DATA "Import"
290 DATA "Export"
300 DATA "End"
310 :
320 FOR I= 1 TO MAX.MENU
330   FOR K= 1 TO 3
340     READ X$
350     MENU.HELP$(I,K) = X$ + SPACE$(70-(LEN(X$)))
360   NEXT K
370 NEXT I
380 :
```

In the loop, starting at line 320, the text for the menu help is read from the data lines (starting at line 390) into the MENU.HELP$() array. Each line remains the same length (line 350) so that, during later displays, there won't be any characters from the previous display. Instead, they're overwritten by spaces.

```
390 DATA "Prepare a mask to input data. At the same time the"
400 DATA "file is created for saving the data."
410 DATA " "
420 :
430 DATA "Adds new data/records to the file. Also tests file"
440 DATA "to prevent double entries."
450 DATA " "
460 :
470 DATA "Searches for and displays data from the file."
480 DATA "You cannot make changes or delete records in this option."
490 DATA " "
500 :
510 DATA "Displays data/records from the file. You can make changes"
520 DATA "to the data or delete entire records."
530 DATA " "
540 :
550 DATA "Use this option for a hardcopy according to"
560 DATA "various criteria. You can also determine"
565 DATA "search and sort sequences using this option."
570 DATA " "
580 :
590 DATA "Import (read-in) data from other databases or other "
600 DATA "file management programs. You can specify how"
610 DATA "the foreign file is read using this option."
620 :
630 DATA "Export (send) data to other databases or other "
640 DATA "file management programs. The record format is preset."
650 DATA " "
660 :
670 DATA "Terminate the program. The program saves any changes or"
680 DATA "additions you make to the file."
690 DATA " "
700 :
```

In these data lines you'll find text for the menu help. A maximum of three lines has been provided for each menu option. For clarity, blank lines have been created with a blank string "" instead of blank characters.

```
710 WD.ROW= 1: WD.COLM= 1: WD.LGTH= 80: WD.HGT= 25
720 GOSUB 1560 'initialize background
730 RW= 1: CL= 1: X$= " File Management V1.00 (C) 1987 H.-J. Bomanns "
740 DEF SEG: CALL FASTSCRN(RW,CL,MESSG.BKG,X$)
750 :
760 GOSUB 1090 'menu-selection
770 IF MENU= 0 THEN MENU = 8 '<Shift> <End>
780 GOSUB 1910 'store screen display
790 ON MENU GOSUB 830,850,870,980,1000,1020,1040,1060
800 GOSUB 1980 'restore screen display
810 GOTO 760 'query menu again
820 :
830 '----- input mask -----
840 RETURN
```

```
850 '----- add records -----
860 RETURN
870 '----- search -----
880 WD.ROW= 8: WD.COLM= 30: WD.LGTH= 40: WD.HGT= 3:WD.SHADOW= TRUE
890 WD.HEAD$= MENU$(MENU): WD.FOOT$= "<F1> = Help"
900 GOSUB 1640 'display window
910 RW= WD.ROW+2: CL= WD.COLM+2: X$= "Search criteria:"
920 DEF SEG:CALL FASTSCRN(RW,CL,WNDW.BKG,X$)
930 LOCATE WD.ROW+2,WD.COLM+18,1
940 RW=25: CL= 1: X$= "Input search criteria, <Return> to begin search <Esc> to
    end": X$= X$+SPACE$(80-LEN(X$))
950 DEF SEG:CALL FASTSCRN(RW,CL,MESSG.BKG,X$)
960 IF INKEY$= "" THEN 960
970 RETURN
980 '----- change -----
990 RETURN
1000 '----- list -----
1010 RETURN
1020 '----- import -----
1030 RETURN
1040 '----- export -----
1050 RETURN
1060 '----- end -----
1070 COLOR 7,0:CLS:PRINT "*** END ***":PRINT:END
1080 :
1090 '----- display menu and control selection -----
1100 :
1110 MAX.LGTH= 0
1120 FOR I=0 TO MAX.MENU
1130   IF LEN(MENU$(I)) > MAX.LGTH THEN MAX.LGTH= LEN(MENU$(I))
1140 NEXT I
1150 WD.ROW= 5: WD.COLM= 10: WD.SHADOW= FALSE
1160 WD.LGTH= MAX.LGTH+6: WD.HGT= MAX.MENU+2
1170 WD.HEAD$= MENU$(0):WD.FOOT$= "<F1> = help"
1180 GOSUB 1640 'display window
1190 CL= WD.COLM+3
1200 FOR I= 1 TO MAX.MENU
1210   RW= WD.ROW+I+1
1220   DEF SEG:CALL FASTSCRN(RW,CL,WNDW.BKG,MENU$(I))
1230 NEXT I
1240 RW=25: CL= 1: X$= "Use <Cursor Up> and <Cursor Down> to select, <Return>
     to execute <Esc> to end": X$= X$+SPACE$(80-LEN(X$))
1250 DEF SEG:CALL FASTSCRN(RW,CL,MESSG.BKG,X$)
1260 HDFT.ROW= 1: CL= WD.COLM+1: ONKEY$= "": LOCATE ,,0
1270 GOSUB 1910 'store screen display
```

Before the keyboard query, the (still empty) screen is saved. By doing this, a new screen doesn't have to be created after a routine is completed. Otherwise the previous menu help text would remain visible.

```
1280 WHILE ONKEY$<> CHR$(27) AND ONKEY$<> CHR$(13)
1290   RW= WD.ROW+HDFT.ROW+1
1300   Y$= "  "+MENU$(HDFT.ROW) : Y$= Y$+SPACE$(MAX.LGTH+6-LEN(Y$))
1310   DEF SEG:CALL FASTSCRN(RW,CL,HDFT.TXT,Y$)
1320   GOSUB 1480 'display menu-Help
```

After the cursor is located on the current menu option, the routine for displaying the menu help (line 1320) is called.

```
1330   ONKEY$= INKEY$:IF ONKEY$= "" THEN 1330
1340   DEF SEG:CALL FASTSCRN(RW,CL,WNDW.BKG,Y$)
1350   IF ONKEY$= CHR$(27) THEN MENU= 0
1360   IF ONKEY$= CHR$(13) THEN MENU= HDFT.ROW
1370   ONKEY= ASC(RIGHT$(ONKEY$,1))
1380   IF ONKEY= 72 THEN HDFT.ROW= HDFT.ROW-1 'Cursor up
1390   IF ONKEY= 80 THEN HDFT.ROW= HDFT.ROW+1 'Cursor down
1400   IF ONKEY= 71 THEN HDFT.ROW= 1 '<Home>
1410   IF ONKEY= 79 THEN HDFT.ROW= MAX.MENU
1420   IF HDFT.ROW < 1 THEN HDFT.ROW= MAX.MENU
1430   IF HDFT.ROW > MAX.MENU THEN HDFT.ROW= 1
1440 WEND
1450 GOSUB 1980 'restore screen display
```

The screen display is restored again once the "End" option or other menu option is selected. This clears the previous menu help and immediately displays the next template.

```
1460 RETURN
1470 :
1480 '----- menu-Help display -----
1490 :
1500 MH.CL= 3
1510 FOR I= 1 TO 3
1520   MH.RW= I+20
1530   CALL FASTSCRN(MH.RW,MH.CL,WDW.HELP,MENU.HELP$(HDFT.ROW,I))
1540 NEXT I
1550 RETURN
```

The routine starting at line 1480 takes over the output of the menu help. Since all lines are brought to the same length (line 350), all possible lines (in this case, three) can be sequentially output in a loop.

```
1560 '----- initialize background -----
1570 :
1580 X$= STRING$(WD.LGTH,BKG.CHAR$)
1590 FOR RW= WD.ROW TO WD.ROW+WD.HGT
1600   CALL FASTSCRN(RW,WD.COLM,BKG.COLR,X$)
1610 NEXT RW
1620 RETURN
1630 :
1640 '----- Universal-Routine for window -----
```

```
1650 :
1660 X$= CHR$(218)+STRING$(WD.LGTH%,CHR$(196))+CHR$(191)
1670 DEF SEG:CALL FASTSCRN(WD.ROW,WD.COLM,WNDW.BKG,X$)
1680 X$= CHR$(179)+STRING$(WD.LGTH%," ")+CHR$(179)
1690 IF WD.SHADOW THEN X$= X$+CHR$(178)+CHR$(178)
1700 FOR W.RW= WD.ROW+1 TO WD.ROW+WD.HGT
1710   DEF SEG:CALL FASTSCRN(W.RW,WD.COLM,WNDW.BKG,X$)
1720 NEXT W.RW
1730 X$= CHR$(192)+STRING$(WD.LGTH%,CHR$(196))+CHR$(217)
1740 IF WD.SHADOW THEN X$= X$+CHR$(178)+CHR$(178)
1750 RW= WD.ROW+WD.HGT+1
1760 DEF SEG:CALL FASTSCRN(RW,WD.COLM,WNDW.BKG,X$)
1770 IF WD.HEAD$= "" THEN 1810 'continue with footer
1780   X$= " "+WD.HEAD$+" "
1790   W.CL= WD.COLM+3
1800   CALL FASTSCRN(WD.ROW,W.CL,HDFT.TXT,X$)
1810 IF WD.FOOT$= "" THEN 1850 'continue with WD.SHADOW
1820   X$= " "+WD.FOOT$+" "
1830   W.RW= WD.ROW+WD.HGT+1:W.CL= WD.COLM+3
1840   CALL FASTSCRN(W.RW,W.CL,HDFT.TXT,X$)
1850 IF NOT WD.SHADOW THEN 1890 'back
1860   X$= STRING$(WD.LGTH+2,CHR$(178))
1870   W.RW= WD.ROW+WD.HGT+2:W.CL= WD.COLM+2
1880   CALL FASTSCRN(W.RW,W.CL,WNDW.BKG,X$)
1890 RETURN
1900 :
1910 '----- store current screen display -----
1920 :
1930 IF CUR.SCN= MAX.SCN THEN BEEP:RETURN
1940 DEF SEG:BUFFER.OFS%= VARPTR(BUFFER%(CUR.SCN*2000)):CALL
     SAVESCRN(BUFFER.OFS%)
1950 CUR.SCN= CUR.SCN+1
1960 RETURN
1970 :
1980 '----- restore last screen display -----
1990 :
2000 IF CUR.SCN= 0 THEN BEEP:RETURN
2010 CUR.SCN= CUR.SCN-1
2020 DEF SEG:BUFFER.OFS%= VARPTR(BUFFER%(CUR.SCN*2000)):CALL
     RESTSCRN(BUFFER.OFS%)
2030 RETURN
2040 :
2050 'data-lines from COM-file: screen.com
2060 :
2070 RESTORE 2090
2080 DEF SEG:FOR I=1 TO  227:READ X:POKE MP.START+I-1,X: NEXT I
2090 DATA 235,109,144,235,109,144, 85,139,236, 30,  6
2100 DATA 139,118, 12,138, 28,176,160,246,227, 45,160
2110 DATA   0, 80,139,118, 10,138, 28,176,  2,246,227
2120 DATA  91,  3,195, 72, 72, 80,139,118,  8,138, 36
2130 DATA 139,118,  6,138, 12,181,  0,139,116,  1, 80
2140 DATA 191,  0,176,179,  0,205, 17, 37, 48,  0, 61
2150 DATA  48,  0,116,  6,129,199,  0,  8,179,  1,142
```

```
2160 DATA 199,  88,  95,252,186,218,   3,128,251,   0,116
2170 DATA  11,236,208,216,114,246,250,236,208,216,115
2180 DATA 251,172,251,171,226,235,   7, 31, 93,202,  8
2190 DATA   0,235,  41,144,  85,139,236, 30,   6,139,118
2200 DATA   6,139,   4,139,240,191,   0,176,179,   0,205
2210 DATA  17,  37,  48,   0,  61,  48,   0,116,   6,129,199
2220 DATA   0,   8,179,   1,142,199,  51,255,235,  40,144
2230 DATA  85,139,236,  30,   6,139,118,   6,139,   4,139
2240 DATA 248,  30,   7,190,   0,176,179,   0,205,  17,  37
2250 DATA  48,   0,  61,  48,   0,116,   6,129,198,   0,  8
2260 DATA 179,   1,142,222,  51,246,185,208,   7,252,186
2270 DATA 218,   3,128,251,   0,116,  11,236,208,216,114
2280 DATA 246,250,236,208,216,115,251,173,251,171,226
2290 DATA 235,   7,  31,  93,202,   2,   0
2300 RETURN
```

16.2.5 Help in the Status Line

The status line, which is usually the last screen line (25), provides additional automatic help. This line displays suggestions for various procedures. This is the location where many applications display the current program status. There are times when the program executes in the background without the user knowing that any action is occurring. Some actions are very fast and others require several seconds or perhaps even minutes. This is the time when the user may wonder whether the program is still working or if it has crashed.

A simple message in the status line can prevent any confusion. For example, if a large file is being loaded or saved, the user can be informed of this with the message:

```
One moment please, file loading ...
```

Such messages can also be used in other applications in which the user may think that the program could have crashed. Implementing this is simple. The text for the status line is stored, for example, in a variable named STATUS$. A subroutine displays the text:

```
100 .....
110 STATUS$= "One moment please, file loading ..."
120 GOSUB 500 'Status-Line display
130 OPEN "ADDRESS.DAT" FOR INPUT AS #2
140 I= 1
150 WHILE NOT EOF(2)
160   INPUT#2, TEXT$(I)
170   I=I+1
180 WEND
190 CLOSE #2
200 STATUS$= "" 'erase Status-Line
210 GOSUB 500 'display Status-Line
220 .....
500 '----- display Status-Line -----
510 :
```

```
520 LOCATE 25,1,0
530 PRINT STATUS$;SPACE$(80-POS(0));
540 RETURN
550 :
560 .....
```

You can use the status line to display not only the current program status but also input instructions, important keys or other information:

```
Please input a number between 1 and 99
```

or

```
<F1> = Help, <F10> = store, <Esc> = terminate function
```

16.2.6 Plausibility Test

A help function that is often overlooked is the *plausibility test*. Often you may have wondered about the strange results produced by some calculations. A plausibility test checks for certain conditions. If there's a problem or inconsistency, the test informs the user so that they can correct the problem. As an example, let's use a program that calculates the total price for finished plywood sheets based on thickness, price per square foot and the dimensions of the sheet:

```
Wood: sheet raw, 3" thick, price for square foot $14.95
Cut:  32 inches by 53 inches.
```

This is actually a simple calculation. However, if you forget to enter the decimal point while entering the square foot price, the result will be very expensive sheets of wood. These errors are avoided with a simple plausibility test and a note to the user:

```
10 '---------------------------------------------------
20 'PLAUSIBL.BAS  Plausibility Test Demo
30 '---------------------------------------------------
40 :
50 CLS:KEY OFF
60 MAX.TYPES= 5
70 DIM WOOD$(MAX.TYPES),PRICE!(MAX.TYPES)
80 RESTORE 100
90 FOR I= 1 TO MAX.TYPES:READ WOOD$(I),PRICE!(I):NEXT I
100 DATA "1.5",8.95,"2.0",12.95,"2.5",14.95,"2.75",17.45,"3.0",21.35
110 :
120 PRINT "Calculation for cutting sheets "
130 LOCATE 5,5:INPUT "Thickness of the plate (1.5" to 3")";THICK$
140 FOR I=1 TO MAX.TYPES
150   IF THICK$= WOOD$(I) THEN 200 'Everything OK, continue
160 NEXT I
170 LOCATE 25,1:PRINT "Wrong thickness indicated ...";:BEEP
180 GOTO 130
190 :
200 SIZE= I
```

```
210 LOCATE 7,5:INPUT "Price per square foot:";INP.PRICE!
220 IF (INP.PRICE! >= PRICE!(SIZE)-2.5) AND (INP.PRICE! <= PRICE!(SIZE)+2.5) THEN
280
230 LOCATE 25,1
240 PRINT "Price isn't within allowable limits: ";
250 PRINT USING "##.## - ##.## - ##.##";PRICE!(SIZE)-
2.5;PRICE!(SIZE);PRICE!(SIZE)+2.5;
260 BEEP:GOTO 210
270 :
280 '----- calculation starts here... -----
290 :
```

This routine stores the possible thickness of the sheets and the normal price for each square foot. The values are stored in data lines and starting at line 90 read into the WOOD$ and PRICE! arrays with a loop. After line 140 the first plausibility test is performed on the thickness of the sheet in line 130. If it's determined, in the FOR...NEXT loop, that the correct thickness was entered, the square foot price is queried at line 200. Otherwise a message is displayed and the input is requested again (lines 170/180).

The price from line 210 is tested for plausibility. A price of $2.50 more or less than $14.95 will be accepted. It's also possible that the sheet could be scratched or a corner broken off. If there is some damage to the wood, the price may be reduced. The calculation/query occurs in line 220. If the entered price is within the acceptable range (+/- $2.50), the branch to the calculation routine occurs. Otherwise, another message, which lists the limits and the standard price for the sheets, is displayed. These plausibility tests should be used in applications in which figures are important (i.e., inventory control, sales figures).

16.3   Implementing a Help Function

In this section we'll discuss implementing user-friendly help functions in your own programs. However, first we'll give you some background information on help functions. We'll use a context-sensitive help. As an example, let's use a database for addresses which contain the following fields:

last name
first name
street
city/state
ZIP code
country code
telephone

The data input for the individual fields occurs in a common input routine, as discussed in Chapter 12.

Help Key

Which key is defined as a help key is the programmer's decision. However, you should consider what keys are available. Most of the major software manufacturers use the <F1> key. In some cases, the combinations <Alt><H> or <Alt></?> are used for the help key. In programs using a mouse, a symbol to call the help function should be available at a fixed location on the screen. This symbol is usually a question mark. By using these keys, users will be able to access the help function in your program easily.

Now let's return to the input routine. The interception of the help key and the subsequent call of the help function are critical to the entire program. The only remaining task is to tell the help function which help screen to display. This is easily accomplished. All that is needed for the entire program is one global variable to store a number. Every function that is called receives an incremented number, called HELP.NUMBER, which it stores in this variable. If the help function is called, it can recognize, on the basis of the number stored in HELP.NUMBER, which function is now active and display the appropriate help screen.

Querying the help key with ON KEY GOSUB

You may be wondering why the query of the help key doesn't occur through the interrupt programming of ON KEY GOSUB. This is because each program, whether ON KEY, ON COM or something similar, results in PC-BASIC having to perform some tests. Obviously this takes time. Since the universal input routine could be used under another editor, it could interrupt the input, at least on a slow PC. In other words, if a long line is entered, the INKEY$ function is frequently interrupted by the interrupt query. This could delay the display of characters on the screen.

Assigning the Help Text

Now we must assign the help text. There are two ways to do this:

1.   As in the example for menu help, the text can be stored in the two-dimensional array, HELP.TEXT$(). On the basis of HELP.NUMBER, the needed lines are read from the array and displayed. This solution is only practical with smaller programs. Usually three lines aren't enough for a help function. There are certain situations where up to twenty lines are needed; although this many lines would require too much memory.

2.   The second, and better, solution consists of storing the individual help messages in a random file. HELP.NUMBER acts as access criterion since it corresponds to the record number. During the programming, every function, including every field entry, is assigned a number. In order to do this you should create a flow chart (refer to Chapter 10), in which all the functions are recorded. After this the functions are numbered. The help file is created after the programming is completed (and eventual changes in the numbers). We'll present more information about this later (Section 16.3.1).

Let's review what we've discussed:

•   Help is always called with the same key for all functions. We'll use the <F1> key.

•   The query of the help key must occur at a central location in the program. It's best to use a global variable.

•   In order to access help, every function is assigned its own number. This number is stored in the HELP.NUMBER variable. Each function must contain a statement which sets this number.

•   The help text is prepared and displayed through one central help function.

•   The individual help texts are stored in a random file. The record number is identical to the HELP.NUMBER in the program. A special editor is used for the input of the text into this help file (see Section 16.3.1).

The following graphic should illustrate this process:

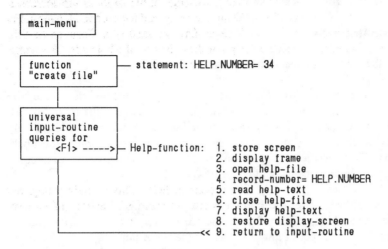

Fig. 37: Help Function Design

The "create file" function is called from the main menu. This function sets the HELP.NUMBER to 34 and calls the universal input routine so the user can enter the name of the file to be created. If the user needs help, he/she activates the <F1> key. In the input routine, the last activated key is tested. If it was <F1>, the help function is called; otherwise the key is treated like any other input. After <F1>, the input routine calls the central help function through a GOSUB <line-number>.

The help function first stores the current screen display. Then a window for the display of the help text is constructed. At the same time, HELP.NUMBER represents the record number for the access to the random file, in which the help text is stored. The record that is needed is now read and displayed. Then a wait occurs for the activation of a key. The screen display is restored again and, through the RETURN, a return is made to the input routine, which continues its work.

Although this process may seem very complicated, you'll see that it isn't really that difficult. It's very rewarding when your help function is utilized more than the reference manuals. Before looking at a concrete example, first we must establish the structure of the help file and gather the information needed for the help text.

16.3.1 Editor for the Help File

As we explained earlier, the help text is stored in a random file. This enables you to use the HELP.NUMBER, which in the program was assigned to a function, as a record number for the random file.

When deciding how much help text to include, remember the target audience for the program. The size of help increases as the assumed knowledge of the target group decreases. Generally for each help screen between 10 and 20 lines are required for each explanation. For programs aimed at professionals, as few as 3 lines may be adequate. Because of this, variable page sizes were provided during the design of the editor for the help file. The width, or actual line length, for the help text is set at 60 characters.

Structure of the Help File

Every record of the help file consists of two parts:

1.   Title for the help screen

This part is designed to inform the user of the purpose of help. This is mainly required when parts of the input template are covered by the window for the help screen and the user may not be able to see this information.

2.   Help text

This is the actual text for help. As mentioned, the size of the help screen, in relation to the lines to be displayed, varies. We used an increment of four: either 4, 8, 12, 16 or 20 lines can be selected. We did this because 4 lines, each with up to 60 characters, are gathered in the FIELD statement into a block of 240 bytes. If other values are used, the programming becomes even more complicated.

A control record must exist

The first record of the random file is used as a *control record*. The number of lines of the help texts are recorded in it so the window can be properly constructed during the display of this information.

The number of records currently in the help file are also stored in the control record. This number is important because during access to a record that doesn't exist yet in a random file, PC-BASIC returns random content. This random content can consist of non-printable characters. These characters could destroy the screen content. Therefore, you need to first create a help file consisting of 10 empty records. As soon as an access occurs to a non-existing record, a special process occurs in the editor. This process ensures that only initialized (empty) records are displayed for processing. We'll present details on this in the listing. The following graphic helps explain this:

rec.1	HELP.LINES $0D0A	MAX.HELP $0D0A
rec.2	TITLE$	HELP.TEXT$()
rec.3	TITLE$	HELP.TEXT$()
rec.4	TITLE$	HELP.TEXT$()
.....	TITLE$	HELP.TEXT$()
rec.n	TITLE$	HELP.TEXT$()

Fig. 38: Construction of the Help File

The number of lines provided for the help screen (4, 8, 12, 16 or 20) are stored in the HELP.LINES variable. The number of records currently stored in the help file are stored in the MAX.HELP variable. Arrays cannot be used in a FIELD statement. But since it's easier and faster to create a display from an array, a conversion occurs inside the editor.

Note: In Section 16.4 we'll discuss error handling in detail. The way error messages are handled and assigned is similar to the help function. So the editor is used for both the texts of the help file and for the text of the error file.

Some parts of the program listing, such as the universal window routine, the routines for saving and restoring the screen display and the input routine, were taken from previous chapters. So you will find explanations for them in the appropriate chapters. Otherwise, the required comments are in the listing:

Note: To execute the following program correctly, you must call PC-BASIC with the /M switch as follows:

```
GWBASIC /M:54000/S:1000
```

```
10 '---------------------------------------------------
20 'HF_EDIT.BAS   Editor for Help-/Error File
30 '---------------------------------------------------
40 :
50 DEFINT A-Z
60 OPTION BASE 0
70 CLS:KEY OFF:FOR I=1 TO 10:KEY I,"":NEXT I:LOCATE,,0
80 MP.START= &HE000
90 FALSE= 0: TRUE= NOT FALSE
100 MAX.SCN= 3:DIM BUFFER%(2000*MAX.SCN)
110 CUR.SCN= 0
120 WNDW.BKG= 112: MESSG.BKG= 127: HDFT.TXT= 7
130 BKG.CHAR$= CHR$(177): BKG.COLR= 15
140 DIM HELP.TEXT$(20) ' 1-20= help-texts
```

506

The text for help is sent from the FIELD buffer into the HELP.TEXT$() array for easier and faster processing. It's dimensioned in line 140.

```
150 :
160 'data lines from COM file: screen.com
170 :
180 RESTORE 200
190 DEF SEG:FOR I=1 TO  227:READ X:POKE MP.START+I-1,X: NEXT I
200 DATA 235,109,144,235,109,144, 85,139,236, 30,  6
210 DATA 139,118, 12,138, 28,176,160,246,227, 45,160
220 DATA   0, 80,139,118, 10,138, 28,176,  2,246,227
230 DATA  91,  3,195, 72, 72, 80,139,118,  8,138, 36
240 DATA 139,118,  6,138, 12,181,  0,139,116,  1, 80
250 DATA 191,  0,176,179,  0,205, 17, 37, 48,  0, 61
260 DATA  48,  0,116,  6,129,199,  0,  8,179,  1,142
270 DATA 199, 88, 95,252,186,218,  3,128,251,  0,116
280 DATA  11,236,208,216,114,246,250,236,208,216,115
290 DATA 251,172,251,171,226,235,  7, 31, 93,202,  8
300 DATA   0,235, 41,144, 85,139,236, 30,  6,139,118
310 DATA   6,139,  4,139,240,191,  0,176,179,  0,205
320 DATA  17, 37, 48,  0, 61, 48,  0,116,  6,129,199
330 DATA   0,  8,179,  1,142,199, 51,255,235, 40,144
340 DATA  85,139,236, 30,  6,139,118,  6,139,  4,139
350 DATA 248, 30,  7,190,  0,176,179,  0,205, 17, 37
360 DATA  48,  0, 61, 48,  0,116,  6,129,198,  0,  8
370 DATA 179,  1,142,222, 51,246,185,208,  7,252,186
380 DATA 218,  3,128,251,  0,116, 11,236,208,216,114
390 DATA 246,250,236,208,216,115,251,173,251,171,226
400 DATA 235,  7, 31, 93,202,  2,  0
410 :
420 SAVESCRN= MP.START
430 RESTSCRN= MP.START+3
440 FASTSCRN= MP.START+6
450 :
460 DEF FNUP$(SMALL$)= CHR$(ASC(SMALL$) AND 223)
470 GOTO 1700 'skip subroutines
```

Line 460 defines a function for the conversion of a single character into an uppercase letter. Line 470 skips the subsequent subroutines and moves directly to the main program.

```
480 :
490 '----- Output Note -----
500 :
510 GOSUB 1020 'store screen display
520 RW= 25: CL= 1: MESSG$= " "+MESSG$+SPACE$(80-LEN(MESSG$)-1)
530 CALL FASTSCRN(RW,CL,MESSG.BKG,MESSG$)
540 LOCATE 25,79:PRINT CHR$(254);: LOCATE 25,79,1
550 SOUND 895,1: SOUND 695,1
560 X$= INKEY$:IF X$= "" THEN 560
570 GOSUB 1090 'restore screen display
580 LOCATE ,,0
590 RETURN
600 :
```

Notes or error messages are displayed in line 520. Then a wait occurs until a key is activated. The current screen display is saved before the output of the note (line 510) or restored after a key is activated (line 570).

```
610 '----- display status line -----
620 :
630 RW= 25: CL= 1: STATUS$= " "+STATUS$+SPACE$(80-LEN(STATUS$)-1)
640 CALL FASTSCRN(RW,CL,MESSG.BKG,STATUS$)
650 RETURN
660 :
```

The status of the program (load file, etc.) or notes on the input, are displayed in line 630. This routine (starting at line 610) prepares and displays the text. The following routines: background, window, screen store/restore and input are explained in Chapters 11 and 12.

```
670 '----- initialize background -----
680 :
690 X$= STRING$(WD.LGTH,BKG.CHAR$)
700 FOR RW= WD.ROW TO WD.ROW+WD.HGT
710    CALL FASTSCRN(RW,WD.COLM,BKG.COLR,X$)
720 NEXT RW
730 RETURN
740 :
750 '----- Universal Routine for window -----
760 :
770 X$= CHR$(218)+STRING$(WD.LGTH%,CHR$(196))+CHR$(191)
780 DEF SEG:CALL FASTSCRN(WD.ROW,WD.COLM,WNDW.BKG,X$)
790 X$= CHR$(179)+STRING$(WD.LGTH%," ")+CHR$(179)
800 IF WD.SHADOW THEN X$= X$+CHR$(178)+CHR$(178)
810 FOR WRW= WD.ROW+1 TO WD.ROW+WD.HGT
820    DEF SEG:CALL FASTSCRN(WRW,WD.COLM,WNDW.BKG,X$)
830 NEXT WRW
840 X$= CHR$(192)+STRING$(WD.LGTH%,CHR$(196))+CHR$(217)
850 IF WD.SHADOW THEN X$= X$+CHR$(178)+CHR$(178)
860 WRW= WD.ROW+WD.HGT+1
870 DEF SEG:CALL FASTSCRN(WRW,WD.COLM,WNDW.BKG,X$)
880 IF WD.HEAD$= "" THEN 920 'continue with footer$
890    X$= " "+WD.HEAD$+" "
900    WCL= WD.COLM+3
910    CALL FASTSCRN(WD.ROW,WCL,HDFT.TXT,X$)
920 IF WD.FOOT$= "" THEN 960 'continue with shadow
930    X$= " "+WD.FOOT$+" "
940    WRW= WD.ROW+WD.HGT+1:WCL= WD.COLM+3
950    CALL FASTSCRN(WRW,WCL,HDFT.TXT,X$)
960 IF NOT WD.SHADOW THEN 1000 'back
970    X$= STRING$(WD.LGTH+2,CHR$(178))
980    WRW= WD.ROW+WD.HGT+2:WCL= WD.COLM+2
990    CALL FASTSCRN(WRW,WCL,WNDW.BKG,X$)
1000 RETURN
1010 :
1020 '----- store current screen display -----
```

```
1030 :
1040 IF CUR.SCN= MAX.SCN THEN BEEP:RETURN
1050 DEF SEG:BUFFER.OFS%= VARPTR(BUFFER%(CUR.SCN*2000)):CALL
     SAVESCRN(BUFFER.OFS%)
1060 CUR.SCN= CUR.SCN+1
1070 RETURN
1080 :
1090 '----- restore last screen display -----
1100 :
1110 IF CUR.SCN= 0 THEN BEEP:RETURN
1120 CUR.SCN= CUR.SCN-1
1130 DEF SEG:BUFFER.OFS%= VARPTR(BUFFER%(CUR.SCN*2000)):CALL
     RESTSCRN(BUFFER.OFS%)
1140 RETURN
1150 :
1160 '----- read subroutine -----
1170 :
1180 GOSUB 610 'display Status-Line for the input according to STATUS$
1190 X$="":ONKEY= 0:ANYCHANGE= FALSE
1200 Y$= INSTRING$+SPACE$(LNGTH-LEN(INSTRING$))
1210 CALL FASTSCRN(ROWNO,COLMNO,HDFT.TXT,Y$)
1220 LOCATE ROWNO,COLMNO,1: CRSR.POS= 1
1230 X$= INKEY$:IF X$="" THEN 1230 'wait for key
1240 IF X$= CHR$( 8) AND POS(0)> COLMNO THEN GOSUB 1370:GOTO 1230 '<Backspace>
1250 IF X$= CHR$(27) THEN ANYCHANGE= FALSE:LOCATE ,,0:RETURN
1260 IF X$= CHR$(13) THEN LOCATE ,,0:RETURN
1270 IF LEN(X$)= 2 THEN 1550 'control and function keys
1280 '
1290 IF X$< " " THEN BEEP:GOTO 1230 'kill characters smaller than BLANK
1300 IF MAKE.CAPS THEN IF X$>= "a" AND X$<= "z" THEN X$= CHR$(ASC(X$)-32)
1310 PRINT X$;:ANYCHANGE= TRUE
1320 IF CRSR.POS<= LEN(INSTRING$) THEN MID$(INSTRING$,CRSR.POS,1)= X$ ELSE
     INSTRING$= INSTRING$+X$
1330 CRSR.POS= CRSR.POS+1
1340 IF POS(0)> COLMNO+LNGTH-1 THEN LOCATE ROWNO,COLMNO:CRSR.POS= 1:GOTO 1230
1350 GOTO 1230 'continue to query keyboard
1360 '
1370 '----- BACKSPACE and DEL key -----
1380 '
1390 IF X$=CHR$(8) THEN INSTRING$= LEFT$(INSTRING$,CRSR.POS-
     2)+MID$(INSTRING$,CRSR.POS)
1400 IF ONKEY= 83  THEN INSTRING$= LEFT$(INSTRING$,CRSR.POS-
     1)+MID$(INSTRING$,CRSR.POS+1) '<Del>
1410 LOCATE ROWNO,COLMNO:PRINT INSTRING$;" ";
1420 IF X$=CHR$(8) THEN CRSR.POS= CRSR.POS-1
1430 LOCATE CSRLIN,COLMNO+CRSR.POS-1
1440 ONKEY= 0: X$="":ANYCHANGE= TRUE
1450 RETURN
1460 '
1470 '----- INS key -----
1480 '
1490 INSTRING$= LEFT$(INSTRING$,CRSR.POS-1)+" "+MID$(INSTRING$,CRSR.POS)
1500 PRINT " ";MID$(INSTRING$,CRSR.POS+1);
```

```
1510 LOCATE CSRLIN,COLUMN+CRSR.POS-1
1520 ANYCHANGE= TRUE
1530 RETURN
1540 '
1550 '----- control and function keys -----
1560 '
1570 ONKEY= ASC(RIGHT$(X$,1))
1580 IF ONKEY= 68 OR ONKEY= 63 THEN LOCATE ,,0:RETURN '<F5> and <F10>
1590 IF ONKEY= 72 OR ONKEY= 80 THEN LOCATE ,,0:RETURN 'Cursor up and down
1600 IF ONKEY= 73 OR ONKEY= 81 THEN LOCATE ,,0:RETURN '<PgUp> and <PgDn>
1610 IF ONKEY= 75 AND POS(0)> COLMNO THEN LOCATE CSRLIN,POS(0)-1:CRSR.POS=
     CRSR.POS-1:GOTO 1230 'Cursor <--
1620 IF ONKEY= 77 AND POS(0)< COLMNO+LNGTH-1 THEN IF CRSR.POS<= LEN(INSTRING$)
     THEN LOCATE CSRLIN,POS(0)+1:CRSR.POS= CRSR.POS+1:GOTO 1230 'Cursor -->
1630 IF ONKEY= 83 AND CRSR.POS <= LEN(INSTRING$) THEN GOSUB 1370:GOTO 1230 '<Del>
     treated like <Backspace>
1640 IF ONKEY= 71 THEN LOCATE ROWNO,COLMNO:GOTO 1230 '<Home>, start of field
1650 IF ONKEY= 79 THEN LOCATE CSRLIN,COLMNO+LEN(INSTRING$)-1:CRSR.POS=
     LEN(INSTRING$):GOTO 1230 '<End>, set to last character s
1660 IF ONKEY= 117 THEN INSTRING$= LEFT$(INSTRING$,CRSR.POS-1):PRINT
     SPACE$(LNGTH-CRSR.POS);:LOCATE CSRLIN,COLMNO+ CRSR.POS-1: ANYCHANGE=
     TRUE:GOTO 1230 '<Ctrl> <End>, erase to end of field
1670 IF ONKEY= 82 AND CRSR.POS<= LEN(INSTRING$) AND LEN(INSTRING$)< LNGTH THEN
     GOSUB 1470:GOTO 1230 '<Ins>
1680 BEEP:GOTO 1230 'continue to query keyboard
1690 :
1700 '----- main-program -----
1710 :
1720 WD.ROW= 1: WD.COLM= 1: WD.LGTH= 80: WD.HGT= 25
1730 GOSUB 670 'initialize background
1740 RW= 1: CL= 1
1750 X$= " HF-EDIT V1.00    Editor for Help/Error File                (C)
     1987 H.J. Bomanns "
1760 CALL FASTSCRN(RW,CL,MESSG.BKG,X$)
1770 :
1780 '----- read filename and dimension help
1790 :
1800 GOSUB 1020 'store screen display
1810 :
1820 WD.ROW= 5: WD.COLM= 5: WD.LGTH= 70: WD.HGT= 4: WD.SHADOW= TRUE
1830 WD.HEAD$= "Data for error/help file:": WD.FOOT$= "<F10> = OK or <Esc> =
     End"
1840 GOSUB 750 'display window
1850 :
1860 FIL.NAM$= "TEST.HLP"      'default for filename
1870 HELP.LINES= 12            'default for number of help lines
1880 :
1890 RW= WD.ROW+2: CL= WD.COLM+2: X$= "Name  :": Y$= FIL.NAM$
1900 CALL FASTSCRN(RW,CL,WNDW.BKG,X$): CL= CL+8
1910 CALL FASTSCRN(RW,CL,MESSG.BKG,Y$)
1920 RW= WD.ROW+3: CL= WD.COLM+2: X$= "Lines:": Y$= "12"
1930 CALL FASTSCRN(RW,CL,WNDW.BKG,X$): CL= CL+8
1940 CALL FASTSCRN(RW,CL,MESSG.BKG,Y$)
```

```
1950 :
1960 COUNTER= 1              'counter for current input field
1970 MAKE.CAPS= TRUE         'default for input routine
1980 X$= "": ONKEY= 0        'same
1990 :
2000 WHILE X$<> CHR$(27) AND ONKEY<> 68 '68= <F10>
2010   ROWNO= WD.ROW+COUNTER+1: COLMNO= WD.COLM+10
2020   IF COUNTER<> 1 THEN 2070 'otherwise first field "Name"
2030     STATUS$= "Please input the name for the file ..."
2040     INSTRING$= FIL.NAM$: LNGTH= 12: GOSUB 1160 'input routine
2050     IF X$= CHR$(27) THEN  2220 '<Esc> = End
2060     FIL.NAM$= INSTRING$
2070   IF COUNTER<> 2 THEN 2160 'otherwise second field "lines"
2080     STATUS$= "Please input number of lines for each help page ..."
2090     INSTRING$= STR$(HELP.LINES):INSTRING$= MID$(INSTRING$,2,99)
2100     LNGTH= 2: GOSUB 1160 'input routine
2110     IF X$= CHR$(27) THEN  2220 '<Esc>= End
2120     HELP.LINES= VAL(INSTRING$)
2130     IF HELP.LINES MOD 4= 0 THEN 2160 'Everything OK
2140     MESSG$= "NUMBER OD LINES MUST BE 4, 8, 12, 16 or 20 ...":GOSUB 490
2150     ONKEY= 0: X$= "": GOTO 2220 'continue in the loop
2160     Y$= INSTRING$+SPACE$(LNGTH-LEN(INSTRING$))
2170     CALL FASTSCRN(ROWNO,COLMNO,MESSG.BKG,Y$)
2180   IF ONKEY= 80 OR X$= CHR$(13) THEN COUNTER= COUNTER+1
2190   IF ONKEY= 72 THEN COUNTER= COUNTER-1
2200   IF COUNTER< 1 THEN COUNTER= 2
2210   IF COUNTER> 2 THEN COUNTER= 1
2220 WEND
2230 :
2240 IF X$= CHR$(27) THEN CLS:END
2250 GOSUB 1090 'restore screen display
2260 :
```

The data for the help file is read, starting at line 1780. Besides the name for the file, this also includes the number of lines per help screen. We selected an increment of four. Only the values 4, 8, 12, 16 and 20 can be entered. Other values cause an error message and the input must be repeated (line 2130).

```
2270 '----------------------------------------------
2280 ' open file or create one if none available
2290 '----------------------------------------------
2300 :
2310 IF INSTR(FIL.NAM$,".")= 0 THEN FIL.NAM$= FIL.NAM$+".HLP"
2320 SET.LNGTH= (HELP.LINES+1)*60
2330 'number of lines * line length plus one line as headline
2340 :
```

The record length for the random file is computed from the selected number of lines per page, multiplied by 60 (characters per line) plus one line (60 characters) for the headline.

```
2350 ON ERROR GOTO 3760 'error-handling
2360 :
2370 STATUS$= "One moment please, initiating file...":GOSUB 610
2380 OPEN FIL.NAM$ FOR INPUT AS #1 'open file for sequential access
2390 LINE INPUT #1,X$ 'first record/first line contains HELP.LINES
2400 HELP.LINES= VAL(X$)
2410 LINE INPUT#1,X$ 'first record/second line contains MAX.HELP
2420 MAX.HELP= VAL(X$)
2430 SET.LNGTH= (HELP.LINES+1)*60
2440 CLOSE #1
2450 GOTO 4000 'file found, continue normally
2460 :
```

First a test is made to determine whether the file already exists. If it does, the values, for HELP.LINES and MAX.HELP, which are stored in the control record, are read (line 2390/2410) and the record length is calculated accordingly (line 2430). A jump then occurs to line 4000 to initialize random file and help pages display.

If the file doesn't exist, a jump occurs, on the basis of the ON ERROR GOTO in line 2350, to the error handling. A test is made there to determine whether it was error 53 (File not found). If it was, the file is created after a query and initialized. If it was another error (disk full, write-protect etc.), that particular error is indicated and the filename must be selected again.

```
2470 '----- open random-file, initialize FIELDs -----
2480 :
2490 OPEN "R",#1,FIL.NAM$,SET.LNGTH
2500 ON HELP.LINES GOTO 0,0,0,2520,0,0,0,2540,0,0,0,2560,0,0,0,2580,0,0,0,2600
2510 'according to HELP.LINES:      4        8        12        16
     20
2520 FIELD#1,60 AS PAGE.TITLE$,240 AS TEXT1$
2530 RETURN 'continue in text
2540 FIELD#1,60 AS PAGE.TITLE$,240 AS TEXT1$,240 AS TEXT2$
2550 RETURN 'continue in the text
2560 FIELD#1,60 AS PAGE.TITLE$,240 AS TEXT1$,240 AS TEXT2$,240 AS TEXT3$
2570 RETURN 'continue in the text
2580 FIELD#1,60 AS PAGE.TITLE$,240 AS TEXT1$,240 AS TEXT2$,240 AS TEXT3$,240 AS
     TEXT4$
2590 RETURN 'continue in the text
2600 FIELD#1,60 AS PAGE.TITLE$,240 AS TEXT1$,240 AS TEXT2$,240 AS TEXT3$,240 AS
     TEXT4$,240 AS TEXT5$
2610 RETURN 'continue in the text
2620 :
```

This somewhat awkward construction initializes the random file. Unfortunately, there isn't another way to do this. As we already mentioned, a block of the help text consists of 4 lines of 60 characters each. These blocks are prepared according to the selection of HELP.LINES. The ON HELP.LINES GOTO in line 2500 is responsible for the correct branching. Starting at line 2520, besides the TITLE$, either 1, 2, 3, 4 or 5 blocks of 240 characters each are set as TEXT<n>$ in the FIELD statement.

Warning: If you make changes in the program, and execute a RENUM, line 2510 will generate an error message because line 0 doesn't exist. You can ignore this error message because a jump to line 0 doesn't occur. The HELP.LINES variable can only have the values 4, 8, 12, 16 or 20.

```
2630 '----- read help-texts -----
2640 :
2650 GET#1,HELP.NUMBER 'read current help page
2660 Z= 1
2670 FOR I=1 TO 240 STEP 60 'read four lines from TEXT1$
2680    HELP.TEXT$(Z)= MID$(TEXT1$,I,60)
2690    Z=Z+1
2700 NEXT I
2710 IF HELP.LINES= 4 THEN 2920 '4 lines for Help
2720 FOR I=1 TO 240 STEP 60 'read four lines from TEXT2$
2730    HELP.TEXT$(Z)= MID$(TEXT2$,I,60)
2740    Z=Z+1
2750 NEXT I
2760 IF HELP.LINES= 8 THEN 2920 '8 lines for Help
2770 FOR I=1 TO 240 STEP 60 'read four lines from TEXT3$
2780    HELP.TEXT$(Z)= MID$(TEXT3$,I,60)
2790    Z=Z+1
2800 NEXT I
2810 IF HELP.LINES= 12 THEN 2920 '12 lines for Help
2820 FOR I=1 TO 240 STEP 60 'read four lines from TEXT4$
2830    HELP.TEXT$(Z)= MID$(TEXT4$,I,60)
2840    Z=Z+1
2850 NEXT I
2860 IF HELP.LINES= 16 THEN 2920 '16 lines for Help
2870 FOR I=1 TO 240 STEP 60 'read four lines from TEXT5$
2880    HELP.TEXT$(Z)= MID$(TEXT5$,I,60)
2890    Z=Z+1
2900 NEXT I
2910 :
2920 FOR I=1 TO HELP.LINES
2930    IF RIGHT$(HELP.TEXT$(I),1)<> CHR$(0) THEN 2950
2940    HELP.TEXT$(I)= LEFT$(HELP.TEXT$(I),INSTR(HELP.TEXT$(I),CHR$(0))-1)
2950 NEXT I
2960 RETURN '20 lines for Help
2970 :
```

In the routine starting at line 2630, the record is read, according to HELP.NUMBER, from the random file and the help texts are received from the TEXT<n>$ blocks into the HELP.TEXT$() array. In a FOR...NEXT loop, 60 characters (STEP 60) are sent into the HELP.TEXT$() array. The Z variable is used as a counter.

After the blocks have been sent into the array, the text is prepared again in the array starting at line 2920. During this procedure, the extra characters following the actual text are erased. With the saving through LSET and PUT#, the fields are usually filled with spaces (CHR$(32)) according to the FIELD statement. If the variable contains 30 characters and the field is 60 characters long, LSET fills the last 30 characters with spaces. To erase the spaces again after the reading would require a slow and complicated routine. So when the records are created and saved, the remaining characters to the right of the actual text are filled with the CHR$(0) character.

Because of this, you can use the INSTR function as shown in line 2940. This wouldn't work with CHR$(32) because spaces occur in the text between the words. You'll need to remember this when making changes. In line 2930 a test is made to determine whether the line is completely filled with text. If it is, processing isn't required and the loop continues. Without this test, an error message appears because a CHR$(0) wouldn't be available for INSTR to find in a full line. Depending on the content of HELP.LINES, up to five blocks are prepared in this way.

```
2980 '----- save help-texts -----
2990 :
3000 IF NOT FIL.SAVE THEN RETURN
3010 GOSUB 3690 'set all FIELDs to CHR$(0)
3020 Z= 1
3030 Y$= ""
3040 FOR I=1 TO 4 'save four lines in TEXT1$
3050    GOSUB 3370 'construct Y$ from HELP.TEXT$(I)
3060 NEXT I
3070 LSET TEXT1$= Y$
3080 IF HELP.LINES= 4 THEN 3330 'save and restore
3090 Y$= ""
3100 FOR I=1 TO 4 'save four lines in TEXT2$
3110    GOSUB 3370 'same
3120 NEXT I
3130 LSET TEXT2$= Y$
3140 IF HELP.LINES= 8 THEN 3330 'save and restore
3150 Y$= ""
3160 FOR I=1 TO 4 'save four lines in TEXT3$
3170    GOSUB 3370 'same
3180 NEXT I
3190 LSET TEXT3$= Y$
3200 IF HELP.LINES= 12 THEN 3330 'save and back
3210 Y$= ""
3220 FOR I=1 TO 4 'save four lines in TEXT4$
3230    GOSUB 3370 'same
3240 NEXT I
3250 LSET TEXT4$= Y$
3260 IF HELP.LINES= 16 THEN 3330 'save and back
3270 Y$= ""
3280 FOR I=1 TO 4 'save four lines in TEXT5$
3290    GOSUB 3370 'same
3300 NEXT I
```

```
3310 LSET TEXT5$= Y$
3320 :
3330 PUT#1,HELP.NUMBER 'save
3340 FIL.SAVE= FALSE
3350 RETURN 'save help-texts
3360 :
3370 '----- save subroutine for Help -----
3380 :
3390 Y$= Y$+HELP.TEXT$(Z)+STRING$(60-LEN(HELP.TEXT$(Z)),CHR$(0))
3400 Z=Z+1
3410 RETURN
3420 :
```

Starting at line 2980, the help texts are prepared and saved. As we already mentioned, the blocks are filled with CHR$(0) (subroutine starting at line 3370) so that working with the INSTR function will be easier during the reading. Also, depending on HELP.LINES, either 1, 2, 3, 4 or 5 blocks are processed.

```
3430 '----- display help-texts -----
3440 :
3450 H.RW= WD.ROW: H.CL= WD.COLM+2
3460 CALL FASTSCRN(H.RW,H.CL,MESSG.BKG,PAGE.TITLE$)
3470 FOR I=1 TO HELP.LINES
3480    H.RW= WD.ROW+I+1:Y$= HELP.TEXT$(I)+SPACE$( 60-LEN(HELP.TEXT$(I)))
3490    CALL FASTSCRN(H.RW,H.CL,MESSG.BKG,Y$)
3500 NEXT I
3510 COUNTER= 1 'input starting at first line (headline)
3520 PAGE.SAVE= FALSE
3530 RETURN 'display page
3540 :
```

Starting at line 3430, the routine accepts the display of the help texts from the HELP.TEXT$() array. Before this, the title of the help screen is displayed separately (line 3450/3460). The COUNTER variable for the current input line is set to 1 in order to process the screen from the beginning. The PAGE.SAVE variable is used as a flag for the "store help texts" subroutine (see line 3000). If a screen is skipped, a change isn't made and the record won't be saved.

```
3550 '----- create new page ? -----
3560 :
3570 MESSG$= "Create new help page? (Y/N)":GOSUB 490
3580 IF FNUP$(X$)= "N" OR X$= CHR$(27) THEN X$= "":ONKEY= 0:RETURN
3590 HELP.NUMBER= HELP.NUMBER+1
3600 MAX.HELP= MAX.HELP+1
3610 LSET PAGE.TITLE$= " Help number:"+STR$(HELP.NUMBER)
3620 GOSUB 3690 'set FIELD to CHR$(0)
3630 PUT#1,HELP.NUMBER
3640 GOSUB 2660 'read help-text
3650 GOSUB 3430 'and display
3660 X$= "": ONKEY= 0
3670 RETURN 'create new page
3680 :
```

The MAX.HELP variable contains the number of previously created help screens in the file. If, during scrolling, the last page is exceeded, the new record is initiated in this subroutine (starting at line 3550) and in the variables (HELP.NUMBER+1, MAX.HELP+1). All TEXT<n>$ blocks are set to CHR$(0), as explained above (line 3620). The title is assigned the text "help number:" and the current help screen. The query (line 3570/3580) acts as a safety precaution if the paging goes too far.

```
3690 '----- set FIELDs to CHR$80) -----
3700 :
3710 LSET TEXT1$= STRING$(240,CHR$(0)): LSET TEXT2$= STRING$(240,CHR$(0))
3720 LSET TEXT3$= STRING$(240,CHR$(0)): LSET TEXT4$= STRING$(240,CHR$(0))
3730 LSET TEXT5$= STRING$(240,CHR$(0)) 'set all FIELDs to CHR$(0)
3740 RETURN
3750 :
3760 '----- error-handling "file-access" -----
3770 :
3780 IF ERR<> 53 THEN 3960 'general error display
3790    CLOSE 'close all files
3800    MESSG$= "Help file not found, create one? (Y/N)":GOSUB 490
3810    IF X$= CHR$(27) OR FNUP$(X$)= "N" THEN RESUME 1780 'read new name
3820    :
3830    GOSUB 2470 'open random-file and initialize FIELD
3840    Y$= STR$(HELP.LINES)+CHR$(13)+CHR$(10)+"10"+CHR$(13)+CHR$(10)
3850    LSET PAGE.TITLE$=Y$   'write dimension/MAX.HELP in FIELD-buffer
3860    LSET TEXT1$="!!! CTRL-RECRD !!!" 'identify control-record
3870    PUT#1,1 'write first record (control-record)
3880    GOSUB 3690 'set all FIELDs to CHR$(0)
3890    FOR I= 2 TO 11 'write 10 empty records
3900      LSET PAGE.TITLE$= " Help number:"+STR$(I)
3910      PUT#1,I
3920    NEXT I
3930    CLOSE #1: MAX.HELP= 10 'close file again, set MAX.HELP
3940    RESUME 4000 'continue in the text
3950 :
3960 CLOSE 'close all file(s)
3970 MESSG$="error "+STR$(ERR)+" in line "+STR$(ERL)+"...":GOSUB 490
3980 RESUME 1780 'from the beginning
3990 :
```

Error handling begins at line 3760. A test is made to determine whether error 53 (File not found) occurred. If it did, a new help file is initialized after a query. The control record is generated, according to HELP.LINES, for 10 records (line 3840 ff). The file is created with 10 empty records (line 3890 ff). If it wasn't error 53, a general error message is issued (starting at line 3960) and the input of the filename, etc. is repeated.

```
4000 '- initialize random-file and help-pages display -
4010 :
4020 GOSUB 2470        'open random-file and initialize FIELDs
4030 HELP.NUMBER= 2    'first help-page, 1 is control-record
4040 COUNTER= 1        'for current input-line
```

```
4050 MAKE.CAPS= FALSE 'default for input-routine
4060 X$="": ONKEY= 0  'same
4070 :
4080 GOSUB 1020 'save screen display
4090 WD.ROW= 5: WD.COLM= 9: WD.LGTH= 62: WD.HGT= HELP.LINES+2: WD.SHADOW= FALSE
4100 WD.HEAD$= "": WD.FOOT$= "<F5> = page 'x', <F10> = new file, <Esc> = end"
4110 GOSUB 750  'display window for Help
4120 GOSUB 2630 'read help-texts
4130 GOSUB 3430 'display help-texts
4140 :
```

Starting after line 4000, the display and the collection/change of the help screen is controlled. First the random file is initialized (line 4020). Two is set as the first HELP.NUMBER; the control record is 1. Lines 4040 to 4060 initialize the variables used by the input routine. Finally the window for the help screen is constructed (starting at line 4090) and the first screen (line 4120/4130) is read and displayed. In line 4080 the current screen is stored (or restored in line 4720) so that a new screen won't have to be constructed after the text is collected.

```
4150 WHILE X$<> CHR$(27) AND ONKEY<> 68 'until <Esc><F10> have been activated
4160   COLMNO= WD.COLM+2:LNGTH= 60
4170   IF COUNTER<> 1 THEN 4260
4180     INSTRING$= PAGE.TITLE$
4190     STATUS$="Please input title for help page ..."
4200     ROWNO= WD.ROW
4210     GOSUB 1160 'input-routine
4220     IF X$= CHR$(27) THEN 4650 '<Esc>= terminate
4230     IF ANYCHANGE THEN FIL.SAVE= TRUE
4240     LSET PAGE.TITLE$=INSTRING$
4250     COLR= HDFT.TXT: GOTO 4350 'display input
4260   IF COUNTER <2 OR COUNTER >20 THEN 4350
4270     INSTRING$= HELP.TEXT$(COUNTER-1)
4280     STATUS$="Please input help text ..."
4290     ROWNO= WD.ROW+COUNTER
4300     GOSUB 1160 'input-routine
4310     IF X$= CHR$(27) THEN 4650 '<Esc>= terminate
4320     IF ANYCHANGE THEN FIL.SAVE= TRUE
4330     HELP.TEXT$(COUNTER-1)= INSTRING$
4340     COLR= MESSG.BKG
4350   Y$= INSTRING$+SPACE$(LNGTH-LEN(INSTRING$))
4360   CALL FASTSCRN(ROWNO,COLMNO,COLR,Y$)
4370   IF ONKEY<> 73 THEN 4440 'test PgUp
4380     IF HELP.NUMBER < 3 THEN BEEP:GOTO 4650 'is first page
4390     GOSUB 2980 'save current page
4400     HELP.NUMBER= HELP.NUMBER-1 'one page back
4410     GOSUB 2630 'read help-text
4420     GOSUB 3430 'display help-text
4430     GOTO 4650  'continue in the text
4440   IF ONKEY<> 81 THEN 4510 'test for PgDn
4450     GOSUB 2980 'save current page
4460     IF HELP.NUMBER = MAX.HELP THEN GOSUB 3550:GOTO 4650 'new page?
```

```
4470      HELP.NUMBER= HELP.NUMBER+1 'one page before
4480      GOSUB 2630 'read help-text
4490      GOSUB 3430 'display help-text
4500      GOTO 4650 'continue in the text
4510   IF ONKEY<> 63 THEN 4610 'process <F5>= Help 'x'
4520      STATUS$= "Help number:"
4530      ROWNO= 25: COLMNO= 13: LNGTH= 3
4540      INSTRING$= MID$ (STR$ (HELP.NUMBER),2,99)
4550      GOSUB 1160 'input-routine
4560      IF X$= CHR$ (27) THEN X$= "": GOTO 4650 'continue in the text
4570      I= VAL(INSTRING$): X$= "": ONKEY= 0
4580      IF I> 2 AND I<= MAX.HELP THEN HELP.NUMBER= I:GOTO 4480 'read/display
4590      MESSG$= "Invalid help number, try again...": GOSUB 490
4600      GOTO 4520 'try again
4610   IF ONKEY= 80 OR X$= CHR$(13) THEN COUNTER= COUNTER+1
4620   IF ONKEY= 72 THEN COUNTER= COUNTER-1
4630   IF COUNTER< 1 THEN COUNTER= HELP.LINES+1 'last line
4640   IF COUNTER> HELP.LINES+1 THEN COUNTER= 1 'first line
4650 WEND
```

This WHILE...WEND loop reads the title and the individual lines of the help text. The COUNTER variable provides information if the title (COUNTER= 1) or a help line (COUNTER= 2-21) are immediately available for processing. Besides the "normal" keys (cursor keys, etc.) for positioning the input line (lines 4610/4620), the <PgUp> and <PgDn> keys (lines 4370/4440) are also used. These keys are used to scroll through the help screens. A test needs to be made to determine whether the first or last screen is already displayed. For the last displayed line, a test must be made to determine whether a new screen should be created. If the first page is displayed, a warning tone is emitted. If the user is in the middle of the screen page, it's advanced with <PgDn> or the previous page is displayed with <PgUp>.

The <F5> key also has a special purpose (line 4510). With this key, a jump can be made to a certain help number. The desired line must be entered in the status line (line 25). For an incorrect number (line 4580), an error message is displayed and the input must be repeated.

```
4660 Y$= STR$(HELP.LINES) +CHR$(13) +CHR$(10) +STR$ (MAX.HELP) +CHR$(13) +CHR$(10)
4670 LSET PAGE.TITLE$=Y$    'write dimension/MAX.HELP in FIELD-buffer
4680 LSET TEXT1$="!!! CTRL-RECRD !!!" 'mark as control-record
4690 PUT#1,1 'write first record (control-record)
4700 CLOSE
4710 :
4720 GOSUB 1090 'restore screen display
4730 GOTO 1780 'if necessary work on other file
```

In the last lines, the control record is initialized again (if records were added) and the file is then closed after pressing the <Esc> or <F10> key. In line 4720 the previous screen display is again restored. Line 4730 calls the input for the file data again. Here another file can be processed or the program can be terminated with <Esc>.

16.3.2 Using HF_EDIT

After the start of the program, a window appears in which the name of the help/error file and the number of lines per page must be entered. The input lines can be 4, 8, 12, 16 or 20. An error message appears in the bottom line if you enter other values. You must use 4, 8, 12, 16 or 20 for the number of input lines. The program can be terminated at any time with <Esc>.

After pressing <F10>, the program tests to determine whether the file already exists. If the file does exist, it's displayed so that additions and/or changes can be made to it. If the file doesn't yet exist, a message appears asking whether a file should be created. This query is done for safety reasons because the user could have made a mistake while entering the name of an existing file. If the reply is "Y", a help/error file, with 10 empty records, is created. Then the first screen is displayed and the user can enter text. If you enter "N" or <Esc>, the window appears again so you can enter another name.

You can scroll through the help/error screens by using the <PgUp> to scroll one page back and <PgDn> to scroll one page forward. A beep is sounded if you're already on the first page and press <PgUp>. If you're on the last screen page and press <PgDn>, you'll receive a prompt asking whether a new screen page should be created. If the reply is "Y", a new page is created and displayed. New text may be entered. For "N" or <Esc>, the last screen page remains active and the program does not create a new page. With <F5>, a jump can be made to a specific help/error number. In the status line, you're asked to enter the desired number. This number must be at least 2 but not larger than the last created help/error screen page. The input is accepted by pressing the <Return> key. An error message is displayed ("Invalid help number, try again...") for incorrect input. This function can be terminated with the <Esc> key. The displayed screen remains active.

You can move up and down using the cursor keys in the individual text lines. If, during the input of the text, the <Return> key is pressed, the input is automatically advanced one line. The <Ins> key adds a space to the current cursor position. With the <Del> and <Backspace> keys the user can delete characters, as in the PC-BASIC editor. During a file or diskette error, a general error message is displayed in the following format:

```
error <xxx> in line <yyy>
```

Consult the Appendix for the definition of this error and how to correct it. Since HF_EDIT is a utility intended for programmers, we did not include a user-friendly error handling.

Changing the program and messages

This program should be easy to change because of its construction. We suggest implementing a function that displays an overview, according to titles, of the available help/error texts. This could be very helpful with large files. However, we didn't use this with our program because the flow chart provided an overview. Here is a brief excerpt:

Help-/record-number	function/description
2	select menu-point
3	input last-name
4	input first-name (include title),
5	input street (include P.O.Box),

and so on...

Fig. 39: Chart "help assignment"

The method of saving is very important as changes are made to the program. As we mentioned earlier, the fields aren't filled by using LSET and CHR$(32), but in their own routines with CHR$(0). Remember that this may also apply to other functions and INSTR.

As you can see in the listing, there aren't any limits for the record numbers for the random file. The function "<F5>/jump to number" allows a three digit number (which seems to limit the number of records to 999) to be entered. However, as you can see in line 4530, the LENGTH variable is simply changed from 3 to 4 or 5. You should remember that, with 20 lines for each help screen, 1,260 bytes (including the title) are needed for each record. With 100 help screens, that would be 126,000 bytes (126K). So for an application which uses the diskette drive, not much memory would be available for the program and data files.

16.3.3 Help Functions in Applications

In this section we'll discuss using the help function in applications. In the previous section we created a special editor that will help us do this. Now we'll see how the files created with the editor can be used with an application program. We're using the B_MENU program (menu bars) from Chapter 11 again as a base. A template, a special input routine and control were added to the "add data" function. A query of the help key, <F1>, was built into the subroutine for the menu control to permit the help function in the menu selection.

In the "Delete" template, the <F1> help key can be activated in every field. This causes a context-sensitive help to appear for the specific field.

This program will also demonstrate how a help screen can also be "misused" for purposes other than context-sensitive help. After the activation of the <F10> key for "save", the checking of the input is "simulated" and a message is displayed. The text in the help file doesn't have to be called through a help key, but can be displayed as messages during a plausibility check. Details on this can be found in the following listing. For explanations on the basic routines, refer to the appropriate chapters.

You must create a help file before using the HELP.BAS program. You'll receive an error message if there are no help files available. See Section 16.3.4 for more information.

Note: In order to execute the following program correctly, you must call PC-BASIC with the switch /M as follows:

```
GWBASIC /M:54000/S:1000
```

```
10 '---------------------------------------------------
20 'HELP.BAS demonstration of the help function
30 '---------------------------------------------------
40 :
50 DEFINT A-Z
60 OPTION BASE 0
70 CLS:KEY OFF:FOR I=1 TO 10:KEY I,"":NEXT I
80 :
90 DEF FNUP$(SMALL$)= CHR$(ASC(SMALL$) AND 223)
100 :
110 MP.START= &HE000
120 GOSUB 2050 'initialize MP
130 SAVESCRN= MP.START
140 RESTSCRN= MP.START+3
150 FASTSCRN= MP.START+6
160 FALSE= 0: TRUE= NOT FALSE
170 MAX.SCN= 3:DIM BUFFER%(2000*MAX.SCN)
180 MAX.MENU= 8: DIM MENU$(MAX.MENU)
190 CUR.SCN= 0
200 WNDW.BKG= 112: MESSG.BKG= 127: HDFT.TXT= 7
210 BKG.CHAR$= CHR$(177): BKG.COLR= 15
220 DIM HELP.TEXT$(20)
230 :
240 RESTORE 260
250 FOR I= 0 TO MAX.MENU:READ MENU$(I):NEXT I
260 DATA " MAIN MENU "
270 DATA "prepare"
280 DATA "add"
290 DATA "search"
300 DATA "change"
310 DATA "list"
320 DATA "import"
330 DATA "export"
340 DATA "End"
350 :
360 RESTORE 380
370 FOR I=1 TO 7:READ MASK$(I):NEXT I
380 DATA "Last name"
390 DATA "First name"
400 DATA "Street"
410 DATA "City"
420 DATA "ZIP code"
430 DATA "Country code"
440 DATA "Remark"
450 :
```

Starting at line 360, the MASK$() array is initialized. This is used later for a fast display in a FOR...NEXT loop. Individual statements would be too slow.

```
460 WD.ROW= 1: WD.COLM= 1: WD.LGTH= 80: WD.HGT= 25
470 GOSUB 1560 'initialize background
480 RW= 1: CL= 1: X$= " File Administration V1.00 (C) 1987 H.J. Bomanns "
490 DEF SEG: CALL FASTSCRN(RW,CL,MESSG.BKG,X$)
500 :
510 GOSUB 1130 'menu-selection
520 IF MENU= 0 THEN MENU = 8 '<Shift> <End>
530 GOSUB 1910 'store screen display
540 ON MENU GOSUB 580,600,980,1000,1020,1040,1060,1080 'execute function
550 GOSUB 1980 'restore screen display
560 GOTO 510 'query menu again
570 :
580 '----- arrange -----
590 GOSUB 1110: RETURN
600 '----- add -----
610 :
620 WD.ROW= 8: WD.COLM= 20: WD.LGTH= 50: WD.HGT= 9: WD.SHADOW= TRUE
630 WD.HEAD$= "add data:"
640 WD.FOOT$= "<F1> = Help, <F10> = save, <Esc> = back"
650 GOSUB 1640 'display window
660 :
670 CL= WD.COLM+2
680 FOR I=1 TO 7
690    RW= WD.ROW+I+1
700    DEF SEG:CALL FASTSCRN(RW,CL,WNDW.BKG,MASK$(I))
710 NEXT I
720 :
730 COUNTER= 1 'for current input-field
740 :
750 WHILE X$<> CHR$(27) 'until <Esc> is activated
760    STATUS$= "Please input "+MASK$(COUNTER)+" ..."
770    HELP.NUMBER= 2+COUNTER
780    ROWNO= WD.ROW+COUNTER+1: COLMNO= WD.COLM+16
790    INSTRING$= CONTENTS$(COUNTER)
800    LNGTH= 20:GOSUB 2500 'input-routine
810    CONTENTS$(COUNTER)= INSTRING$
820    Y$= CONTENTS$(COUNTER)+SPACE$(20-LEN(CONTENTS$(COUNTER)))
830    CALL FASTSCRN(ROWNO,COLMNO,MESSG.BKG,Y$)
840    IF ONKEY<> 68 THEN 900 'otherwise process <F10>
850      AHELP.NUMBER= HELP.NUMBER 'save HELP.NUMBER
860      HELP.NUMBER= 10 'note about duplicate customer
870      GOSUB 3050 'display note as "help-page"
880      HELP.NUMBER= AHELP.NUMBER 'HELP.NUMBER back again
890    COUNTER= 1 'set to field "last-name"
900    IF X$= CHR$(13) OR ONKEY= 80 THEN COUNTER= COUNTER+1
910    IF ONKEY= 72 THEN COUNTER= COUNTER-1
920    IF COUNTER <1 THEN COUNTER= 7
930    IF COUNTER >7 THEN COUNTER= 1
940 WEND
950 :
960 RETURN
970 :
```

Line 600 starts the addition to the "add data" routine. In lines 620 to 650, the window for the input is initialized. In lines 670 to 710 the field names from MASK$() are displayed in a FOR...NEXT loop. The COUNTER variable is used to position the input field. In the WHILE...WEND loop (line 750 to 940) the individual fields are initialized according to COUNTER (line 760/790) and its input routine is called.

Line 770, in which the HELP.NUMBER is set, is significant. In our example, the help number 2 is provided for the menu selection so that, from this point on, the number 3 can be assigned. This is done by adding the current content of the COUNTER variable to the value 2. So: 2+1= 3, 2+2= 4, 2+3= 5, etc. The actual call of the help routine doesn't occur here, but in the universal input routine (starting at line 2500). This is done so that this routine can be called from all functions. The query in each individual function routine (add data, search, change, etc.) would require more memory space and, in case of changes, more lines would have to be modified. The <F10> key (line 840) is also important. A plausibility test is simulated and a help screen is displayed at the end. It's not always necessary to display a help screen when the help key is activated. Several help screens can also be "misused" for such messages.

```
980  '----- search -----
990  GOSUB 1110: RETURN
1000 '----- change -----
1010 GOSUB 1110: RETURN
1020 '----- list -----
1030 GOSUB 1110: RETURN
1040 '----- import -----
1050 GOSUB 1110: RETURN
1060 '----- export -----
1070 GOSUB 1110: RETURN
1080 '----- End -----
1090 COLOR 7,0:CLS:PRINT "*** END ***":PRINT:END
1100 :
1110 MESSG$= "FUNCTION NOT AVAILABLE...":GOSUB 2320:RETURN
1120 :
1130 '---- menu display and selection control ----
1140 :
1150 MAX.LNGTH= 0
1160 FOR I=0 TO MAX.MENU
1170    IF LEN(MENU$(I)) > MAX.LNGTH THEN MAX.LNGTH= LEN(MENU$(I))
1180 NEXT I
1190 :
1200 WD.ROW= 5: WD.COLM= 10: WD.SHADOW= FALSE
1210 WD.LGTH= MAX.LNGTH+6: WD.HGT= MAX.MENU+2
1220 WD.HEAD$= MENU$(0):WD.FOOT$= "<F1> = Help"
1230 GOSUB 1640 'display window
1240 :
1250 CL= WD.COLM+3
1260 FOR I= 1 TO MAX.MENU
1270    RW= WD.ROW+I+1
1280    DEF SEG:CALL FASTSCRN(RW,CL,WNDW.BKG,MENU$(I))
```

```
1290 NEXT I
1300 :
1310 STATUS$=" Use <"+CHR$(24)+"> and <"+CHR$(25)+"> to select, <Return> to
     execute  <Esc> to End"
1320 GOSUB 2440 'display Status-Line
1330 HDFT.ROW= 1: ONKEY$= "": LOCATE ,,0
1340 HELP.NUMBER= 2 'for Help-function
1350 :
1360 WHILE ONKEY$<> CHR$(27) AND ONKEY$<> CHR$(13)
1370   LOCATE ,,0 'switch Cursor off
1380   RW= WD.ROW+HDFT.ROW+1: CL= WD.COLM+1
1390   X$= "  "+MENU$(HDFT.ROW): X$= X$+SPACE$(MAX.LNGTH+6-LEN(X$))
1400   DEF SEG:CALL FASTSCRN(RW,CL,HDFT.TXT,X$)
1410   ONKEY$= INKEY$:IF ONKEY$= "" THEN 1410
1420   DEF SEG:CALL FASTSCRN(RW,CL,WNDW.BKG,X$)
1430   IF ONKEY$= CHR$(27) THEN MENU= 0
1440   IF ONKEY$= CHR$(13) THEN MENU= HDFT.ROW
1450   ONKEY= ASC(RIGHT$(ONKEY$,1))
1460   IF ONKEY= 72 THEN HDFT.ROW= HDFT.ROW-1 'Cursor up
1470   IF ONKEY= 80 THEN HDFT.ROW= HDFT.ROW+1 'Cursor down
1480   IF ONKEY= 71 THEN HDFT.ROW= 1 '<Home>
1490   IF ONKEY= 79 THEN HDFT.ROW= MAX.MENU
1500   IF ONKEY= 59 THEN GOSUB 3050 'Help display
1510   IF HDFT.ROW < 1 THEN HDFT.ROW= MAX.MENU
1520   IF HDFT.ROW > MAX.MENU THEN HDFT.ROW= 1
1530 WEND
1540 RETURN
1550 :
```

In the routine for the menu control, the lines 1340 and 1500 have been added. Line 1340 sets the HELP.NUMBER to the value 2. Line 1500 calls the help routine after line 3050, after the <F1> key is activated. The value stored in HELP.NUMBER is used as a record number for the access to the help file and the special help is displayed.

```
1560 '----- initialize background -----
1570 :
1580 X$= STRING$(WD.LGTH,BKG.CHAR$)
1590 FOR H.RW= WD.ROW TO WD.ROW+WD.HGT
1600   CALL FASTSCRN(H.RW,WD.COLM,BKG.COLR,X$)
1610 NEXT H.RW
1620 RETURN
1630 :
1640 '----- Universal-Routine for window -----
1650 :
1660 X$= CHR$(218)+STRING$(WD.LGTH%,CHR$(196))+CHR$(191)
1670 DEF SEG:CALL FASTSCRN(WD.ROW,WD.COLM,WNDW.BKG,X$)
1680 X$= CHR$(179)+STRING$(WD.LGTH%," ")+CHR$(179)
1690 IF WD.SHADOW THEN X$= X$+CHR$(178)+CHR$(178)
1700 FOR W.RW= WD.ROW+1 TO WD.ROW+WD.HGT
1710   DEF SEG:CALL FASTSCRN(W.RW,WD.COLM,WNDW.BKG,X$)
1720 NEXT W.RW
1730 X$= CHR$(192)+STRING$(WD.LGTH%,CHR$(196))+CHR$(217)
1740 IF WD.SHADOW THEN X$= X$+CHR$(178)+CHR$(178)
```

```
1750 W.RW= WD.ROW+WD.HGT+1
1760 DEF SEG:CALL FASTSCRN(W.RW,WD.COLM,WNDW.BKG,X$)
1770 IF WD.HEAD$= "" THEN 1810 'continue with footer$
1780   X$= " "+WD.HEAD$+" "
1790   W.CL= WD.COLM+3
1800   CALL FASTSCRN(WD.ROW,W.CL,HDFT.TXT,X$)
1810 IF WD.FOOT$= "" THEN 1850 'continue with shadow
1820   X$= " "+WD.FOOT$+" "
1830   W.RW= WD.ROW+WD.HGT+1: W.CL= WD.COLM+3
1840   CALL FASTSCRN(W.RW,W.CL,HDFT.TXT,X$)
1850 IF NOT WD.SHADOW THEN 1890 'return
1860   X$= STRING$(WD.LGTH+2,CHR$(178))
1870   W.RW= WD.ROW+WD.HGT+2:W.CL= WD.COLM+2
1880   CALL FASTSCRN(W.RW,W.CL,WNDW.BKG,X$)
1890 RETURN
1900 :
1910 '----- store current screen display -----
1920 :
1930 IF CUR.SCN= MAX.SCN THEN BEEP:RETURN
1940 DEF SEG:BUFFER.OFS%= VARPTR(BUFFER%(CUR.SCN*2000)):CALL
     SAVESCRN(BUFFER.OFS%)
1950 CUR.SCN= CUR.SCN+1
1960 RETURN
1970 :
1980 '----- restore last screen display -----
1990 :
2000 IF CUR.SCN= 0 THEN BEEP:RETURN
2010 CUR.SCN= CUR.SCN-1
2020 DEF SEG:BUFFER.OFS%= VARPTR(BUFFER%(CUR.SCN*2000)):CALL
     RESTSCRN(BUFFER.OFS%)
2030 RETURN
2040 :
2050 'Data-lines from COM-file: screen.com
2060 :
2070 RESTORE 2090
2080 DEF SEG:FOR I=1 TO  227:READ X:POKE MP.START+I-1,X: NEXT I
2090 DATA 235,109,144,235,109,144, 85,139,236, 30,  6
2100 DATA 139,118, 12,138, 28,176,160,246,227, 45,160
2110 DATA   0, 80,139,118, 10,138, 28,176,  2,246,227
2120 DATA  91,  3,195, 72, 72, 80,139,118,  8,138, 36
2130 DATA 139,118,  6,138, 12,181,  0,139,116,  1, 80
2140 DATA 191,  0,176,179,  0,205, 17, 37, 48,  0, 61
2150 DATA  48,  0,116,  6,129,199,  0,  8,179,  1,142
2160 DATA 199, 88, 95,252,186,218,  3,128,251,  0,116
2170 DATA  11,236,208,216,114,246,250,236,208,216,115
2180 DATA 251,172,251,171,226,235,  7, 31, 93,202,  8
2190 DATA   0,235, 41,144, 85,139,236, 30,  6,139,118
2200 DATA   6,139,  4,139,240,191,  0,176,179,  0,205
2210 DATA  17, 37, 48,  0, 61, 48,  0,116,  6,129,199
2220 DATA   0,  8,179,  1,142,199, 51,255,235, 40,144
2230 DATA  85,139,236, 30,  6,139,118,  6,139,  4,139
2240 DATA 248, 30,  7,190,  0,176,179,  0,205, 17, 37
2250 DATA  48,  0, 61, 48,  0,116,  6,129,198,  0,  8
```

```
2260 DATA 179,  1,142,222, 51,246,185,208,  7,252,186
2270 DATA 218,  3,128,251,  0,116, 11,236,208,216,114
2280 DATA 246,250,236,208,216,115,251,173,251,171,226
2290 DATA 235,  7, 31, 93,202,  2,  0
2300 RETURN
2310 :
2320 '----- output message -----
2330 :
2340 GOSUB 1910 'store screen display
2350 RW= 25: CL= 1: MESSG$= " "+MESSG$+SPACE$(80-LEN(MESSG$)-1)
2360 CALL FASTSCRN(RW,CL,MESSG.BKG,MESSG$)
2370 LOCATE 25,79:PRINT CHR$(254);: LOCATE 25,79,1
2380 SOUND 895,1: SOUND 695,1
2390 X$= INKEY$:IF X$= "" THEN 2390
2400 GOSUB 1980 'restore screen display
2410 LOCATE ,,0
2420 RETURN
2430 :
2440 '----- display Status-Line -----
2450 :
2460 RW= 25: CL= 1: STATUS$= " "+STATUS$+SPACE$(80-LEN(STATUS$)-1)
2470 CALL FASTSCRN(RW,CL,MESSG.BKG,STATUS$)
2480 RETURN
2490 :
2500 '----- read subroutine -----
2510 :
2520 GOSUB 2440 'display Status-Line for the input according to STATUS$
2530 X$="":ONKEY= 0:ANYCHANGE= FALSE
2540 Y$= INSTRING$+SPACE$(LNGTH-LEN(INSTRING$))
2550 CALL FASTSCRN(ROWNO,COLMNO,HDFT.TXT,Y$)
2560 LOCATE ROWNO,COLMNO,1: CRSR.POS= 1
2570 X$= INKEY$:IF X$="" THEN 2570 'wait for key
2580 IF X$= CHR$( 8) AND POS(0)> COLMNO THEN GOSUB 2710:GOTO 2570 '<Backspace>
2590 IF X$= CHR$(27) THEN ANYCHANGE= FALSE:LOCATE ,,0:RETURN
2600 IF X$= CHR$(13) THEN LOCATE ,,0:RETURN
2610 IF LEN(X$)= 2 THEN 2890 'control and function keys
2620 '
2630 IF X$< " " THEN BEEP:GOTO 2570 'kill characters smaller than BLANK
2640 IF MAKE.CAPS THEN IF X$>= "a" AND X$<= "z" THEN X$= CHR$(ASC(X$)-32)
2650 PRINT X$;:ANYCHANGE= TRUE
2660 IF CRSR.POS<= LEN(INSTRING$) THEN MID$(INSTRING$,CRSR.POS,1)= X$ ELSE
     INSTRING$= INSTRING$+X$
2670 CRSR.POS= CRSR.POS+1
2680 IF POS(0)> COLMNO+LNGTH-1 THEN LOCATE ROWNO,COLMNO:CRSR.POS= 1:GOTO 2570
2690 GOTO 2570 'continue to query keyboard
2700 '
2710 '----- BACKSPACE and DEL keys -----
2720 '
2730 IF X$=CHR$(8) THEN INSTRING$= LEFT$(INSTRING$,CRSR.POS-
     2)+MID$(INSTRING$,CRSR.POS)
2740 IF ONKEY= 83  THEN INSTRING$= LEFT$(INSTRING$,CRSR.POS-
     1)+MID$(INSTRING$,CRSR.POS+1) '<Del>
2750 LOCATE ROWNO,COLMNO:PRINT INSTRING$;" ";
```

```
2760 IF X$=CHR$(8) THEN CRSR.POS= CRSR.POS-1
2770 LOCATE CSRLIN,COLMNO+CRSR.POS-1
2780 ONKEY= 0: X$="":ANYCHANGE= TRUE
2790 RETURN
2800 '
2810 '----- INSERT key -----
2820 '
2830 INSTRING$= LEFT$(INSTRING$,CRSR.POS-1)+" "+MID$(INSTRING$,CRSR.POS)
2840 PRINT " ";MID$(INSTRING$,CRSR.POS+1);
2850 LOCATE CSRLIN,COLMNO+CRSR.POS-1
2860 ANYCHANGE= TRUE
2870 RETURN
2880 '
2890 '----- control and function keys -----
2900 '
2910 ONKEY= ASC(RIGHT$(X$,1))
2920 IF ONKEY= 59 THEN GOSUB 3050:GOTO 2570 'Help/continue to 2930 IF ONKEY= 68
     OR ONKEY= 63 THEN LOCATE ,,0:RETURN '<F5> and <F10>
```

In the universal input routine the <F1> key is also significant and the help routine is called when it's activated (starting at line 3050). No HELP.NUMBER is set, but this must be done in the function/routine which calls the input routine. This occurs in line 770 in this example and before the input routine is called. You can easily avoid the problem that this presents.

Suppose that you forget to set the HELP.NUMBER in a function/routine and call the input routine. If <F1> is activated here, the help routine is called, but in the HELP.NUMBER variable it finds an old and, therefore, incorrect help number. Since the routine doesn't know this, the incorrect help is also displayed. The user could be confused, if, for the "ZIP code" field, the help "menu selection" is displayed. As we mentioned, this can be avoided if, during programming, everything is recorded properly in a flow chart (see Section 16.3.2) and once the programming is completed, all the help features are properly tested.

```
2940 IF ONKEY= 72 OR ONKEY= 80 THEN LOCATE ,,0:RETURN 'Cursor up and down
2950 IF ONKEY= 73 OR ONKEY= 81 THEN LOCATE ,,0:RETURN '<PgUp> and <PgDn>
2960 IF ONKEY= 75 AND POS(0)> COLMNO THEN LOCATE CSRLIN,POS(0)-1:CRSR.POS=
     CRSR.POS-1:GOTO 2570 'Cursor <--
2970 IF ONKEY= 77 AND POS(0)< COLMNO+LNGTH-1 THEN IF CRSR.POS<= LEN(INSTRING$)
     THEN LOCATE CSRLIN,POS(0)+1:CRSR.POS= CRSR.POS+1:GOTO 2570 'Cursor -->
2980 IF ONKEY= 83 AND CRSR.POS <= LEN(INSTRING$) THEN GOSUB 2710:GOTO 2570 '<Del>
     handled similar to <Backspace>
2990 IF ONKEY= 71 THEN LOCATE ROWNO,COLMNO:GOTO 2570 '<Home>, beginning of field
3000 IF ONKEY= 79 THEN LOCATE CSRLIN,COLMNO+LEN(INSTRING$)-1:CRSR.POS=
     LEN(INSTRING$):GOTO 2570 '<End>, set to last character
3010 IF ONKEY= 117 THEN INSTRING$= LEFT$(INSTRING$,CRSR.POS-1):PRINT
     SPACE$(LNGTH-CRSR.POS);:LOCATE CSRLIN,COLMNO+CRSR.POS-1:ANYCHANGE= TRUE:GOTO
     2570 '<Ctrl> <End> erase to end of field
3020 IF ONKEY= 82 AND CRSR.POS<= LEN(INSTRING$) AND LEN(INSTRING$)< LNGTH THEN
     GOSUB 2810:GOTO 2570 '<Ins>
3030 BEEP:GOTO 2570 'continue to query keyboard
```

```
3040 :
3050 '----- subroutine for Help-function -----
3060 :
3070 AWD.ROW= WD.ROW: AWD.COLM= WD.COLM: AWD.LGTH= WD.LGTH: AWD.HGT= WD.HGT
3080 AWD.SHADOW= WD.SHADOW 'store data of the window Variables
3090 ACRSR.ROWNO= CSRLIN: ACRSR.COLMNO= POS(0) 'store Cursor position
3100 LOCATE ,,0
3110 :
```

In the help routine the window variables and the cursor position are stored first. The window variable is needed here for the help window. The cursor position is stored to ensure that the cursor can be returned to its previous position.

```
3120 GOSUB 1910   'store screen display
```

Storing the screen display is especially important so that the user can quickly continue his/her work.

```
3130 :
3140 FIL.NAM$= "TEST.HLP"
```

The filename should always agree with HF_EDIT. The following routines were explained in Section 16.3.2. The routines for the creation and storage aren't needed here.

```
3150 ON ERROR GOTO 3880 'error-handling
3160 :
3170 STATUS$= "a moment please, reading Help...":GOSUB 2440
3180 OPEN FIL.NAM$ FOR INPUT AS #1 'open file for sequential access
3190 LINE INPUT #1,X$ 'first record/first line contains HELP.LINES
3200 HELP.LINES= VAL(X$)
3210 LINE INPUT#1,X$ 'first record/second line contains MAX.HELP
3220 MAX.HELP= VAL(X$)
3230 SET.LNGTH= (HELP.LINES+1)*60
3240 CLOSE #1
3250 GOTO 3990 'file found, continue normally
3260 :
3270 '----- open Random-File, initialize FIELDs ---
3280 :
3290 OPEN "R",#1,FIL.NAM$,SET.LNGTH
3300 ON HELP.LINES GOTO 0,0,0,3320,0,0,0,3340,0,0,0,3360,0,0,0,3380,0,0,0,3400
3310 'according to HELP.LINES:        4        8        12        16
     20
3320 FIELD#1,60 AS PAGE.TITLE$,240 AS TEXT1$
3330 RETURN 'continue in the text
3340 FIELD#1,60 AS PAGE.TITLE$,240 AS TEXT1$,240 AS TEXT2$
3350 RETURN 'continue in the text
3360 FIELD#1,60 AS PAGE.TITLE$,240 AS TEXT1$,240 AS TEXT2$,240 AS TEXT3$
3370 RETURN 'continue in the text
3380 FIELD#1,60 AS PAGE.TITLE$,240 AS TEXT1$,240 AS TEXT2$,240 AS TEXT3$,240 AS
     TEXT4$
```

```
3390 RETURN 'continue in the text
3400 FIELD#1,60 AS PAGE.TITLE$,240 AS TEXT1$,240 AS TEXT2$,240 AS TEXT3$,240 AS
     TEXT4$,240 AS TEXT5$
3410 RETURN 'continue in the text
3420 :
3430 '----- read help-texts -----
3440 :
3450 GET#1,HELP.NUMBER 'read current help-page
3460 Z= 1
3470 FOR I=1 TO 240 STEP 60 'read four lines from TEXT1$
3480    HELP.TEXT$(Z)= MID$(TEXT1$,I,60)
3490    Z=Z+1
3500 NEXT I
3510 IF HELP.LINES= 4 THEN 3720 '4 lines for Help
3520 FOR I=1 TO 240 STEP 60 'read four lines from TEXT2$
3530    HELP.TEXT$(Z)= MID$(TEXT2$,I,60)
3540    Z=Z+1
3550 NEXT I
3560 IF HELP.LINES= 8 THEN 3720 '8 lines for Help
3570 FOR I=1 TO 240 STEP 60 'read four lines from TEXT3$
3580    HELP.TEXT$(Z)= MID$(TEXT3$,I,60)
3590    Z=Z+1
3600 NEXT I
3610 IF HELP.LINES= 12 THEN 3720 '12 lines for Help
3620 FOR I=1 TO 240 STEP 60 'read four lines from TEXT4$
3630    HELP.TEXT$(Z)= MID$(TEXT4$,I,60)
3640    Z=Z+1
3650 NEXT I
3660 IF HELP.LINES= 16 THEN 3720 '16 lines for Help
3670 FOR I=1 TO 240 STEP 60 'read four lines from TEXT5$
3680    HELP.TEXT$(Z)= MID$(TEXT5$,I,60)
3690    Z=Z+1
3700 NEXT I
3710 :
3720 FOR I=1 TO HELP.LINES
3730    IF RIGHT$(HELP.TEXT$(I),1)<> CHR$(0) THEN 3750
3740    HELP.TEXT$(I)= LEFT$(HELP.TEXT$(I),INSTR(HELP.TEXT$(I),CHR$(0))-1)
3750 NEXT I
3760 RETURN '20 lines for Help
3770 :
3780 '----- display help-texts -----
3790 :
3800 H.RW= WD.ROW: H.CL= WD.COLM+2
3810 CALL FASTSCRN(H.RW,H.CL,HDFT.TXT,PAGE.TITLE$)
3820 FOR I=1 TO HELP.LINES
3830    H.RW= WD.ROW+I+1:Y$= HELP.TEXT$(I)+SPACE$( 60-LEN(HELP.TEXT$(I)))
3840    CALL FASTSCRN(H.RW,H.CL,MESSG.BKG,Y$)
3850 NEXT I
3860 RETURN 'page display
3870 :
3880 '----- error-handling "file-access" -----
3890 :
3900 IF ERR<> 53 THEN 3950 'general error display
```

```
3910   CLOSE 'close all files
3920   MESSG$= "help-file not found, check page 348 of the reference manual..."
       :GOSUB 2320
3930   RESUME 4110 'back to calling function
3940   :
```

Line 3920 displays a message if the help file wasn't found or wasn't created yet. In this example, there is a reference to the manual containing an explanation of this error message. Then there is a return to the calling function/routine.

```
3950 CLOSE 'close all files
3960 MESSG$="error "+STR$(ERR)+" in line "+STR$(ERL)+"...":GOSUB 2320
3970 RESUME 4110 'back to calling function
3980 :
3990 '----- initialize random-file and help-page display -----
4000 :
4010 GOSUB 3270 'open random-file and initialize FIELDs
4020 WD.ROW= 5:WD.COLM= 9:WD.LGTH= 62:WD.HGT= HELP.LINES+2:WD.SHADOW= TRUE
4030 WD.HEAD$= "": WD.FOOT$= "<Esc> = back"
4040 GOSUB 1640  'display window for Help
4050 GOSUB 3430 'read help-texts
4060 GOSUB 3780 'display help-texts
4070 STATUS$= " ":GOSUB 2440
4080 X$= INKEY$: IF X$= "" THEN 4080
4090 CLOSE
4100 :
4110 GOSUB 1980 'restore screen display
4120 WD.ROW= AWD.ROW: WD.COLM= AWD.COLM: WD.LGTH= AWD.LGTH: WD.HGT= AWD.HGT
4130 WD.SHADOW= AWD.SHADOW
4140 LOCATE ACRSR.ROWNO,ACRSR.COLMNO,1
4150 X$= "": ONKEY= 0
4160 RETURN
```

The screen display is restored and the window variables, as well as the cursor position, are returned to their original values. Then a return is made to the calling function.

16.3.4 Suggestions for HELP.BAS

You must create a help file before using the HELP.BAS program. You'll receive an error message if there are no help files available. We'll provide more information on this shortly.

A menu bar containing several options is displayed after the start of the program. We're using only the "add" function for this example. You'll receive a "FUNCTION NOT AVAILABLE" error message if you try accessing any of the other options.

Press the <F1> key and to see an example of the help function. After selecting the "add" option, an input template is displayed in a window and an input is requested in the first field. Move through the fields with the cursor keys and press the <F1> key in every field. The help specifically designed for that field immediately appears.

Press the <F10> key when you're finished. A plausibility test is simulated and the result appears as a message.

Expanding the Program

You can easily adapt the above code to your own programming needs. You should add a help function to programs that anyone other than yourself will use. This extended help function includes a routine that reads help screen data from a random file and displays a set of help topics in the form of a menu bar. When the user selects a topic from the menu bar, the program displays the appropriate help screen. This can be particularly helpful to users who don't have any documentation for the program and want a general overview of program commands. This is just a suggestion that you could implement on your own.

Important Note

For the program above, you must create a help file; otherwise you'll receive an error message. First copy the HF_EDIT program (unless this has already been done). Then create the TEST.DAT file with 12 lines per page (simply accept default values by pressing <F10>).

Then enter the following help texts. The numbers in parentheses (1) (2) (3) represent the help numbers and don't have to be entered. The first line is always the title of the help screen. The rest is the actual help text. Since the lines separating the text are only used for clarity, they can be omitted:

```
-------------------------------------------------------------
(2) select menu option...

Use the cursor keys to move the inverted cursor to
the desired menu option. Strike the <Return>-
key to execute the desired function.
-------------------------------------------------------------
(3) last name...

Please enter the last name of the customer.
This name is needed for the mail merge function.
It appears in the address and also the salutation:

Mr.
<first-name> <last-name>
etc.

Dear Mr. <last-name>,
etc.
```

```
-----------------------------------------------------------
(4) first name...
```

Please enter the first name of the customer. The
first name is required for the example of the mail merge function.
It appears in the address:

Mr.<first-name> <last-name>

If the customer has a title, it will be indicated here:

```
first-name :   Dr. Michael
last-name:   Miller
-----------------------------------------------------------
(5) street...
```

Please enter the complete address where the
customer resides. You should include the house number, apartment number or PO Box
number:

113 Main Street

This input is required for the function "serial-letter-
and is used in the address.


```
--------------------------------------------------
(6) city...
```

Enter the name of the city where the customer
resides. The ZIP code may have to reflect the suburb.

Philadelphia

This input is required for the address in the mail merge function.
```
-----------------------------------------------------------
(7) ZIP code...
```

Enter the ZIP code of the location where the customer lives. This input is
required for the address in the mail merge function:

```
Mr.
<first-name> <last-name>
<street>
<city> <ZIP>
```

Geographical relationships can be evaluated on the basis of the ZIP-code.
```
-----------------------------------------------------------
(8) country code...
```

You must enter a proper country code for foreign customers.

Examples:

```
Aus   - Australia
I   - Italy
NZ-New Zealand
```

A more detailed listing appears in the reference manual,
Appendix -D-, "country codes", starting at page 378
----
(9) remark...

You can enter any text which provides more information about the customer:

examples:

```
Hobbies: sailing
Birthday: 2/2/56
Sales 1989: $23,789,560
Appointment to discuss Abacus book line: Monday, 10/12/90
```

and so on ...
----
(10) Note:

A customer with the same name already exists in the file.

Please check if this is the same customer or somebody with a similar name.

For double entries, The customer gets two letters from the mail merge function if he/she is entered twice.

16.4   What Error Handling Capabilities are Available?

As with the help function, error handling can also be used in various ways. Again, this depends on the target audience. Experienced PC users probably only require short messages. For users working with a more complicated program, for example a CAD system, this message can be much shorter. Since this type of user probably has more experience with a PC, the following message is appropriate:

```
Diskette is write-protected,
correct and strike <Return> key
```

However, if you're developing a word processing application, the target audience probably won't have much computer experience. So, the error messages for this program should be extensive. The following message for a write-protect error is an example of this:

```
While trying to save your text on the diskette, it was discovered that this
diskette is write-protected. This is a tag affixed to the left side of the
diskette. Remove this tag, re-insert the diskette and close the door on the
drive. Strike the <Return> key.
```

16.4.1 General Error Handling

There are two definitions for general error handling:

1.   With the ON ERROR GOTO statement you can jump to a universal routine which simply displays a brief message and the error number:

```
file-error 53, see reference manual page 351
```

The user is also directed to a detailed explanation found in the reference manual.

2.   Another way to present general error handling is to present a message that indicates that an error has occurred and include a brief explanation of how to correct it. In the status line, a simple message appears. For example:

```
Diskette full - insert another diskette
```

As we explained at the beginning of this section, these two capabilities are mainly suited for advanced users requiring only a brief message to correct their mistakes.

The programming needed for this type of error handling is simple. Usually at the beginning of the program the ON ERROR GOTO <line number> statement is given. In this routine the system variable ERR and, if necessary, ERL are prepared and displayed in the status line or a small window. Then a wait occurs for a key activation. The statement causing the error is executed again with a RESUME until the error has been corrected or the user switches off the computer. The following program demonstrates a simple routine of this type:

```
10 '------------------------------------------------------
20 'ERROR1.BAS    Simple Error-handling
30 '------------------------------------------------------
40 :
50 CLS:KEY OFF
60 :
70 ON ERROR GOTO 180
80 :
90 PRINT SPC(5);"Insert a diskette into drive A: "
100 PRINT SPC(5);" but do not close the drive door !!!"
110 PRINT:PRINT:PRINT "Strike any key when ready...";
120 IF INKEY$= "" THEN 120
130 :
140 OPEN "A:TEST.DAT" FOR INPUT AS #1
150 CLOSE #1
160 CLS:END
170 :
180 '----- error-handling -----
190 :
200 X$= "Error:"+STR$(ERR)+" in line "+STR$(ERL)+". Correct and strike key "
210 LOCATE 25,1:PRINT X$;SPACE$(80-POS(0));
220 BEEP
230 IF INKEY$= "" THEN 230
240 LOCATE 25,1:PRINT SPACE$(79);
250 RESUME
```

As we already mentioned, the error handling routine is simply prepared with ON ERROR GOTO (line 70), in which the system variables ERR and ERL are processed (line 200) and displayed with a reference to the manual (line 210). The line causing the error is called again with a RESUME.

This type of message, since it isn't very comprehensive, should only be used for utilities. These utilities are used mainly by programmers. The following example is more informative:

```
10 '------------------------------------------------------
20 'ERROR_2.BAS   demonstration of a simple error handling
30 '------------------------------------------------------
40 :
50 CLS:KEY OFF
60 :
70 NUM.OF.ERRORS= 19: DIM ERR.NUM(NUM.OF.ERRORS), ERR.MESSG$(NUM.OF.ERRORS)
80 RESTORE 100
90 FOR I=1 TO NUM.OF.ERRORS:READ ERR.NUM(I),ERR.MESSG$(I):NEXT I
100 DATA 11,"Division by zero - check input "
110 DATA 13,"Wrong data type - check input "
```

```
120 DATA 14,"Insufficient memory for character strings - file can not be
    enlarged"
130 DATA 15,"Character string is too long - shorten input "
140 DATA 18,"Undefined function - please inform programmer "
150 DATA 24,"Invalid drive specification - please check drive"
160 DATA 25,"Device does not respond - please check device"
170 DATA 27,"Printer is out of paper - please insert paper"
180 DATA 51,"Internal error in the interpreter - please inform programmer"
190 DATA 53,"File not found - please check filename "
200 DATA 57,"Input/Output error - please check printer or diskette "
210 DATA 61,"Diskette is full - please insert a new diskette "
220 DATA 67,"No space for the file on this diskette - insert another diskette"
230 DATA 68,"Device not present or does not answer - please check device"
240 DATA 70,"Diskette is write-protected - please remove write-protect"
250 DATA 71,"Drive not ready - please check drive and if disk is fully inserted"
260 DATA 72,"Diskette error, may not be properly formatted - please check
    diskette"
270 DATA 75,"Invalid or non-existent path was indicated - please check input"
280 DATA 76,"Indicated path not found - please check input "
290 ON ERROR GOTO 400
300 :
310 PRINT SPC(5);"Insert a diskette into drive A: "
320 PRINT SPC(5);"but do not close the drive door !!!"
330 PRINT:PRINT:PRINT "Strike any key when ready ...";
340 IF INKEY$= "" THEN 340
350 :
360 OPEN "A:TEST.DAT" FOR INPUT AS #1
370 CLOSE #1
380 CLS:END
390 :
400 '----- error-handling -----
410 :
420 X$= ""
430 FOR I=1 TO NUM.OF.ERRORS
440    IF ERR.NUM(I)= ERR THEN X$= ERR.MESSG$(I)
450 NEXT I
460 IF X$<> "" THEN 480
470 X$= "General error: "+STR$(ERR)+" in line: "+STR$(ERL)
480 LOCATE 25,1:PRINT X$;SPACE$(80-POS(0));:BEEP
490 IF INKEY$= "" THEN 490
500 LOCATE 25,1:PRINT SPACE$(79);
510 RESUME
```

Again the ON ERROR GOTO is used to implement an error handling routine (line 290).
The difference is that the error number and texts for the most important errors are stored in
two arrays (line 90). A test is made starting at line 400 for the error correction in a loop to
determine whether the error reported in ERR is available as text (lines 430 to 450). If it is,
the text is transmitted to the output variable X$ (line 440) and displayed. If text isn't
available for the error number (test in line 460), the output variable is initialized with the
message "general error" and the values from ERR and ERL (line 470) are displayed (line
480). As you can see, this routine should only be used for an advanced PC user.

16.4.2 Context-Sensitive Error Handling

The user receives answers to the following questions using context-sensitive error handling:

- What error has occurred?

- Why did this error occur?

- How can this error be corrected?

A more complete and comprehensive explanation must be displayed instead of the short messages we used previously.

The context-sensitive error handling is now used in almost every application. Almost all software manufacturers consider it a standard. We'll thoroughly discuss this in Section 16.5.

16.4.3 Preventive Error Handling

Many errors are caused by the user's carelessness. Both beginners and experienced users make these types of mistakes. These errors can be avoided with preventive error handling.

As an example, let's use a word processing program and the "save text" function. Before calling the actual save routine, go to a routine which displays the following message:

```
┌─ Text Store: ──────────────────────┐
│ Please insert a diskette into drive "A:" │
│ and close the drive door.                │
│ Strike the <F10> key.                    │
└─ With <Esc> return to the text ──────┘
```

Fig. 40: Preventive Error Handling

The preventive error handling messages provide the user with helpful information and avoid the potential for future errors. In most cases, these types of messages are more of a reminder to the user not to forget to do something important. In this example, it's a reminder to the user to have a diskette in the drive before saving the word processor file.

16.5   Implementing Error Handling

In this section we'll discuss context-sensitive error handling in detail. First we'll discuss "error analysis".

16.5.1 Analyzing Errors

You must know the following three things to design an effective error handling routine:

- What error has occurred?

- Where in the program did the error occur?

- How can the error be corrected?

It's necessary to analyze the error in an error handling routine. You must and, depending on the results, inform the user of what happened and how to proceed. Let's review the statements and variables which PC-BASIC has for analyzing and correcting errors:

ON ERROR GOTO

Determines to which line number a jump should be made when an error occurs.

RESUME

After the error handling, RESUME calls the statement causing the error. A RESUME can be used when the "Drive not ready" or "Printer out of paper" error occurs. These errors are easy to correct. For other errors, such as "Device not present", an endless loop can be programmed with RESUME.

RESUME NEXT

Calls the statement which follows the statement that caused the error. You should be careful using this statement because it can perform calculations using false values (i.e., division with zero). So, after a RESUME NEXT, be prepared for incorrect results.

RESUME <line>

Continues the program, in the indicated line, after the error handling. This is mainly suited for the query "File available or not". If the file doesn't exist, the user can jump to a routine after error 53 and RESUME <line> creates the file. Refer to the HF_EDIT program for an example. This statement is, however, difficult to use in large programs. For example, it's difficult to execute if there is a handling routine in line 9980. It's better to branch inside the error handling routine and locate the routine to create a file.

ERR

The number of the last error that occurred is stored in this system variable. This variable is never set to 0 by PC-BASIC, even if the last action occurred without an error. So the following query is dangerous:

```
IF ERR<> 0 THEN error
```

ERL

The number of the line, in which the last error occurred, is stored in this system variable. This variable is also never set to 0 by PC-BASIC.

ERDEV$

The name of the device causing the error is stored, in text form, in this system variable. If, for example, the diskette in drive A isn't formatted, ERDEV$ returns the following if displayed after an error:

```
A:
```

PRN and LPTx for printer or AUX and COMx for the V.24 interface could also be displayed.

ERDEV

After an error, this system variable returns the DOS error code in the LowByte and the bits 8 to 15 of the device header attribute field in the HighByte.

The DOS error code basically corresponds to the error numbers of PC-BASIC. A listing of possible DOS errors can be found in the Appendix.

The device header attribute field provides information about the attributes of a device driver:

```
Bit 15: 0= character-driver (for example printer)
        1= Block-driver (for example diskette)
Bit 14: 0= IOCTL not supported
        1= IOCTL is supported
Bit 13: 0= IBM-format (Block-driver)
        1= no IBM-Format (Block-driver)
Bit 12:    not used
Bit 11: 0= does not support diskettes
        1= supports diskettes
Bit 10:
  to
Bit  4:    reserved for DOS
Bit  3: 0= device is not a clock driver
        1= device is a clock-driver
Bit  2: 0= device is not a null driver
        1= device is a null driver
Bit  1: 0= device is not a Standard-Output
        1= device is a Standard-Output
Bit  0: 0= device is not a Standard-Input
        1= device is a Standard-Input
```

As you already know, the bits 8 to 15 are returned in the HighByte. Since this information isn't needed by the user, the error message, "Printer out of paper" is sufficient.

EXTERR

Starting with PC-BASIC Version 3.xx or MS-/PC-DOS Version 3.xx, enhanced error codes, which are designed to simplify identifying and correcting errors, were introduced. PC-BASIC provides the EXTERR function for this. We've already discussed this function in Section 4.8.

ERROR <n>

ERROR <n> can be used to simulate an error or to enable the user to define error codes. It can be used to check plausibility tests or to have these tests trap specific errors. As an example, let's consider an application which has several masks and several fields. A test for acceptable values must be performed. This test must be performed for each field individually and according to the established limits.

The error messages can be read in a central location in your program. The specific message can then be displayed on the screen. This way, the message is only displayed in one place saving program space and allowing you to make changes quickly.

The following small program highlights the importance of ERDEV and ERDEV$.

```
10 '-------------------------------------------------
20 'ERROR_3.BAS    ERDEV and ERDEV$ demonstration
30 '-------------------------------------------------
40 :
50 CLS:KEY OFF
60 PRINT "Attempt to print on LPT1: failed ...":PRINT:PRINT
70 ON ERROR GOTO 180
80 :
90 OPEN "lpt1:" FOR OUTPUT AS #1
100 PRINT #1,"Test"
110 CLOSE
120 :
130 PRINT "Attempt to open a file on A: failed...":PRINT:PRINT
140 OPEN "A:test.dat" FOR INPUT AS #1
150 CLOSE
160 END
170 :
180 '----- error-correction -----
190 :
200 PRINT "Device: ";ERDEV$
210 HI= INT(ERDEV/256)
220 LO= INT(ERDEV-HI*256)
230 PRINT USING "DOS-error: ###";LO
240 PRINT "Device-Attribute: ";
250 FOR I= 7 TO 0 STEP -1
260    IF (2^I AND HI)<> 0 THEN PRINT "1"; ELSE PRINT "0";
270 NEXT I
280 PRINT:PRINT:PRINT
290 RESUME NEXT 'next error
```

Before executing this program, either switch off the printer (or switch it to Off-Line) and remove the diskette from drive A. The program first attempts to send output to the printer. The error handling shows the evaluation of the DOS code and displays the bits 15 to 8 of the attribute field.

Now let's return to the error analysis. First convert the error into text. An example for this was already demonstrated in the ERROR_2.BAS program. Enhancements are required for a user-friendly error handling. We'll discuss this in more detail later. Three possibilities exist concerning where and why the error occurred:

1.   The error occurred in the program because of incorrect programming. Errors such as "RETURN without GOSUB" or "Subscript out of range" are programming errors and not the fault of the user.

2.   The error was caused by incorrect input. "Division by zero" indicates, for example, that the entered values weren't subjected to a plausibility test. This also applies to "Type mismatch" or "String too long".

3.   The error was caused by a hardware problem. A "Drive not ready" or "Out of Paper" error message is, for example, a typical hardware error.

If the first type of error occurs, you should be honest and admit it in the error message. For example:

```
Error in the program! Please inform programmer ...
```

This immediately informs the user that he/she didn't cause the error.

For the second type of error, the program should display the following message:

```
Error in the input. Please input only <correct values>.
```

For <correct values>, indicate the range of characters or possibilities which are permitted in this field.

For the third type of error, the message should be more comprehensive:

```
The printer is out of paper ! Please insert more paper into the printer,
switch the device On-Line and then strike the <F10> key.
```

The source of the error must be as specific as possible. Telling the user that the printer is out of paper doesn't provide enough information. Which printer is involved should also be indicated. Many times several printers are connected to one PC so that various paper types can easily be used. With ERDEV$, you can determine if the error occurred on LPT1 or LPT2.

Differentiating between errors

PC-BASIC helps distinguish between errors by separating the error numbers into groups.

error 1 to 30

These errors generally indicate an error exists in the program or there is a syntax error. The exceptions are errors 24 (Device timeout), 25 (Device fault) and 27 (Out of Paper). These errors must be handled differently.

error 50 to 76

These errors indicate a file or diskette error exists. It can be determined in an error handling routine whether it's a programming error or an error caused by the user. This determination is based on the error number.

Error Message Construction

An error message must indicate what error has occurred (i.e., "Diskette is full" or "Printer out of paper"). The location of the error must also be indicated (i.e., "drive "A:" or "printer on LPT2:"). Finally, there must be an indication of what action the user should take (i.e., "Please insert paper" or "Please insert another diskette"). So the following information must be known:

- What error?

- Where did it occur?

- What should be done now?

When indicating what error occurred, you should also include when the error occurred. Although this isn't necessary, it increases the user's understanding of the error handling process.

Displaying Error Messages

As we previously mentioned, at least three points must be covered in an error message. The error messages cannot be displayed in the status line because of the amount of information required for the message.

As in the help function, the text for the error message can also be initialized from an array, which was previously initialized from the data lines. As we already know, this would require too much memory space. PC-BASIC displays about 50 error numbers. With only 10 lines of 60 characters each for each message, that would require about 30K just for the array. So the only alternative is to construct a random file, as we did for the help function.

16.5.2 Assigning error text

We'll encounter some problems with the error handling we didn't face with the help function. With the help function we could use the assigned HELP.NUMBER as a record number for the random file. This isn't possible with error messages because only the error number from PC-BASIC can be used as access criteria. Unfortunately, these error numbers aren't numbered in sequence.

In order to use these numbers, we must use the first record of the random file as a control record. So the first available record for the error text is 2. With an assignment table we can create a connection between the error number and the record number. For this we construct a two dimensional array to store the error number and the record number to which it corresponds:

```
 90 .....
100 DIM ASSIGN.TAB(50,2)
110 RESTORE 170
120 FOR I= 1 TO 50
130    READ ASSIGN.TAB(I,1) 'read error-number from data-line
140    READ ASSIGN.TAB(I,2) 'add record-number to it
150 NEXT I
160 :
170 DATA 1,2 ,2,3 ,3,4 ,4,5 ,5,6 and so on ...
180 .....
```

Later, during the evaluation of the ERR variable, the table is searched for the value according to ERR and the record number which belongs to it is determined:

```
490 .....
500 FOR I=1 TO 50
510    IF ASSIGN.TAB(I,1)= ERR THEN SIZE.NUMBER= ASSIGN.TAB(I,2)
520 NEXT I
530 .....
```

You may be wondering why a one-dimensional array couldn't be used for ASSIGN.TAB(). It's possible to increment the I counter by one (first record is 2), which would also produce the correct record number. However, empty error screens would have to be created for the error numbers that aren't assigned. Also, it wouldn't be possible to use error screens for any purposes other than displaying error messages.

For example, in the demonstration program, we used screen 10 as an indicator for a duplicate customer name. However, in order to use this function with the error screens, the assignment must remain flexible in the data lines. By doing this, it's possible to use screen page 6 as a warning instead of using it for error number 5. Instead, screen page 7, for example, could be used for error 5. Obviously, in order to do this, an error handling routine must be activated with ON ERROR GOTO at the beginning of the program.

Construction of the error text file

The construction of the file for the error text corresponds to the construction of the help text files. The first record is again a control record, which indicates how many lines are provided for the error text and how many records have already been collected. Even though the numbers of records could be limited, we'll keep this flexible. As we mentioned earlier, any number of screens can be used as a message. Also, later PC-BASIC versions may provide additional error numbers so that the file can be enhanced as needed.

The error text, which is stored in the individual lines, indicates when and where the error occurred and what can be done to correct it.

16.5.3 Editor for the error file

The editor that was used for the help text is also used for the error text. So the information given in Section 16.3.1 also applies to the error file. Also for the error messages, the size of the error text must be flexible so that the error handling can be tailored according to the proper target audience. For the listing and the explanations or comments refer to Section 16.3.1.

Note: The execution of the HF_EDIT was also explained in the help function in Section 16.3.2. Refer to this section for information about HF_EDIT.

16.6   Help Functions and Error Handling in Applications

We'll present an example to conclude our discussion of help functions and error handling routines. Both topics have been combined in the program so that you can easily see the importance of a user-friendly approach to such a program. We enhanced the demonstration program from the help function with a context-sensitive error handling routine. We've included some of the most common errors and their handling in the program.

The existing routines for the file access from the help function are reused for the enhancement of the context-sensitive error handling. The files are identical and the display can easily be changed. As we mentioned, this program corresponds in many ways to the HELP.BAS program from Section 16.5. Basic explanations for the program can be found in that section. Only comments on error handling were included in this listing.

Important Note

You must create an error file before executing this program. First enter the HF_EDIT program (if you haven't already done so). Then create a file named TEST.ERR with 12 lines per screen page (simply accept the default values with <F10>). Consult Appendix C and D for the correct error messages. The text of each message (i.e., RETURN without GOSUB), should be used as a title. You can modify the explanations in the Appendix and use them as error text. We've listed other required examples at the end of this section.

Note: To execute the following program correctly, you must call PC-BASIC with the /M switch as follows:

```
GWBASIC /M:54000/S:1000
```

```
10 '--------------------------------------------------
20 'HLPERR.BAS  Help function/error-handling demonstration
22 'This program uses the files TEST.HLP and TEST.ERR.  You should create
23 'both of these with 16HFEDIT.BAS.
30 '--------------------------------------------------
40 :
50 DEFINT A-Z
60 OPTION BASE 0
70 CLS:KEY OFF:FOR I=1 TO 10:KEY I,"":NEXT I
80 ON ERROR GOTO 4180
90 :
```

If an error occurs line 80 indicates a jump to line 4180. This line is the location for the error handling routine.

```
100 DEF FNUP$(SMALL$)= CHR$(ASC(SMALL$) AND 223)
110 :
120 MP.START= &HE000
130 GOSUB 2160 'initialize MP
140 SAVESCRN= MP.START
150 RESTSCRN= MP.START+3
160 FASTSCRN= MP.START+6
170 FALSE= 0: TRUE= NOT FALSE
180 MAX.SCN= 3:DIM BUFFER%(2000*MAX.SCN)
190 MAX.MENU= 8: DIM MENU$(MAX.MENU)
200 MAX.ERROR= 51: DIM ERR.TAB(MAX.ERROR,2)
```

PC-BASIC issues 51 defined error numbers (line 200). The ERR.TAB() array is dimensioned accordingly. You can change this line to adjust the program for PC-BASIC versions with different error numbers.

```
210 CUR.SCN= 0
220 WNDW.BKG= 112: MESSG.BKG= 127: HDFT.TXT= 7
230 BKG.CHAR$= CHR$(177): BKG.COLR= 15
240 DIM HELP.TEXT$(20)
250 :
260 RESTORE 280
270 FOR I= 0 TO MAX.MENU:READ MENU$(I):NEXT I
280 DATA " MAIN MENU "
290 DATA "Arrange"
300 DATA "Add"
310 DATA "Search"
320 DATA "Change"
330 DATA "List"
340 DATA "Import"
350 DATA "Export"
360 DATA "End"
370 :
380 RESTORE 400
390 FOR I=1 TO 7:READ MASK$(I):NEXT I
400 DATA "Last name"
410 DATA "First name"
420 DATA "Street"
430 DATA "City/ST"
440 DATA "ZIP code"
450 DATA "Country code"
460 DATA "Remark"
470 :
480 RESTORE 500
490 FOR I=1 TO MAX.ERROR:READ ERR.TAB(I,1),ERR.TAB(I,2):NEXT I
500 DATA   1,2 ,2,3   ,3,4   ,4,5   ,5,6   ,6,7   ,7,8   ,8,9   ,9,10
510 DATA 10,11 ,11,12 ,12,13 ,13,14 ,14,15 ,15,16 ,16,17 ,17,18 ,18,19
520 DATA 19,20 ,20,21 ,22,22, 23,23 ,24,24 ,25,25 ,26,26 ,27,27 ,29,28 ,30,29
530 :
540 DATA 50,30 ,51,31 ,52,32 ,53,33 ,54,34 ,55,35 ,57,36 ,58,37 ,61,38
550 DATA 62,39 ,63,40 ,64,41 ,66,42 ,67,43 ,68,44 ,69,45 ,70,46 ,71,47
560 DATA 72,48 ,74,49 ,75,50 ,76,51
570 :
```

Starting at line 480, the ERR.TAB() array is initialized with the values from the data lines. In line 520/530 it becomes obvious that this array is necessary because of the jump from error number 20 to 22 or 30 to 50.

The data statements starting with line 500 control which error message is displayed. You may want to change these statements to fit your program requirements.

```
580 WD.ROW= 1: WD.COLM= 1: WD.LGTH= 80: WD.HGT= 25
590 GOSUB 1670 'initialize background
600 RW= 1: CL= 1: X$= " File Management V1.00 (C) 1987 H.J. Bomanns "
610 DEF SEG: CALL FASTSCRN(RW,CL,MESSG.BKG,X$)
620 :
630 GOSUB 1240 'menu-selection
640 IF MENU= 0 THEN MENU = 8 '<Shift> end
650 GOSUB 2020 'save screen display
660 ON MENU GOSUB 700,720,1110,1130,1150,1170,1190,1210 'execute function
670 GOSUB 2090 'restore screen display
680 GOTO 630 'query menu again
690 :
700 '----- arrange -----
710 ERROR 61: RETURN
720 '----- add -----
730 :
740 WD.ROW= 8: WD.COLM= 20: WD.LGTH= 50: WD.HGT= 9: WD.SHADOW= TRUE
750 WD.HEAD$= "Add data:"
760 WD.FOOT$= "<F1> = Help  <F10> = save  <Esc> = back"
770 GOSUB 1750 'display window
780 :
790 CL= WD.COLM+2
800 FOR I=1 TO 7
810   RW= WD.ROW+I+1
820   DEF SEG:CALL FASTSCRN(RW,CL,WNDW.BKG,MASK$(I))
830 NEXT I
840 :
850 COUNTER= 1 'for current input-field
860 :
870 WHILE X$<> CHR$(27) 'until <Esc> is activated
880   STATUS$= "Please input "+MASK$(COUNTER)+" ..."
890   HELP.NUMBER= 2+COUNTER
900   ROWNO= WD.ROW+COUNTER+1: COLMNO= WD.COLM+16
910   INSTRING$= CONTENT$(COUNTER)
920   LNGTH= 20:GOSUB 2610 'input-routine
930   CONTENT$(COUNTER) = INSTRING$
940   Y$= CONTENT$(COUNTER)+SPACE$(20-LEN(CONTENT$(COUNTER)))
950   CALL FASTSCRN(ROWNO,COLMNO,MESSG.BKG,Y$)
960   IF ONKEY<> 68 THEN 1030 'process <F10> here
970     AHELP.NUMBER= HELP.NUMBER 'save HELP.NUMBER
980     HELP.NUMBER= 10 'alert for duplicate customer
990     GOSUB 3160 'message as "help-page" display
1000    HELP.NUMBER= AHELP.NUMBER 'HELP.NUMBER back again
1010    ERROR 99 'simulate general error
```

Line 1010 simulates a general error. This error is displayed if the content of ERR in the error handling routine cannot be assigned a record number from ERR.TAB().

```
1020   COUNTER= 1 'set to field "last-name"
1030   IF X$= CHR$(13) OR ONKEY= 80 THEN COUNTER= COUNTER+1
1040   IF ONKEY= 72 THEN COUNTER= COUNTER-1
1050   IF COUNTER <1 THEN COUNTER= 7
1060   IF COUNTER >7 THEN COUNTER= 1
1070 WEND
1080 :
1090 RETURN
1100 :
1110 '----- search -----
1120 ERROR 3: RETURN
1130 '----- change -----
1140 ERROR 4: RETURN
1150 '----- list -----
1160 ERROR 5: RETURN
1170 '----- Import -----
1180 ERROR 6: RETURN
1190 '----- Export -----
1200 ERROR 7: RETURN
1210 '----- End -----
1220 COLOR 7,0:CLS:PRINT "*** END ***":PRINT:END
```

Every menu option except "Arrange" and "Add" generates an error.

```
1240 '---- control menu display and selection ----
1250 :
1260 MAX.LGTH= 0
1270 FOR I=0 TO MAX.MENU
1280    IF LEN(MENU$(I)) > MAX.LGTH THEN MAX.LGTH= LEN(MENU$(I))
1290 NEXT I
1300 :
1310 WD.ROW= 5: WD.COLM= 10: WD.SHADOW= FALSE
1320 WD.LGTH= MAX.LGTH+6: WD.HGT= MAX.MENU+2
1330 WD.HEAD$= MENU$(0):WD.FOOT$= "<F1> = Help"
1340 GOSUB 1750 'display window
1350 :
1360 CL= WD.COLM+3
1370 FOR I= 1 TO MAX.MENU
1380    RW= WD.ROW+I+1
1390    DEF SEG:CALL FASTSCRN(RW,CL,WNDW.BKG,MENU$(I))
1400 NEXT I
1410 :
1420 STATUS$=" Use <"+CHR$(24)+"> and <"+CHR$(25)+"> to select and <Return> to
     execute or <Esc> to End"
1430 GOSUB 2550 'display Status-Line
1440 HDFT.RW= 1: ONKEY$= "": LOCATE ,,0
1450 HELP.NUMBER= 2 'for Help-function
1460 :
1470 WHILE ONKEY$<> CHR$(27) AND ONKEY$<> CHR$(13)
```

```
1480    LOCATE ,,0 'switch Cursor off
1490    RW= WD.ROW+HDFT.RW+1: CL= WD.COLM+1
1500    X$= "  "+MENU$(HDFT.RW): X$= X$+SPACE$(MAX.LGTH+6-LEN(X$))
1510    DEF SEG:CALL FASTSCRN(RW,CL,HDFT.TXT,X$)
1520    ONKEY$= INKEY$:IF ONKEY$= "" THEN 1520
1530    DEF SEG:CALL FASTSCRN(RW,CL,WNDW.BKG,X$)
1540    IF ONKEY$= CHR$(27) THEN MENU= 0
1550    IF ONKEY$= CHR$(13) THEN MENU= HDFT.RW
1560    ONKEY= ASC(RIGHT$(ONKEY$,1))
1570    IF ONKEY= 72 THEN HDFT.RW= HDFT.RW-1 'Cursor up
1580    IF ONKEY= 80 THEN HDFT.RW= HDFT.RW+1 'Cursor down
1590    IF ONKEY= 71 THEN HDFT.RW= 1 '<Home>
1600    IF ONKEY= 79 THEN HDFT.RW= MAX.MENU
1610    IF ONKEY= 59 THEN GOSUB 3160 'Help display
1620    IF HDFT.RW < 1 THEN HDFT.RW= MAX.MENU
1630    IF HDFT.RW > MAX.MENU THEN HDFT.RW= 1
1640 WEND
1650 RETURN
1660 :
1670 '----- initialize background -----
1680 :
1690 X$= STRING$(WD.LGTH,BKG.CHAR$)
1700 FOR H.RW= WD.ROW TO WD.ROW+WD.HGT
1710    CALL FASTSCRN(H.RW,WD.COLM,BKG.COLR,X$)
1720 NEXT H.RW
1730 RETURN
1740 :
1750 '----- Universal-Routine for window -----
1760 :
1770 X$= CHR$(218)+STRING$(WD.LGTH%,CHR$(196))+CHR$(191)
1780 DEF SEG:CALL FASTSCRN(WD.ROW,WD.COLM,WNDW.BKG,X$)
1790 X$= CHR$(179)+STRING$(WD.LGTH%," ")+CHR$(179)
1800 IF WD.SHADOW THEN X$= X$+CHR$(178)+CHR$(178)
1810 FOR W.RW= WD.ROW+1 TO WD.ROW+WD.HGT
1820    DEF SEG:CALL FASTSCRN(W.RW,WD.COLM,WNDW.BKG,X$)
1830 NEXT W.RW
1840 X$= CHR$(192)+STRING$(WD.LGTH%,CHR$(196))+CHR$(217)
1850 IF WD.SHADOW THEN X$= X$+CHR$(178)+CHR$(178)
1860 W.RW= WD.ROW+WD.HGT+1
1870 DEF SEG:CALL FASTSCRN(W.RW,WD.COLM,WNDW.BKG,X$)
1880 IF WD.HEAD$= "" THEN 1920 'continue with footer
1890    X$= " "+WD.HEAD$+" "
1900    W.CL= WD.COLM+3
1910    CALL FASTSCRN(WD.ROW,W.CL,HDFT.TXT,X$)
1920 IF WD.FOOT$= "" THEN 1960 'continue with shadow
1930    X$= " "+WD.FOOT$+" "
1940    W.RW= WD.ROW+WD.HGT+1: W.CL= WD.COLM+3
1950    CALL FASTSCRN(W.RW,W.CL,HDFT.TXT,X$)
1960 IF NOT WD.SHADOW THEN 2000 'back
1970    X$= STRING$(WD.LGTH+2,CHR$(178))
1980    W.RW= WD.ROW+WD.HGT+2:W.CL= WD.COLM+2
1990    CALL FASTSCRN(W.RW,W.CL,WNDW.BKG,X$)
2000 RETURN
```

```
2010 :
2020 '----- store current screen display -----
2030 :
2040 IF CUR.SCN= MAX.SCN THEN BEEP:RETURN
2050 DEF SEG:BUFFER.OFS%= VARPTR(BUFFER%(CUR.SCN*2000)):CALL
     SAVESCRN(BUFFER.OFS%)
2060 CUR.SCN= CUR.SCN+1
2070 RETURN
2080 :
2090 '----- restore last screen display -----
2100 :
2110 IF CUR.SCN= 0 THEN BEEP:RETURN
2120 CUR.SCN= CUR.SCN-1
2130 DEF SEG:BUFFER.OFS%= VARPTR(BUFFER%(CUR.SCN*2000)):CALL
     RESTSCRN(BUFFER.OFS%)
2140 RETURN
2150 :
2160 'Data-lines from COM-file: screen.com
2170 :
2180 RESTORE 2200
2190 DEF SEG:FOR I=1 TO  227:READ X:POKE MP.START+I-1,X: NEXT I
2200 DATA 235,109,144,235,109,144, 85,139,236, 30,  6
2210 DATA 139,118, 12,138, 28,176,160,246,227, 45,160
2220 DATA   0, 80,139,118, 10,138, 28,176,  2,246,227
2230 DATA  91,  3,195, 72, 72, 80,139,118,  8,138, 36
2240 DATA 139,118,  6,138, 12,181,  0,139,116,  1, 80
2250 DATA 191,  0,176,179,  0,205, 17, 37, 48,  0, 61
2260 DATA  48,  0,116,  6,129,199,  0,  8,179,  1,142
2270 DATA 199, 88, 95,252,186,218,  3,128,251,  0,116
2280 DATA  11,236,208,216,114,246,250,236,208,216,115
2290 DATA 251,172,251,171,226,235,  7, 31, 93,202,  8
2300 DATA   0,235, 41,144, 85,139,236, 30,  6,139,118
2310 DATA   6,139,  4,139,240,191,  0,176,179,  0,205
2320 DATA  17, 37, 48,  0, 61, 48,  0,116,  6,129,199
2330 DATA   0,  8,179,  1,142,199, 51,255,235, 40,144
2340 DATA  85,139,236, 30,  6,139,118,  6,139,  4,139
2350 DATA 248, 30,  7,190,  0,176,179,  0,205, 17, 37
2360 DATA  48,  0, 61, 48,  0,116,  6,129,198,  0,  8
2370 DATA 179,  1,142,222, 51,246,185,208,  7,252,186
2380 DATA 218,  3,128,251,  0,116, 11,236,208,216,114
2390 DATA 246,250,236,208,216,115,251,173,251,171,226
2400 DATA 235,  7, 31, 93,202,  2,  0
2410 RETURN
2420 :
2430 '----- message output -----
2440 :
2450 GOSUB 2020 'save screen display
2460 RW= 25: CL= 1: MSG$= " "+MSG$+SPACE$(80-LEN(MSG$)-1)
2470 CALL FASTSCRN(RW,CL,MESSG.BKG,MSG$)
2480 LOCATE 25,79:PRINT CHR$(254);: LOCATE 25,79,1
2490 SOUND 895,1: SOUND 695,1
2500 X$= INKEY$:IF X$= "" THEN 2500
2510 GOSUB 2090 'restore screen display
```

```
2520 LOCATE ,,0
2530 RETURN
2540 :
2550 '----- display Status-Line -----
2560 :
2570 RW= 25: CL= 1: STATUS$= " "+STATUS$+SPACE$(80-LEN(STATUS$)-1)
2580 CALL FASTSCRN(RW,CL,MESSG.BKG,STATUS$)
2590 RETURN
2600 :
2610 '----- read subroutine -----
2620 :
2630 GOSUB 2550 'Status-Line for the input, according to STATUS$ display
2640 X$="":ONKEY= 0:ANYCHANGE= FALSE
2650 Y$= INSTRING$+SPACE$(LNGTH-LEN(INSTRING$))
2660 CALL FASTSCRN(ROWNO,COLMNO,HDFT.TXT,Y$)
2670 LOCATE ROWNO,COLMNO,1: CRSR.POS= 1
2680 X$= INKEY$:IF X$="" THEN 2680 'wait for key
2690 IF X$= CHR$( 8) AND POS(0)> COLMNO THEN GOSUB 2820:GOTO 2680 '<Backspace>
2700 IF X$= CHR$(27) THEN ANYCHANGE= FALSE:LOCATE ,,0:RETURN
2710 IF X$= CHR$(13) THEN LOCATE ,,0:RETURN
2720 IF LEN(X$)= 2 THEN 3000 'control and function keys
2730 '
2740 IF X$< " " THEN BEEP:GOTO 2680 'kill characters smaller than BLANK
2750 IF MAK.CAPS THEN IF X$>= "a" AND X$<= "z" THEN X$= CHR$(ASC(X$)-32)
2760 PRINT X$;:ANYCHANGE= TRUE
2770 IF CRSR.POS<= LEN(INSTRING$) THEN MID$(INSTRING$,CRSR.POS,1)= X$ ELSE
     INSTRING$= INSTRING$+X$
2780 CRSR.POS= CRSR.POS+1
2790 IF POS(0)> COLMNO+LNGTH-1 THEN LOCATE ROWNO,COLMNO:CRSR.POS= 1:GOTO 2680
2800 GOTO 2680 'continue to query keyboard
2810 '
2820 '----- BACKSPACE and DEL keys -----
2830 '
2840 IF X$=CHR$(8) THEN INSTRING$= LEFT$(INSTRING$,CRSR.POS-
     2)+MID$(INSTRING$,CRSR.POS)
2850 IF ONKEY= 83   THEN INSTRING$= LEFT$(INSTRING$,CRSR.POS-
     1)+MID$(INSTRING$,CRSR.POS+1) '<Del> key
2860 LOCATE ROWNO,COLMNO:PRINT INSTRING$;" ";
2870 IF X$=CHR$(8) THEN CRSR.POS= CRSR.POS-1
2880 LOCATE CSRLIN,COLMNO+CRSR.POS-1
2890 ONKEY= 0: X$="":ANYCHANGE= TRUE
2900 RETURN
2910 '
2920 '----- INS key -----
2930 '
2940 INSTRING$= LEFT$(INSTRING$,CRSR.POS-1)+" "+MID$(INSTRING$,CRSR.POS)
2950 PRINT " ";MID$(INSTRING$,CRSR.POS+1);
2960 LOCATE CSRLIN,COLMNO+CRSR.POS-1
2970 ANYCHANGE= TRUE
2980 RETURN
2990 '
3000 '----- control and function keys -----
3010 '
```

```
3020 ONKEY= ASC(RIGHT$(X$,1))
3030 IF ONKEY= 59 THEN GOSUB 3160:GOTO 2680 'Help/continue to query keyboard
3040 IF ONKEY= 68 OR ONKEY= 63 THEN LOCATE ,,0:RETURN '<F5> and <F10>
3050 IF ONKEY= 72 OR ONKEY= 80 THEN LOCATE ,,0:RETURN 'Cursor up and down
3060 IF ONKEY= 73 OR ONKEY= 81 THEN LOCATE ,,0:RETURN '<PgUp> and <PgDn>
3070 IF ONKEY= 75 AND POS(0)> COLMNO THEN LOCATE CSRLIN,POS(0)-1:CRSR.POS=
     CRSR.POS-1:GOTO 2680 'Cursor <--
3080 IF ONKEY= 77 AND POS(0)< COLMNO+LNGTH-1 THEN IF CRSR.POS<= LEN(INSTRING$)
     THEN LOCATE CSRLIN,POS(0)+1:CRSR.POS= CRSR.POS+1:GOTO 2680 'Cursor -->
3090 IF ONKEY= 83 AND CRSR.POS <= LEN(INSTRING$) THEN GOSUB 2820:GOTO 2680 '<Del>
     handled like <Backspace>
3100 IF ONKEY= 71 THEN LOCATE ROWNO,COLMNO:GOTO 2680 '<Home>, start of field
3110 IF ONKEY= 79 THEN LOCATE CSRLIN,COLMNO+LEN(INSTRING$)-1:CRSR.POS=
     LEN(INSTRING$):GOTO 2680 '<End>, set to last character
3120 IF ONKEY= 117 THEN INSTRING$= LEFT$(INSTRING$,CRSR.POS-1):PRINT
     SPACE$(LNGTH-CRSR.POS);:LOCATE CSRLIN,COLMNO+CRSR.POS-1:ANYCHANGE= TRUE:GOTO
     2680 '<Ctrl><End>, erase to end of field
3130 IF ONKEY= 82 AND CRSR.POS<= LEN(INSTRING$) AND LEN(INSTRING$)< LNGTH THEN
     GOSUB 2920:GOTO 2680 '<Ins>
3140 BEEP:GOTO 2680 'continue to query keyboard
3150 :
3160 '----- Help-function -----
3170 :
3180 FIL$= "TEST.HLP"
3190 :
```

The routine for the help function was only slightly changed. The only difference is now the error handling routine also accesses it. The name for the help file is assigned after line 3180. The name for the error file is assigned in the error handling routine. The beginning of the jump occurs in line 3200 (see line 4290).

```
3200 AWD.ROW= WD.ROW: AWD.COLM= WD.COLM: AWD.LGTH= WD.LGTH: AWD.HGT= WD.HGT
3210 AWD.SHADOW= WD.SHADOW 'store data of the window Variable
3220 ACRSR.ROWNO= CSRLIN: ACRSR.COLMNO= POS(0) 'store Cursor-Position
3230 LOCATE ,,0
3240 :
3250 GOSUB 2020 'save screen display
3260 :
3270 IF INSTR(FIL$,".ERR")= 0 THEN STATUS$= "One moment please, reading
     help...":GOSUB 2550
```

The status line only displays the message, "One moment please..." in the help function. This message is suppressed if, based on the filename in FIL$, it's determined that an error should be displayed (line 3270).

```
3280 OPEN FIL$ FOR INPUT AS #1 'open file for sequential access
3290 LINE INPUT #1,X$ 'first record/first line contains HELP.LINES
3300 HELP.LINES= VAL(X$)
3310 LINE INPUT#1,X$ 'first record/second line contains MAX.HELP
3320 MAX.HELP= VAL(X$)
3330 SET.LNGTH= (HELP.LINES+1)*60
```

```
3340 CLOSE #1
3350 GOTO 3980 'skip subroutines
3360 :
3370 '--- open Random-file, initialize FIELDs ---
3380 :
3390 OPEN "R",#1,FIL$,SET.LNGTH
3400 ON HELP.LINES GOTO 0,0,0,3420,0,0,0,3440,0,0,0,3460,0,0,0,3480,0,0,0,3500
3410 'according to HELP.LINES:    4          8          12          16          20
3420 FIELD#1,60 AS PAGE.TITLE$,240 AS TEXT1$
3430 RETURN 'continue in the text
3440 FIELD#1,60 AS PAGE.TITLE$,240 AS TEXT1$,240 AS TEXT2$
3450 RETURN 'continue in the text
3460 FIELD#1,60 AS PAGE.TITLE$,240 AS TEXT1$,240 AS TEXT2$,240 AS TEXT3$
3470 RETURN 'continue in the text
3480 FIELD#1,60 AS PAGE.TITLE$,240 AS TEXT1$,240 AS TEXT2$,240 AS TEXT3$,240 AS
     TEXT4$
3490 RETURN 'continue in the text
3500 FIELD#1,60 AS PAGE.TITLE$,240 AS TEXT1$,240 AS TEXT2$,240 AS TEXT3$,240 AS
     TEXT4$,240 AS TEXT5$
3510 RETURN 'continue in the text
3520 :
3530 '----- read help-text -----
3540 :
3550 GET#1,HELP.NUMBER 'read current help-page
3560 C= 1
3570 FOR I=1 TO 240 STEP 60 'read four lines from TEXT1$
3580    HELP.TEXT$(C)= MID$(TEXT1$,I,60)
3590    C=C+1
3600 NEXT I
3610 IF HELP.LINES= 4 THEN 3820 '4 lines for Help
3620 FOR I=1 TO 240 STEP 60 'read four lines from TEXT2$
3630    HELP.TEXT$(C)= MID$(TEXT2$,I,60)
3640    C=C+1
3650 NEXT I
3660 IF HELP.LINES= 8 THEN 3820 '8 lines for Help
3670 FOR I=1 TO 240 STEP 60 'read four lines from TEXT3$
3680    HELP.TEXT$(C)= MID$(TEXT3$,I,60)
3690    C=C+1
3700 NEXT I
3710 IF HELP.LINES= 12 THEN 3820 '12 lines for Help
3720 FOR I=1 TO 240 STEP 60 'read four lines from TEXT4$
3730    HELP.TEXT$(C)= MID$(TEXT4$,I,60)
3740    C=C+1
3750 NEXT I
3760 IF HELP.LINES= 16 THEN 3820 '16 lines for Help
3770 FOR I=1 TO 240 STEP 60 'read four lines from TEXT5$
3780    HELP.TEXT$(C)= MID$(TEXT5$,I,60)
3790    C=C+1
3800 NEXT I
3810 :
3820 FOR I=1 TO HELP.LINES
3830    IF RIGHT$(HELP.TEXT$(I),1)<> CHR$(0) THEN 3850
3840    HELP.TEXT$(I)= LEFT$(HELP.TEXT$(I),INSTR(HELP.TEXT$(I),CHR$(0))-1)
```

```
3850 NEXT I
3860 RETURN '20 lines for Help
3870 :
3880 '----- display help-text -----
3890 :
3900 H.RW= WD.ROW: H.CL= WD.COLM+2
3910 CALL FASTSCRN(H.RW,H.CL,HDFT.TXT,PAGE.TITLE$)
3920 FOR I=1 TO HELP.LINES
3930    H.RW= WD.ROW+I+1:Y$= HELP.TEXT$(I)+SPACE$( 60-LEN(HELP.TEXT$(I)))
3940    CALL FASTSCRN(H.RW,H.CL,MESSG.BKG,Y$)
3950 NEXT I
3960 RETURN 'display page
3970 :
3980 '----- initialize random-file and display help-page -----
3990 :
4000 GOSUB 3370 'open random-file and initialize FIELDs
4010 WD.ROW= 5:WD.COLM= 9:WD.LGTH= 62:WD.HGT= HELP.LINES+2:WD.SHADOW= TRUE
4020 WD.HEAD$= "": WD.FOOT$= "Strike <Esc> to return to main menu"
4030 GOSUB 1750  'display window for Help
4040 GOSUB 3530 'read help-text
4050 GOSUB 3880 'display help-text
4060 STATUS$= " ":GOSUB 2550
4070 IF INSTR(FIL$,".ERR")<> 0 THEN RETURN 'continue with error-handling
```

If, on the basis of the filenames, it's determined that an error was displayed, a return jump (line 4070) to the error handling occurs so that additional data (file, device) is displayed.

```
4080 X$= INKEY$: IF X$= "" THEN 4080
4090 CLOSE
4100 :
4110 GOSUB 2090 'restore screen display
4120 WD.ROW= AWD.ROW: WD.COLM= AWD.COLM: WD.LGTH= AWD.LGTH: WD.HGT= AWD.HGT
4130 WD.SHADOW= AWD.SHADOW 'restore data of the window-Variable
4140 LOCATE ACRSR.ROWNO,ACRSR.COLMNO,1 'restore Cursor position
4150 X$= "": ONKEY= 0
4160 RETURN
4170 :
4180 '----- error-handling -----
4190 :
4200 AHELP.NUMBER= HELP.NUMBER 'save current help-number
4210 HELP.NUMBER= 0
4220 ERROR.FIL$= FIL$
4230 FIL$= "TEST.ERR"
4240 :
```

The error handling uses the routines from the help function. For this, the current HELP.NUMBER is stored (line 4200) and the HELP.NUMBER is set to 0 as a flag for a general error (line 4210). The name of the FIL$ variable is assigned to ERROR.FIL$, which is in the display of the additional data (line 4320). In line 4230, FIL$ is assigned the name of the error file so that it can operate normally in the help function routines.

```
4250 FOR I=1 TO MAX.ERROR
4260   IF ERR.TAB(I,1)= ERR THEN HELP.NUMBER= ERR.TAB(I,2)
4270 NEXT I
4280 IF HELP.NUMBER= 0 THEN HELP.NUMBER= 52 'general message
```

In this loop, starting at line 4250, a test is performed to determine whether, in the ERR.TAB() array, an error text has been assigned for the error reported in ERR (line 4260). If it has, the record number of the error text is sent to the HELP.NUMBER for the display in the help function (line 4260). In line 4280 a test is made to determine whether HELP.NUMBER is 0. If it is, there was no error text in the ERR.TAB() array and a "general error" is displayed.

```
4290 GOSUB 3200 'display error-text in the routine "Help-function"
4300 :
```

Line 4290 calls the help function, in which the error text is displayed. The HELP.NUMBER variable was already given the correct values, as shown above.

```
4310 W.RW= WD.ROW+12: W.CL= WD.COLM+5
4320 X$= "Access occurred on file: "
4330 IF ERROR.FIL$= "" THEN ERROR.FIL$= "TEST.DAT"
4340 X$= X$+ERROR.FIL$
4350 IF (ERR<31) AND (ERR <> 24 AND ERR<> 25 AND ERR<> 27) THEN X$= "ERROR IN THE
     PROGRAM"
4360 CALL FASTSCRN(W.RW,W.CL,MESSG.BKG,X$)
4370 W.RW= WD.ROW+13: W.CL= WD.COLM+5
4380 X$= "Access occurred to device: "
4390 IF ERDEV$= "" THEN X$= X$+ "A:" ELSE X$= X$+ERDEV$
4400 IF (ERR<31) AND (ERR <> 24 AND ERR<> 25 AND ERR<> 27) THEN X$= "Please
     notify the programmer"
4410 CALL FASTSCRN(W.RW,W.CL,MESSG.BKG,X$)
4420 :
```

Starting at line 4310, the additional data is prepared and displayed. For file accesses the name of the file is stored in ERROR.FIL$, which is then displayed here (line 4320). The ERDEV$ variable, which contains the name of the device that is causing the error, is also displayed in the error message (line 4380). A test is also made to determine whether a program or operating error has occurred (lines 4350 and 4400). The content of the display variable X$ is changed accordingly.

```
4430 SOUND 895,1: SOUND 695,1
4440 IF INKEY$= "" THEN 4440
4450 GOSUB 4090 'restore original condition
4460 HELP.NUMBER= AHELP.NUMBER 'restore current help-number
4470 :
4480 IF ERR= 53 THEN RESUME 4110 'help-file not found, back
4490 RESUME NEXT 'For all other errors (only in this demonstration program !!!)
```

A note is sounded (line 4430) and the keyboard queried (line 4440). After a key has been activated, a part of the help function is called again (line 4450) in order to restore the original appearance. The AHELP.NUMBER is set to its old value so that the help function will work properly.

The lines starting at 4480 are also important. Here a query is made on how to continue after an error. In this demonstration program, there is only a query for error 53. This error is generated when the help file cannot be found. The RESUME in line 4480 jumps to the line to which it pertains. All other errors are processed here with a RESUME NEXT. Remember that, for changes, the queries and branches will be different, depending on your program.

16.6.1 Suggestions for HLPERR.BAS

After the start of the program, you can select a menu option. An error to demonstrate the error handling is assigned to every menu option except the "add" option. If you select the "add" option after activating the <F10> key, the display will notify you of a duplicate customer name (see the help function). Then a "general error" is displayed with ERROR 99.

The help function can be used again with the <F1> key. Using the routine for the error handling doesn't limit the help function's capabilities.

Program Changes

You can make any changes quickly and easily in this program. However, remember that you cannot call help if the error handling routine is active. This is because the routines are used by the error handling and a query for the keys doesn't occur during the error handling. If you want to change this aspect of the program, you must provide your own routine for the error handling and a keyboard query must be included. The routines are simply "duplicated" by the help function. Don't forget to change the name of the variables used; otherwise the screen will become unreadable because of double assignments. The query of the keyboard must be enhanced with a query of the <F1> key.

Note: Starting at line 4, the text for the error text is collected. Additional data on the error is provided by the program in lines 1 and 2. Line 3 remains empty so that the text can be read easily. If this isn't done, your text may be overwritten.

The following error text must be available for the demonstration program HLPERR.BAS. You must also include the numbers in parentheses (1) (2) (3) which represent the error numbers (in the title). The first line is the title of the error screen page and the remainder is the actual error text. We included the separation lines only for clarity; you should omit them from the input:

```
-----------------------------------------------------------------
(4) RETURN without GOSUB...




You're not responsible for this error.
It's a programming error!

Please notify the programmer to correct this error.
Also note the exact sequence of events preceding this error.

Thanks for your support and suggestions
-----------------------------------------------------------------
(38) Diskette is full...




There is insufficient space remaining on this diskette.

Please remove the diskette from the drive and
insert another diskette with sufficient space.

Strike the <F10> key after inserting the diskette.
-----------------------------------------------------------------
(41) Wrong filename ...




Wrong characters were used when entering the filename.
Only the following characters are valid:

        letters    "A" to "Z"
        numbers    "0" to "9"
        characters "!$%&_"

Strike <F10> to repeat the input...
-----------------------------------------------------------------
(46) Diskette is write protected...




The diskette you're using is write protected. You cannot save to a write
protected diskette.

Remove the write protect tab before saving.
Strike <F10> after removing the tab.

You can also insert another diskette and then strike <F10>.
-----------------------------------------------------------------
(47) Drive not Ready...
```

It has been determined that this drive is not operational.
Please check:
- if a diskette is properly inserted
- if the door is closed
- if the diskette was formatted

After the check/handling, please strike the <F10> key.
----
(48) error during access on diskette/hard disk ...

During your attempt to save data on the drive,
it was determined that the drive did not
perform properly.
Please insert another diskette and try again.

Diagnosis and repair from the LAV Division may
be required.
----
(52) general error...

An undefined error was detected ...

Please notify the programmer on extension XXX.

Also note the exact sequence of events preceding this error.

Thank you very much for your support.

17. Graphics in Applications

As you probably already know, your PC isn't capable of truly complex graphics. The PC was, after all, designed primarily for "serious" applications, such as accounting, word processing and databases. The CGA (Color Graphics Adapter) color graphic card was designed after the PC was introduced. It soon became apparent that advanced capabilities were needed for some graphic applications. Also, the Hercules Corporation created some interest in graphics with its popular monochrome graphic card.

In this chapter we'll show you some examples of graphics programming. Then we'll discuss CGA emulation.

17.1 Creating Moving Text

The color graphics of the PC can be used in many ways. We'll demonstrate one of these capabilities with a program for moving text across the screen. This program displays a line of continuous text. The individual words first appear on the right side of the screen and then slowly move to the left and off the screen.

Before describing the program in detail, study the listing or try it for yourself:

```
10 '-----------------------------------------------------
20 ' MOVETEXT.BAS          1988 (C) H.J. Bomanns
30 '-----------------------------------------------------
40 :
50 CLS:KEY OFF
60 NUM.OF.LINES= 3
70 DIM TEXT$(NUM.OF.LINES) 'for the output of text
80 DIM BUFFER%(1000)
90 X.MAX= 319: Y.MAX= 199 'maximum coordinates
100 RESTORE 110:FOR I=1 TO NUM.OF.LINES:READ TEXT$(I):NEXT
110 DATA "This is a test demonstrating moving text on your PC."
120 DATA " This demonstration continues until you're tired of it "
130 DATA "and strike any key to quit. "
140 :
150 SCREEN 1 'resolution 320*200 pixels
160 LOCATE 5,5:PRINT "A DEMONSTRATION OF MOVING TEXT"
170 LOCATE 6,10:PRINT "ON YOUR PC"
180 '
190 LOCATE 20,1:PRINT "<+> text forward    <-> text backward";
200 LINE (0,108)-(X.MAX,110),1,BF
210 LINE (0,120)-(X.MAX,122),1,BF
220 :
230 FOR ROWNO= 1 TO NUM.OF.LINES
240    FOR CHAR= 1 TO LEN(TEXT$(ROWNO))
```

```
250      LOCATE 15,39:PRINT MID$(TEXT$(ROWNO),CHAR,1);
260      GET (8,119)-(X.MAX-8,111),BUFFER% 'read content of the line
270      LOCATE 15,39:PRINT " ";
280      PUT (0,111),BUFFER%,PSET
290      X$= INKEY$:IF X$<>"" THEN 480
300      FOR DELAY= 1 TO 100:NEXT DELAY
310    NEXT CHAR
320 NEXT ROWNO
330 X$=INKEY$:IF X$="" THEN 230
340 GOTO 480
350 :
360 FOR ROWNO= NUM.OF.LINES TO 1 STEP-1
370   FOR CHAR= LEN(TEXT$(ROWNO)) TO 1 STEP-1
380      LOCATE 15,1:PRINT MID$(TEXT$(ROWNO),CHAR,1);
390      GET (0,119)-(X.MAX-8,111),BUFFER% 'read content of the line
400      LOCATE 15,1:PRINT " ";
410      PUT (8,111),BUFFER%,PSET
420      X$= INKEY$:IF X$<>"" THEN 480
430      FOR DELAY= 1 TO 100:NEXT DELAY
440    NEXT CHAR
450 NEXT ROWNO
460 X$=INKEY$:IF X$="" THEN 360
470 :
480 LINE (0,111)-(X.MAX,119),0,BF 'erase line
490 IF X$="+" THEN 150 'forward
500 IF X$="-" THEN 360 'backward
510 SCREEN 0:WIDTH 80
520 PRINT "Finished?":PRINT:PRINT
```

The listing for this program is fairly easy to follow. The text from lines 110 to 130 is read character by character in a loop (lines 230 to 320). The first character moves to the next column as the subsequent characters are displayed (line 250). With PUT(X,Y) the complete line, from the second to last column, is read into the BUFFER%() variable in line 80. In line 270 the character in the position located before the previous column is erased again to prevent a double image during the next output with GET(X,Y). In line 280 the content of BUFFER%() is moved exactly one character to the left and displayed again. Then the previously displayed character in the first column is overwritten and the complete line is moved by one character.

The <-> key reverses the program. This means that the text then moves from left to right. You'll find that the routine for this (line 360) operates similar to the routine for the normal output from right to left except that the content of the line is moved by one character from left to right. During the output you can terminate the program by striking any other key.

17.2   Turn your PC into a Clock

Many programmers like to display the current time on the screen. Most of us are familiar with time being displayed on either an analog or digital clock. However, we've decided to try something different. The following program, called "The Time Barometer", is the result:

```
10 '-------------------------------------------------
20 ' CLOCK.BAS              1988 (C) H.J.Bomanns
30 '-------------------------------------------------
40 :
50 CLS:KEY OFF
60 X.MAX= 319:Y.MAX= 199
70 DIM BUFFER%(1000)
80 :
90 SCREEN 1 'resolution 320*200 pixels
100 :
110 '----- frame for display -----
120 :
130 X.ST= 30 'X-Position
140 Y.ST=  0 'Y-Position
150 WDTH= 50
160 FOR I=1 TO 3
170   LINE (X.ST,Y.ST)-(X.ST+WDTH,Y.MAX),1,B
180 X.ST= X.ST+WDTH
190 NEXT I
200 LOCATE 22,
210 LOCATE ,25:PRINT " The Abacus PC":PRINT
220 LOCATE ,25:PRINT " Time Barometer";
230 LINE (190,192)-(319,166),1,B
240 GET(190,192)-(319,166),BUFFER%
250 COUNTER= 40
260 FOR Y= 166 TO 20 STEP-1
270   LINE(190,Y+27)-(319,Y),0,BF
280   PUT(190,Y),BUFFER%,PSET
290   FOR DELAY= 1 TO COUNTER:NEXT DELAY:COUNTER= COUNTER-.5
300 NEXT Y
310 :
320 '----- scale for hour display -----
330 :
340 X.ST= 30 'X-Position
350 Y.ST=  0 'Y-Position
360 STD.ABST= INT((Y.MAX-Y.ST)/25)+.5 'scale for hour display
370 FOR I= Y.MAX-STD.ABST TO Y.ST+15 STEP-STD.ABST
380   LINE(X.ST,I)-(X.ST+10,I),1
390 NEXT I
400 :
410 '----- scale for minutes/seconds display -----
420 :
430 X.ST= X.ST+WDTH
440 SM.ABST= INT((Y.MAX-Y.ST)/60) 'scale for minutes/seconds display
450 FOR I= Y.MAX-SM.ABST TO Y.ST+15 STEP-SM.ABST
```

```
460    LINE(X.ST,I)-(X.ST+10,I),1
470    LINE(X.ST+WDTH,I)-(X.ST+WDTH+10,I),1
480 NEXT I
490 :
500 '----- time display -----
510 :
520 STD= VAL(LEFT$(TIME$,2)):MIN= VAL(MID$(TIME$,4,2)):SEK= VAL(RIGHT$(TIME$,2))
530 GOSUB 890:GOSUB 800:GOSUB 730 'first display after call
540 STD= VAL(LEFT$(TIME$,2))
550 A.STD= STD
560 WHILE A.STD= STD
570    MIN= VAL(MID$(TIME$,4,2))
580    A.MIN= MIN
590    WHILE A.MIN= MIN
600      SEK= VAL(RIGHT$(TIME$,2)):MIN= VAL(MID$(TIME$,4,2))
610      GOSUB 730 'seconds display
620    WEND
630    MIN= VAL(MID$(TIME$,4,2)):STD= VAL(LEFT$(TIME$,2))
640    BEEP:GOSUB 800 'minutes display
650 WEND
660 STD= VAL(LEFT$(TIME$,2))
670 GOSUB 890 'hours display
680 GOSUB 800 'minutes display
690 GOTO 540
700 :
710 '----- seconds display -----
720 :
730 X.ST= (WDTH*2)+30:SEK.START= (SEK)*SM.ABST
740 LINE (X.ST+12,Y.MAX-1)-(X.ST+42,Y.MAX-SEK.START-SM.ABST),2,BF
750 LOCATE 2,20:PRINT RIGHT$(TIME$,2);
760 IF INKEY$="" THEN RETURN ELSE SCREEN 0:WIDTH 80:END
770 :
780 '----- minutes display -----
790 :
800 X.ST= (WDTH*2)+30
810 LINE(X.ST+12,Y.MAX-1)-(X.ST+42,Y.ST+16),0,BF 'erase second display
820 X.ST= WDTH+30:MIN.START= (MIN)*SM.ABST
830 LINE (X.ST+12,Y.MAX-1)-(X.ST+42,Y.MAX-MIN.START-SM.ABST),2,BF
840 LOCATE 2,14:PRINT MID$(TIME$,4,2);
850 IF INKEY$="" THEN RETURN ELSE SCREEN 0:WIDTH 80:END
860 :
870 '----- hours display -----
880 :
890 X.ST= WDTH+30
900 LINE(X.ST+12,Y.MAX-1)-(X.ST+42,Y.ST+16),0,BF 'erase minute display
910 X.ST= 30:STD.START= (STD)*STD.ABST
920 LINE(X.ST+12,Y.MAX-1)-(X.ST+42,Y.ST+16),0,BF 'erase hour display
930 LINE (X.ST+12,Y.MAX-1)-(X.ST+42,Y.MAX-STD.START-STD.ABST),2,BF
940 LOCATE 2,7:PRINT LEFT$(TIME$,2);
950 IF INKEY$="" THEN RETURN ELSE SCREEN 0:WIDTH 80:END
```

The Program

The main idea for this program was to show the current time on the screen without using "hands" or numbers. In other words, we did not want either a digital or analog clock but instead a new type of clock. We came up with the time-barometer clock.

The time appears digitally over each bar so that you don't have to count the tick marks to determine the time. Lines 50 to 90 initialize the program. The three column frame is drawn in lines 130 to 190. Lines 200 to 230 display the short title which is read into the BUFFER%() variable with GET(X,Y). The content of this variable is then moved from the lower screen to the top with a loop (lines 250 to 300). A counter, which is decremented after each output, controls the speed of the movement of the title as it approaches the top of the screen.

The individual bars are scaled in the program section. This starts at line 410. The first two lines of the display for the time in numbers remain unaffected. At the same time, the distance between the individual lines is retained in the STD.ABST and SM.ABST variables (lines 360/440).

The control of the display occurs after line 500. After the call, the display is completely constructed in line 530. From that point the display is only active during a change in minutes or hours. This occurs inside two WHILE...WEND loops. The first loop (lines 560 to 650) runs until the hour changes. The second loop (lines 590 to 620) runs until the minute changes. This loop displays the seconds. During the time display (starting in line 710), the current value of the system variable TIME$ is used as an index in the bar and multiplied with the previously calculated distance (lines 360/440 and 730/820/910). Finally, the bar is displayed again (lines 740/830/930) and the time is displayed in numbers over the columns (lines 750/840/940).

When a minute has passed, the seconds display is erased (line 810). When an hour has elapsed, the minutes display and the hour are both erased (lines 900/920). The program can be interrupted at any time by activating any key. The individual output routines contain a suitable test (lines 760/850/950).

17.3   Graphics Instead of Plain Numbers

After the color/monochrome graphic cards were introduced, the ability to represent numbers and data graphically has been offered in many application programs. Previously, it was only possible to present numbers in columns that were often very difficult to read.

However, today there are many ways to graphically present information. An application can use, for example, a pie chart, bar chart or line chart to display data. These charts enable the user to easily visualize a particularly high or low value. Using charts and graphics with PC-BASIC is fairly simple. Several commands and functions are available for this purpose. The best example of this is the CIRCLE statement. This statement enables you to draw full circles, ellipses and pie charts.

The following program shows how to graphically represent numeric values in pie charts, bar charts and line charts. The program starts with a table where you enter the values and items. We've added comments directly into the listing:

```
 10 '----------------------------------------------------
 20 'BUSINESS.BAS    business graphics demonstration
 30 '----------------------------------------------------
 40 :
 50 KEY OFF:FOR I=1 TO 10:KEY I,"":NEXT I
 60 MAX.ENTRYS= 12
 70 DIM DAT(MAX.ENTRYS), GDAT(MAX.ENTRYS+1), ITEM$(MAX.ENTRYS)
 80  SL= 5      'start-line for table and later input
 90 TITLE$= "groceries"
100 RESTORE 120
110 FOR I=1 TO MAX.ENTRYS:READ DAT(I),ITEM$(I): NEXT I 'only for demonstration
120 DATA 12.56,"bread",13.57,"milk",17.68,"butter",21.45,"potatoes"
130 DATA  8.97,"margarine",12.87,"sausage",11.91,"cheese",13.29,"soda water"
140 DATA  7.82,"pickles", 9.20,"radishes",15.82,"yogurt",14.97,"mustard"
150 :
```

The program is capable of processing twelve values. This allows you to create a monthly report for a yearly overview. In lines 100 to 140 the VALUE() and ITEM$() arrays are initialized with data for this demonstration program. You can change or delete these lines for your own applications.

```
160 COLOR 7,0:CLS
170 COLOR 0,7
180 PRINT " BUSINESS.BAS             1988 (C) H.J. Bomanns ";
190 :
200 COLOR 7,0: LOCATE 3,2: PRINT "name of the data:     ";
210 COLOR 0,7: PRINT " "+TITLE$+" ";
220 :
230 :
240 FOR I= 1 TO 12
250    COLOR  7,0:LOCATE SL+I, 2:PRINT USING "Amount ##:";I;
```

```
260    COLOR  0,7:LOCATE SL+I,14:PRINT USING " ######.## ";DAT(I);
270    COLOR  7,0:LOCATE SL+I,33:PRINT "Item:";
280    COLOR  0,7:LOCATE SL+I,40:PRINT ITEM$(I);
290 NEXT I
300 :
310 COLMNO = 23: ROWNO= 3: LNGTH= 30: INSTRING$= TITLE$
320 COLOR 0,7:LOCATE 25,1
330 PRINT " Press <Return> to accept name or <Esc> to end";SPACE$(80-POS(0));
340 GOSUB 1660 'read subroutine
350 IF X$= CHR$(27) THEN CLS:COLOR 7,0:END
360 TITLE$= INSTRING$
370 COLOR 0,7: LOCATE 3,23: PRINT " "+TITLE$+" ";
380 :
```

The program title appears in the top line and then the name of the data appears. This starts in line 160. We chose "groceries" for the data name. You can change this data name for your own applications in TITLE$= "" (line 90).

In the FOR...NEXT loop in line 240, the amounts and labels are displayed from the VALUE() and ITEM$() arrays with field names. Starting at line 310, the name of the table is read. You can terminate the program anytime by pressing the <Esc> key.

```
390 COUNTER= 1: INP.COLMNO= 1
400 COLM.POS(1)= 15: COLM.POS(2)= 40
410 COLOR 0,7:LOCATE 25,1
420 PRINT " Press <Tab> for other column, <F10> for charts, <Esc> to change name
    or End";SPACE$(80-POS(0));
430 WHILE X$<> CHR$(27) AND ONKEY<> 68 'until <Esc> or <F10>
440    IF INP.COLMNO= 1 THEN INSTRING$= MID$(STR$(DAT(COUNTER)),2,99)
450    IF INP.COLMNO= 2 THEN INSTRING$= ITEM$(COUNTER)
460    COLMNO= COLM.POS(INP.COLMNO): ROWNO= SL+COUNTER
470    IF INP.COLMNO= 1 THEN LNGTH= 9 ELSE LNGTH= 20
480    GOSUB 1660 'read subroutine
490    IF INP.COLMNO= 1 THEN DAT(COUNTER)= VAL(INSTRING$)
500    IF INP.COLMNO= 2 THEN ITEM$(COUNTER)= INSTRING$
510    COLOR  0,7:LOCATE SL+COUNTER,14:PRINT USING " ######.## ";DAT(COUNTER);
520    COLOR  0,7:LOCATE SL+COUNTER,40:PRINT ITEM$(COUNTER);
530    IF ONKEY= 72 THEN COUNTER= COUNTER-1
540    IF ONKEY= 80 THEN COUNTER= COUNTER+1
550    IF X$= CHR$(13) THEN COUNTER= COUNTER+1
560    IF X$<> CHR$(9) THEN 590
570      IF INP.COLMNO= 1 THEN INP.COLMNO= 2 ELSE INP.COLMNO= 1
580      GOTO 610 'change field column
590    IF COUNTER > MAX.ENTRYS THEN COUNTER= 1
600    IF COUNTER < 1 THEN COUNTER= MAX.ENTRYS
610 WEND
620 IF X$= CHR$(27) THEN 310 'read name or <Esc>= End
630 :
```

The amounts and items are read in the WHILE...WEND loop (line 430 to 610). This input loop is implemented in such a way that first all values are inserted into the left column.

After the last line, the input field again jumps to the first line. Use the <Tab> key to move the cursor to the right column and enter the items.

You can move within the table by using the cursor keys and to change individual values or items. The program jumps back to the data name of the table when you press the <Esc> key. Now you can change the data name or terminate the program by repeatedly pressing the <Esc> key.

```
640 FOR I=1 TO MAX.ENTRYS 'determine how many entries are available
650   IF DAT(I)<> 0 AND ITEM$(I)<> "" THEN NUM.ENTRYS= I
660 NEXT I
670 SUM= 0
680 FOR I = 1 TO NUM.ENTRYS 'calculate the total sum of the values
690   SUM = SUM + DAT(I)
700 NEXT I
710 FOR I = 1 TO NUM.ENTRYS 'calculate part per value
720   GDAT(I) = DAT(I) / SUM
730 NEXT I
740 :
```

The FOR...NEXT loop in line 640 tests how many entries are available in the table. It's possible that less than 12 values can be processed. The NUM.ENTRYS variable is set accordingly and acts as a loop limitation in the following graphic routines. The loops in lines 680 and 710, calculate a sum of all available values and then initialize the GDAT() array with the the individual values. GDAT() is used later in the graphic routines as the basis for the pie sections, the height of the bars and the position of the lines.

```
750 COLOR 0,7:LOCATE 25,1
760 PRINT " Press <P> for pie chart, <B> for bar chart, <L> for line chart, <Esc>
    to end";SPACE$(80-POS(0));
770 LOCATE 25,77,1:BEEP
780 A$= INKEY$: IF A$= "" THEN 780
790 IF A$= "P" OR A$= "p" THEN 850  'pie chart
800 IF A$= "B" OR A$= "b" THEN 1100 'bar chart
810 IF A$= "L" OR A$= "l" THEN 1350 'line chart
820 IF A$= CHR$(27) THEN 160
830 GOTO 770 'continue to query keyboard
840 :
```

A prompt appears in line 750 asking whether the data should be displayed as a pie chart, bar chart or line chart. Then the specific routines are called according to the input (P, B or L).

```
850 '----- values as pie-chart -----
860 :
870 A.ENDE = 0: LR = 50: SR = 44
880 :
890 SCREEN 1 'resolution 320*200, 4 colors
900 LINE (0,0)-(319,199),1,B 'frame
910 LOCATE 2, 20 - LEN(TITLE$) / 2 'center title
```

```
 920 PRINT TITLE$;
 930 LINE(16,17)-(303,17),1 'underline title
 940 FOR PIE = 1 TO NUM.ENTRYS
 950   P.START = P.ENDE
 960   P.ENDE = P.ENDE + GDAT(PIE) * 2 * 3.1415926#
 970   P.MEDIAN = (P.START + P.ENDE) / 2
 980   X.POS = 160 + COS(P.MEDIAN) * (LR - SR)
 990   Y.POS = 100 - SIN(P.MEDIAN) * (LR - SR)
1000   CIRCLE (X.POS,Y.POS), SR, 1, -P.START , -P.ENDE
1010   PAINT (X.POS + COS(P.MEDIAN) * .8 * SR, Y.POS - SIN(P.MEDIAN) * .8 * SR),
       PIE MOD 4, 1
1020   G.COLMNO = (X.POS + COS(P.MEDIAN) * (24 + SR) - 4 * LEN(ITEM$(PIE))) \ 8
1030   G.ROWNO = (Y.POS - SIN(P.MEDIAN) * (SR + 16)) \ 8
1040   IF G.ROWNO= CSRLIN THEN G.ROWNO= G.ROWNO+1
1050   LOCATE 1 + G.ROWNO, 1 + G.COLMNO
1060   PRINT ITEM$(PIE);
1070 NEXT PIE
1080 GOTO 1590 'wait for activation of key
1090 :
```

Line 850 starts the display of the pie chart. The display in this and other routines has a resolution of 320*200 pixels (line 890). Line 900 ensures that the graphic is displayed inside a border. The title is displayed, centered and underlined, in the second line (lines 910 to 930). In the loop, starting at line 940, the individual pie segments are calculated (lines 950 to 990), drawn (line 1000) and filled with color (line 1010). Then the labels are attached to the individual values (lines 1020 to 1060). Finally the jump to the keyboard query occurs (line 1080). You can terminate the program here with the <Esc> key or the input table can be called with another key.

```
1100 '----- values as bar-chart -----
1110 :
1120 FOR I=1 TO NUM.ENTRYS 'prepare content of GDAT() for bar chart
1130   GDAT(I)= GDAT(I)*1000 'provides the absolute height of the bar in pixels
1140 NEXT I
1150 :
1160 SCREEN 1
1170 LINE (0,0)-(319,199),2,B 'frame
1180 LOCATE 2,20-LEN(TITLE$) \ 2 'title center
1190 PRINT TITLE$;
1200 LINE(16,17)-(303,17),1 'title underlined
1210 X.POS= 16: WDTH= 16 '1. column and width for bar
1220 PATTERN$(0)= "ABC": PATTERN$(1)= "DEF": PATTERN$(2)= "GHI": PATTERN$(3)=
     "JKL"
1230 FOR BAR= 1 TO NUM.ENTRYS
1240   LINE(X.POS,198-GDAT(BAR))-(X.POS+WDTH,198),1,B
1250   PAINT (X.POS + 3,198-GDAT(BAR)+3),PATTERN$(BAR MOD 4), 1
1260   RW= 24
1270   X.POS= X.POS+WDTH+8
1280   FOR I= LEN(ITEM$(BAR)) TO 1 STEP -1
1290     LOCATE RW, (X.POS \ 8): PRINT MID$(ITEM$(BAR),I,1);
1300     RW= RW-1
```

```
1310   NEXT I
1320 NEXT  BAR
1330 GOTO 1590 'wait for activation of key
1340 :
```

The values are displayed as a bar chart starting in line 1100. The values in the GDAT() array, starting in line 1120, are multiplied by 1000 to provide the height of the bar in pixels. This value can be used, without additional calculations, in the LINE command. A border and the title are displayed as in the pie chart. The display of the individual bars occurs again in a loop (starting at line 1230) and the bars are filled with a pattern (line 1250). The items corresponding to the individual values are placed vertically to the right of the bars (starting after line 1280). Then the jump to the keyboard query occurs again (line 1330).

```
1350 '----- values as line-chart -----
1360 :
1370 FOR I=1 TO NUM.ENTRYS 'prepare content of GDAT() for lines
1380   GDAT(I)= GDAT(I)*1000 'provides the absolute position of the lines in
         pixels
1390 NEXT I
1400 GDAT(13)= 100
1410 :
1420 SCREEN 1
1430 LINE (0,0)-(319,199),2,B 'frame
1440 LOCATE 2,20-LEN(TITLE$) \ 2 'center title
1450 PRINT TITLE$;
1460 LINE(16,17)-(303,17),1 'underline title
1470 X.POS= 16: DISTANCE= 16 '1. column and distance for bar
1480 FOR LIN= 1 TO NUM.ENTRYS
1490   LINE (X.POS,198-GDAT(LIN))-(X.POS+DISTANCE+8,198-GDAT(LIN+1)),1
1500   CIRCLE (X.POS,198-GDAT(LIN)),2,1
1510   RW= 24
1520   X.POS= X.POS+DISTANCE+8
1530   FOR I= LEN(ITEM$(LIN)) TO 1 STEP -1
1540     LOCATE RW,(X.POS \ 8)-2: PRINT MID$(ITEM$(LIN),I,1);
1550     RW= RW-1
1560   NEXT I
1570 NEXT  LIN
```

Line 1350 starts the display for the line chart. The values in the GDAT() array are multiplied by 1,000 to determine the absolute position, in pixels, for the line (starting at line 1370). The frame and title are also displayed. Starting at line 1480, the lines are output in a loop. This is done by drawing a line from the current position, according to the GDAT(LIN) array, to the next pixel, according to the GDAT(LIN+1) array (line 1490). The items are placed vertically under the lines (starting at line 1530).

```
1580 :
1590 '----- wait for key activation -----
1600 :
1610 A$ = INKEY$: IF A$ = "" THEN 1610
1620 SCREEN 0: WIDTH 80: COLOR 7,0: CLS
```

```
1630 IF A$= CHR$(27) THEN END
1640 GOTO 160 'display table, read values
1650 :
```

A jump is made to this routine after the program displays each graphic. You can terminate the program here with the <Esc> key. Every other key causes the return jump to the input table. The end of the program is the "read subroutine", which has been used in previous chapters.

```
1660 '----- read subroutine -----
1670 '
1680 X$="":ONKRY= 0
1690 LOCATE ROWNO,COLMNO,0:COLOR 15,0:PRINT INSTRING$;SPACE$(LNGTH-
     LEN(INSTRING$));
1700 LOCATE ROWNO,COLMNO,1:CRSR.POS= 1
1710 X$= INKEY$:IF X$="" THEN 1710
1720 IF X$= CHR$(8) AND POS(0)> COLMNO THEN GOSUB 1850:GOTO 1710 'keys-routine
1730 IF X$= CHR$(27) THEN ANYCHANGE= 0:RETURN
1740 IF X$=CHR$(13) OR X$= CHR$(9) THEN RETURN
1750 IF LEN(X$)= 2 THEN 2030 'control and function keys
1760 '
1770 IF X$< " " THEN BEEP:GOTO 1710 'kill characters smaller than BLANK
1780 IF MAKE.CAPS THEN IF X$>= "a" AND X$<= "z" THEN X$= CHR$(ASC(X$)-32)
1790 PRINT X$;:ANYCHANGE= -1
1800 IF CRSR.POS<= LEN(INSTRING$) THEN MID$(INSTRING$,CRSR.POS,1)= X$ ELSE
     INSTRING$= INSTRING$+X$
1810 CRSR.POS= CRSR.POS+1
1820 IF POS(0)> COLMNO+LNGTH-1 THEN BEEP:LOCATE ROWNO,COLMNO:CRSR.POS= 1:GOTO
     1710
1830 GOTO 1710
1840 '
1850 '----- BACKSPACE and DEL keys -----
1860 '
1870 IF X$=CHR$(8) THEN INSTRING$= LEFT$(INSTRING$,CRSR.POS-
     2)+MID$(INSTRING$,CRSR.POS)
1880 IF ONKEY= 83  THEN INSTRING$= LEFT$(INSTRING$,CRSR.POS-
     1)+MID$(INSTRING$,CRSR.POS+1)
1890 LOCATE ROWNO,COLMNO:PRINT INSTRING$;" ";
1900 IF X$=CHR$(8) THEN CRSR.POS= CRSR.POS-1
1910 LOCATE CSRLIN,COLMNO+CRSR.POS-1
1920 ONKEY= 0: X$="":ANYCHANGE= -1
1930 RETURN
1940 '
1950 '----- INS key -----
1960 '
1970 INSTRING$= LEFT$(INSTRING$,CRSR.POS-1)+" "+MID$(INSTRING$,CRSR.POS)
1980 PRINT " ";MID$(INSTRING$,CRSR.POS+1);
1990 LOCATE CSRLIN,COLMNO+CRSR.POS-1
2000 ANYCHANGE= -1
2010 RETURN
2020 '
2030 '----- control and function keys -----
```

```
2040 '
2050 ONKEY= ASC(RIGHT$(X$,1))
2060 IF ONKEY= 63 THEN RETURN '<F5>= selection
2070 IF ONKEY= 68 THEN RETURN '<F10>= input OK
2080 IF ONKEY= 72 OR ONKEY= 80 THEN RETURN 'Cursor up and down
2090 IF ONKEY= 73 OR ONKEY= 81 THEN RETURN '<PgUp> and <PgDn>
2100 IF ONKEY= 75 AND POS(0)> COLMNO THEN LOCATE CSRLIN,POS(0)-1:CRSR.POS=
     CRSR.POS-1:GOTO 1710 'Cursor <--
2110 IF ONKEY= 77 AND POS(0)< COLMNO+LNGTH-1 THEN IF CRSR.POS<= LEN(INSTRING$)
     THEN LOCATE CSRLIN,POS(0)+1:CRSR.POS= CRSR.POS+1:GOTO 1710 'Cursor-->
2120 IF ONKEY= 83 AND CRSR.POS <= LEN(INSTRING$) THEN GOSUB 1850:GOTO 1710 '<Del>
     treated like <Backspace>
2130 IF ONKEY= 71 THEN LOCATE ROWNO,COLMNO:GOTO 1710 '<Home>, start of field
2140 IF ONKEY= 79 THEN LOCATE CSRLIN,COLMNO+LEN(INSTRING$)-1:CRSR.POS=
     LEN(INSTRING$):GOTO 1710 '<End>, set to last character
2150 IF ONKEY= 117 THEN INSTRING$= LEFT$(INSTRING$,CRSR.POS-1):PRINT
     SPACE$(LNGTH-CRSR.POS);:LOCATE CSRLIN,COLMNO+CRSR.POS-1:ANYCHANGE= -1:GOTO
     1710 '<Ctrl><End>, erase to field end
2160 IF ONKEY= 82 AND CRSR.POS<= LEN(INSTRING$) AND LEN(INSTRING$)< LNGTH THEN
     GOSUB 1950:GOTO 1710 '<Ins>
2170 BEEP:GOTO 1710
```

Suggestions for BUSINESS.BAS

You'll need to change the dimensions of the arrays and the individual graphic routines if you want to use the program for processing more than 12 values. The chart most likely to present problems is the pie chart. Although the program is presently limited to 12 values, at least twice the number of values can easily be displayed for bar and line charts. All you need to do is modify the X.POS, WDTH and DISTANCE variables (therefore 24). However, it may be difficult to display because the text would become very crowded. But the 640*200 resolution would help a little.

It's easy to enhance this program. It's possible to include routines for saving or loading graphics. Also colors and patterns could be added by using variables. You can also use the MS-DOS utility program GRAPHICS.COM to print the chart or graphic.

17.4   CGA Card with the Hercules Card

Certain problems exist when executing a CGA graphic application, an application program or a game if a Hercules card is installed in your PC. This is caused by both the hardware and the software. The following are the most important differences between CGA and Hercules cards:

1.   The video RAM starts at segment address &HB800 in the CGA card and at segment address &HB000 in the Hercules card. Graphic routines for CGA execute all commands starting at segment address &HB800. If this was the only difference, nothing would be visible using the Hercules card because the wrong segment is addressed.

2.   The CGA card is able to display four colors but the Hercules card displays only two colors. CGA requires two bits for each pixel and Hercules requires only one bit. So, even if the segment address problems could be solved, the display still wouldn't be recognizable.

3.   The Hercules card has a resolution of 720*348 pixels. Theoretically, a CGA resolution of 320*200 or 640*200 pixels would "fit in". In reality, however, this doesn't work because of the different addressing. Since, in the graphic mode, Hercules uses 720 pixels and CGA uses 320 or 640 pixels per line, the line break wouldn't match.

4.   The control of the 6845 CRT chips occurs in the CGA through the &H03Dx ports and in Hercules through the &H03Bx ports. CGA applications, which directly access the CRT chip, don't find the required hardware environment.

In addition, many CGA applications, before switching on the graphics mode, query the equipment byte at address &H0040:&H0010 or the current video mode, at address &H0040:&H0049. An error message appears if this query indicates that a Hercules card is installed. You may be familiar with this from PC-BASIC, which displays an "Illegal function call" message when graphic commands are used.

CGA Emulation Design

During the design of a CGA emulation, the different addresses of the video segments are significant. From the viewpoint of a CGA card, special provisions don't have to be made since the video memory of the Hercules card covers &HB000 to &HBFFF. As usual, the CGA card finds its segment at &HB800. The video RAM of the Hercules card starts at address &HB000. So it's necessary to transfer the memory content, in regular intervals, from address &HB800 to &HB000. You must also consider the different line length at the same time.

Perhaps you already know that the Hercules card can be operated in two different modes. These are the Page 0 or HALF and Page 1 or FULL modes. In the Page 0 mode the video segment to be displayed is at address &HB000, but in the Page 1 mode it's at address &HB800. You may wonder why the Hercules card couldn't simply be operated in Page 1 mode and the segment displayed starting at &HB800. The answer was already discussed earlier. Hercules requires only one bit for each pixel. Since it can display four colors, CGA requires two bits for each pixel. Also, there is a difference in line length of 720 pixels, as compared with 320 or 640 pixels. So we cannot avoid the transfer of address &HB800 to &HB000 and, at the same time, consider the difference in the line length.

This must be done in regular and brief intervals. The timer Interrupt 1Ch, which is called 18.2 times per second, is used. The emulation "locks" itself into this interrupt and, in a routine, copies the memory from &HB800 to &HB000 with consideration of the line length. Details on this can be found in the following listing. Copying the display isn't enough. Also, during a query of the equipment byte or the CRT mode byte, the proper content must be found. So it's necessary to set interrupt 10h, which, among other things, is responsible for graphics, to routines that perform this task. There are details on this in the listing.

Finally, after completing its job in the graphics mode, the 6845 CRT chip must be set in the text mode. This is also performed in the routines for interrupt 10h. A test is made to determine whether the text or graphics mode should be set. Depending on the test, the values are written into the registers of the 6845 and allow the switch to the graphics or text mode. The following is the assembler listing for the CGA emulation. We've included any necessary comments directly into the listing:

```
Program segment 'CODE'
        assume cs: Program, ds: Program
        org 0100h


Start:  jmp Install
;----------------------------------------
IndexReg        equ 03B4h               ;index Register 6845
ModeControl     equ 03B8h               ;Mode Control Register 6845
ConfigSwitch    equ 03BFh               ;Configuration Switch Register 6845
;----------------------------------------
; RESIDENT part...
;----------------------------------------
INT1C           dd 0,0
INT10           dd 0,0
LineFlag        db 0
;----------------------------------------
INT_1C  proc    far

        cli                             ;no Interrupts
        push    ax                      ;store AX and ES
        push    es
        mov     ax,0040h
```

```
          mov      es,ax                      ;0040h= BIOS-Data-Segment
          cmp      byte ptr es:[49h],4        ;text-mode active ?
          jb       No_INT_1C                  ;if yes, back
          cmp      byte ptr es:[49h],7        ;monochrome-mode active?
          je       No_INT_1C                  ;if yes, back

          pop      es                         ;restore AX and ES again
          pop      ax
          jmp      ScrCopy

No_INT_1C:
          pop      es                         ;restore AX and ES again
          pop      ax
          jmp      OrgINT_1C

ScrCopy:
          push     ds                         ;store Registers
          push     es
          push     ax
          push     bx
          push     cx
          push     dx
          push     si
          push     di

          mov      ax,0B800h                  ;Segment Color
          mov      ds,ax                      ;source= Color-Segment
          mov      bx,0B000h                  ;Mono Segment
          mov      es,bx                      ;destination= Mono-Segment
          mov      ax,16304
          mov      dx,16374

          add      cs:[LineFlag],80h          ;Flag for even/odd lines
          jne      OddLines                   ;is either 0 or 80h

EvenLines:
          xor      si,si                      ;Offset source= 0
          mov      di,1625                    ;Offset destination= display-screen-area
          jmp      MoveLines                  ;move lines
OddLines:
          mov      si,2000h                   ;Offset source= CGA/first line
          mov      di,2000h+1625              ;Offset destination=

MoveLines:
          cld                                 ;direction: forward
          mov      bl,50                      ;50 lines
MoveLoop:
          mov      cx,40                      ;40 characters/line
          rep      movsw                      ;move
          mov      cx,40
          add      di,ax
          rep      movsw
          sub      di,dx
```

```
              dec       bl
              jne       MoveLoop

              pop       di                      ;restore Registers
              pop       si
              pop       dx
              pop       cx
              pop       bx
              pop       ax
              pop       es
              pop       ds

OrgINT_1C:
              sti                               ;Interrupts permitted again
              jmp       cs:[INT1C]              ;call original INT 1Ch

INT_1C   endp
```

In regular intervals the PROC INT_1C takes over the copying of the display from B800h to B000h. During the call of interrupt 1CH, the odd and even lines are copied alternately. Since the copying is only necessary in the graphics mode, first there is a test of the current video mode with the CRT mode byte. The copy routine is simply skipped in the text mode. During the copying of the display, 40 words/640 pixels are sent per line.

```
;-----------------------------------------
INT_10   proc      far

              cmp       ah,0FFh                 ;function 'installed ?'
              jne       Check_AH                ;if not, continue to test
              mov       ax,0ABCDh               ;return message 'I am already installed'
              iret                              ;back from the Interrupt

Check_AH:
              test      ah,ah                   ;function 0 called?
              jz        Set_Mode                ;if yes, test mode
              jmp       cs:[INT10]              ;else, call original INT 10h

Set_Mode:
              push      ax                      ;store Register
              push      bx
              push      dx

              mov       dx,ConfigSwitch
              cmp       al,4                    ;set text or graphic ?
              jb        Set_Text                ;0 to 3= text-mode, continue there
              cmp       al,7                    ;set monochrome-mode ?
              je        Set_Text                ;if yes, continue there

Set_Graphic:
              push      ax                      ;store mode in AL
              mov       al,3                    ;graphic permitted, buffer to B8000:0000
              out       dx,al                   ;write in port
```

```
          call    InitGraphic              ;set 6845 to graphics-mode
          pop     ax                       ;restore mode in AL
          call    SetEQPColor              ;set Equipment-Byte to 'COLOR'
          mov     ah,0Bh                   ;set function 'color-Palette '
          mov     bx,0                     ;BL= color-value, BH= Palette-number
          pushf                            ;INT simulate
          call    cs:[INT10]               ;call old INT 10h
          jmp     INT_10_End

Set_Text:
          push    ax                       ;store mode in AL
          mov     al,0                     ;no graphic, Buffer to B0000:0000
          out     dx,al                    ;write Port
          call    InitText                 ;set 6845 to text-mode
          pop     ax                       ;restore mode in AL
          call    SetEQPMono               ;set Equipment-Byte to 'MONO'

INT_10_End:
          pop     dx                       ;restore Registers
          pop     bx
          pop     ax
          iret                             ;return from Interrupt

INT_10   endp
```

The PROC INT_10 is responsible for intercepting the "set 0/mode " function. Depending on the mode in AL, the 6845 is initialized for graphics or text and the equipment and CRT mode bytes are set. Also, interrupt 10h was enhanced with the function "FFh/installed ?". This function is called during the call of the program and returns the value ABCDh, for already installed emulation, in AX. A corresponding test (see PROC Install) prevents a multiple installation.

```
;----------------------------------------
; set Equipment-Byte to 'COLOR' ...
;----------------------------------------
SetEQPColor:
          push    es                       ;store ES and AX
          push    ax                       ;AL= mode
          mov     ax,0040h
          mov     es,ax                    ;0040h= BIOS-Data Segment
          and     byte ptr es:[10h],0CFh
          or      byte ptr es:[10h],20h
          pop     ax                       ;AL= mode
          mov     byte ptr es:[49h],al     ;set mode
          push    ax
          xor     ax,ax                    ;AX= 0
          mov     es,ax                    ;0000h= Segment Vector-table
          cli                              ;no Interrupts
          mov     word ptr es:[4*1Ch]+0,Offset INT_1C ;set INT 1C
          mov     word ptr es:[4*1Ch]+2,cs
          sti                              ;Interrupts permitted
```

```
            pop     ax                      ;restore ES and AX again
            pop     es
            ret                             ;return
```

The PROC SetEQPColor sets the equipment and CRT mode byte as if a CGA card was installed. Queries of these two bytes always return the necessary results. Also the vector for interrupt 1Ch is set again. This is done in case some application "redirects" the interrupt for its own purposes, which would undermine the emulation.

```
;----------------------------------------
; set Equipment-Byte to 'MONO' ...
;----------------------------------------
SetEQPMono:
            push    es                      ;store Registers
            push    bx
            push    ax                      ;AL= mode
            mov     ax,0040h
            mov     es,ax                   ;0040h= BIOS-Data Segment
            and     byte ptr es:[10h],0CFh
            or      byte ptr es:[10h],30h
            pop     ax                      ;AL= mode
            mov     byte ptr es:[49h],al    ;set mode
            push    ax
            xor     ax,ax                   ;AX= 0
            mov     es,ax                   ;0000h= Segment Vector table
            mov     ax,word ptr cs:[INT1C]+0 ;Offset Original INT 1Ch
            mov     bx,word ptr cs:[INT1C]+2 ;Segment Original INT 1Ch
            cli                             ;no Interrupts
            mov     word ptr es:[4*1Ch]+0,ax ;set Offset Original INT 1Ch
            mov     word ptr es:[4*1Ch]+2,bx ;set Segment Original INT 1Ch
            sti                             ;Interrupts permitted
            pop     ax                      ;restore Registers again
            pop     bx
            pop     es
            ret                             ;return
```

The PROC SetEQPMono sets the equipment byte as if a Hercules card was installed. This ensures the correct text output in monochrome mode. The CRT mode byte remains in mode 2, text 80*25 in black/white to permit output of color text. The vector for the interrupt 1Ch is set to the original address again, since, copying hasn't occurred in the text mode.

```
;----------------------------------------
; set 6845 into graphics-mode ...
;----------------------------------------
InitGraphic:
            push    ax                      ;store Registers
            push    bx
            push    cx
            push    si
            push    ds
```

```
        push    cs
        pop     ds                      ;DS= CS
        mov     al,2                    ;set graphics-mode
        xor     bx,bx                   ;BX= 0, value for 'ClrScr'
        mov     cx,8000h                ;number of Bytes to be erased
        mov     si,offset GValues       ;table of the Init-values for graphic
        call    Init6845                ;initialize 6845

        pop     ds                      ;restore Registers again
        pop     si
        pop     cx
        pop     bx
        pop     ax
        ret                             ;return
```

The PROC InitGraphic sets the 6845 through the PROC Init6845, which immediately follows, to the graphics mode (AL= 2) and erases the complete buffer (CX= 8000h) with null bytes (BX= 0) for the subsequent graphic. SI is a pointer to the table, in which the values for the direct programming of the 6845 for the graphics mode, are recorded.

```
;--------------------------------------
; set 6845 into text-mode ...
;--------------------------------------
InitText:
        push    ax                      ;store Registers
        push    bx
        push    cx
        push    si
        push    ds

        push    cs
        pop     ds                      ;DS= CS
        mov     al,20h                  ;set text-mode
        mov     bx,0720h                ;BH= color, BL= characters for 'ClrScr'
        mov     cx,2000h                ;number of Bytes to be erased
        mov     si,offset TValues       ;table of the Init-values for text
        call    Init6845                ;6845 initialize
        pop     ds                      ;restore Registers again
        pop     si
        pop     cx
        pop     bx
        pop     ax
        ret                             ;return
```

The PROC InitText sets the 6845 through the PROC Init6845, which follows immediately, into the text mode (AL= 20h) and erases the text buffer (CX= 2000h) with the null characters and the color 7 (BX= 0720h) for the subsequent text output. SI is a pointer to the table, in which the values for the direct programming of the 6845 for the text mode are stored.

```
;---------------------------------------
; initialize 6845,
; set Mode Control Register ...
;---------------------------------------
Init6845:
        push    ds                      ;store Registers
        push    es
        push    ax                      ;mode for 6845
        push    bx                      ;erase values
        push    cx                      ;number of characters

        mov     dx,ModeControl
        out     dx,al                   ;set mode, display-screen off

        mov     dx,IndexReg
        mov     cx,12                   ;write 12 values (0-11) into Register
        xor     ah,ah                   ;AH= 0, first Register
InitLoop:
        mov     al,ah                   ;AL= Register
        out     dx,al                   ;write in Port
        inc     dx                      ;DX= 03B5h
        lodsb                           ;read value at table DS:SI to AL
        out     dx,al                   ;write to Port
        inc     ah                      ;AH= AH+1, next Register
        dec     dx                      ;DX= 03B4h
        loop    InitLoop                ;until CX= 0

ClrScr:
        cld                             ;direction: forward
        mov     ax,0B000h               ;Video-Segment Monochrome
        mov     es,ax                   ;ES/destination= Video-Segment Mono
        xor     di,di                   ;DI/destination= 0
        pop     cx                      ;CX= number of Bytes to be erased
        pop     ax                      ;AX= 0 or color/characters for erasing
        rep     stosw                   ;write into display-screen-buffer

        mov     dx,ModeControl
        pop     ax                      ;AX= mode for 6845 (2 or 20h)
        or      al,8                    ;switch display-screen on
        out     dx,al                   ;write into Port

        pop     es                      ;restore remaining Registers
        pop     ds
        ret                             ;return
;---------------------------------------
GValues         db 35h,2dh,2eh,07h,5bh,02h,57h,57h,02h,03h,00h,00h
TValues         db 61h,50h,52h,0fh,19h,06h,19h,19h,02h,0dh,0bh,0ch
```

The PROC 6845 accepts the direct programming of the 6845 according to the parameters passed in AX, BX, CX and SI. First the screen is switched off (Port 03B8h= AL). Then the values from the table are set according to SI (GValues for graphic, TValues for text) through the index register 03B4h and the data register 03B5h. Starting at label ClrScr the screen is cleared, according to CX = number bytes and AX = characters/attribute. Then the screen is switched on again (Port 03B8h= AL or 8).

```
;------------------------------------
; TRANSIENT Part ...
;------------------------------------
Install:
        push    cs
        pop     ds                      ;DS= CS
        mov     ah,0FFh                 ;new function 'installed ?'
        int     10h
        cmp     ax,0ABCDh               ;is already installed ?
        jne     Do_Install              ;if not, install

        mov     ah,9                    ;Print String
        mov     dx,offset Already_da    ;message, since it is already installed
        int     21h
        mov     ah,4ch                  ;terminate program
        int     21h
```

This is the previously mentioned test for multiple installation. Interrupt 10h is called with function FFh. If the result is AX = ABCDh, the emulation is already installed and a message is displayed. Otherwise, the installation occurs, starting at the label Do_Install since AX is unchanged. The "normal" interrupt 10h doesn't recognize the FFh function.

```
Do_Install:
        mov     ah,35h                  ;function 'Get Interrupt Vector'
        mov     al,1Ch                  ;of Interrupt 1Ch
        int     21h                     ;ES:BX= Interrupt-Vector
        mov     word ptr [INT1C]+0,bx   ;store Offset
        mov     word ptr [INT1C]+2,es   ;store Segment

        mov     ah,35h                  ;function 'Get Interrupt Vector'
        mov     al,10h                  ;of Interrupt 10h
        int     21h                     ;ES:BX= Interrupt-Vector
        mov     word ptr [INT10]+0,bx   ;store Offset
        mov     word ptr [INT10]+2,es   ;store Segment

        mov     ah,25h                  ;function 'Set Interrupt Vector'
        mov     al,1Ch                  ;of Interrupt 1Ch
        mov     dx,Offset INT_1C        ;Offset new INT 1Ch-Routine
        cli                             ;no Interrupts
        int     21h                     ;set new INT-Vector
        sti                             ;permit Interrupts again

        mov     ah,25h                  ;function 'Set Interrupt Vector'
        mov     al,10h                  ;of Interrupt 10h
        mov     dx,Offset INT_10        ;Offset new INT 10h-Routine
        cli                             ;no Interrupts
        int     21h                     ;set new INT-Vector
        sti                             ;permit Interrupts again

        mov     ah,0                    ;set Video-Mode
        mov     al,2                    ;mode= text 80*25 B/W
        int     10h
```

```
        mov     ah,9                    ;Print String
        mov     dx,offset Now_da        ;message that it is installed now
        int     21h

        mov     dx,Offset Install       ;make resident to here
        int     27h                     ;TSR-function
```

The installation is divided into three parts: first the addresses of the original interrupts 10h and 1Ch are determined and stored. Then the addresses of the new interrupt routines INT_10 and INT_1C are set. Finally, after a message through interrupt 27h, the program is resident.

```
;-----------------------------------------
Already_da      db 13,10,10
                db 'the CGA-Emulation is already installed ...',7
                db 13,10,10,'$'

Now_da          db 13,10,10
                db 'the CGA-Emulation is now installed ...'
                db 13,10,10,'$'
;-----------------------------------------
Program ends
        end Start
```

Notes on CGAONHGC.ASM

The direct programming of the 6845 CRT chip occurs through the 03B4h and 03B5h ports. The first 12 registers (0 to 11) determine how many characters (or pixels) should be displayed per line and how many lines should be displayed. Also, the horizontal and vertical synchronization is determined. The values in the GValues table and the source/destination addresses in the ScrCopy routine are arranged in such a way that the emulated graphic is placed into the middle of the screen. Through the Configuration Switch register 03BFh, it's determined that the 6845 may operate in graphics mode and allows access to the area starting at address B800h. Through the Mode Control register 03B8h it's determined whether the 6845 should operate in text or graphics mode, which area is displayed (starting at B000h or B800h) and if the screen is switched on or off. Unfortunately, because of space limitations, we cannot explain these registers here. For more information, consult the **PC System Programming for Developers** book by Abacus. To switch on the emulation, simply call the CGAONHGC.COM program. Then any CGA application should be started.

Limitations of the Emulation CGAONHGC

As we mentioned earlier, there is a difference in various port addresses of the CGA and Hercules (CGA= 03Dxh, Hercules= 03Bxh) for controlling the 6845. CGA applications, which write directly into the ports, cannot function under CGAONHGC. Ports cannot be emulated.

A few problems occurred during tests of CGAONHGC on some Hercules compatible cards. The display started to run, flickered or wasn't completed. This could be the result of either the incompatibility of the registers or by the peripheral chips on the cards apparently working differently with the 6845 than in the Hercules card. Unfortunately, these cards are typically sold without schematics, register descriptions and documentation. This makes it impossible to locate the problem.

Some applications use interrupts 10h or 1Ch themselves. This can also create problems. If, for example, interrupt 10h is redirected in an "unclean" manner, and the original address cannot be reached with a jump, the emulation cannot function. The same applies to interrupt 1Ch, which is set by some applications through interrupt 8 (also a timer interrupt which is called before the INT 1Ch) regularly to an IRET, in order to kill off user-routines, such as a clock. The copying of the graphic doesn't occur and the screen remains blank. A condition against which the emulation is also defenseless.

18. PC-BASIC and Compilers

Almost all programmers will eventually want to use a compiler in order to make their programs faster and more user-friendly. Using a compiler has several advantages. The processing and execution speed are significantly faster. Stand alone, executable EXE programs can be used instead of having to use the interpreter. Also, it isn't easy for users to modify a compiled program. In this chapter we'll discuss the currently available compilers. We'll begin with some basic observations.

18.1   General Information

The first BASIC compilers had several limitations. Many commands and functions available with the interpreter couldn't be used in the program to be compiled. The program was simply unable to understand them. Obviously this made programming very complicated. The programmer had to be sure that each line of the program could be processed by the compiler. Because of this, user-friendly commands and functions were omitted and improvised solutions were used instead.

The first QuickBASIC compiler was introduced in 1985 by Microsoft. The only problem with this compiler was that it was missing twelve commands and functions. However, their absence wasn't very significant. Most of these commands were for program input (AUTO, LIST, RENUM etc.). The advantages of this compiler included many new compiler-specific commands and functions that made the programs more user-friendly. Existing PC-BASIC programs could almost be directly transferred. The limitations decreased and the new commands and functions became more user-friendly as new versions of QuickBASIC were released.

Before they can be compiled, PC-BASIC programs must meet two requirements:

1.   The programs cannot contain commands or functions that the compiler is unable to translate.

2.   The program must be available as an ASCII text file so that there aren't any control characters.

You may be wondering how you can test the interpreter for compiler-specific commands and functions (as specified in the first requirement). However, this isn't necessary because the interpreter is no longer required. The powerful compilers that we'll describe in this chapter are very advanced. They're actually *integrated development environment* (IDE) software.

These compilers offer a user-friendly interface, an integrated editor and the ability to compile and start the program from the editor. We'll explain this in more detail later.

You're already familiar with the second requirement. Any program written in PC-BASIC can be saved in ASCII format with the ",A" switch:

```
SAVE "<name>",A
```

and then loaded into the editor of the current system. Besides the IDE type of compiler, there are also *command-line compilers*. These are also known as *batch-mode compilers*. As the name indicates, these compilers are called through the DOS command line. An example is:

```
C> Compiler title [options] source code [options]
```

You can create the source code either with the interpreter or with an ASCII editor. However, using this compiler can be time consuming. This is especially true when developing longer programs because the compiler stops after every error. So you must load the source code into the interpreter or the editor, perform the necessary edits and save the source code again. Then you need to recall the compiler. This process continues until no errors are detected in the program. The entire procedure depends on the skill and patience of the programmers.

18.1.1 Changing the program

Most of the changes you're likely to make in existing programs are limited to the program lines containing commands, statements or functions which the compiler doesn't understand. You must delete or edit these lines with equivalent statements. Unfortunately, this isn't easy to do. For example, recently we developed a program whose help displays were loaded and displayed with BLOAD. However, the first QuickBASIC compiler didn't support BLOAD. So, after two weeks of work, we were able to find a solution.

When working on compiler projects, you must decide whether it's better to modify the existing program or develop a new one. Also, remember that instead of line numbers, compilers use labels. So the statement, GOSUB 500, would become "gosub file.open". For existing programs, this means that numerous line numbers must be erased and the remaining ones converted to labels.

As we already mentioned, compilers provide new commands and functions. However, in order to determine how these new capabilities can be used, the available programs must be analyzed. For large programs, this can be a very tedious task.

Finally, the data types must be checked. PC-BASIC only provides the integer, string and real types with single or double precision. For compilers, in addition to these types, there are extended data types (mainly real) to determine the length of strings or to administer arrays. Again an analysis of the available programs is required to determine which variables or arrays to use in saving memory or increasing the speed of mathematical calculations.

18.1.2 Source Code Tips

If you want to develop programs in the interpreter and then compile them, you must also consider the compiler-specific capabilities. Making changes after completing the program and using GOTO statements disrupts the structure of the program.

Usually you'll develop your programs in the interpreter if you use a command-line compiler. But, since integrated development environment software offers more user-friendliness, using an interpreter to develop the program is rather useless. Using a word processor to create your source code is very helpful. These programs offer editing capabilities, such as search and replace commands for variable names, and can save you a lot of time when you need to erase line numbers or convert them to labels.

18.1.3 Assembler Routines and Compilers

As we discussed in Chapter 8, there are three ways to include assembler routines:

1. Load them into a protected memory area with BLOAD.

2. Use POKE to move them from the data lines to a protected memory area.

3. Save them in a string.

All of these methods cannot be used with a compiler. This is mainly because memory locations cannot be protected since variables are administered differently from an interpreter. The CALL command doesn't operate the same way as the interpreter. A label or the name of the routine to be executed must be given instead of an address for the jump. This routine must be included as an OBJ file during linking as an assembler generated routine.

Also, passing parameters is performed differently with compilers. In PC-BASIC the passing is always "by reference" - as a pointer to the data. In some compilers, for example the new QuickBASIC 4.0, you can control the passing parameters. The parameter is passed either as a value or as a pointer and the assembler routine must be designed accordingly.

18.1.4 Interpreted and Compiled Programs

Another type of rarely used program is interpreted and compiled programs. These programs can run under the interpreter and can also be compiled without changes. However, this capability can cause problems for programmers. Some users may want to be able to access the source code so that they can make their own programming changes while other users may want the program as designed, without any changes. So, the programmer needs to maintain two versions of the program - one for the interpreter and one for the compiler. This obviously creates a lot of extra work. So, from the beginning, the program must be designed to be used in either application area.

The source code cannot contain compiler-specific commands and functions that the interpreter wouldn't understand and that the compiler couldn't translate. This results in an interpreter program that doesn't offer the user-friendliness that would be possible by using additional compiler capabilities. The compiler program can also become difficult to read because the line numbers must be retained since the interpreter cannot use labels.

18.2   QuickBASIC

We believe the current version of QuickBASIC from Microsoft (Version 4) is presently the best development system for PC-BASIC. Besides the excellent user interface, functions and capabilities for program development, which make programming very simple and faster, have been implemented. We'll discuss this in more detail in the next section.

QuickBASIC includes three diskettes and accompanying manuals. The retail cost is around $100. The installation is performed with a batch file. Various directories on the hard disk or diskette can be used to organize files. Then the environment variables, SET LIB=, SET EXE=, tell QuickBASIC where to find the files. The example and utility programs that are included fill an entire diskette.

18.2.1 QuickBASIC Features

In the following section we'll discuss QuickBASIC's most important features.

User Interface
All the functions are called either with pull-down menus or with the key combination <Alt><main menu option><pull-down menu option>. Beginners will probably use the menus and then switch to the key combinations as they become more familiar with the program. QuickBASIC can also be operated with the mouse. This is helpful to programmers who are already working with other mouse controlled programs.

Module Processing
QuickBASIC processes the following source codes:

1.   Module programs are a collection of various procedures and functions. For example, you can create a module (called *modularization*) for screen input/output or for keyboard and mouse handling. This module, once debugged, is then available for use in other programs. Every module program can have a main program part through which the subroutines and functions are called.

2.   Include programs, like module programs, are included in programs and contain repetitive program sequences. These can be used for dimensioning arrays, variable assignments or subroutines and functions.

3.   Documents are true ASCII files included in the program. They can be, for example, imports from other programs or program parts created with another editor.

These programs (or parts) are accessed through menus. For example, to work on a procedure called "keyboard input", it's not necessary to go through the program page by page. The procedure can be selected from the menu. Then QuickBASIC displays its program lines.

You can move, edit or delete procedures, functions, modules or include files through this menu.

Direct Mode

QuickBASIC provides a direct mode in an additional window, called the Immediate window. The content of variables can be checked in this window. For example, while developing a procedure, you can call and execute this procedure from the direct mode. So you can test a function and make any needed changes. This is helpful because you won't have to execute the entire program in order to test only a certain part.

Half Interpreter, Half Compiler

When you enter a program line, it is tested by QuickBASIC for syntax and, if everything was correct, compiled. Since this eliminates the compile time after a RUN command, the program can be immediately started and tested.

Defining Proprietary Data Types

QuickBASIC permits the definition of proprietary data types from the available data types. Suppose that you want to write a program for warehouse inventory control. This was a complicated process in PC-BASIC because random files had to be used. However, by using QuickBASIC, you can define the data record as a data type:

```
TYPE TInventoryrecord
     Itemnumber AS INTEGER
     Description AS STRING * 30
     Price as SINGLE
END TYPE
```

DIM InvRec AS TInventoryrecord

Now you have defined a data type "TInventoryrecord" and created a variable, InvRec, of this type. Access to the individual components of the new data type is as follows:

```
InvRec.Itemnumber= 100200
InvRec.Description= "screwdriver"
InvRec.Price= 12.80
```

Creating a file is also easier because a record length doesn't have to be considered.

```
OPEN "WHOUSE.DAT" FOR RANDOM AS #1, LEN= LEN(InvRec)
```

Of course there are other possibilities for using proprietary data types (i.e., in connection with arrays).

Help

QuickBASIC provides a keyword-oriented help feature. If, for example, you cannot remember the syntax of the PRINT USING command, simply move the cursor on the keyword and press the <Shift><F1> keys. An explanation, example of the syntax and other important information appears in a help window.

If the cursor isn't on a keyword, a listing of all keywords appears on the screen. You can then select, from this list, the statement, command or function for which you need help.

Watching variables

In a separate window called the *watch window*, QuickBASIC displays variable content during the program execution. This allows errors to be detected and corrected quickly on the basis of incorrect variable contents.

Tracing and Single Step Processing

QuickBASIC allows you to set any number of *breakpoints* in the program. A program continues to execute until it reaches a breakpoint. This is a location in the program you set to pause program execution. QuickBASIC then stops and checks certain conditions with the content of variables or branching criteria. The program can be executed in single step mode by using the function keys. In this mode, either a line or a complete procedure is executed each time you press the appropriate function key. Through a separate pull-down menu, the sequence of the procedure calls can be traced back, step by step. For example, suppose that an error is reported in the "keyboard input" procedure, which was called from the "filename.input" procedure. This procedure was called from the "file.open" procedure. The procedure that is part of the call can be displayed and checked to determine if the error originated there or in the calling procedure.

Access through two windows

QuickBASIC allows you to work on the source code in two windows. For example, two cooperating procedures can be modified at the same time, or certain parts can be copied from one window to another.

Assembler and Libraries

QuickBASIC operates with QuickLibs (Lib= Library). These libraries can contain assembler routines or routines generated with QuickBASIC from module programs. QuickBASIC creates programs based on OBJ files. The assembler and the QuickBASIC compiler generate these OBJ files. During the linking, all OBJ files are collected and an EXE program is created from them. The QuickLibs aren't just added during the linking, but can be loaded, as a part of QuickBASIC, during the call. The procedures and functions contained in the QuickLib can then be used like normal commands and functions.

Because of this, assembler routines can be included either separately during linking, or together in a Lib, perhaps with other modules. You can determine whether a runtime module should be included as you create the program. If it isn't included, all programs access it in common. This saves a lot of space on the hard disk or diskette. If you plan on publishing the program, you should also include the runtime module.

18.2.2 How QuickBASIC differs from PC-BASIC

Obviously there are many differences between QuickBASIC and PC-BASIC. In this section we'll discuss the most important differences. For example, the control of the variables is completely different. Strings can be defined with a fixed length; the maximum length of a string has been extended to 32,000 characters (32K). Arrays can be created as both static and dynamic. The indexing limit of arrays can be set with an upper and lower value as follows:

```
DIM year.table(1980 TO 2000)
```

Subroutines are implemented as procedures or functions and called by name; parameters can be passed. Also, the type of parameter passing can be determined before they're used with external modules.

Variables can be defined locally in the subroutines or functions. This makes it possible to use meaningful variable names repeatedly. Variables and arrays can be any size, but individually cannot exceed one segment (64K).

18.2.3 User Interface/Menu Structure

Finally, we'll discuss the user interface and the menu structure. As we mentioned earlier, the call of the individual functions occurs through the main menu bar and pull-down menus.

```
|File|
┌─────────────────────┐
│ New Program         │
│ Open Program...     │
│ Merge...            │
│ Save                │
│ Save As...          │
│ Save All            │
├─────────────────────┤
│ Create File...      │
│ Load File...        │
│ Unload File...      │
├─────────────────────┤
│ Print...            │
├─────────────────────┤
│ DOS Shell           │
├─────────────────────┤
│ Exit                │
└─────────────────────┘
```

New Program

Corresponds to the NEW under PC-BASIC. It erases the RAM and variables existing in memory. QuickBASIC asks if you want to save any changes you have made.

Open Program...

Corresponds to LOAD under PC-BASIC. You use this option to load an existing program for processing. QuickBASIC asks if you want to save any changes you have made.

Merge...

Corresponds to the MERGE statement in PC-BASIC. You use this option to merge two or more programs into one program.

Save

Saves the module or include files, which you're currently working on, to disk under the original name. With this option you don't have to enter the program name as with the "Save as..." option.

Save as...

Use this option to save the current program under a new or different name.

Save all

Saves all program parts belonging to the current project whether or not you made any changes in them.

Create File...

Use this menu option to create a new module, include or document file in your current project.

Load File...

Loads an existing module, include or document file as an addition to the current project.

Unload File...

Deletes a module, include or document file from the current project.

Print...

Prints the current module or selected portions of it, the active window and all modules.

DOS Shell

Corresponds to the SHELL statement in PC-BASIC. You can use this option to return to the DOS command level temporarily in order to execute other programs and access DOS commands without exiting QuickBASIC.

Exit

Terminates QuickBASIC. If you have not saved any changes, QuickBASIC asks if you want these changes saved before returning to DOS.

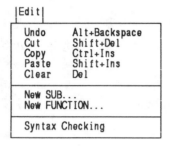

```
|Edit|
 _____
| Undo      Alt+Backspace        |
| Cut       Shift+Del            |
| Copy      Ctrl+Ins             |
| Paste     Shift+Ins            |
| Clear     Del                  |
|_____|
| New SUB...                     |
| New FUNCTION...                |
|_____|
| Syntax Checking                |
|_____|
```

Undo

Reverses all changes in the current line providing the cursor is located in that line.

Cut

Deletes the selected text into a temporary buffer called the Clipboard. You can copy and paste from the Clipboard as often as desired to any location in the program.

Copy

Copies the selected text into the Clipboard. The original text remains unchanged. You can copy and paste from the Clipboard to any location in the program as often as you want.

Paste

Copies a portion of text from the Clipboard to the cursor position.

Clear

Use this option to delete the selected text permanently. This text isn't copied in the Clipboard.

New SUB...

Creates a new procedure (Sub). After selecting this option a dialog box and a prompt requesting a name appear on the screen. The input can be simplified by entering "SUB" and the name of the procedure. This name can be accepted by pressing the <Return> key.

New FUNCTION...

Creates a new function. The name is requested in a dialog box. The input can be simplified by entering "FUNCTION" and the name of the procedure. This name can be accepted by pressing the <Return> key.

Syntax Checking

Switches the automatic syntax checking on or off. The checking should only be switched off when using a slow PC and very long program lines.

```
|View|
┌──────────────────────────┐
│ SUBs...             F2    │
│ Next SUB      SHIFT+F2    │
│ Split                    │
├──────────────────────────┤
│ Next Statement           │
│ Output Screen       F4   │
├──────────────────────────┤
│ Include File             │
│ Included Lines           │
├──────────────────────────┤
│ Options...               │
└──────────────────────────┘
```

SUBs...

Calls a pop-up menu from which the individual modules, include files, procedures and functions for a change or display can be called.

Next SUB

Displays, in alphabetical order, the procedure for a module.

Split

Splits the window into two horizontal screens. This allows you to view, edit or modify two different parts of the same program simultaneously.

Next Statement

Places the cursor at the next statement to be executed.

Output Screen

Displays the result of the last program execution.

Include File

Since include files are included through a compiler statement, they do not appear as program lines in the program. They can only be changed when the editing is switched on.

Include Lines

Displays include files as program lines for easier editing. You can change the include file only when this option is switched off.

Options...

You can change the parameters for the foreground and background colors of the screen display and control the screen construction using this option.

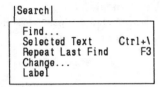

```
|Search|
 _____
| Find...                 |
| Selected Text   Ctrl+\  |
| Repeat Last Find    F3  |
| Change...               |
| Label                   |
|_____|
```

Find...

Searches either the current module or in the active window for a specific search criterion such as a statement or group of characters.

Selected Text

This option is similar to the "Find..." option. It also allows you to search either the current module or in the active window for a specific search criterion.

Repeat Last Find

Repeats the search for the string previously entered in the "Find..." option.

Change...

Use this option when you want to perform a search for a specific string and replace it with another string. You can use this option either in the entire program or the current window.

Label

This option looks for a line label by adding a semicolon to the text that is currently selected.

```
|Run|
 _____
| Start       Shift+F5    |
| Restart                 |
| Continue         F5     |
| Modify COMMAND$...      |
|_____|
| Make EXE File...        |
| Make Library...         |
|_____|
| Set Main Module...      |
|_____|
```

Start

Select this option to execute your BASIC program.

Restart

This option resets all variables to zero or null strings. It also highlights the first executable statement in your BASIC program.

Continue

Continues the program after you stop or break into the program. This corresponds to the CONT command in PC-BASIC.

Modify COMMAND$...

A DOS command line can be "simulated" here. The entered parameters are passed to the program in the COMMAND$ variable and are evaluated there.

Make EXE File...

Compiles and links the current program to an executable EXE program. Your program no longer requires QuickBASIC help after successfully finishing this option.

Make Library...

Makes a QuickLib from the current module.

Set Main module...

Here you determine which of the modules loaded as a main program should be called, after the start, as a control program.

```
|Debug|
┌─────────────────────────┐
│ Add Watch...            │
│ Watchpoint...           │
│ Delete Watch...         │
│ Delete All Watch        │
├─────────────────────────┤
│ Trace On                │
│ History On              │
├─────────────────────────┤
│ Toggle Breakpoint    F9 │
│ Clear All Breakpoints   │
│ Set Next Statement      │
└─────────────────────────┘
```

Add Watch...

When you select this option, a dialog box opens so that you can enter expressions to be included in the Watch window.

Watchpoint...

Here you can indicate under what conditions the program should stop its execution.

Delete Watch...

Removes individual variable displays from a separate variable window.

Delete All Watch

Removes all variable displays from the separate variable window.

TRACE on

Switches on the TRACE mode. The program can be executed in step or procedure mode.

History on

Select this option if you want to trace backwards/forwards through the last 20 statements your program executed.

Toggle Breakpoint

Sets or deletes a breakpoint. The breakpoint always relates to the line in which the cursor is currently located.

Clear all Breakpoints

Clears all breakpoints which are set.

Set Next Statement

Determines the next statement to be executed.

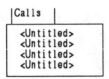

After the execution of the program, the calls are displayed in this menu. The last procedure or function is at the top. The procedure or functions which were called by this function are listed below this.

18.3   Turbo Basic

When Turbo Basic was released by Borland it was considered as direct competition to QuickBASIC. However, it was soon obvious that both products could co-exist. Although the current version of Turbo Basic is called PowerBASIC (released from SPECTRA Publishing, with an approximate retail price of $130), we'll discuss Turbo Basic in this section because it is more widely used. If you're already using PowerBASIC, refer to the PowerBASIC Reference Guide for information concerning differences between it and Turbo Basic.

Turbo Basic includes two diskettes and two manuals. It's easy and quick to install by following the instructions in the manual. Turbo Basic administers various directories on the hard disk and diskette.

18.3.1 Turbo Basic Features

Turbo Basic is designed so that the editor, compiler and linker are collected into one program under a single user interface.

Many Windows

Each function features its own window so that you can observe the program execution. So instead of being randomly displayed on the screen, error messages or input always appear in the intended window. Turbo Basic operates with a total of four windows:

Edit window

You create or change your programs in this window.

Message window

This window displays error messages, prompts and program statistics.

Run window

Shows the results of program execution.

Trace window

This window displays the current line numbers, label and procedure/function names as they're executed by your program.

You can change the size, color and position of each window. Also switching between windows or deleting windows is possible. The windows are controlled through the Window menu option. The sequence of the windows can also be determined here. They can be positioned sequentially like file cards or symmetrically, with all windows being the same size.

The system is controlled through a main menu line and pull-down menus. From here programs are loaded and stored, directories are displayed and changed or Turbo Basic is terminated. For functions requiring a filename, you can select a name from a directory. The DOS Shell function, through which the normal MS-DOS commands can be executed and the COMMAND.COM can be called without terminating Turbo Basic, is also available.

Help

Turbo Basic provides a context-sensitive help function. This means that after the help key is activated, only help information, which is relevant to the user's location in Turbo Basic, is displayed. However, this doesn't apply to keywords.

Ideal System Setup

Through the SETUP menu option the names of the available directories for Turbo Basic, the include files and the completed programs are determined. This enables the various programs on the hard disk and diskette to be organized for easy access. The colors for the system, including the menus, window, messages and input/output boxes can be set individually.

Every SETUP can be saved or loaded from its own file. So if several programmers are using the same PC, each one can have an individual Turbo Basic. To save SETUP permanently, store it in the program file. In this way the set values are immediately active after loading and don't have to be initialized separately.

An excellent editor

The editor is a very important part of a program. The best user interface is worthless if entering the program is tedious and time consuming. Turbo Basic provides an excellent solution for this problem. Its editor will be familiar to you if you've already worked with Turbo PASCAL or Turbo PROLOG. The same user-friendly (and WordStar compatible) editor is used in Turbo Basic. All functions are called through the key combination <Ctrl> + one or two other keys.

Module editing

Turbo Basic differentiates between work and main files in the source codes. You must enter a name in the "main file" option in the File menu option in order to use the include function. You can include various work files by using this option. The program is also a work file. The actual main program is a main file. This makes the work easier since the name of the main program doesn't have to be entered before compilation.

Only Compiler

After the source text has been entered, the program can be immediately executed and tested. This is started through the Run menu option. Since the individual program lines aren't pre-compiled, the entire program must be translated each time. Normally the program is compiled in memory, stored there and then executed. If the compiler finds a syntax error, the error message is displayed in the message window. After the <Esc> key is activated, the cursor in the editor is placed on the statement which has caused the error. So it's not necessary to page through the program in search of the problem. Also, the error message can be called again at any time with a key combination.

Programs for every application

The compilation is determined with the Options menu option. You can compile directly into memory during program development and the test phase. Alternatively, you can create an executable EXE program. Other options include a mathematical co-processor (8087), querying the key combination <Ctrl> <Break>, or testing the limits of an array. The Autosave function, which stores a program before every Run, is also important. This is especially useful during the development phase or during experiments with assembler routines because, with many computers, a system crash or an endless loop occurs.

Program with Overlays

It's possible to generate a chain file from the current program. These chain files are loaded as overlays by the executing program. Since the runtime library, which is already in memory, is used, these files are much smaller than completely executable programs. So they require much less space on the diskette or hard disk. This also enables you to store larger, seldom-used routines as chain files and load them only when needed.

Error Correction

Turbo Basic differentiates between compile and runtime errors. The compile errors are handled during the compilation as described above. You can switch on trace in the Debug menu option to detect consistent errors. This displays the currently executing line number in the Trace window. The program execution can be followed step by step until an error occurs. However, unfortunately there is a problem with this feature. Although Turbo Basic permits BASIC programs without line numbers, Trace can only work on programs with line numbers.

Turbo Basic displays an error number and the address where the error occurred if a runtime error occurs during program execution. This address is used to locate the error in the source text. The runtime function error can be called through the Debug menu option. After the address is entered, the cursor is moved, in the source text, to the statement that corresponds to the address.

18.3.2 How Turbo Basic differs from PC-BASIC

Now we'll discuss the most important differences between Turbo Basic and PC-BASIC. First let's discuss the new data types in Turbo Basic. A string can be up to 32,768 bytes long and the Long Integer data type has been added. In contrast with the interpreters, the floating point numbers are stored by Turbo Basic in the IEEE format instead of in a special

Microsoft format. Turbo Basic provides functions that can convert to and from both formats.

Turbo Basic permits the use of integer constants which are declared separately and are addressed through their name. These constants cannot be changed through an assignment or editing. Therefore constants remain constants. In some systems a constant may become a variable. This makes searching for errors more difficult.

Variables are used and handled as in the interpreter. The only difference in Turbo Basic is that individual variables can be declared as local for functions or procedures. These variables then exist in the functions or procedures for the current execution only.

The OPTION BASE statement, used to set the minimum value for array subscript, has been extended. A value between 0 and 32,767 can now be used. However, occasionally, even this may be large enough. The DIM command permits the individual arrays to be increased and decreased similar to QuickBASIC. For example, displaying an error message from a string array with a loop could appear as follows in the interpreter:

```
10 DIM error-message$(4)
.....
115 FOR I= 10 to 14
120  LOCATE I,5
125  PRINT error-message$(I-10)
130 NEXT I
With Turbo-BASIC the same task would appear as follows:
DIM error-message$(10|14)
.....
FOR I= 10 to 14
  LOCATE I,5
  PRINT error-message$(I)
NEXT I
```

Notice the DIM command and how PRINT displays the message in both listings. We selected a simple example. Actually, you can omit calculations similar to the one in line 120 of the first example. Also, the arrays can be dimensioned as static or dynamic in Turbo Basic. Static means that the array is initially created during compilation with fixed dimensions. An array, which is dimensioned dynamically, is created only during the program execution. This allows you to reserve only the memory space that is actually used.

Besides the familiar file administration for sequential and direct access files, Turbo Basic also provides the binary access method. The file isn't confined to a fixed record format, but access is possible to every byte of the file through a file pointer. It doesn't matter whether the file was previously created as a sequential or a direct access file. Also field or record separators aren't considered when the file is read. This enables you to read damage files.

Subroutines are handled with GOSUB and RETURN, as in the interpreter. In contrast to the interpreter, user-defined functions can be created over several lines in Turbo Basic. The return jump from one of these functions can occur at any location. Passing variables occur as a constant value or as a variable, as in the interpreter. Procedures are a new feature in Turbo Basic. Parameters can also be passed to these procedures. Functions and procedures are fully recursive, which means that they can call themselves.

We prefer a programming language which, through interfaces, allows full access to the entire system (BIOS/DOS) and, therefore, provides complete control of the PC. Turbo Basic supports this in two ways:

CALL ABSOLUTE

Assembler routines can be stored at the end of the free memory and called through their offset address. The segment is defined through the DEF SEG. Variables are passed with a parameter list through the stack.

CALL INTERRUPT

A BIOS or DOS interrupt is called through its number. The registers are loaded from an internal buffer, which is supplied with the data through a command (REG X,value). After the return from the interrupt, the current register content is stored in this buffer and can be read through a function (value = REG X).

18.3.3 User Interface and Menu Structure

We'll conclude this section by discussing the user interface and the menu structure. As we mentioned, you select the individual functions through a main menu bar and pull-down menus.

```
┌─────────────────────────────────────────────────────────────────────────┐
│ File       Edit      Run     Compile     Options     Setup    Window  Debug│
├──────────────┐
│ Load         │
│ New          │
│ Save         │
│ Write to     │
│ Main file    │
│ Directory    │
│ Change dir   │
│ OS shell     │
│ Quit         │
└──────────────┘
```

Load

Loads an existing program for editing. If a program is in memory, Turbo Basic asks whether you want to save any changes you made in it.

601

New

Deletes the RAM, current projects and all variables. If a program is in memory, Turbo Basic asks whether you want to save any changes you made in it.

Save

Saves the program, which you're currently working on, to file under the original name. With this option you don't have to enter the program name as with the "Write to" option.

Write to

Use this option to save the current program under a new or different name.

Main file

This option allows you to separate the source code into smaller sections. This is especially useful in large programs exceeding the capacity of the editor.

Directory

This option displays the directory so you can search subdirectories and enter extensions (i.e., *.BAS or *.ICL).

Change dir

Select this option to change the directory.

OS shell

Corresponds to the SHELL statement in PC-BASIC. You can use this option to return to the DOS command level temporarily in order to execute other programs and access DOS commands without exiting Turbo Basic.

Quit

Terminates Turbo Basic. If you have not saved any changes, Turbo Basic asks if you want these changes saved before returning to DOS.

File	**Edit**	Run	Compile	Options	Setup	Window	Debug

Changes from the menu mode to the editor.

File	Edit	**Run**	Compile	Options	Setup	Window	Debug

Compiles the current program and then executes it.

File	Edit	Run	**Compile**	Options	Setup	Window	Debug

Compiles but doesn't execute the current program. This menu option is called when you create an EXE program or want to test for errors quickly.

File	Edit	Run	Compile	Options	Setup	Window	Debug

Compile to	Memory
8087 required	OFF
Keyboard break	OFF
Bounds	OFF
Overflow	OFF
Stack test	OFF
Parameter line	
Metastatements	

Compile to <destination>

This enables you to create the program as an EXE or CHN program. You can also save the program in memory for further testing.

8087 required {OFF/ON}

Determines whether the program should operate with a mathematical co-processor. If you select ON and the program doesn't find a co-processor, it terminates with an error message. For OFF, the routines are implemented with software.

Keyboard break {OFF/ON}

(ON) selects whether the program can be interrupted with the <Ctrl><C> or <Ctrl><Break> keys. If it can't, select (OFF).

Bounds {OFF/ON}

Select (ON) if the array limits should be tested and (OFF) if a test shouldn't occur. It's possible that, during OFF, program or data portions may be overwritten if incorrect indexing was used.

Overflow {OFF/ON}

Determines whether, during mathematical operations, an overflow should be reported (ON) or ignored (OFF).

Stack test {OFF/ON}

Turbo Basic is fully recursive, which means that each procedure can call itself as often as necessary. If the stack is too small, a program crash can occur. If this happens and you've selected ON, the program will terminate with a message.

Parameter line

Permits the "simulation" of the DOS command line. The parameters indicated here are passed to the program, as if the user had actually entered them.

Metastatements

Determines the stack and buffer size for the PLAY command and the serial interface.

```
┌──────────────────────────────────────────────────────────────────────────┐
│ File      Edit      Run      Compile      Options      Setup    Window   Debug │
└──────────────────────────────────────────────────────────────────────────┘
                                              ┌────────────────────────────┐
                                              │ Colors                     │
                                              │ Directories                │
                                              │ Miscellaneous              │
                                              │ Load Options/Window/Setup  │
                                              │ Save Options/Window/Setup  │
                                              └────────────────────────────┘
```

Colors

All colors used for the individual functions, menus and boxes are set with this option.

Directories

Here you can indicate the directories in which Turbo Basic should search for include files, or where to store the EXE programs.

Miscellaneous

Includes miscellaneous control parameters, such as AUTOSAVE ON/OFF, for the complete system.

Load Options/Window/Setup

The settings selected for the options and windows can be stored in a file. This allows individual versions of Turbo Basic to be implemented on one PC. One of these files can be selected here for loading.

Save Options/Window/Setup

The settings selected for the options and windows can be stored in a file. One of these files can be stored here.

```
┌──────────────────────────────────────────────────────────────────────────┐
│ File      Edit      Run      Compile      Options      Setup    Window   Debug │
└──────────────────────────────────────────────────────────────────────────┘
                                                           ┌──────────┐
                                                           │ Open     │
                                                           │ Close    │
                                                           │ Next     │
                                                           │ Goto     │
                                                           │ Tile     │
                                                           │ Stack    │
                                                           │ Zoom     │
                                                           └──────────┘
```

Open

Opens a window for the editor, Debug, Message or Run.

Close

Closes a window for the editor, Debug, Message or Run.

Next

Jumps from the current window into the next open window.

Goto

Jumps from the current window into one of the windows for the editor, Debug, Message or Run.

Tile

Places the open windows either side by side or underneath each other.

Stack

Stacks the open windows like file cards.

Zoom

Changes one of the windows for the editor, Debug, Message or Run, to full size on the screen.

```
┌───────────────────────────────────────────────────────────────────────────┐
│ File      Edit      Run      Compile      Options      Setup      Window  Debug │
└───────────────────────────────────────────────────────────────────────────┘
                                                    ┌──────────────────────────┐
                                                    │ Trace               OFF  │
                                                    │ Run-time error           │
                                                    └──────────────────────────┘
```

Trace {ON/OFF}

You can switch the step mode on or off. In the Trace mode program execution occurs through the function keys.

Run-time error

If Turbo Basic encounters a run-time error, its number and the address, where the error was discovered, are displayed. You can enter both and Turbo Basic moves the cursor to the statement, which caused the error, in the source code.

18.4   BASIC Version 7.0

Microsoft recently released its new BASIC Professional Development compiler, Version 7.0. This compiler can develop programs for the new OS/2 or PS/2 operating system. However, it's also possible to use this version on a normal PC or AT under DOS. Although a discussion of this compiler isn't vital to this chapter, we'll discuss it so that you have some general information.

The compiler is delivered on 12 diskettes; some of these are intended to be used only with OS/2, while others are only for MS-DOS. The installation occurs through a special installation program (which asks numerous questions). Three manuals are also included. Besides the actual compiler, there is also a version of QuickBASIC on the diskettes. The program includes a special utility, named CodeView, allowing you to search for errors.

One disadvantage of this program is that it can take a long time to learn how all of its functions work. However, QuickBASIC does offer error tracing capabilities that are unmatched in the industry. For example, the source code and the assembler code can be displayed simultaneously and executed in single step mode. Control of all registers and variable content, as well as breakpoint setting, has been implemented.

The new menu-driven Microsoft Editor and Microsoft CodeView window orientated debugging system makes developing professional BASIC application fast and easy for MS-DOS and OS/2 computers.

The manuals are divided into the following topics: BASIC and QuickBASIC in general, Utilities and a reference manual for all commands and functions.

18.4.1 BASIC Version 7.0 Features

BASIC Version 7.0 can create programs that execute under OS/2, but also fully utilize the available multiuser/multitasking capabilities. It's also capable of executing the programs in the protected mode of the processor or performing OS/2 function calls directly. Since "dynamic linking" under OS/2 is supported, it's possible to call such routines.

Compared to QuickBASIC, the error correction in Version 7.0 has been improved so that a single correction can be made on the procedure and function level. Until now the program always had to be continued in the main program after an error, regardless of where the error had occurred. BASIC programs can be made "dormant" in a multitasking environment by suppressing their call for a period of time. This prevents any unnecessary use of the processor.

A few of the features of BASIC 7.0 include:

- Integrated ISAM (indexed sequential access method) files were added for lightning fast databases with multiple index keys.

- Three new statements, DIR$, CURDIR$ and CHDRIVE make it easy to manage DOS files form BASIC.

- The currency data type speed up you calculation for super fast program operation.

- Structured error handling allows procedure and module level error routines

- Improved handing of timeouts on the communication ports.

- New libraries have been added that support Date/Time, Financial and Formatting options to give your BASIC programs spreadsheet style calculations and formatting.

- New toolboxes are available that allows math matrix calculation, easy presentation graphics and excellent user interface routines.

The Microsoft BASIC Professional Development package is the top of the line BASIC development system.

18.5   Input/Output Comparison

In this section we'll discuss the execution speed of compilers.

We'll compare a small benchmark program. This program is executed in the interpreter and the compilers. They're compared under the same conditions and without any changes in the source code.

The following is the listing for the benchmark program:

```
10 '-------------------------------------------------------------
20 'BENCH.BAS    speed comparison Interpreter/Compiler
30 '-------------------------------------------------------------
40 :
50 CLS:KEY OFF
60 :
70 '----- mathematical calculations ... -----
80 :
90 PRINT "Mathematical Operations....."
100 MATH.START= TIMER
110 FOR I=1 TO 1000
120    A= I*2
130    A= I^2
140    A= SQR(I)
150 NEXT I
160 MATH.ENDE= TIMER
170 :
180 '----- screen display output ... -----
190 :
200 SCREEN.START= TIMER
210 CLS
220 FOR I=1 TO 2000
230    COLOR I MOD 15,0
240    PRINT "X";
250 NEXT I
260 SCREEN.ENDE= TIMER
270 COLOR 7,0
280 :
290 '----- string operations -----
300 :
310 CLS
320 PRINT "String Operations..."
330 STRING.START= TIMER
340 FOR I=1 TO 255
350    X$= X$+ CHR$(I)
360    Y$= LEFT$(X$,I)
370    Z$= MID$(X$,1,I)
380 NEXT I
390 STRING.ENDE= TIMER
400 :
410 '----- Diskette-/hard-disk access -----
420 :
```

```
430 PRINT "Diskette-/hard-disk access..."
440 DISK.START= TIMER
450 OPEN "test.dat" FOR OUTPUT AS #1
460 FOR I=1 TO 100
470   PRINT#1,STRING$(255,"X")
480 NEXT I
490 CLOSE
500 OPEN "test.dat" FOR INPUT AS #1
510 FOR I=1 TO 100
520    INPUT#1,X$
530 NEXT I
540 CLOSE
550 DISK.ENDE= TIMER
560 :
570 CLS
580 PRINT USING "Mathematical Operations ####.##";MATH.ENDE-MATH.START
590 PRINT USING "Screen display output   ####.##";SCREEN.ENDE-SCREEN.START
600 PRINT USING "String Operations       ####.##";STRING.ENDE-STRING.START
610 PRINT USING "Disk Operations         ####.##";DISK.ENDE-DISK.START
620 PRINT:PRINT
```

The program executes the most important operations in a loop and displays the results. The following table shows the results of the comparison:

Action / System	PCB	TB	QB	B7
Mathematical Operations	2.42	1.98	8.41	8.24
display output	5.93	4.56	2.58	2.03
String-Operations	1.15	0.49	0.55	0.44
Disk accesses	5.82	2.19	5.05	4.94

PCB = PC-BASIC, TB = Turbo-BASIC, QB = QuickBASIC, B7 = BASIC V7.0

Fig. 41: Speed Comparison Interpreter/Compiler

The program was executed in memory mode and also as an EXE program on the compilers. The results differed only slightly. Only in Turbo Basic was the screen display output almost twice as fast for the compiled program (2.03).

19. PC-BASIC Quick Reference

The following is an overview of all PC-BASIC commands and functions. This chapter will help you quickly find the proper syntax and all required parameters. The first part of this chapter is organized according to application area. The second is organized alphabetically.

19.1   Application Area

Variables

Screen Output

Data Output

Data Input

String Operations

Data Conversion

Mathematical Operations

Print Output

Error Correction

Sound

Graphic

Interfaces

Accessing Memory Areas

Interrupt Programming

19.2   Alphabetical Order

Appendix A: <Alt> Key Shortcuts

In this appendix you'll find an overview of the keywords that can be entered with the following key combination:

```
<Alt>+<one of the following keys>
```

Simultaneously press the <Alt> key and the additional key. After the keys are released, the keyword appears on the screen.

Key	Result:	Key	Result:
<A>	AUTO	<N>	NEXT
<B>	BSAVE	<O>	OPEN
<C>	COLOR	<P>	PRINT
<D>	DELETE	<Q>	nothing
<E>	ELSE	<R>	RETURN
<F>	FOR	<S>	SCREEN
<G>	GOTO|GOSUB	<T>	THEN
<H>	HEX$	<U>	USING
<I>	INPUT	<V>	VAL
<J>	nothing	<W>	WIDTH|WINDOW
<K>	KEY	<X>	XOR
<L>	LOCATE	<Y>	nothing
<M>	MERGE|MOTOR	<Z>	nothing

Note: Since this table isn't valid for all versions of PC-BASIC, there may be some differences with your version.

625

Appendix B: PC-BASIC Error Messages

The PC-BASIC error messages are divided into the following groups:

Errors 01 to 30	program-/syntax errors
Errors 50 to 76	file-management and peripherals

The following error numbers, which aren't assigned, generate an "Unprintable error" message:

    21, 28, 56, 59, 60, 65, 78 to 255

The following error numbers also are not assigned. They produce different messages depending on the version of PC-BASIC you are using:

Error 73	mostly advanced feature
Error 77	mostly deadlock

The following error messages don't have error numbers:

Can't continue after SHELL

This message is sent to the program or data area if PC-BASIC crashes after executing a program in SHELL. Unless the operating system was also affected, the MS-DOS prompt appears again.

Can't run BASIC as a child from BASIC

You'll receive this message with some versions of PC-BASIC if you call the interpreter again while in SHELL.

01   NEXT without FOR

A NEXT statement was discovered without a corresponding FOR statement. This error usually occurs in nested FOR...NEXT loops from which FOR was deleted.

02   Syntax Error (input error)

The interpreter cannot identify the instruction to be performed. There are several different causes of this error: a keyword was entered incorrectly, invalid parameter is used or too many characters were entered in one program line. Other possibilities include forgetting to enter special characters such as parentheses, commas or semicolons.

03 RETURN without GOSUB

During the program execution the interpreter encountered a RETURN without first having executed a GOSUB. Most of the time this error occurs in nested GOSUB/RETURN sequences.

04 Out of data

READ attempted to read more data than was available in DATA statements. Check the DATA lines. Also, RESTORE could have been specified with an incorrect line.

05 Illegal function call

This error has various causes:

- The record number for GET#/PUT# for a random-access file is zero or negative.

- USR command without a previous DEF USR.

- The value of a mathematical operation was illegal.

- An invalid parameter was passed to a function.

- You tried to index an array with a negative number.

- Some graphics commands report this error if the coordinates aren't correctly stated.

06 Overflow

The result of a calculation is too large. Check the arguments.

07 Out of memory

Two causes are possible for this error message. Your program may be so large there isn't sufficient memory for the variables and stack. It's also possible that the statements are nested too deeply and are too complex. This means that too many FOR...NEXTs, WHILE...WENDs or GOSUB...RETURNs are open at one time. Make sure that the subroutines are exited using GOTO, that FOR...NEXT and WHILE...WEND loops are terminated and the calculations and expressions are as simple as possible. Perform garbage collection regularly with FRE("") when you use several string operations at one time.

08 Undefined line number

You are trying to reference a non-existent line number in a statement such as GOTO or GOSUB. Check the line number that your program is calling.

09   *Subscript out of range*

You attempted to address an array element that is either beyond the dimension set with DIM or less than the lower index boundary set by OPTION BASE. Check the call.

10   *Duplicate definition*

An array was redefined with DIM, or an array being used with default dimensioning was redimensioned with DIM. It's also possible that OPTION BASE was used after arrays were referenced. You must first use ERASE to delete an array before redimensioning. You must use OPTION BASE before all DIMs at the beginning of the program.

11   *Division by zero*

You cannot divide a value by zero. Check the value before the division to see if it is zero.

12   *Illegal direct*

You tried to execute a command in direct mode that can only be permitted in program mode. Use the command within a program only.

13   *Type mismatch*

The variable types used in a string or mathematical operation do not match. Check the variable types.

14   *Out of string space*

String memory will overflow when you use too many string operations and insufficient garbage collection. Keep these string operations to a minimum and use more garbage collections with FRE("").

15   *String too long*

The maximum number of characters in a string is 255. Check the operation and the contents of the variables you're using.

16   *String formula too complex*

The string operation you tried to perform is too complex for the interpreter. Divide the operation into several smaller operations.

17   *Can't continue*

You cannot execute a CONT without a previous STOP or change the program or variable contents after a STOP.

18   *Undefined user function*

A function was called in the program with FN or USR that has not been defined with DEF FN or DEF USR.

19   *No RESUME*

After an ON ERROR GOTO the interpreter discovered that your error handling routine didn't contain a RESUME.

20   *RESUME without ERROR*

A RESUME was discovered in the program but an error did not occur. Check the routine.

22   *Missing operand*

An operand within an operation is missing.

23   *Line buffer overflow*

You entered a line, in direct mode, that contains more than 255 characters. Shorten the line or write a small program to execute the line.

24   *Device timeout*

The expected answer from a peripheral unit was not received within the specified time. Check the unit to see if it is available and switched on. For COM operations you can specify longer delay times for CS<Time>, DS<Time> and CD<Time>. You can also trap the error with ON ERROR GOTO and IF ERR=24 THEN RESUME. In the worst case, an endless loop will be generated.

25   *Device fault*

The addressed device does not exist. Check the call.

26   *FOR without NEXT*

A corresponding NEXT isn't available for the FOR to execute. Also loops may not be nested correctly.

27   *Out of paper*

Your printer is out of paper. This error is sent by the printer.

29   *WHILE without WEND*

A WHILE occurred in the program without a corresponding WEND.

30   *WEND without WHILE*

A WEND was encountered without a WHILE having been executed.

50   *FIELD overflow*

You tried to make the FIELD larger than the record length indicated during OPEN. Check the specified variable lengths or the LEN=<record length> parameter.

51   *Internal Error*

An error occurred within the interpreter that was the interpreter's fault.

52   *Bad file number*

There are usually three causes of this error: the file you tried to access was not previously opened with OPEN, the file number lies outside the range 1 to 15 or the maximum number of files is already open. Check your input or the /F parameter when calling GW-BASIC or the entry in CONFIG.SYS.

53   *File not found*

The file addressed cannot be found. Check the drive, path, filename and extension. If all of these are correct, you may have inserted the wrong diskette.

54   *Bad file mode*

You tried to use a file that does not correspond with its mode. This means that you tried to use PUT# or GET# on a sequential file or change its name with NAME.

55   *File already open*

You tried to use a file number that is currently in use in another OPEN command. Choose a different file number or close the other file. The same error is printed if you try to KILL an open file or change its name with NAME. In these cases the file must first be closed.

57   *Device I/O error*

An error occurred during output to the diskette or printer. It is possible that a diskette isn't formatted, is write-protected or cannot be written for other reasons. If this error occurs with a hard disk, there can be a problem with the disk itself. For a printer, either the device is not switched on, is not online or sent an error code that cannot be interpreted. Check the printer.

58   *File already exists*

When you changed the name of a file with NAME, you entered an existing filename as new_filespec. Choose another name.

61   *Disk full*

Your diskette or hard disk is full. Insert a new diskette or delete unnecessary files for more disk space.

62   *Input past end*

You tried to read past the end of a sequential file. Use EOF to check for the end of the file.

63   *Bad record number*

The specified record number is either 0, negative or larger than the maximum record number (16,777,215).

64   *Bad file name*

The filename used contains illegal characters or has too many characters. See the MS-DOS reference manual for valid characters or shorten the name.

66   *Direct statement in file*

While loading an ASCII file, a statement without a line number was discovered. The loading process is terminated. Check the program and insert line numbers as needed.

67   *Too many files*

There is not enough space in the directory of the diskette or hard disk to store the entry for the file. Use a different diskette or subdirectory.

68   *Device unavailable*

During OPEN, an attempt was made to access a nonexistent device.

69   *Communication buffer overflow*

The receive buffer for the COM interface has exceeded its limit. You'll need to create a larger buffer with /C:<buffer> when calling PC-BASIC, select a lower baud rate if the data cannot be processed quickly enough or use ON ERROR GOTO.

70   *Disk write protected*

During file output it was discovered that the diskette is write-protected. Remove the write-protect tab or use another diskette.

71   *Disk not ready*

A diskette isn't in the drive or the drive door is open. Insert a new diskette and/or lock the drive.

72   *Disk media error*

The disk controller has discovered irregularities during data transfer. There are several reasons for this:

•   The diskette is defective.

•   The read/write head cannot be positioned properly.

•   The diskette contains defective sectors.

•   The read/write head is dirty.

Check the diskette with CHKDSK, copy the files, if necessary, to another diskette and then reformat the defective diskette.

74   *Rename across disks*

You specified different drives in the file specifications for renaming.

75   *Path/file access error*

The given path/file specification contains an error.

76   *Path not found*

The path specified for a file access is not correct.

Appendix C: MS-DOS Error Messages

The MS-DOS functions return an error number in the AX register after an error in parameter passing or for an incorrect call. An error is usually signaled with a set carry flag. The following is a listing of error numbers and messages:

01H   *Invalid function code*

02H   *File not found*

03H   *Path not found*

04H   *Too many open files*

05H   *Access denied*

06H   *Invalid handle*

07H   *Memory control blocks destroyed*

08H   *Insufficient memory*

09H   *Invalid memory block address*

0AH   *Invalid environment*

0BH   *Invalid format*

0CH   *Invalid access code*

0DH   *Invalid data*

0EH   *Reserved*

0FH   *Invalid drive*

10H   *Attempt to remove current directory*

11H   *Not same device*

12H	*No more files*
13H	*Disk is write-protected*
14H	*Bad disk unit*
15H	*Drive not ready*
16H	*Invalid disk command*
17H	*CRC error*
18H	*Invalid length*
19H	*Seek error*
1AH	*No MS-DOS diskette*
1BH	*Sector not found*
1CH	*Out of paper*
1DH	*Write fault*
1EH	*Read fault*
1FH	*General failure*
22H	*Wrong disk*
23H	*FCB unavailable* (File Control Block)

You can query an extended error code through function 59h of the PC-BASIC function EXTERR. This adds the following information:

MS-DOS return message

BH = error class

BL = suggested action on error

CH = localization of error

EXTERR(<n>) return message

<n> = 1	error class
<n> = 2	suggested action on error
<n> = 3	localization of error

Error Class

01H   Access is outside the permitted options. For example, in a network, access to a device which isn't assigned.

02H   Not actually an error but a temporary situation. For example, if a record or a file is temporarily protected from access.

03H   Access not permitted. In a network, an attempt was made to access a file which wasn't released yet.

04H   Internal error in the system software.

05H   Error in the hardware.

06H   A system software error which wasn't caused by the last function but, for example, by the wrong configuration.

07H   Unspecified error in the applications software.

08H   File or device wasn't found.

09H   File or device doesn't have a valid DOS format, is the wrong type, invalid or lost.

0AH   File or device isn't available because of denied access.

0BH   Wrong diskette in drive, diskette defective or other problems with the diskette.

0CH   Other error which cannot be specified.

Suggested Action

01H Retry, then prompt user.

02H Retry after a pause.

03H Prompt the user again for data they may have entered such as a drive letter or filename.

04H Function call cannot be executed, terminate with cleanup.

05H Function call cannot be executed. The system is in an uncontrolled condition. Terminate program immediately; it may not be possible to close files correctly.

06H Informational error.

07H Prompt the user to perform some action. Then try the operation again.

Localization

01H Unknown cause for the error.

02H Error is related to random-access block devices (i.e., disk drive).

03H Error in network.

04H Error at the serial interface (printer, modem, etc.).

05H Error in the main memory (RAM).

Appendix D: PC Character Set and ASCII Codes

PC Character Set

32		33	!	34	"	35	#	36	$	37	%	38	&	39	'	40	(	41	)	42	*	43	+
44	,	45	-	46	.	47	/	48	0	49	1	50	2	51	3	52	4	53	5	54	6	55	7
56	8	57	9	58	:	59	;	60	<	61	=	62	>	63	?	64	@	65	A	66	B	67	C
68	D	69	E	70	F	71	G	72	H	73	I	74	J	75	K	76	L	77	M	78	N	79	O
80	P	81	Q	82	R	83	S	84	T	85	U	86	V	87	W	88	X	89	Y	90	Z	91	[
92	\	93	]	94	^	95	_	96	`	97	a	98	b	99	c	100	d	101	e	102	f	103	g
104	h	105	i	106	j	107	k	108	l	109	m	110	n	111	o	112	p	113	q	114	r	115	s
116	t	117	u	118	v	119	w	120	x	121	y	122	z	123	{	124	|	125	}	126	~	127	⌂
128	Ç	129	ü	130	é	131	â	132	ä	133	à	134	å	135	ç	136	ê	137	ë	138	è	139	ï
140	î	141	ì	142	Ä	143	Å	144	É	145	æ	146	Æ	147	ô	148	ö	149	ò	150	û	151	ù
152	ÿ	153	Ö	154	Ü	155	¢	156	£	157	¥	158	₧	159	ƒ	160	á	161	í	162	ó	163	ú
164	ñ	165	Ñ	166	ª	167	º	168	¿	169	⌐	170	¬	171	½	172	¼	173	¡	174	«	175	»
176	░	177	▒	178	▓	179	│	180	┤	181	╡	182	╢	183	╖	184	╕	185	╣	186	║	187	╗
188	╝	189	╜	190	╛	191	┐	192	└	193	┴	194	┬	195	├	196	─	197	┼	198	╞	199	╟
200	╚	201	╔	202	╩	203	╦	204	╠	205	═	206	╬	207	╧	208	╨	209	╤	210	╥	211	╙
212	╘	213	╒	214	╓	215	╫	216	╪	217	┘	218	┌	219	█	220	▄	221	▌	222	▐	223	▀
224	α	225	ß	226	Γ	227	π	228	Σ	229	σ	230	µ	231	τ	232	Φ	233	θ	234	Ω	235	δ
236	∞	237	ø	238	∈	239	∩	240	≡	241	±	242	≥	243	≤	244	⌠	245	⌡	246	÷	247	≈
248	°	249	•	250	·	251	√	252	ⁿ	253	²	254	■	255											

ASCII Codes 0 - 127

Dec	Hex	Char	Dec	Hex	Char	Dec	Hex	Char	Dec	Hex	Char
0	00		32	20		64	40	@	96	60	`
1	01	☺	33	21	!	65	41	A	97	61	a
2	02	●	34	22	"	66	42	B	98	62	b
3	03	♥	35	23	#	67	43	C	99	63	c
4	04	♦	36	24	$	68	44	D	100	64	d
5	05	♣	37	25	%	69	45	E	101	65	e
6	06	♠	38	26	&	70	46	F	102	66	f
7	07	•	39	27	'	71	47	G	103	67	g
8	08	□	40	28	(	72	48	H	104	68	h
9	09	o	41	29	)	73	49	I	105	69	i
10	0A	j	42	2A	*	74	4A	J	106	6A	j
11	0B	k	43	2B	+	75	4B	K	107	6B	k
12	0C	l	44	2C	,	76	4C	L	108	6C	l
13	0D	m	45	2D	-	77	4D	M	109	6D	m
14	0E	♫	46	2E	.	78	4E	N	110	6E	n
15	0F	☼	47	2F	/	79	4F	O	111	6F	o
16	10	►	48	30	0	80	50	P	112	70	p
17	11	◄	49	31	1	81	51	Q	113	71	q
18	12	↕	50	32	2	82	52	R	114	72	r
19	13	‼	51	33	3	83	53	S	115	73	s
20	14	¶	52	34	4	84	54	T	116	74	t
21	15	§	53	35	5	85	55	U	117	75	u
22	16	▬	54	36	6	86	56	V	118	76	v
23	17	↨	55	37	7	87	57	W	119	77	w
24	18	↑	56	38	8	88	58	X	120	78	x
25	19	↓	57	39	9	89	59	Y	121	79	y
26	1A	→	58	3A	:	90	5A	Z	122	7A	z
27	1B	←	59	3B	;	91	5B	[	123	7B	{
28	1C	∟	60	3C	<	92	5C	\	124	7C		
29	1D	↔	61	3D	=	93	5D	]	125	7D	}
30	1E	▲	62	3E	>	94	5E	^	126	7E	~
31	1F		63	3F	?	95	5F	_	127	7F	⌂

ASCII Codes 128 - 255

Dec	Hex	Char	Dec	Hex	Char	Dec	Hex	Char	Dec	Hex	Char
128	80	Ç	160	A0	á	192	C0	└	224	E0	α
129	81	ü	161	A1	í	193	C1	┴	225	E1	β
130	82	é	162	A2	ó	194	C2	┬	226	E2	Γ
131	83	â	163	A3	ú	195	C3	├	227	E3	π
132	84	ä	164	A4	ñ	196	C4	─	228	E4	Σ
133	85	à	165	A5	Ñ	197	C5	┼	229	E5	σ
134	86	å	166	A6	ª	198	C6	╞	230	E6	µ
135	87	ç	167	A7	º	199	C7	╟	231	E7	τ
136	88	ê	168	A8	¿	200	C8	╚	232	E8	Φ
137	89	ë	169	A9	⌐	201	C9	╔	233	E9	Θ
138	8A	è	170	AA	¬	202	CA	╩	234	EA	Ω
139	8B	ï	171	AB	½	203	CB	╦	235	EB	δ
140	8C	î	172	AC	¼	204	CC	╠	236	EC	∞
141	8D	ì	173	AD	¡	205	CD	═	237	ED	Ø
142	8E	Ä	174	AE	«	206	CE	╬	238	EE	∈
143	8F	Å	175	AF	»	207	CF	╧	239	EF	∩
144	90	É	176	B0	░	208	D0	╨	240	F0	≡
145	91	æ	177	B1	▒	209	D1	╤	241	F1	±
146	92	Æ	178	B2	▓	210	D2	╥	242	F2	≥
147	93	ô	179	B3	│	211	D3	╙	243	F3	≤
148	94	ö	180	B4	┤	212	D4	╘	244	F4	⌠
149	95	ò	181	B5	╡	213	D5	╒	245	F5	⌡
150	96	û	182	B6	╢	214	D6	╓	246	F6	÷
151	97	ù	183	B7	╖	215	D7	╫	247	F7	≈
152	98	ÿ	184	B8	╕	216	D8	╪	248	F8	°
153	99	Ö	185	B9	╣	217	D9	┘	249	F9	∙
154	9A	Ü	186	BA	║	218	DA	┌	250	FA	·
155	9B	¢	187	BB	╗	219	DB	█	251	FB	√
156	9C	£	188	BC	╝	220	DC	▄	252	FC	ⁿ
157	9D	¥	189	BD	╜	221	DD	▌	253	FD	²
158	9E	₧	190	BE	╛	222	DE	▐	254	FE	■
159	9F	ƒ	191	BF	┐	223	DF	▀	255	FF	

Appendix E: Hexadecimal and Decimal Conversions

First Digit		Second Digit		Third Digit		Fourth Digit	
Hex	Dec.	Hex	Dec.	Hex	Dec.	Hex	Dec.
0	0	0	0	0	0	0	0
1	4096	1	256	1	16	1	1
2	8192	2	512	2	32	2	2
3	12288	3	768	3	48	3	3
4	16384	4	1024	4	64	4	4
5	20480	5	1280	5	80	5	5
6	24576	6	1536	6	96	6	6
7	28672	7	1792	7	112	7	7
8	32768	8	2048	8	128	8	8
9	36864	9	2304	9	144	9	9
A	40960	A	2560	A	160	A	10
B	45056	B	2816	B	176	B	11
C	49152	C	3072	C	192	C	12
D	53248	D	3328	D	208	D	13
E	57344	E	3584	E	224	E	14
F	61440	F	3840	F	240	F	15

You should use this table to convert hexadecimal into decimal numbers. For example:

```
HEX = A5B4
        4th digit          4
        3rd digit        176
        2nd digit       1280
        1st digit      40960
        Result         42420
```

Conversion of two 8-bit pointers into a 16-bit address:

```
address= INT(LowByte + (256 * HighByte))
```

Conversion of a 16-bit address into two 8-bit pointers:

```
HighByte = INT(address/256):
LowByte = address-HighByte*256
```

Appendix F: BIOS and DOS Interrupts

BIOS Interrupts and Functions

INT 5 (BIOS)	hardcopy routine

BIOS calls this interrupt when the user simultaneously presses the <Shift> and <PrtScr> keys. The system then creates a hardcopy by sending the current screen display to the printer. The PC-BASIC command LCOPY performs the same task.

Input:

No parameters

Output:

None. With errors, the normal error messages from MS-DOS ("Error during Write on Unit PRN", etc.) are displayed and there is a return jump to DOS.

Note: If GRAPHICS.COM is loaded, the output is made as graphic hardcopy; otherwise it is text hardcopy.

INT 10, function 00 select video mode

During SCREEN, this call is made by PC-BASIC with the WIDTH command.

Input:

AH = 00H
AL = Video mode
AL = 0   40*25 text mode, monochrome (color card)
AL = 1   40*25 text mode, color (color card)
AL = 2   80*25 text mode, monochrome (mono card)
AL = 3   80*25 text mode, color (color card)
AL = 4   320*200 4-color graphics (color card)
AL = 5   320*200 4-color graphics (color card)
          (colors displayed in monochrome)
AL = 6   640*200 2-color graphics (color card)
AL = 7   Internal mode (mono card)

Output:
None

INT 10, function 01 define cursor type

With PC-BASIC the starting and ending lines of the cursor can be determined during the LOCATE command.

Input:

AH =   01H
CH =   Bits 0-4 = Starting line of the cursor
CL =   Bits 0-4 = Ending line of the cursor

Based on the character matrix (e.g., 8*8 (0-7) or 9*16 (0-15)).

Output:
None

INT 10, function 02 cursor positioning

The PC-BASIC LOCATE command can access this function.

Input:
AH = 02H
BH = display page number
DH = screen line (0 to 24)
DL = screen column (0 to 79)

0 to 3 for 80*25 or 7 for 40*25, for graphics always 0

Output:
None

INT 10, function 03 determine cursor position

The CSRLIN and POS(0) functions obtain their results through this call.

Input:
AH = 03H
BH = display page number

display page= 0 to 3 for 80*25 or 7 for 40*25, for graphics always 0

Output:
DX = position (see function 02)
CX = cursor size (see function 01)

INT 10, function 04 determine lightpen position

Input:
AH = 04H

Output:

AH = 0 lightpen isn't connected or not active
AH = 1 lightpen is connected, values in DX, CH and BX

DX = position in text mode (see function 02)
CH = line in graphics mode (Y = 0 to 199)
BX = column in graphics mode (X = 0 to 319/639)

INT 10, function 05   select display page

The SCREEN command allows you to select a display page (text mode only) that will be
displayed.

Input:

AH = 05H
AL = display page number (0 to 3 for 80*25, to 7 for 40*25)

Output:
None

INT 10, function 06   scrolling a window upwards

This can be used with the next function (INT 10, function 07) for word processing or
displaying lists.

[handwritten:]
0 = BLACK —— (+8) GREY
1 BLUE —— LT BLU
2 GREEN —— LT GRN
3 CYAN —— LT CYAN
4 RED —— LT RED
5 MAGENTA —— LT MAGENTA
6 BROWN —— YELLOW
7 WHITE —— HI INT WHITE

Input:

AH = 06H
AL = number of lines to be scrolled
CX = position the window upper-left (line, column)
DX = position the window lower-right (line, column)
BH = attribute for the following lines:

Bit 0, 1 and 2	foreground- color
Bit 3 double	brightness 1l0
Bit 4, 5 and 6	background color
Bit 7	blink 1l0 *(FOREGROUND)*

Output:
None

[handwritten:] BH = FOREGROUND + 16* BACKGROUND + 128 * BLINK

[handwritten:] FOREGROUND   0 to 15
BACKGROUND   0 to 7

INT 10, function 07
scrolling a window downward

Input:

AH = 07H

The rest is the same as for function 06.

Output:

None

INT 10, function 08
read character/attribute

This delivers the results to the SCREEN function.

Input:

AH = 08H
BH = display page number

Output:

AL = ASCII code of character according to PC character set
AH = color (attribute)

INT 10, function 09
write character/attribute

Input:

AH = 09H
AL = ASCII code of character according to PC character set
BH = display page number (0 to 3 for 80*25 or to 7 for 40*25)
CX = number of times to write the character
BL = attribute (see table for function 06)

Output:

None

Note: BH can only be called in text mode.

INT 10, function 0A

Input:

AH = 0AH
BH = display page number (0 to 3 for 80*25 or to 7 for 40*25, not in graphics mode)
CX = number of times to write the character
AL = ASCII code of character according to PC character set

Output:

None

Note: The attribute remains unchanged.

INT 10, function 0B

Important for color graphics in 320*200 mode.

Input:

AH = 0BH
BH = number of the palette (0-127)
BL = border/background color:
          0 = green/red/yellow
          1 = Cyan/Magenta/white

Output:

None

INT 10, function 0C

This function applies to all PC-BASIC graphic commands.

Input:

AH = 0CH
AL: bits 0 to 6 = color of the pixel
AL: bit 7 = XOR with potentially set pixel 1|0
BH = graphics page
DX = screen line (Y = 0 to 199)
CX = screen column (X = 0 to 319/639)

Output:

None

INT 10, function 0D   read graphic pixel

Input:

AH = 0DH
DX = screen line (Y = 0 to 199)
CX = screen column (X = 0 to 319/639)

Output:

AL = color of the pixel (0 = background color)

INT 10, function 0E   write character

Input:

AH = 0EH
AL = ASCII code of the character according to PC character set
BL = foreground color of the character (graphics mode only)

Output:

None

INT 10, function 0F | read display mode

Input:

AH = 0FH

Output:

AL = display screen mode (see function 00)
AH = number columns (40 or 80)
BH = current display page (0 to 3 for 80*25 or 7 for 40*25)

INT 11 | determine configuration

This is very helpful if programs must run on various computers with different configurations. With one call you'll know the total configuration.

Input:

No parameters

Output:

AX returns a 16-bit value consisting of 00, 01, 11, etc., with these values representing set or unset bits:

Bit 0: 1 if the system has one or more disk drives

Bit 1: not used

Bit 2 and 3: RAM available on the main circuit board
00 = 16K, 01 = 32K, 10 = 48K, 11 = 64K

Bit 4 and 5: display screen mode during start-up
00 = unused
01 = color 40*25,
10 = color 80*25,
11 = monochrome 80*25

Bit 6 and 7: number of disk drives in the system if bit 0 is equal to 1
00 = 1, 01 = 2, 10 = 3, 11 = 4

Bit 8: 0 when a DMA chip is present

Bit 9, 10 and 11: number of RS232 cards connected
00 = none, 01 = 1, 10 =2, 11 = 3

Bit 12: game adapter (joystick) available
0 = no joystick
1 = joystick available

Bit 13: not used

Bit 14 and 15: number of printers available
00 = none, 01 = 1, 10 = 2, 11 = 3

INT 12 — determine memory size

Input:
No parameters

Output:
AX = size of the memory in KBytes

INT 13 — disk controller

Input and output can be bundled on the basis of the standardized parameters for the various functions:

Input:

AH = 0	resets controller
AH = 1	status of controller, move to AL
AH = 2	reads sectors
AH = 3	writes to sectors
AH = 4	verifies sectors
AH = 5	formats track

DL = drive (0 = A:, 1 = B:, 3 = C:)
DH = head (0|1)
CH = track (0 to 39)
CL = sector (1 to 8|9)
AL = number sectors (8|9)
ES:BX = buffer for read/write

Output:

AL = number of sectors read
AH = 00   no errors, operation completed

When carry flag set, then:

AH = 01	wrong command
AH = 02	mark not found
AH = 03	write error
AH = 04	sector not found
AH = 08	DMA reports error
AH = 09	DMA reports segment exceeded
AH = 10	CRC error
AH = 20	controller chip reports error
AH = 40	error during search
AH = 80	time out error

For details on error messages, consult the manual for the controller. The control of the hard disk also goes through interrupt 13h. This is a very complex topic and it's possible that data will be lost.

INT 14   handling the serial port

Input:

AH = 00	initializing according to value in AL
AH = 01	sends character in AL to serial port
AH = 02	reads character from serial port
AH = 03	determines status of the serial port

DX = number of the port:

0 = COM1:
1 = COM2:
etc.

AL = initial value for AH = 0

00, 01, 11, etc. are to be interpreted as set or reset bits:

Bit 0 and 1: word length in bits
10 = 7 bits
11 = 8 bits

Bit 2: stop bits
00 = 1 stop bit
1 = 2 stop bits

Bit 3 and 4: Parity
00 = none
01 = odd
11 = even

Bit 5, 6 and 7: Baud rate
000 = 110 ,   001 = 150,   010 = 300, 011 = 600
100 = 1200, 101 = 2400, 110 = 4800, 111 = 9600

Output:
AL = status for AH = 3
AH = status of the port:

Bit 0: receiving status
0 = no data
1 = data received

Bit 1: overrun
0 = no overrun
1 = overrun error

Bit 2: parity
0 = no error
1 = parity error

Bit 3: framing
0 = no error
1 = framing error

Bit 4: break
0 = no break
1 = break discovered

Bit 5: hold register
0 = empty
1 = occupied

Bit 6: shift register
0 = empty
1 = occupied

Bit 7: time out
0 = everything OK
1 = time out error

INT 16, function 00   read character

Input:
AH = 00H

Output:
AL = ASCII code of the character according to the PC character set
AH = keyboard scan code of the key

Note: The character is removed from the keyboard buffer.

INT 16, function 01   read keyboard for character

Input:
AH = 01H

Output:
Zero-Flag = 1: character is available in the keyboard buffer

Zero-Flag = 0: character is available in the keyboard buffer
ASCII code and scan code are passed in AX (see function 00). The character remains in the buffer.

INT 16, function 02   read keyboard status

Input:
AH = 02H

Output:
AL = keyboard status

Bit reset, key not activated
Bit set, key activated

Bit 0 = Right <Shift> key
Bit 1 = Left <Shift> key
Bit 2 = <Ctrl> key
Bit 3 = <Alt> key
Bit 4 = <Scroll Lock> key
Bit 5 = <Num Lock> key
Bit 6 = <Caps Lock> key
Bit 7 = <Ins> key

INT 17
handling the Centronics parallel interface

Input:

AH = 00H	writes character to one of the printers interfaced to PC
AH = 01H	initializes printer interfaced to PC (reset)
AH = 02	determines status of the printer interfaced to PC

DX = printer number:

00 = LPT1:
01 = LPT2:
02 = LPT3:

Output:

The status of the printer is returned as a 16-bit value that has the following meanings:

Bit 0: time out

0 = everything OK
1 = time out error

Bit 1: not used

Bit 2: not used

Bit 3: transfer

0 = everything OK
1 = transfer error

Bit 4: printer selection (ON/OFF line)

0 = printer offline
1 = printer online

Bit 5: paper

0 = everything OK
1 = printer out of paper

Bit 6: receive

0 = no response
1 = everything OK

Bit 7: busy/ready

0 = printer busy
1 = printer ready

INT 1B   controlling the <Ctrl><Break> keys

This interrupt is called when a user activates the <Ctrl><Break> keys. After the keys have been activated, the vector points to a dummy routine which has no effect. From a program this vector must be set to point to your own routine. PC-BASIC handles <Ctrl><Break> in its own way and the key combination cannot be switched off with this INT. For additional ways to do this, refer to Chapter 12.

INT 1C   periodic interrupt

This interrupt is called by the system at every pulse of the timer (18 times per second). After being switched on, the vector points to a dummy routine which doesn't do anything. The program can set the vector to a routine which is then executed at every system clock.

INT 1F   character table

In graphics mode during text output, only the characters with an ASCII code up to 128 are displayed. Characters that exceed this are displayed as space characters (CHR$(32)). Through this interrupt, a character set can be installed which permits the display of characters beyond ASCII 128. On the system diskette you'll find the GRAPHTABL.COM or GRAPHPAT.COM program, which installs the character set for the graphics mode through this interrupt.

Dos Interrupts and Functions

| INT 20 | end program |

Input:
CS = segment address of the PSP of the executing program

Output:
None

Note: The executing program is terminated and the higher level process (for example a .BAT-File or COMMAND.COM) is called. All open files are closed.

| INT 21, function 00 | End program |

Also refer to interrupt 20.

Input:
AH = 00H
CS = segment address of the PSP of the executing program

Output:
None

Note: In contrast with INT 20, the files remain open and must be closed before the call of this function.

| INT 21, function 01 | character input with echo |

Input:
AH = 01H

Output:
AL = ASCII code of the character according to PC character set

INT 21, function 02 — character output

Input:

AH = 02H

DL = ASCII code of the character to be displayed, according to PC character set

Output:

None

INT 21, function 05 — output character on the printer

Input:

AH = 05H

DL = ASCII code of the character to be printed, according to PC character set

Output:

None

Note: Unless otherwise indicated, the character is always output on LPT1:.

INT 21, function 06 — Input/Output on standard I/O-devices

Input:

AH = 06H
DL = 0-254: send character code
DL = 255: read a character

Output:

If DL = FF, then the ASCII code of the character conformed to the PC character set in AL.

INT 21, function 07   input through standard input device

Input:
AH = 07H

Output:
AL = ASCII code of the character read, according to PC character set

INT 21, function 08   input through keyboard, no display

Input:
AH = 08H

Output:
AL = ASCII code of the character read, according to PC character set

INT 21, function 09   output character string

Input:
AH = 09H
DS = string segment address
DX = string offset address

Output:
None

Note: The string must end with the $ character. The function recognizes the end of the string with this character.

INT 21, function 0A   buffered input

Input:

AH = 0AH
DS = buffer segment address
DX = buffer offset address

Byte 1 of the input buffer defines the maximum length of the input, including the
<Return> key.

Output:

None

INT 21, function 0B   determine keyboard status

Input:
AH = 0BH

Output:

AL = 0: no character available in the buffer
AL = 255: one or more characters available in the buffer

INT 21, function 0C   reset input buffer, then input

Input:

AH = 0CH
AL = function to be called during call of function 10
DS = input buffer address
DX = input buffer offset address

Output:

Functions 1,6,7 and 8: AL = character to be read
Function 10: no output

INT 21, function 0D   reset disk

Input:
AH = 0DH

Output:
None

Note: This function does not close any files.

INT 21, function 0E   select default disk drive

Input:
AH = 0EH
DL = drive number
        0 = A:, 1 = B:, 2 = C:, etc.

Output:
AL = number of installed drives or volumes

Note: You should check the output message carefully. A total of five drives were
                 reported on the PC we were using but it actually has only two disk drives, a
                 hard disk and a RAM disk.

INT 21, function 0F   open file

Input:
AH = 0FH
DS = FCB segment address of the file
DX = FCB offset address of the file

Output:

AL = 0: file found and opened
AL = 255: file not found

Found no entry in the directory, indicating that the file has the hidden attribute or system attribute.

The FCB is modified for AL = 00 as follows:

If (0) is indicated as drive in FCB, it will be set to the actual number (1 = A:, 2 = B: etc.).

The current block is set to 0.
The record length is set to the standard value of 128.

File size and date/time of the last access are transmitted from the directory entry into the FCB.

INT 21, function 10   close file

Input:

AH = 10H
DS = FCB segment address of the file
DX = FCB offset address of the file

Output:

AL = 0: file closed and directory entry revised
AL = 255: file not found in directory

INT 21, function 11   search for first match (FCB)

Input:

AH = 11H
DS = FCB segment address
DX = FCB offset address

DS:DX = pointer to unopened FCB. In the FCB a filename must be indicated as a selection template (for example, *.EXE). If a search should be conducted for hidden or system files or for volume-ID or directories, an extended FCB, with the proper attribute bytes, must be provided.

Output:

AL = 0: file found
AL = 255: file not found

For AL = 00 and a normal FCB, the Disk Transfer Area (DTA), which is constructed like a normal FCB, is modified as follows:

> Byte 1 contains the drive number (1 = A, 2 = B etc.).
> Starting at byte 2, is the directory entry with a length of 32 bytes.

With AL = 00 and an extended FCB, the Disk Transfer Area (DTA), which is constructed like an extended FCB, is modified as follows:

> Byte 1 is set to FF. The next 5 bytes are set to 00.
> The following byte contains the attribute of the file, the next byte the drive number (1 = A:, 2 = B: etc.), and the next 32 bytes contain the directory entry.

INT 21, function 12 — search for next match

Input:

AH = 12H
DS = FCB segment address
DX = FCB offset address

Output:

see function 11

INT 21, function 13 — delete file

Input:

AH = 13H
DS = FCB segment address
DX = FCB offset address

Output:

AL = 0: file(s) erased
AL = 255: no file(s) found or file(s) assigned Read Only attribute (undeletable)

INT 21, function 14   sequential read (FCB)

Input:

AH = 14H
DS = FCB segment address
DX = FCB offset address

Output:

AL = 0: block read
AL = 1: EOF reached
AL = 2: segment wrap
AL = 3: partial record read

Data stored in the Disk Transfer Area (DTA).

INT 21, function 15   sequential write (FCB)

Input:

AH = 15H
DS = FCB segment address
DX = FCB offset address

Data must be stored in the DTA.

Output:

AL = 0: block written
AL = 1: medium (disk/hard disk) full
AL = 2: segment overflow

INT 21, function 16   create file

Input:

AH = 16H
DS = FCB segment address
DX = FCB offset address

Output:

AL = 0: file created
AL = 255: file could not be created, no space in the directory

Note: If a file with this name already exists, it will be erased.

INT 21, function 17   rename file

Input:

AH = 17H
DS = FCB segment address
DX = FCB offset address

DS:DX = pointer to modified FCB. As filename in FCB, the name of the file to be renamed is indicated. The new name of the file (without drive number) must be available starting at offset 11h of the FCB.

Output:

AL = 0: File(s) renamed
AL = 255: no file found, or new filename matches old filename

---

INT 21, function 19   get default disk drive

Input:

AH = 19H

Output:

AL = number of the current drive
        0 = A, 1 = B, 2 = C, etc.

INT 21, function 1AH | set address of DTA

Input:

AH = 1AH
DS = New DTA segment address
DX = New DTA offset address

Output:

None

INT 21, function 1B | allocation info for default drive

Input:

AH = 1BH

Output:

AL = number of sectors per cluster
DS = media descriptor segment address
BX = media descriptor offset address
DX = number of clusters per drive

The total capacity of the unit is calculated as follows: bytes = (CX*AL)*DX

DS:DX = pointer to ID byte:

FFH   disk drive: double-sided, 8 sectors per track,
FEH   disk drive: single-sided, 8 sectors per track
FDH   disk drive: double-sided, 9 sectors per track
FCH   disk drive: single-sided, 9 sectors per track
F9H   disk drive: double-sided, 15 sectors per track (AT only)
F8H   hard disk

INT 21, function 1C

allocation info for specified drive

Input:
AH = 1CH
DL = drive number:

0 = current drive, 1 = A, 2 = B, 3 = C, etc.

Output:
see function 1B

INT 21, function 21

random read

Input:
AH = 21H
DS = FCB segment address
DX = FCB offset address

In the FCB, the record number must be indicated at offset 21h (see function 24).

Output:
AL = 0: record read
AL = 1: EOF reached, record is empty
AL = 2: segment overflow
AL = 3: partial record read

Data stored in the DTA.

INT 21, function 22

random write

Input:
AH = 22H

Similar to function 21. Data must be stored in DTA.

Output:

AL = 0: record written successfully
AL = 1: diskette/hard disk full
AL = 2: segment overflow

INT 21, function 23   get file size in records (FCB)

Input:

AH = 23H
DS = FCB segment address
DX = FCB offset address

Output:

AL = 0: number of records found starting at FCB address 21h
AL = 255: file not found

At offset 21h of the FCB, the size of the file is stored, divided by the record length.

INT 21, function 24   set random record number

Input:

AH = 24H
DS = FCB segment address
DX = FCB offset address

DS:DX = pointer to opened FCB. In FCB, at offset 21h, the record number or, at offset 20h, the block number must be stored.

Output:

None

INT 21, function 25   set interrupt vector

Input:
AH = 25H
AL = interrupt number
DS = new interrupt routine segment address
DX = new interrupt routine offset address

Output:
None

INT 21, function 27   random block read (FCB)

Input:
AH = 27H
CX = number of records to be read
DS = FCB segment address
DX = FCB offset address

Output:
see function 21

INT 21, function 28   random block write

Input:
AH = 28H
CX = number of records to be written
DS = FCB segment address
DX = FCB offset address

Same as in function 22.

Output:
see function 22

INT 21, function 2A — determine system date

Input:
AH = 2AH

Output:
CX = year (1980 to 2099)
DH = month (1 to 12)
DL = day (1 to 31)
AL = day of the week (0 = Sunday, 1 = Monday, etc.)

INT 21, function 2B — set system date

Input:
AH = 2BH
CX = year (1980 to 2099)
DH = month (1 to 12)
DL = day (1 to 31)

Output:
AL = 00: o.k.
AL = 255: date incorrect

INT 21, function 2C — determine system time

Input:
AH = 2CH

Output:
CH = hours (0 to 24)
CL = minutes (0 to 59)
DH = seconds (0 to 59)
DL = hundredths of a second (0 to 99)

INT 21, function 2D   set system time

Input:
AH = 2DH
CH = hours (0 to 24)
CL = minutes (0 to 59)
DH = seconds (0 to 59)
DL = hundredths of a second (0 to 99)

Output:
AL = 0: O.K.
AL = 255: incorrect time

INT 21, function 2E   set verify flag

Input:
AH = 2EH
DL = 0
AL = 1: verify data
AL = 0: don't verify data

Output:
None

INT 21, function 2F   get DTA address

Input:
AH = 2FH

Output:
ES = DTA segment address
BX = DTA offset address

INT 21, function 30   determine MS-DOS version number

Input:
AH = 30H

Output:
AL = major version number (e.g., version 2.01 = 2)
AH = minor version (e.g., version 3.01 = 0)
BH = serial number of a license version
BL = serial number of a user version

INT 21, function 31   terminate and stay resident

This function is required for interrupt routines, for example (keyboard driver, printer driver, etc.) and should only be used by experienced assembler programmers. Use this function only if you have extensive knowledge of this material.

Input:
AH = 31H
AL = return code
DX = number of paragraphs to be reserved

Output:
None

Note: See interrupt 27.

INT 21, function 33   get <Ctrl><Break> flag

Input:
AH = 33H
AL = 1
DL = 0: test only during character input/output
DL = 1: test on every function call

Output:

If AL = 00, then status is in DL:

        DL = 0: test only during character input/output

        DL = 1: test on every function call

        AL = FF, AL was neither 0 nor 1 during call

INT 21, function 35   determine interrupt vector

Input:

AH = 35H

AL = interrupt number

Output:

ES:BX = pointer to the entry point of the interrupt routine

INT 21, function 36   determine free disk space

Input:

AH = 36H

DL = drive number:

0 = current drive, 1 = A, 2 = B, 3 = C, etc.

Output:

AX = 65535: device unavailable

AX < 65535: number of sectors per cluster

BX = number of available clusters

CX = number of bytes per sector

DX = total number clusters of the drive

Free disk space = (CX*AX)*BX

INT 21, function 39   create subdirectory

Input:

AH = 39H
DS = subdirectory path segment address
DX = subdirectory path offset address

Output:

If Carry-Flag is set, then error number is in AX:
AX = 3: path not found or incorrect
AX = 5: access denied (a directory with that name already exists)

INT 21, function 3A   erase directory

Input:

AH = 3AH
DS = subdirectory path segment address
DX = subdirectory path offset address

Output:

When Carry-Flag is set, then error number is in AX:
AX = 3: path not found or incorrect
AX = 5: access denied (i.e., directory contains subdirectories)
AX = 6: directory to be deleted is the current directory

INT 21, function 3B   change directory

Input:

AH = 3BH
DS = subdirectory path segment address
DX = subdirectory path offset address

Output:

When carry flag is set, then error number is in AX:

AX = 3: path not found or incorrect

INT 21, function 43, sub-function 0   get file attributes

Input:

AH = 43H

AL = 0: determine file attribute

DS = filename segment address

DX = filename offset address

Output:

Carry flag = 0: O.K. (CX = file attribute)

Bit 0 = 1: file can only be read

Bit 1 = 1: file hidden

Bit 2 = 1: file is a system file

Bit 3 = 1: file is the volume name

Bit 4 = 1: file is a subdirectory

Bit 5 = 1: file was changed since the last date/time

Carry flag = 1: error (AX = error code)

        AX = 1: unknown function code

        AX = 2: file not found

        AX = 3: path not found

INT 21, function 43, sub-function 1   set file attributes

Input:

AH = 43H

AL = 1

CX = file attributes

Bit 0 = 1: file can be read but not written

Bit 1 = 1: file hidden

Bit 2 = 1: file is a system file

Bit 3 = 0

Bit 4 = 0

Bit 5 = 1: file was change since the last date/time

DS = filename segment address

DX filename offset address

Output:
Carry flag = 0: O.K.
Carry flag = 1: error (AX = error code)
   AX = 1: unknown function code
   AX = 2: file not found
   AX = 3: path not found
   AX = 5: attribute cannot be changed.

INT 21, function 47   determine current directory

Input:
AH = 47H
DL = device designation
   0 = current drive, 1 = A, 2 = B, 3 = C, etc.
DS = buffer segment address
SI = buffer offset address

Output:
If carry flag is set, then error number is in AX:
   AX = 15: invalid drive number

INT 21, function 4E   search for first match

Input:
AH = 4EH
CX = file attribute
DS = filename segment address
DX = filename offset address

Output:
When carry flag is set, then error number is in AX:
AX = 2: path not found or incorrect path indicated
AX = 18: no file with the attribute found

The directory entry is stored in DTA as follows:

The offset is given in hexadecimal/decimal, the length in decimal (also refer to function 11h):

Offset	Length	Meaning
00/00	21	reserved for function 4F
15/21	1	file-Attribute
16/22	2	time of last access
18/24	2	date of last access
1A/26	2	file-size (Low-Word)
1C/28	2	file-size (High-Word)
1E/30	13	file-name in format "name.Extension"+CHR$(0)

INT 21, function 4F   search for next match

Input:

AH = 4FH

Output:

see function 4E

Note: See function 12h.

INT 21, function 54   get verify flag

This flag provides information to MS-DOS. It determines whether data transmitted to a medium (floppy disk or hard disk) should be verified after the transmission. This is important during the Copy command.

Input:

AH = 54H

Output:

AL = 0: verify off
AL = 1: verify on

INT 21, function 56   rename file (handle)

This function renames a file or moves the file to another directory of a block device. Moving is possible only within the different directories of one particular device (i.e., you can't move a file from a hard disk directory to a floppy disk directory).

Input:

AH = 56H
DS = old filename segment address
DX = old filename offset address
ES = new filename segment address
DI = new filename offset address

Output:

If the carry flag is set, then error number is in AX:
AX = 2: file not found according to first path name
AX = 3: path not found
AX = 5: access denied
AX = 11: different drives indicated

INT 25   read sectors from diskette/hard disk

Input:

AL = drive number:
       0 = A, 1 = B, 2 = C, etc.
CX = number of sectors to be read
DX = first sector to be read
DS = buffer segment address
BX = buffer offset address

Output:

If carry flag is set, then DOS error number is in AL.
Carry flag = 0: O.K.
Carry flag = 1: error (AX = error code)
       AX = 1: bad command
       AX = 2: bad address
       AX = 4: sector not found
       AX = 8: DMA error
       AX = 16: CRC error
       AX = 32: disk controller error

AX = 64: seek error
AX = 128: device doesn't respond

Note: The parameters passed aren't sufficiently checked. So, a system crash could occur with erroneous entries.

INT 26   write sector to diskette/hard disk

Input:
As in INT 25H

Output:
As in INT 25H

Note: The parameters passed aren't sufficiently checked. So, with erroneous entries, a system crash could occur.

INT 27   terminate and stay resident

Input:
CS = PSP segment address
DX = number of bytes +1 to be reserved

Output:
None

Note: Also see function 31h of interrupt 21h.

Appendix G: Mouse Function Calls

This appendix covers an overview of mouse functions. Remember that the functions are intended for a Microsoft or compatible mouse driver.

The listings in this paragraph indicate the mouse function number, expressed as an integer (i.e., FUNCTION%). The function number is often followed by parameters, also expressed as integers (i.e., PARA1%, PARA2% and PARA3%). The excerpt of program code listed below shows how you might call a mouse routine in BASIC:

```
420 :
430 '----- call mouse-function -----
440 :
450 DEF SEG= MOUSE.SEGMENT:CALL MOUSE (FUNCTION%, PARA1%, PARA2%,
    PARA3%)
460 RETURN
```

The following is a description of the functions:

Function% = 0   test for hardware error

Test the hardware, if error, then FUNCTION% <> 1. At the same time the mouse-system is initialized with default-values.

Input:
Function% = 0

Output:
None

Function% = 1   display mouse pointer

Input:
Function% = 1

Output:
None

Function% = 2   remove mouse pointer

Input:
Function% = 2

Output:
None

Function% = 3   determine mouse position and status

Input:
Function% = 3

PARA 1% = BUTTON STATUS
LEFT = 1
RIGHT = 2
CENTER = 3

Output:
PARA2% = status of the buttons

Bit 0 = 1: left button activated
Bit 1 = 1: right button activated
Bit 2 = 1: center mouse button activated
Bits 3-15: unused

PARA 2% = HORIZ POS
PARA 3% = VERT POS

Function% = 4   set cursor positioning

The coordinates relate to the resolution 640*200 pixels.

OR TO SCREEN COORDINATES
SCREEN 9 = 640 X 350

Input:
PARA2% = horizontal position - column or X coordinate
PARA3% = vertical position - line or coordinate

681

Output:

None

Function% = 5   test if a mouse button is activated

This function determines how often a button was activated since the last call of this function. It also informs the calling program of the pointer's location on the screen when the button was last activated.

Input:

PARA1% = 0: left button, = 1: right button, = 2: center button ∴ 3

Output:

FUNCTION% = status of the buttons:

       Bit 0 = left button activated

       Bit 1 = right button activated

       Bit 2 = center button activated

PARA1% = counter, how often activated, is in area 0 to 32,767

PARA2% = horizontal cursor position - column or X coordinate

PARA3% = vertical cursor position - line or Y coordinate

Function% = 6   number of times button was released

Determines how often a mouse button has been released since the last call of this function. It also informs the calling program of the pointer's location on the screen when the button was last activated.

Input:

PARA1% = 0 left button, = 1 right button, = 2 center button

Output:

FUNCTION% = status of the buttons:

        Bit 0 = 1: left button

        Bit 1 = 1: right button

        Bit 2 = 1: center button

PARA1% = counter, how often released, is in the area 0 to 32,767

PARA2% = horizontal cursor position - column or X coordinate

PARA3% = vertical cursor position - line or Y coordinate

Function% = 7   set horizontal cursor area

Sets the horizontal area in which the cursor can be moved.

Input:

PARA2% = minimal horizontal pointer position

PARA3% = maximum horizontal pointer position

Output:

None

Function% = 8   set vertical cursor area

Sets the vertical area in which the cursor can be moved.

Input:

PARA2% = minimum vertical pointer position

PARA3% = maximum vertical pointer position

Output:

None

Function% = 9   set mouse pointer (graphics mode)

This function sets the "hot spots" of the cursor within the cursor matrix (16*16 pixels). This is the pixel in the matrix whose screen coordinates are reported by some functions. The appearance of the cursor can also be defined. In order to do this, a two-dimensional array must be created. In the first part, the template for connecting the cursor with the background is defined. In the second part, the appearance of the cursor is defined.

```
'template:
CURSOR%( 0,0)= &HFFFF '1111111111111111
...
CURSOR%(15,0)= &HFFFF '1111111111111111

'Cursor-appearance:

CURSOR%( 0,1)= &H8000 '1000000000000000
CURSOR%( 1,1)= &HE000 '1110000000000000
CURSOR%( 2,1)= &HF800 '1111100000000000
CURSOR%( 3,1)= &HFE00 '1111111000000000
CURSOR%( 4,1)= &HD800 '1101100000000000
CURSOR%( 5,1)= &H0C00 '0000110000000000
CURSOR%( 6,1)= &H0600 '0000011000000000
CURSOR%( 7,1)= &H0300 '0000001100000000
CURSOR%( 8,1)= &H0000 '0000000000000000
...
CURSOR%(15,1)= &H0000 '0000000000000000
```

Input:

PARA1% = HotSpot horizontal - X position
PARA2% = HotSpot vertical - Y position
PARA3% = Array-name/Pointer, for example CURSOR%(0,0)

All values in the array must be 16 bit values. This function is for graphics mode only.

Output:

None

Function% = 10   set mouse pointer (text mode)

Input:

PARA1% = pointer type
      0: software pointer
      1 = hardware pointer
PARA2% = template for connecting the cursor with the screen background
PARA3% = display attribute for the character under the cursor

Output:

None

Function% = 11   determine movement values

This function determines the distance between the current mouse position and the mouse position during the last call of function 11.

Input:

Function% = 11

Output:

PARA2% = horizontal distance
PARA3% = vertical distance

The result returned is in the area from -32,768 to +32,767. Negative values indicate movement toward the top or left border of the screen; positive values indicate a movement to the bottom or right border of the screen.

Function% = 12   set event handler

Sets the address of an event handler called by the mouse driver when a particular mouse event occurs.

Input:

PARA2% = event definition
Bit 0 = mouse movement
Bit 1 = left button activated
Bit 3 = right button activated
Bit 4 = right button released
Bit 5 = center button activated
Bit 6 = center button released

If the routine should be called on the activation of the left button, bit 1 in PARA2% must be set. Several events can be combined and every event query can be terminated through the resetting of the corresponding bit. Function 0 resets all queries.

PARA3% = variable with offset to assembler routine in the current segment.

Output:

None

Function% = 13/14 enable/disable lightpen emulation

The mouse can be used as a lightpen. Both buttons activated means "pen down"; otherwise the mouse can be moved like a lightpen across the screen.

Input:

Function% = 13: switch on mode
Function% = 14: switch off mode

Output:

None

Note: Function 0 erases the emulation.

Function% = 15   set pointer speed

Defines the relationship between the mouse movement on the desk and the movement of the cursor on the screen.

Input:

PARA2% = horizontal relationship
PARA3% = vertical relationship

The values are between 1 to 32,767.

Output:

None

Function% = 16   exclusion area

Designates any area of the screen as an exclusion area. The mouse pointer disappears if moved into the exclusion area. This enables the screen to be constructed faster because the cursor doesn't have to be displayed continuously. This also eliminates the flickering of the cursor. After the screen is constructed, the cursor must be switched on again with function 1.

Note: This function can only be called through an assembler routine. The registers must be loaded as follows:

Input:

AX = 16d
CX = top X coordinate, upper left corner of exclusion area
DX = top Y coordinate, upper left corner of exclusion area
SI = bottom X coordinate, lower right corner of exclusion area
DI = bottom Y coordinate, lower right corner of exclusion area

Output:

None

Function% = 19   set maximum for mouse speed doubling

Sets the maximum limit for doubling mouse speed. If the speed of the mouse movement exceeds a certain limit, the mouse driver doubles the mouse pointer speed by doubling the movement's relationship between points and mickeys.

Input:

PARA3% = factor

The factor can be indicated with a value between 1 and 32,767.

Output:

None

Appendix H: ANSI Escape Codes

The ANSI.SYS driver is designed for the unified control of the screen and keyboard functions in MS-DOS computers. The ANSI escape codes control the cursor, the graphic display and the keyboard assignment. In this Appendix we'll describe how to use the codes and discuss their syntax. They can only be used when the ANSI driver is loaded. The following line:

```
DEVICE= ANSI.SYS
```

must be available in the CONFIG.SYS file. The default values provided by the driver are used if a parameter isn't provided or a "0" is used.

An ANSI code is preceded by the value 27 (decimal) or 1B (hexadecimal) and the character [. Through this character sequence the ANSI driver interprets the subsequent characters as sequence for the execution of the previously mentioned tasks. The expression ESC represent the decimal value 27 or the hexadecimal value 1B.

Define cursor position

```
ESC [<line>;<column>H
ESC [<line>;<column>f
```

Positions the cursor in column x, line y. If one or both of the parameters are omitted, the default is 1. If a value isn't indicated, ANSI moves the cursor to the upper left corner of the screen (1,1).

Moves cursor up

```
ESC [<lines>A
```

Moves the cursor up the number of lines indicated in <lines>. The column position remains unchanged. If <lines> is omitted, the cursor is moved one line. The cursor cannot be moved past the top of the screen.

Move cursor down

```
ESC [<lines>B
```

Moves the cursor down the number of lines indicated in <lines>. The column position remains unchanged. If <lines> is omitted, the cursor is moved one line. The cursor cannot be moved past the bottom of the screen.

Move cursor right

```
ESC [<columns>C
```

Moves the cursor to the right by the number indicated in <columns>. If <columns> is omitted, the cursor is moved one character. The line remains unchanged. If the cursor is already in the rightmost column, the command has no effect.

Move cursor left

```
ESC [<columns>D
```

Moves the cursor to the left by the number indicated in <columns>. If <columns> is omitted, the cursor is moved one character. The line remains unchanged. If the cursor is already located in the leftmost column, the command has no effect.

Save current cursor position

```
ESC [s
```

The values for line and column of the current cursor position are saved.

Send cursor to saved position

```
ESC [u
```

Moves the cursor to the position saved with "ESC [s".

Clear the screen

```
ESC [2J
```

The screen is completely erased and the cursor is moved to the upper left corner.

Clear to end of line

```
ESC [K
```

Erases the remainder of a line, from the cursor position to the end of the line.

Set screen attribute

```
ESC [<Attribute>;<Attribute>m
```

Sets the screen attribute for the characters. For <attribute> the following values can be used:

0	None
1	Bold
2	Normal
3	Italic
4	Underlined (only monochrome screen)
5	Blinking
6	Fast blinking
7	Reverse video
8	Invisible
30	Black foreground
31	Red foreground
32	Green foreground
33	Yellow foreground
34	Blue foreground
35	Magenta foreground
36	Cyan foreground
37	White foreground
40	Black background
41	Red background
42	Green background
43	Yellow background
44	Blue background
45	Magenta background
46	Cyan background
47	White background
48	Superscript
49	Subscript

Set screen mode

```
ESC [=<mode>h
```

Sets the graphics mode or the number of characters that can be displayed per line on the screen. For <mode> the following values can be used:

0	40x25 monochrome
1	40x25 color
2	80x25 monochrome
3	80x25 color
4	320*200 color
5	320*200 monochrome
6	640*200 monochrome
7	Word wrap

Reset mode

```
ESC [=<mode>l
```

Returns to the mode previously set with "ESC [<mode>h". The parameter for <mode> corresponds to the above list.

Keyboard reassignment

With the ANSI driver individual keys can be reassigned, or character sequences can be assigned. Some standard programs use their own keyboard drivers. In these instances, the reassignment may not always work. A buffer of 200 bytes can be used for the assignment/reassignment. The sequence is created as follows:

```
ESC [<old_key>;<new_key>p
ESC [<key>;"character-sequence"p
```

With the first parameter <old_key> the key, which will be assigned, is defined. With "character-sequence" the text, which should be displayed when this key is activated, is defined. The value <new_key> defines the character to be displayed when activating this key. The <old_key>, <new_key> and <key> parameters can be composed of two characters to assign extended keyboard codes to the key. This is necessary, for example, with function keys.

For example, the following line assigns the function, for displaying the directory from drive A, to the <F10> function key:

```
ESC [0;68;"DIR A:/P";13p
```

The 13 parameter represents the <Return> key.

```
ESC [90;89p
ESC [122;121p
```

When the <Z> key is activated, the Y character is displayed.

Appendix I

Scan codes PC/XT and AT keyboards

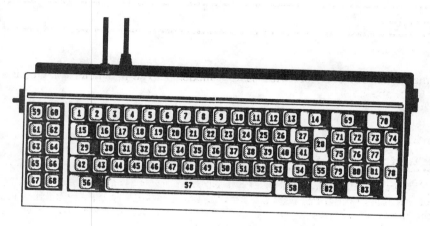

PC/XT keyboard scan codes

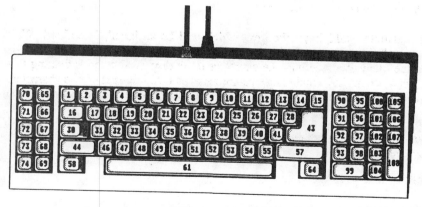

AT keyboard scan codes

Program Index

The following is a listing to the programs and utilities in this book. We've included most of these programs on the companion diskette accompanying this book. Remember that you must create files before using some of the programs. You'll find information on these files and how to create them in the appropriate chapters.

Programs in the Book

The following are example routines from the first section of the book (Chapter 2 to 7).

The following programs demonstrate how to create and include assembler routines. They also show how to use assembler routines in a PC-BASIC program:

The following utilities convert assembler routines into COM files so that they can be used in various initialization and call routines:

These programs are examples of an interface between PC-BASIC and either the operating system or the BIOS. DIRECTOR.BAS shows how an interface is used in an application.

The following programs demonstrate how to use function keys and how to display the current line and column in the editor. They also demonstrate the development of a simple template generator and how to save protected programs.

The following routines determine which monitor (color or monochrome) and which graphic card is installed in the PC/AT. These routines then set the appropriate colors and attributes for the screen display.

Fast output and the ability to save and restore the screen content are essential for a user-friendly screen display. The following programs demonstrate how to do this:

Windows are a very important feature of today's programs. The following programs demonstrate how to develop windows:

The first interfaces the user encounters in a program are the menus. The following programs demonstrate how to create selection, bar and pull-down menus.

This program is used for displaying lists. It shows how screen areas can be scrolled up and down to make displaying lists user-friendly.

The following programs concern the keyboard. They demonstrate how to read "invisible passwords", how to use a universal input routine for templates, how to suppress the termination of <Ctrl><C> or <Ctrl><Break>, and how to continuously display the status of the keyboard.

The following programs provide tips on using the mouse instead of the keyboard:

The following programs demonstrate bubble sort, quick sort and assembler sort:

These programs show how to develop an assembler routine and how to simplify the input of data through the keyboard with an assembler interface:

The following programs contain useful utilities for printing. They show how text can be printed in columns, printed sideways or how to create disk labels in various sizes, fonts and frames.

The following programs demonstrate how to implement a simple context-sensitive help function and a user-friendly error correction routine.

The following programs show several ways graphics can be used in PC-BASIC. The topics include moving text on the PC, the PC as a clock and the evaluation and display of numbers as graphics. There is also a program that demonstrates how CGA graphics can be displayed on a Hercules card by using an emulator:

The following program is used to compare the speed of the interpreter and the compiler:

Index

Abacus

pc catalog

Order Toll Free 1-800-451-4319

5370 52nd Street SE • Grand Rapids, MI 49512
Phone: (616) 698-0330 • Fax: (616) 698-0325

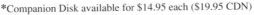

Programming VGA Graphics

VGA is now the standard display mode among the top selling PC software packages. If you develop software and want to support VGA mode, **Programming VGA Graphics** will help you write for almost any VGA video card. Programming VGA Graphics is a collection of language extensions for the Turbo Pascal and Turbo BASIC programmer.

Programming VGA Graphics also includes real world applications - a game called "The search for alien planet Earth" and a multicolor fractal demonstration for video mode 19. Beginning programmers and professional developers alike can profit from **Programming VGA Graphics**. What can YOU do with VGA? Find out with our **Programming VGA Graphics**. 670 pages. W/2 companion disks. Item # B099 ISBN 1-55755-099-9. $39.95
Canada: 57908 $51.95

QuickBASIC Toolbox

is for all QuickBASIC programmers who want professional results with minimum effort. It's packed with powerful, ready-to-use programs and routines you can use in your own programs to get professional results quickly.

Some of the topics include:
- Complete routines for SAA, interfacing mouse support, pull-down menus, windows, dialog boxes and file requestors
- Descriptions of QuickBASIC routines
- A BASIC Scanner program for printing completed project listings and more

This book/disk combination will teach you how to write even better QuickBASIC code. 130 pages.

QuickBASIC Toolbox, with companion disk.
Item # B104 ISBN 1-55755-104-9 $34.95
Canada: 57911 $45.95

Productivity Series books are for the user who wants to become more productive sooner with their PC.

Tips & Tricks for your PC Printer
Describes how printers work, basic printer configurations using DIP switches, using MS-DOS commands for simple printer control, includes utilities on a 5.25" companion diskette to demonstrate popular software commands. Useful printer accessories, font editor, and printing tricks and tips. 400 pp. with companion disk containing essential printer utilities.
ISBN 1-55755-075-1. $34.95
Canada: 53903 $45.95

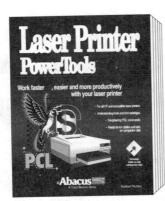

Laser Printer Powertools
shows you how to harness all the capabilities built into your HP-compatible laser printer quickly and easily. You'll learn about both the built-in and add-on fonts, the whys and hows of printing graphics, understanding the Printer Control Language (PCL) and how to set up dozens of applications to get the most from your laser printer. The companion disk includes programs for printing ASCII files, initializing margins and fonts; printing soft fonts, using Word printer drivers, converting ASCII files to print characters. It also includes many sample files you can use to get the most out of your printer. 350 pages.

Laser Printer Powertools with companion disk
Item #B095 ISBN 1-55755-095-6 $34.95
Canada: 53925 $45.95

DOS 5.0 Complete

Not just another reference book - **DOS 5.0 Complete** is a practical user's guide to learning and using Microsoft's new DOS. It's an encyclopedia of DOS knowledge not only for the computer whiz but for the everyday user.

DOS 5.0 Complete is loaded with helpful hints for outfitting any computer with MS-DOS 5.0. From installing DOS 5.0 to using the new features for file, directory and storage maintenance you'll find techniques and hints here.

DOS 5.0 Complete has dozens of easy to follow examples. This book explains AUTOEXEC.BAT and CONFIG.SYS. The detailed explanations make this the most authoritative DOS book available. The friendly, easy to understand writing style insures that even beginners will grasp the fundamentals quickly and easily. And you'll find a complete DOS command reference.

Topics include:

- Learn the "ins and outs" of using the new MS-DOS 5.0
- Boost your productivity with these practical techniques
- Discover ways to solve your own DOS problems
- Save valuable time with the ready-to-run companion disk.
- Browse the extensive MS-DOS reference section
- Using DOS' new memory management features
- Using the improved SHELL ;for performing your computer housekeeping ;chores
- Using the new DOSKEY utility for faster command line editing and macro power.
- Using EDIT, the new full-screen editor
- Using QBASIC, DOS' new BASIC programming language
- Complete DOS command reference.

DOS 5.0 Complete includes a companion disk with example batch files, detailed explanations, and powerful tips and tricks to help you get the most out of MS-DOS 5.0. **DOS 5.0 Complete** will become THE source for reference information about DOS 5.0.

DOS 5.0 Complete
Authors: Michael Tornsdorf, Helmut Tornsdorf
ISBN 1-55755-109-X.
Suggested retail price $34.95 with companion disk.

Stepping up to DR DOS 5.0

DR DOS 5.0 is a new alternative operating system to MS-DOS. Its many new features overcome some of the limitations that users are finding in MS-DOS.

This fast paced guide shows you the most important features of DR DOS 5.0. It presents practical examples to get you going quickly with DR DOS 5.0. It takes you step-by-step through the world of DR DOS 5.0. You'll find clear explanations and many "hands on" examples on using DR DOS. Learn the information you'll need to become more productive with DR DOS. 210 pages.
Item # B106 ISBN 1-55755-106-5. $14.95
Canada: 57913 $19.95

Novell NetWare Simplified

answers many questions about file servers and workstations using the most popular LAN system. **Novell NetWare Simplified** is your first step to understanding and using Novell NetWare more effectively.

Some of the topics include:
• Installing extra printers and PC workstations.
• Memory requirements for each user.
• Sending messages through your systems.
• Developing a user-friendly menu system and more.

Novell NetWare Simplified.
Item #B105 ISBN 1-55755-105-7 $24.95. Available June.
Canada: 57910 $3395

Assembly Language Step by Step

For lightning execution speed, no computer language beats assembly language. This book teaches you PC assembly and machine language the right way - one step at a time. The companion diskette contains a unique simulator which shows you how each instruction looks as the PC executes it. Includes companion diskette containing assembly language simulator. Available September 1990. ISBN 1-55755-096-4. $34.95
Canada: 53927 $45.95

Upgrading & Maintaining your PC

Your PC represents a major investment. This book shows you how to turn your PC into a high performance computing machine. It describes what you'll see when you open the "hood" and how all of the parts work together. Whether you want to add a hard drive, increase your memory, upgrade to a higher resolution monitor, or turn your XT into a fast AT or 386 screamer, you'll

see how to do it easily and econom-ically, without having to be an electronics wizard. Available September 1990. ISBN 1-55755-092-1. $24.95
Canada: 53926 $33.95

To order direct call Toll Free 1-800-451-4319
In US and Canada add $4.00 shipping and handling. Foreign orders add $12.00 per item. Michigan residents add 4% sales tax.

Paradox 3.5 Now!
introduces you to this quality relational database without any ifs, ands or buts - from installation to actual operation. Three examples show you how easy it is to work directly with Paradox: an accounting database, a sales report and a library database. You'll learn how to create forms; enter data; edit, sort and search change database structures; generate and print reports; and a lot more. You'll also find tips for importing data, important information about PAL and the Engine.
Available August.
Author: M. Bohmer
ISBN 1-55755-121-9. $12.95

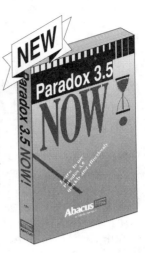

Toolbook Now!
is the effective and fast way to learn about Toolbook's environment and capabilities. Shows you how to manage data; get help through practical examples. You'll learn how to develop new applications and edit existing ones using the OpenScript system included in ToolBook. OpenScript makes it easier to create your own applications to run under Windows. You'll find development will take less time with this book. Includes helpful hints for installation, sample books (applications) like the Quick Tour, Buttons, Pages, Books, Fields, Graphics.
Available August.
Authors: V. Sasse and P. Shulz
ISBN 1-55755-119-7. $12.95

Virus Secure for Windows

Eliminate potential valuable data loss and minimize your risks with Virus Secure.

Don't give viruses the chance to ruin your data when you're using Windows. Avoid virus infection and potential valuable data loss. **Virus Secure for Windows** provides complete data protection for your hard and/or floppy disks from computer virus infection. **Virus Secure** is written by virus authority Ralf Burger (author of <u>Computer Viruses and Data Protection</u>). This is security that will keep your data alive and your PC operations productive.

Virus Secure can be run by both beginning and experienced users. Beginners will like the clear user interface and detailed error system. Experts will like the numerous options offered by **Virus Secure.** Beginning and advanced users will learn how to protect their diskettes and hard drives from unwanted data loss caused by viruses.

Virus Secure can detect over 200 known viruses and has built-in power for recognizing new or unknown viruses. It can also distinguish "normal" changes from "unusual" changes that viruses can make. **Virus Secure** can also be expanded. You can easily expand the recognition of viruses using a standard word processor. **Virus Secure** allows you to stay up to date as new viruses appear in the PC community.

Item #S108, ISBN 1-55755-108-1. Retail price $95.00.
System requirements: PC AT, 386 or compatible, hard drive and Windows 3.0.
Windows not included.

Author Ralf Burger

Windows is a trademark of Microsoft Corporation.

MICROSOFT WINDOWS
Version 3.0 Compatible Product

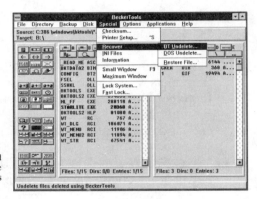